MANUAL OF BIOGENIC HOUSE SECTIONS

MANUAL OF BIOGENIC HOUSE SECTIONS

Lewis.Tsurumaki.Lewis

PAUL LEWIS, MARC TSURUMAKI, DAVID J. LEWIS

Introduction

SECTION

This book is both a sequel to and a critique of our 2016 publication, *Manual of Section*,[1] in which our intent was to change the way in which the practice and discipline of architecture understood and used the section as drawing type and site of design. Recognizing that a clear language for the communication about the section did not yet exist, we used the organization of that book, broken into eight types of section, to develop a heuristic structure serving as shorthand for discourse and design processes. We generated 63 one-point sectional perspectives to re-examine well-known buildings, and by cutting each project vertically, shifted the focus from building as object to a simultaneous examination of space, light, site, and proportion as well as the less-visible attributes of structure, thermal forces, and social exchanges. While inevitable in the walls of the section cut, the detail of the materiality shown in any given drawing was more often the by-product of the size of the project. Large-scale projects, with more complex spatial sections, generated representations that did not show their materiality.

Although this publication also advances our commitment to the section as a form of knowledge and site of architectural design innovation, *Manual of Biogenic House Sections* has a different ambition. It is intended to act as a catalyst for changing both how we build as well as the materials we use to build in order to address our climate crisis. This manual examines the intersection between better, and healthier materials and their potential to create dynamic building sections. We simultaneously argue for the use of carbon sequestering or low-carbon materials while demonstrating through the selection of houses that these materials can create spatial and formal play. Therefore, the majority of the houses, carefully curated for this book, use plant-based or biogenic materials to articulate new approaches to section. Moreover, these 55 houses testify that the future of architectural innovation is through regenerative materials, is revealed in the section, and can and should be elegant and seductive.

We focus on houses for two reasons. First, section drawings of houses within the constraints of a two-page spread allow the visualization of material details. And second, the house is a ubiquitous global building type and the historic site of experimentation and innovation which form the basis of entire economies. If we want to significantly decrease embodied carbon as a global society, we need to change how and why buildings are built, and the house provides an accessible proving ground for scalable and rapid innovation. This book also joins the clarion call for architects, developers, homebuilders, and homeowners to raise fundamental questions about conventional practices, while drawing upon the familiar and known characteristics of dwellings to inspire everyday change.

EMBODIED CARBON

As of 2022 and the writing of this book, the environmental arguments concerning what is required to preserve life on this planet are well known and unequivocal. To have any chance of keeping below a 1.5-degree-Celsius increase in global temperatures requires a 45% reduction in global carbon emissions by 2030, and zero net global carbon emissions by 2050.[2] The building industry accounts for approximately 39% of global emissions of which the making of the materials of buildings comprises about 11%.[3] Since the OPEC oil embargo of 1973, a focus of architecture, the building industry, and government regulation has been the reduction and limiting of operational energy, which is primarily related to heating and cooling of buildings. These remain important aspects of a system-wide approach to environmental performance. Advances in energy-efficient mechanical systems and thermal envelope performance combined with restrictive energy codes lead to significant reductions in building operation energy uses. Integrated with an expansion of renewable sources and a commitment to all electric systems, operational energy's impact on global warming has a probable path to zero.

This is not, however, the case for those building and construction materials that are excluded from most energy codes, and which were, until recently, overlooked and downplayed in professional education and practice, especially in North America. Compared to the enormous impact of the heating and cooling of uninsulated buildings, the energy involved in their manufacture was seen as an unavoidable but seemingly minor cost of doing business. Yet as the operational energy of buildings is reduced through high-performing building practices, a greater proportion of energy is used in the materials, making, and disassembly of our constructed environments. The amount of greenhouse gases, tracked in terms of the equivalent kilograms of carbon dioxide ($kgCO_2e$) used in the assembly, renovation, and demolition of any given project is its embodied carbon, and that embodied carbon is spent up front. Once a material is made or a building built, there is no way to reclaim that released carbon dioxide and other greenhouse gases. Therefore, if we are to significantly reduce global greenhouse gas emissions by 2030, there is even greater urgency to address these emissions now. By 2060 an estimated 2.4 trillion sq ft (230 billion sq m) of new construction is anticipated globally to meet population growth and aging building stock.[4] Eliminating all greenhouse gas emissions in little under three decades means finding and engaging building materials that have little to no embodied carbon. To put this in perspective, the making of cement alone constitutes 6% of all global emissions,[5] so getting to no carbon means no substantial use of conventionally made portland cement.

We also know that embodied carbon is not distributed evenly in a building. The structure, foundation, and envelope accounts for upwards of 80% of the total carbon. This is due in part to our current reliance on concrete, steel, and aluminum. These three materials are responsible for 23% of global emissions.[6] The chemical processes required to make them release huge quantities of global warming gases which are independent from the energy needed for their manufacture. Alternatively, biogenic materials that grow through photosynthesis have the capacity to sequester carbon dioxide in their cell structure. Once formed into a building, the carbon that makes trees and plants is captured and stored. While the long-term legacy of stored carbon must be accounted for by anticipating recycling, reuse, and redeployment, the tight time frame for reducing upfront carbon provides a greater incentive and an increased urgency to embracing plant-based building materials.

HEALTH

Addressing global warming also means understanding the unintended health consequences of modernity. Conventional building materials, many of which are made through petrochemical processes, present a danger both to the environment and to humans. These materials pose potential toxicity issues at every stage of their linear life cycles, from extraction, to use, to waste.[7] The abundance of chemical additives integrated into the petroleum products we encounter in our everyday lives is known to contribute to health problems from asthma to diabetes, and to impact human fertility at alarming rates.[8] Not surprisingly, simple, minimally processed, raw materials and those grown through photosynthesis do not come with the same level of health risks.

In the search for higher-performing buildings that reduce operational energy, exterior façades have increasingly become complex assemblies of lightweight processed materials. A typical residential assembly can easily top six different layers in which each strata is assigned a unique purpose, and often their intended benefits come with unintended consequences. Air barriers on the inside of exterior walls restrict movement of heat, but trap moisture behind other membranes. Polyurethane insulation resists thermal change, but requires unhealthy flame retardant chemicals aimed at controlling the spread of fire fueled by the air channel they can sponsor.[9] With increasingly complex and material-intensive assemblies, the carbon emissions in the materials used to achieve added performance can outweigh the energy savings over the life of the building, especially if the energy source is renewable.[10] Simply not building at all or reusing existing buildings and their components is a possible avenue of change. Similarly, building smaller with less stuff is a necessary shift. But these approaches are qualified by the anticipated global need for new buildings, often characterized as one New York City being built every month.[11]

The processes of construction, when left unregulated or ill-considered, can lead to environmental degradation, which is itself distributed inequitably in an inverse relationship to economic and political power, reinforcing existing environmental and racial injustices. The intertwined crises of climate, ecological devastation, and justice are intrinsically linked through the extraction, pollution, disposal, and associated global warming consequences of the materials that go into the making of a building. The implications of these challenges are not simple and there is no single solution. Rather, multiple trajectories and approaches are required. One central tenet of this book is that we must consider materials in their full life cycle. We must question and understand where the things we use originate and where they will go after their relatively short life in the form of buildings is over. As such we are keenly interested in visualizing the life cycles of these materials, and we hope to raise through these diagrams an enhanced awareness of the profound impact that they have—an impact which will exist well beyond their temporary gathering into architecture.

Our insistence that we examine, understand, and engage building materials that minimize harmful environmental impact throughout the life cycle leads to the selection and promotion of regenerative materials and design practices. Regenerative and circular practices are the antithesis of the conventional linear and extractive systems that underscore most conventional building assemblies today. Seen in this light, this book embraces a new optimism brought about by plant-based materials. If carefully cultivated in all stages of their lives, regenerative materials have the capacity, through their full life cycle, to sequester carbon, reduce toxicity, rejuvenate environments, and enhance human health and global biodiversity.

HOUSEKEEPING

We acknowledge and recognize that using the house as a site of examination raises issues of the significant environmental pitfalls that accompany suburbia, its associated culture of consumption and the transportation, energy, and land use it demands. Yet, the over one million homes which are built each year in North America[12] are increasingly assembled and glued together from petrochemical-based materials throughout, from vinyl floors and siding to plastic lumber, acrylic paint, and asphalt shingles. The home is a primary locus of our carbon-intensive economy. Changing the material basis of houses while incorporating innovative design derived from the exploration of the spatial, structural, and assembly potentials of regenerative materials, not only offers a better way to build, but it will also shift global economic systems. The unitized nature of houses means that new material systems can be imagined, tested, and quickly brought to a large scale of adaptation. In this sense, the focus on the house is equally an economic unit that needs change as well as one in which the necessary experimentation required for that change can extend into other building types and systems.

Redesigning the house based on embodied carbon criteria, offers a transformation equal to that brought about by the industrial revolution. The spatial and formal possibilities afforded by steel and concrete are inseparable from modern architecture. Yet, the unintended global warming consequence from the production of these materials has set the foundation for an entirely different approach to architecture, one that is informed by contemporary moral and ethical obligations. In order to move away from highly processed, industrialized materials, we must embrace a multivalent approach that can lead to systemic and enduring change. Examining alternative, regenerative materials while also examining how designing in creative play with those materials will inspire new ways of thinking about the shape, size, and configuration of dwellings.

When approaching the challenge of reducing the embodied carbon of a project, or house, the easiest solution is one of substitution. In this practice, one material simply replaces another with limited if any impact on the overall house or building system. Recycled denim insulation, for example, can substitute for fiberglass, and wood shingles can replace vinyl siding. Embracing substitution can lead to the creation of new market demands and the introduction of better, healthier products. Such practices, however, are ultimately limited in their capacity to lead to zero carbon emissions, and do not substantially change the underlying logic of the construction assembly nor the conception of the house. Moreover, substitution alone as the sole answer runs the risk of perpetuating an underlying problem, namely the sheer size and scale of today's residential buildings. While the average North American home in 1950 was 1,000 sq ft, by 2021 the average new house was over 2,500,[13] representing an increase of 150%. Swapping a handful of carbon-intensive materials with regenerative ones is a good first step but will not provide the wholesale transformation at the scale that is needed.

Similarly, using vast amounts of carbon sequestering material in the manufacture of enormous houses is also not a sustainable and equitable approach to preserving the planet.[14]

A different approach would be to return to traditional, pre-industrial building technologies in which the limited access to energy resources and transportation systems reinforced local building practices and used available materials. A significant number of the materials that are the focus of this publication have such a lineage, whether stone or earth or straw, yet the historic legacy of pre-modern materials presents a potential liability. The resuscitation of these older materials and construction practices brings with them expectations of nostalgia, if not overt regression, in the associated image of the houses. In this sense, the conflation of traditional materials with conventional building forms may undercut the capacity to address the full range of global identities, familial structures, cultural and environmental contexts that define dwelling today.

We advocate through the selection of houses in this *Manual* for an expanded use of low-carbon and carbon-sequestering materials. Moreover, we are interested in the intersection of material assembly and architectural seduction and have identified projects where this play is on display. In this sense we underscore architecture's role in galvanizing the imagination as a key component of embracing change. This is not to be mistaken for the pursuit of newness as an independent goal. Rather, the selected projects have the capacity to excite, motivate, and engage, thus expanding the interest in and use of regenerative materials. While we recognize that none of these projects is perfect, we have sought out houses throughout the globe that are typically smaller and address a variety of climatic zones. Some have concrete foundations, others rely on steel connectors, or avoid using insulation to illustrate new assembly systems as prototype houses. In curating this collection, which includes only built houses, we argue that the perfect should not be the enemy of good and see in each of these projects opportunities for ongoing discovery and improvement.

BOOK STRUCTURE

This book organizes the selected houses according to a primary material—wood framing, mass timber, bamboo, straw, hemp, cork, earth, brick, stone, and reuse—rather than by section type. A diagram at the introduction of each chapter illustrates the circular life cycle process of a given material. While simplified and abstracted, this illustration is essential for reinforcing a conceptual approach to building and architecture that considers where materials come from, how they are made, and where they will end up. The subsequent page shows the processing of the material, demonstrating the cradle to gate sequence that transforms a raw material into a component ready for the making of architecture. Like our food system, the complex industrialized processes that make our modern building materials, which are often guarded as trade secrets, have effectively rendered this knowledge inaccessible to most people, including architects, builders, and owners.

An early step toward awareness and subsequent responsibility is making processes visible through both a diagram of each material's life cycle as well as an overview of how each raw material is formed into building products. Individual house projects based on the given material follow, using a standard four-page arrangement. Overall axonometrics start each new project illustrating the interplay between plan and site. Construction photographs help to clarify the process of assembly, while exterior and interior images capture the material qualities of the project. Regional climate data aid in locating the project in its specific context, acknowledging that each house reflects a unique climatic condition. A single section with one-point perspective offers a simultaneous view into technical assembly of the materials, the interior life of the house, and the engagement with the site. Scale-figure entourage is intentionally staged to animate the section, with the section cut forming the equivalent of a proscenium for domestic life.

The Manual of Biogenic House Sections ends with two important chapters in the Appendix. Acknowledging that the full-house sections may not have sufficient detail to illustrate precisely the nature of the building assembly, we have generated detailed section-axonometrics with material labels. These serve as biopsy-like extractions from the house to provide comparison within and between material classifications in order to help understand the overall building tectonic system. This is not a comprehensive inventory of all possible ways of building with these materials, but rather a snapshot of the assembled houses for comparison within a given material and between them.

The second part of the Appendix documents the embodied carbon associated with one house from each material chapter. This area of the *Manual* requires qualification to understand its intent and limitations. Quantitative life cycle assessments are complicated, involved, and detailed processes used to ascertain a range of environmental impacts associated with a whole building. For our purposes, we have focused on the greenhouse gas emissions ($kgCO_2e$) involved in the production stage only, including the extraction of raw materials, transportation to processing, and their fabrication. Otherwise known as cradle-to-gate, the embodied carbon associated with this phase of a life cycle is consistent with data available on environmental product declarations (EPDs). It does not involve the specifics of a project's site, its distance from the material source, or the end-of-life concerns as those are as yet unknown for each of these projects.[15] This approach to embodied carbon data also underscores the material-specific nature of this *Manual*, providing a comparison between impacts by removing other variables associated with the global nature of individual projects.

We acknowledge that the embodied carbon data presented do not reflect the specific whole-building life cycle for each individual project, and we want to make clear that we are not presenting this information as a set of absolute facts, despite the seeming specificity that accompanies hard numbers. Identifying an approximate embodied carbon for selected projects is intended to build practical knowledge and a commonsense understanding while remaining transparent about sources. It is imperative that we have a solid understanding of the environmental impact of material decisions, but we are cautious about the need to balance data precision with data obfuscation. In other words, methodological requirements that underscore absolute data precision require enormous specialization and time that are out of reach for most practices and clients.

It is our goal to strike a balance between information precision and actionable knowledge. Debates over proper methodology and system boundaries can be used as a way of distracting and deflecting from the underlying intent of evaluating the environmental impact of buildings. Whether or not to include sequestered carbon in the production stage, for example, is a contested and highly political debate. Carbon-intensive materials compare more favorably and therefore look "greener" when one is not allowed to include the sequestered carbon in alternative plant-based materials in calculations. On the other hand, forest stewardship practices are fundamental to the net carbon impact of the use of trees. As a matter of transparency, we do include in this *Manual* the biogenic carbon sequestered in the production stage, as it is a key criterion to track, especially in order to impact our immediate future. Make no mistake, the pursuit of increasingly accurate and transparent data is a laudable and necessary goal, but it is also one that should in turn reinforce and inform holistic, common-sense design practices. This stance frames this publication's approach to embodied carbon data, and it is precisely the comparative information derived about the environmental impact of building materials and architectural choices that underscores the simple phrase that echoes the noted writer Michael Pollan's approach to food: *Live in delightful spaces. Not too big. Made from plants.*

HOUSE CONSTRUCTION

House construction systems, particularly in the United States, have been motivated by six interlinked values or trajectories. The first is that lighter is better than heavier. This belief is based on an alignment between weight, material quantity, and cost. Lighter building parts are usually easier to assemble, and therefore require less labor, which reduces cost. Second, thinner is better than thicker. When each material is made to be as light as possible, it's not surprising that a wall is seen as an assembly of thin materials. Each layer can then be marketed for its unique and essential contribution to the sandwich and its necessary inclusion within building codes. This leads to the third trajectory, which asserts that each layer does primarily one thing, and the logical consequence of that trajectory is that standard methods of house construction require multiple layers to achieve the air, water, vapor, and thermal controls. The need for multi-layered construction is the fourth trajectory. These layers are almost exclusively sandwiched and thought of as a singular element in support of the fifth trajectory which is the strict binary between interior and exterior, enabled and facilitated by post–World War II mechanical systems.[16] In parallel to this binary is the sixth value. Materials must appear to be hygienic and maintenance free, and must resist natural entropy. Plastics have extraordinary performative qualities in very thin sheets at low cost and align well with curated aesthetics of hygiene. As such, conventional construction is now defined by multiple, thin, lightweight, hygienic, and mostly plastic layers, each with a discrete performance, all assembled into a single compressed wall that maintains a strict distinction between the exterior and interior. Only the very thin veneer of interior paint and exterior cladding is typically visible, while the multiple layered ingredients are hidden in the sandwich. Unfortunately, some of the more visible failures of recent house construction have been the unintended impact that these layers have upon each one another, most notably the growth of mold. While external issues such as mold can be seen, the invisible toxicity and high levels of carbon emissions these layers can create are those that this book seeks to address.

In addition to using plant-based and other earth-based materials in the pursuit of lower toxicity and embodied carbon, many of the houses in this book also exhibit characteristics that resist if not contradict these six implicit and explicit trajectories. Most of the selected houses do not repress but rather embrace natural materials as the aesthetic for the house, and those characteristics are the basis for their inclusion. Furthermore, the way those materials change over time is viewed as an asset and not a liability. Wood and stone are allowed to age, developing depth and character over the seasons and years. Earthen materials' tendency to erode is designed into the system, and successive rains reveal the articulation of that system, adding detail and shadow. Changes of weather are anticipated in the shaping and forming of the materials, as in the example of a roof being converted into a ski launch after a heavy snowfall.

Rather than form a binary between the exterior and interior, some of the houses deploy a gradient of spaces with a range of thermal and climatic qualities. Multiple layers of skins are not compressed into an invisible sandwich, but are expanded or exfoliated into layers of space, allowing those interstitial spaces to be used for both programmatic and performative purposes. In contrast to a rigid assumption of a single optimal interior temperature, these projects explore the pleasures of thermal contrasts, while also nesting buildings within buildings to maximize passive sources of energy and reduce the need for artificial heating and cooling. Strategies of reuse of existing buildings especially lend themselves to these nested section benefits.

In contrast to multiple discrete layers, many of the houses use a single material that does multiple things. Earthen walls act as structure, exterior sheathing, and water and air barriers. Cross-laminated timber (CLT) is not only the structure but can also be the air barrier; part of the insulation; and the interior surface, thereby removing drywall, joint compound, and paint from the system. CLT's capacity can be pushed further allowing it to be the *only* material in the wall section, replacing insulation and cladding. Given their complex properties, plant-based biogenic materials often reduce the number of layers and create elegant multivalent systems. Cork, straw, and hemp work as thermal-resistant layers: straw has the capacity to be the structure, cork can act as the water and air resistive barrier, and hemp can provide the suitable substrate for lime and clay plasters. More interestingly, rather than atomize performance of each individual building product, the material assemblies in this book exhibit mutual coexistence, in which the whole is greater than the sum of the parts. Hemp and lime form a fire-proof, rot-resistant, insulating, and semi-rigid layer. Similarly, straw-bales support their clay or lime skins, which provide additional structural capacity and resist fire and vermin, while serving as water and air barriers.

Many of the houses selected have unusually thick walls. In certain cases, this is to increase the insulating capacity of those walls. Straw, hemp, bamboo, and wood, all biogenic materials, are much less dense than steel or concrete, which accounts for their insulative capacities. Their thickness therefore is not incompatible with being lightweight, and their ability to be both undermines false binaries between weight and depth. Passive house standards, which seek to minimize operational energy, advocate for super-insulated and air-tight walls. This logic is at play in several houses in this *Manual*. As noted previously, carbon-intensive, petroleum-based insulations (expanded polystyrene, extruded polystyrene, polyurethane foam, and polyisocyanurate insulation), offer limits to the benefits of that thickness, since the energy savings from each additional increment of insulation decreases asymptotically, and cannot offset their up-front linear carbon expenditure.[17] Alternatively, biogenic materials such as straw, hemp, seagrass, and local earthen materials in the form of loam and stones, avoid these initial carbon costs, with biogenic materials able to store more carbon through each increment of thickness. Moreover, their structural capacity is often generated through that very mass.

The value of lightweight construction is in part predicated on the desire for global distribution of uniform materials. Lighter is simply cheaper to transport. Particularly in the case of concrete and metals that require large amounts of processing, less material is assumed to equate to less energy. This seemingly sacrosanct edict of modernism, as invoked by Buckminster Fuller's question, "How much does your building weigh?" is countered by projects that ask, "How locally sourced are the building's materials?" Blocks or walls made from the very soil excavated for the building, or harvested from adjacent farms, forests, or coastlines, restructure the presumed linear equation between weight, costs, and environmental impact. Furthermore, in more extreme climates, mass is often a critical component of the thermal performance of the house, enabling the optimization of solar gain, and offsetting diurnal temperature swings.

Reducing embodied carbon and using biogenic materials demand a radical reassessment of the trajectory of conventional building assemblies that promote lightweight, thin, single-performing, multiple, hygienic layers to enact strict demarcation of the interior. In its place we argue for a messier, productive embrace of the sometimes heavy, thick, multivalent, singular, and entropic with gradients of enclosure. To provide clarity to this more heterogeneous approach to buildings, we have organized the book according to material-specific chapters, recognizing that each material can be pursued in myriad ways.

WOOD FRAMING

Lightweight stick framing is not only the most common structural system used in houses in the Americas, it is fundamental to the evolution of the multiple-thin-layer system that currently holds sway. Stud-based framing, which efficiently used the bulk of a softwood trunk cut into a range of decreasing sizes, allowed for more of the tree to be of value, thereby decreasing waste. Furthermore, lightweight framing is mass-produced and easily distributed through railroad and highway networks and it offers a uniform, simple to assemble, and cheaper alternative to either its heavy timber post and beam or solid wood predecessors. This iterative framing also allowed for a lightweight structure to disappear within the very veneers it held up—veneers that could take many forms precisely because of their independence from structural responsibilities. The cavity space between the studs was a consequence of reducing the mass of the structure. In other words, its use as a site for insulation is a response to, and not a cause of the resulting cavity. Thermal bridging resulting from the use of studs account for a weakness in the performance of the envelope, and wood's susceptibility to rot demands waterproofing layers of exterior sheathing, membranes, and cladding. Because these skins have developed over time, the resulting sandwich is not only composed of multiple, single-use layers, but those layers are not in optimum order. Insulation placed between structural members is not as effective as encasing the structure in a thermal envelope.

Wood is one of the most important structural alternatives to concrete and steel, but because building with wood begins with the harvesting of trees, there are opposing factors that must be accounted for relative to carbon impacts. When dry, wood is composed of about 50% carbon, which is stored or sequestered for the duration of the building's life. But accessing wood means removing living trees, which can disturb the additional carbon stored in a forest's soils and the biomass independent from trees. Careful forest stewardship, which is attentive to the quantity and frequency of harvest cycles, to erosion management, to robust replanting strategies, and to the full forest ecosystem and biodiversity, is essential. Without it, the production of lumber can have serious detrimental effects that far exceed its carbon storage.[18] Ensuring proper chain of custody verifications for timber, such as those provided by the Forest Stewardship Council, is a critical part of engaging the full life cycle of timber.

The projects in our chapter on wood framing remain attentive to the sources of the wood itself while exemplifying distinctly different approaches to both stick structural construction and its cladding. In contrast to the stacked section of platform framing, Gago House uses a fully three-dimensional framing system augmented by a central column to disperse rooms with great freedom within the spiraling section. In embedding a frame within an exterior blanket of wood fiber insulation, Zilvar House uses thickness as a virtue, sculpting space through deflections and attenuations of that skin. Similarly, Thunder Top Cabin uses a shaped section, but places the wood framing fully within the interior, forming ribs that mark contours within the topographic roof. This desire to reveal the wood framing, rather than conceal it within the walls, defines Helio Olga House, House in Itsuura, Ogimachi House, and Radic's Wood House. Each invents specific wood joinery details that have ripple effects not only on the form of the buildings and their relationship to the ground, but also on the very materials that enclose these skeletons. With little to no drywall, these houses incorporate their enclosures into the joinery, blurring distinctions between skin and structure.

MASS TIMBER

Mass timber is composed of aggregations of smaller wood members that constitute beams, such as glue-laminated beams (glulam) or laminated veneer lumber (LVL), or structural plates. The plates are characterized by the orientation of their component parts and their means of assembly, including nail-laminated timber (NLT), dowel-laminated timber (DLT), and mass plywood. The most prominent mass timber assembly is cross-laminated timber (CLT). Similar to plywood, CLT is made up of multiple layers of wood which are adhered perpendicularly to each other so that they produce a structural stable composite. But unlike plywood, CLT increases its scale in all three directions, with 10' x 50' x 6 7/8" a typical size for a plank. CLT is most frequently used as a structural system, with an ability to sequester carbon, based on other material logics, primarily steel post and beam or concrete slabs. Particularly in larger-scale apartment and office buildings, CLT can replace concrete slabs, often with glulam columns and beams, and because it blends well with existing structural systems, CLT and steel hybrids are not uncommon. Given its limited ability to resist footfalls and associated noise, CLT slab is typically covered with a robust topping, leaving its underside visible as wood. Yet as a plate that has the capacity to span in two directions and can be precisely milled, CLT also presents unique architectural possibilities. As a sheet, it can have distinct apertures subtracted with great ease, and can also be used as the interior finish, eliminating interior layers. Although mass timber is used on increasingly large projects, many of its distinctive qualities have been tested more effectively in smaller-scale residential projects.

The projects in the mass timber chapter all explore the specific qualities of this structural material that go beyond mere substitution. The porosity, articulation of volumes, and floating mass in House W are all possible because of CLT. Similarly, the play between surface and very large apertures in Sunken House hints at its use of CLT, which is otherwise invisible. Haus Gables uses CLT's alignment between form and surface to rethink the roof geometry as the generator of a complex interior section, with an equal attention given to how the required surfacing of the CLT floor might transform interior material aesthetics. In using two nested layers of CLT with a very large void between, Meteorite tests whether a house can be produced using only one material, with its cavity forming the insulation, and a simple stain augmenting its exterior weather resistant layer. The two skins have distinctly different geometries, and precise cuts to the CLT panels' edges produce an intricate section both within and between the layers. This precision informs the unique overlaps between Kostner House and Studio's glulam perimeter trusses and the CLT twin volumes it both holds aloft and envelopes. In an equally bespoke, albeit more reserved form, House Köris weaves multiple types of wood assemblies together, such that the very details and articulation of the house are inextricable from mass timber's union of structure and interior skin.

BAMBOO

Among the world's fastest growing plants, bamboo is an arborescent grass characterized by a rhizomatic root system and straight woody stems. It can be readily cultivated or harvested from the wild, has a wide distribution globally and an enormous diversity of uses from food to fabrics to structures, particularly in the cultures of Southeast and East Asia.[19] Bamboo's rapidity of growth, regenerative capacity, ability to inhabit degraded land and frequent cultivation cycle (typically three to seven years) can contribute to carbon mitigation through afforestation. Bamboo has been shown in studies to sequester carbon more efficiently and faster than trees, and unlike wood timber its harvesting does not release carbon to the atmosphere.[20]

For architectural purposes and depending on species and size, bamboo can be deployed in its unprocessed form, known as culms, or transformed into a variety of building products, from bamboo plywood to flooring. In their raw state, which still requires initial treatment to forestall decay, the linear culms provide flexibility and a varying scale that allows for a breadth of spatial possibilities, textural effects, and uses, ranging from structure to enclosure to surface. When performing as primary structure and due to inherent limitations of scale, bamboo culms are often clustered to function as beams, purlins, or columns, necessitating various techniques for joining and assembly or bent-to-form arches and vaults, taking advantage of their inherent elasticity. As culms vary and elude precise structural calculation, construction is partly dependent on empirical methods and hands-on experience, often necessitating mockups or large-scale models. In this sense the use of bamboo challenges contemporary notions of standardization arising from the synthetic predictability of processed and modularized building products. This potential to shift the methodology of how we design buildings away from a quantitatively driven, predictive approach to one that embraces contingency and experimentation is one of the more compelling implications of this material. It is also one of the distinct limits to the widespread use of bamboo in its integral form, since professional responsibilities are tied to legal obligations that depend on verifiable data. Bamboo, however, can also be machined into strips or strands and laminated or woven into surfaces and planks, providing a plentiful biogenic resource for an array of architectural elements that can be incorporated into more conventional construction.

The selected projects primarily use culms in their minimally modified state since such works amplify the intrinsic qualities of bamboo to become a primary driver in the design expression. While most of these houses deploy varying combinations of bamboo culms as primary structural components, they take divergent approaches to their sectional dialogue with other material systems. Energy Efficient Bamboo House restricts the use of the culms to the primary structural frame held together with custom metal joints, while at Cabañón DLPM, culms are used not only as beams and purlins, but also form the integrated formwork for the sloping concrete floors. From the Territory to the Dweller and Trika Villa create more or less complex roof canopies that shelter the domestic spaces below. The nature of these roof assemblies, which tend toward a dense porosity based on the interweaving of the linear stems, is compatible with the climatic demands put upon these buildings. Constructed in tropical or semi-tropical regions where the plant flourishes, these assemblies facilitate natural ventilation and mitigate the need for mechanical cooling, thus establishing a reciprocity between biogenic tectonics and environmental performance. In the Bamboo Hostels project, this permeability results in the reduction of conditioned space, with a woven netting of bamboo strips enclosing a semi-outdoor space around a heated earthen core. Blooming Bamboo Home takes the use of the material to an extreme, arraying and combining varying scales of bamboo culms to function as both structure and skin, resulting in a monolithic architecture paradoxically based on aggregated parts.

STRAW

Two of wood's critical limitations are the decades needed to grow a tree to maturity and the inevitable cutting down of those same trees. Straw and other agricultural residues avoid these temporal limitations. By contrast, not only are these agricultural fibers extremely fast growing, they also already exist as a largely untapped source for carbon sequestration for use in building materials. Primarily considered waste, the stocks of grain seed are typically burned or left to decompose, allowing their carbon to be re-released. In addition to its capacity to draw down atmospheric carbon, straw is ubiquitous, inexpensive, lightweight, and its tubular structure provides an ideal shape for insulation. Moreover, straw can be load bearing as was the case in its earliest use in building in the plains of Nebraska in the 1890s, when it was mechanically formed into compressed bales. When combined with clay, lime, or cement coatings, which adhere well to straw's coarse irregular surface, straw-bale assemblies are fire, air, water, and vermin resistant, and also remain vapor permeable, thereby regulating excesses of interior humidity. Although their insulative value is about R-1.5 to 2 per inch, the thickness of the bales produces a highly insulated wall and allows for distinctive architectural qualities as a result of that depth.

There are four primary methods by which straw-bales are used in building, based largely on how instrumental they are to the structure and how the straw is assembled into a useful unit. They are: a full load bearing or Nebraska-style approach; an insulative infill within a timber frame; an infill within a prefabricated wood box that is skinned on site;[21] and a fully prefabricated and skinned structural insulated panel. Prefabrication provides precision and protection from weather that can negatively impact onsite assembly of these otherwise crude building blocks. Nevertheless, Gartist GmbH House, which is one of the most intriguing buildings made from straw in this book, maximizes the capacity of very large, highly compressed bales to carry structural load. With each block offset 30 cm horizontally, the tall, elongated section of the space is a consequence of the corbeled bales themselves, whose interior clay surface follows and accentuates the inverted ziggurat of the ready-made agricultural units.

The other four projects in the *Manual's* straw chapter illustrate different ways besides bales that straw, reeds, or seagrass fibers can provide insulative value. Media Perra House capitalizes on straw's lightweight quality as well as the mild climate of Guadalupe. Here, straw is packed into the stud cavity in judicious amounts, allowing the house to perch delicately above the land. Dune House and Modern Seagrass House reinvigorate specific thatch traditions by using locally harvested materials, and each extends the tectonics of densely packed fibers down the entire enclosure, producing idiosyncratic buildings rooted in local, historic building techniques. Also based on vernacular traditions, albeit transplanted from Morocco to Scandinavia, Mauritzberg Test House is an experimental cob construction in which loam and straw are formed into air-dried blocks, creating long, thick parallel walls which capture interior courtyards while maintaining privacy. As these five examples demonstrate, straw's role in a building is modified through its relationship to how it is aggregated into units, and in which the design of the unit prefigures its architectural consequences.

HEMP

Considering its robust regenerative processes, hemp is an exceptionally compelling plant for use in buildings.[22] Used primarily as insulation, the inner core of hemp, called the hurd, is combined with lime as a mineral binder activated by water. The combination of lime and water coheres the hurd, creating a monolithic material that, while self-supporting, has ample air pockets and a rough surface which allow it to support a direct lime plaster coating without metal mesh. This combination is often called hempcrete but is more accurately described as hemp-lime as it has limited structural properties when compared to concrete. When used in combination with timber framing and coated with lime plaster on both inside and outside, hemp-lime can simultaneously act as the air barrier, thermal barrier, and acoustic absorber; all while being non-toxic, non-flammable, and breathable. Moreover, industrialized hemp sequesters a high amount of carbon (110 $kgCO_2/m^3$) and generates more biomass per acre than other plants currently used in construction.[23] Hemp can also grow in a range of climatic zones and requires limited watering, fertilizer, and pesticides. It is also used as a rotational crop to remediate soil through phytoremediation by pulling contaminants out of degraded soil while stabilizing against erosion through a deep root system.

Most hemp in North America is grown for seed and CBD extraction, or for the fiber stripped from the exterior layer of the tall stalks that make textiles, rope, and other fiber-based products. As such, the inner core used in hemp-lime is currently an underutilized part of the plant. However, using this hemp hurd with lime requires knowledge and care in the mixing and installation to ensure proper compaction, drying, and performance. It can also be labor intensive to install and is subject to the impact of weather during construction owing to the need to dry the thick walls. The insulation value of hemp-lime is also not high, roughly R-1.25 to R-2.3 per inch depending on the precise mix used. A thick wall of 10 to 20 inches is required, depending on local energy code or desired performance and this additional mass does increase the amount of sequestered carbon in a hemp-based wall assembly. But if installed properly, hemp-lime walls offer an elegant monolithic shell that respirates, regulates the indoor air humidity, and absorbs pollutants with naturally occurring antifungal properties that resist the mold that plague multilayer assemblies.

While they employ different approaches to interior and exterior finishes, the four projects in our chapter on hemp all use hemp-lime as a through-wall insulation in combination with wood assemblies as the primary structure. The house project Clay Field illustrates a hemp-based wall within double-stud framing to support a wood and stucco finish. Low Energy House in Uccle is built using site-casting of hemp-lime with shutters or formwork and rendered on the interior with lime plaster. Built within an area prone to brush fires, Mudgee Hempcrete House 2 illustrates another unique and beneficial property of hemp-lime. Despite being made from a carbon-based plant material, it is highly fire-resistant. Flat House fully embraces the versatility and challenges of using hemp as a building material. It has a prefabricated wood frame which creates a panelized assembly system that can be filled with hemp-lime in a factory setting where drying conditions can be controlled, thereby speeding erection, and minimizing unwanted site-based construction contingencies. The exterior wall of Flat House is also made of hemp that has been pressed into corrugated wood boards with plant-based resins. The interior is protected with clay paint, which brings the texture and materiality of the hemp-plant forward and creates an enticing backdrop for domestic life.

CORK

Cork is derived from the bark of cork oak trees and has been valued for thousands of years for its water resistance and buoyancy.[24] The outer bark of mature, living oaks is harvested by hand every nine to twelve years using age-old methods that do not damage the tree itself. The cultivation of these oaks supports a unique woodland ecosystem (known in Portugal as *montados*), forestalls deforestation, and sponsors a rich agrarian culture, principally on the Iberian Peninsula.[25] Due to its directional cellular structure, cork has unique, waterproof, antifungal, and insulating properties; is lightweight; and has a unique odor and texture. Although the limited geographic growing range of cork oaks constrains material availability and most high-quality cork bark is used in the wine industry, the byproducts from cork stopper production can be transformed into a variety of building products that capitalize on its beneficial properties and carbon sequestering potential. While sheet goods like flooring may contain added adhesives, many cork products, such as cork insulation, capitalize on naturally occurring binders in the cork granules activated when exposed to heat.

While the most common use of cork in standard building practices is as an interior finish, in which its mass is often minimized, its moisture retardant and thermal properties also make it a viable insulating and exterior sheathing material, particularly when used in thicker applications. Cork Screw House and Two Cork Houses demonstrate this ability of solid cork to substitute for the layering of monofunctional synthetic layers and act as a highly performing skin that reduces the need for additive assemblies. At the same time, these projects exhibit a monolithic appearance achievable despite the modularity of the cork since the lightweight and elastic nature of the material allows for tight construction tolerances. Beyond its use as an exterior skin, cork can also function as a primary structural material and integrated wall assembly, fully replacing more layered systems, and although such uses remain rare, Cork House demonstrates the potential of such an approach, resulting in a thickened organic masonry that performs both as a climatic barrier and tectonic system at once. In addition to these performative and even structural capacities, the exposed cork exhibits unique olfactory, acoustical, and tactile effects that contribute to both the sensory qualities and healthfulness of the house's interior environment.

EARTH

Earth is one of the oldest and most widely used building materials on the planet. Composed of a mixture of clay, silt, sand, and sometimes aggregate in the form of stones, the material used in earth building is also called loam.[26] Topsoil is rich with organic matter and therefore cannot be used, so it is the earth below fertile ground that is typically sourced for building purposes. Organizing earth into architectural form takes many processes, from rammed earthen walls set within formwork, to directly worked wet loam, to unitized sunbaked blocks which can be stacked and layered. The advantages of loam or earth buildings are numerous and overlapping. Earth constructions are hydroscopic in that they regulate moisture and breath, creating indoor environments of consistent humidity. Walls of earth are monolithic and often thick thus absorbing and regulating temperature through their inherent thermal mass. If used without stabilizers or additives, earth is a fundamentally circular material, easily returning to the ground at end of life. Earth is also inexpensive and does not require highly capitalized industrial processes to make, raising opportunities for localized work and labor to meet housing demand on a global scale. These structures are of their place, bringing into view terrestrial matter made through the geological history that formed each specific site.

Earth is global, ubiquitous, and accessible. These qualities are, however, its potential Achilles' heel, as earth-based buildings are seen as crude, temporary, and unrefined, the antithesis of the conventional western teleological direction of human development. Yet recent projects as well as examples throughout the history of building, demonstrate that this reductive way of thinking represents a limited understanding of earth's rich potential.[27] Moreover, the unintended global warming consequences brought about by a blind belief in technological progress raises interesting questions about the opportunity to recast the value and aesthetics of earth building, precisely because they are relegated to hegemonic linear concepts of historical progression.

The selection of houses made of earth join in the call to recast earth as a viable contemporary and future building material, one that offers rich aesthetic possibility and environmental performance.[28] House Rauch exemplifies current research in earth building and transforms one of the significant challenges of the material into a defining aesthetic feature. Earth buildings are subject to erosion. House Rauch deploys regular courses of hardened earth to slow the flow of water over the exterior surface, gradually revealing larger aggregates in the earth that are left as protection. Other projects approach these issues with cement or lime stabilizers, such as Dong Anh House or TECLA - Technology and Clay; or modified cladding materials as in Gando Teachers' Housing. Wohnhaus Flury isolates the earthwork through raised foundations and extensive roof overhangs thereby replacing ordinary interior walls with thick earthen art installations, putting on display the local geology of the site.

BRICK

A brick is a modular building material made from earthen clay or shale that is formed, dried, and heated through fusion and vitrification into a durable and hard object. Given the simplicity of brick making, availability of earth-based source materials, and their durability, bricks are found throughout the globe and a staple of many architecture and construction cultures. The long history of brick in architecture is storied and rich and the inherent modularity of brick lends itself to a diverse array of aggregation strategies and patterns. But the push toward thin, multi-layered wall systems has relegated brick to something it likely does not want to be. The dominant way in which bricks are used currently in North American residential construction is as a single-wythe veneer clipped to a lightweight structural frame, supported by steel angles, and perforated with weep holes. This assembly does not take advantage of brick's structural capacities nor its ability to act as a thermal mass.

Unfortunately, the firing process used in the making of most modern bricks requires a considerable amount of energy. Almost all kilns rely on fossil fuels as their heat source and the creation of each standard-sized brick releases approximately one pound of CO_2.[29] The global need for a simple, available, durable building material demands that earth bricks be made with lower embodied energy, and this need has inspired a great deal of ongoing research. The principle ecological concern is in the fuel for firing brick, rather than in its simple, earth-based source. The conversion of kilns to renewable fuel sources is clearly needed.[30] Alternatively, using conversion processes that harden clay or stabilize without heat are also possible, as those used in the project Earth Bricks demonstrate.

Once we recognize that the way bricks are fired carries with it embodied carbon costs, we must begin to consider how this durable material can and should be reused and repurposed in order to maximize the life of the inherent spent carbon. Aalto's own experimental house at Muuratsalo, which was the testing ground for larger projects, clearly illustrates a playful aggregation of dissimilar brick and tiles. Given their durability, bricks can be reused again, and dnA House exemplifies the way in which bricks with a history can be repurposed to suit a contemporary aesthetic. Iturbide Studio deploys thin assemblies of brick to create dynamic, shade-producing skins and structures in dense urban settings, creating seductive spaces through this earth-derived material. LETH + GORI's Brick House is an intentional counterpoint to the ubiquitous thin brick façade, clipped onto the front of a house. The entire wall of this project is one single material: clay brick. At over 22 in (560 mm thick), this mass wall provides thermal resistance, breathes, regulates moisture, and is designed to last for 150 years before either being rebuilt into another structure or crushed and recycled. Here, the tectonics of the wall assembly celebrates the full performance of brick and embraces its durability, designed in alignment with its inherent material properties.

STONE

Stone's brief treatment in this publication belies its significance as one of the most ancient and varied materials in the history of human construction. As referenced in *Manual of Section*, a vast portion of architecture in the west comprises the evolution of buildings exhibiting a sectional morphology derived from the structural and assembly logics of stone masonry. As we have previously discussed, one of the implications of this tectonic approach was an architecture of thicknesses, whose spatial properties were based on monolithic mass, with a single material dividing inside from out. By the mid-20th century however, most stone in buildings had been reduced to thin veneers, often applied as interior or exterior finishes, and usually divorced from structural, thermal, or other performative functions except as an outermost weatherproofing layer. This contemporary use of stone offers the illusion of solidity and permanence onto what are in fact complex, multilayered envelopes and assemblies. The projects included here, however, employ stone for more multivalent purposes rather than exclusively for its surface effects, and revitalize its potential as a structural thickness or a porous thermal mass.

Stone itself is a highly variable material, exhibiting a broad range of characteristics, appearances, and performative qualities, from the durability of igneous granite to the readily carved surface of metamorphic marble. And while stone offers a plentiful, naturally occurring resource, several critical factors impact its use in the context of low carbon construction, namely the location and method of extraction, degree of processing, and its appropriateness to its intended use. Stone is heavy, making transportation more cumbersome than for lighter weight materials; therefore, locally sourced indigenous stone is used in all of the projects detailed in this *Manual*. Most stone is obtained from quarries, and while this process results in less waste than in mining, it leads to the degradation of the surrounding landscape, which can have long-term deleterious effects on the environment.[31] Stone House in Shimane, Japan uses local stone gathered from the bed of a nearby river, while Jacobs House II employs limestone indigenous to its midwestern site, minimizing the negative effects of quarrying and transport. The dressing of stone once it has left the quarry usually involves industrial processing in a factory setting, incurring both more transportation and energetic carbon costs. Using a less processed stone, like the rough-hewn limestone blocks of Hill Country Jacal allows for a reduction of these environmental impacts while still capitalizing on the material's rich visual and tactile qualities. Utzon's Can Lis incorporates local sandstone taken directly from the quarry, and purposefully retains the circular traces of the masonry saws to create delicate shadow effects on both the building's interior and exterior surfaces.

While the use of stone can signal a potentially nostalgic appeal to historic precedent, building with stone needn't be reduced to architectural atavism. Can Lis employs a tectonic language of stone masonry that nevertheless weaves together interior and exterior spaces, combining a modernist spatial sensibility with a careful integration of site. Stone House in Shimane, Japan nests a timber house in an aerosolized berm of river stones, treating stone simultaneously as mass and void to generate both thermal and spatial effects. These projects manage to be both attentive to the attributes of stone while evidencing inventive new performative and formal possibilities for this age-old architectural material.

REUSE

Reuse refers to both the repurposing of extant structures, in whole or in part, as well as the reclamation of materials taken from demolished buildings and subsequently used in new construction. The former is arguably one of the most effective means of reducing the environmental impacts of building processes, as it leverages the investment of resources and carbon already expended during the original construction. Reuse of buildings typically involves modification through addition or renovation to accommodate new programs and to increase utility or performance, extending the use value of buildings. Alternatively, materials are recuperated in the demolition processes and are redeployed in new construction, treating outmoded buildings as a storehouse for anthropogenic resources. Varying degrees of processing are required to render recovered materials useful. They range from downcycling, for example, the conversion of wood members into wood pulp, to recycling of materials into equivalent products as in the case of metals, to the reuse of durable components like brick or stone. In the case of direct reuse, the effects of wear, weathering, and handling reduce the predictability of previously used materials, introducing contingency and challenging expectations of standardization often in compelling ways.

Reuse requires that buildings are conceived not as static artifacts but rather as dynamic and evolving systems subject to entropy, transformation, and revitalization. The rate of replacement of architectural elements varies, meaning that all buildings are continually in flux, shedding or adding layers, decaying and being repaired.[32] And while historically architecture has been predicated on notions of durability and permanence, in reality, particularly beginning in the 20th century, buildings have become increasingly subject to accelerating cycles of consumption, outmoding, and disposal.[33] Not only does reuse put the emphasis on the productive dialogue between old and new, it renders visible the temporal dimensions of architecture as the play of material and spatial conditions. Reuse also shifts the focus to the extended life cycle of our constructions, giving rise to strategies like design for disassembly and urban mining that consciously take stock of the afterlives of the materials we use.

Given the range of approaches to reuse of buildings and materials, we selected projects for this publication that drew their design trajectory from the generative interchange between existing and new, and which vary widely in the extent and nature of the reuse. Half-Slope House starts with an existing wall and uses it to sponsor an entire house, amplifying the tensions of the site through a vertically sheared section. Verbiest converts an industrial building into a residence and studio, modifying as little as possible with an eye toward an economy of means and occupying only a portion of the structure. House Renovation in Scudellate inserts a new timber house within the masonry shell of an old stable, taking advantage of the stone walls as both climatic protection and historic image while retaining the mutual independence of the nested spaces as revealed by the section. By contrast, House Simma wraps a new straw coat around a mid-century house to increase its thermal performance, radically altering the exterior expression of the building through its organic thickened skin. In all cases, the encounter between new and pre-existing becomes the basis for the design trajectory, intensifying rather than erasing the tension between material, spatial, and tectonic systems.

BEING PRESENT

In focusing on these ten material strategies, we are seeking to call attention to the key role that a material-based architecture can have on global ecology and future architectural practice now. This is not to say that there are not other building sources or future approaches that can be explored or might be pursued. Rather in curating the following set of 55 innovative houses, we are seeking to accelerate the full embrace of more vital and circular design practices with known, available, and immediately implementable sources. Research into alternative low-carbon production practices, bio-engineered materials, and alternative plant-based products are rich in possibility and potential. Yet, the challenge with some is that they may not be ready in the time frame we need them.

By focusing on commonplace, readily available and scalable material strategies, we seek to not only amplify the call to rethink architecture to mitigate climate change, but to assert that the means to do so are already at hand. Moreover, these material approaches should be catalysts for new inventive ways of building that are attentive not only to the quantitative effects of embodied carbon but also to the qualitative aspects of our constructed environment. Building with biogenic materials does not need to come at the expense of architectural imagination and experimentation but quite the reverse, it should sponsor new spatial, formal, and experiential possibilities. This book is testament to different ways of dwelling on this earth that are already here. All three of us are architects, educators, and parents, and it is from that perspective that we are writing and working, with optimism for designing and realizing a vibrant, transformative, and regenerative future.

Paul Lewis, Marc Tsurumaki, David J. Lewis
New York, 2022

1 Paul Lewis, Marc Tsurumaki, and David J. Lewis, *Manual of Section* (New York: Princeton Architectural Press, 2016).

2 IPCC, *Climate Change 2022: Mitigation of Climate Change. Contribution of Working Group III to the Sixth Assessment Report of the Intergovernmental Panel on Climate Change*, P.R. Shukla, J. Skea, R. Slade, A. Al Khourdajie, R. van Diemen, D. McCollum, M. Pathak, S. Some, P. Vyas, R. Fradera, M. Belkacemi, A. Hasija, G. Lisboa, S. Luz, J. Malley, eds. (New York: Cambridge University Press, 2022). www.ipcc.ch/report/ar6/wg3/

3 Architecture 2030, *Why the Building Sector: We Must Eliminate All CO_2 Emissions from the Built Environment by 2040 to Meet 1.5°Climate Targets* (March 15, 2022). https://architecture2030.org/why-the-building-sector/ See also reports from the Carbon Leadership Forum. https://carbonleadershipforum.org/

4 Thibaut Abergel, Brian Dean, John Dulac, and International Energy Agency for the Global Alliance for Buildings and Construction, *Global Status Report: Towards a Zero-Emission, Efficient, and Resilient Building and Construction Sector* (2017): 8.

5 Bill Gates, *How to Avoid a Climate Disaster: The Solutions We Have and the Breakthroughs We Need* (New York: Alfred A. Knopf, 2021). Architecture 2030 draws on estimates that concrete production is responsible for 11%.

6 Abergel, "Global Status Report."

7 See the repository of resources and references on the intersection of human health and building materials, at the Healthy Materials Lab, Parsons School of Design. https://healthymaterialslab.org/

8 Shanna H. Swan and Stacey Colino, *How Our Modern World Is Threatening Sperm Counts, Altering Male and Female Reproductive Development, and Imperiling the Future of the Human Race* (New York: Simon & Schuster, 2022).

9 The 2017 fire that engulfed Grenfell Tower killing 72 people was attributed to the combination of plastic insulation products and their exterior building envelope assembly. See "Grenfell Tower: What Happened," *BBC News* (October 29, 2019). https://www.bbc.com/news/uk-40301289

10 Gianluca Grazieschi, Francesco Asdrubali, and Guilhem Thomas, "Embodied Energy and Carbon of Building Insulating Materials: A Critical Review," *Cleaner Environmental Systems* 2 (2021). https://doi.org/10.1016/j.cesys.2021.100032

11 Abergel, "Global Status Report."

12 "Housing Starts End 2020 Strong; Risks Ahead," Press Release, *National Association of Home Builders* (January 21, 2021). https://www.nahb.org/news-and-economics/industry-news/press-releases/2021/01/Housing-Starts-End-2020-Strong-Risks-Ahead

13 "Single-Family Home Size Continues to Trend Higher," *NAHB Now. National Association of Home Builders* (December 2, 2021). https://nahbnow.com/2021/12/single-family-home-size-continues-to-trend-higher

14 Fred A. Bernstein, "Taking Credit for Trees Planted Elsewhere Is a Whole Lot of Embodied Irony," *Dezeen* (June 18, 2021). https://www.dezeen.com/2021/06/18/carbon-negative-solo-house-perkins-will-fred-bernstein-opinion/

15 See Kathrina Simonen, *Life Cycle Assessment* (New York: Taylor & Francis Group, 2014) and John Cays, *An Environmental Life Cycle Approach to Design: LCA for Designers and the Design Market.* (Cham: Springer, 2021).

16 See Kiel Moe, *Insulating Modernism: Isolated and Non-Isolated Thermodynamics in Architecture* (Basel: Birkhäuser Verlag GmbH, 2014) and Daniel A Barber, *Modern Architecture and Climate: Design before Air Conditioning* (Princeton: Princeton University Press, 2020).

17 Forrest Meggers, "Use-Full: Embodied Entropy in an Architecture of Moving Parts," in *Embodied Energy and Design*, ed. Andrew Benjamin (Zurich: Lars Muller Publishers, 2017): 116-127.

18 Daniel Ibanez, Jane Hutton, and Kiel Moe, eds., *Wood Urbanism: From the Molecular to the Territorial* (New York: Actar Publishers, 2019).

19 Pablo van der Lugt, *Booming Bamboo: The (Re)Discovery of a Sustainable Material with Endless Possibilities* (Naarden: Materia Exhibitions B.V., 2017) and Oscar Hidalgo-López, *Bamboo: The Gift of the Gods* (Oscar Hidalgo-López, 2003).

20 Peter Edwards and Yvonne Edwards-Widmer, "The Ecological Impact of Industrially Cultivated

Bamboo," *Cultivated Building Materials: Industrialized Natural Resources for Architecture and Construction* (Basel: Birkhäuser Verlag GmbH, 2017): 80-85.

21 See for example the commercial products, Ecococon and ModCell.

22 Alison Mears, Jonsara Ruth, Irshaad Malloy, Mariana Gonzalez, and Tina Le, *Hemp + Lime: Examining the Feasibility of Building with Hemp and Lime in the USA*, Parsons Healthy Materials Lab (2020). https://healthymaterialslab.org/tool-guides/hemp-lime-1

23 Chris Magwood, *Essential Hempcrete Construction: The Complete Step-by-Step Guide* (Gabriola Island: New Society Publishers, 2016): 7.

24 James Aronson, João Santos Pereira, and Juli G. Pausas, eds., *Cork Oak Woodlands on the Edge: Ecology, Adaptive Management, and Restoration* (Washington, DC: Island Press, 2009).

25 Eduardo Goncalves, T*he Cork Report: A Study on the Economics of Cork* (Royal Society for the Protection of Birds, 2000).

26 Gernot Minke, *Building with Earth: Design and Technology of Sustainable Architecture*, 3rd ed. (Basel: Birkhäuser Verlag GmbH, 2013): 11.

27 Jean Dethier, ed., *The Art of Earth Architecture: Past, Present, Future* (New York: Princeton Architectural Press, 2020).

28 Anna Heringer, Lindsay Blair Howe, and Martin Rauch, *Upscaling Earth: Material, Process, Catalyst* (Zurich: gta Verlag ETH Zurich, 2019).

29 Peter J. Aresenault, "Reducing Embodied Energy in Masonry Construction," *Continuing Education Center: Architecture + Construction* (BNP Media, February 2012). https://continuingeducation.bnpmedia.com/article_print.php?L=219&C=878

30 Akhtar Abbas, et al., "Assessment of Long-Term Energy and Environmental Impacts of the Cleaner Technologies for Brick Production," *Energy Reports* 7 (2021): 7157-69.

31 Ansgar Schulz and Benedikt Schulz, *Manual of Natural Stone* (Munich: Detail Business Information GmbH, 2020).

32 Steward Brand, *How Buildings Learn: What Happens after They're Built* (New York: Penguin Books, 1995).

33 Daniel Abramson, *Obsolescence: An Architectural History* (Chicago: University of Chicago Press, 2016).

SELECTED BIBLIOGRAPHY

Abbas, Akhtar, et al. "Assessment of Long-Term Energy and Environmental Impacts of the Cleaner Technologies for Brick Production." *Energy Reports* 7 (2021): 7157-69.

Abergel, Thibaut, et al. *Global Status Report: Towards a Zero-Emission, Efficient, and Resilient Building and Construction Sector*, 2017.

Abergel, Thibaut, et al. *Global Status Report: Towards a Zero-Emission, Efficient and Relient Buildings and Construction Sector*: United Nations Environmental Programme, 2018.

Barber, Daniel A. *Modern Architecture and Climate: Design before Air Conditioning*. Princeton: Princeton University Press, 2020.

Benjamin, David, ed. *Embodied Energy and Design*. Zurich: Lars Muller Publishers, 2017.

Bryce, Katy, and Adam Weismann. *Clay & Lime Renders Plasters & Paints*. Cambridge: Green Books, 2018.

Cays, John. *An Environmental Life Cycle Approach to Design: Lca for Designers and the Design Market*. Cham: Springer 2021.

Churkina, Galina, et al. "Buildings as a Global Carbon Sink." *Nature Sustainability* 3.4 (2020): 269-76.

Grazieschi, Gianluca, Francesco Asdrubali, and Guilhem Thomas. "Embodied Energy and Carbon of Building Insulating Materials: A Critical Review." *Cleaner Environmental Systems* 2 (2021): 100032.

Henry, Michael, and Tina Therrien. *Essential Natural Plasters: A Guide to Materials, Recipes, and Use*. Gabriola Island: New Society Publishers, 2018.

Hill, Callum, et al. "A Comparison of the Environmental Impacts of Different Categories of Insulation Materials." *Energy and Buildings*, 2018. 12-20. Vol. 162 of 3 vols.

IPCC. *Climate Change 2021: The Physical Science Basis. Contributions of Working Group 1 to the Sixth Assessment Report of the Intergovernmental Panel on Climate Change*. Ed. V. Masson-Delmotte, P. Zhai, A. Pirani, S.L. Connors, C. Péan, S. Berger, N. Caud, Y. Chen, L. Goldfarb, M.I. Gomis, M. Huang, K. Leitzell, E. Lonnoy, J.B.R. Matthews, T.K. Maycock, T. Waterfield, O. Yelekçi, R. Yu, and B. Zhou. Cambridge: Cambridge University Press, 2021.

IPCC. *Climate Change 2022: Impacts, Adaptation, and Vulnerability. Contribution of Working Group II to the Sixth Assessment Report of the Intergovernmental Panel on Climate Change.* H.-O. Pörtner, D.C. Roberts, M. Tignor, E.S. Poloczanska, K. Mintenbeck, A. Alegría, M. Craig, S. Langsdorf, S. Löschke, V. Möller, A. Okem, B. Rama, eds. New York: Cambridge University Press, 2022.

IPCC. *Climate Change 2022: Mitigation of Climate Change. Contribution of Working Group III to the Sixth Assessment Report of the Intergovernmental Panel on Climate Change*. P.R. Shukla, J. Skea, R. Slade, A. Al Khourdajie, R. van Diemen, D. McCollum, M. Pathak, S. Some, P. Vyas, R. Fradera, M. Belkacemi, A. Hasija, G. Lisboa, S. Luz, J. Malley, eds. New York: Cambridge University Press, 2022.

King, Bruce. *The New Carbon Architecture*. Gabriola Island, BC: New Society Publishers, 2017.

Lewis, Meghan, et al. *AIA-CLF Embodied Carbon Toolkit for Architects*, 2021.

Magwood, Chris. *Making Better Buildings: A Comparative Guide to Sustainable Construction for Homeowners and Contractors*. Gabriola Island: New Society Publishers, 2014.

Moe, Kiel. *Empire, State & Building*. New York: Actar Publishers, 2017.

Moe, Kiel. *Insulating Modernism: Isolated and Non-Isolated Thermodynamics in Architecture*. Basel: Birkhäuser Verlag GmbH, 2014.

Moe, Kiel. *Unless*. New York: Actar Publishers, 2020.

Pomponi, Francesco, Catherine De Wolf, and Alice Moncaster, eds. *Embodied Carbon in Buildings: Measurement, Management and Mitigation*. Charm: Springer, 2018.

Racusin, Jacob Deva, and Ace McArleton. *The Natural Building Companion*. White River Junction: Chelsea Green Publishing, 2012.

Simonen, Kathrina. *Life Cycle Assessment*. New York: Taylor & Francis Group, 2014.

WOOD Bernheimer, Andrew, ed. *Timber in the City: Design and Construction in Mass Timber.* San Rafael: ORO Editions, 2015.

Bonner, Jennifer, and Hanif Kara, eds. *Blank: Speculations on Clt.* San Rafael: Applied Research & Design/ORO Editions, 2022.

Herzog, Thomas, et al. *Timber Construction Manual.* Trans. Gerd Soffker and Philip Thrift. Basel: Birkhäuser Verlag GmbH, 2004.

Huss, Wolfgang, Matthias Kaufmann, and Knorad Mertz. *Building in Timber: Room Modules.* Munich: Detail Business Information GmbH, 2019.

Ibanez, Daniel, Jane Hutton, and Kiel Moe, eds. *Wood Urbanism: From the Molecular to the Territorial.* New York: Actar Publishers, 2019.

Kaufmann, Hermann, and Winfried Nerdinger, eds. *Building with Timber Paths into the Future.* New York: Prestel Publishing, 2012.

Lugt, Pablo van der. *Tomorrow's Timber: Towards the Next Building Revolution.* Naarden: Material District, 2020.

Mayo, Joseph. *Solid Wood: Case Studies in Mass Timber Architecture, Technology and Design.* New York: Routledge, 2015.

McLeod, Virginia. *Detail in Contemporary Timber Architecture.* London: Laurence King Publishing Ltd, 2009.

Merz, Konrad, Anne Niemann, and Stefan Torno. *Building with Hardwood.* Munich: Detail Business Information GmbH, 2021.

BAMBOO Hebel, Dirk E. and Heisel, Felix, *Cultivated Building Materials: Industrialized Natural Resources for Architecture and Construction.* Basel: Birkhäuser Verlag GmbH, 2017.

Hidalgo-López, Oscar. *Bamboo: The Gift of the Gods.* Oscar Hidalgo-López, 2003.

Lugt, Pablo van der. *Booming Bamboo: The (Re)Discovery of a Sustainable Material with Endless Possibilities.* Naarden: Materia Exhibitions B.V., 2017.

Minke, Gernot. *Building with Bamboo: Design and Technology of a Sustainable Architecture.* Basel: Birkhäuser Verlag GmbH, 2016.

STRAW Association, California Straw Building. *Straw Bale Building Details.* Gabriola Island: New Society Publishers, 2019.

Guarneri, Andrea Bocco. *Werner Schmidt Architect: Ecology Craft Invention.* Vienna: Springer, 2013.

King, Bruce. *Design of Straw Bale Buildings: The State of the Art.* San Rafael: Green Building Press, 2006.

Magwood, Chris. *Essential Prefab Straw Bale Building.* Gabriola Island: New Society Publishers. 2016.

Minke, Gernot, and Benjamin Krick. *Straw Bale Construction Manual: Design and Technology of a Sustainable Architecture.* Basel: Birkhäuser Verlag GmbH, 2020.

HEMP Allin, Steve. *Building with Hemp.* Rusheens, Kenmare: Seedpress, 2012.

Magwood, Chris. *Essential Hempcrete Construction: The Complete Step-by-Step Guide.* Gabriola Island: New Society Publishers, 2016.

Mears, Alison, Jonsara Ruth, Irshaad Malloy, Mariana Gonzalez, Tina Le. *Hemp + Lime: Examining the Feasibility of Building with Hemp and Lime in USA.* New York: Parsons Healthy Materials Lab. 2020. https://healthymaterialslab.org/tool-guides/hemp-lime-1

Stanwix, William, and Alex Sparrow. *The Hempcrete Book: Designing and Building with Hemp-Lime.* Cambridge: Green Books, 2014.

CORK Aronson, James, João Santos Pereira, and Juli G. Pausas, eds. *Cork Oak Woodlands on the Edge: Ecology, Adaptive Management, and Restoration.* Washington, DC: Island Press, 2009.

Bounaoure, Guillaume, and Chloe Genevaux. *Cork: In Architecture, Design, Fashion, Art.* Berkeley, CA: Gingko Press, 2020.

Goncalves, Eduardo. *The Cork Report: A Study on the Economics of Cork.* Royal Society for the Protection of Birds, 2000.

EARTH Dethier, Jean, ed. *The Art of Earth Architecture: Past, Present, Future.* New York: Princeton Architectural Press, 2020.

Heringer, Anna, Lindsay Blair Howe, and Martin Rauch. *Upscaling Earth: Material, Process, Catalyst.* Zurich: gta Verlag ETH Zurich, 2019.

Minke, Gernot. *Building with Earth: Design and Technology of Sustainable Architecture.* 3rd ed. Basel: Birkhäuser Verlag GmbH, 2013.

Rael, Ronald. *Earth Architecture.* New York: Princeton Architectural Press, 2008.

Rauch, Martin. *Refined Earth Construction & Design with Rammed Earth.* Munich: Detail Business Information GmbH, 2015.

BRICK Abbas, Akhtar, et al. "Assessment of Long-Term Energy and Environmental Impacts of the Cleaner Technologies for Brick Production." *Energy Reports* 7 (2021): 7157-69.

Campbell, James W. P. *Brick: A World History.* London: Thames & Hudson, 2016.

Cartwright, Peter. *Bricklaying.* New York: McGraw Hill, 2002.

Hall, William. *Brick.* London: Phaidon Press, 2015.

Ham, Robert Benjamin. *Residential Construction Academy: Masonry, Brick and Block Construction.* Independence, KY: Cengage Learning, 2007

STONE Dernie, David. *New Stone Architecture.* New York: McGraw Hill, 2003.

Hall, William. *Stone.* London: Phaidon Press, 2019.

Schulz, Ansgar, and Benedikt Schulz. *Manual of Natural Stone.* Munich: Detail, 2020.

REUSE Abramson, Daniel. *Obsolescence: An Architectural History.* Chicago: University of Chicago Press, 2016.

Brand, Steward. *How Buildings Learn: What Happens After They're Built.* New York: Penguin Books, 1995.

Hebel, Dirk, Marta Wisniewska, and Felix Heisel. *Building from Waste.* Basel: Birkhäuser Verlag GmbH, 2014.

Hillebrandt, Annette, et al. *Manual of Recycling: Building as Sources of Materials.* Munich: Detail, 2019.

SELECTED ORGANIZATIONS

Architects Declare https://www.architectsdeclare.com/ and https://us.architectsdeclare.com
Architecture 2030 https://architecture2030.org/
Builders for Climate Action https://www.buildersforclimateaction.org/
Carbon Leadership Forum https://carbonleadershipforum.org/
Climate Justice Alliance https://climatejusticealliance.org/
Decarbonize Design https://www.decarbonizedesign.com/
Ecological Building Network https://www.ecobuildnetwork.org/
Green Science Policy Institute https://greensciencepolicy.org/
Healthy Building Network https://healthybuilding.net/
Healthy Materials Lab at Parsons School of Design https://healthymaterialslab.org/
The Intergovernmental Panel on Climate Change https://www.ipcc.ch/
The International Living Future Institute https://living-future.org/
Project Drawdown https://drawdown.org/
Regeneration https://regeneration.org/
Rocky Mountain Institute https://rmi.org/
We Act for Environmental Justice https://www.weact.org/
World Green Building Council https://www.worldgbc.org/embodied-carbon

STANDARD HOUSE

Most of the materials used in the standard house are based on a linear take, make, waste process. Many of these are extracted from the earth and are not renewable. The drilling and mining processes can have detrimental effects on the sites of extraction. The standard house contains a wide range of plastic and petro-chemical building materials.

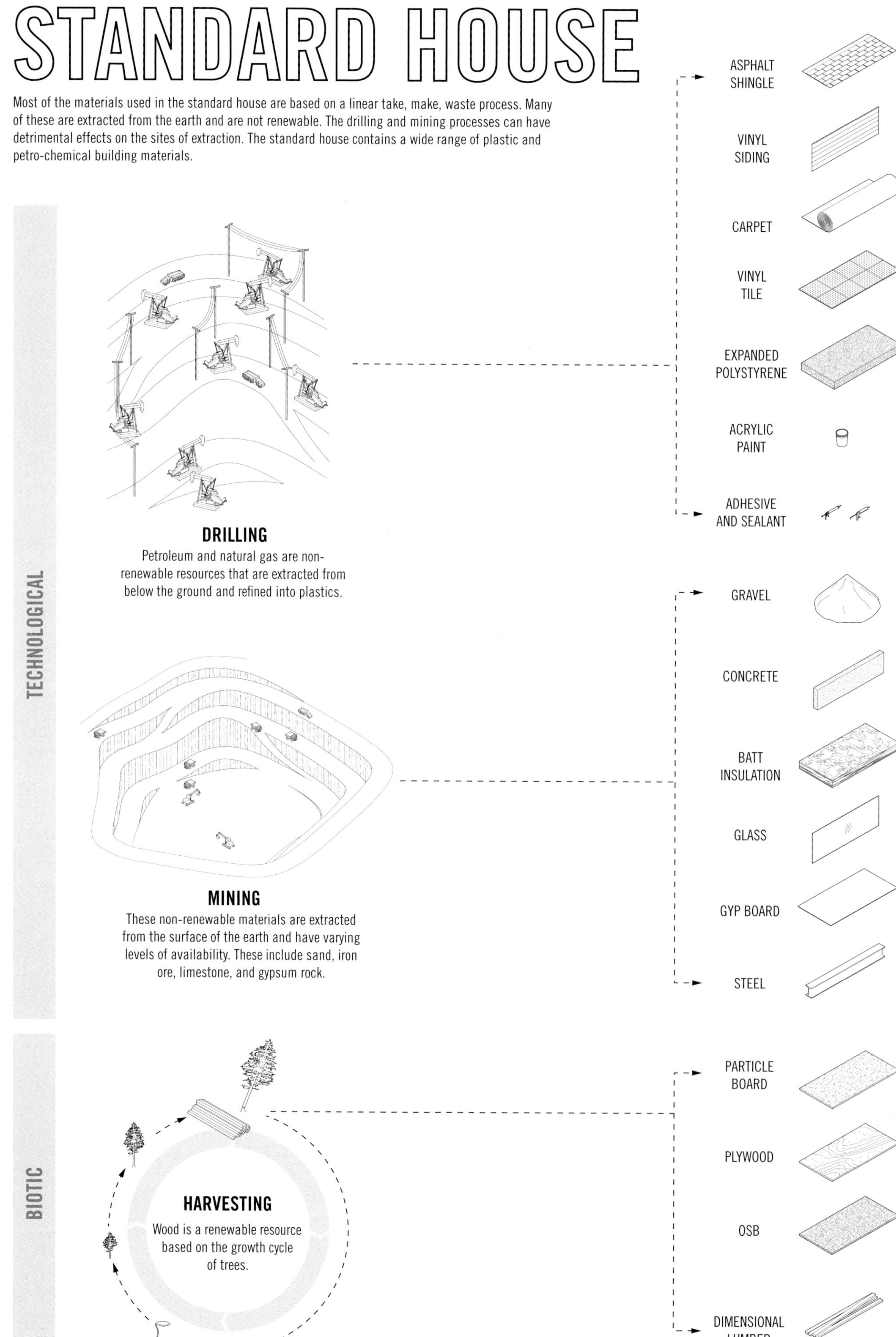

Conventional house construction produces waste at every stage of its life, from construction to renovation to demolition. A significant amount of the materials are not able to be reused or recycled and end up in landfills.

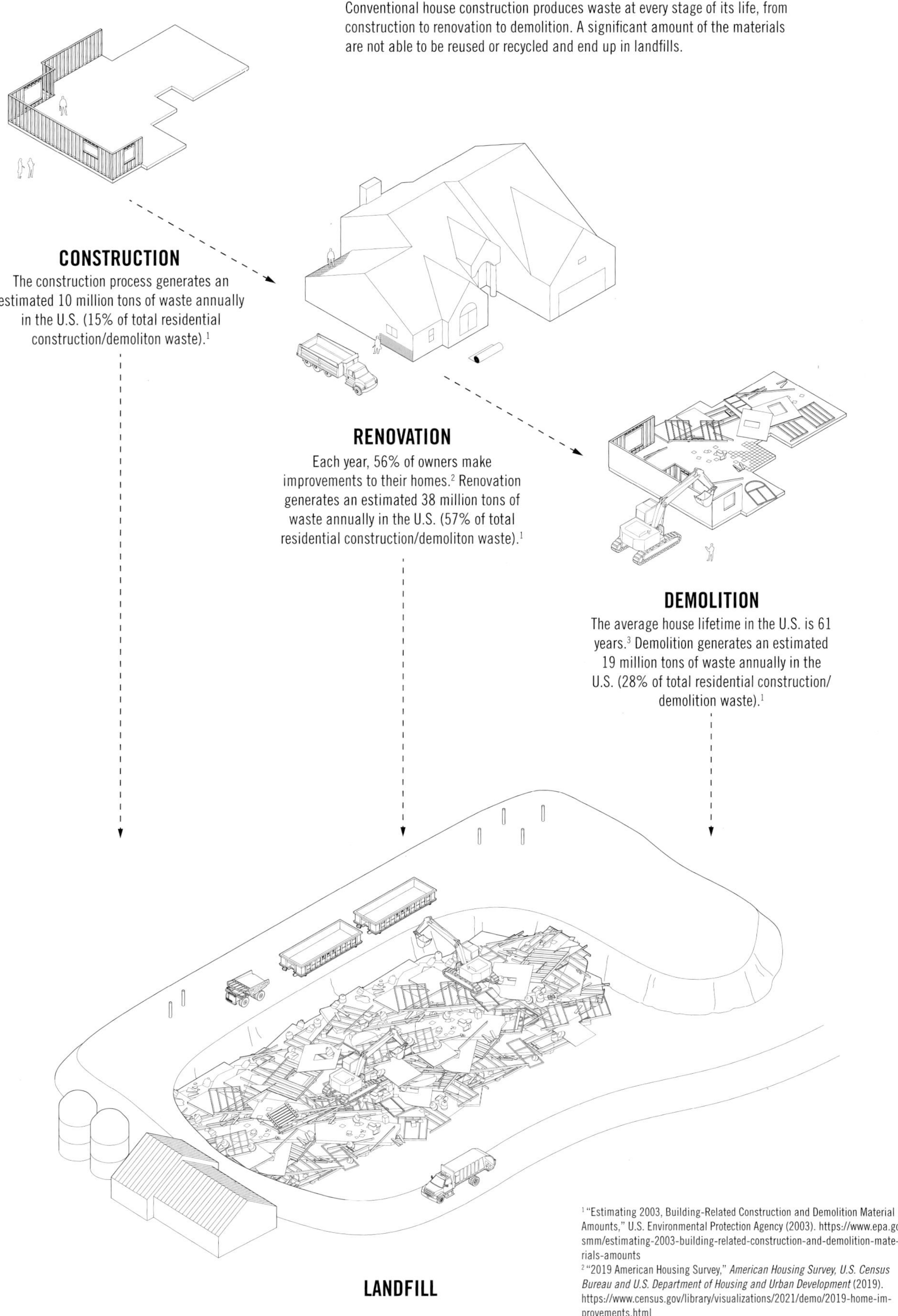

[1] "Estimating 2003, Building-Related Construction and Demolition Material Amounts," U.S. Environmental Protection Agency (2003). https://www.epa.gov/smm/estimating-2003-building-related-construction-and-demolition-materials-amounts

[2] "2019 American Housing Survey," *American Housing Survey, U.S. Census Bureau and U.S. Department of Housing and Urban Development* (2019). https://www.census.gov/library/visualizations/2021/demo/2019-home-improvements.html

[3] Can B. Aktar and M.M. Bilec, "Impact of Lifetime on U.S. Residential Building LCA Results," *The International Journal of Life Cycle Assessment*, 17.3 (2012): 337-349. doi: 10.1007/s11367-011-0363-x

STANDARD HOUSE

HIGH EMBODIED CARBON MATERIALS

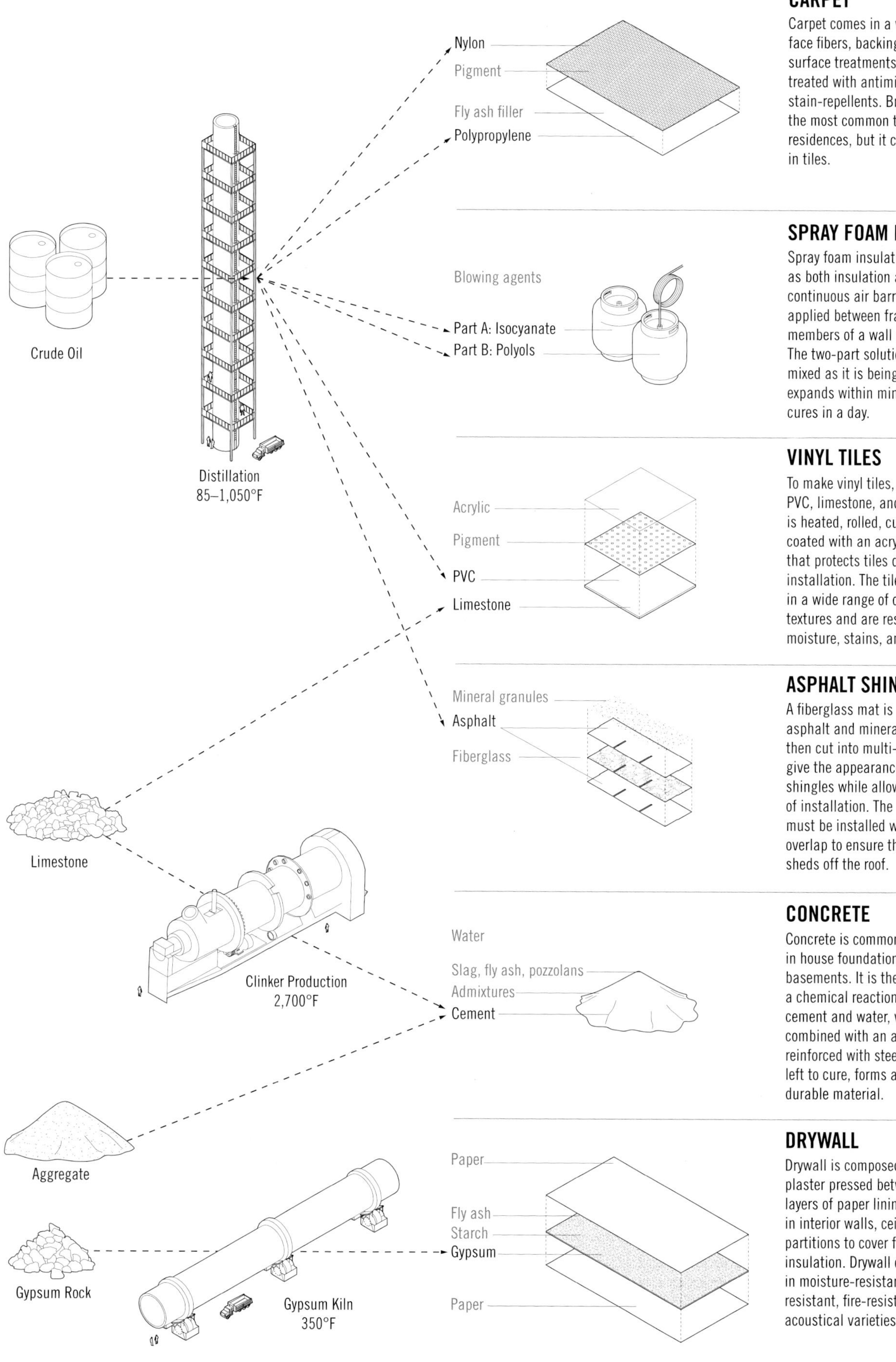

CARPET

Carpet comes in a variety of face fibers, backings, and surface treatments. It is often treated with antimicrobials and stain-repellents. Broadloom is the most common type used in residences, but it can also come in tiles.

SPRAY FOAM INSULATION

Spray foam insulation acts as both insulation and as a continuous air barrier when applied between framing members of a wall or ceiling. The two-part solution gets mixed as it is being sprayed, expands within minutes, and cures in a day.

VINYL TILES

To make vinyl tiles, a mixture of PVC, limestone, and plasticizer is heated, rolled, cut, and coated with an acrylic finish that protects tiles during installation. The tiles come in a wide range of colors and textures and are resistant to moisture, stains, and abrasion.

ASPHALT SHINGLES

A fiberglass mat is coated in asphalt and mineral granules, then cut into multi-tab strips to give the appearance of separate shingles while allowing for ease of installation. The shingles must be installed with an overlap to ensure that water sheds off the roof.

CONCRETE

Concrete is commonly used in house foundations and basements. It is the result of a chemical reaction between cement and water, which, when combined with an aggregate, reinforced with steel bars, and left to cure, forms a strong and durable material.

DRYWALL

Drywall is composed of gypsum plaster pressed between two layers of paper lining. It is used in interior walls, ceilings, and partitions to cover framing and insulation. Drywall can come in moisture-resistant, mold-resistant, fire-resistant, and acoustical varieties.

INSTALLATION	END-OF-LIFE	HUMAN HEALTH RISKS
Carpet Carpet padding	• Landfill • Some carpet manufacturers offer to take back their own product to be recycled or reused • Facing fibers can be reused in new products	• Vinyl or polypropylene backing contain hazardous organotins and phthalates • Fly ash used as filler in backings may contain heavy metals • PFAs used in stain-resistant treatments are associated with health impacts such as cancer and thyroid disease
Wood framing Sheathing Sprayed insulation	• Landfill	• Exposes installers and inhabitants to isocyanates, an asthmagen • Toxic emissions can persist past the 24 -hour curing time • Flame retardants may cause cancer and impair neurological and reproductive development
Tiles Adhesive	• Landfill • Some flooring manufacturers offer to take back their vinyl tiles to be recycled or reused	• The processing of chlorine, a key ingredient in PVC, releases chlorine gas as well as mercury, asbestos, or PFAs depending on the process used • The chemical byproducts of PVC production build up in the ecosystem locally at production facilities and globally wherever PVC is transported and used • Recycled vinyl may contain lead, arsenic, PCBs, and plasticizers
Asphalt shingles Underlayment Sheathing	• Landfill • Can be ground down, screened, and remelted for use in paving and new roofing • Can be reused as aggregate	• Worker exposure to asphalt fumes can result in headaches, rashes, fatigue, coughing, and skin cancer
Rebar	• Landfill • Can be crushed, screened, and sorted for use as aggregate	• Fly ash, which is recycled from industrial processes for use in concrete, may contain heavy metals • Cement can cause injury to the skin and lungs of workers
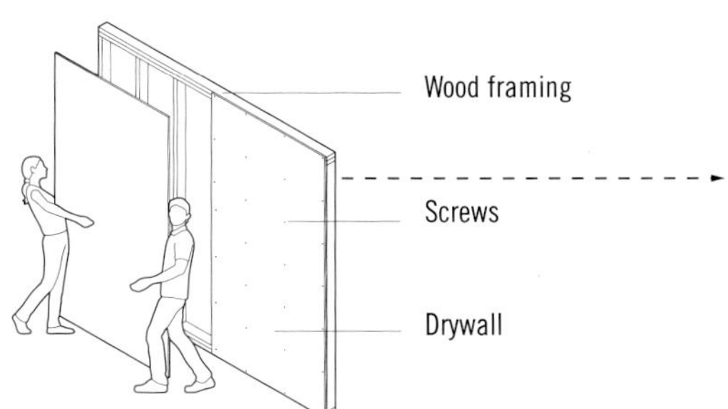	• Landfill • Gypsum can be reused in the production of new drywall or in the production of cement • Used for soil amendment to improve drainage and plant growth	• Fly ash used in recycled gypsum products may contain heavy metals that can leach out • Antimicrobials used in mold-resistant treatments may be toxic • Gypsum breaking down in landfills releases poisonous hydrogen sulfide

Standard Single-Family House

The standard single-family house, particularly in the United States, is characterized by three interlinked problems. First, they are mostly constructed of multiple, thin, lightweight layers of inexpensive material, many only doing one thing within the building assembly. Only the very thin veneers of exterior cladding and interior paint are visible, hiding these multiple layers. Second, with the exception of the wood frame, many of those materials are petroleum based, have high levels of embodied carbon, and similar levels of toxicity. Third, the average house has increased in size from 1,000 sq ft (93 sq m) in 1950 to 2,500 sq ft (232 sq m) in 2021. The embodied carbon of this illustrated standard single-family house is

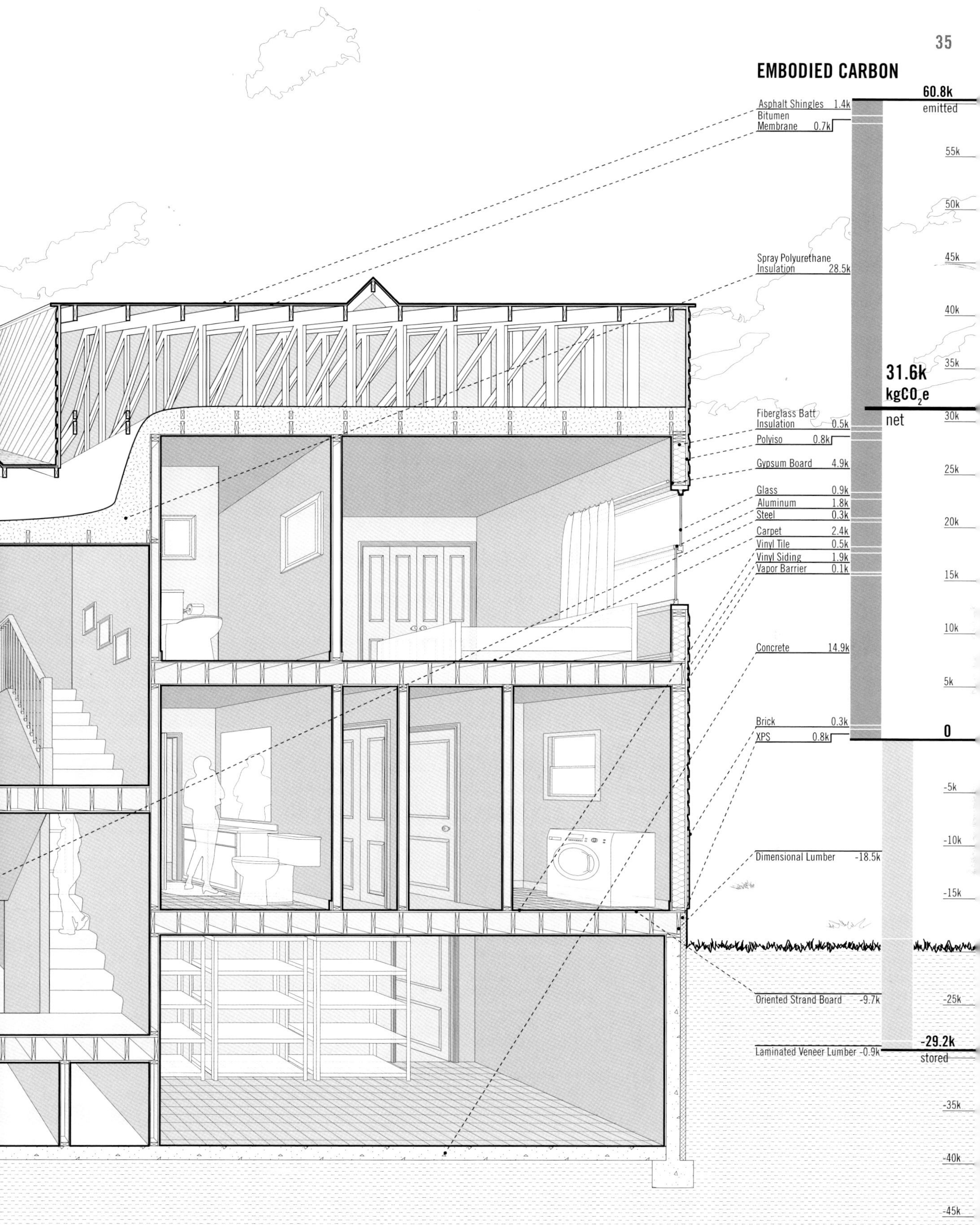

31,600 kgCO_2e. The quantity is driven by the substantial use of concrete in the foundation and basement; by the insulation made from plastics (XPS, EPS, Polyiso), fiberglass and mineral wool; by the exterior cladding such as fired brick, vinyl siding and asphalt shingles; and by the plastic interior finishes, synthetic carpets, and vinyl floors. These materials are often difficult to reuse and usually end up in a landfill. The short-term economic benefits of these inexpensive materials is countered by the longer-term health consequence of the poor interior air quality and the global environmental impacts, of which global warming is just one problem.

WOOD FRAME

800

600

400

Brick

200

Stone

Earth

0

Cork
Hemp
Straw

-200

-400

Bamboo

Wood Frame

Mass Timber

-600

-615 $kgCO_2e/m^3$

ICE

-739 $kgCO_2e/m^3$

Ökobaudat

-800

WOOD FRAME

Wood frames are the most common form of North American house construction, using standardized lumber dimensions and conventional 16 in to 24 in stud spacing. Although most wood frame construction is based on platform framing, with each floor resting on the walls below, other approaches include continuous vertical balloon framing and heavy timber post and beam. In each type, the stick construction is combined with lateral bracing, typically a stress skin of plywood or oriented-strand board. Although trees sequester carbon during their growth with about 50% of the dry weight of wood composed of carbon, lumber's value as a carbon sink is qualified by industrial harvesting, potential damage to forests, and the release of carbon stored in its soils and ecosystems. Responsible forest stewardship is a critical factor in lumber's net carbon benefits.

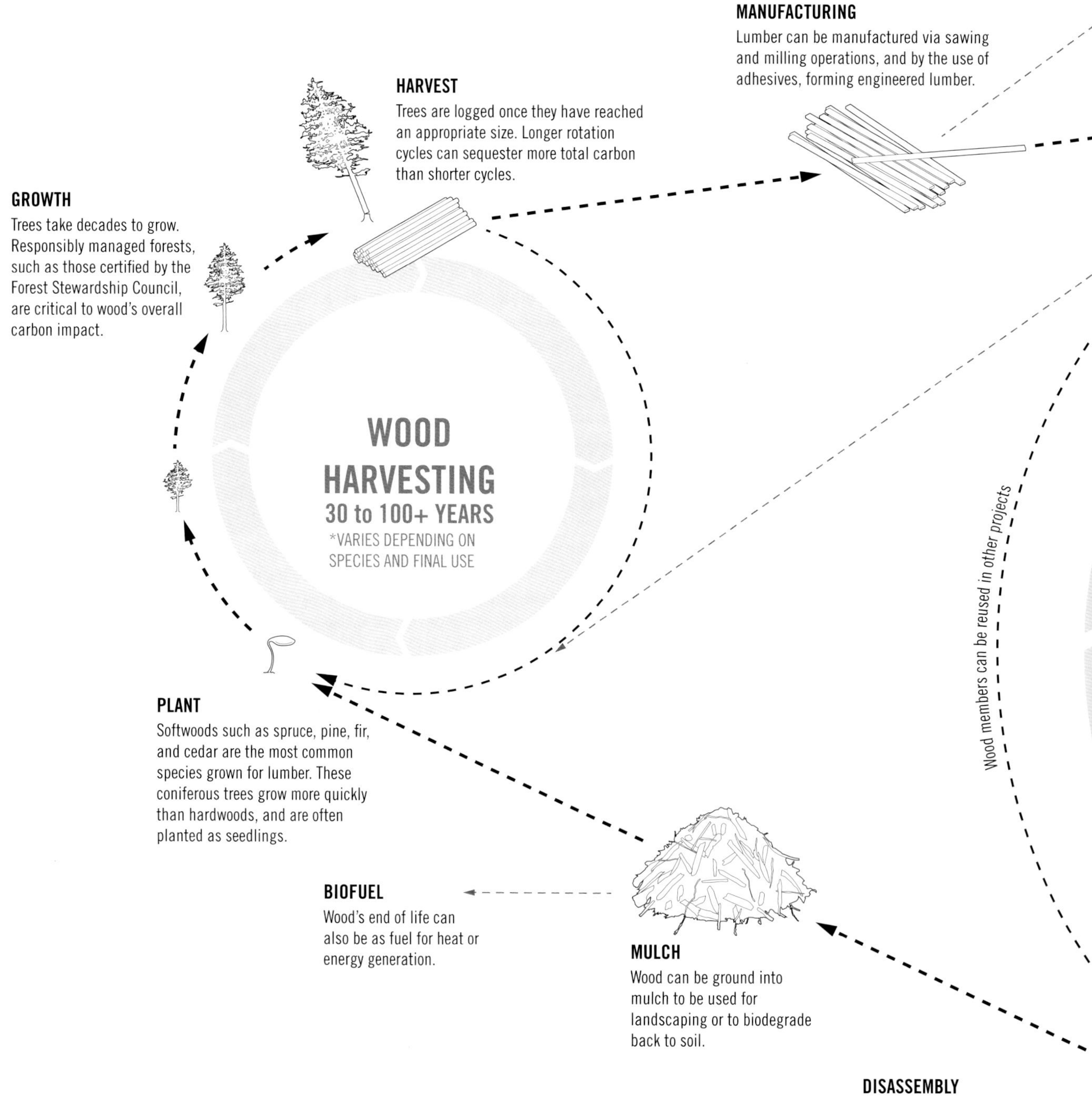

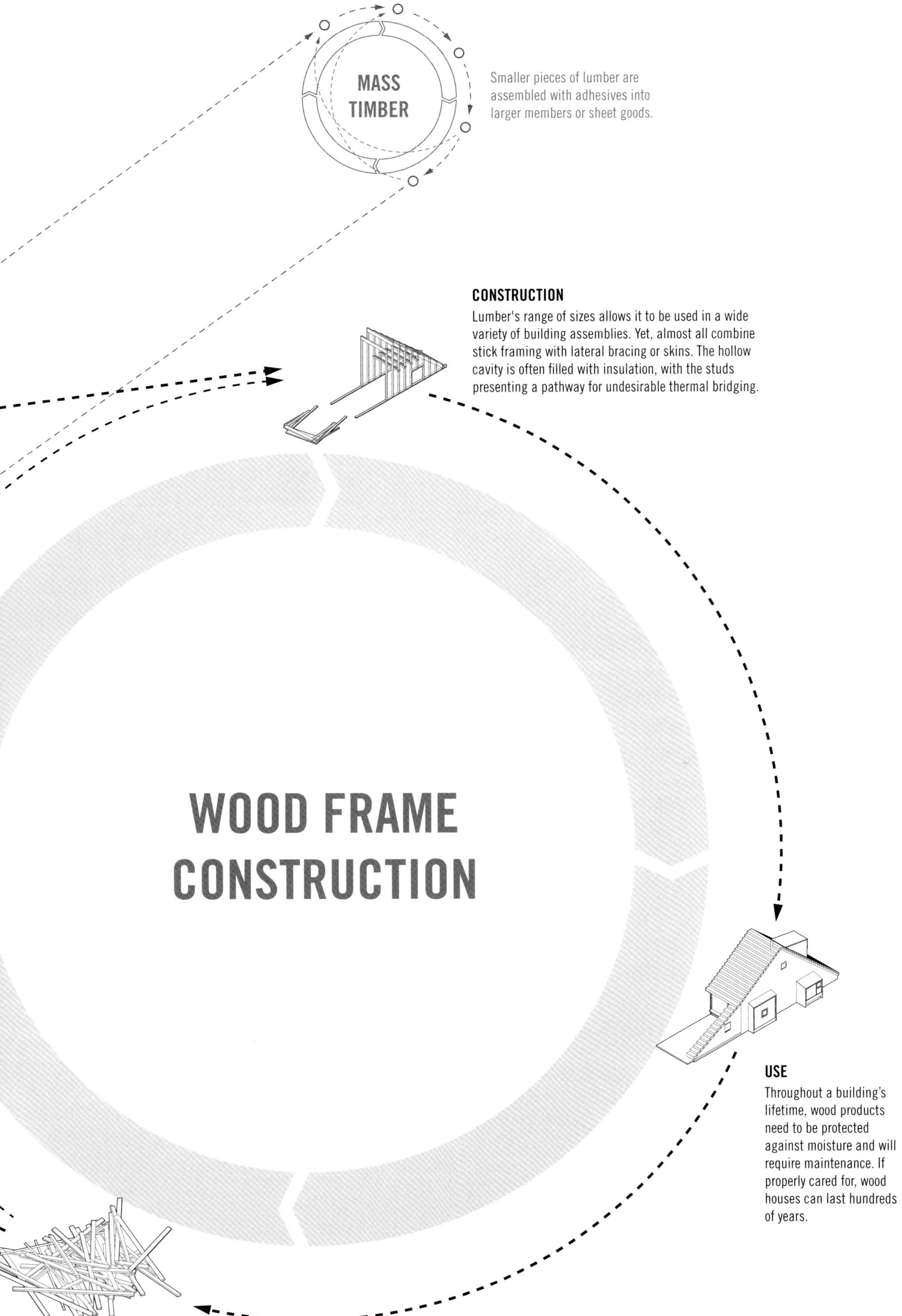
MASS
TIMBER
Smaller pieces of lumber are assembled with adhesives into larger members or sheet goods.
CONSTRUCTION
Lumber's range of sizes allows it to be used in a wide variety of building assemblies. Yet, almost all combine stick framing with lateral bracing or skins. The hollow cavity is often filled with insulation, with the studs presenting a pathway for undesirable thermal bridging.
WOOD FRAME
CONSTRUCTION
USE
Throughout a building's lifetime, wood products need to be protected against moisture and will require maintenance. If properly cared for, wood houses can last hundreds of years.

WOOD FRAME

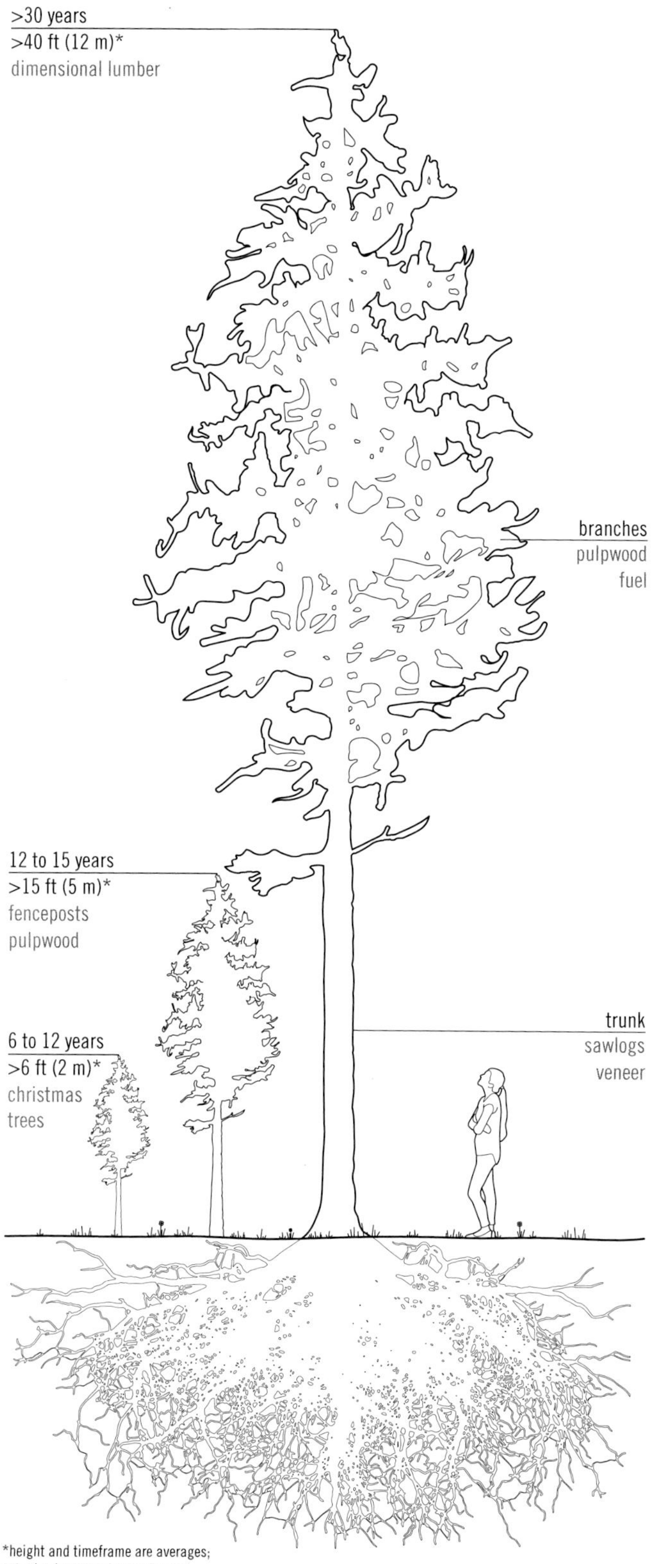

>30 years
>40 ft (12 m)*
dimensional lumber
branches
pulpwood
fuel
12 to 15 years
>15 ft (5 m)*
fenceposts
pulpwood
trunk
sawlogs
veneer
6 to 12 years
>6 ft (2 m)*
christmas
trees

*height and timeframe are averages; actual values vary by species and environmental factors

LOGGING

Essential to wood's overall carbon and environmental impact, forest stewardship standards include longer growth cycles and time between harvest, smaller clear cuts, wider waterway buffers, and limits on herbicide use.

LOGGING STRATEGIES

Clear Cut
0% Remains
Initial Planting
Vertical Thinning
First Harvest
50% Remains
Vertical Thinning
Second Harvest
25% Remains
Diagonal Thinning
First Harvest
50% Remains
Diagonal Thinning
Second Harvest
25% Remains

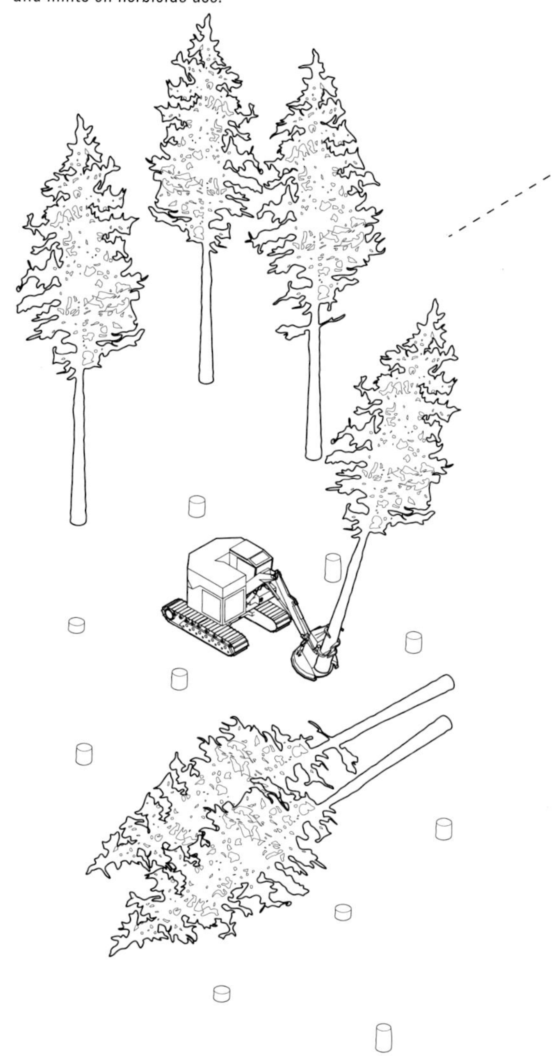

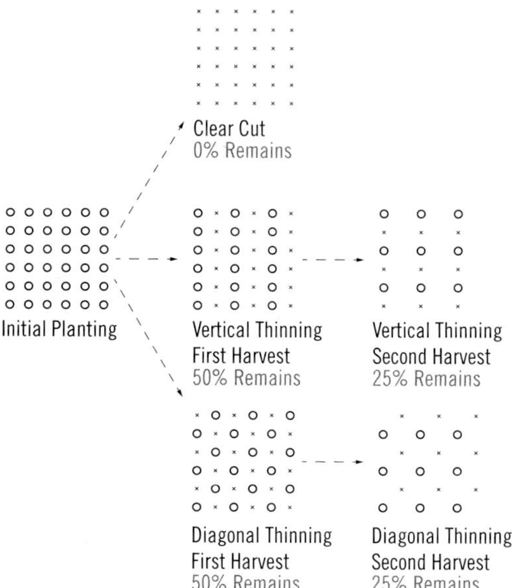

DEBARKING

The tree trunk is stripped of its bark to achieve a consistent cylindrical shape.

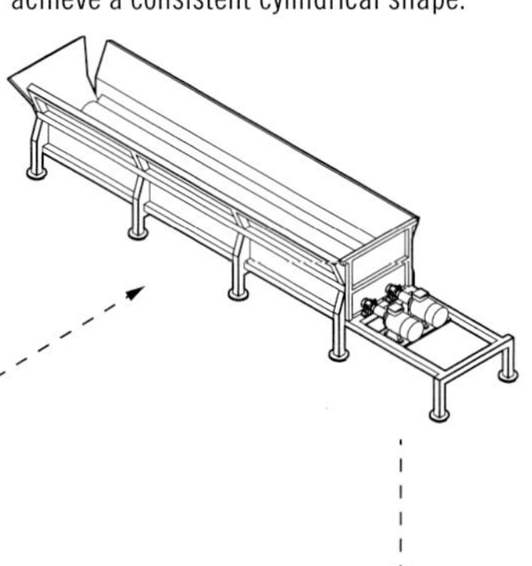

CUTTING

Logs are cut according to the desired grain pattern.

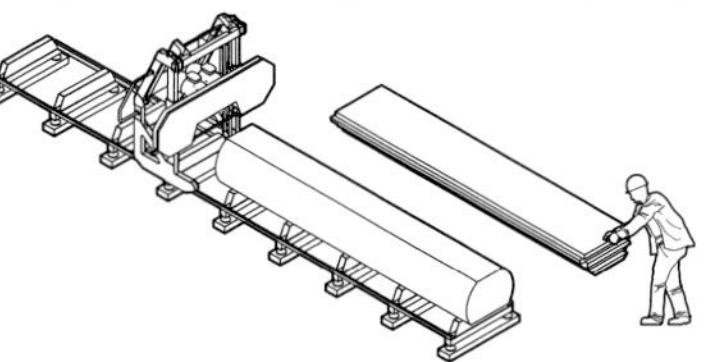

plain

quarter

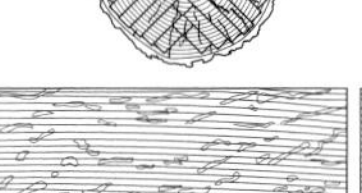

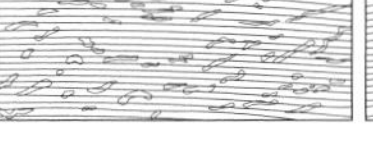

rift

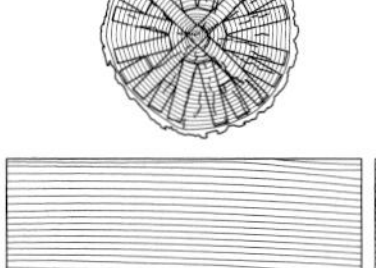

EDGING

The edges of boards are trimmed leaving clean perpendicular corners.

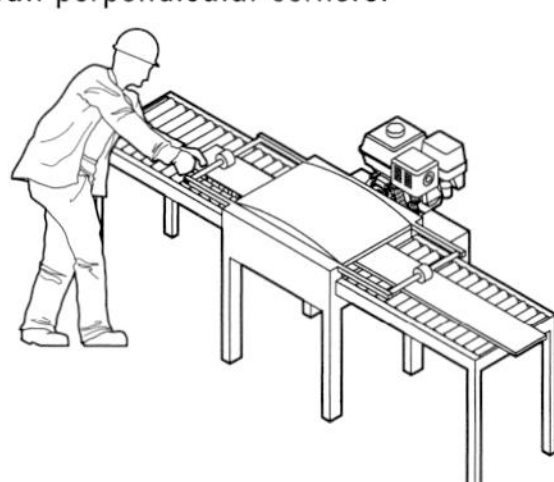

INSULATING

Wood framed walls leave a void between the studs which is often filled with insulation. More insulation can be added as a continuous layer outside of the studs which also provides a thermal break to the studs. Biogenic insulation includes cellulose, wood fiber, hemp, straw, wool, denim, and seagrass.

AIR DRYING

Boards are left to dry via natural means, which may take a year or longer. Drying is necessary to increase dimensional stability.

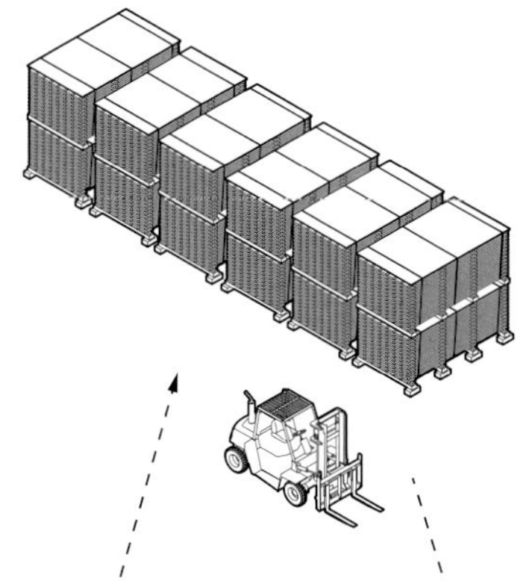

FINISHING

Planing and routing of the edges of each board produces their final dimensional profile.

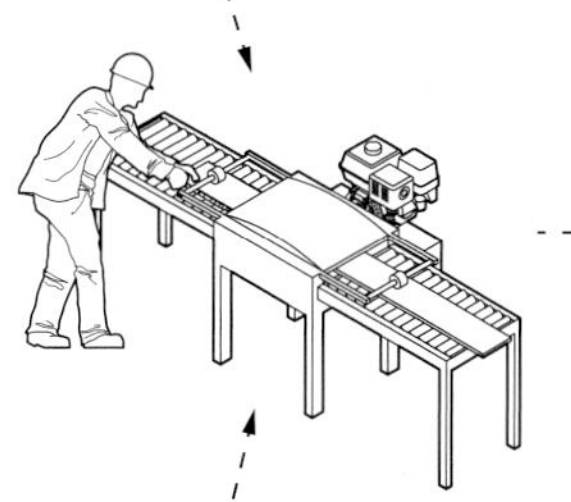

KILN DRYING

Large buildings dry the lumber via mechanical means. Drying is necessary to increase dimensional stability. Although much faster than air drying, kiln drying increases carbon emissions.

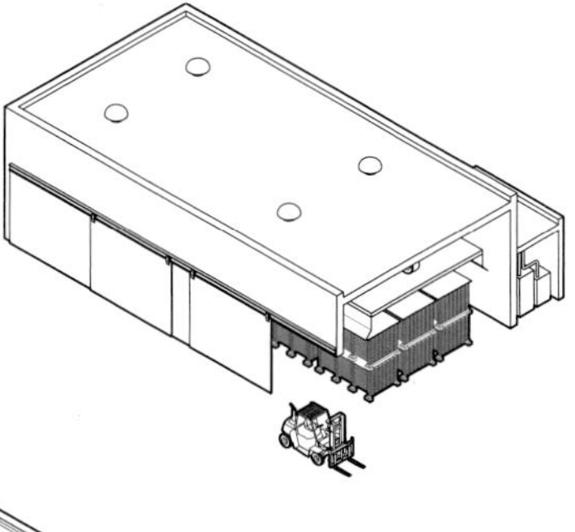

HALF TIMBER

MOMENT FRAME

LIGHT FRAMING

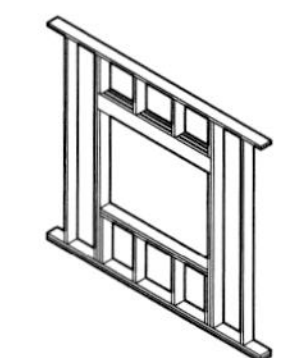

TRUSS

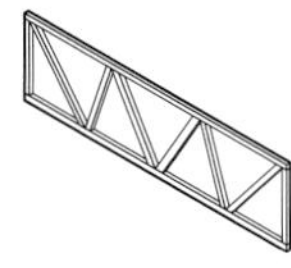

JOINERY

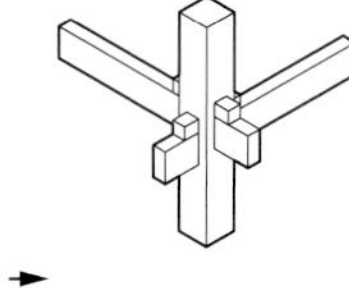

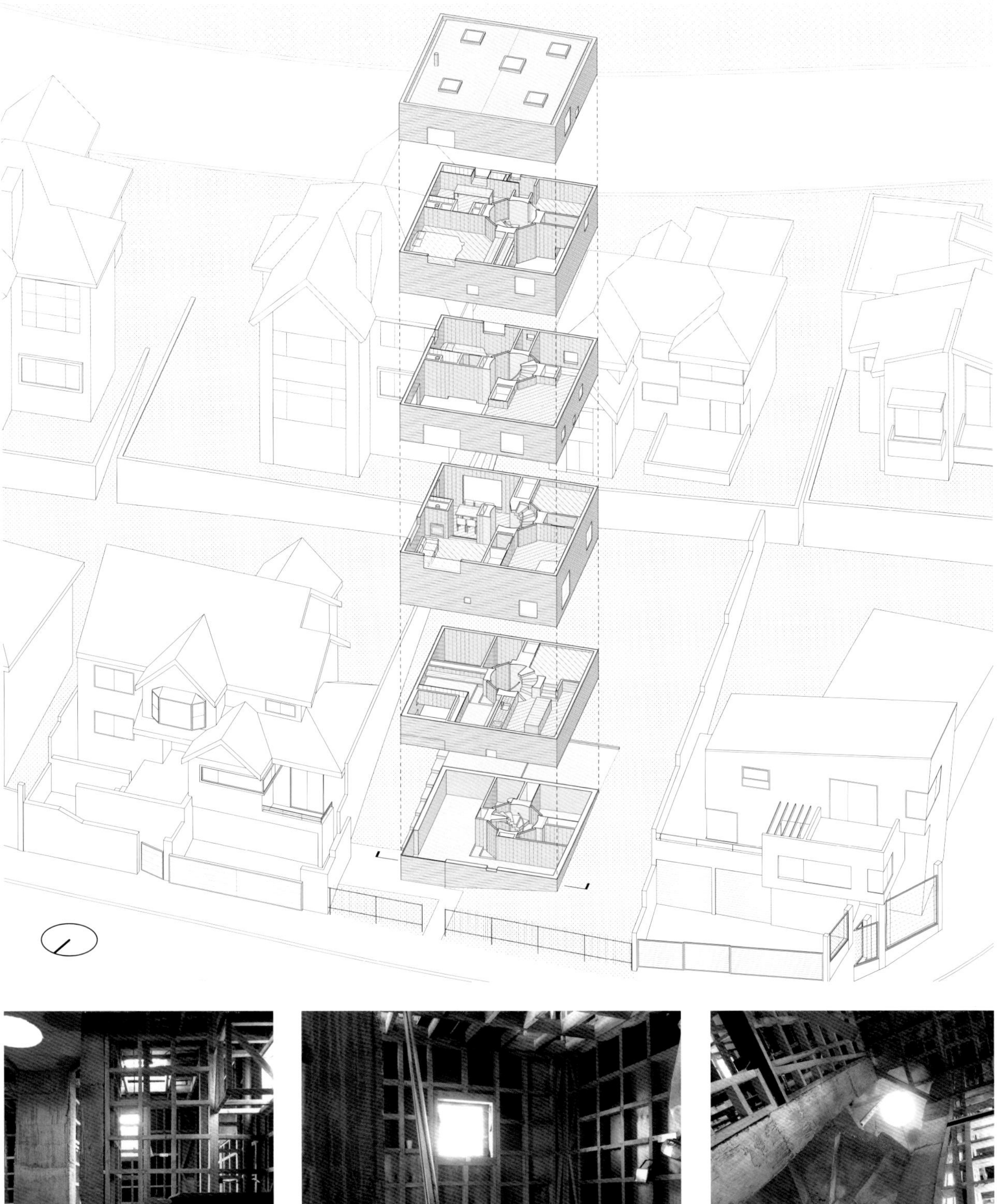

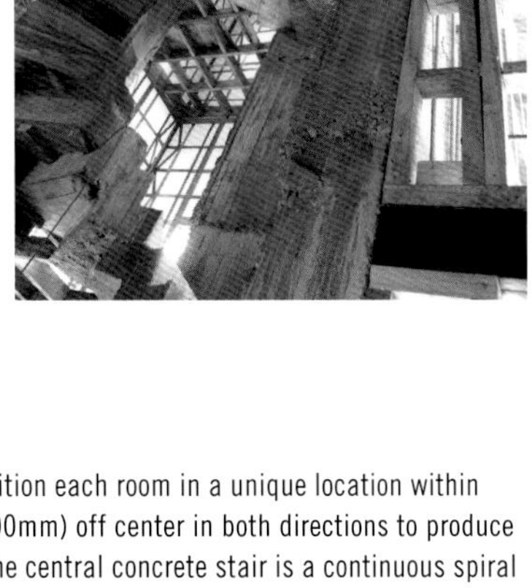

Gago House | Pezo von Ellrichshausen

In this spatially intricate house, a canonical nine-square plan is combined with a spiral of rooms in section. Evoking Adolf Loos' *Raumplan*, the volumetric relationship between the rooms activates the whole interior, whose complexity is only hinted at on the exterior through the irregular pattern of the punched windows. The robust and adaptable capacity of lightweight wood framing is used to position each room in a unique location within the section. Placed 20 in (500mm) off center in both directions to produce three different room sizes, the central concrete stair is a continuous spiral without landings. The stair is also a porous oversized column linking and supporting all the rooms at their corners enabling quick movement

San Pedro, Chile | 2012

throughout the house. On the lower floors, a kitchen, two dining rooms, and a main double-height living area are also connected to each other through partial flights of steps installed in the thickness between the rooms. Bedrooms and other more private rooms are located at the top of the spiral.

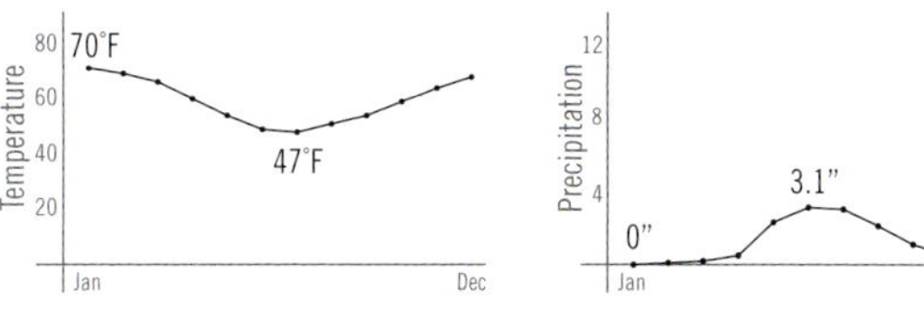

Gago House

The section reveals the complex relationship between this building's space and structure. The concrete spiral stair, positioned slightly offset in the plan, forms a central core or column, itself divided into four facets in plan aligned with the poché service zones. The walls and floors of every room are framed in a flush grid of wood, surfaced on both sides in pine boards. This self-similarity of all surfaces reinforces the volumetric focus of the design, and is enabled by the tactical quality of lightweight wood framing. Small steel beams flush with the wood joists are used sparingly toward

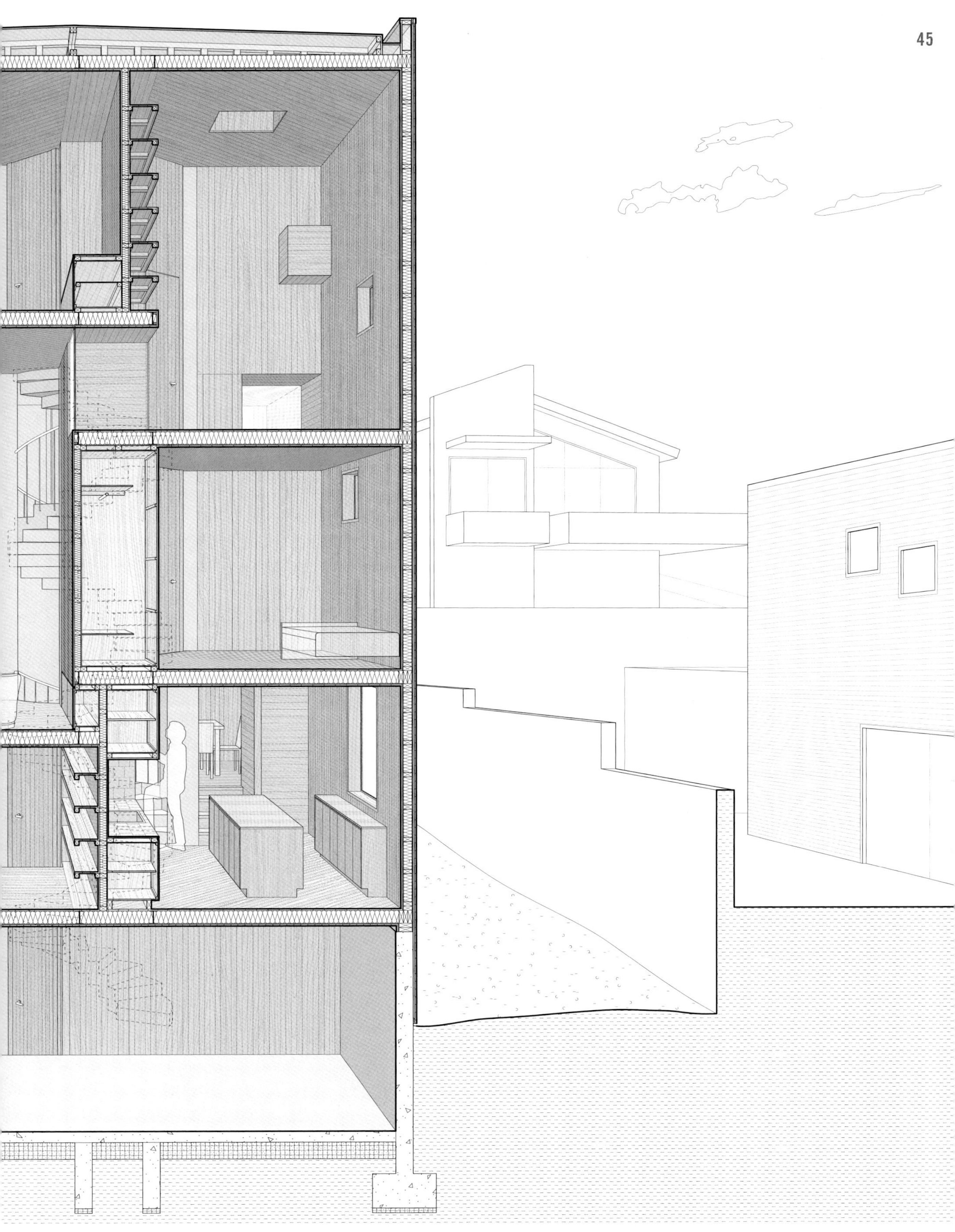

the corners of the room volumes, primarily spanning between the concrete stair and exterior load-bearing wall. Openings both from room to room, and also through the space of the hollow stair, activate the dynamic space that unfolds within the building. With minimal frames, the glass of the square windows appears flush with the exterior wood cladding. The thinness of these punched apertures contrasts with the more volumetric quality of the interior, and allows light to activate Gago House's intricate spaces.

Zilvar House | ASGK Design

Located at the edge of a small residential community in the Czech countryside, this 980 sq ft (91 sq m) house appears as a figural solid volume floating above the ground. The rectangular form of the house is sculpted in plan on its ground floor to produce covered exterior porches directly linked to the interior; the largest one to the east can be covered with large sliding panels. In plan, space is activated by editing away from the rectangular perimeter, while in section, the house is torqued to extend upward at opposite corners to provide sleeping loft spaces on either side of the central living room. This oblique movement is reinforced by two different staircases accessing the loft spaces. Although built with wood

Lodín, Czech Republic | 2013

framing, the house reads as a playful experiment with mass, reinforced by the uniform wood cladding of the interior and exterior and the thickness of the well-insulated enclosure.

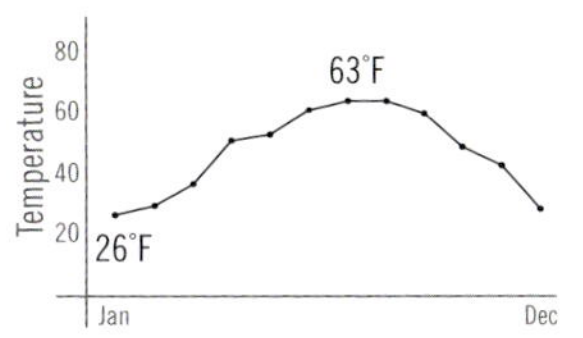

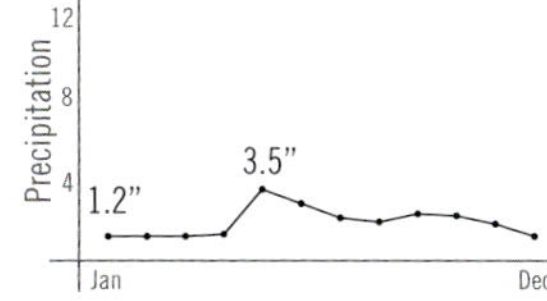

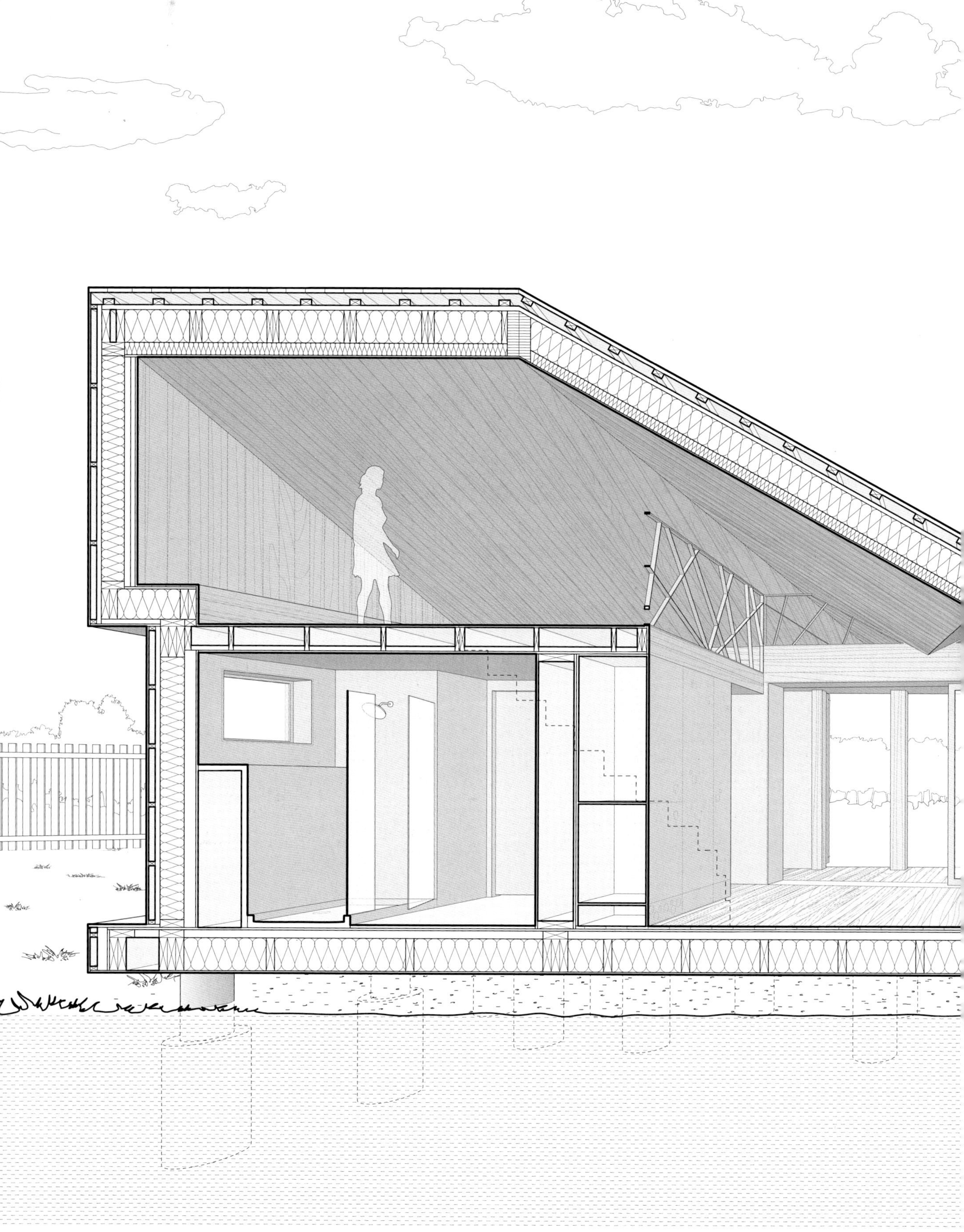

Zilvar House

Four of the distinctive qualities of this house are legible in the section perspective. First, the hierarchy of the wood framing registers the faceting of the roof, which is contoured for sleeping lofts and used to link the house to specific features in the landscape through carefully placed apertures. Positioned oblique to the rectilinear perimeter, larger structural wood beams are located at the folds of the roof, spanning to the load-bearing walls. Second, using both fiberboard and mineral wool, the walls and ceiling contain 9 and 12 in (220 and 300 mm) of insulation respectively, and their thickness is accentuated by the additional space of the ventilated wood rainscreen. This robust enclosure provides a substantial cocoon for

this modest interior, heated by radiant panels and a single central stove. Third, the walls, floors, and roof, on their interior and exterior, are all clad in wood boards. On the exterior, the wood is charred and stained to increase its durability in weather. The consistency of this material allows for the shifts in the directionality of the wood boards to subtly mark the faceting that defines the building's form. And lastly, the whole volume of the house rests on a series of concrete piers, lifting its distinctive figural form above the often damp ground.

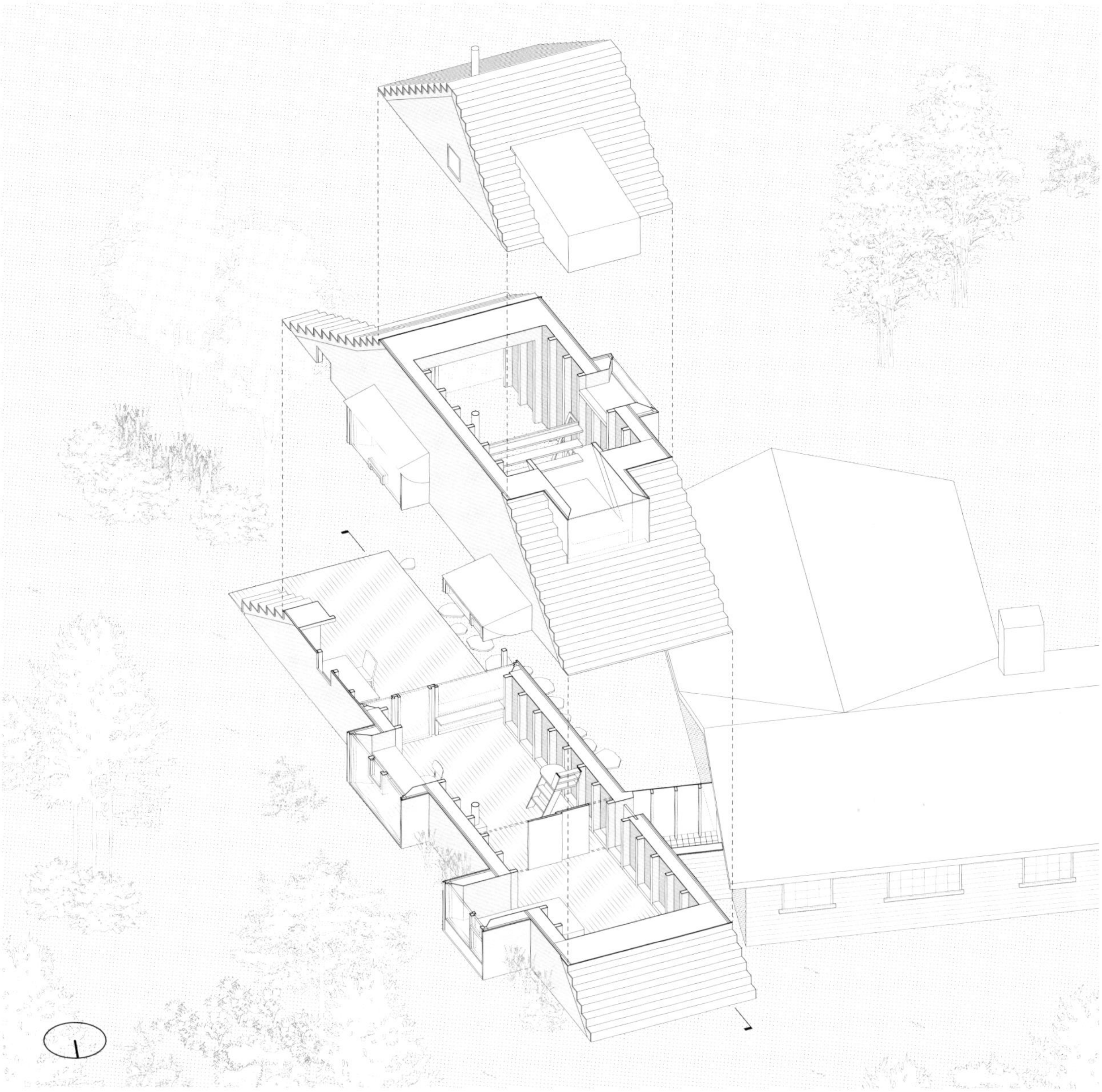

Thunder Top Cabin | Gartnerfuglen Arkitekter

Built as an addition to a Norwegian house, this cabin uses a stepped roof to embed the house in the often-snow-covered landscape, while also reflecting the stacked log structure of the existing building. The cabin's shape allows it to be buried by snow each winter and, over many seasons, to be slowly reabsorbed by its natural context through entropy and the accumulation of plant matter. Capable of being both climbed up or skied down, the shape of the roof reaches almost 20 ft (7 m) high providing an elevated panorama. The shape also protects an outside patio to the south from northern winds. The interior is conceived as a single room heated by a central wood burning stove. With their full depth inboard of the walls, the

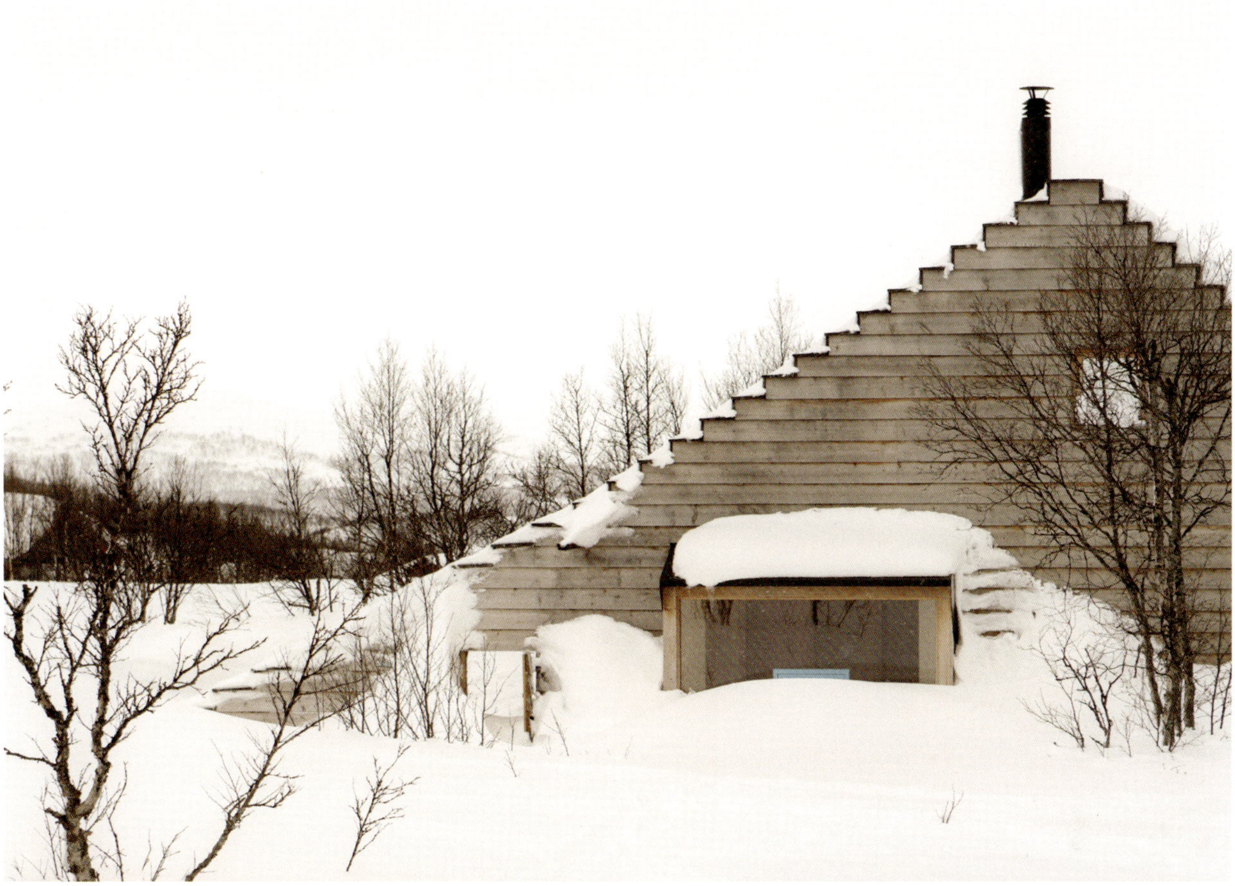

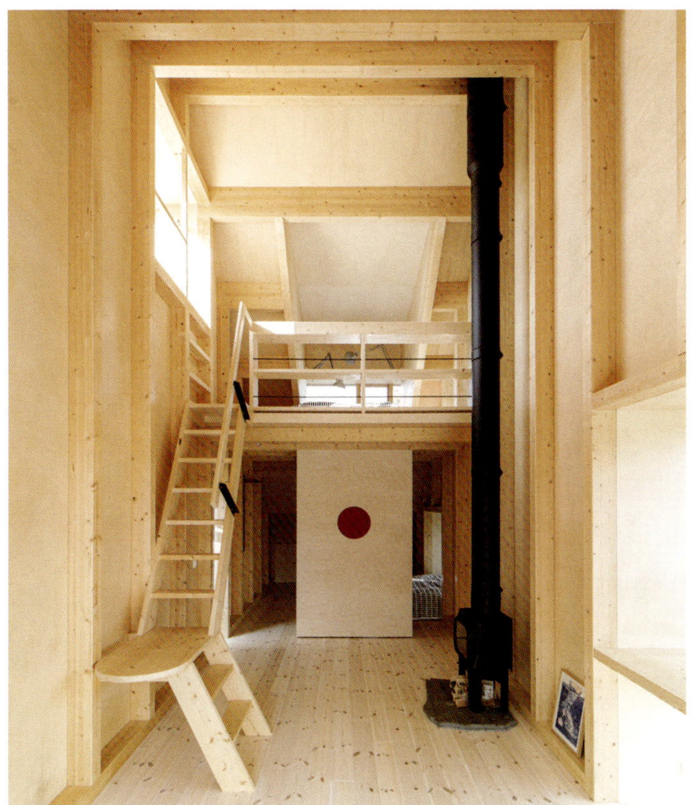

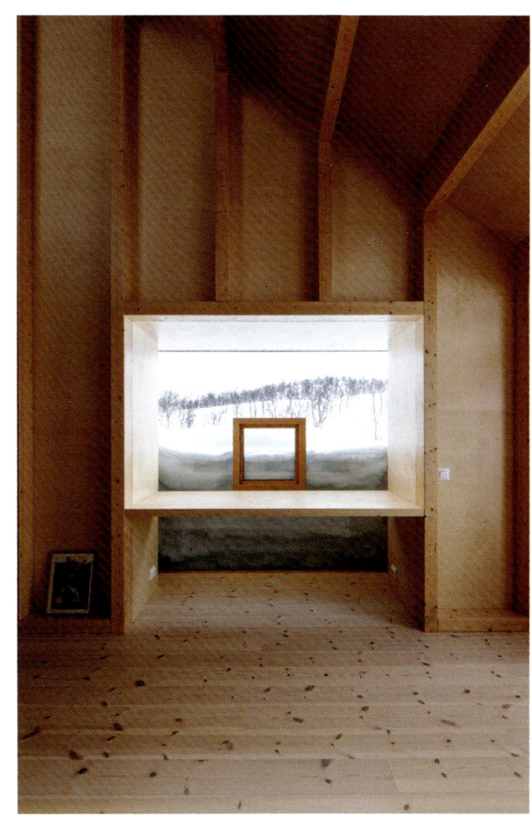

Telemark, Norway | 2018

structural ribs of pine mark the changes in the building's stepped section and support a sleeping loft at one end. The thickness of the insulated walls is intensified through even deeper niches that allow one to sleep in or otherwise inhabit the walls.

Temperature
80
60
40
20
60°F
20°F
Jan
Dec

Precipitation
12
8
4
1.5"
4.1"
Jan
Dec

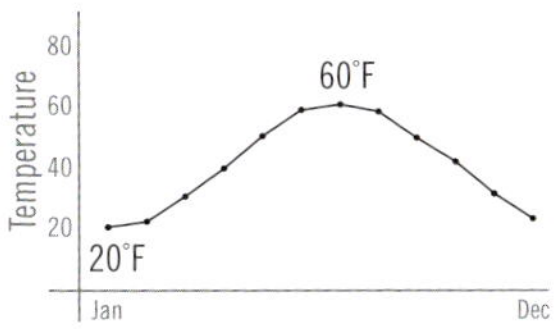

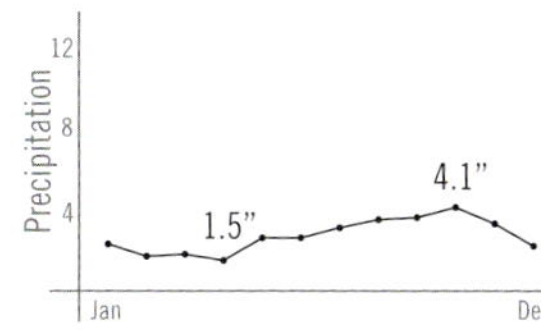

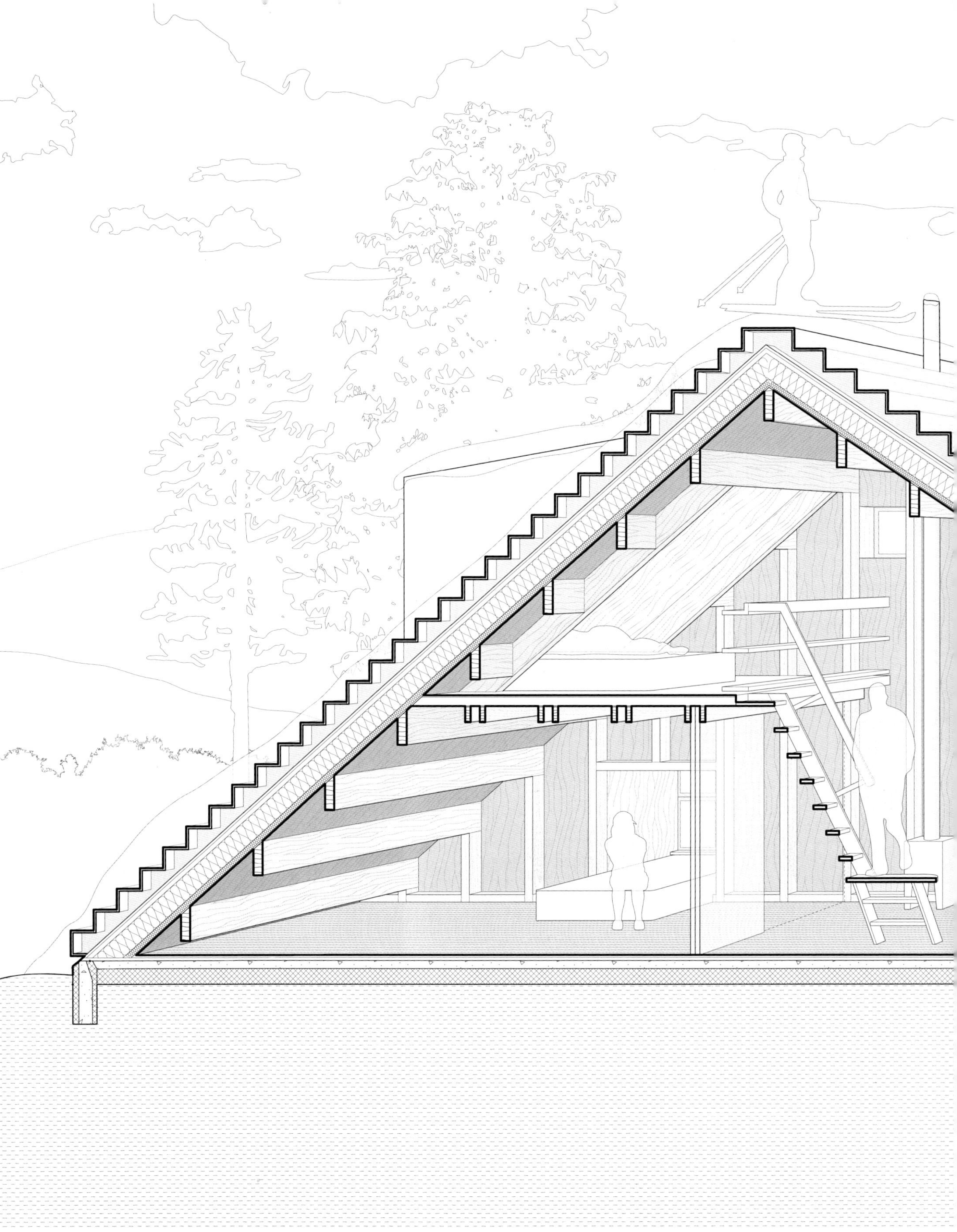

Thunder Top Cabin

Both the exterior walls and the roof of the cabin are clad in untreated heartwood ore pine, which reinforces the reading of the building as a coherent and symmetrical monolithic figure within the Hardangervidda National Park landscape. However, the angles of the 30 steps on either side of the building are slightly different, with the northern side steeper than the south to better orient the building relative to winter winds. The mass of the southern incline is eroded by an exterior courtyard, which is connected to the elongated interior through a glass wall and door. Rather than embed the structural frame in the wall, the pine ribs are fully expressed on the interior, and matched in thickness by the stringers and steps on the

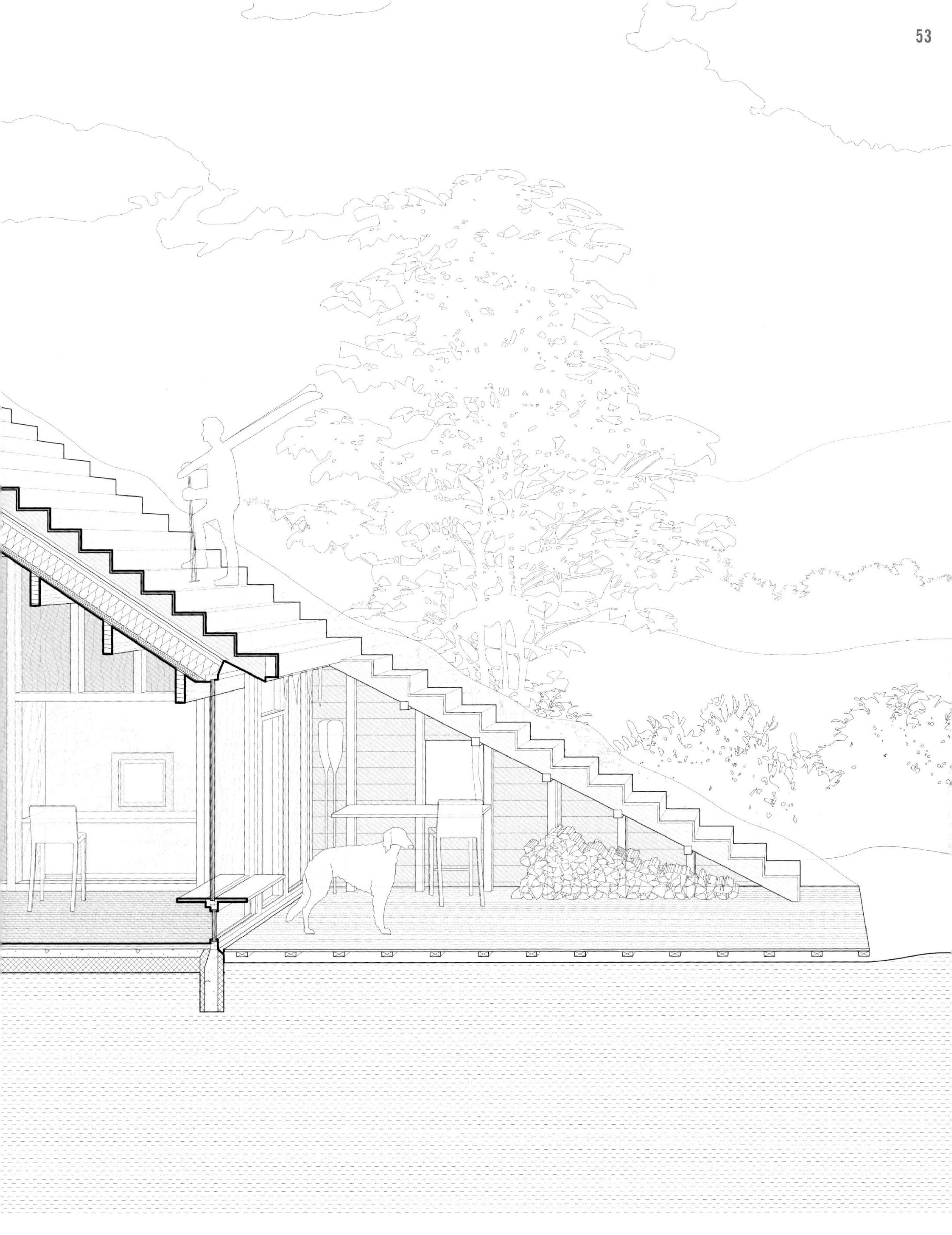

exterior. Between these two outboard layers is an insulating sandwich of two zones of mineral wool about 10 in (250 mm) thick, air and water barriers, and interior and exterior plywood sheathing. This depth enables this wood structure to be conceived as a form of poché, a characteristic more often associated with load-bearing masonry. This quality is made legible through the position and detailing of the sleeping niches, facilitating the ability to occupy this wood poché. This depth is further intensified when the cabin is enveloped by many feet of snow.

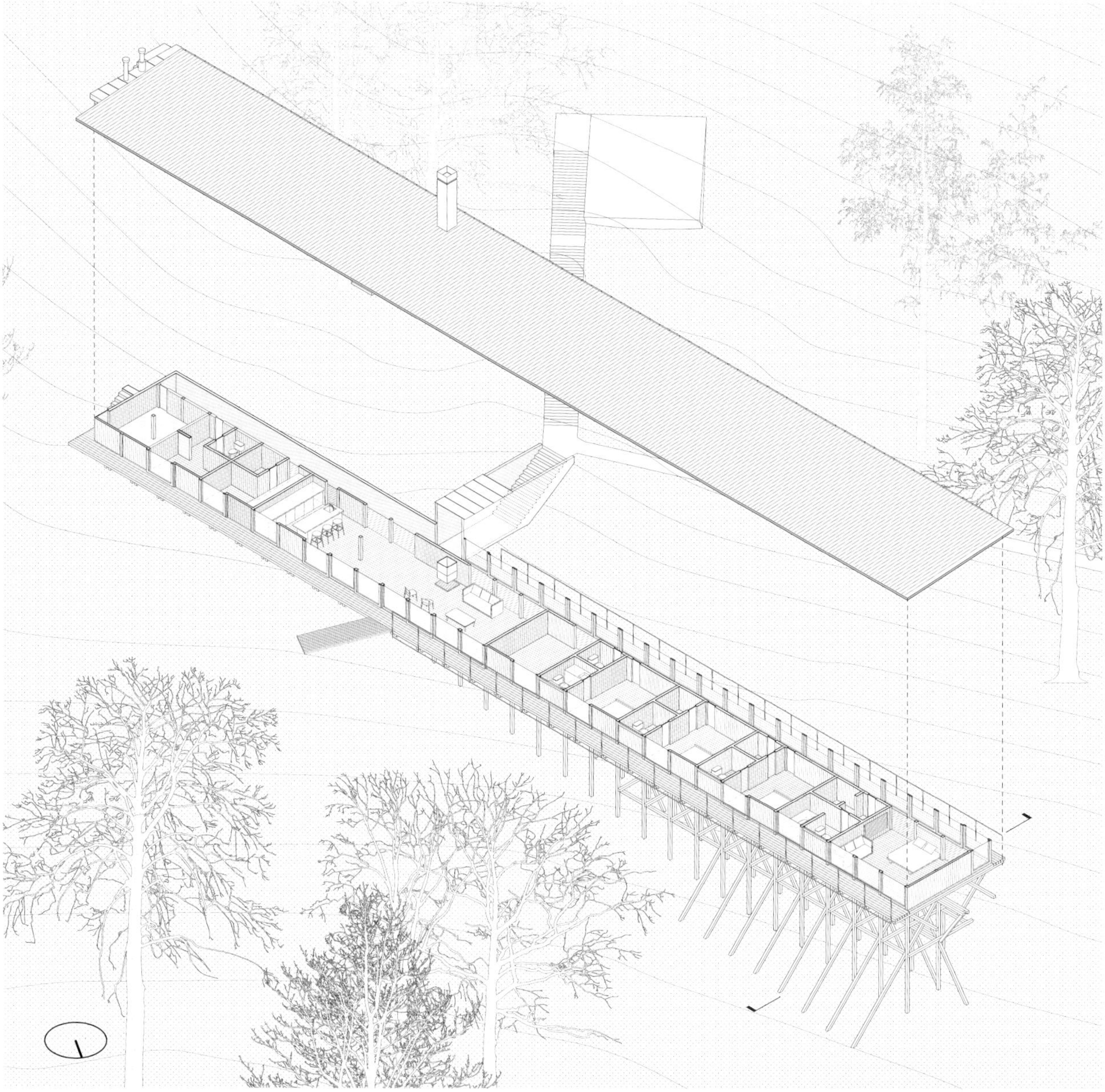

Wood House | Smiljan Radic

This house is located parallel to the edge of a lake in the foothills of the Andes Mountains. At approximately 28.5 ft (8.7 m) wide by 200 ft (61 m) long, the house is stretched very thin allowing all rooms views toward the lake and up toward the hill. Positioned slightly oblique to the slope of the hill, the single long floor is held aloft by increasingly tall stilts, which acquire more cross-bracing as the height increases. Similar to railroad trestles, the house uses self-similar wood members at different quantities to support a continuous horizontal above the topography. One enters the

Colico Lake, Chile | 2015

house by descending into the ground as part of the house is lodged into the hillside. An enfilade series of rooms is flanked by one interior and two exterior corridors, underscoring the elongation of the house, and allowing one to emerge among the tops of trees.

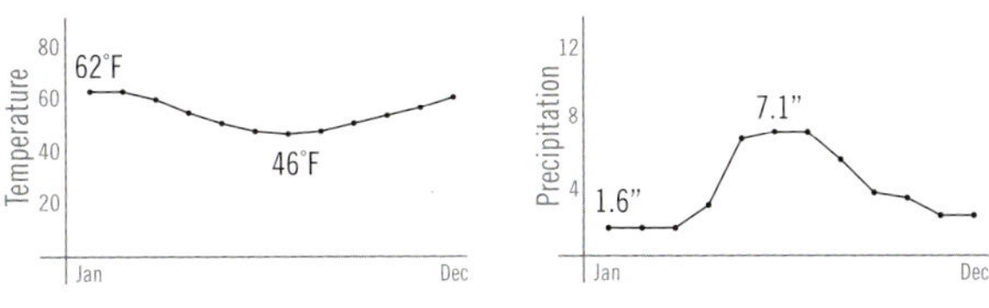

Wood House

The structure is almost entirely composed of 5.5 in (140 mm) square wood members, whose lengths are continuous, not spliced from multiple pieces. In contrast to the convention of hiding joists by aligning them as thin planes or with walls, the framing is fully expressed three-dimensionally as pairs of beams that are bolted to posts. Furthermore, the use of the wood resists typical typological limits, for while the scale and cadence of the individual members is closer to stick framing, the spacing of structural elements is more akin to timber framing. This inventive approach is also

reflected in a subtle inversion at the roof. Here two heavy beams running the length of the house are notched at their base to suspend the paired joists that support the overhanging eaves and the smaller roof over the interior corridor. Although the exposed structure below the house is nearly symmetrical, the floor is shifted to the south, while the roof is offset in the other direction, extending shading toward the north. By staining all the wood black, the material's surface effects are also transformed, consistent with the enigmatic and inventive tectonic quality of the house.

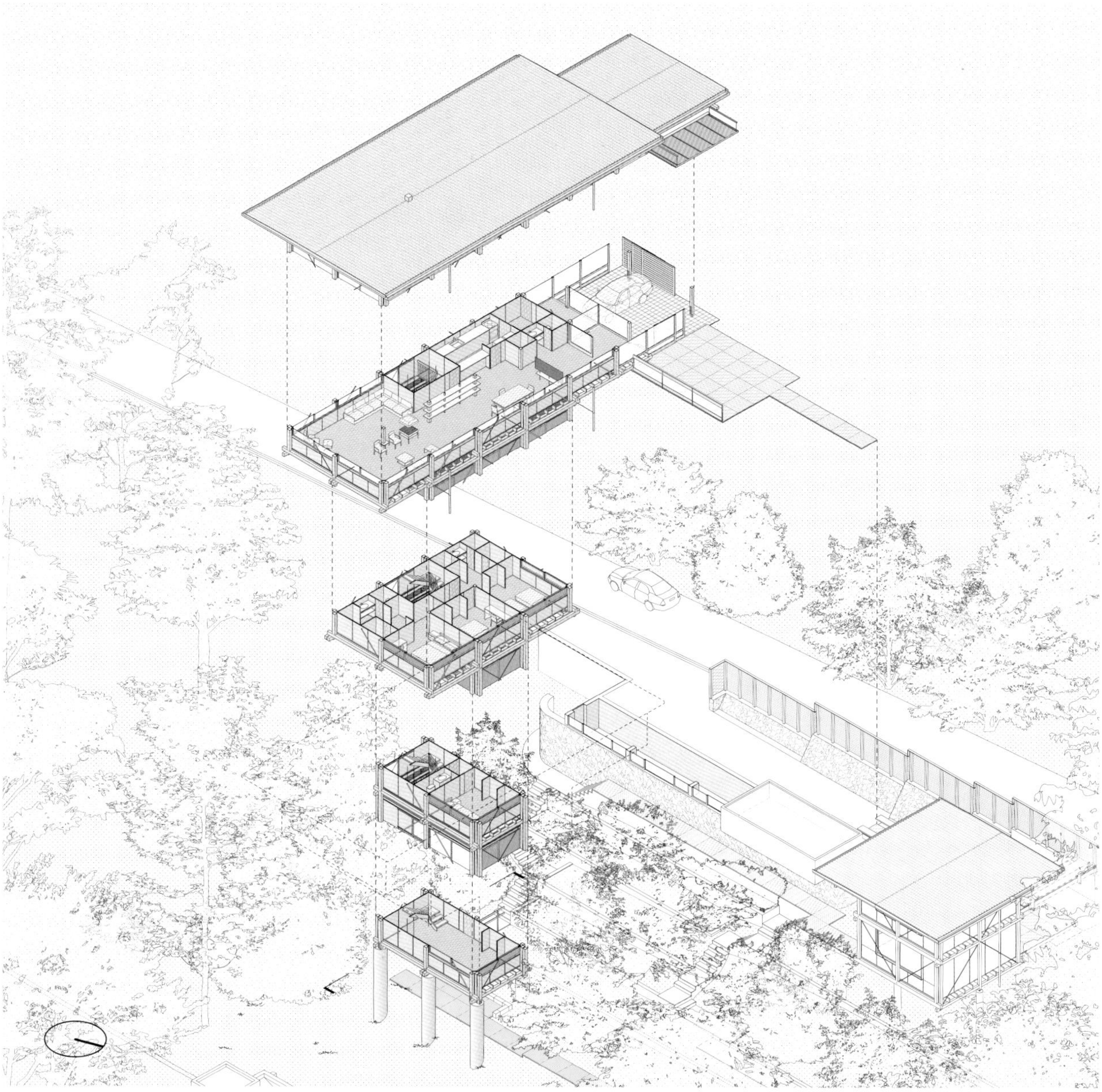

Helio Olga House | Marcos Acayaba Arquitetos

Built as a more efficient and less expensive way to inhabit a steep slope, this house is constructed from a wood frame in an inverted stepped pyramidal section. As such, the house is supported by only six slender concrete piers at its base, but expands to a large living area on the top level contiguous with the upper elevation of the site. With its wood structure positioned on the exterior, the interior of the house comprises 20 cubes of space, with 10 forming the main living, kitchen, and dining floor; six on the floor below housing three bedrooms; and two additional levels

São Paulo, Brazil | 1990

of two volumes containing a guest bedroom and den. A single stair on the southern side connects vertically between all the levels. Continuous ribbon windows on each level provide panoramic views of the city to the east.

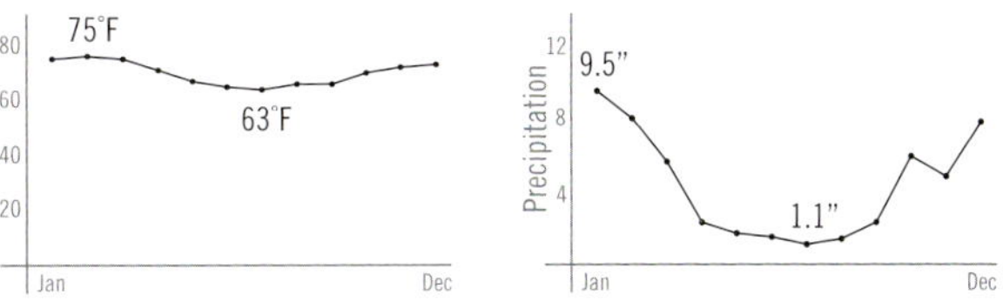

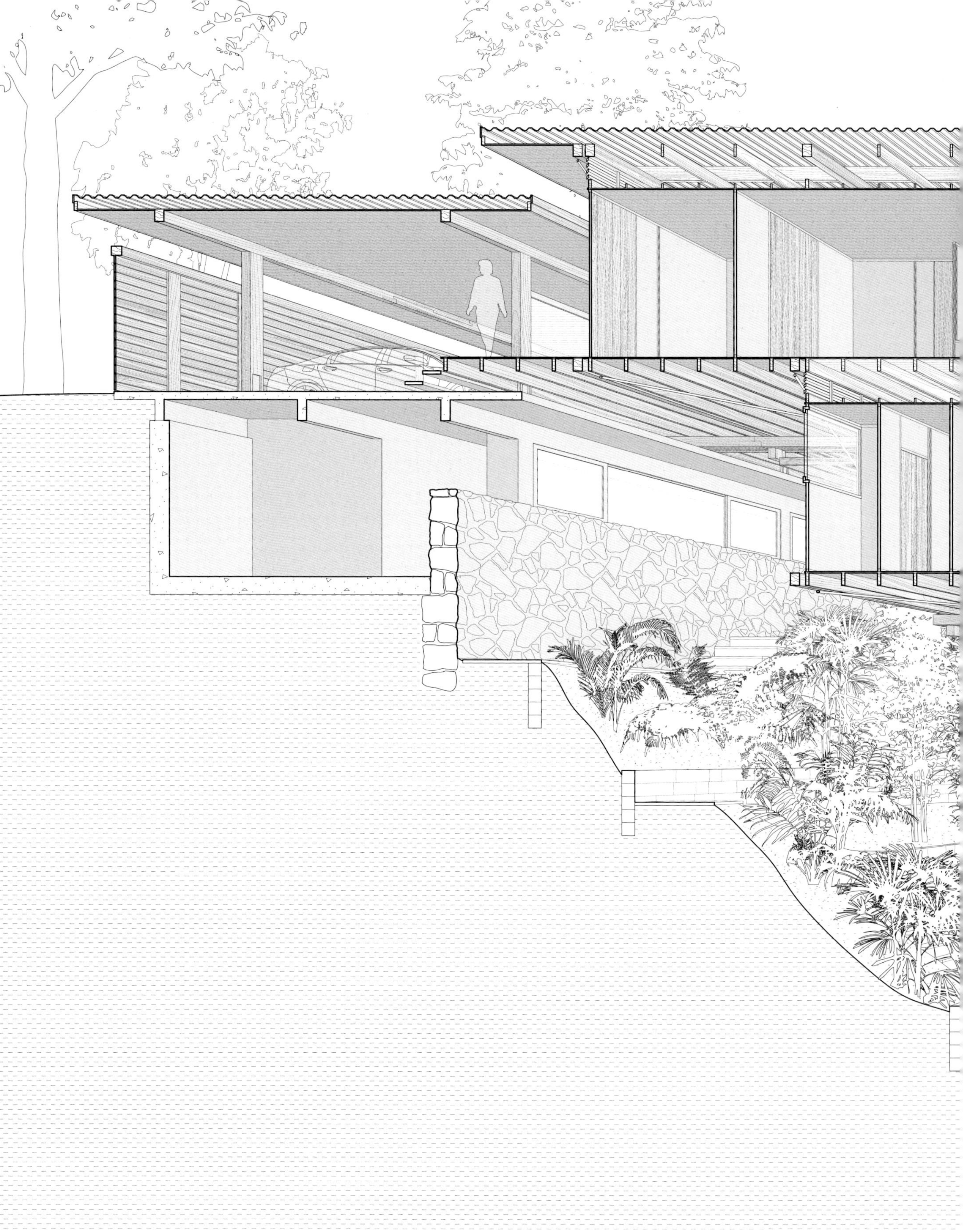

Helio Olga House

The house was constructed with prefabricated components, and its wood frame used as an exoskeletal structure. The corner joints were designed with intricate wood joinery, with as many as 10 separate wood members connecting through an interlocking array of bridal, mortise and tenon joints. The system allows additional posts to be added to the central columns without changing the thin profile of the grid. Wood members extend slightly beyond the joint, emphasizing the autonomy of the parts, while diagonal steel struts reinforce and visually register the structural

cantilevers. The beams under the upper floor anchor to the top surface of the driveway, additionally securing the top portion of the house to the hill. Lighter-weight joists span above and below the frames, supporting smooth surfaces of wood floors and ceilings, and the gap between provides a ventilated cavity above and below each room. Lightweight walls internal to the frame produce a smooth, gossamer surface, much of which is glass. Wide roof overhangs shade the building, and continue the cascading form of this distinctive and tectonically explicit house.

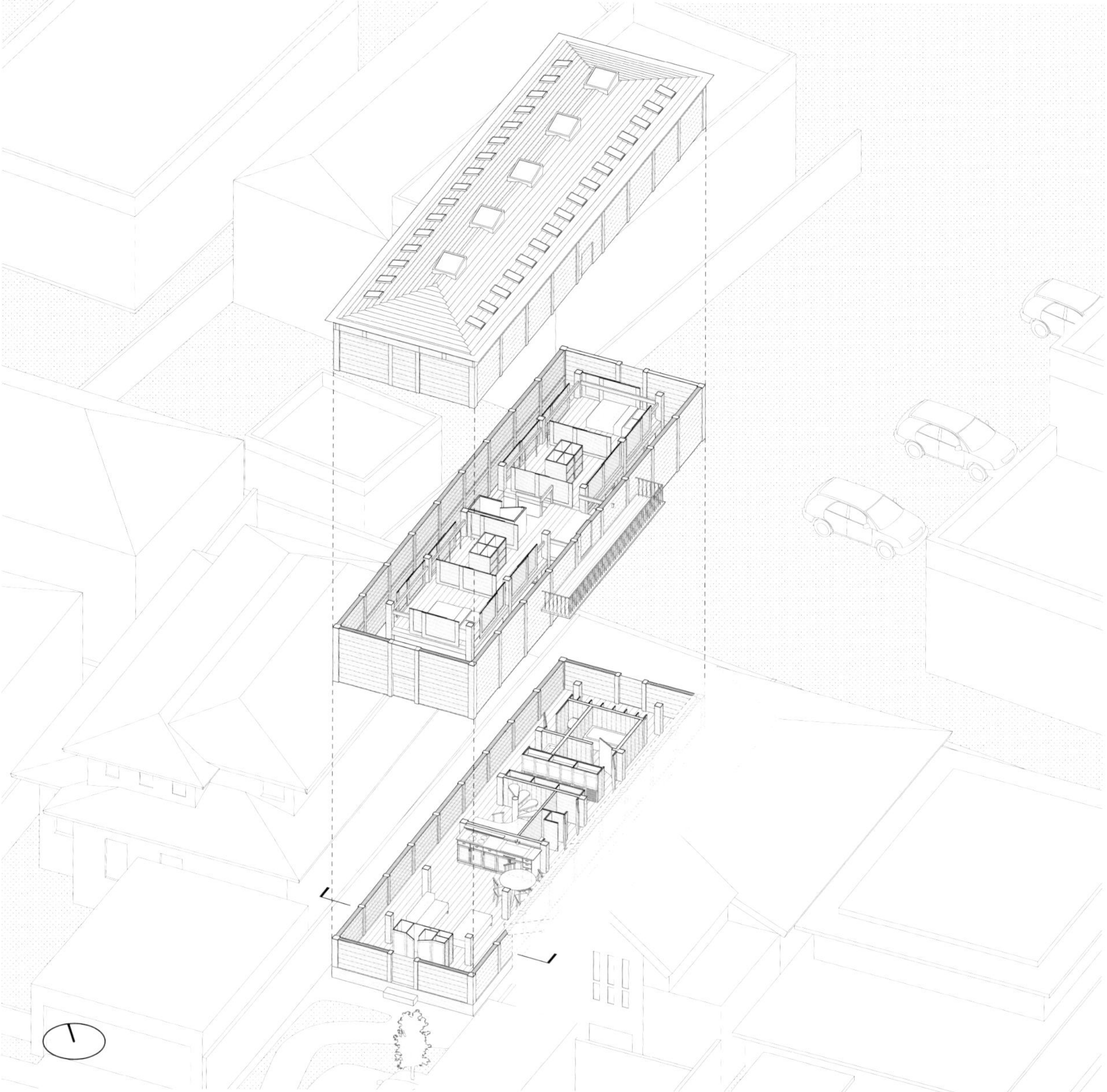

Ogimachi House | Tomoaki Uno Architects

This precisely detailed and meticulously constructed house has three defining features. First, it is almost entirely constructed from wood, according to the Itakura construction method where thick solid boards and heavy timbers are assembled through intricate joinery without metal fasteners. Second, it contains a building nested within a building, producing an interstitial double-height space around the whole house, which is illuminated by 37 skylights. Third, the house has no windows, but rather fosters a sense of privacy distinct from its dense residential context. All three contribute to the house's intended purpose to be a space for the client to heal from an illness. The 1,200 sq ft (112 sq m) house contains a living

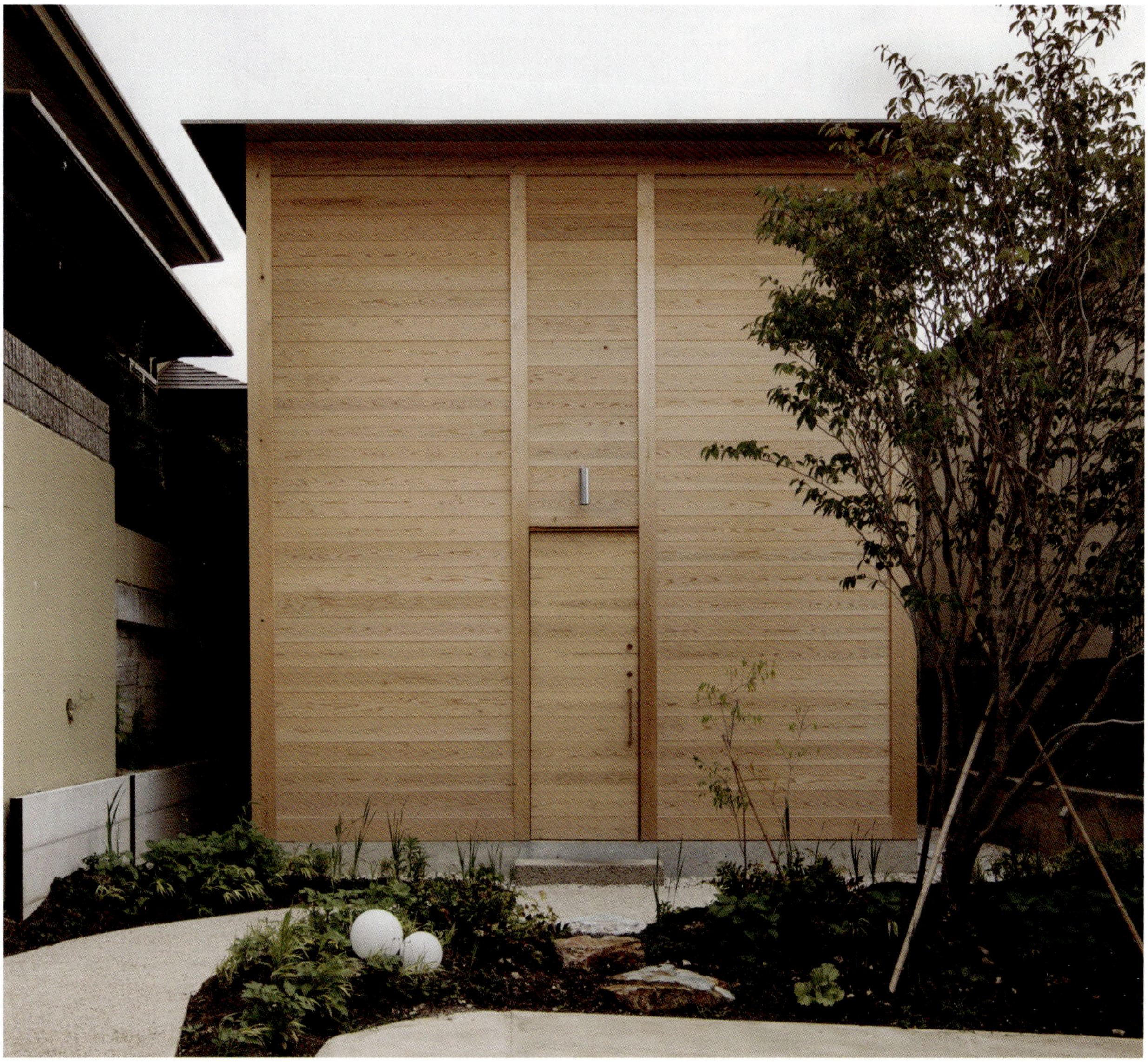

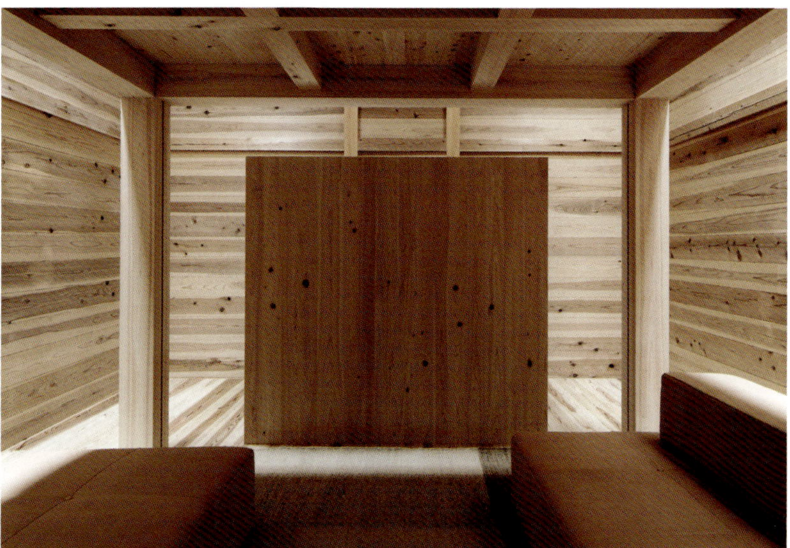

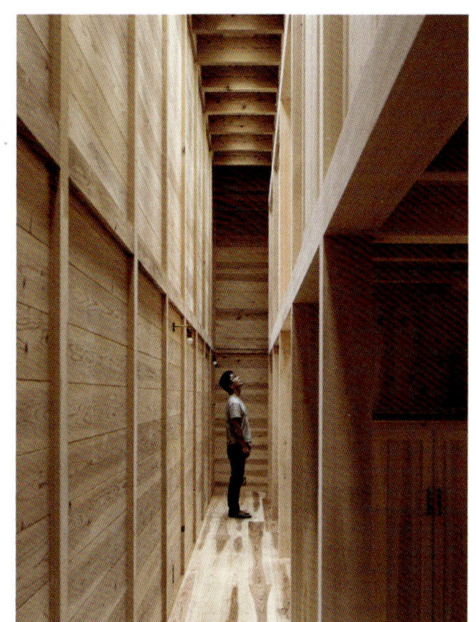

Nagoya, Japan | 2019

area, kitchen, and bathrooms on the ground floor and two bedroom suites positioned symmetrically off a circular stair. Sliding wood walls can enclose the bedrooms, which are otherwise open to the double-height perimeter.

82°F
80
60
40
20
Temperature
40°F
Jan
Dec

9.2"
12
8
4
Precipitation
1.9"
Jan
Dec

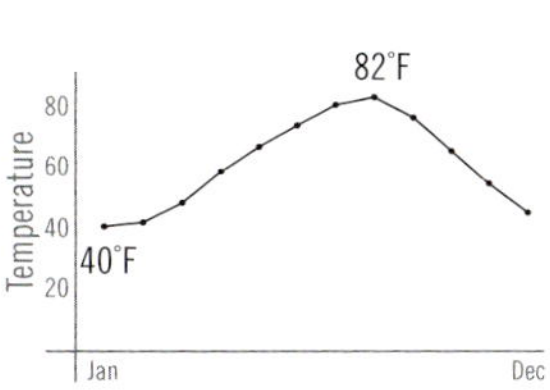

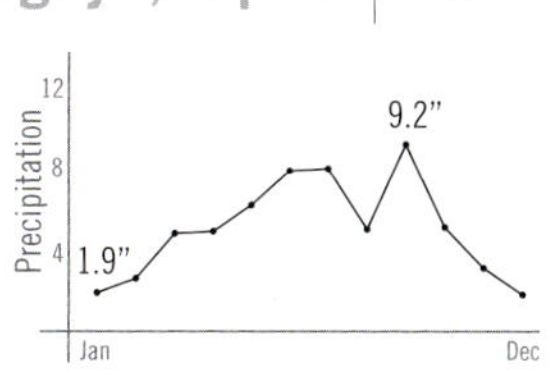

Ogimachi House

The section reveals the unique spatial and tectonic qualities of this house, which was fabricated with a level of precision and tight tolerances more often associated with bespoke furniture. Although sharing a single concrete foundation, the house is made up of two independent wood frames. The outer frame is composed of cedar columns, slotted to accept two rows of stacked 1.2 in (30 mm) thick cedar boards, with wood fiber insulation between. The roof is comprised of beams and purlins interlocked through dovetail lap joints. The interior volume contains larger 7 in (180 mm) cypress posts and beams that form the frames infilled by rooms on the ground floor and by sliding panels on the upper floor. Heat is provided

in the floor cavity, although rarely needed, while air conditioning is distributed from above in the plenum space of the roof. Not only has this design removed the multiple plastic skins found in conventional house construction, and integrated fasteners into the very form of the wood components, but the complexity of those details is concealed within the walls and frames, producing a sublime, understated space exhibiting one material to great effect.

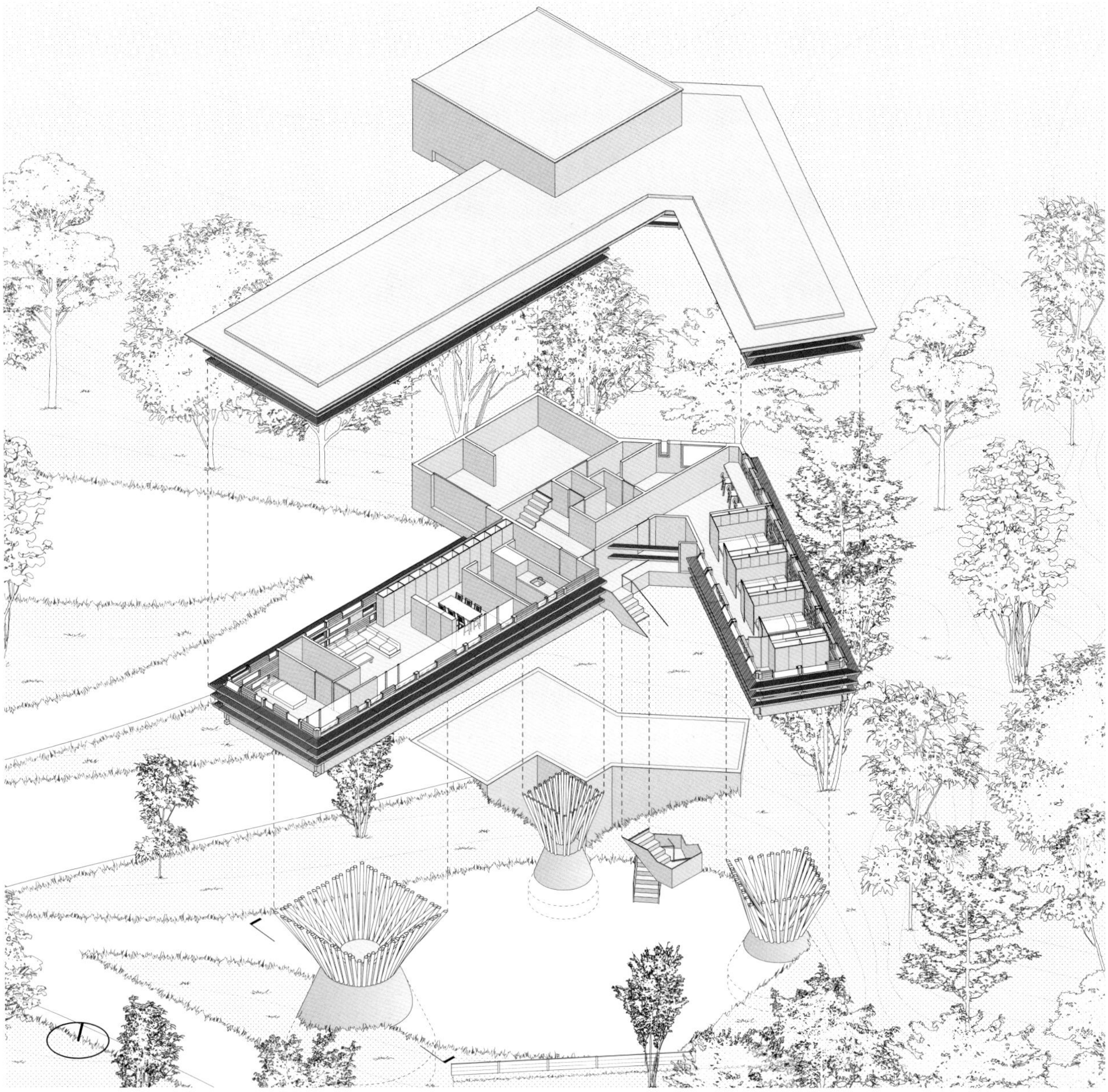

House in Itsuura | ADX

This house for a fisherman is located on tree-covered hilly terrain along Japan's eastern coastline. It is accessed from the street at the base of the site, which transforms the underside of the cantilevered house into its most visible public face. The primary floor of the house is supported by three massive columns, each made from a conical ring of small tree trunks. Opening toward the south, the V-shaped plan consists of a longer bar with the living, dining, and main bedroom joined to a shorter bar of smaller rooms defined by adjustable furniture. The joint between the two wings contains an entry, bathroom, and an adjacent work room. The depth of the wood joists visible below the house, combined with the multiple

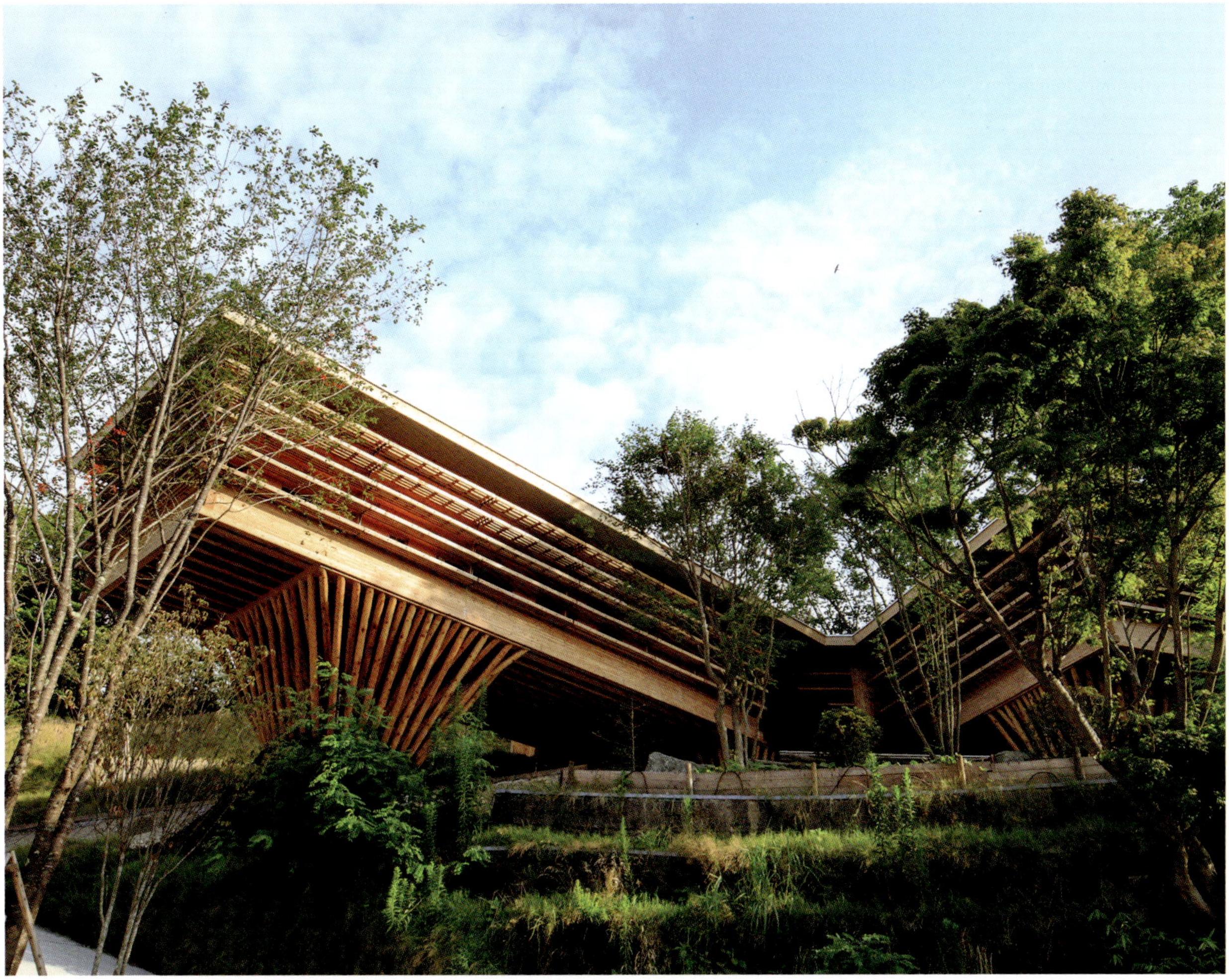

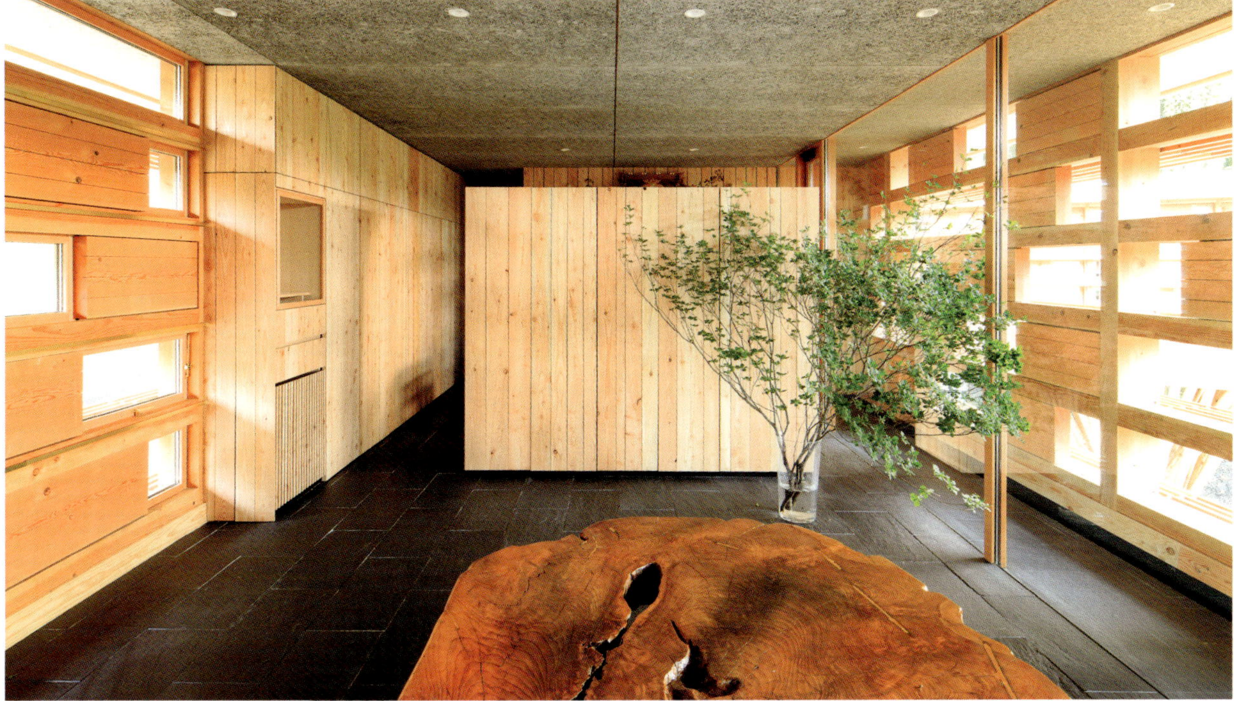

Kitaibaraki-Shi, Japan | 2014

sun-shading louvers on the elevation wrap the house in a protective thickness of wood members, which accentuates the muscular cantilever and substantial columns.

Temperature
80
60
40
20
75°F
37°F
Jan
Dec

Precipitation
12
8
4
9.5"
3.2"
Jan
Dec

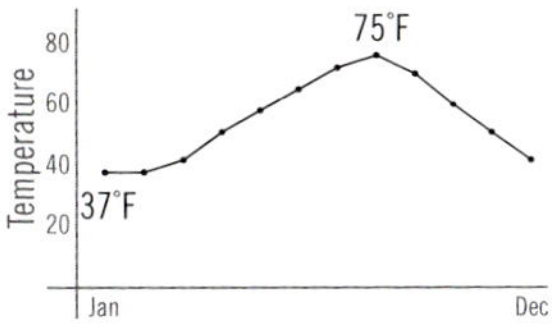

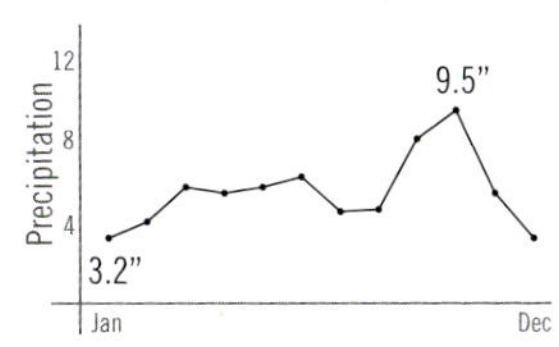

House in Itsuura

This house is composed of wood framing members used as robust exterior skins, whose inventive assembly is the very heart of the building. Each of the three large columns is composed of small 5.5 in (140 mm) diameter wood logs, which spread outward from two concentric rings into a square platform. The thin logs are embedded into a concrete footing that extends to bedrock. 17.75 in (450 mm) deep laminated joists of Oregon pine span between those platforms, with larger 31.5 in (800 mm) deep beams at the perimeter carrying the load of the walls above. Laminated pine post and beam frames of the house are infilled with lateral cedar sun louvers resting on vertical wood blocks, which are scored to control splitting. These

five bands are punctuated by horizontal windows, filling the space with light, but providing privacy from the road. The diagonal arrangement of the wood blocks in the exterior walls provides lateral bracing. One side of the longer bar is not infilled with windows, but is instead an open-air terrace and walkway within the thickness of this distinctive wood structure. A wall of nearly frameless glass separates this walkway from the interior, underscoring the depth and intricacy of the exterior wood enclosure by contrast.

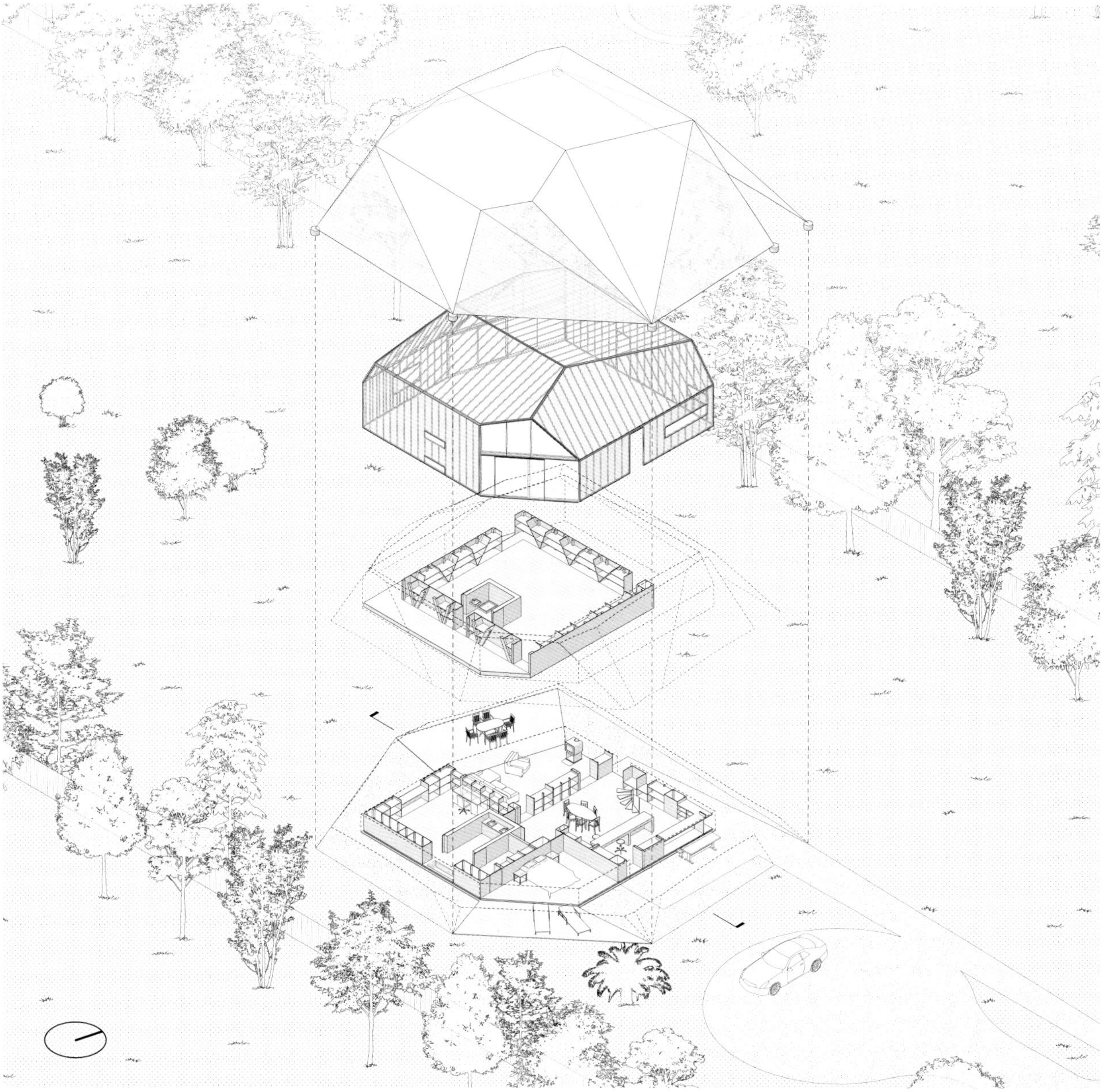

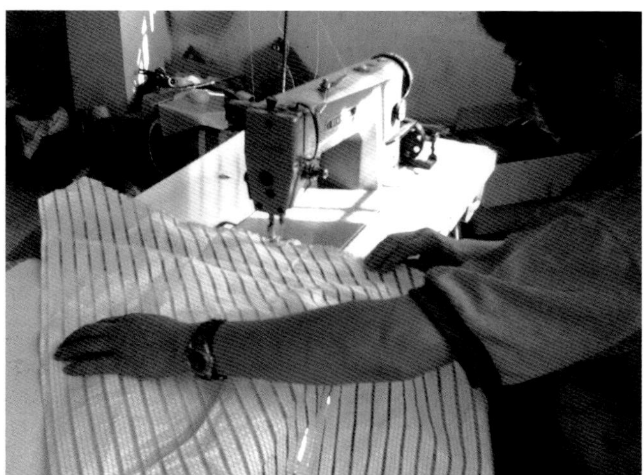

Wall House | FAR frohn&rojas

In contrast to the conventional use of a building's enclosure to define a binary between an interior and an exterior, this innovative house is composed of four different skins that transform the entire depth of the house into a gradient of thermal and programmatic zones. The innermost layer is a central concrete volume, which acts as a heat source with its thermal mass and efficiently concentrates the plumbing for two stacked bathrooms. Wood bookshelves, used as porous walls, define the next layer. On the ground floor these are configured into two intersected rectangles, comprising a kitchen, dining area, and, on their exterior, two bedrooms. A study is placed above, with prefabricated wood shelving fused into cantilever

Santiago, Chile | 2007

trusses. Enveloping these two layers is a polycarbonate and glass weather enclosure, which itself is covered with a fabric skin. The fabric is composed of both insect screening and a translucent fabric embedded with reflective aluminum strips, capable of being opened with zippers. The house is defined by the interstitial space between these permeable layers.

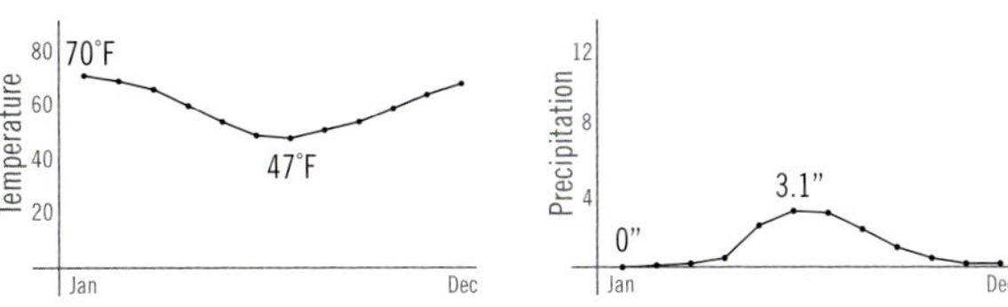

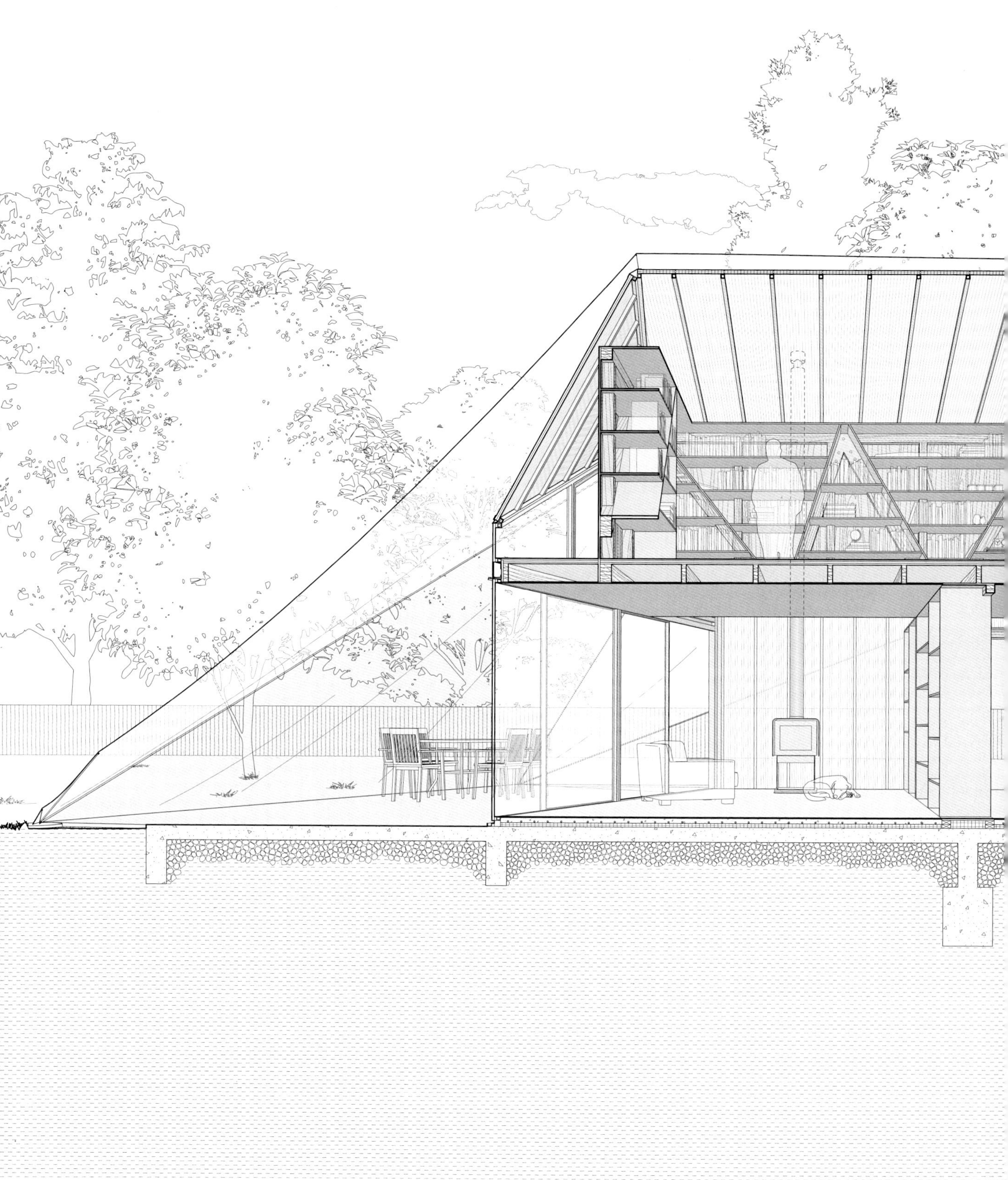

Wall House

Exhibiting a range of geometric and material properties from square to faceted, hard to soft, and opaque to permeable, each of the four exfoliating layers of the house is dependent on the other layers to produce the performative and spatial qualities of this unique house. The form of the house relies on the structural connections between the concrete bathroom core, the engineered wood and plywood shelving walls, and the metal frames of the translucent polycarbonate and glass enclosure. The exterior fabric skin reflects over 50% of the solar radiation, and is displaced 17.7 in (450 mm)

above the milky skin to vent excess heat. Peeled away from the polycarbonate skin by up to four meters, the space between skins are shaded porches in the summer. In the winter, they function like a greenhouse with the concrete slab providing a thermal mass augmented by radiant heating.

These interstitial layers provide a mix of rooms for the house to expand and contract depending on the time of day and season. Moreover, the optical porosity between the layers enables an aesthetic complexity that transcends the sum of its skins.

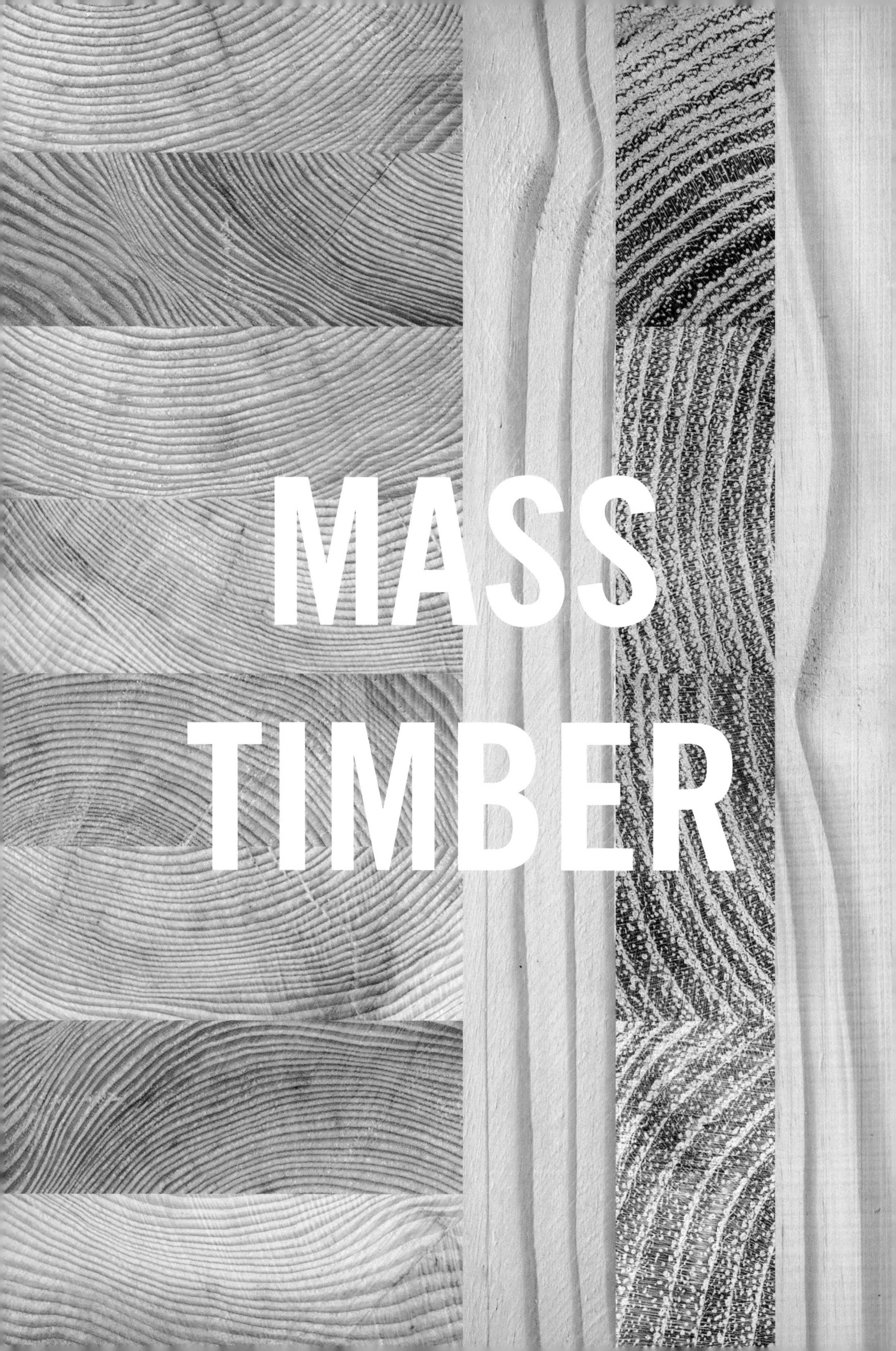
MASS
TIMBER

-418 $kgCO_2e/m^3$	LVL; Ökobaudat
-608 $kgCO_2e/m^3$	CLT; ICE
-667 $kgCO_2e/m^3$	Glulam; Ökobaudat

Mass Timber

800

600

400

Brick

200

Stone

Earth

0

Cork

Hemp

Straw

-200

-400

Bamboo

-600

Wood Frame

-800

MASS TIMBER

Mass timber is composed of aggregations of smaller wood members or veneers adhered together in layers to form structural beams, columns, or thick sheets. The sheet good is made by adhering overlapping layers of wood to form structural plates able to span as a floor or a wall. They are characterized by the orientation of the layers and their means of assembly, with cross-laminated timber the most common type. As with wood framing, mass timber's ability to sequester carbon is qualified by its source forest's management practices. Unlike stick construction, mass timber is defined by off-site prefabrication, where precise computer controlled cutting tools remove material to produce exacting parts to allow for more rapid, on-site assembly. As a sheet good, mass timber is often also the interior finish, but typically needs to be protected against exterior weathering and moisture.

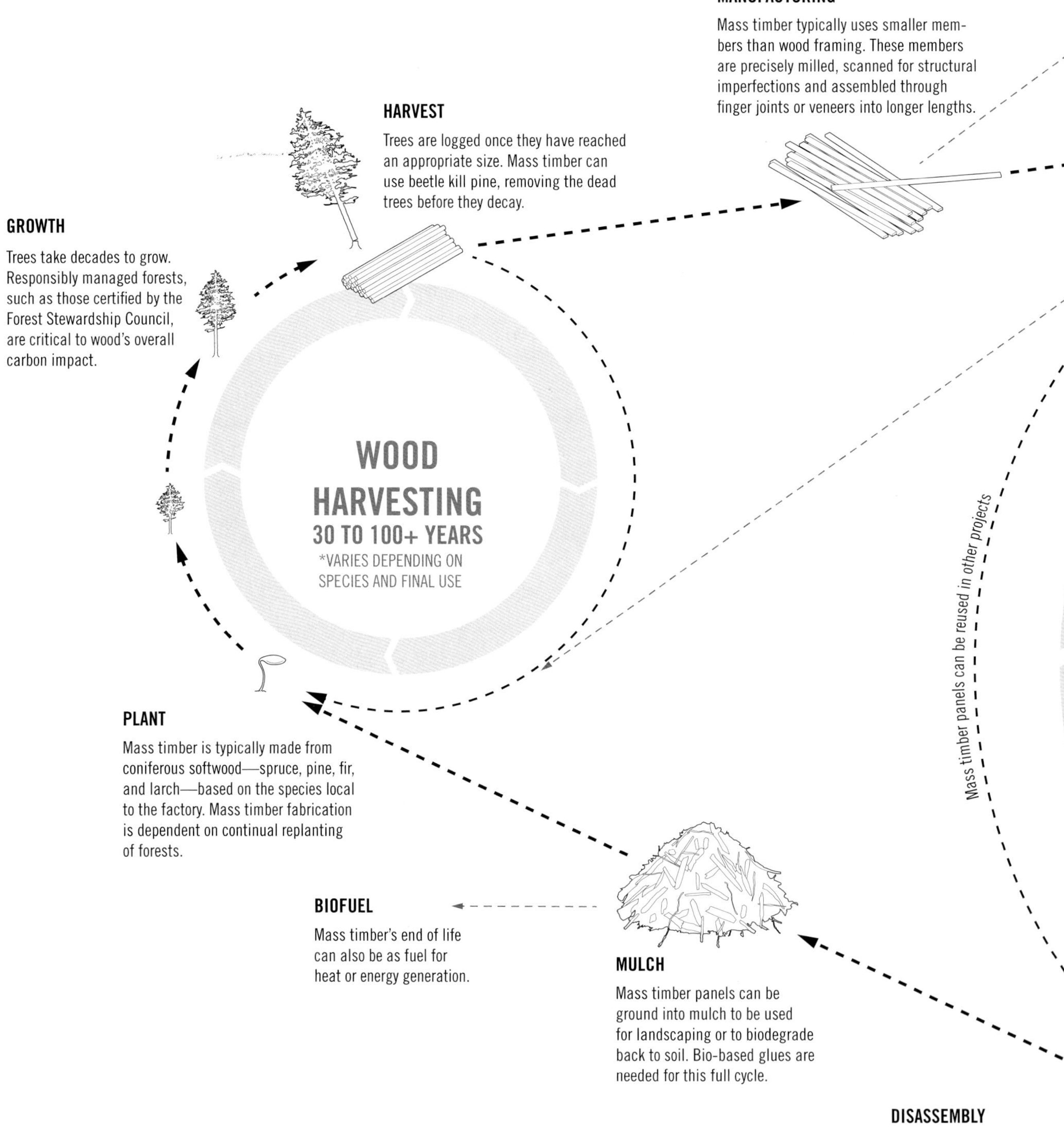

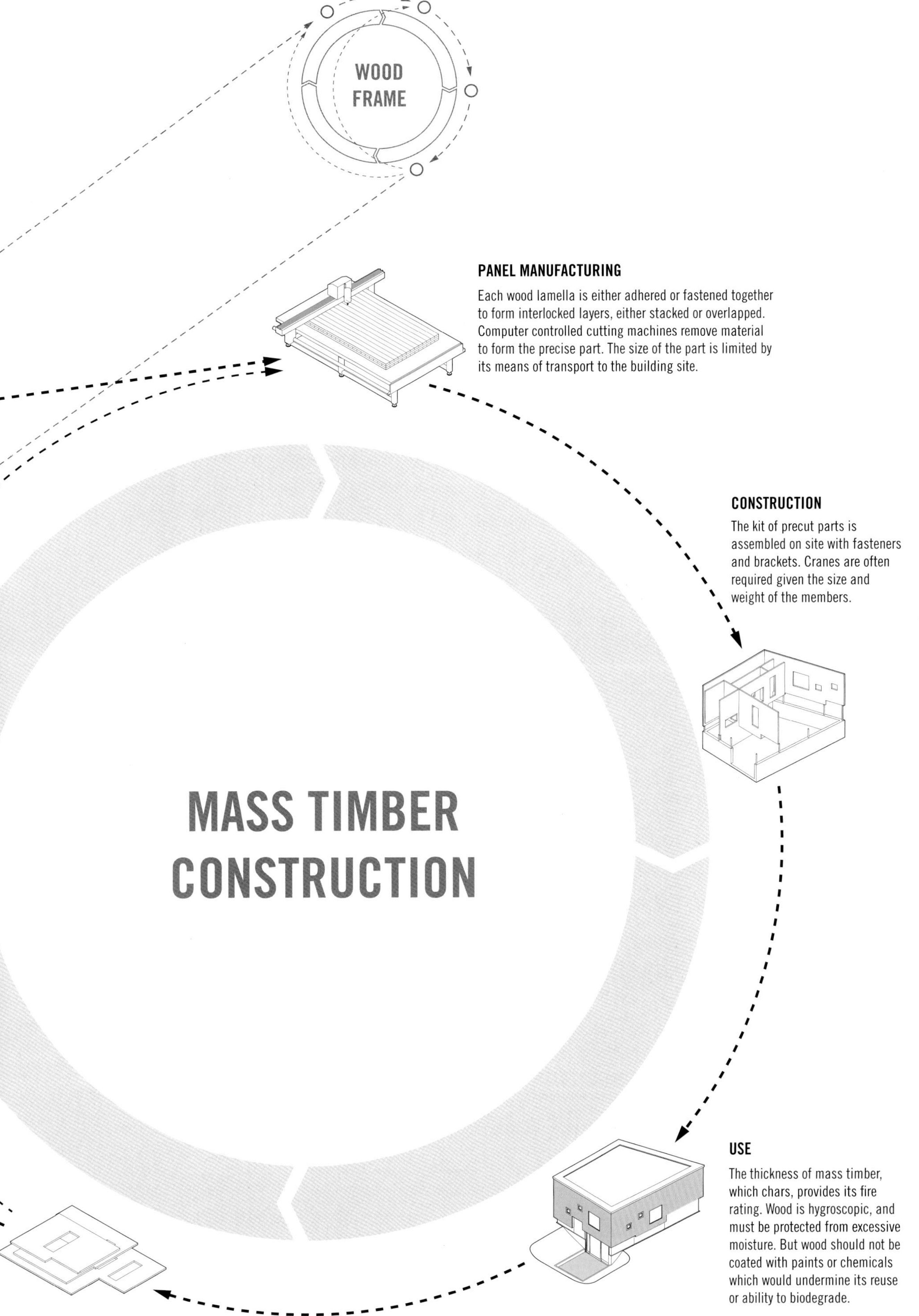
WOOD
FRAME
PANEL MANUFACTURING
Each wood lamella is either adhered or fastened together to form interlocked layers, either stacked or overlapped. Computer controlled cutting machines remove material to form the precise part. The size of the part is limited by its means of transport to the building site.
CONSTRUCTION
The kit of precut parts is assembled on site with fasteners and brackets. Cranes are often required given the size and weight of the members.
MASS TIMBER
CONSTRUCTION
USE
The thickness of mass timber, which chars, provides its fire rating. Wood is hygroscopic, and must be protected from excessive moisture. But wood should not be coated with paints or chemicals which would undermine its reuse or ability to biodegrade.

MASS TIMBER

TIMBER

Many of the types of engineered mass timber are made from laminations of solid-sawn softwood lumber. Finger joints are used to extend the length of each lamination, which are bonded through adhesives or fasteners into larger solid structural members.

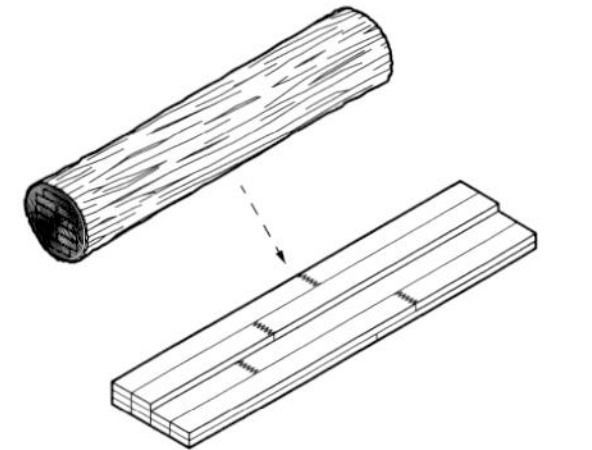

ADHESIVES

Most mass timber products use adhesives to bond the individual wood pieces into larger structural units. The most common adhesives are polyurethane, phenol formaldehyde, melamine formaldehyde, phenol formaldehyde or isocyanate-based. Bio-based adhesives from lignin or soy are less frequently available.

VENEER

Extracted by rotary cutting thin sheets from logs, veneers are laminated with adhesives to form larger solid structural members.

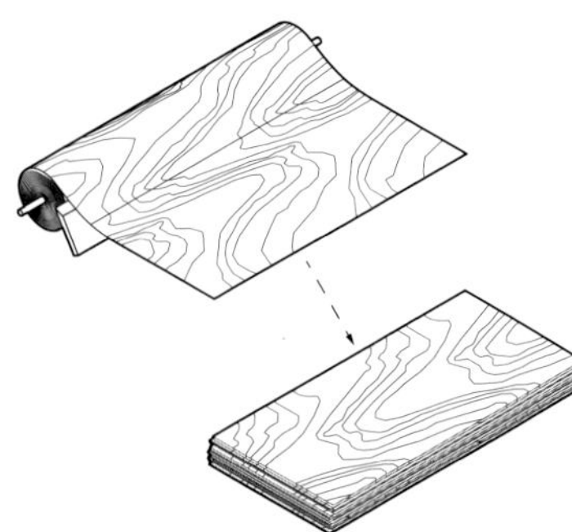

CROSS-LAMINATED TIMBER

Cross-laminated timber (CLT) is made from an odd number of layers of softwood lamellas (usually 3, 5 or 7), each adhered perpendicularly, to form a very structurally stable composite sheet. A typical CLT panel can be 10 by 50 ft (3 by 15 m) and range in thickness from 2 to 20 in (50 to 500 mm).

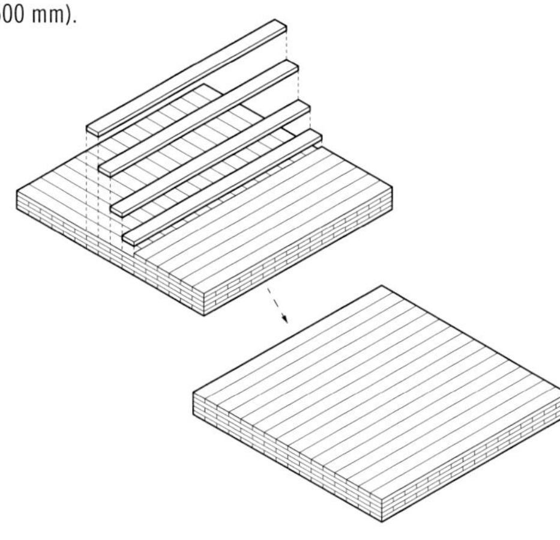

GLULAM

Glulam beams and columns (and less frequently panels) are formed from individual wood elements bonded on their wide edges with adhesives. The specific layers can be tailored to particular performance demands in a member's cross-section. The grain of all the layers runs parallel, allowing custom curvilinear shapes, and long lengths.

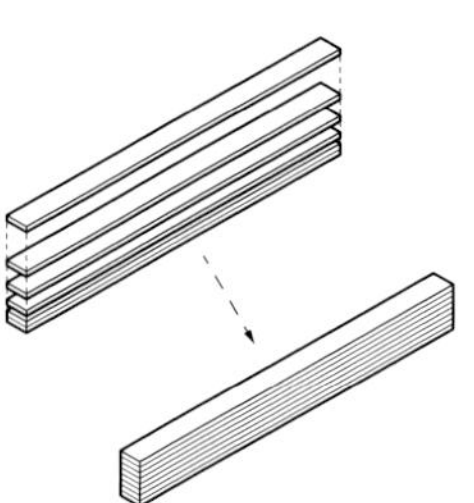

MASS PLYWOOD

Mass plywood panels use roughly 1 in (25 mm) thick sheets of veneer plywood as their base unit, which is then overlapped, adhered and pressed into a single large panel.

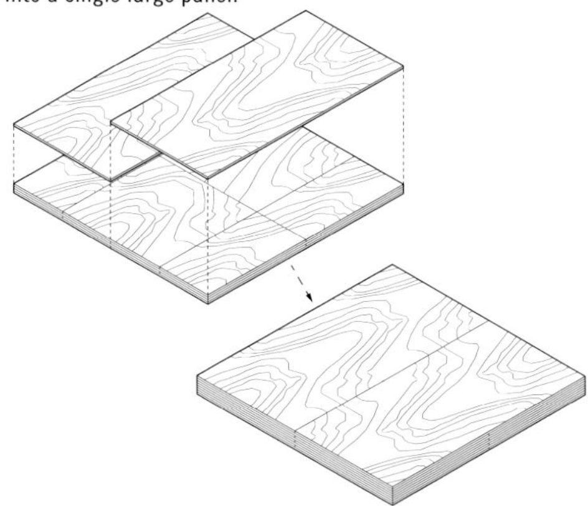

CROSS DOWEL-LAMINATED TIMBER

Cross dowel-laminated timber (CDLT or DCLT), a variation of CLT and DLT, uses a field of dowels to adhere the cross layered lamellas to each other with friction rather than adhesives.

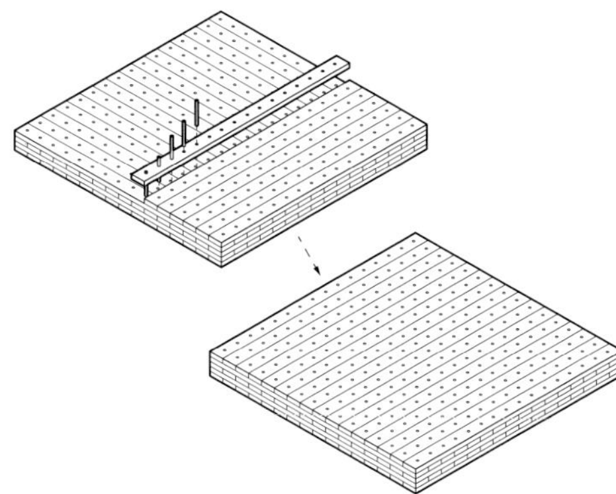

INTERLOCKING CROSS-LAMINATED TIMBER

Unlike CLT which relies on glues to adhere the lamellas, interlocking cross-laminated timber (ICLT) uses extruded dovetail and tongue and groove joints to mechanically bond layers to each other.

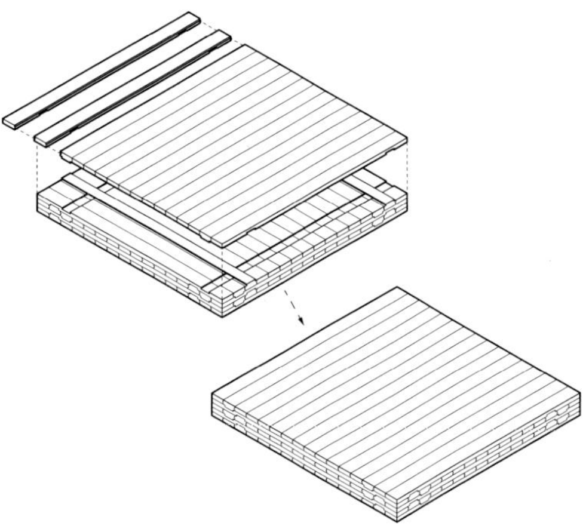

DOWEL-LAMINATED TIMBER

Dowel-laminated timber (DLT) is made from dimensional lumber, typically 2x4, 2x6, 2x8, etc., which are stacked into a sheet and held together through friction by hardwood dowels. Dowels are often dried to moisture levels below the softwood to swell after being placed into position. Unlike CLT, which can span in two directions, DLT spans in one direction.

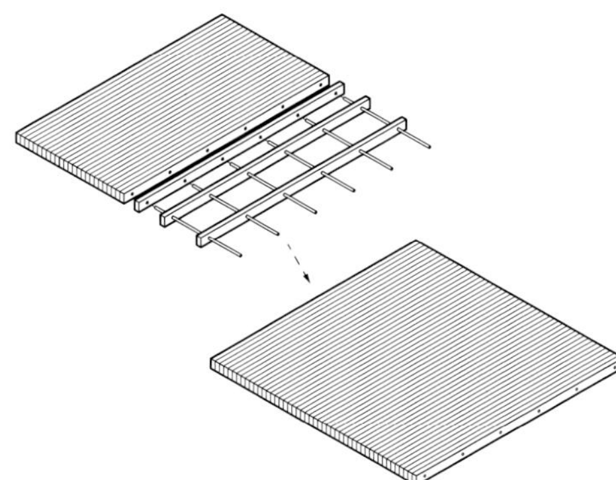

NAIL-LAMINATED TIMBER

Nail-laminated timber (NLT) is made from softwood dimensional lumber (2x and 4x) which are stacked into a sheet and held together through friction by nails or, less frequently, screws. Unlike CLT, which can span in two directions, NLT spans in one direction.

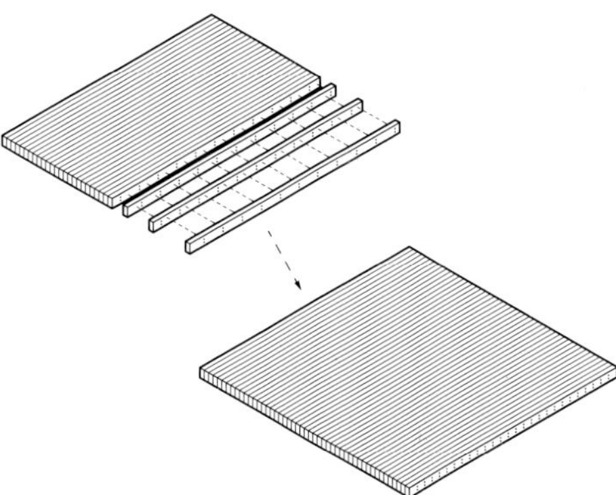

LAMINATED VENEER LUMBER

Laminated veneer lumber (LVL) is formed by adhering thin veneers of softwood to each other with structural glues. The grain of the veneer typically runs parallel to the long axis of the member.

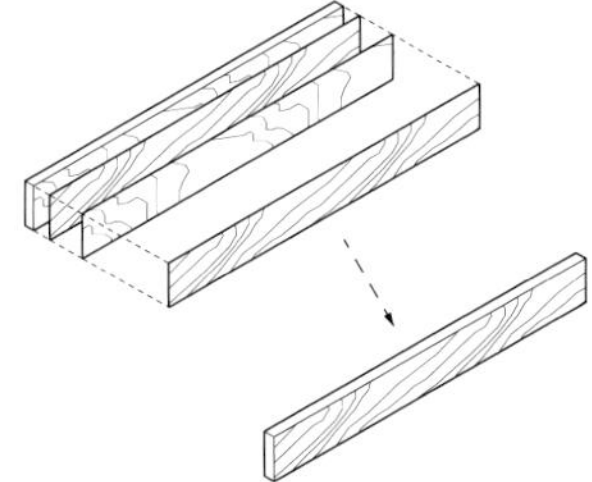

PARALLEL STRAND LUMBER

Parallel strand lumber (PSL) is a variant of LVL using narrower veneer strips of wood adhered and pressed into a structural member. The orientation of the strands aligns with the long axis of the member.

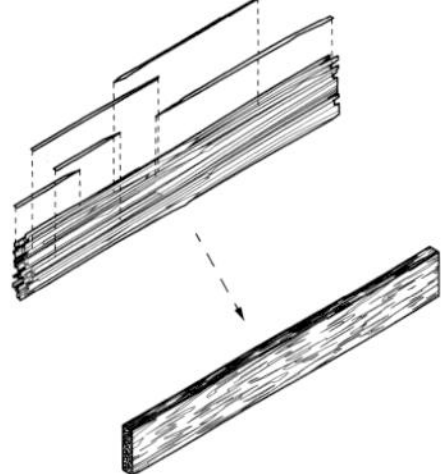

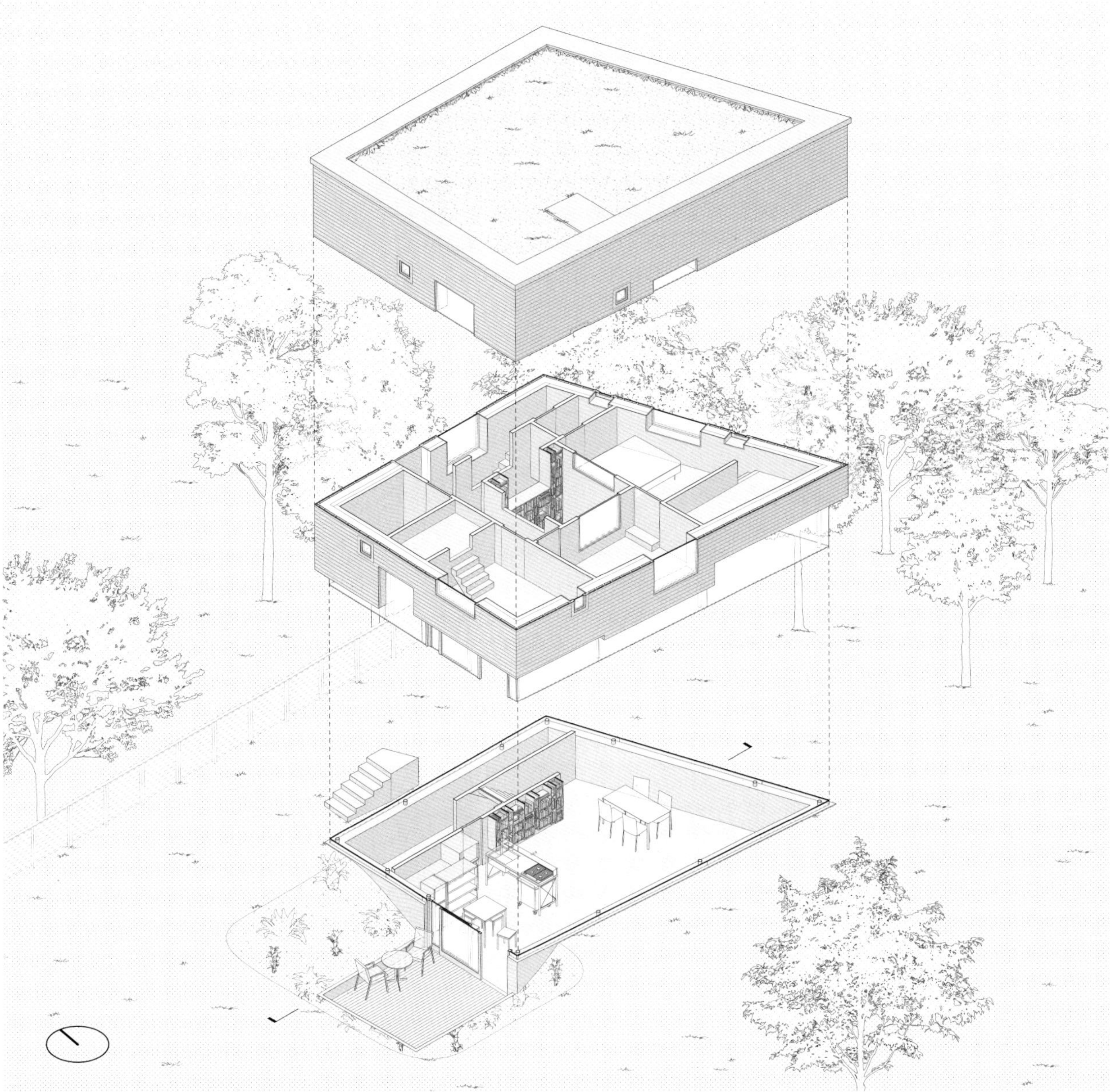

House W | Kraus Schönberg Architects

Creatively sidestepping the local suburban building zoning which limited houses to a single story, the lower level is lodged 5 ft (1.5 m) into the ground. This splits the house into a partially submerged open living level and a single upper volume comprising bedrooms, bathrooms, dressing room, and play areas. Where the lower level has a uniform continuous floor, the floors of the rooms above are at multiple levels producing a stepped ceiling. Glass infills the wall atop the concrete wall providing views out to the site, while making the house appear to float. The upper volume is

Hamburg, Germany | 2007

made from cross-laminated timber, which is painted white on the inside, visually aligning it with the board-formed concrete embedded into the site. Painted exterior wood cladding continues this aesthetic on the exterior of this subtle yet intricate nesting of spaces into a singular form.

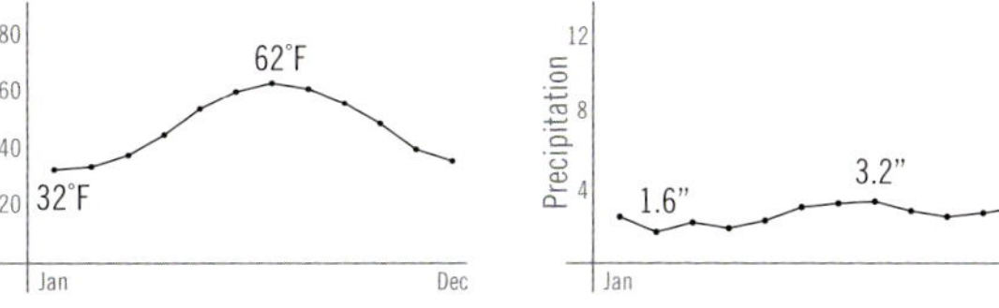

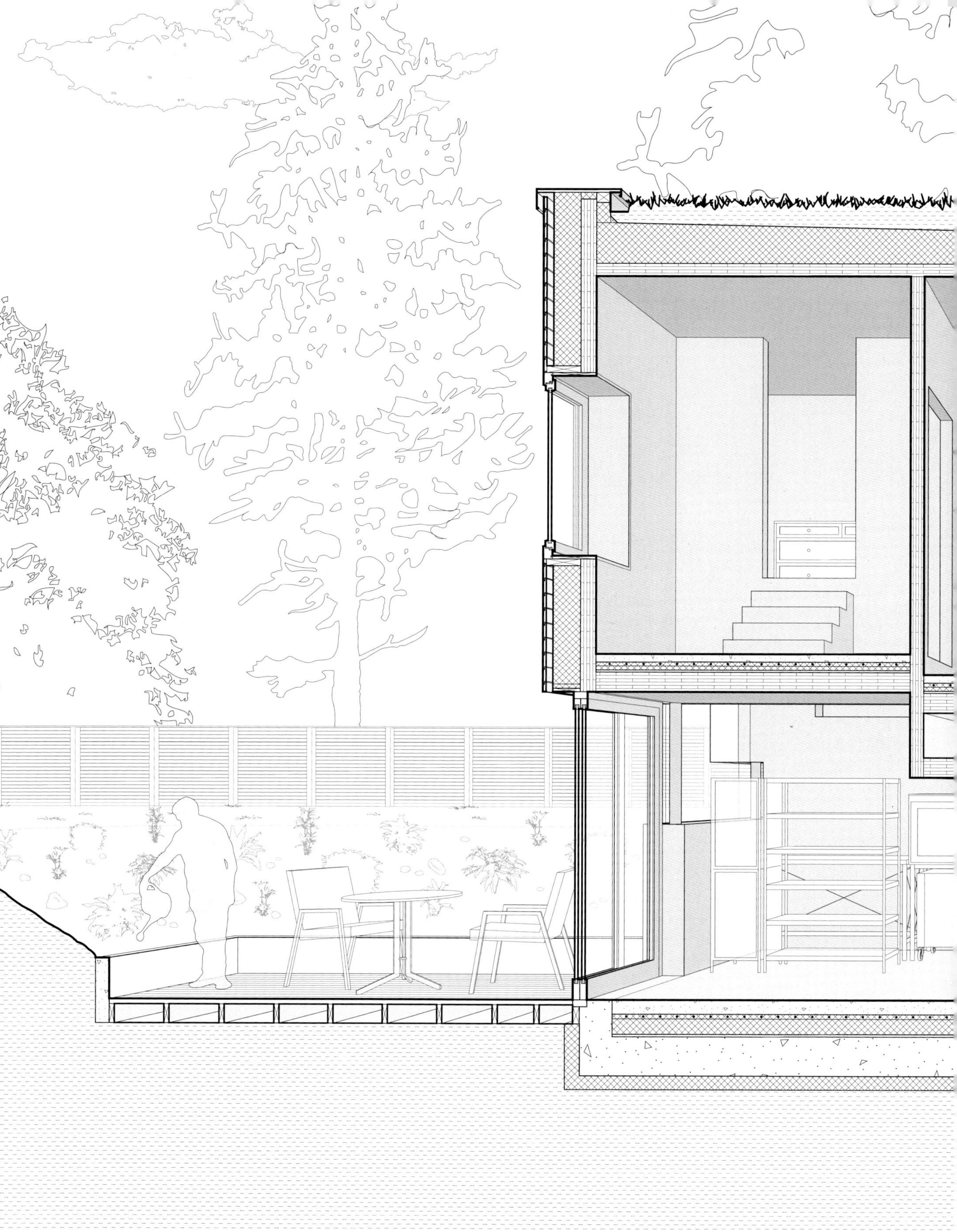

House W

Taking advantage of the small footprint, the structural approach to this house is to use extensively perforated cross-laminated timber to construct all the walls and floors of the upper-floor volume. Both perimeter walls and interior walls span the width of the plan and rest atop 12 round steel columns, themselves cast into the concrete base. The bottom edge of these walls were notched according to the different levels of the rooms, with windows cut from within the panels to allow views through the house and to the exterior. These subtractions from the CLT planks were optimized to keep the vertical panels relatively thin at 4.6 in (117 mm). This porosity is enhanced by both continuous voids that extend horizontally through the middle of the house and a central atrium, which is lined on one side with a 20 ft (6 m) tall bookcase. With a flat green roof, this house inverts the conventional figural quality of a house, shifting it from a roof silhouette to the underbelly of its floating upper floor. Adding to this effect, the CLT floor panels were installed by lowering them down into the grid of walls, effectively suspending them from the walls.

Sunken House | Adjaye Associates

This house's distinctive spatial approach combines a full-story site excavation with the insertion of a cross-laminated timber box within that volume. The space between the larger excavated void and the house allows the space of the house to expand into the exterior, while retaining a sense of privacy from the relatively dense Victorian residential neighborhood.

Although the CLT is only left exposed on the top-floor ceiling, its ability to span and be perforated for a range of apertures enabled the particular windows and wide expanses of glass that animate the house and its connection to its site. One can enter the house by descending down in to the wood-clad yards which connect to the dining area, open kitchen, and

London, England | 2007

study. Bedrooms are located at street level with a large living room on the top floor. A retractable ladder allows access to the roof, which contains a recessed seating area with views across East London.

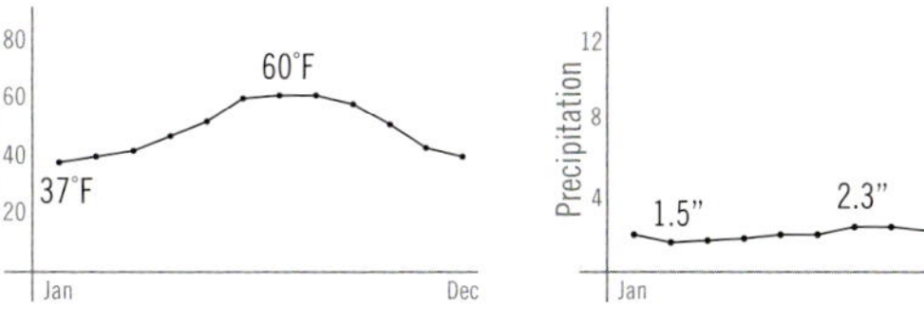

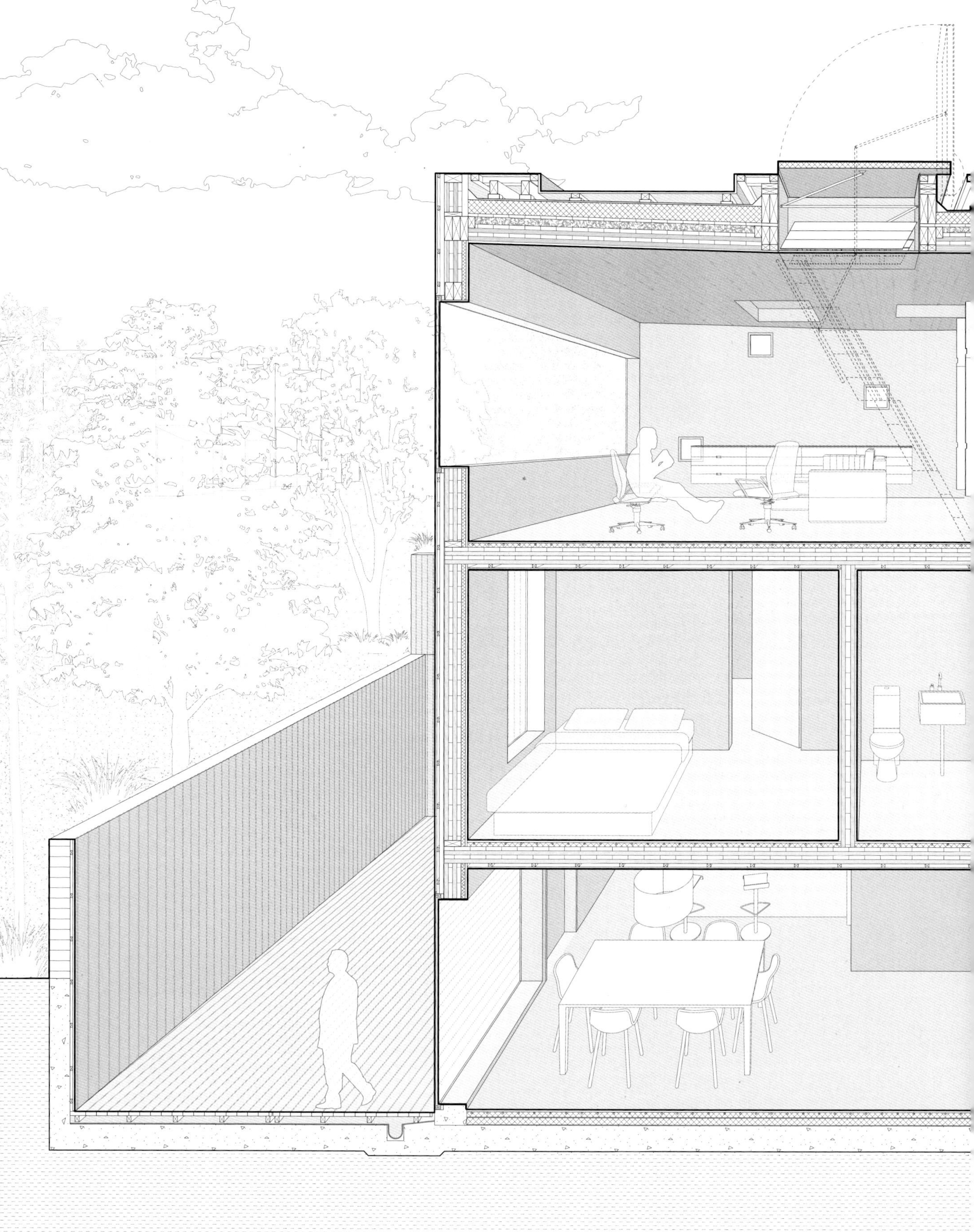

Sunken House

While it has increasingly become the norm to utilize cross-laminated timber for its aesthetic impact on the interior, this house—a relatively early use of CLT in house construction—relied on its structural capacity to form crisp walls capable of having windows of almost any shape without compromising its ability to span. As such the house exhibits very large horizontal expanses of glass, apertures that fold from the wall into the roof, as well as a myriad of carefully positioned small windows and skylights on all sides of the building's skin. Similarly, large openings in the floors

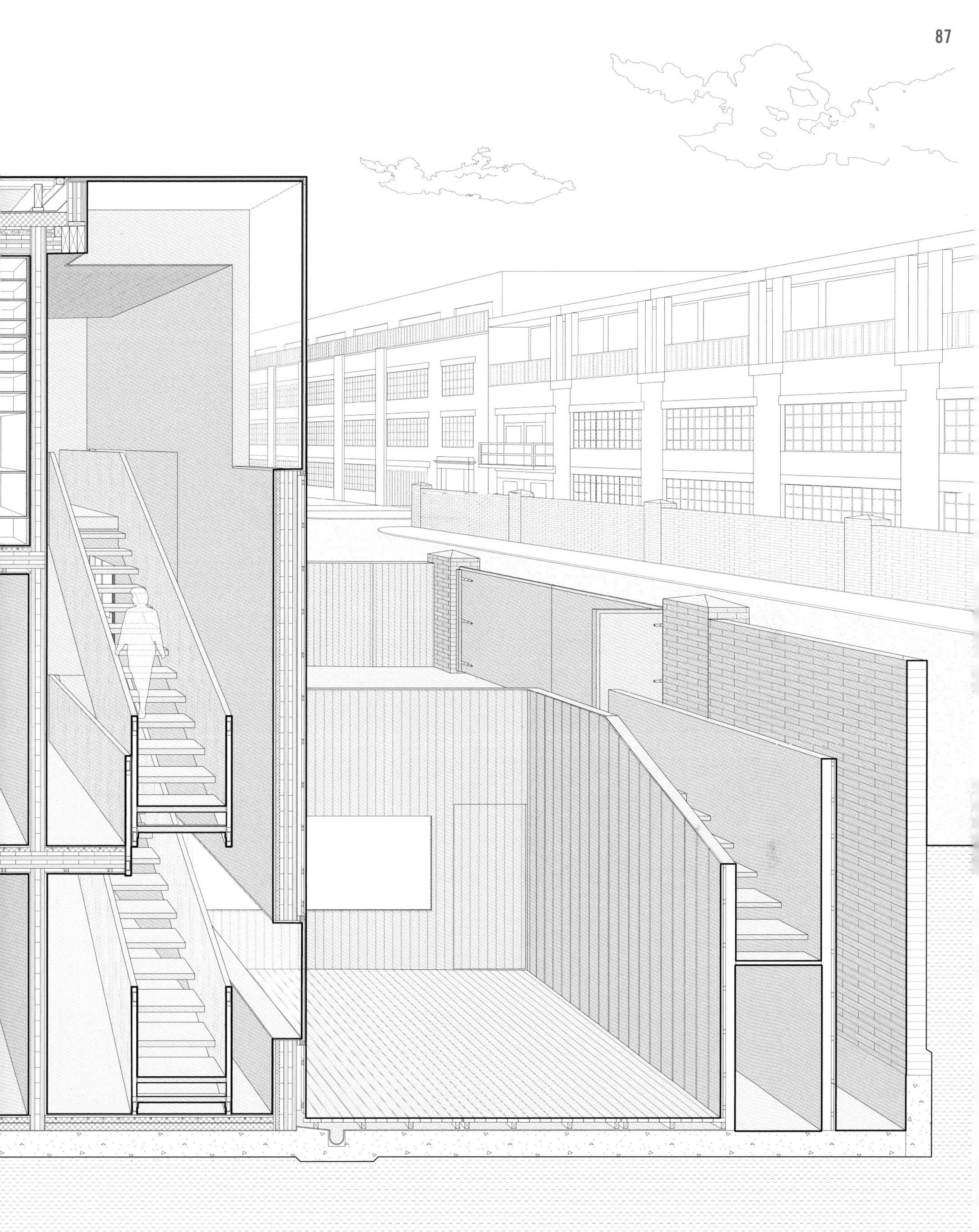

frame a stair and a triple-height volume just inside the front elevation. The interior of the CLT is clad in wall board or plywood floors and painted white to intensify the abstract play of light. On the exterior, ribbed cedar board stained black clads every surface including the roof, and is used in specific locations as flush pivoting panels to help modulate views and light. The precision of the cladding on the interior and exterior of the cross-laminated timber produces the unique architectural qualities of the house.

Haus Gables | Jennifer Bonner / MALL

Located on a narrow 24 ft (7.3 m) wide site in a dense residential neighborhood, this house reworks basic assumptions about construction systems, interior organization, and material finishes. Cross-laminated timber is used to produce a complex assembly of faceted overlapping planes and steeply pitched volumes throughout the whole space of this three-story house, exploiting the specific capacity of this planar structural material. The six intersecting gables of the roof generate the form and the plan of the house with double-height voids extending beneath the gables through

Atlanta, Georgia | 2018

the depth of the section. Floor finishes are extended up walls to produce wainscotting which terminates at raked angles, echoing and intensifying the geometry of the ceiling and contrasting with the natural finish of the CLT interior.

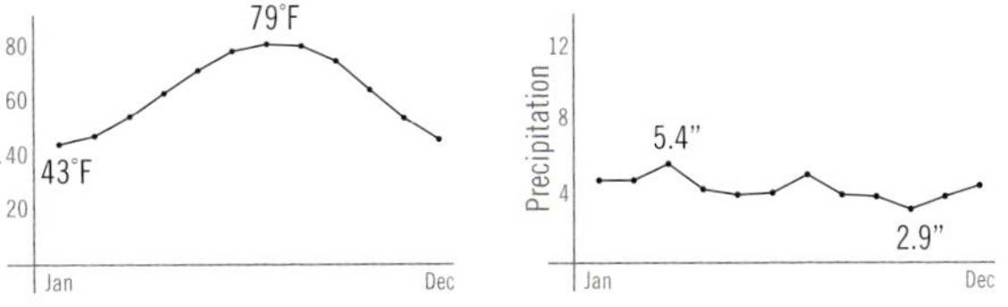

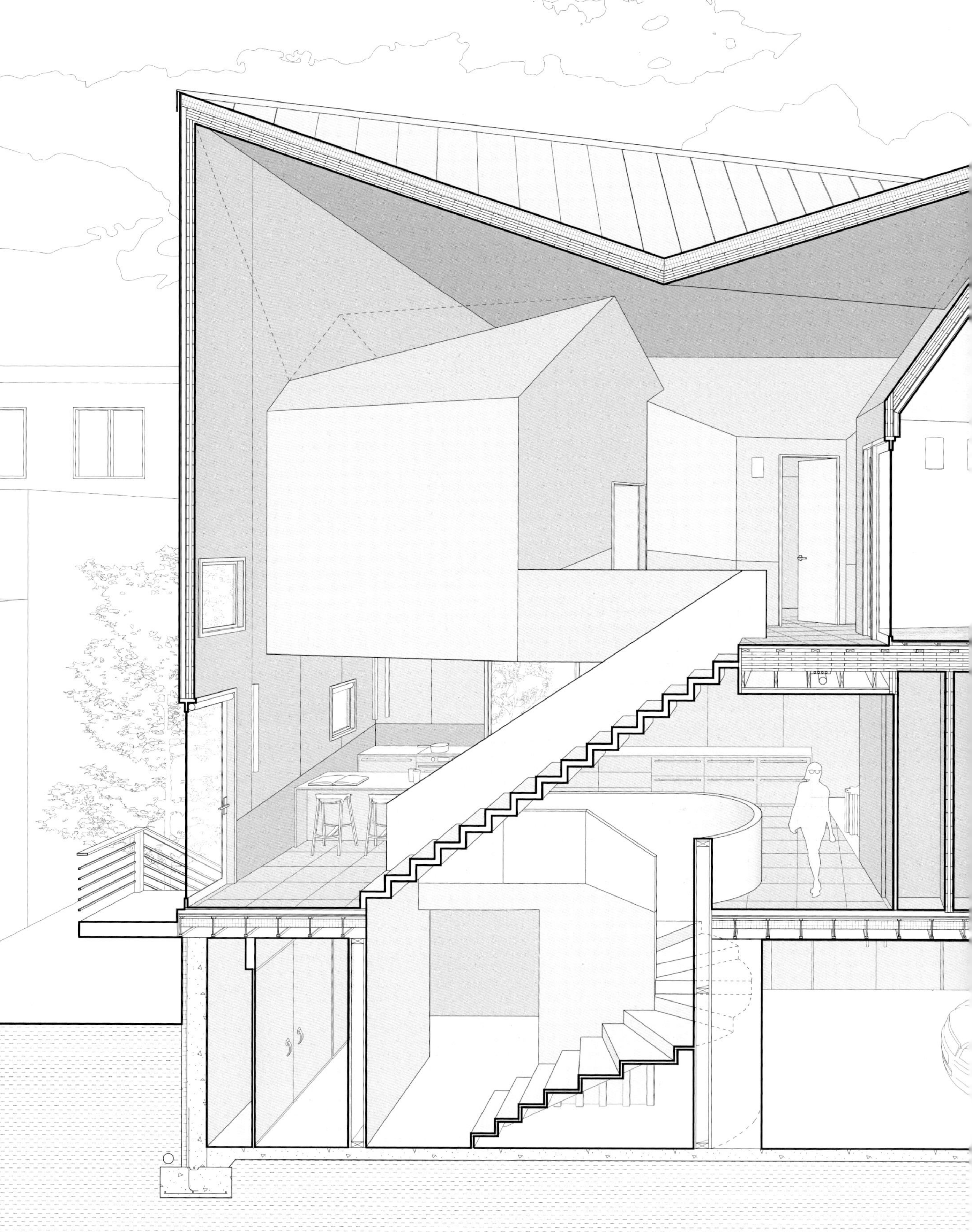

Haus Gables

This house convincingly utilizes CLT for its own architectural capacities, rather than as a material substitute within a steel, concrete, or stick-framing logic. The intricate spaces of this house and the interior effects were a direct result of CLT's ability to span in any orientation, and to be precisely cut into any shape complete with tapered edges. The house is composed of 87 panels, installed in 14 days with a crew of four. The walls, roof, and floor are made with three-, five-, and seven-ply CLT respectively. On the exterior, the CLT is sheathed in rigid insulation with

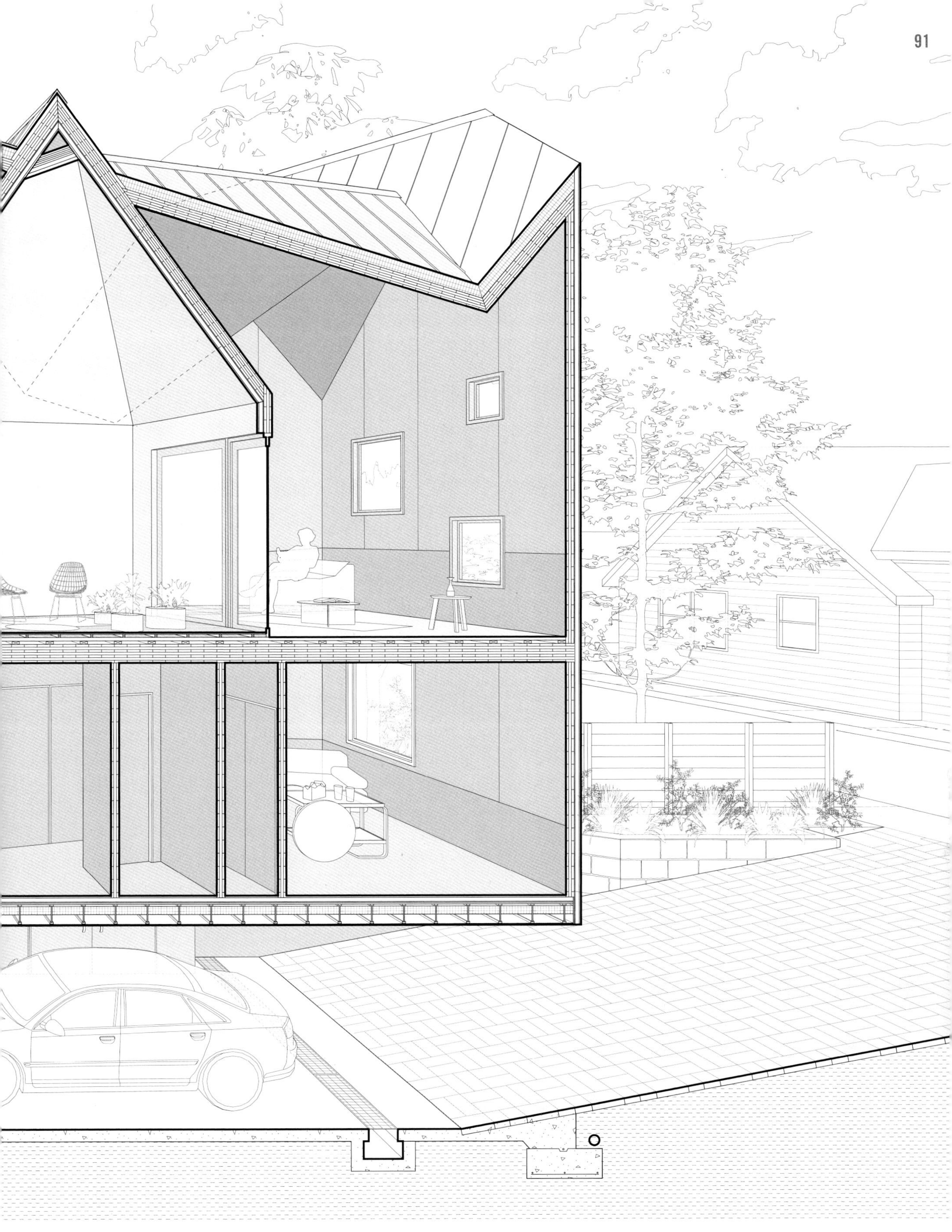

inexpensive commercial metal on the roof, while the walls are coated in glass-bead-infused stucco and faux-finished with a brick pattern adding to the enigmatic quality of this house. The white mass of the house floats above the gray concrete foundation, which doubles as a carport or gallery accessed through an inclined drive. On the upper floor, one of the gable spaces is constructed as an exterior porch and appears as a smaller house extracted from, or alternately, embedded in the mass of the full building.

Meteorite | Ateljé Sotamaa

By using two different skins of cross-laminated timber nested inside each other, this peculiar house is able to present different characteristics on its interior and its exterior. As implied by its name, the house is a faceted object positioned to contrast with its forested site in eastern Finland. While the exterior is an inscrutable oiled black polyhedron, the interior is exposed natural wood with rectilinear logic. The interior volumes are stacked and expand to pierce the irregular exterior skin with apertures. At just over 800 sq ft (75 sq m), the house's floor area is small in comparison to its volume. This is due to the fact that not only is the heart of the house an open three-story void that activates all the spaces that spiral around it,

Kontiolahti, Finland | 2018

but, more importantly, the space between the two CLT skins is an empty insulating cavity. This quantity of poché space is unprecedented in mass timber construction, and enables the complex and diverse architectural qualities achieved with a single material.

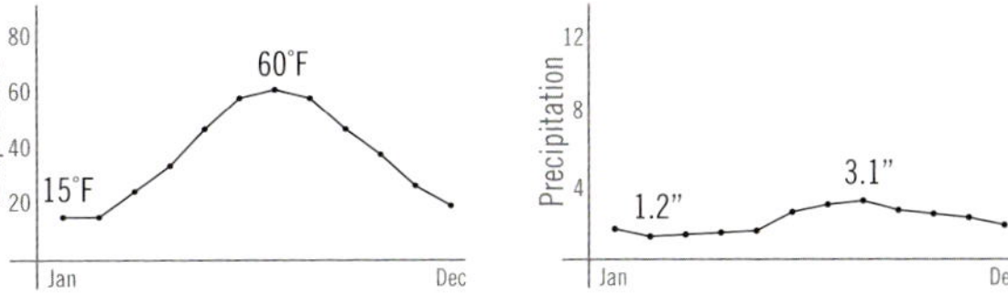

Meteorite

This experimental house tests the capacity of using two skins of the same material to produce distinctly different interior and exterior qualities. Built first, the interior CLT layer is composed of stacking hundreds of rectilinear panels forming a loose aggregation of living areas, sleeping surfaces, inhabitable window nooks, and vertiginous voids complete with a floating mesh net floor. These interior spaces, which vary in scale, interlock physically and are tied together aesthetically through the uniformity of the natural wood finish. The exterior skin is supported by the interior geometry, through its stacked volumes, but also with tube-like extrusions that terminate in punched windows. The outer skin was built second, and consists

of seven lateral rings of triangulated panels, a top plate, and a skylight. Despite the problem of heat loss through convection, the up-to-four-meter-thick voids between the skin functions as additional insulation. The voids also provide pathways for the distribution of services. Rather than clad the mass timber in another layer of siding, the outer CLT skin is simply coated with a black natural sealer. By both removing the conventional layers of typical mass timber wall construction, and in doubling the thick structural skins, this house proposes a fundamentally different approach to the use of mass timber.

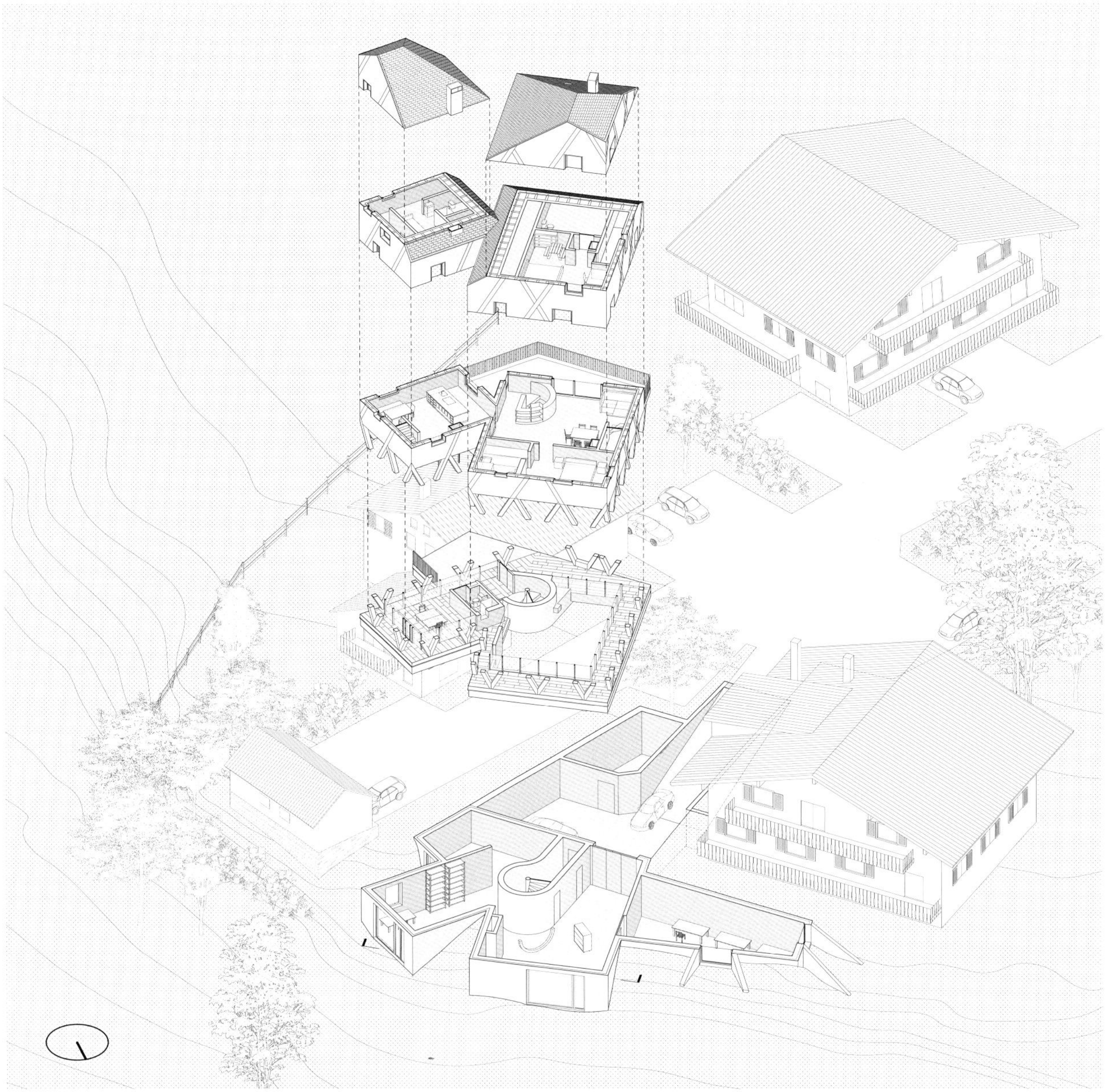

Kostner House and Studio | MoDus Architects

Located near the edge of a picturesque village in the South Tyrol province, this house's intricate section is produced by interlocking spaces and material systems. A partially submerged concrete lower-level, containing a studio and gallery, connects obliquely up a driveway to the street, allowing delivery of heavy art objects. In addition, it extends vertically into a double-height space lined with a clerestory of glass. A diagrid of glulam members overlaps the volume of the studio producing an exterior colonnade and continues wrapping up and around the surface of the upper stories of the house. The mass of the house is two wood figures, hinged internally through a central circular staircase, but splitting apart at the

Castelrotto, Italy | 2013

roof. Evoking Louis Kahn's Fisher House plan, the main living floor abuts a kitchen and dining room with a living area and main bedroom. On the floor above, two bedrooms inhabit distinctly different roofs, whose shapes reflect the mountainous context.

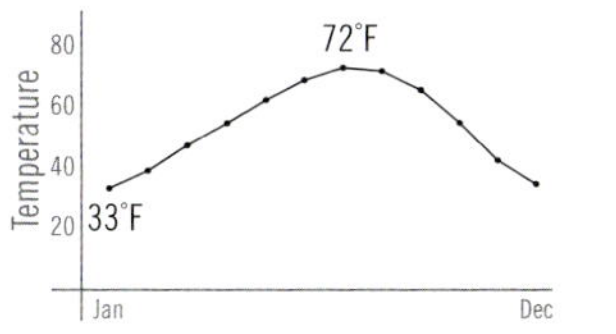

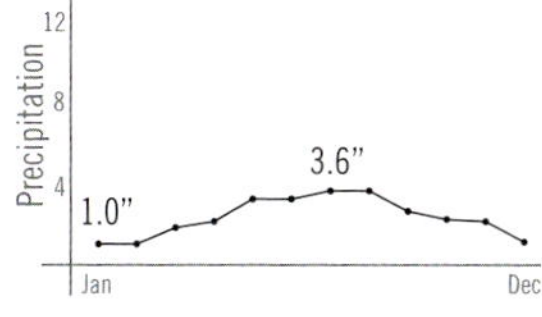

Kostner House and Studio

The section reveals the three structural systems that are stacked to constitute this four-story house. In order to allow views to pass through the building, the ground floor hosts a perimeter wood glulam truss, separated by a corridor from an interior glass skin. The second-story ring beam is the top cord of the truss and is notched to hold the cross-laminated timber floor, while the concrete foundation doubles as the bottom cord of the truss. Given the slope of the site, one side of this lowest level is fully submerged while the other side opens to views of the valley. The upper two

stories are built from cross-laminated timber, with glulam roofing members. Through careful lapping of the outer layer of the glulam, the ground-floor truss is extended into a diagrid that wraps the upper two floors, but is thermally separated from the CLT by a sandwich of insulation. This oscillation between structure and skin, between oblique and rectilinear, intensifies the dynamic between the building's two entangled figures.

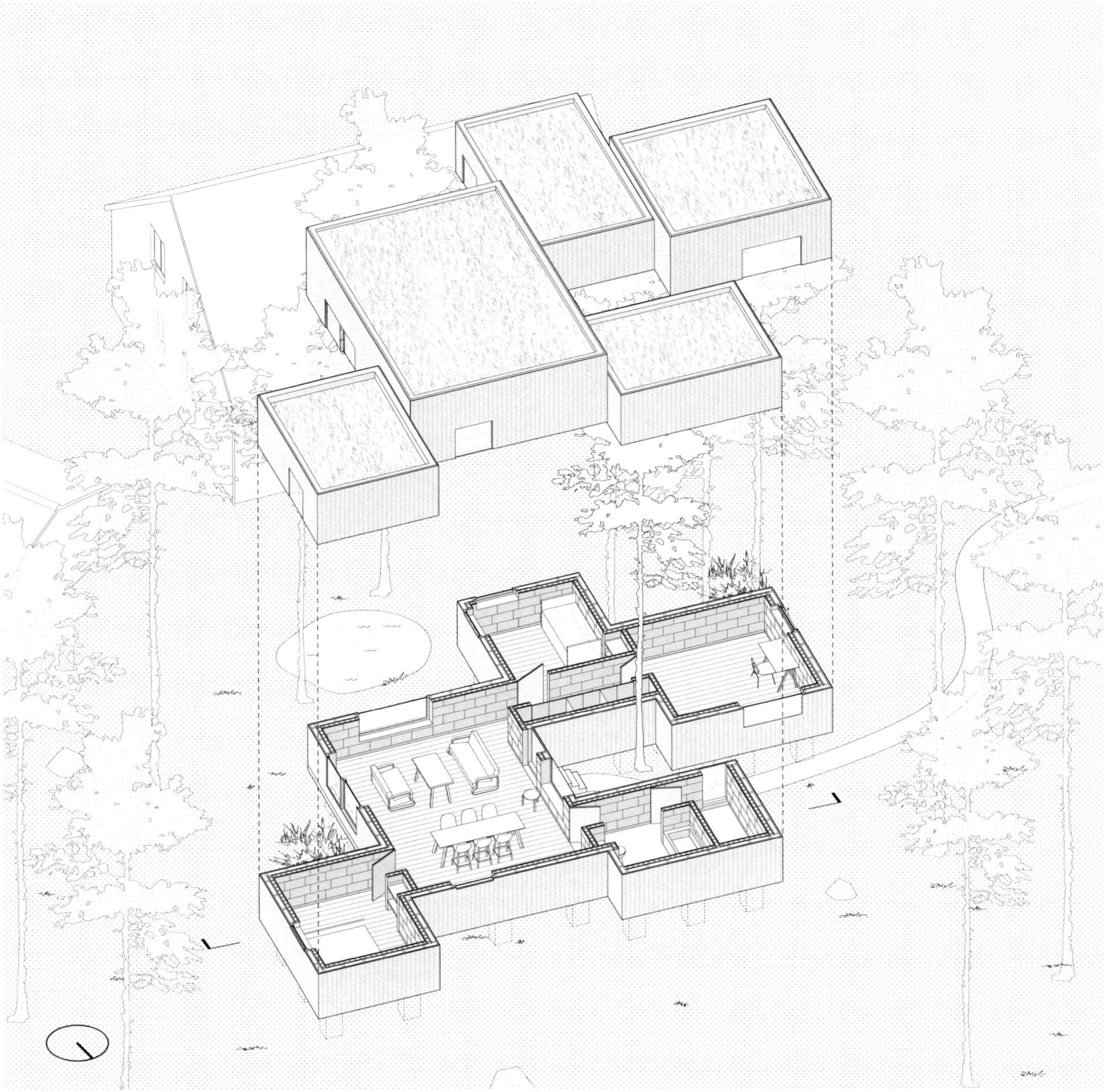

House Köris | Zeller & Moye

Located near a lake in a forested region south of Berlin, this house is an assembly of five volumes almost entirely constructed from wood. In section the house floats above the seasonally damp ground, while the plan of the house is designed to negotiate around the existing tall pine trees and their roots. The front entry courtyard is marked by a single pine tree. Based on a prefabricated hollow wood block as the primary wall structure, the volumes of the house have distinct heights using either six, seven, or eight courses. The units of the house each contain a discrete program, with the largest being a collective living and dining area, the smallest a bathroom. The three mid-sized units are adaptable into bedrooms, studios, or guest

Klein Köris, Germany | 2020

rooms. While the massing and program emphasize the house as a collection of parts, the material is singular and uniform, with both the exterior and interior clad in locally sourced spruce.

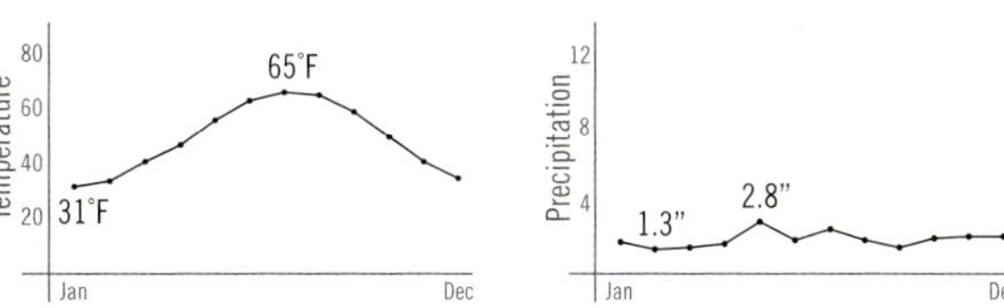

House Köris

Although the house is only 1400 sq ft (130 sq m), it uses four different wood assembly systems all made from spruce to achieve its specific performance and aesthetic characteristics. First, the floor and ceiling systems are laminated mass timber 5.5 in (140 mm) and 6.3 in (160 mm) deep respectively, with the floor planks resting on wood beams, themselves spanning across concrete piles that extend above the ground. Second, the primary wall structure is hollow custom wood block units, staggered like brick in a common bond pattern and infilled with wood fiber insulation. Solid wood members cap the bottom and top of each wall, milled to notch into the blocks. Third, wood sleepers and exterior joists thicken both the

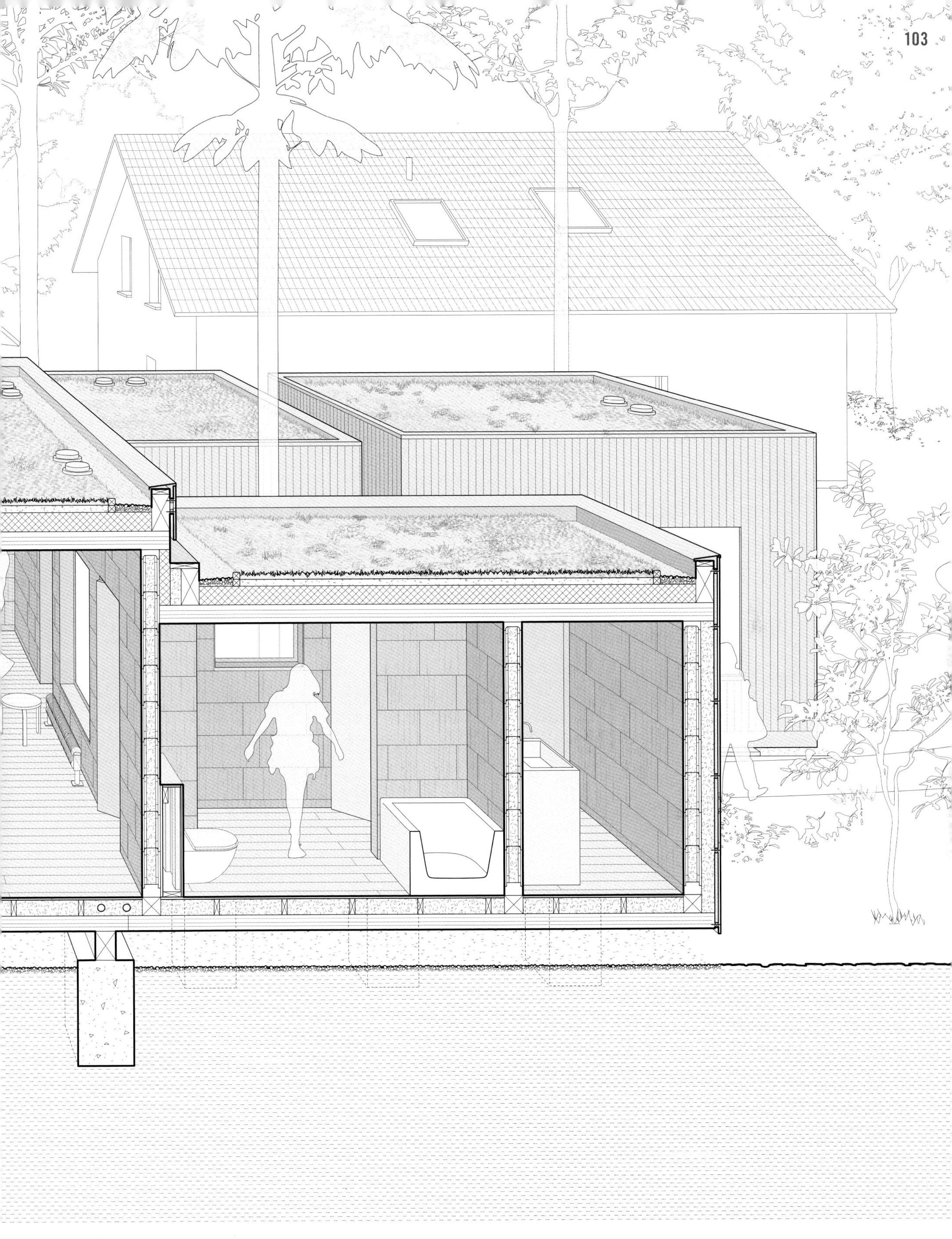

horizontal and vertical surfaces adding room for more insulation, and providing a plenum for the distribution of services in the floor. Finally, a fourth system of wood planks is used to surface the floor and the exterior skin, with the vertical cladding lapping over the window frames making a seamless transition from the wood to the large glass panes. With the exception of the green roof, the entire house displays spruce as its surface, with the pattern of the walls and ceiling also exhibiting the joints of their distinctly different structural and fabrication systems.

BAMBOO

-418 $kgCO_2e/m^3$

Plywood; INBAR

Bamboo

-608 $kgCO_2e/m^3$

Culms; INBAR

BAMBOO

Among the world's fastest growing plants, bamboo is a woody grass with significant carbon mitigation and architectural potential. Bamboo has a vast array of uses historically and a flexibility and strength that make it a versatile construction material. Used in their minimally processed state, full culms can act as primary structure, can be aggregated into surfaces, or transformed into strips and laminated or woven into a variety of building products.

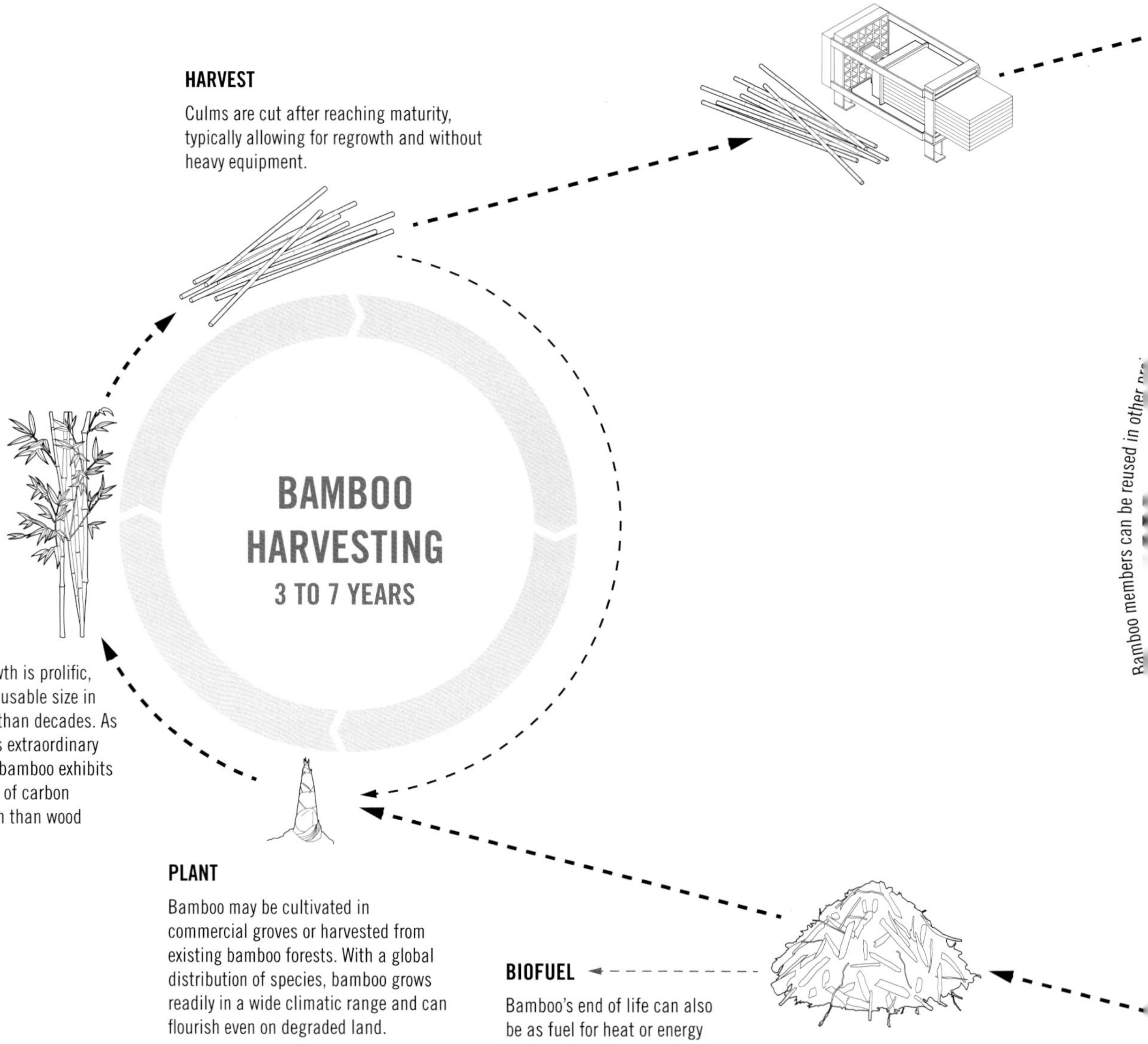

PROCESSING + MANUFACTURING

Full culms are treated with preservatives to ensure greater longevity for direct use or cut into strips and further processed into laminated or strand woven products.

HARVEST

Culms are cut after reaching maturity, typically allowing for regrowth and without heavy equipment.

BAMBOO HARVESTING
3 TO 7 YEARS

Bamboo members can be reused in other

GROWTH

Bamboo growth is prolific, growing to a usable size in years rather than decades. As a result of its extraordinary growth rate, bamboo exhibits a higher rate of carbon sequestration than wood timber.

PLANT

Bamboo may be cultivated in commercial groves or harvested from existing bamboo forests. With a global distribution of species, bamboo grows readily in a wide climatic range and can flourish even on degraded land.

BIOFUEL

Bamboo's end of life can also be as fuel for heat or energy generation.

MULCH

Salvaged bamboo can be ground into mulch for landscaping or to biodegrade and enrich soil.

CONSTRUCTION

Full culms may be used as primary structural elements or aggregated into surfaces and enclosure systems. Building with bamboo culms often requires specialized construction techniques and empirical methods due to the natural variability of the material. Alternately, more conventional construction may employ bamboo in the form of sheet goods such as flooring and plywood or even laminated beams.

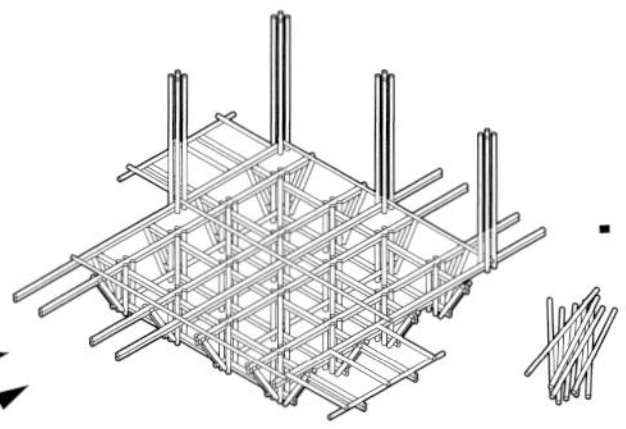

BAMBOO CONSTRUCTION

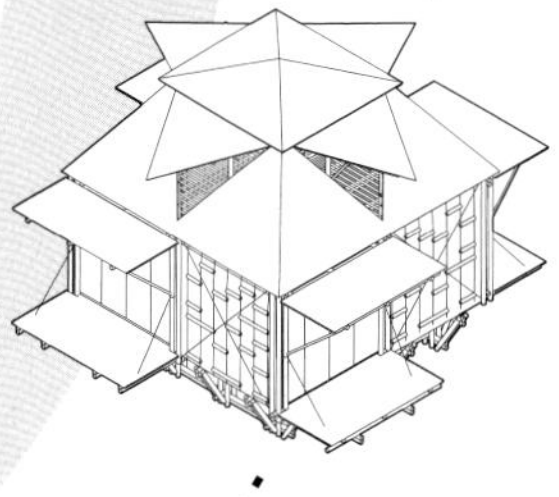

USE

Bamboo relies on proper processing to protect against the effects of insects and fungus. If properly treated and maintained, its durability can be in the range of decades and comparable to certain types of wood structure.

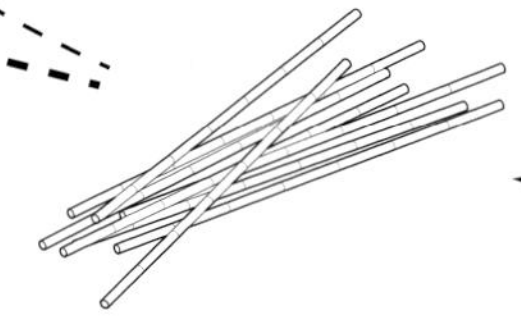

DISASSEMBLY

Depending on joining techniques and the presence of added materials like concrete, bamboo can be reclaimed for reuse or downcycled into bamboo products or mulch.

BAMBOO

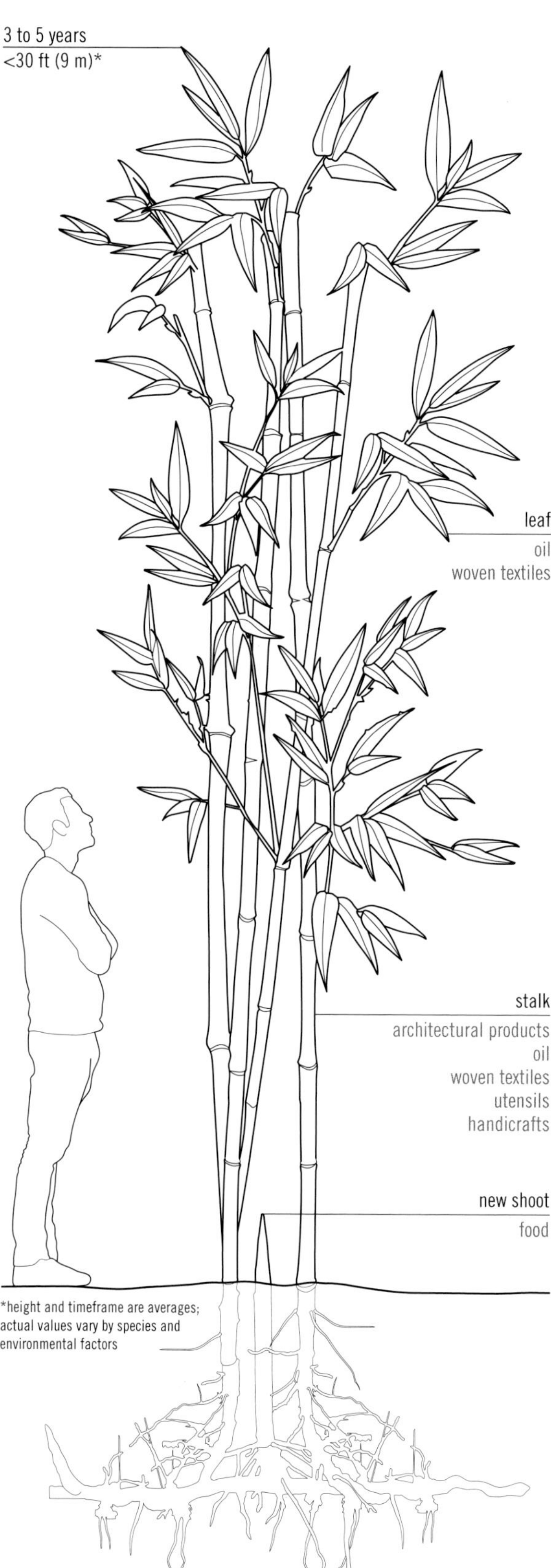

PRIMARY SPECIES AND GROWING REGIONS

Chusquea and Guadua: Amazon Basin and the tropical Americas
Dendrocalamus and Gigantochloa: India, Indonesia, South Asia
Phyllostachys: China, Himalayas, Japan

HARVESTING

Bamboo poles, or culms, with a suitable diameter are selected and harvested from the forest or plantation, with most species used for construction maturing in three to seven years. Unlike timber, harvesting allows regeneration and is frequently accomplished without heavy machinery.

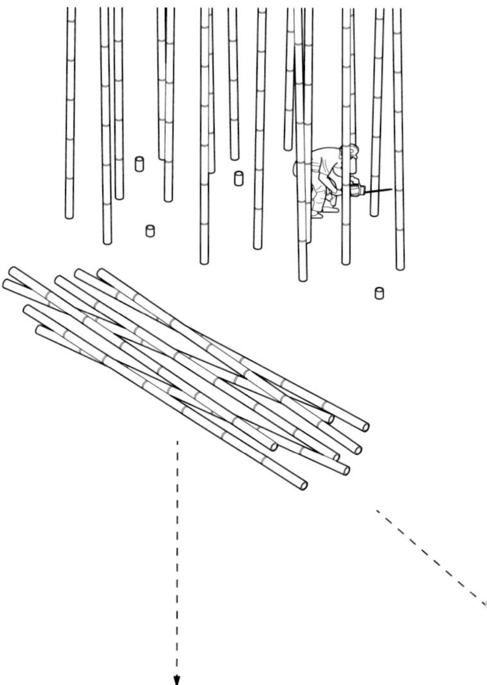

PUNCTURING

Culms are cleaned and a metal rod is used to break the interior partitions so that liquid preservative can flow to all parts.

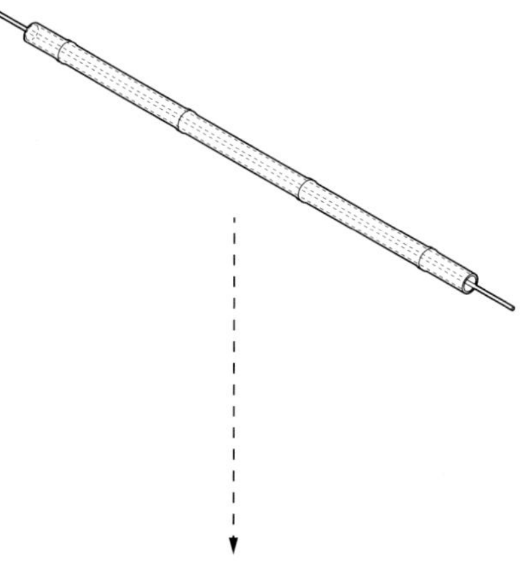

TREATING OR PRESERVING

Culms are submerged in a borax solution to protect them from mold, termites, and other insects.

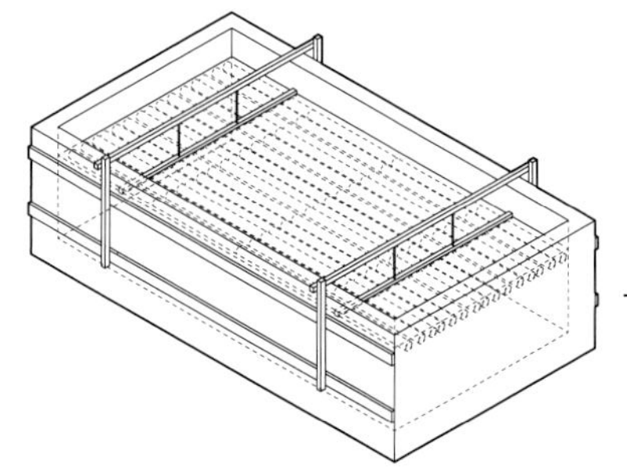

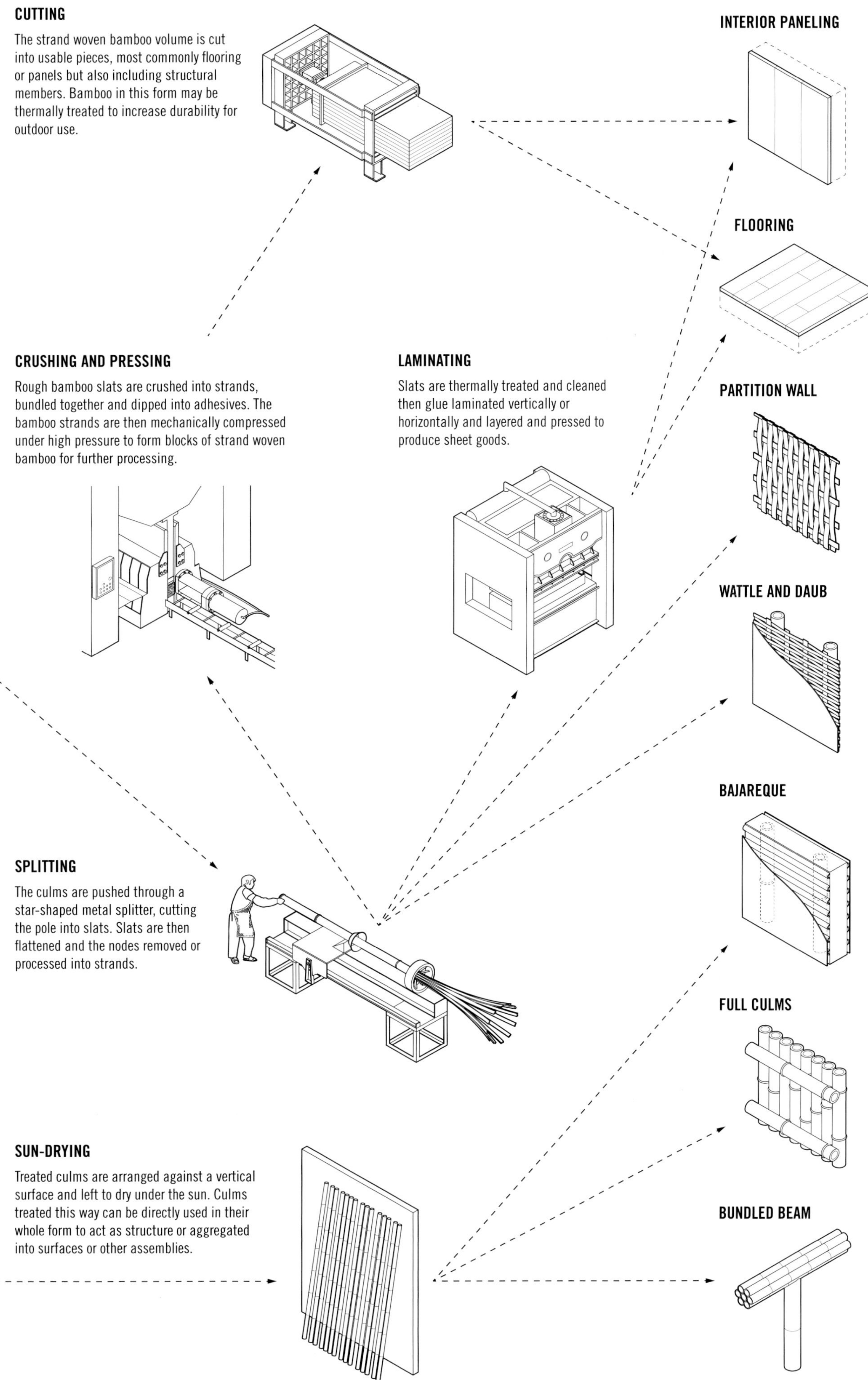
CUTTING
The strand woven bamboo volume is cut into usable pieces, most commonly flooring or panels but also including structural members. Bamboo in this form may be thermally treated to increase durability for outdoor use.
CRUSHING AND PRESSING
Rough bamboo slats are crushed into strands, bundled together and dipped into adhesives. The bamboo strands are then mechanically compressed under high pressure to form blocks of strand woven bamboo for further processing.
LAMINATING
Slats are thermally treated and cleaned then glue laminated vertically or horizontally and layered and pressed to produce sheet goods.
SPLITTING
The culms are pushed through a star-shaped metal splitter, cutting the pole into slats. Slats are then flattened and the nodes removed or processed into strands.
SUN-DRYING
Treated culms are arranged against a vertical surface and left to dry under the sun. Culms treated this way can be directly used in their whole form to act as structure or aggregated into surfaces or other assemblies.
INTERIOR PANELING
FLOORING
PARTITION WALL
WATTLE AND DAUB
BAJAREQUE
FULL CULMS
BUNDLED BEAM

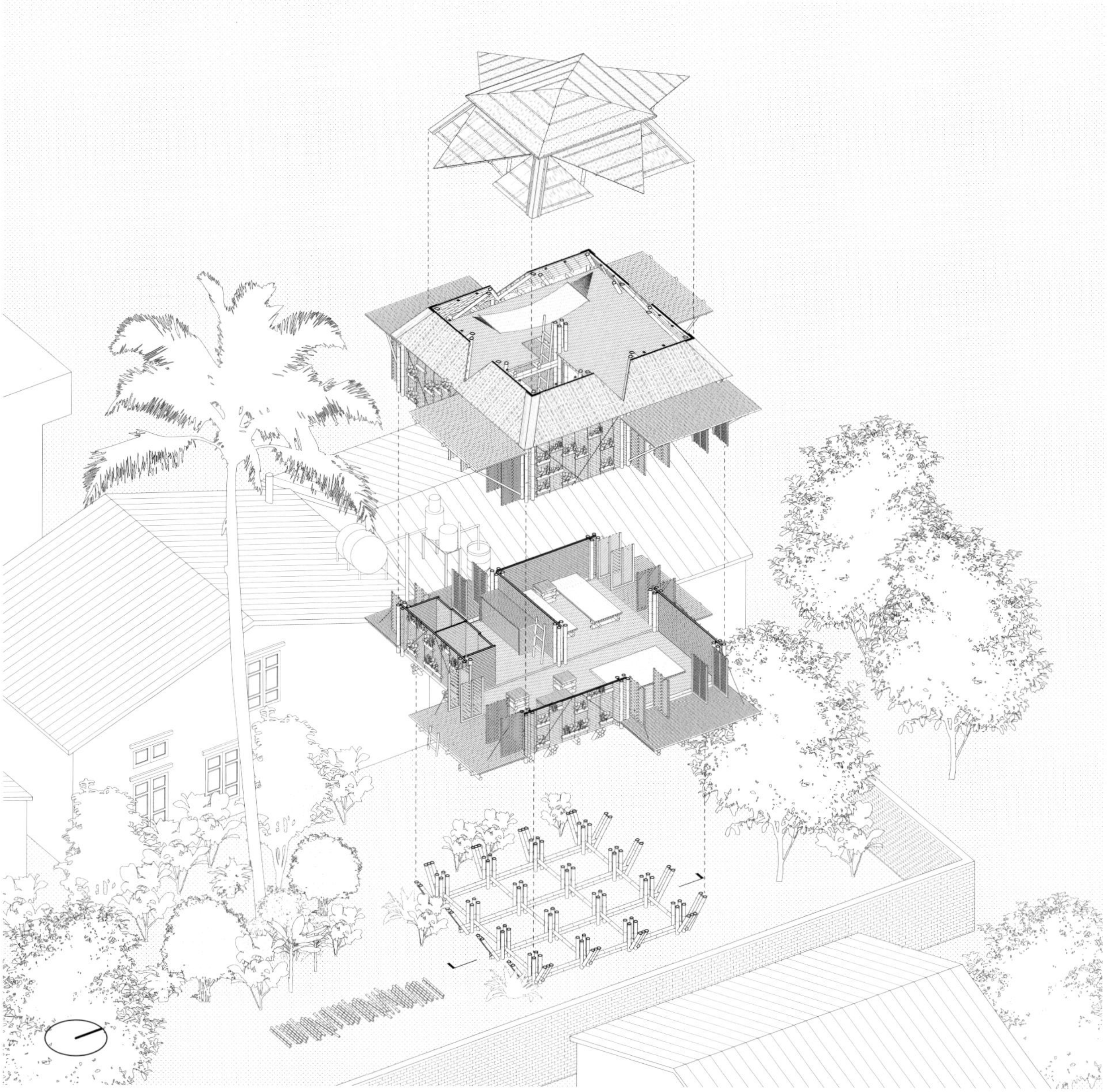

Blooming Bamboo Home | H&P Architects

The project proposes a modular prototype for self-built houses in Vietnam based on the ready availability of indigenous bamboo. Given the high incidence of floods and other natural disasters in the region, the structure is elevated, and built almost entirely of different sizes of lightweight bamboo culms variously clustered, bolted, stacked, and arrayed to create both structure and enclosing surface. The four square plan is intended to accommodate a family of six and can be scaled up for eight. Alternatively, the plan can accommodate a variety of uses, from education to medical facility to community center. The operable nature of the roof and walls are designed to take advantage of natural ventilation and, along with small

Hanoi, Vietnam | 2013

porch-like extensions, open the house to the surrounding site. Relentless in its deployment of bamboo, this modular house demonstrates the capacity of a single, biogenic material to create a density of tectonic, textural, and spatial conditions.

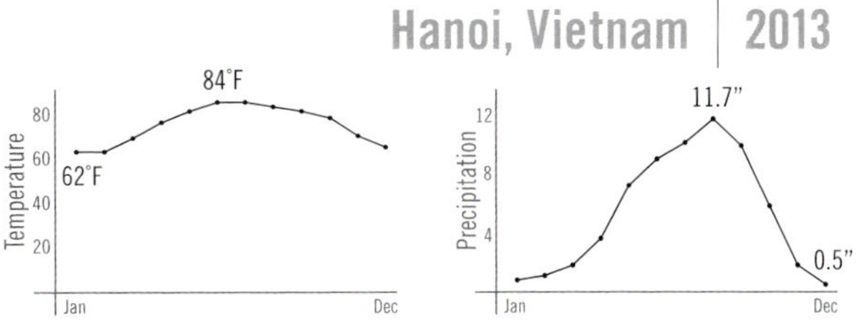

Blooming Bamboo Home

A repeatable module based on culm lengths of 3.3 or 6.6 meters forms the basis for this experiment in the potentials of a full-building approach to bamboo construction. Four cubic bays are lifted above the ground on bamboo stilts and are topped by an inhabitable roof. In addition to the primary structure, all surfaces of the house are comprised of tightly stacked assemblies of bamboo cane in different dimensions, arrayed to form floors, walls, doors, roofs, and even the interior furniture. The shifting scales of the linear bamboo components create variety in their repetition, generating a diversity of visual and textural effects. Pivoting, lattice-like doors and triangular panels in the roof open the house to breezes and

facilitate stack effect ventilation. The house's elevation above the ground plane is a response to the prevalence of regional flooding, allowing the lightweight construction to withstand floods up to 1.5 meters (4.9 feet). During more placid conditions the undercroft allows for the sheltering of small livestock. A variant of the prototype is designed to float in even higher water. Integrated bamboo planters on the project's façade give the house its name.

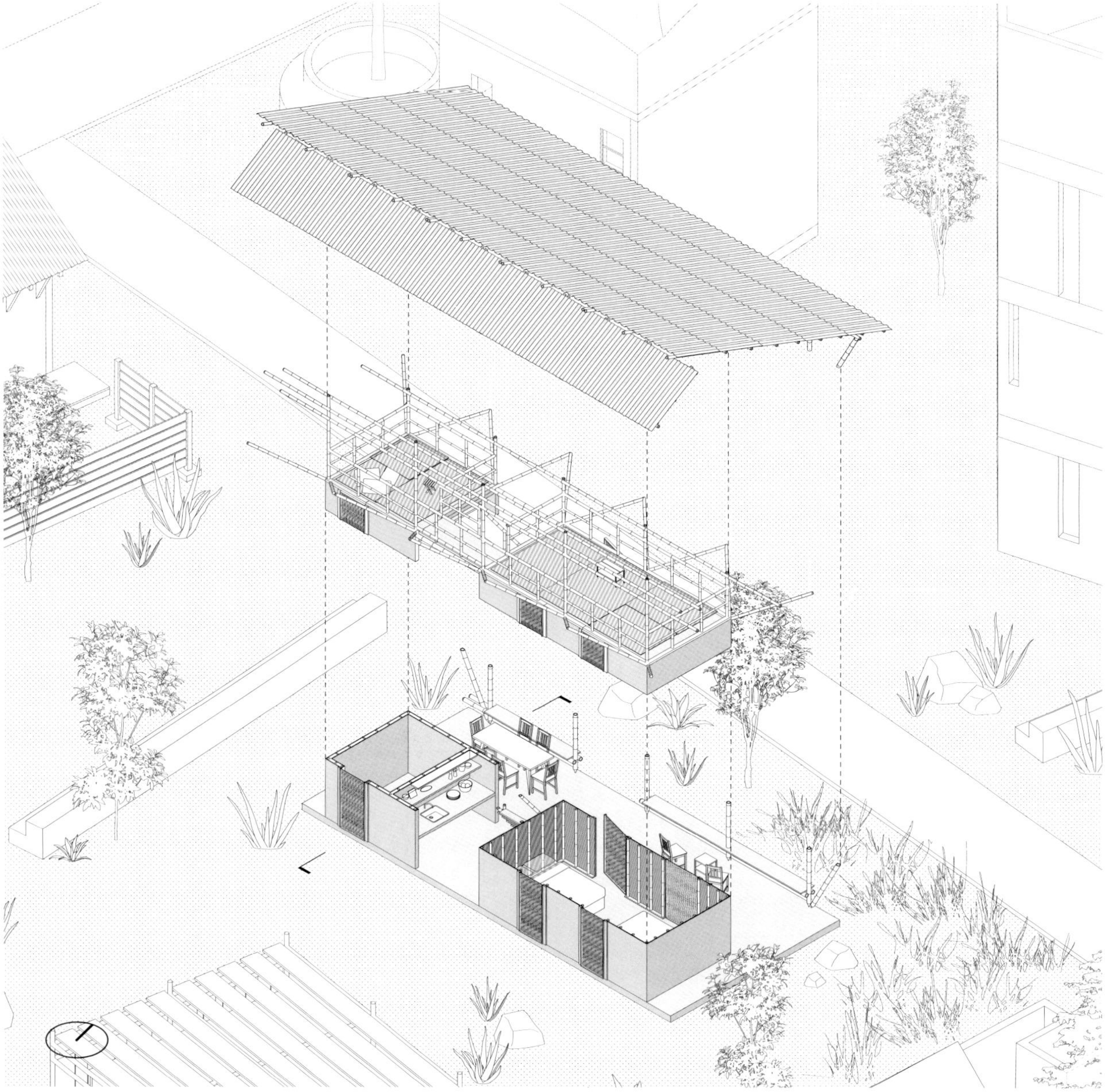

From the Territory to the Dweller | Rozana Montiel Estudio de Arquitectura

This experimental prototype is part of a research initiative to improve the quality of assisted self-constructed housing. The project seeks to redefine the traditional house type of the region, lifting the roof and creating an interplay between enclosed and semi-open spaces linked to the surrounding vegetation and site. Two ground-floor volumes, containing the private bedroom and bath, support extended, elevated, and sloping roof planes which also define a series of partially exterior rooms. These generous, multi-functional spaces, including a large, sheltered porch,

Xochitepec, Mexico | 2020

provide for the social and communal life of the inhabitants, opening to the surrounding landscape of fruit trees. The space between the roof and lower volumes act as sleeping lofts accessible via a stair at the center of the plan and promotes natural ventilation.

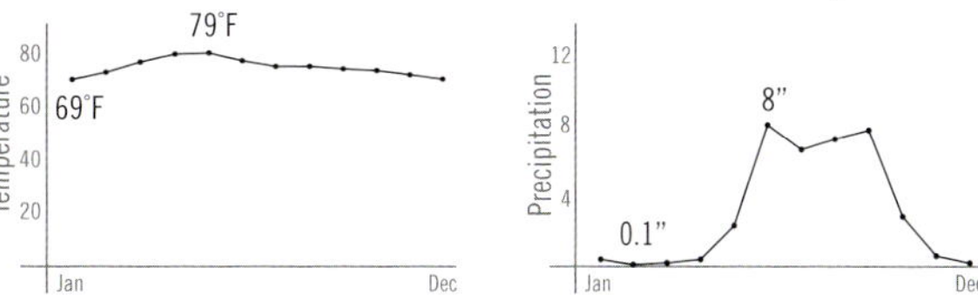

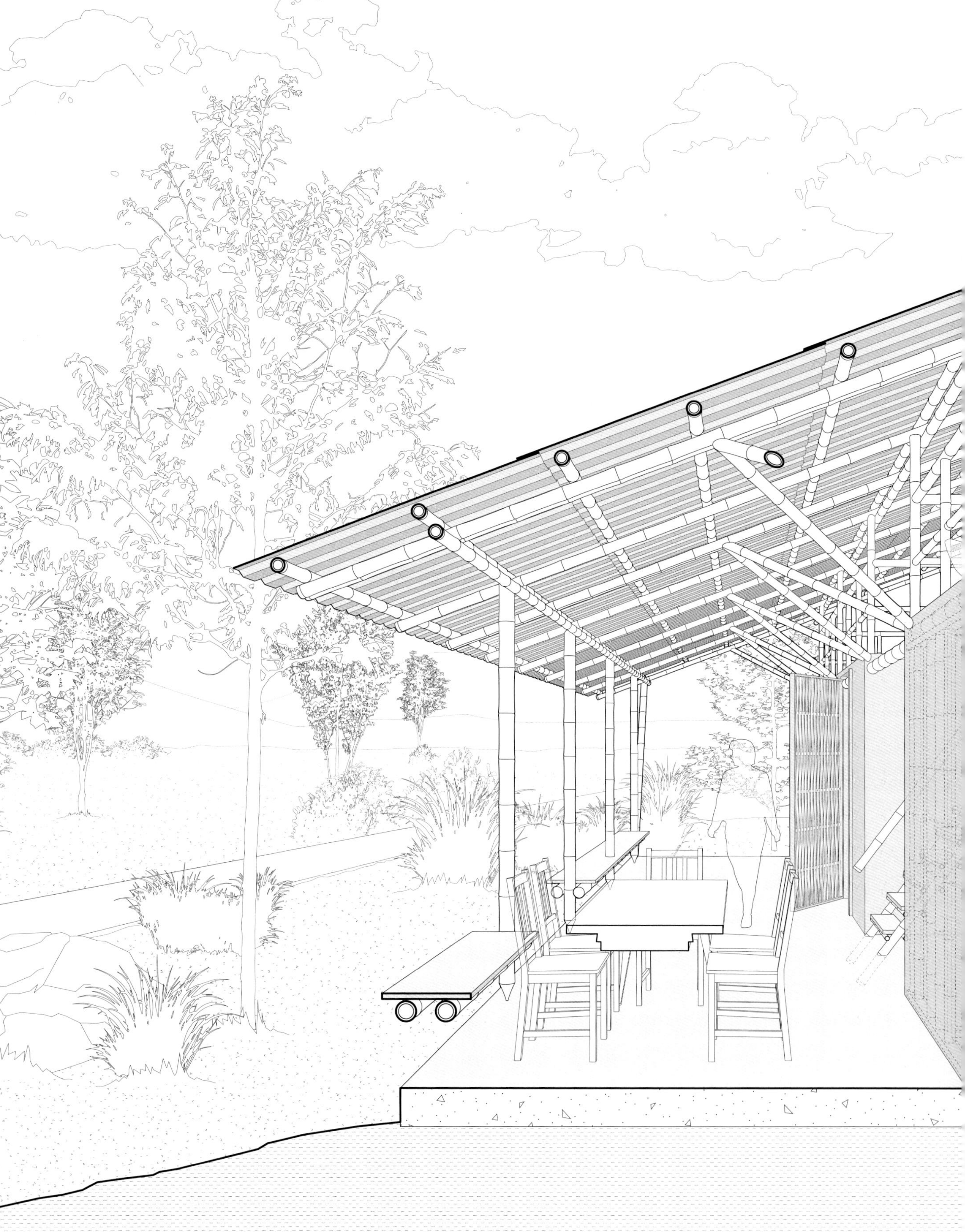

From the Territory to the Dweller

A lightweight roof supported by a framework of bamboo culms hovers over two solid enclosures, capturing a series of semi-enclosed rooms between and below. An expansive porch formed where the roof extends past the primary enclosure expands the usable space of this prototype house and connects it to its surrounding site. Defined by the structural bamboo verticals that support the roof, the multi-functional porch includes the kitchen and dining areas and accommodates the social life of the inhabitants. The area between the articulated roof and the top of the enclosed box-like room serves as additional sleeping lofts with natural ventilation, accessible via a bamboo ship ladder. The roof is clad with recycled poly-aluminum sheets and insulated beneath to minimize heat absorption and transfer. The more enclosed rooms are framed in bamboo and surfaced with bamboo bio-panel walls with a plaster finish and fitted with permeable woven bamboo doors. Creating a dialogue between the solidity of the enclosed rooms and the openness of the hovering roof planes, this minimal house provides a low-cost, efficient, and elegantly simple structural expression of bamboo.

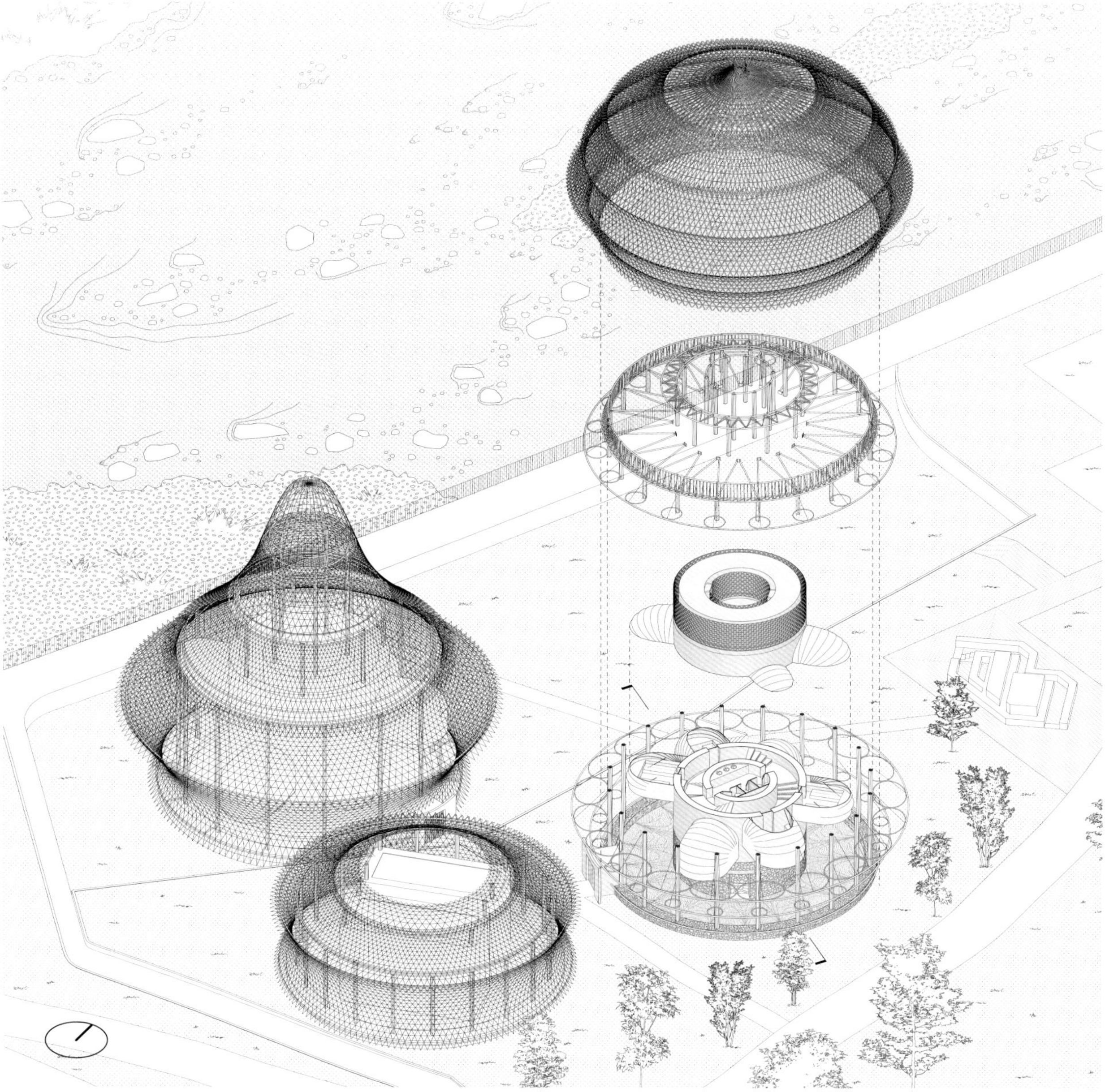

Bamboo Hostels | Studio Anna Heringer

The Bamboo Hostels, located in Baoxi, China, was developed for the International Bamboo Architecture Biennale. One of a series of three prototypical structures, each with contrasting shapes alluding to the area's tradition of ceramic vessels, the youth hostel for women explores the characteristics of natural, non-standardized, locally available materials: bamboo, earth, and stone. Drawing on local craft practices of basket weaving, the project comprises a series of nested volumes. A central core of stone and rammed earth is enveloped in a lattice of woven bamboo that creates a partially protected environment for a series of cantilevered sleeping cocoons. Juxtaposing the solidity and mass of the earthen core

Baoxi, China | 2016

with the ephemeral quality of the textile-like bamboo netting, the project intensifies the expressive potential of these disparate materials for this experimental temporary dwelling.

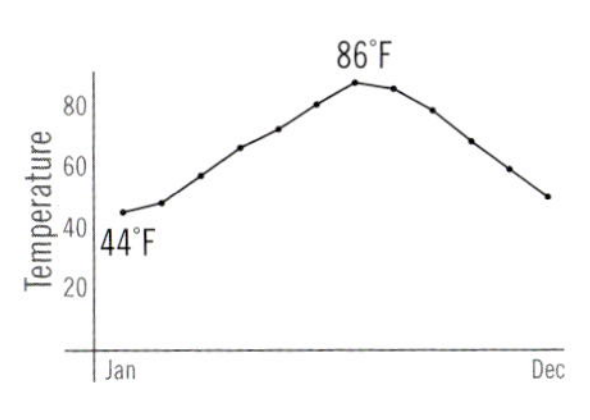

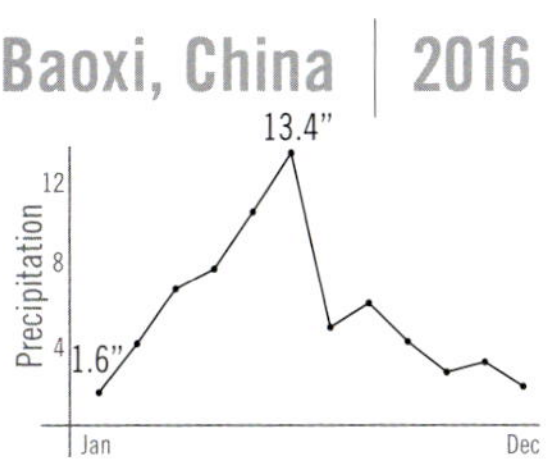

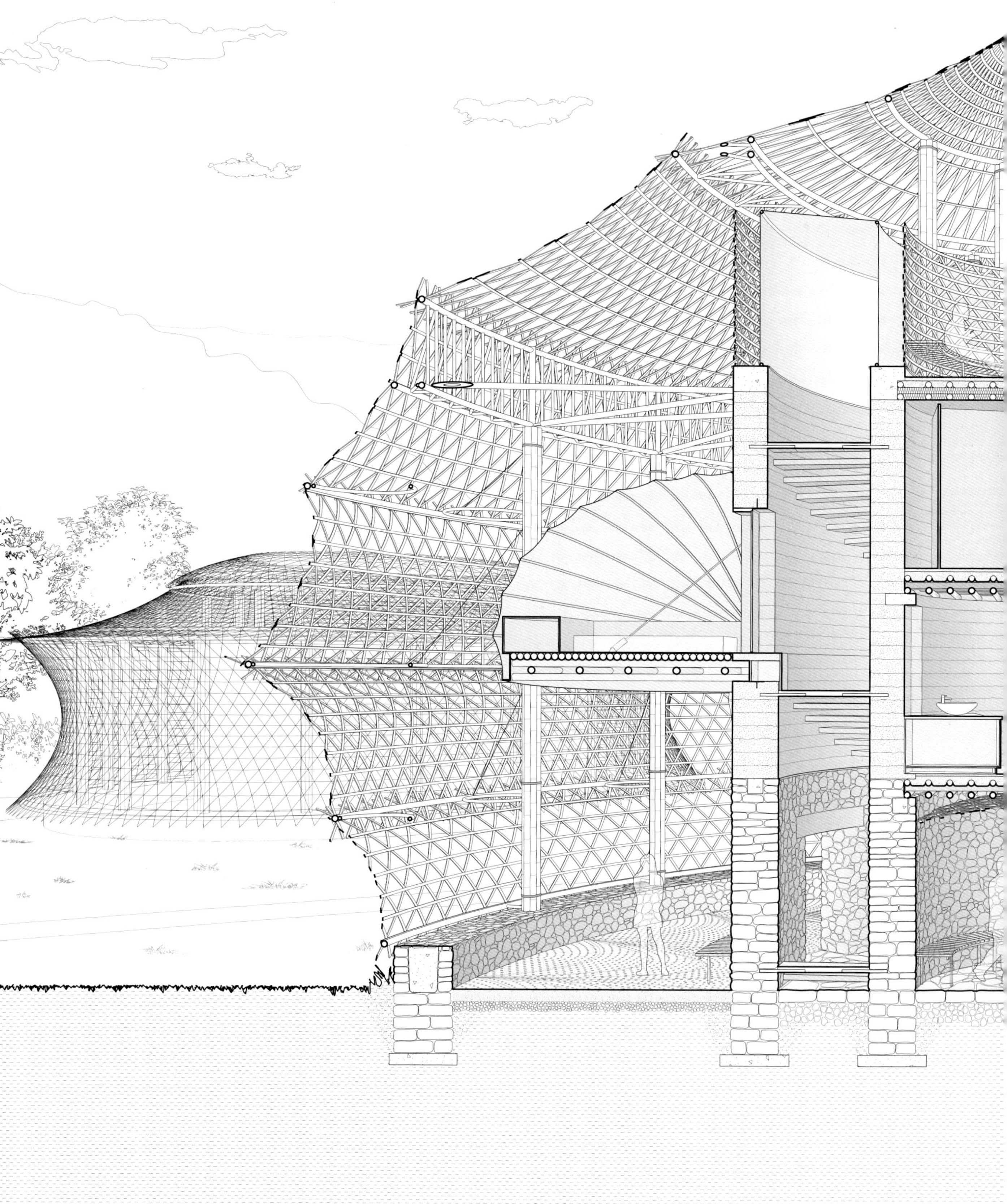

Bamboo Hostels

A cylindrical volume of stone and rammed earth is nested within a net-like enclosure of woven bamboo strips. The central volume, designed in consultation with Martin Rauch, houses bathing facilities, utility spaces, and a spiraling staircase that accesses a series of suspended sleeping platforms. The core, an exposed stone base with rammed earth wall above, is the only conditioned portion of the project. The sleeping pods, shrouded in fabric, cantilever from the solid core into the interstitial space between the contrasting enclosures, partly sheltered from rain and wind.

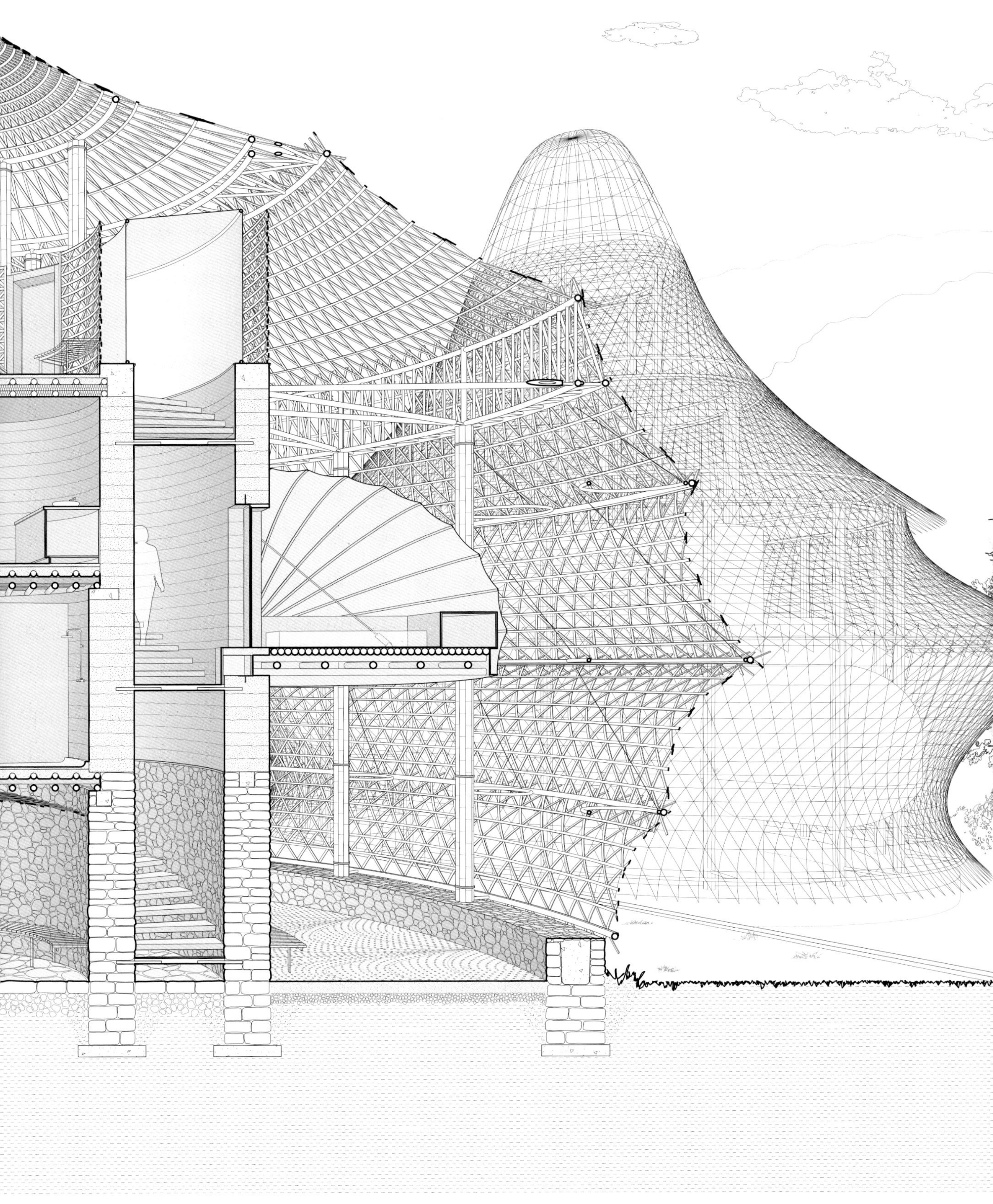

The outer structure of clustered bamboo culms and steel columns and trusses support a woven bamboo lattice that defines a permeable zone of collective social space. A series of steel hoops attached to the vertical structure induce tension in the outer membrane, while the bamboo lattice filters light and view, and casts complex shadows on the inner volume's textured surface. Exploiting the inherent characteristics of bamboo and earthen materials, the project creates a series of layered and nested environments with contrasting spatial and experiential qualities.

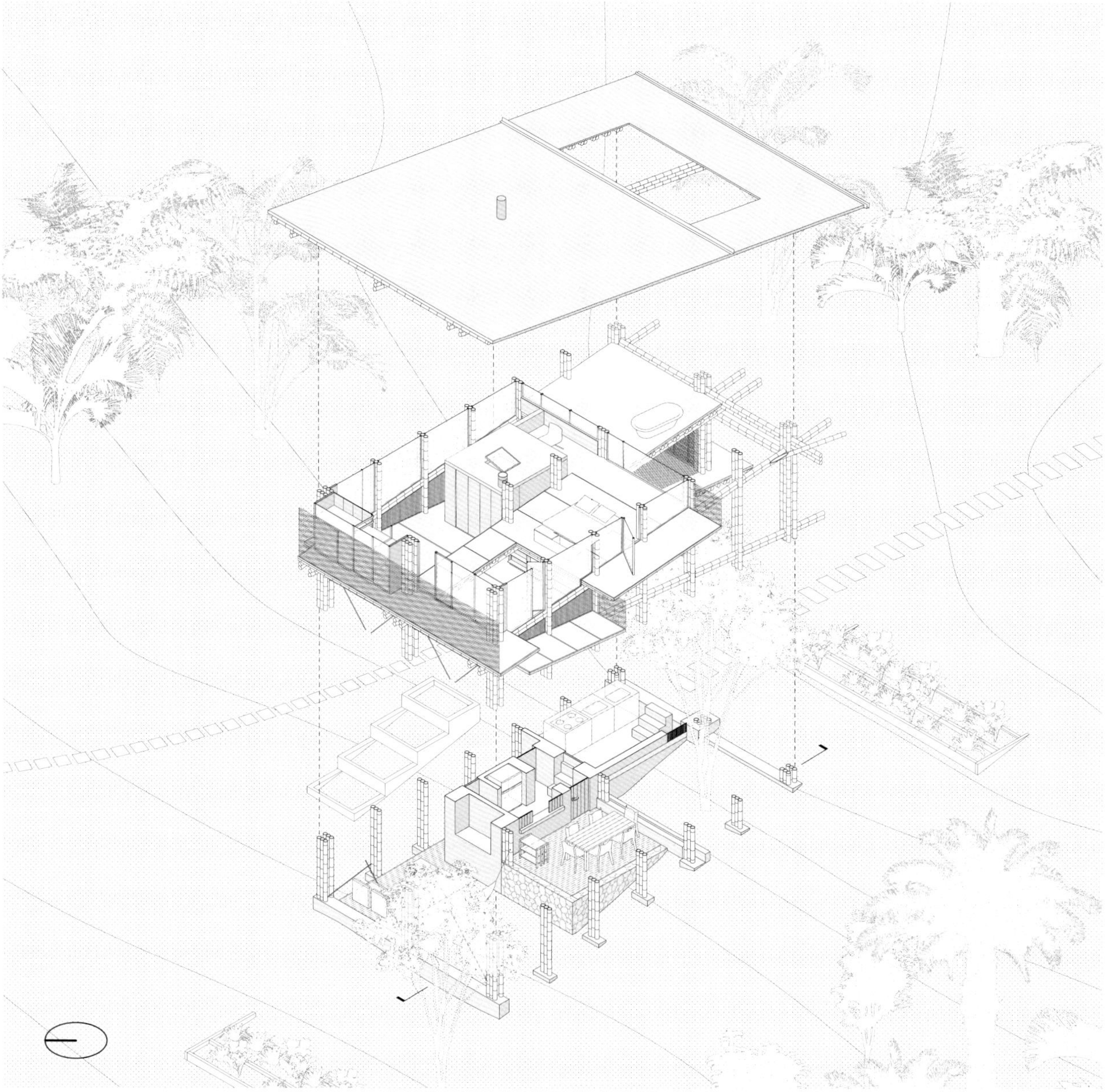

Cabañón DLPM | Juan Carlos Bamba + Ignacio de Teresa + Alejandro González

This small house, conceived as an observation platform for the surrounding landscape, is positioned between two existing trees on a rural site in a mountainous region. Composed of three inclined and perforated planes that comprise the floors and roof, the house eschews expectations of level surfaces for a continuous slope that rises from the angled terrain.

Sheltered below these diagonal planes are exterior dining and living patios, while a brick volume containing service spaces extends vertically through the floors. The *cabañón* is constructed primarily with clusters of large indigenous bamboo culms, forming the structural frame of beams and purlins. Layers of mosquito netting, glass, and polycarbonate provide

Las Tunas, Ecuador | 2016

for weather and insect enclosure while maximizing views to the surrounding gardens and site. Playfully rigorous, the house deploys a dynamic spatial logic derived from the landscape and delineated in a natural material from the local ecology.

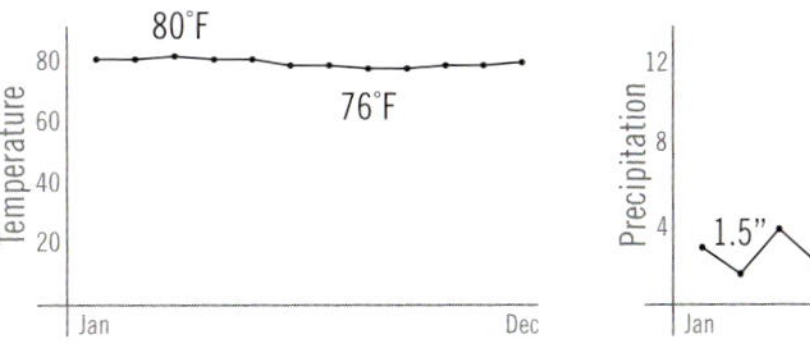

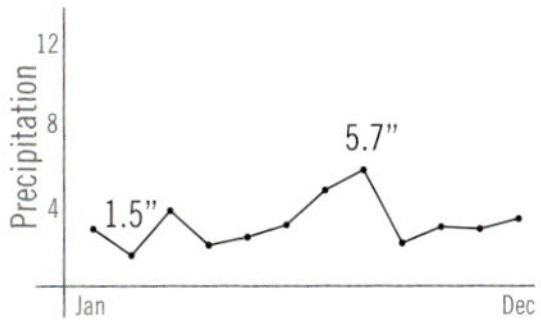

Cabañón DLPM

Three primary sloped surfaces—lower and upper floor plates and roof at angles of 8%, 10%, and 16% respectively—are stacked in zig-zag fashion above a sloping terrain. The section reveals the interplay of these inclined surfaces which are perforated to accommodate vertical voids that weave through the primary bamboo structure. Bamboo culms running in different orientation and clustered as columns, purlins, or beams articulate the diagonal system of the ramping floors, while stepped dry-laid brick terraces and a brick core—a mini-building within a building—provide a series of sheltered exterior patio rooms and more enclosed kitchen and bath areas. The roof is made from concrete poured over split bamboo,

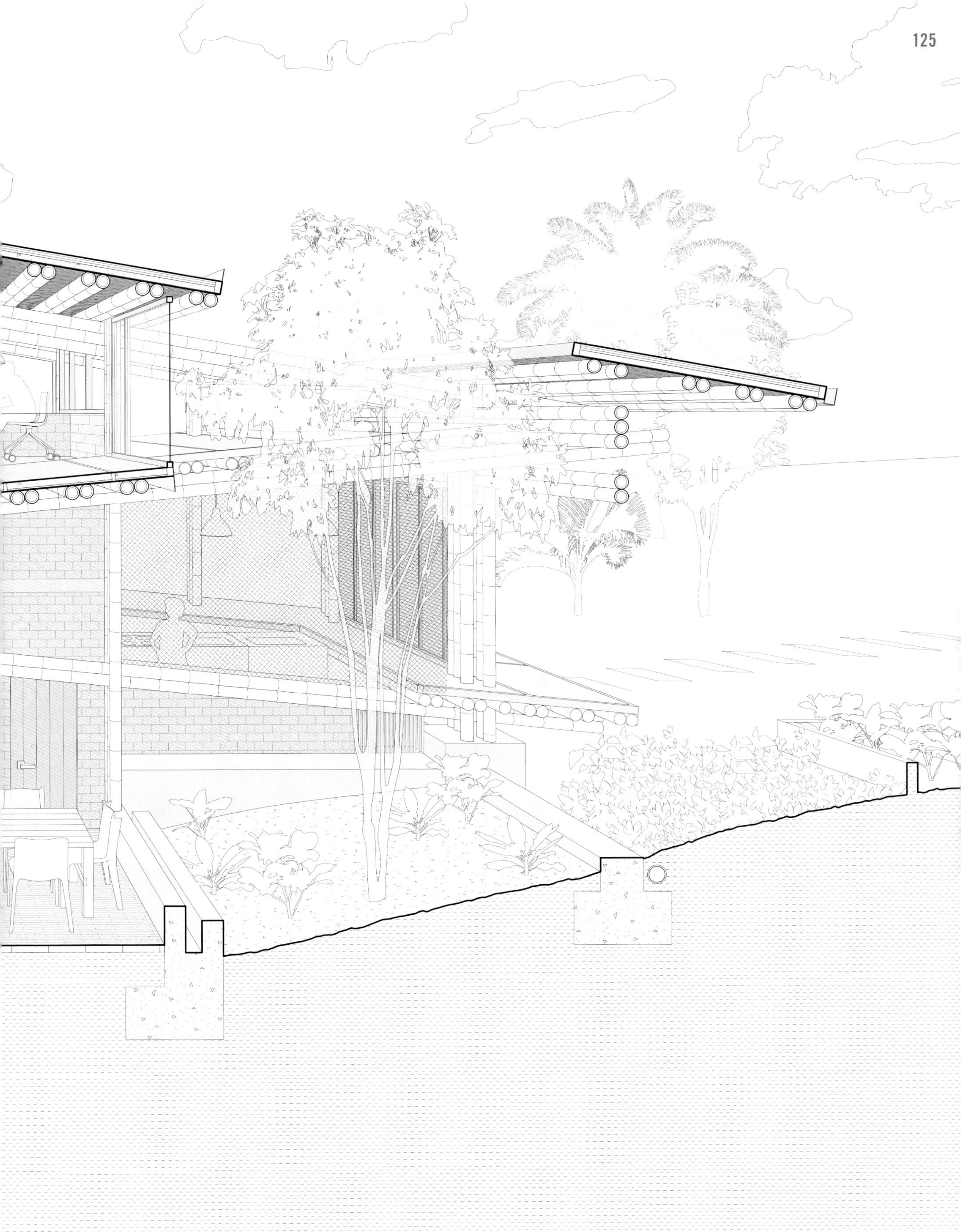

lightened by the addition of rice husks. The sloping interior floors accommodate the sleeping areas and ramping circulation. A study is situated atop the brick volume and an exterior bath is located at the topmost accessible point of the bamboo ramps. Built-in furniture responds to the angled geometry of the floors and provides ergonomic accommodation for sleeping.

A large cabinet-like element on the exterior façade acts as inhabitable furniture and accommodates bunk beds for children. Large windows frame views to the exterior and operable panels access net-enclosed porches.

Trika Villa | Chiangmai Life Architects

This house responds to the climatic demands of its tropical setting through a functional disconnection between the roof and walls. Three semi-enclosed clusters of rooms are organized around a series of partly exterior spaces and sheltered beneath a large bamboo roof. The suspended roof, supported by bundles of bamboo culms sprouting from columns in the plastered adobe brick walls, provides protection from the sun and rain and allows for natural ventilative cooling. Each of the more enclosed bedroom spaces is 'roofed' by a canopy of mosquito netting to mitigate insects while allowing for air flow and mitigating the need for air conditioning. The roof is formed by a complex assemblage of bamboo members, including

Chiangmai, Thailand | 2014

full, split, and clustered culms of several diameters comprising both structure and membrane. While most houses are defined by their plan, this environmentally responsive house is defined by the shaped section of its bamboo roof.

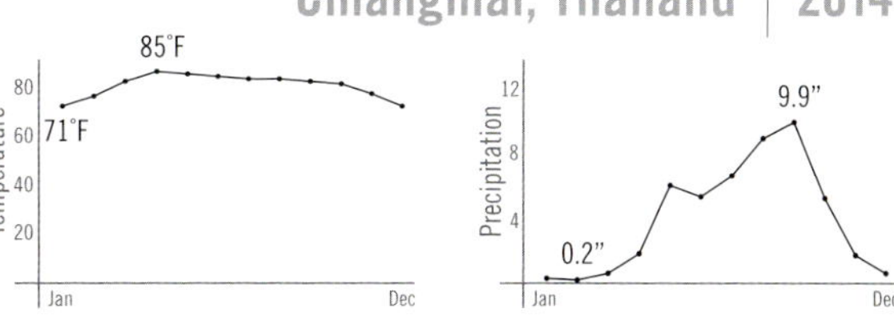

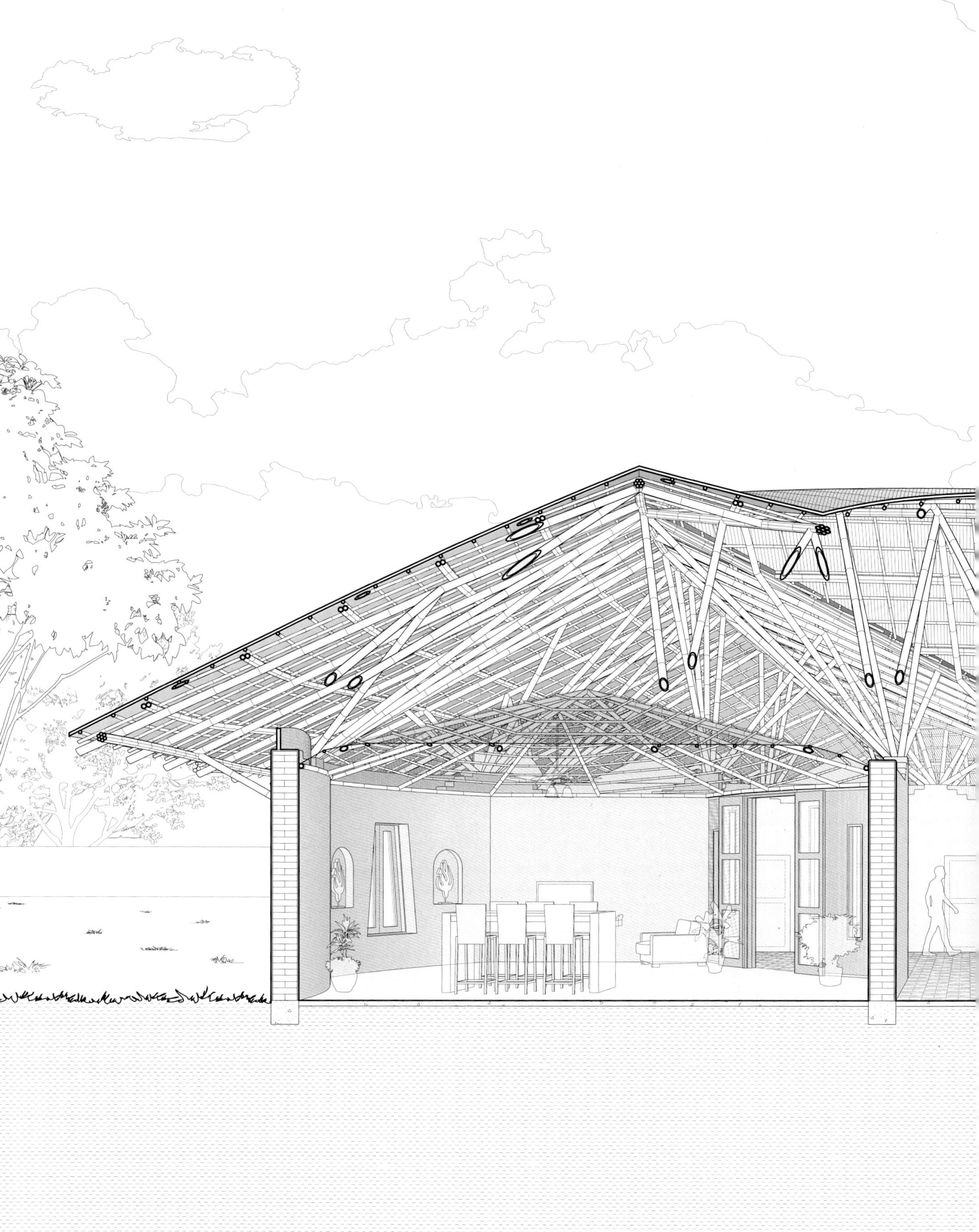

Trika Villa

An expansive bamboo roof is suspended above a series of adobe brick enclosed rooms clustered around an exterior living area and courtyard. Woven of variously scaled bamboo culms and sheathed in a skin of split bamboo shakes, the roof is propped up by bundles of bamboo diagonals that sprout from the solid walls below. Capped only by a transparent mesh of mosquito netting, the rooms are thermally open to the larger roof, allowing for ventilative cooling as air flows through the gap between the umbrella-like canopy and more solid walls. This intentionally unsealed condition, counter to the environmental logic of most house designs, mitigates the need for mechanical cooling while sheltering the inhabitants from sun, wind, and rain. While the room interiors, with finished fine earthen plaster walls and rammed earth floors, are more conventional, the strategically porous condition of the house renders its sheltered assemblage of partial enclosures appropriate to the tropical environs of its site. As a result, the complex geometry of the roof structure, visible throughout the house, provides both the primary architectural expression and performative logic of the house.

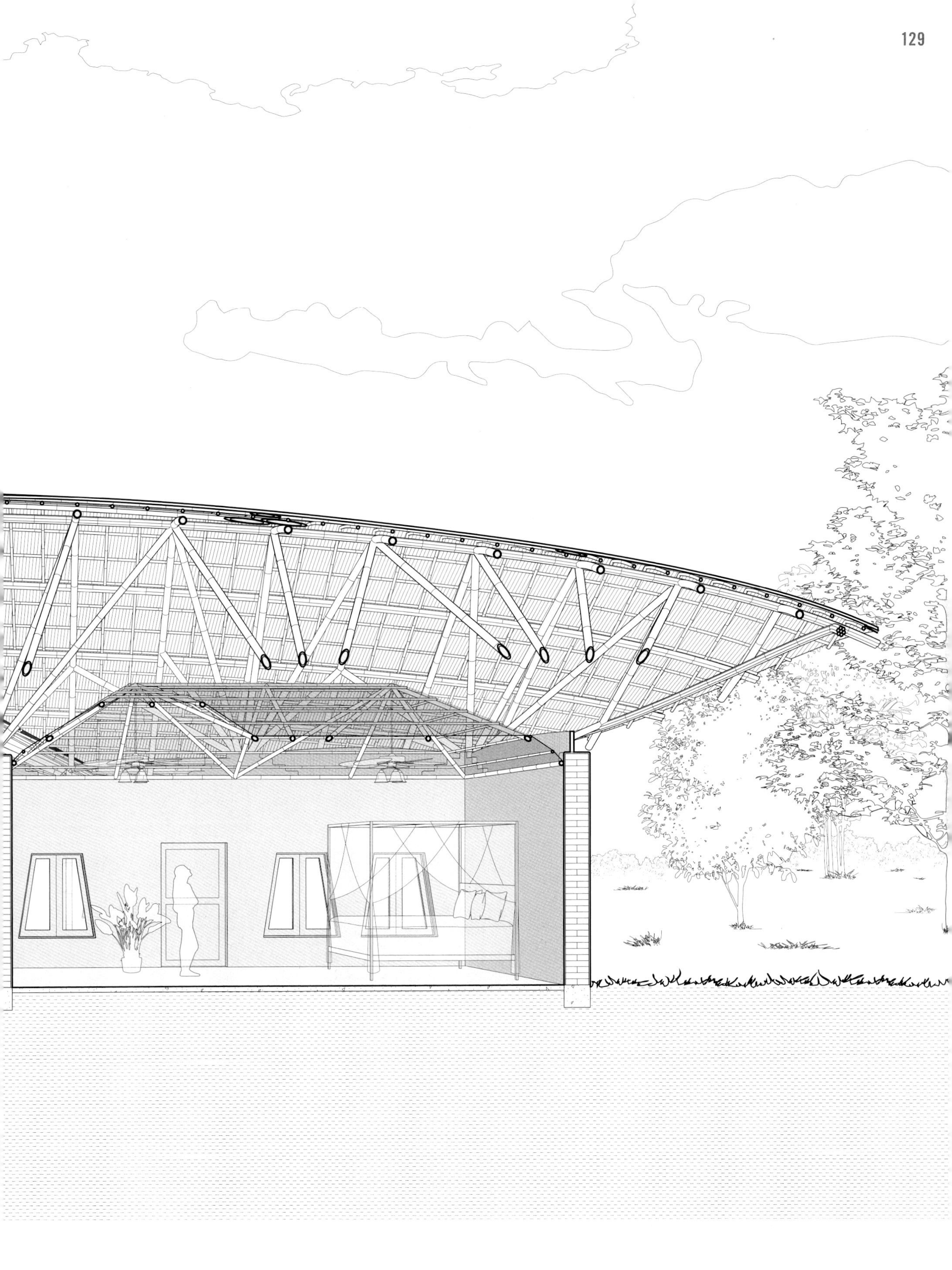

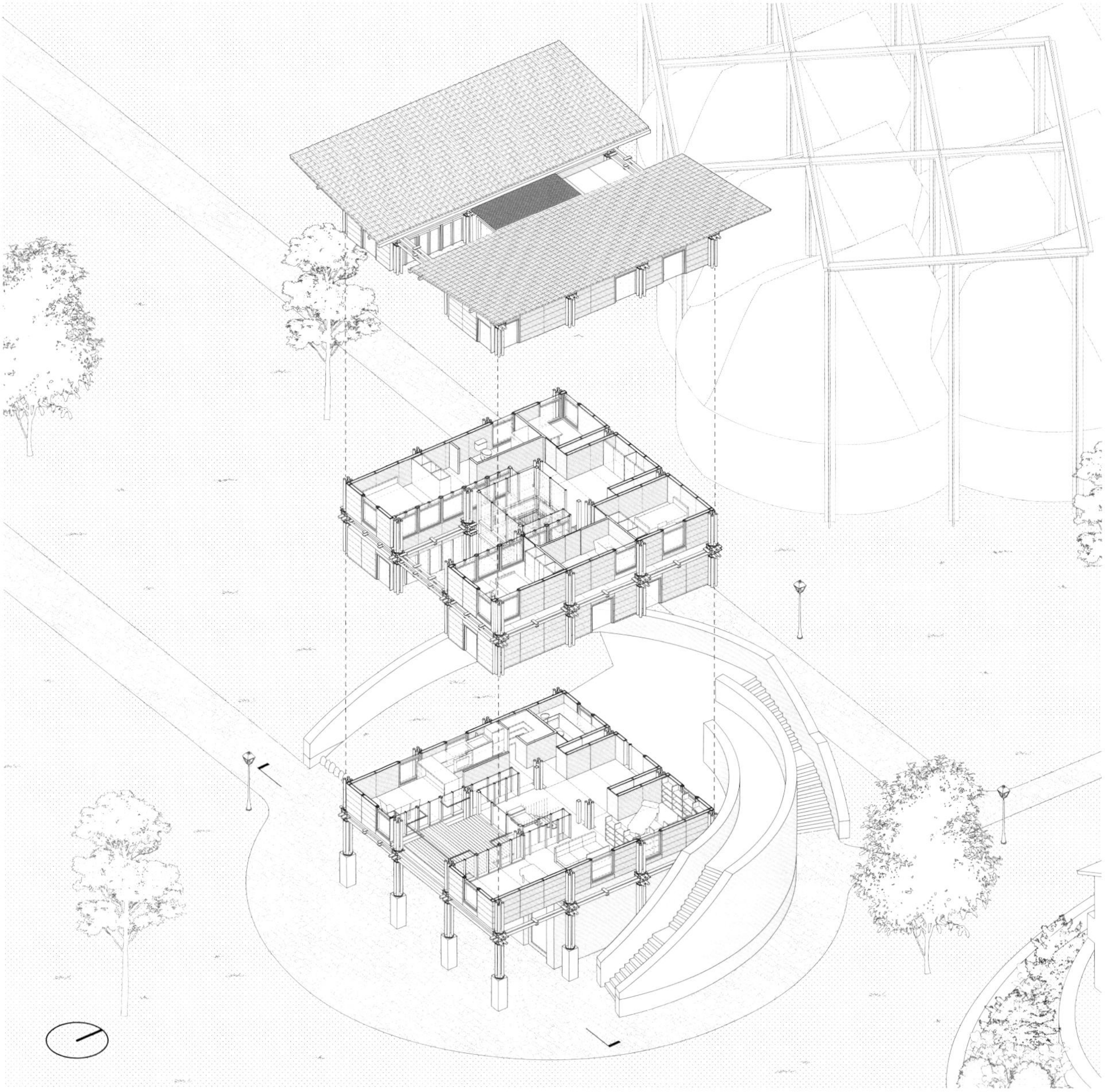

Energy Efficient Bamboo House | Studio Cardenas Conscious Design

This house, constructed for the International Bamboo Architecture Biennale in Baoxi, China, focuses on the benefits of this versatile biogenic building material. The project was intended as a housing prototype that combined local material practices with more industrialized modular means of construction. A nine-square grid in plan, the house is a three-story frame of conjoined bamboo culms straddling a rammed earth base. Customized metal joinery allowed the architects to connect horizontal and vertical clusters of bamboo poles without the negative effects of mechanical

Baoxi, China | 2016

fasteners. The three-dimensional grid is open at the center, responding to principles of Feng Shui, and filled at the perimeter with a modularized CLT enclosure system that defines the primary spaces of the house.

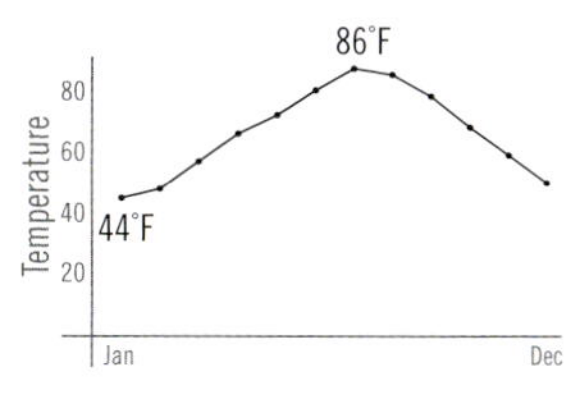

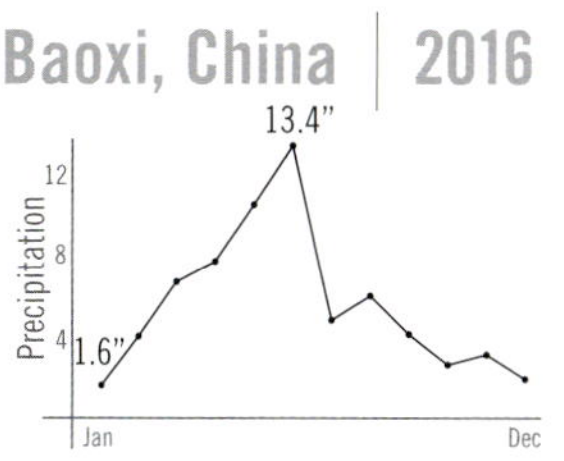

Energy Efficient Bamboo House

A three-dimensional grid of clustered bamboo culms provides the spatial and structural framework of this prototype house. Enclosed at the perimeter by a modularized system of CLT panels, the rooms of the house are expressed as independent volumes suspended within the bamboo matrix. The open center allows for natural ventilation, infiltration of daylight, and access to the suspended wood and steel stair. The vertical and horizontal framing comprises clusters of identically-sized bamboo culms interlinked by custom aluminum compression joints that alleviate the need for mechanical penetrations that would weaken the material, avoid added concrete often used to reinforce structural joints, and allow for potential

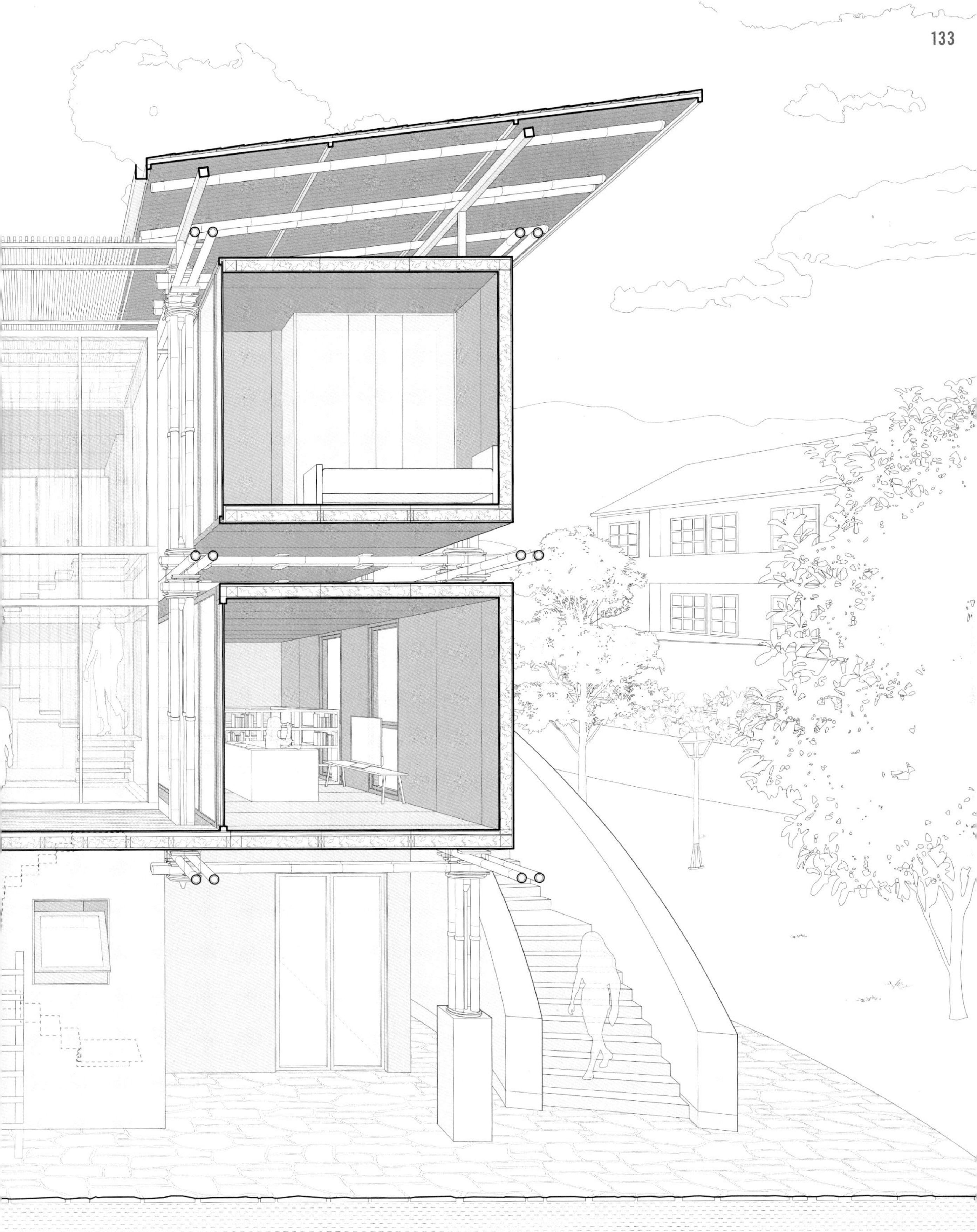

replacement of the vegetal elements. The CLT modules are insulated with recycled fabric and clad on the interior with bamboo finishes. In addition to the carbon sequestering properties of the bamboo, the project utilizes a rudimentary geothermal system for heating and cooling and graywater circulation. A semi-cylindrical base of rammed earth houses utility spaces while a floating bamboo roof is covered in local Luoquan clay tile. Both high and low tech, standardized and locally derived, the project combines natural materials with industrialized techniques to create a new low-carbon housing prototype.

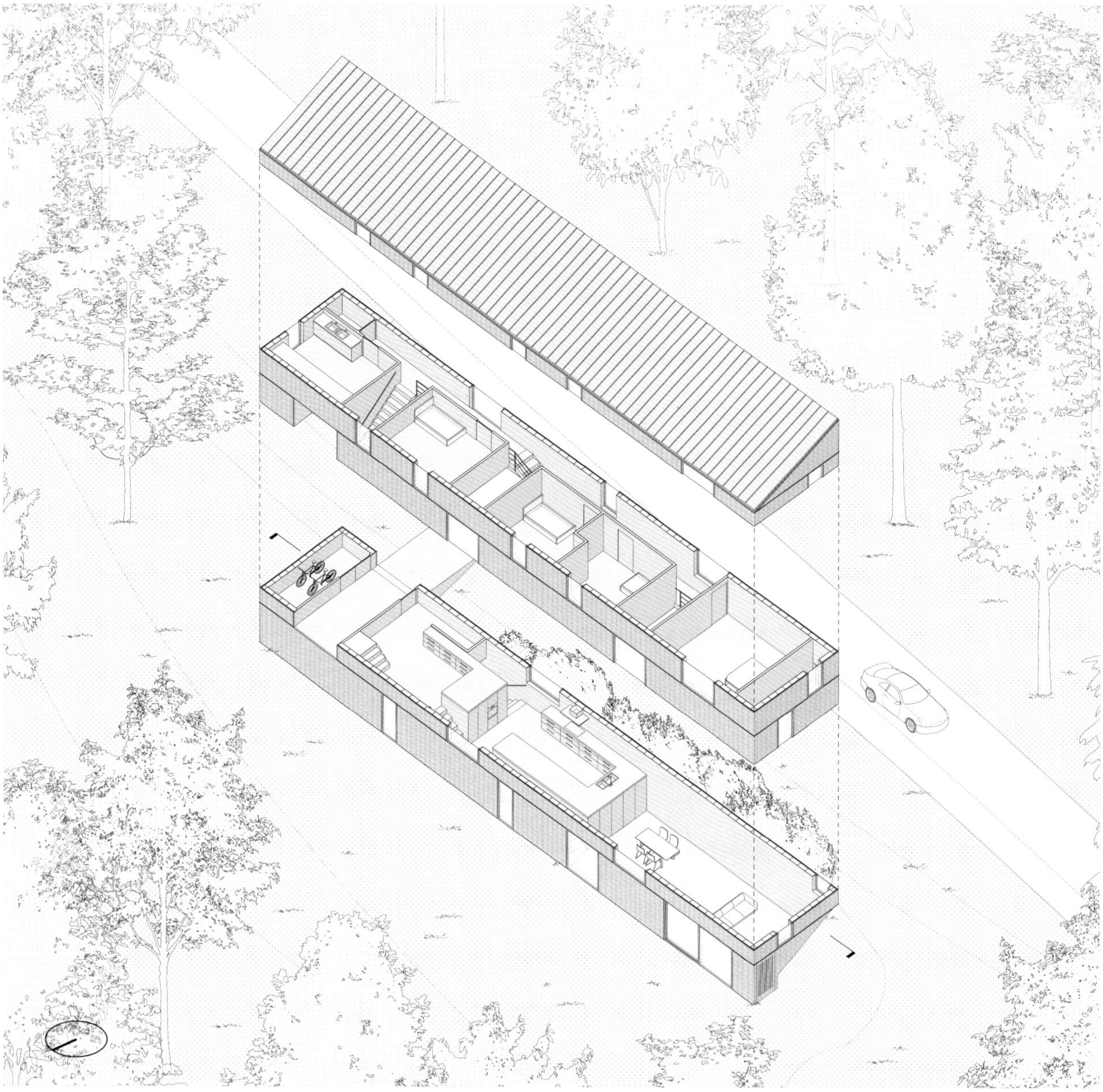

House Rotselaar | AST 77 Architecten

While bamboo is typically associated with warmer climates, the design of this house adapts the material for use in the northern European context. Nestling against an existing retaining wall on the forested, steeply sloping site, the house is a simple rectangle in plan that stretches east to west parallel to the contours of the terrain. Internally, it reveals a more complex section, with a series of sheared terraces for the main living areas and the suspended volumes of bedrooms above punctuated by double height voids. While the house is timber frame and well insulated, bamboo is primarily used on the long façades of the house. Here, three bands of bamboo verticals alternate with large glazed areas and an entry terrace. Acting as

Rotselaar, Belgium | 2011

a rain screen and fitted to black steel frames, the bamboo elements create a linear cadence of vertical lines that provide scale, shadow, and organic warmth to the attenuated façades.

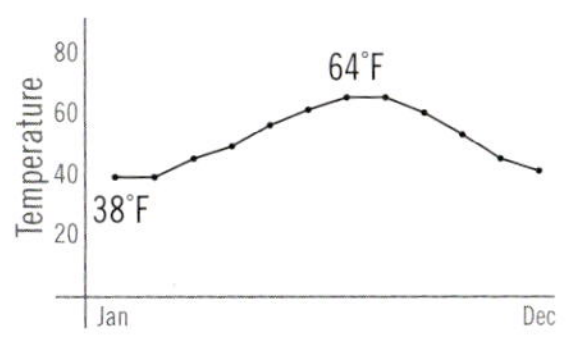

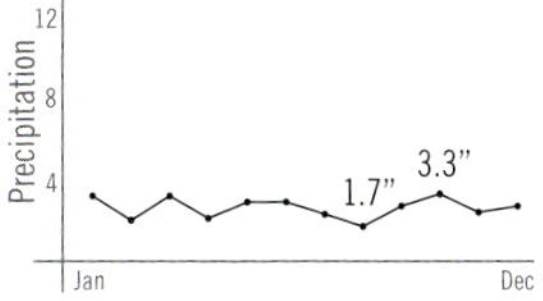

House Rotselaar

A simple, elongated, timber-framed volume conceals an intricate interior section within a skin of vertical bamboo. A series of stepping levels arrayed along the long axis of the house defines the primary collective spaces: living and dining, kitchen, and a workspace. This domestic landscape terraces down from the entry and allows for visual connections between the vertically sheared programmatic zones. Secreted into the space under the staggered section are systems for rain-water recapture, while high-efficiency heating and ventilation, extensive insulation, and solar orientation optimize energy performance. Above, the bedrooms are articulated as a series of discrete volumes with intervening voids linked by a continuous

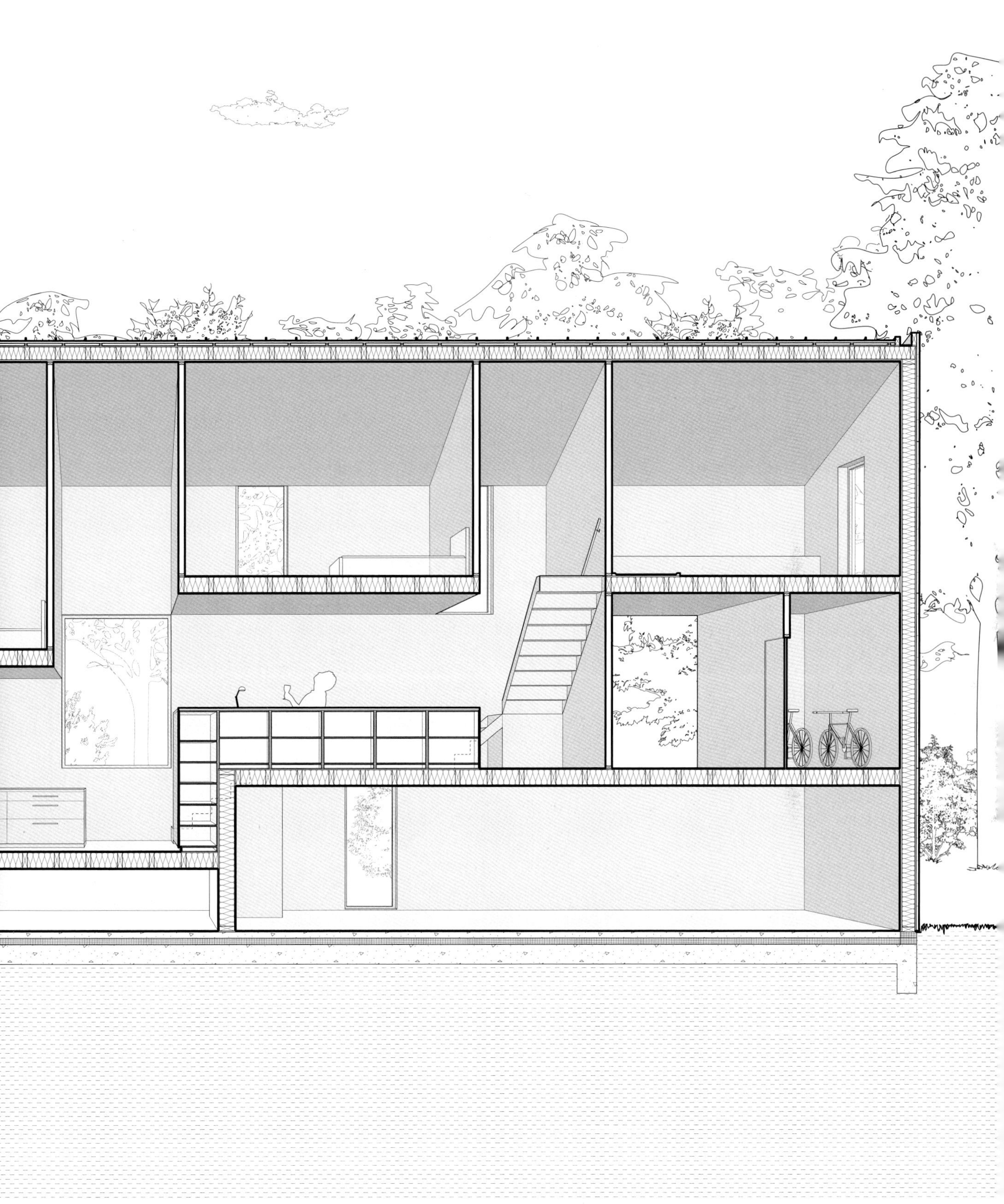

circulation path. The voids between the rooms, lined with exposed strand-board, align with large windows along both façades that provide light and views to the surrounding trees and allow southern light to fall into the living areas below. While the bamboo defines the warmth and cadence of the exterior façade, the building section deploys a variety of shearing and perforation strategies to negotiate the site, optimize daylighting, and create visual and spatial interaction between levels.

STRAW

800

600

400

Brick

200

Stone

Earth

0

Cork
Hemp

Straw

-128 $kgCO_2e/m^3$ Ökobaudat

-165 $kgCO_2e/m^3$ BEAM

-200

-400

Bamboo

-600

Mass Timber
Wood Frame

-800

STRAW

Straw is a byproduct of critical food sources (wheat, rice, oats, barley, rye) and can be found throughout the world. After the seeds have been harvested, straw is the residual stock and not to be confused with hay, which is feedstock. Straw is about 40% carbon, and is transformed into a more useful form for construction by baling machines. Although globally it absorbs a massive amount of carbon dioxide each year, straw is left to decompose or is burned returning the CO_2 to the atmosphere. As a fast growing, inexpensive, ubiquitous, minimally processed, agricultural byproduct, straw has enormous capacity to sequester carbon as a building material. Primarily used as insulation with an R-value of 1.5 to 2 per inch, it can also be a load bearing material. In either condition, its clay, lime, or cementitious plaster skin is critical to its performance and aesthetic, and the source of much of its labor and cost as a building system.

BALING

The size of the bales is contingent on the type of baler. These can range in size from a two-string rectangle weighing about 50 lbs (22 kg), to large round bales that can weigh over a ton. Larger bales can be compressed to much higher density, beneficial to being used as a load bearing structure.

HARVEST

Cut close to the ground, straw is the stock remnant after the seeds have been removed by harvesting equipment. Mechanical hay baling machines compress and strap straw into rectangular or circular units for easier distribution and use.

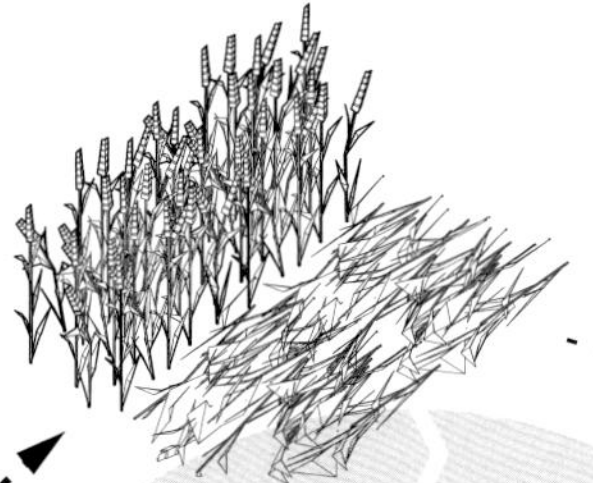

STRAW HARVESTING
4 TO 8 MONTHS

GROWTH

The growth cycle of all cereal grains is less than a year, significantly shorter than any other plant used in building. More importantly, straw is the waste product of these food grains.

PLANT

The impact of straw is directly related to its place in larger agricultural practices, and their impacts. The industrial farming of wheat and other cereal grains often involves the use of fertilizers, herbicides, and pesticides.

BIOFUEL

Straw's end of life can also be as fuel for heat or energy generation.

MULCH

Straw can be ground into mulch, to be used for landscaping or to biodegrade back to soil.

PREFABRICATION

Straw as insulation can be combined with wood frames into prefabricated units in more controlled off-site factories. This avoids some of the moisture challenges of on-site construction with straw. Dry or wet skins can be applied off-site.

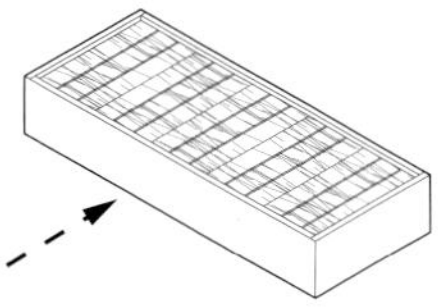

PLASTERING

Clay, lime, and/or cement is frequently used as a plaster skin, applied directly to the rough surface of both sides of straw-bales. Plaster skins are typically the air, water, and vapor controls of the assembly, as well as integral to the structural capacity of the straw wall.

CONSTRUCTION

Straw can be used as a load bearing structure, as infill to a structural frame, or within prefabricated units. The size and type of bale or prefabricated cassette has a significant impact on the geometry of the building.

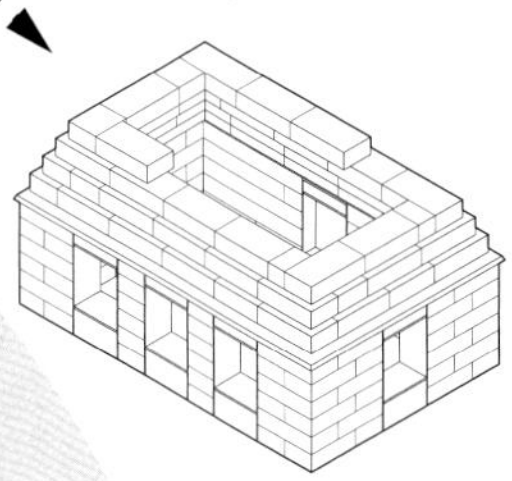

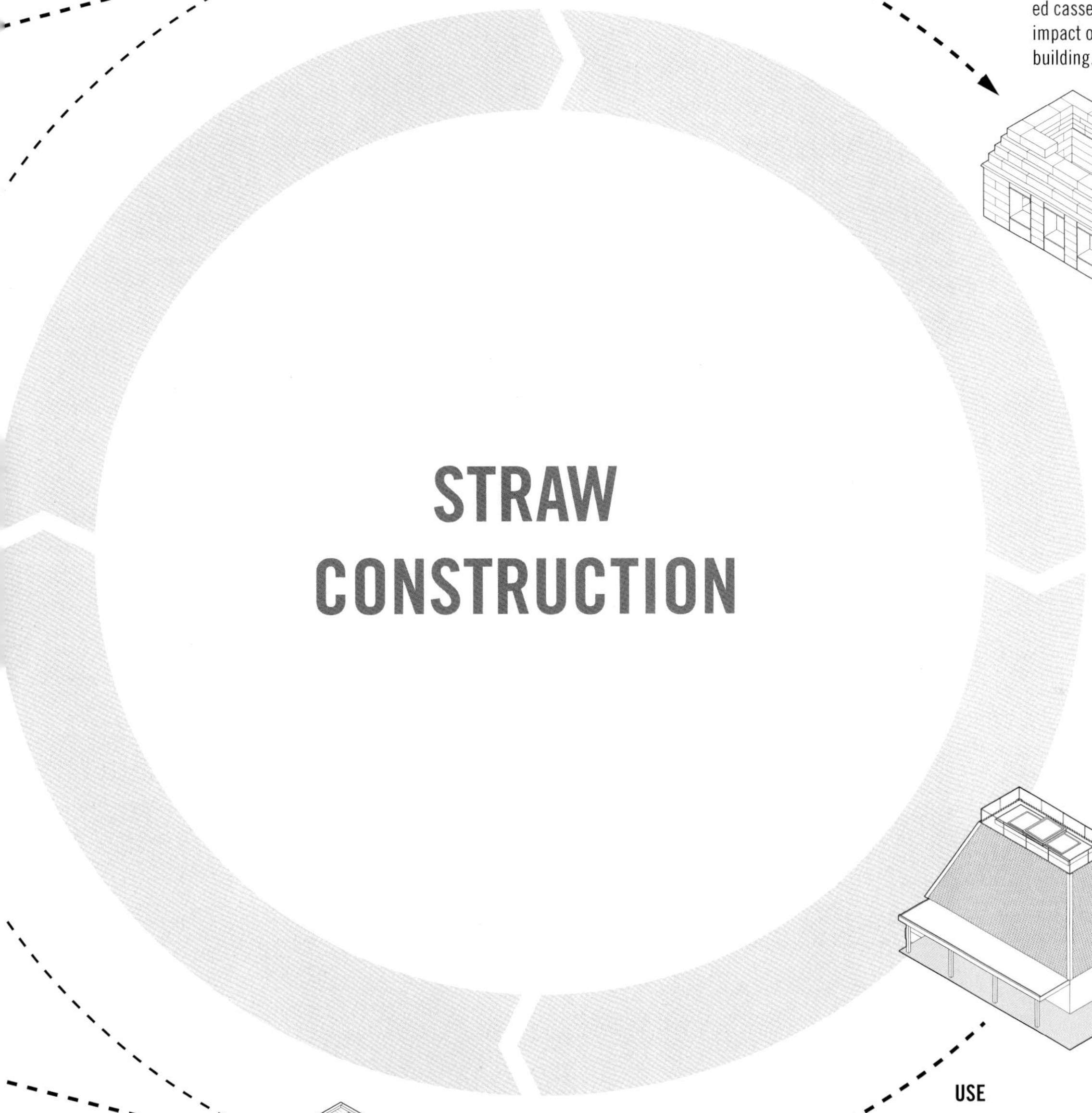

STRAW CONSTRUCTION

USE

Given their thickness, straw-bale walls have excellent thermal values (approximately R-25 to 35), while their hygroscopic attributes helps balance interior humidity. With careful selection of the material for their skins, straw-bale walls can improve indoor air quality, and can have many times the thermal mass of a conventional stick framed wall.

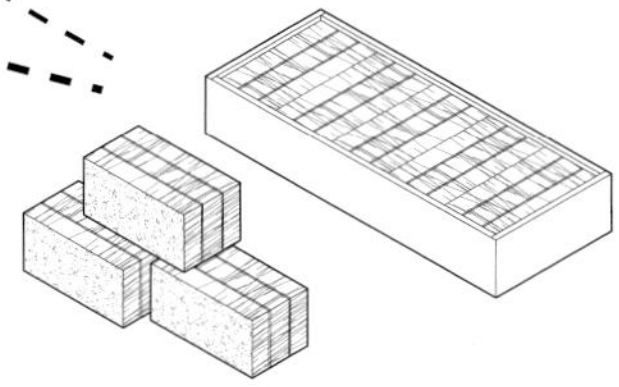

DISASSEMBLY

Prefabricated panels can be designed to be detachable and reused. Straw-bale walls can decompose, particularly if their skins are clay-based or removable.

STRAW

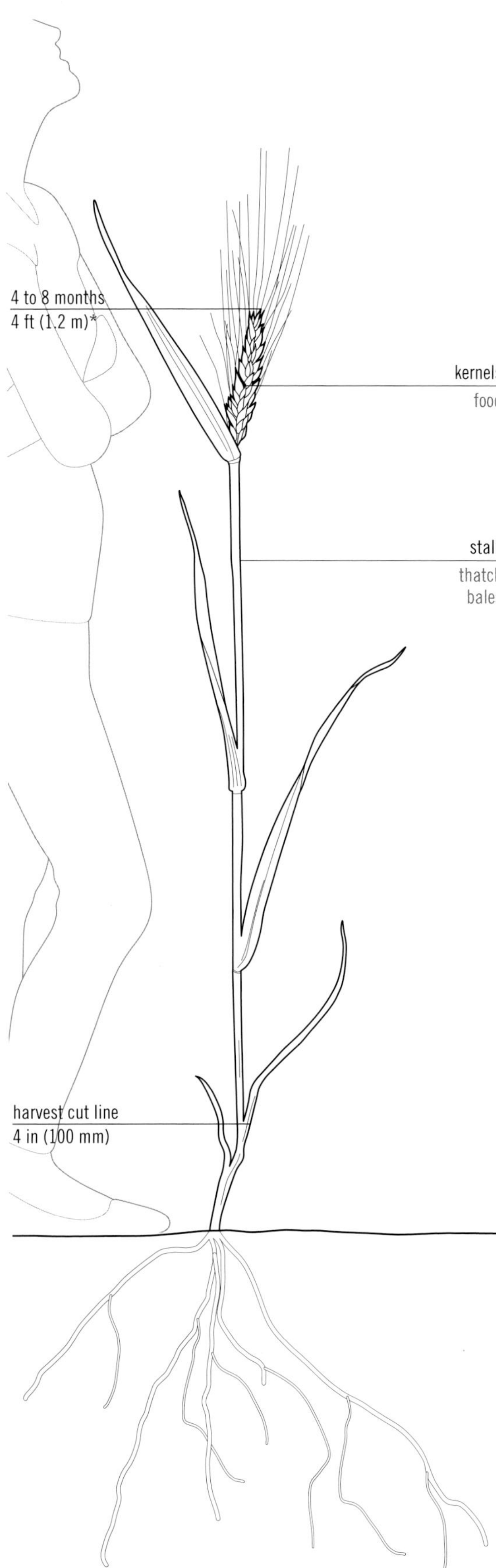

*height and timeframe are averages; actual values vary by planting season and environmental factors

HARVESTING

Reeds for thatching are harvested into carefully formed bundles, while sea grasses are gathered from the shoreline. Straw is typically gleened from fields after the cereal grains have been removed.

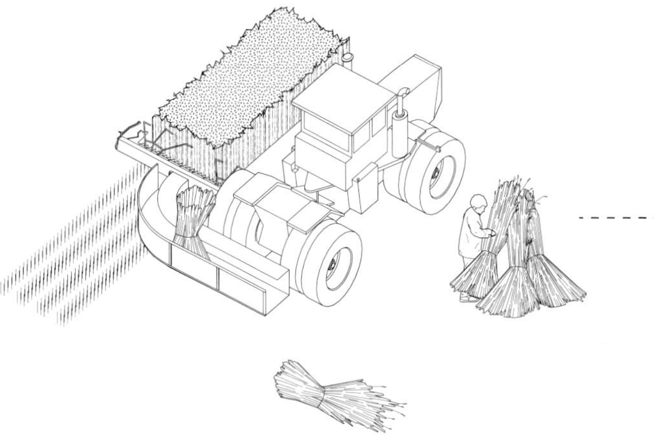

BALING

The most common grains used to make straw-bales are wheat and rice. Both are harvested and formed into bales after the seed kernels have been extracted and the stocks are sufficiently dry.
Although bale sizes vary depending on the baling equipment, two-string bales are roughly 14 by 18 by 36 in (360 by 460 by 910 mm) while three-string bales are roughly 16 by 23 by 46 in (410 by 580 by 1170 mm). Jumbo rectangular and circular bales can also be used. Most commonly, the bales are positioned flat with the strings within the walls, allowing the outer sides to be notched for posts.

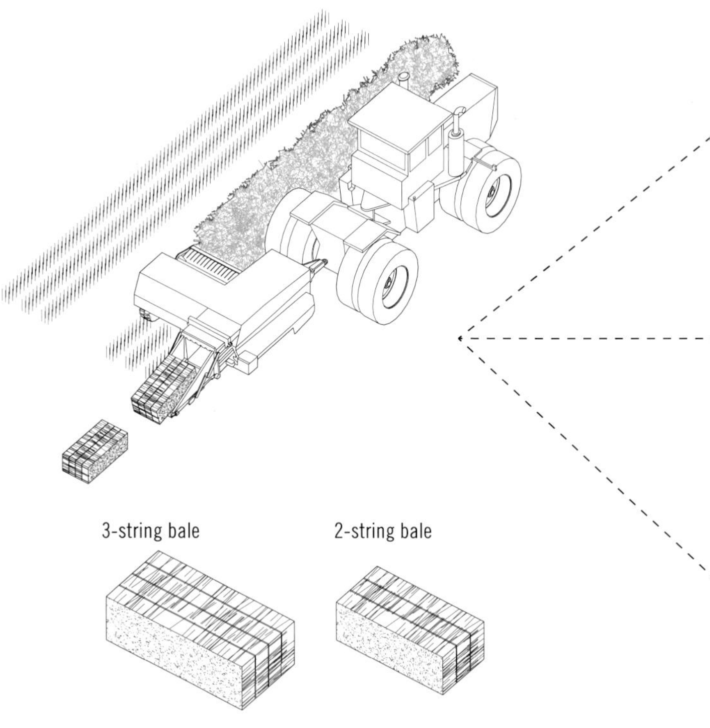

PLASTERING

The plaster skin is a crucial component of straw-bale construction, contributing significantly to its structural capacity, and its resistance to fire, moisture, and vermin. Although slower drying, clay and lime plasters avoid the higher carbon emissions of portland cement-based plasters.

THATCH

Tightly-packed long reeds or straw are fastened in overlapping bundles to a steeply pitched roof with horizontal straps producing a thickness that sheds water and can serve as insulation.

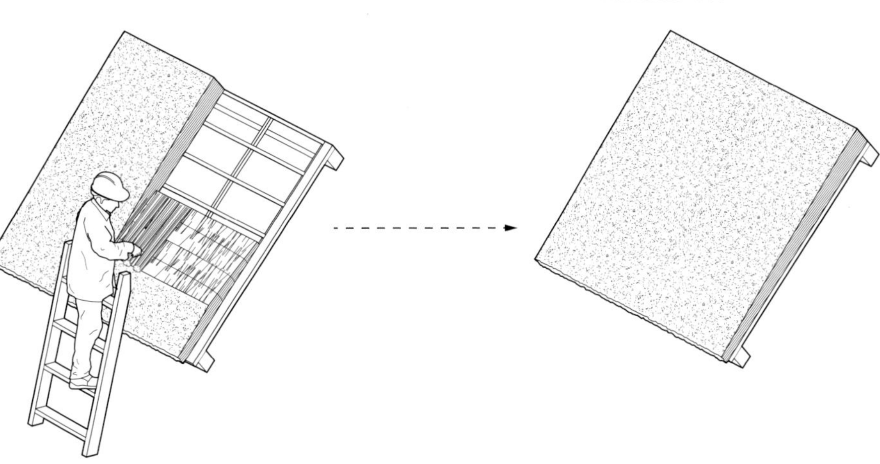

THATCHED ROOF

PRE-FABRICATED PANELS

Straw-bales can be inserted into structural wooden frames to make pre-fabricated panels, increasing moisture control and construction precision. Skins can be added off-site or on-site.

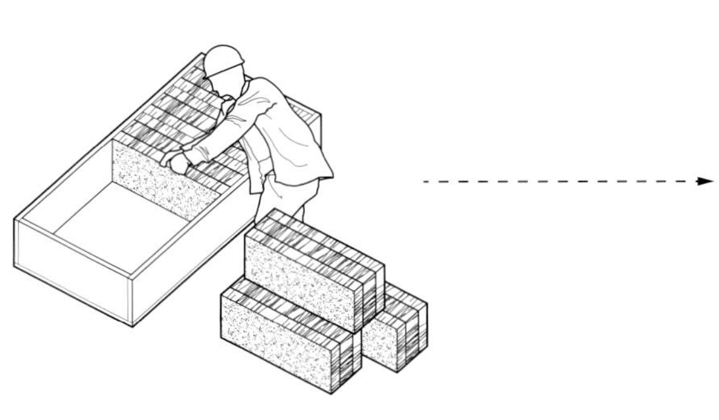

PREFABRICATED ASSEMBLY

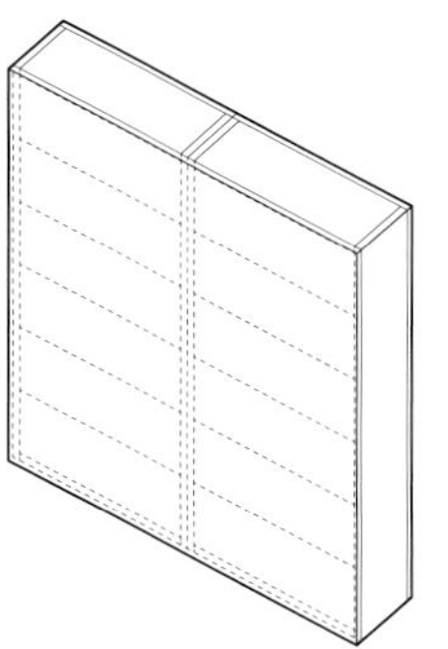

WOOD FRAME INFILL

The most common approach, straw-bales are stacked around or within a structural wood frame, serving primarily as insulation. With proper treatment of the skin, the straw-bale walls can also provide lateral bracing.

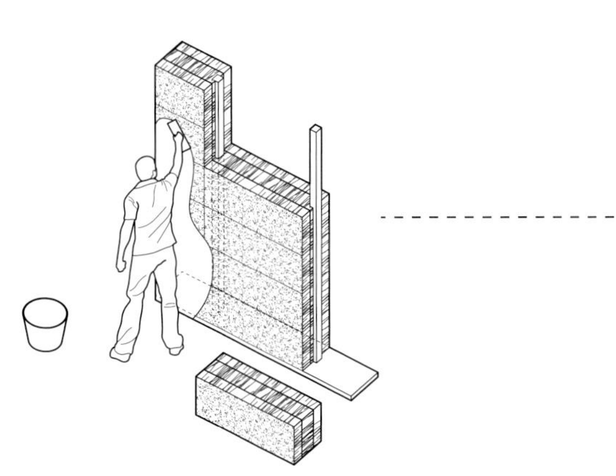

INFILL WALL

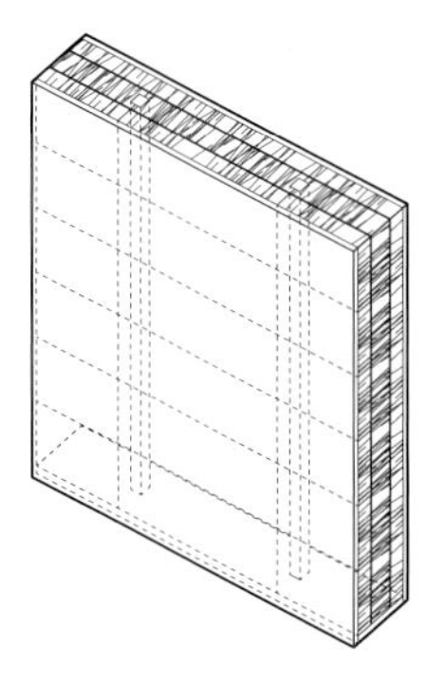

NEBRASKA LOAD-BEARING

Referencing the location of its first use in the late 1800s, Nebraska-style walls use the combined sandwich of thick plaster skins and straw-bales to be the load bearing structure. Typically just a single story, the straw-bale walls are compressed before the plaster is applied. A wooden top plate or ring beam transfers the roof load to the plaster skins which carry it to the foundations.

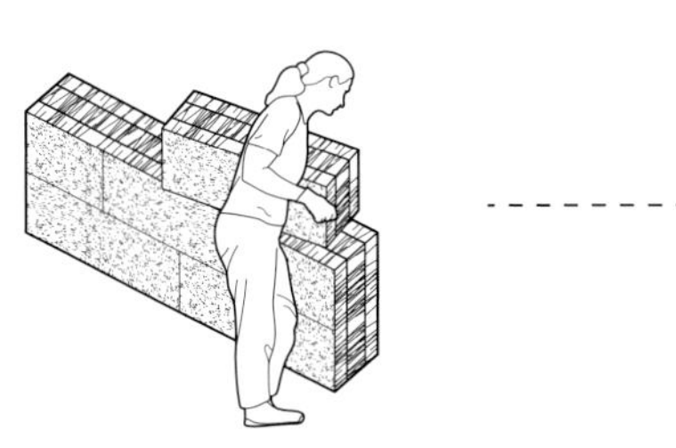

STACKED WALL

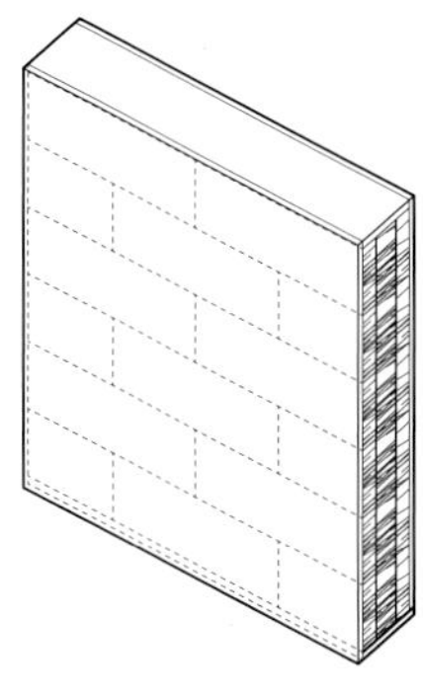

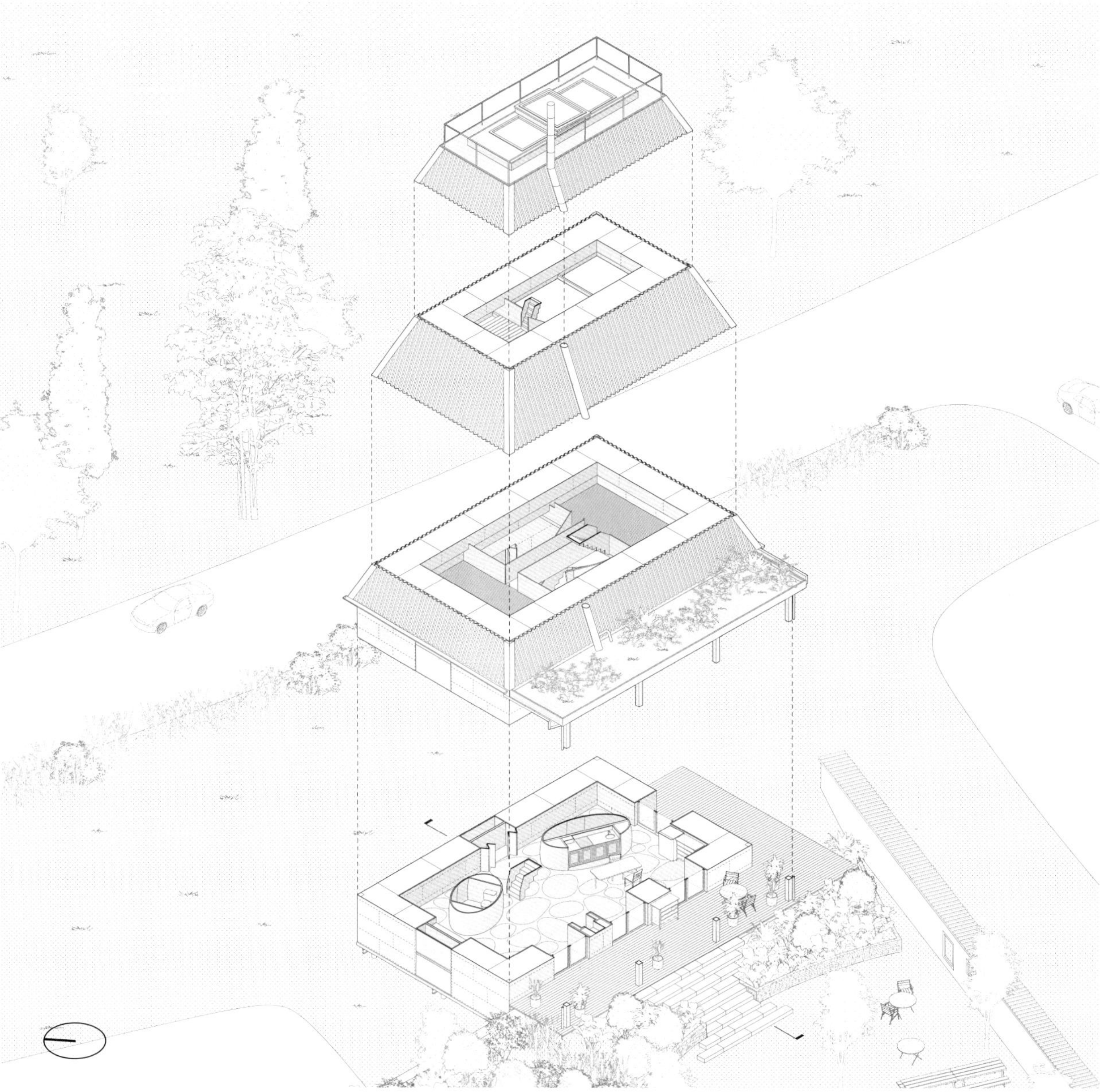

Gartist GmbH House | Atelier Werner Schmidt

This pavilion is an ingeniously simple and consequential use of straw-bales as a building material, taking full advantage of their thermal, structural, volumetric, material, and ecological qualities. The floor, walls, and roof of this house are all constructed of very large and heavily compacted straw-bales. They are the load-bearing structure in the walls and the corbeled roof, augmented only through selective planes of larch wood that frame the windows and form horizontal ring beams in the roof. Lime plaster on the outside and white clay plaster on the inside of the straw adds to the bales' structural capacity and protects against water, fire, and vermin. The thickness of the straw achieves high thermal resistance,

Zurich, Switzerland | 2016

while also absorbing excess humidity. A small wood burning stove is rarely used. Bathroom and kitchen services are contained in lime-coated pods independent from the structural walls.

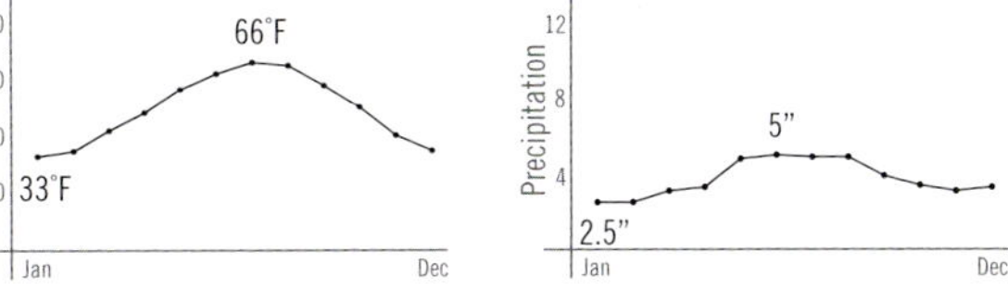

Gartist GmbH House

Raised on stilt piles and a solid wood raft above the damp ground, the thick floor is made from a grid of timber panels infilled with straw and topped with gravel, a radiant heating system, and 2.4 in (60 mm) slices of moraine stones. The load-bearing walls are comprised of 30 by 47 by 98 in (750 by 1200 by 2500 mm) bales, each weighing 661 lb (300 kg), erected by crane in about a week. These extremely thick walls allow the shape of the roof to be made by offsetting the upper eight rows of bales about 1 ft (300 mm) each, forming a corbeled structure. The keystone is a large skylight, filtering light down through the cascading thickness of this distinctive section. Stairs connect to lofted lounge areas nested inside

the inverted ziggurat and permit roof access. The surface of the straw is enhanced by the smooth undulations of the interior clay plaster, allowing the different edges of the bales to be visible. Corrugated metal attached to vertical wood battens, and a layer of clay protects the outside of the staggered roof bales. This house pavilion celebrates the thickness of an inexpensive and minimally processed natural material and in the process stores the carbon contained in 75 metric tons of an agricultural residue within its envelope.

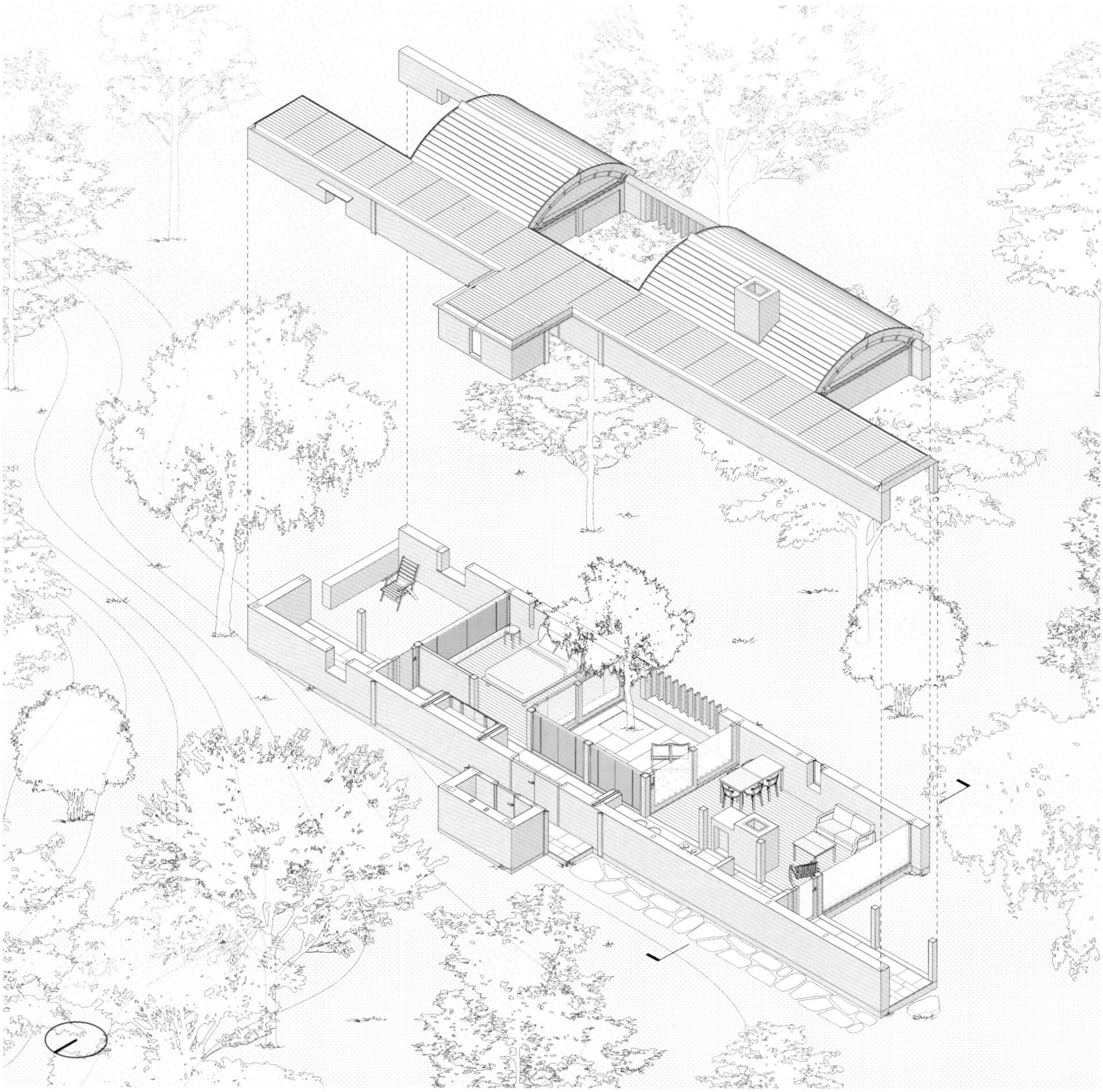

Mauritzberg Test House | Sverre Fehn

This house was part of a larger competition-winning design for a development of approximately 250 vacation units on the Baltic coast of Sweden. Lining the edges between a golf course and a forest, each unit is defined by two thick straw and clay block walls allowing the units to be closely positioned next to each other while maintaining an interior privacy. Within the walls, interior rooms and exterior courtyards are interspersed, linked by a long hallway and service wall containing the kitchen, bathrooms, and closets. Glass connects the interior rooms to the courtyard spaces, and to the adjacent landscape at either end. Although the full development was not realized, this 500 sq ft (46 sq m) house was built by architects Mikko

Norrköping, Sweden | 1991

Heikkinen, Markku Komonen, Henrik Hille, and Professor Beng Ludsten with Technological University of Helsinki students under the direction of Fehn, in eight weeks. It is an early Scandinavian modern experiment with straw and clay construction, materials more often deployed in warmer, dryer climates.

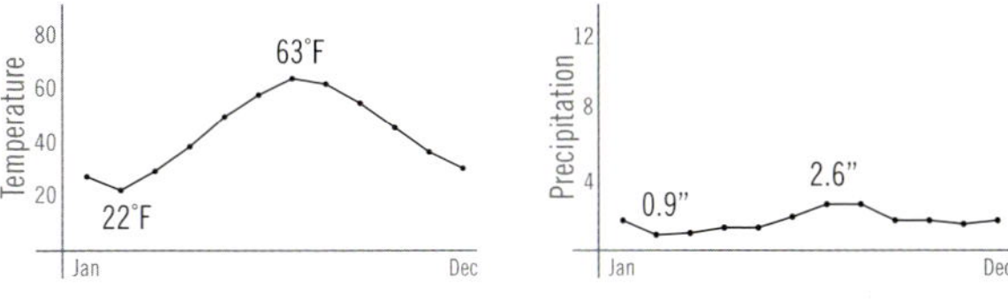

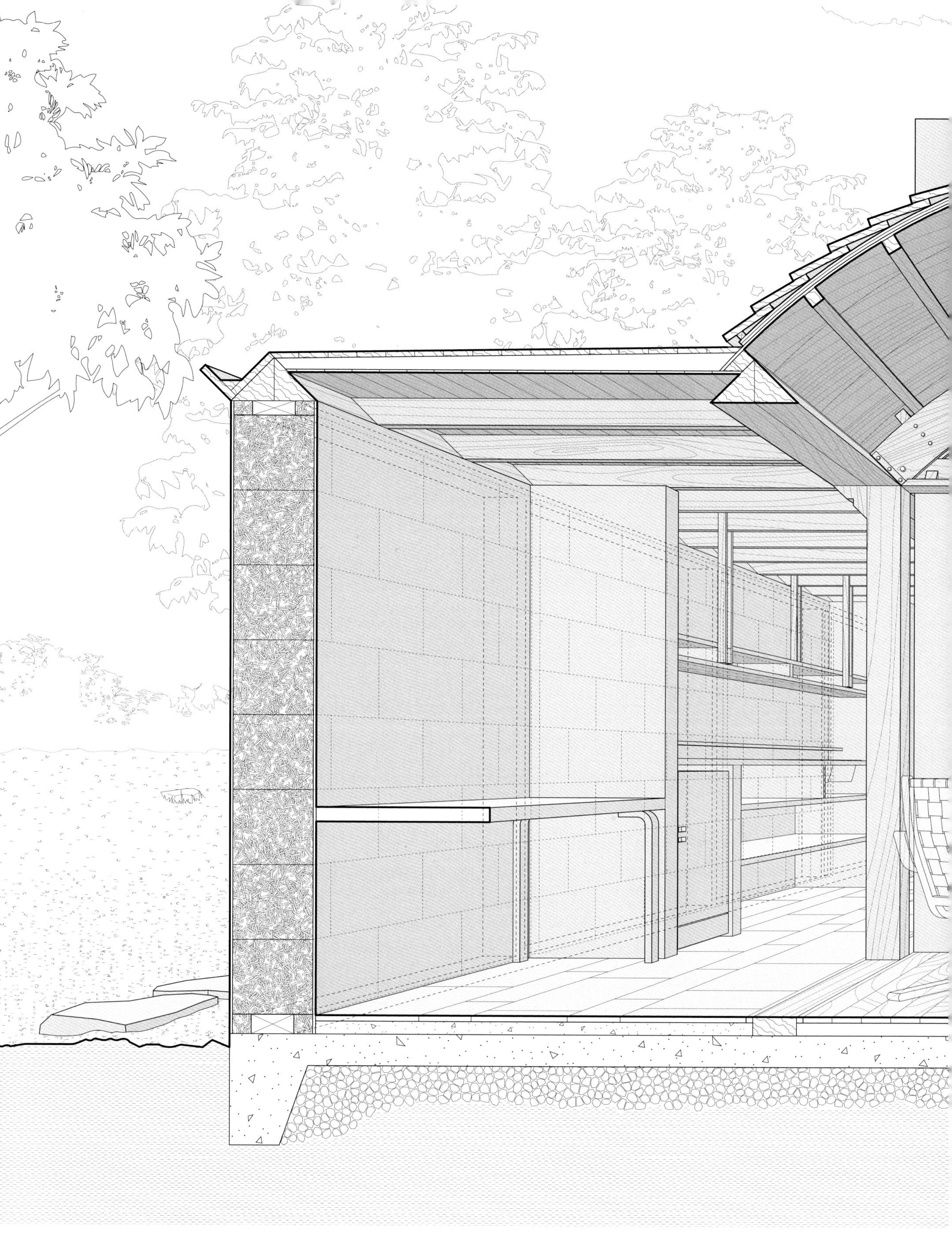

Mauritzberg Test House

The section reveals the architects' exploration of very thin and very thick plant-based material assemblies. The dominant exterior walls are constructed with a load-bearing wood frame, infilled with straw and mud blocks, each measuring 8 by 11 by 21 in (200 by 280 by 530 mm). Although inspired by Moroccan building precedents, these straw walls were specifically configured to deal with the humid and cold Swedish climate. Comprised of 10% clay and 90% straw, the blocks were pressed into wooden forms to remove excess water, then air-dried, stacked, and then surfaced with clay to provide a water- and air-control layer. The mass of a continuous corridor wall was intensified by embedding utility spaces into

its thickness. In contrast, the main rooms are enclosed by glass walls and ceilings composed of pairs of 5/8 inch (15 mm) plywood arches on 6.6 ft (2 m) centers. These arches are skinned with laminated wood and shingles while the flat portions of the roof are surfaced in wood tar. Triangular wood rim joists provide the transition between the earthen walls and the plywood barrel vault. The singular mass of the exterior walls absorbs and hides the wood structural frame, which emerges from the top of the wall into the light-weight, taut arching forms.

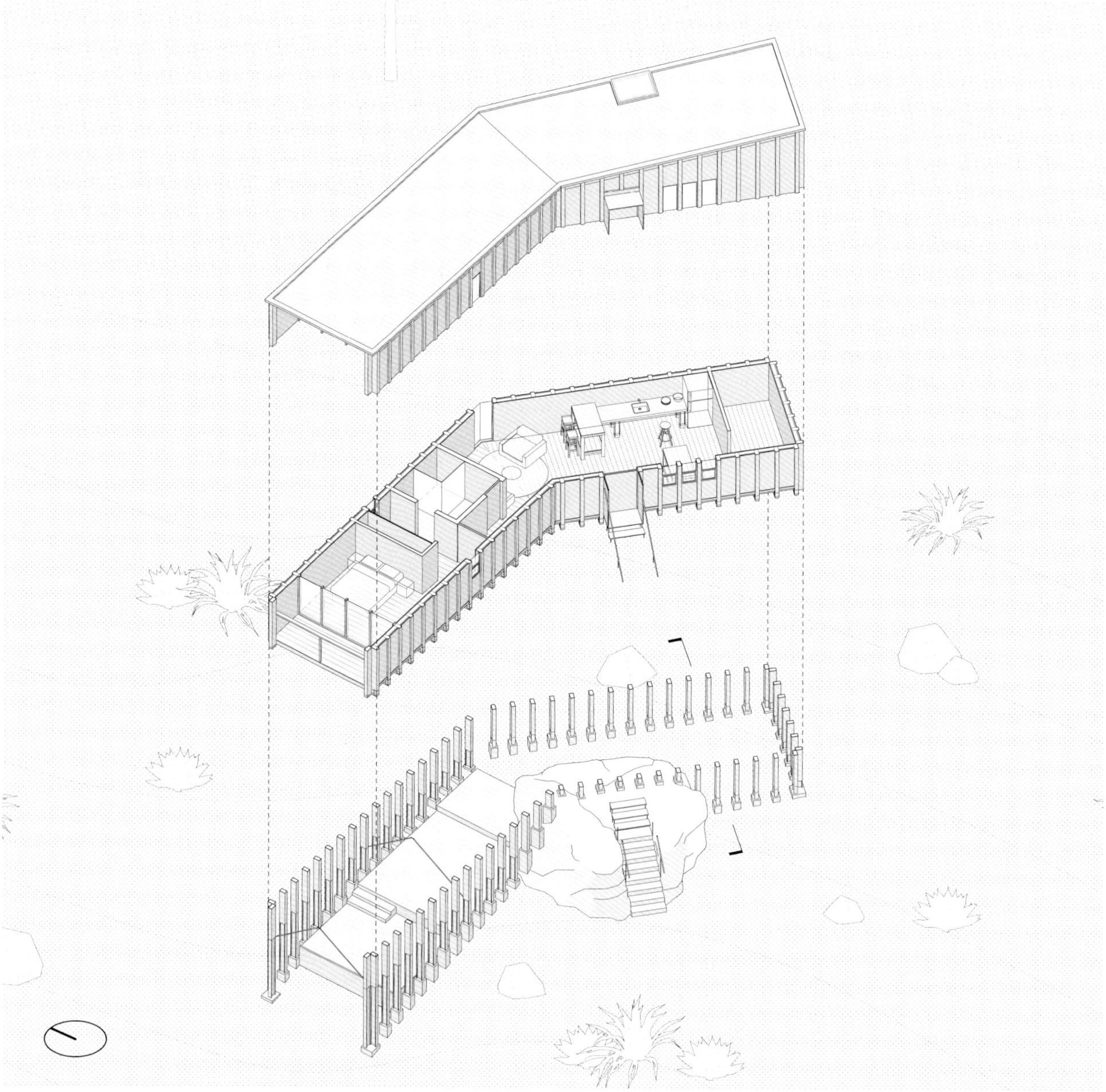

Media Perra House | Santos Bolívar

Located in the wine region of Valle de Guadalupe in northwest Mexico, this house's legible wood frame and relatively thin straw infill insulation engages both the mild warm climate and registers the varied, rocky topography of the site. The underside of the house floats just above a large site boulder, which forms its entry steps and is a catalyst for the building's form. The rectilinear volume is deflected in both plan and section to frame views to either side of the valley. The space between the floating house and the inclined hill, captured between parallel colonnades of wood posts, provides a covered outdoor gathering place. The 750 sq ft (70 sq m) interior above consists of a central living area, flanked on either end by a

Guadalupe, Mexico | 2017

bedroom and a sleeping loft. This modest house, with a minimal footprint, uses iterative wood framing, and straw and earth skins to impressive sculptural effects that activate and reflect its natural context.

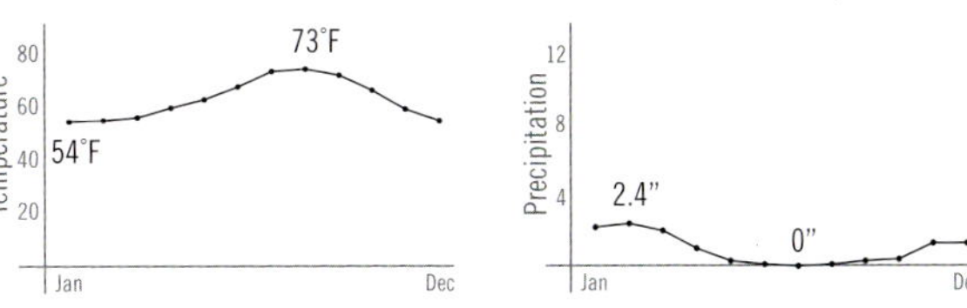

Media Perra House

The house is comprised of 33 4 by 8 in (100 by 200 mm) frames, spaced 2 ft (600 mm) on center, which is the dominant visual characteristic of the house. Connected by steel stitch plates, the legs of each frame extend down to the ground to individual footings, placed with care in the irregular terrain. Given the mild climate, straw insulation infills the wall cavity to about half of the structure's depth. Horizontal wood members span between the joists, supporting the straw in segments. Attached to the horizontal frames, exterior sheathing is then clad in an earth and straw

mixture, visible between the wood frames, while the interior wall has a continuous white plaster surface concealing the frame on the interior. This inverts the more typical position of the frame, more commonly continuously sheathed behind the exterior skin, and reveals the delicacy and lightness of the wood and straw structure on this site. This reading is reinforced by the visible moment frame plates and bolts, implying also that the house is capable of disassembly, and contrasts with the permanence of the large rock, above which this house is perched.

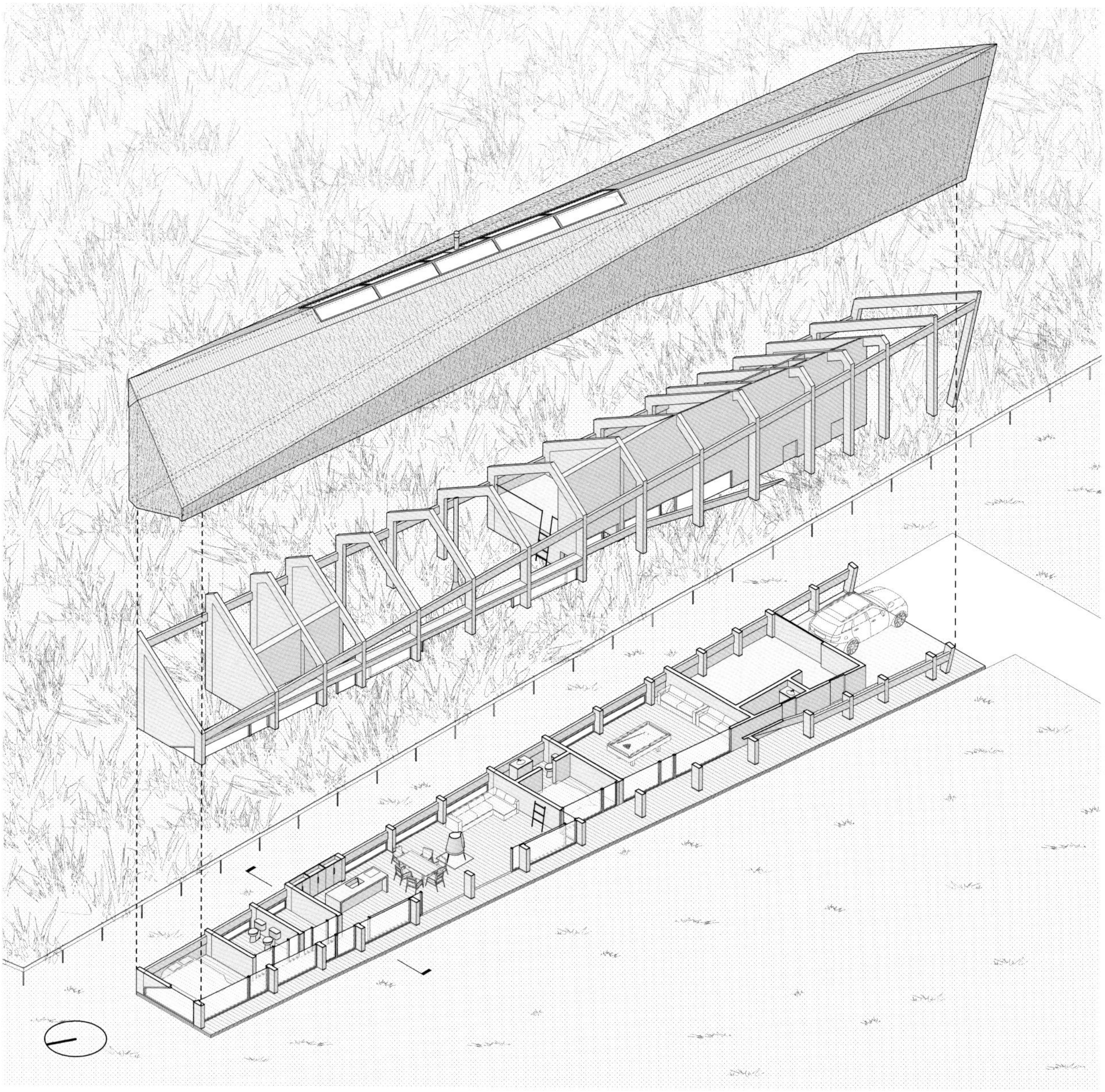

Dune House | Archispektras

Positioned parallel to the coast of the Baltic Sea and just 328 ft (100 m) back from the water's edge, this vacation house is characterized by traditional, local reed roofing thatch configured into unconventional faceted geometries. The house is stretched into an elongated sequence of rooms in order to maximize visual connection with the sea. The width of the house consistently tapers, from the widest end—comprised of a car port, storage, billiard room, and a bedroom—down to an open living, dining, and kitchen area, and culminating in bedrooms at the narrowest portion.

Pape, Latvia | 2016

These rooms are aligned with 16 glulam ribs at irregular spacing. Each rib is unique, reflecting the constantly changing geometry of the house's section, yet every rib extends to the same seven-meter height, and the vertical legs of the ribs always start plumb to the ground.

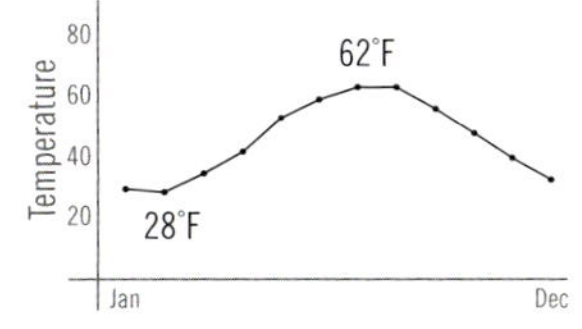

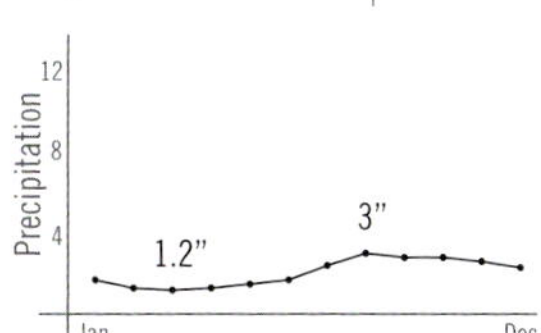

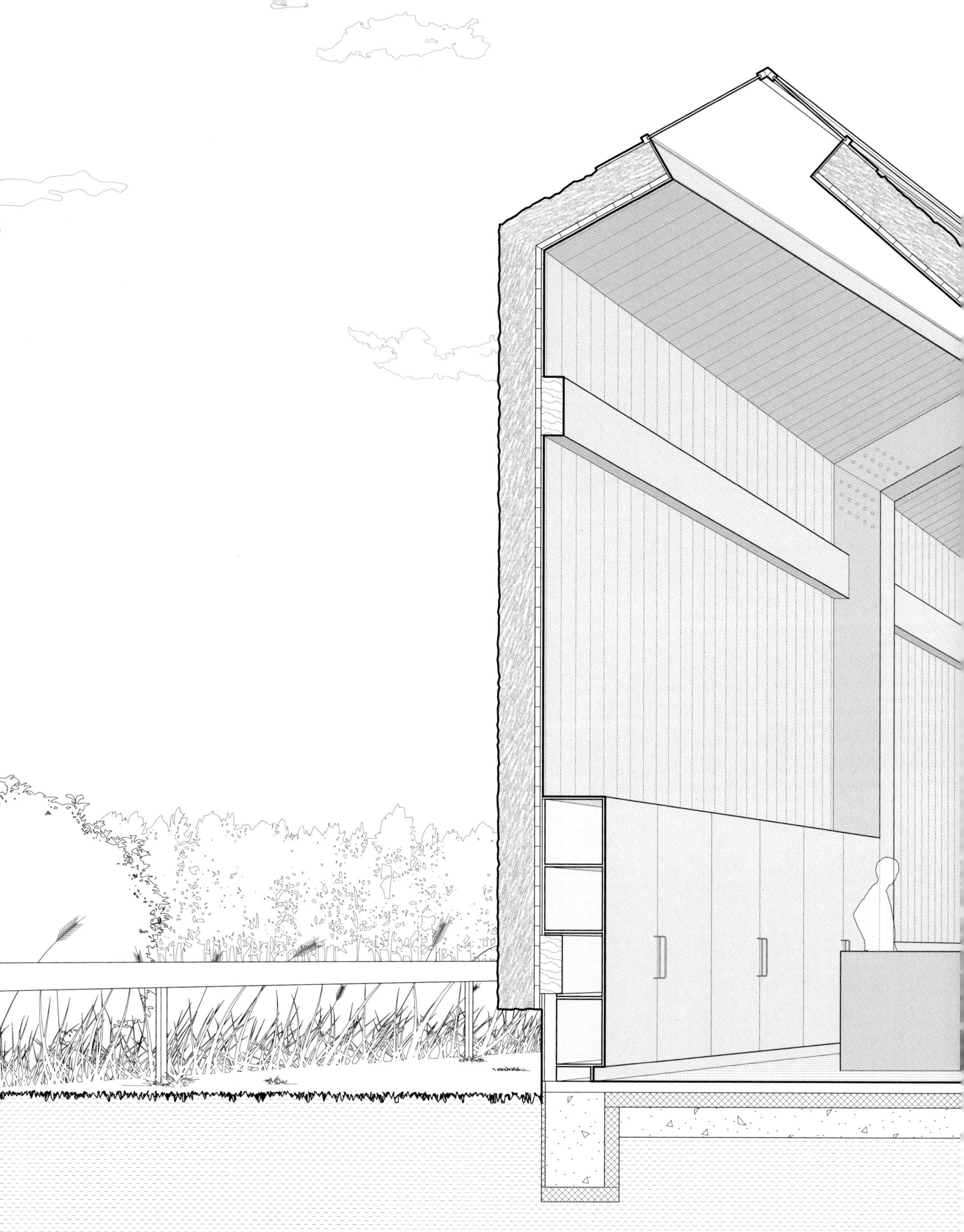

Dune House

The section consists of a laminated wood structural skin spanning between 16 glulam ribs. A roughly 12 in (300 mm) thickness of reed thatching is stapled on to the exterior, while pine boards line the interior. These are aligned vertically with the ribs to accentuate the height of the house. Rather than appearing as a roof placed on top of a house, the thatch wraps to become both roof and wall. This blanket of thatch is then lifted along one side and corner of the house and floats completely above the other side where it reveals wood frame, glazing, or open air slot, in addition to its own material thickness. The large triangular facets of the roof that stretch the length of the house animate the whole building's form, as if

torquing among the coastal dunes. The distinctive insulating skin of the house is also made legible above the car port where it extends beyond the interior volume. The crisp, precise volumetric geometry of the roof is a calculated contrast to the dense aggregation of plants that form the thatch itself, and to the grasses and dunes of the site. Using local biogenic material techniques, this house is embedded in the ecology and culture of its site, without being reduced to simplistic contextualism.

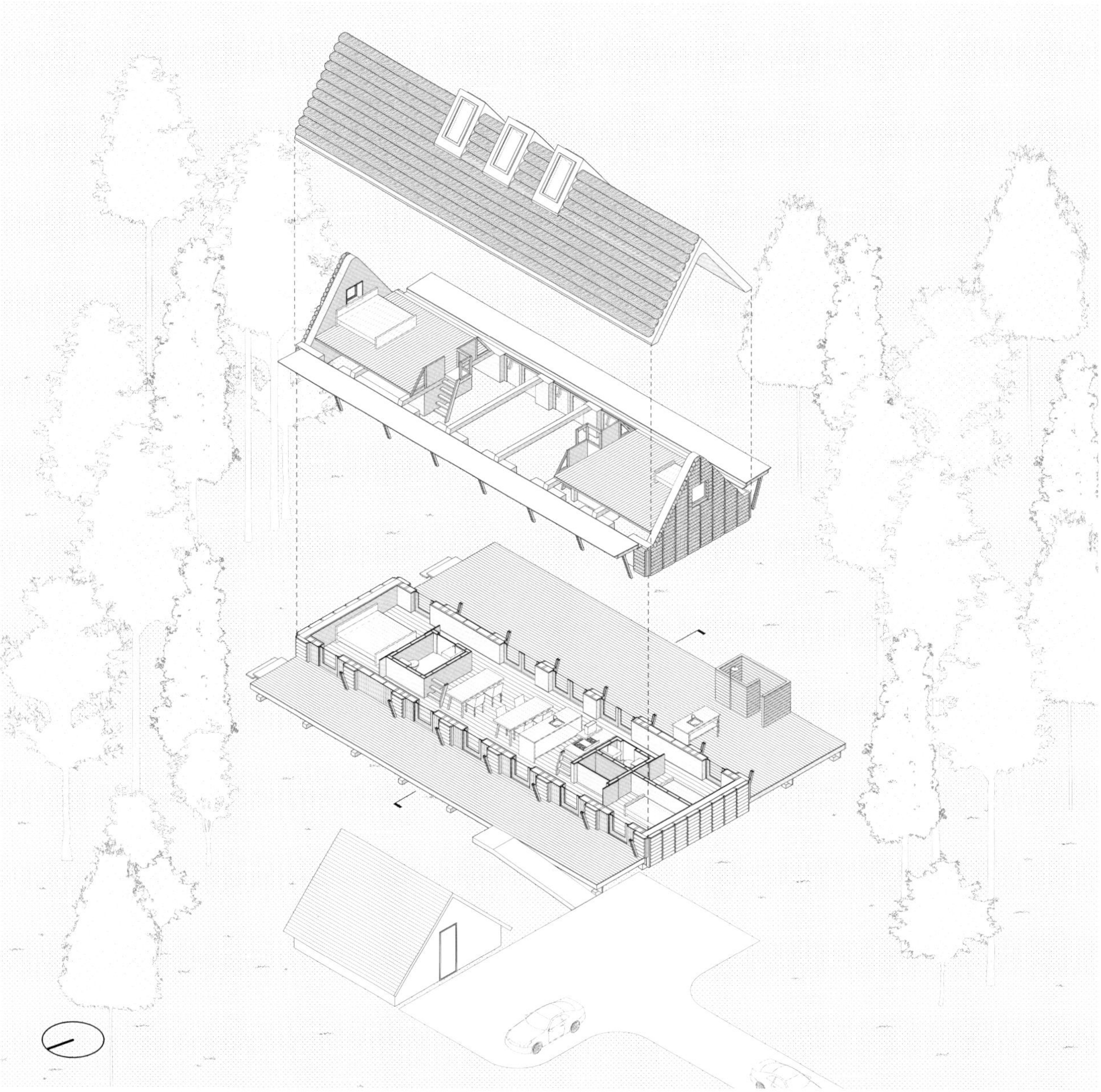

Modern Seagrass House | Vandkunsten Architects

Conceived as both an exploration of historic local building practices and a prototype for experimental tectonics, this small 950 sq ft (90 sq m) vacation house for two families uses seagrass as insulation, cladding, and interior skin. A collaboration between the architects and Realdania Byg, a funding body for the Danish construction industry, the building emerged from a research project to restore centuries-old seagrass thatch buildings on the Danish island of Laesø. Seagrass was once commonly used as a building material on the island out of necessity due to the destruction of forest for fuel by the salt industry, as well as the absence of straw thatch. Eelgrass washes ashore, is cured by salt, and dried by the sun; it

Laesø Island, Denmark | 2013

is non-toxic, fireproof, and has both insulative and acoustic qualities. The wood-framed house is clad on its exterior with bags of the same grass laid in horizontal rows. The house has a central living area, bedrooms at both ends, and lofted sleeping areas on either gabled end. Seagrass-filled panels, clad in cotton and linen fabric, line the interior of the shaped ceiling.

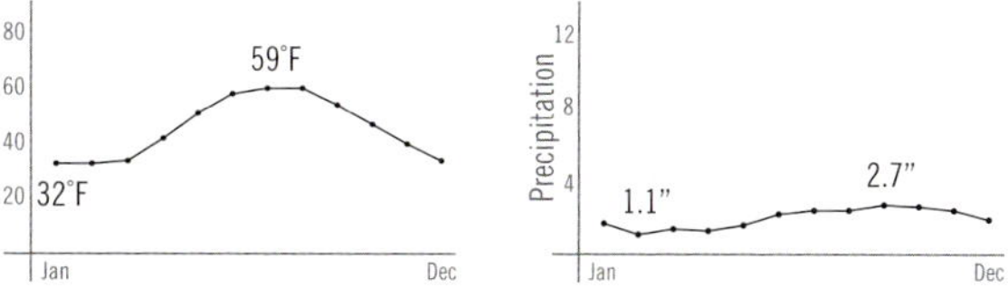

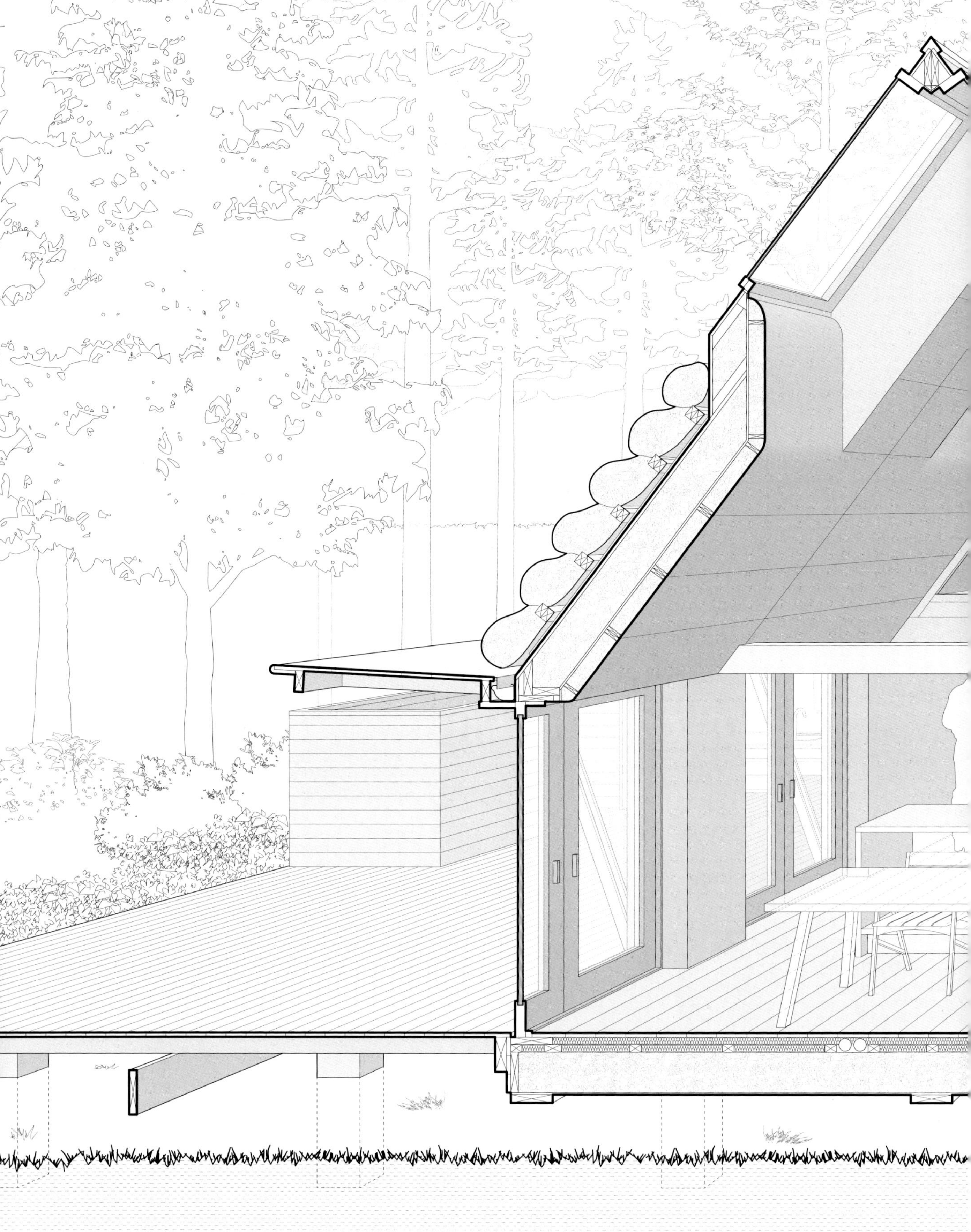

Modern Seagrass House

The section reveals the multiple inventive ways that eelgrass is used in the building, for both aesthetic and performative effects. Hand-stuffed eelgrass-filled mesh sacks, approximately 1 ft (300 mm) in diameter, are attached to horizontal battens on the pitched roof, while an equal thickness of the seagrass is used as insulation between the rafters. Building felt provides the water-resistant layer, while an air cavity between the felt and the sacks allowed for more rapid drying of the grass. Additionally, 4 in (100 mm) thick panels of seagrass-filled frames, lined with fire-treated fabric skins clad the interior of the pitched roof, offering more insulation and acoustic benefits. The vertical walls are clad in 6 in (150 mm)

diameter tubes of seagrass, while the space between the floor and wall framing is also filled with the insulating eelgrass. Through the combination of nine metric tons of seagrass, the wood structure, and minimal use of concrete in the pier foundations, the architect calculates that the building sequesters 8,500 kgCO_2e. The traditional compact gabled form is transformed by the idiosyncratic thick biogenic skins, which reactivate a historic material in new ways. As part of an experimental house, the materials have been evaluated and repaired over time.

HEMP

24 $kgCO_2e/m^3$

Batt; Ökobaudat

Hemp

-106 $kgCO_2e/m^3$

Site Mixed; BEAM

HEMP

Hemp is one of the oldest cultivated plants in recorded human civilization and a member of the Cannabaceae plant family. The common hemp plant used in construction, Cannabis sativa, is distinguished from marijuana in having only trace amounts of the psychoactive drug tetrahydrocannabinol (THC). The hemp plant has a single main stalk, grows to a height of between 6 to 15 ft (1.8 to 4.5 m) and will flower and seed if pollination occurs between male and female plants. The entire plant is usable with the exterior bark or bast of the main stalk harvested for fiber, the interior woody shiv or hurd used in combination with lime and water as a building material, and the seeds crushed to extract oils. Hemp cultivated more for its stalk and seeds is referred to as industrial hemp, and can be grown with limited pesticides, irrigation, and fertilizer. Hemp is used as a rotational crop as it replenishes the soil, and can have two harvests in a year, depending on local climate and soil conditions.

HEMP PROCESSING

Plants are baled and stored under cover after the retting process in the field is complete. The hemp stalk is then processed in a decorticating machine that separates the exterior fibers from the interior hurd.

HARVEST

Industrial hemp grown for fiber and hurd is usually cut before turning to seed, as the flowering of the plant diminishes the quality of the stalk. Once cut it is left on the ground for approximately a month in a drying process called retting, that separates the exterior fibers from the interior hurd.

HEMP HARVESTING
2 TO 4 MONTHS

GROWTH

Hemp plants grow quickly, with a rate of 1 ft (30 cm) per week possible, and reach maturity in approximately 100 days. Plants have a very long root system which aids in the stability and regeneration of soils.

PLANT

Industrial hemp is grown from seed and planted compactly to hinder competing weed growth and to encourage central stalk length over branches and leaves.

BIOFUEL

Hemp's end of life can also be as fuel for heat or energy generation.

MULCH

Hemp can be ground into mulch, to be used for landscaping or to biodegrade back to soil.

LIME PRODUCTION

Lime is derived from limestone, a readily available sedimentary rock made from fossilized animal shells. When heated, limestone or calcium carbonate ($CaCO_3$) transforms into quicklime (CaO). Limestone with clay or other impurities creates hydraulic lime which is often used with hemp.

MIXING

Once separated and cut, the fiber or hurd is combined with additional materials to create a variety of building products. Fibers are combined with other threads and binders to create insulation batts. Hemp-lime is made from the hurd mixed with lime and water.

PREFABRICATION

Hemp-lime products can be manufactured off-site in block or panel formats that allow the necessary drying to occur in a controlled environment.

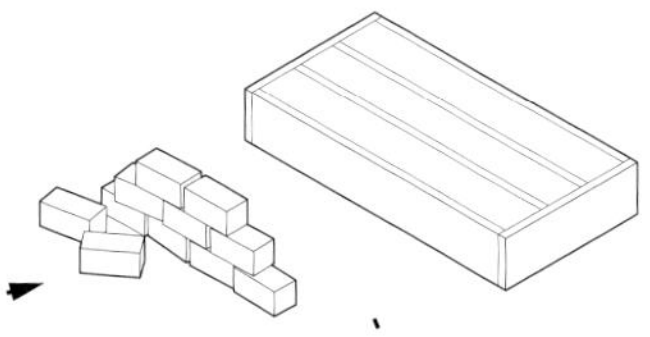

CONSTRUCTION

As hemp-lime materials are non-load bearing, they are typically used in combination with wood framing to form a mass wall system.

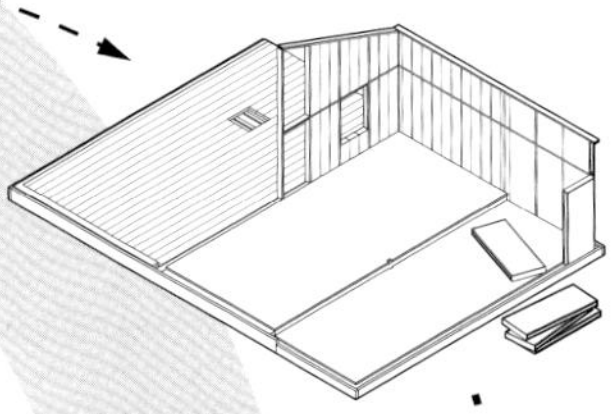

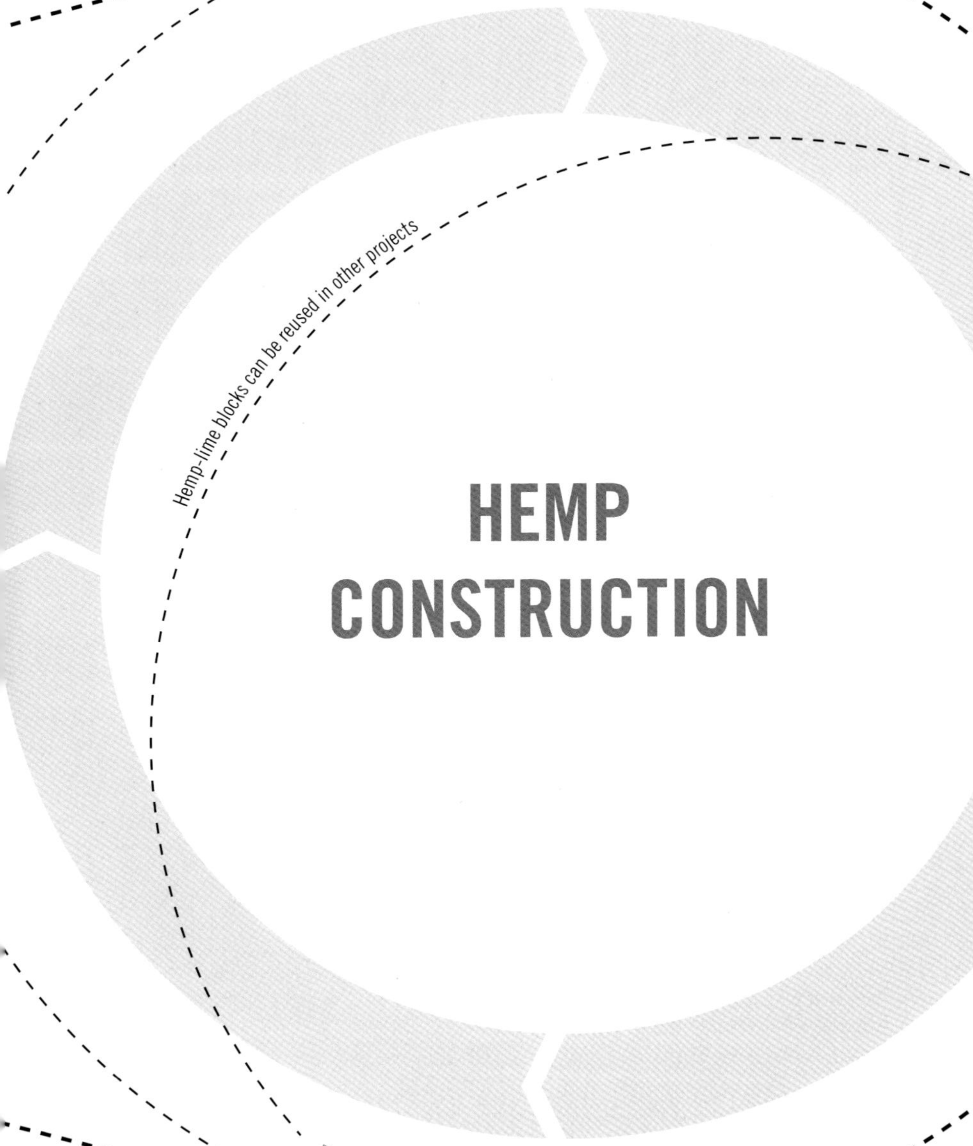

Hemp-lime blocks can be reused in other projects

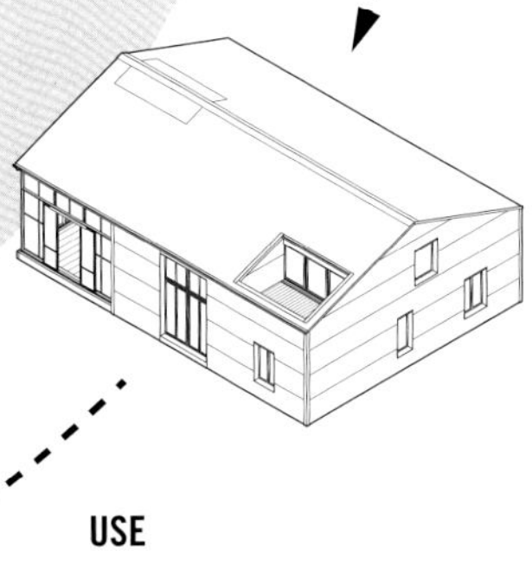

HEMP CONSTRUCTION

USE

If properly detailed to protect from direct contact with water, a hemp-lime assembly is naturally mold, rot, and insect resistant, vapor open and breathable, and requires limited maintenance.

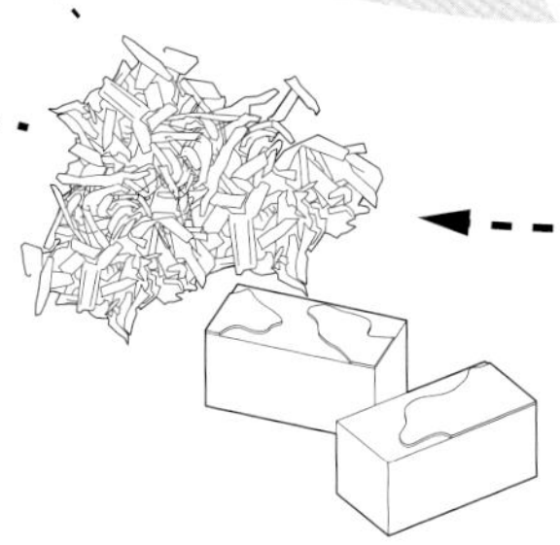

DISASSEMBLY

The constituent elements of a hemp-lime and wood building can be reused, downcycled, or composted as needed with the hemp-lime mixture aiding in the preservation of the wood.

HEMP

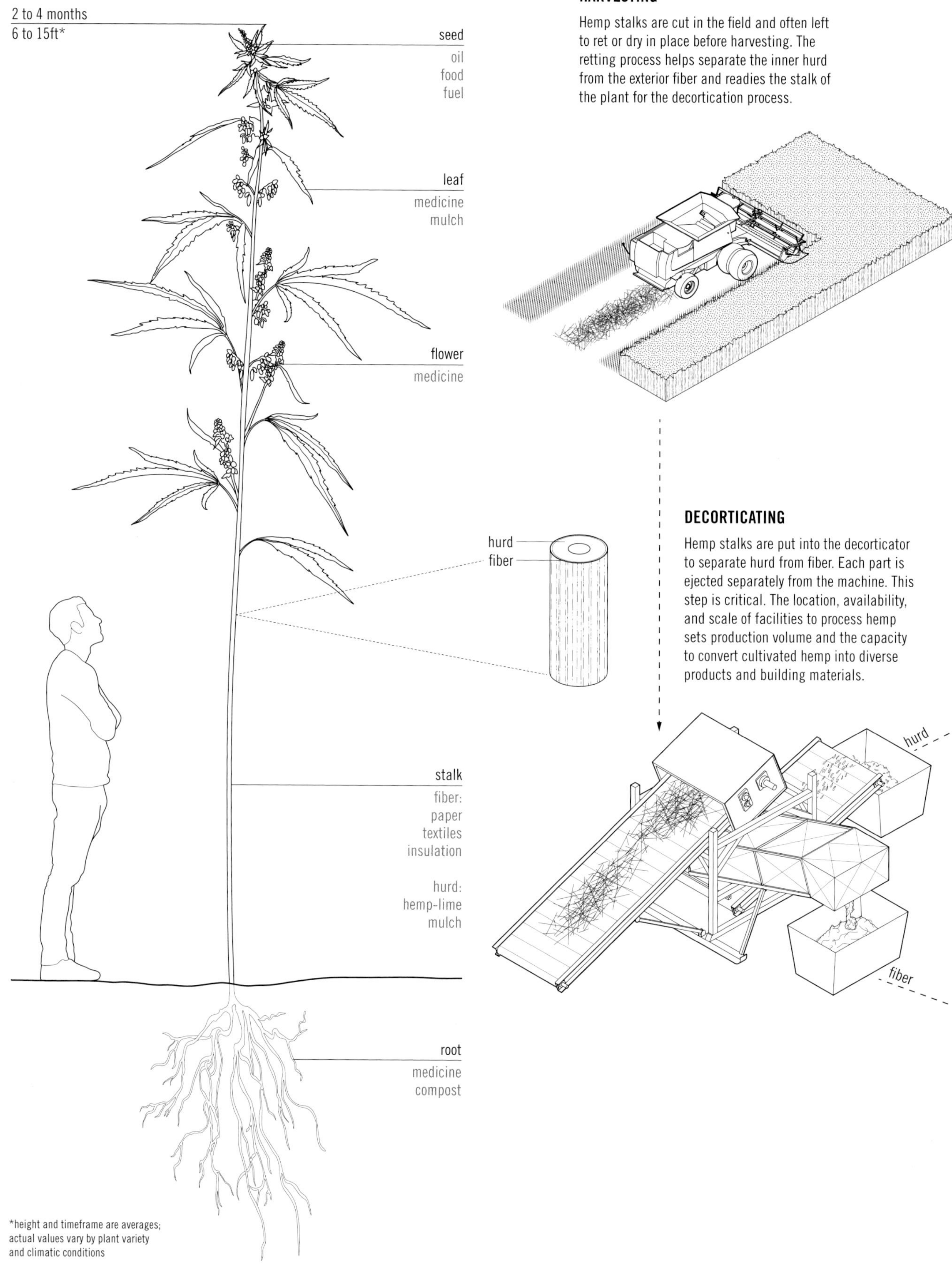

HARVESTING

Hemp stalks are cut in the field and often left to ret or dry in place before harvesting. The retting process helps separate the inner hurd from the exterior fiber and readies the stalk of the plant for the decortication process.

DECORTICATING

Hemp stalks are put into the decorticator to separate hurd from fiber. Each part is ejected separately from the machine. This step is critical. The location, availability, and scale of facilities to process hemp sets production volume and the capacity to convert cultivated hemp into diverse products and building materials.

*height and timeframe are averages; actual values vary by plant variety and climatic conditions

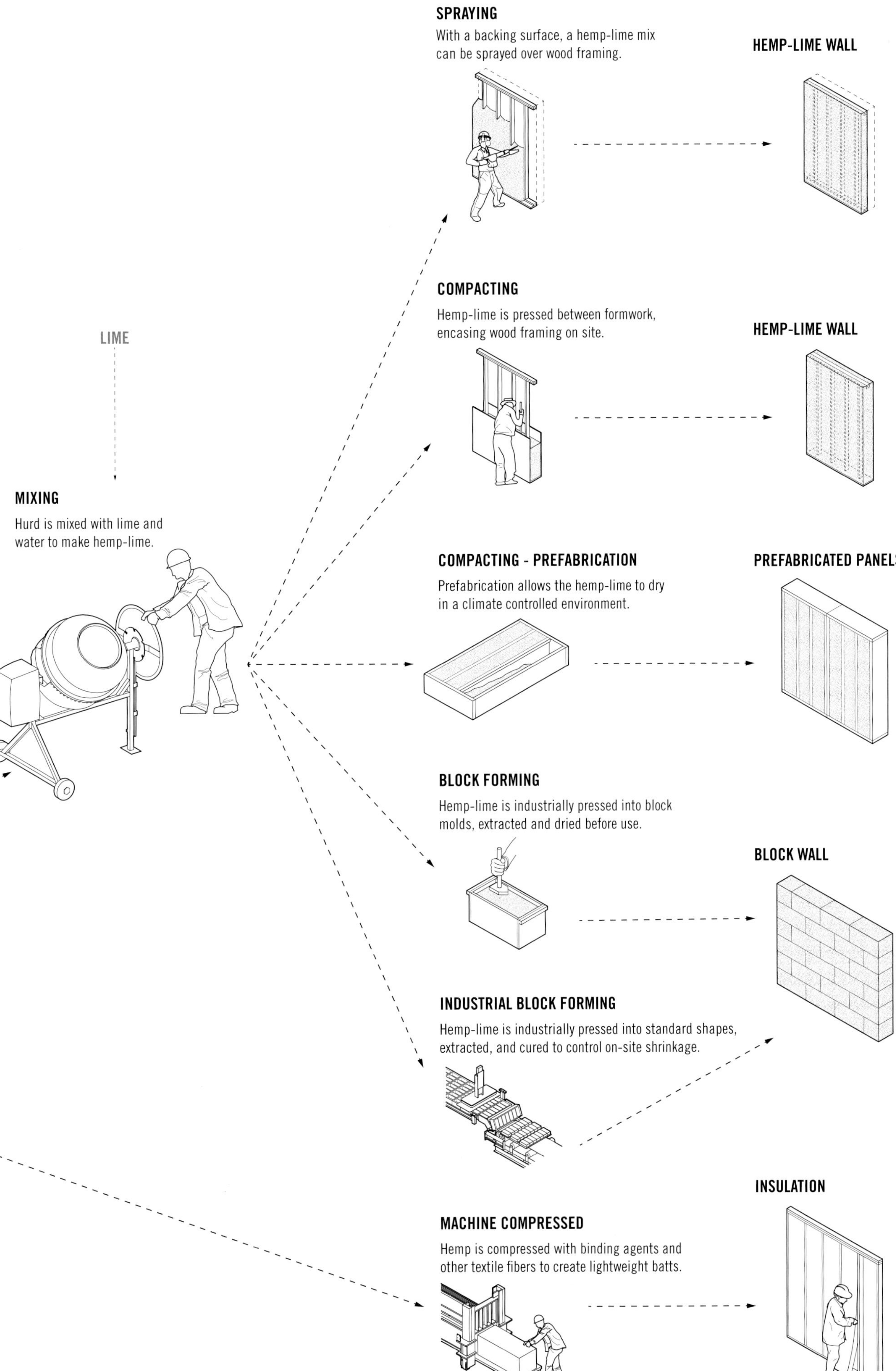
SPRAYING
With a backing surface, a hemp-lime mix can be sprayed over wood framing.
HEMP-LIME WALL
COMPACTING
Hemp-lime is pressed between formwork, encasing wood framing on site.
HEMP-LIME WALL
LIME
MIXING
Hurd is mixed with lime and water to make hemp-lime.
COMPACTING - PREFABRICATION
Prefabrication allows the hemp-lime to dry in a climate controlled environment.
PREFABRICATED PANELS
BLOCK FORMING
Hemp-lime is industrially pressed into block molds, extracted and dried before use.
BLOCK WALL
INDUSTRIAL BLOCK FORMING
Hemp-lime is industrially pressed into standard shapes, extracted, and cured to control on-site shrinkage.
INSULATION
MACHINE COMPRESSED
Hemp is compressed with binding agents and other textile fibers to create lightweight batts.

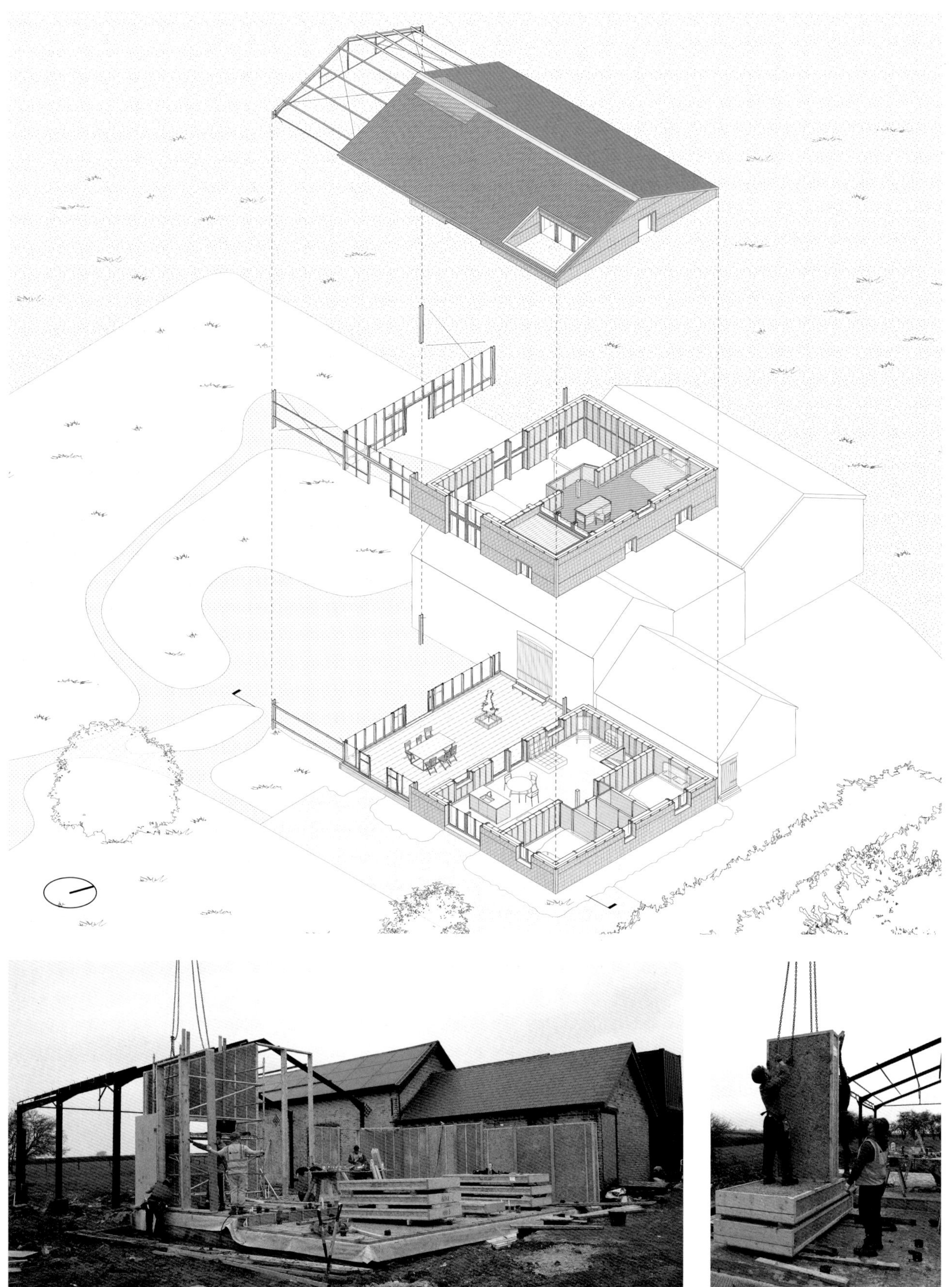

Flat House | Practice Architecture

Built on a 20-acre farm growing hemp, this house uses prefabricated I-joist wood-framed cassettes filled with hemp and lime to prototype an innovative construction and assembly system. At a standard dimension of 4 by 8 ft (1.2 by 2.4 m) panels and 7.6 in (200 mm) thick, these modular units were built offsite, thus enabling the months-long curing time of hemp-lime to occur in a factory-controlled setting prior to the rapid two-day assembly time on site, to exacting tolerances. The interior of the house reveals the innovative framing system with just a clay paint coating over the exposed hemp-lime infill. The new three-bedroom house was designed to the footprint of an existing barn and reused the barn's steel frame for

Cambridgeshire, England | 2019

portions of the structure. This 1,050 sq ft (98 sq m), off-grid residence is clad in corrugated panels of hemp fiber bonded by sugar-based resin, further exploring the hemp's capacity as a building material.

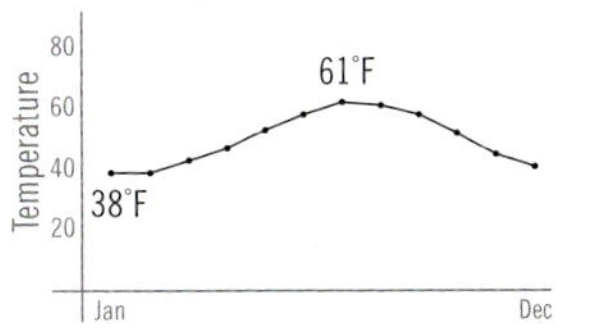

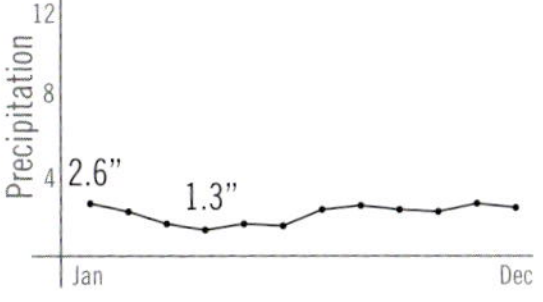

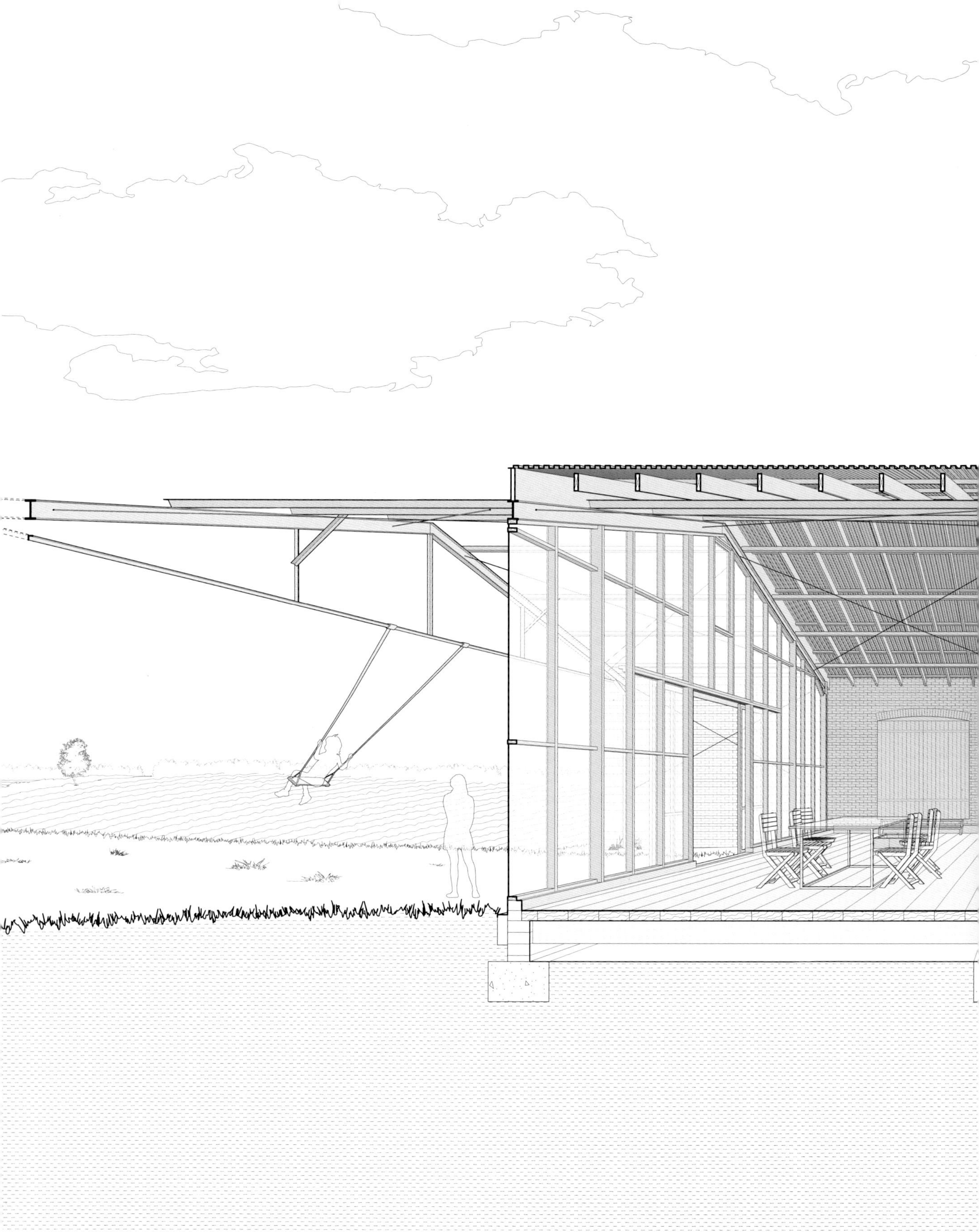

Flat House

Flat House is divided into four distinct areas that maximize the spatial experience and minimize heating demands. A portion of the repurposed steel structure defines the front play area and frames the view toward the hemp fields beyond. The other half of the existing structure is infilled with glass walls on the south and west providing the sun-lit multipurpose room with passive heating. The two fully conditioned sections of the house to the east are structured using the hemp-lime-filled wood cassettes. A double-height kitchen and living space anchors the center of the house with bedrooms, bathroom, and outdoor deck located to the east. Wood fiber provides additional insulation on the exterior and is protected by the hemp

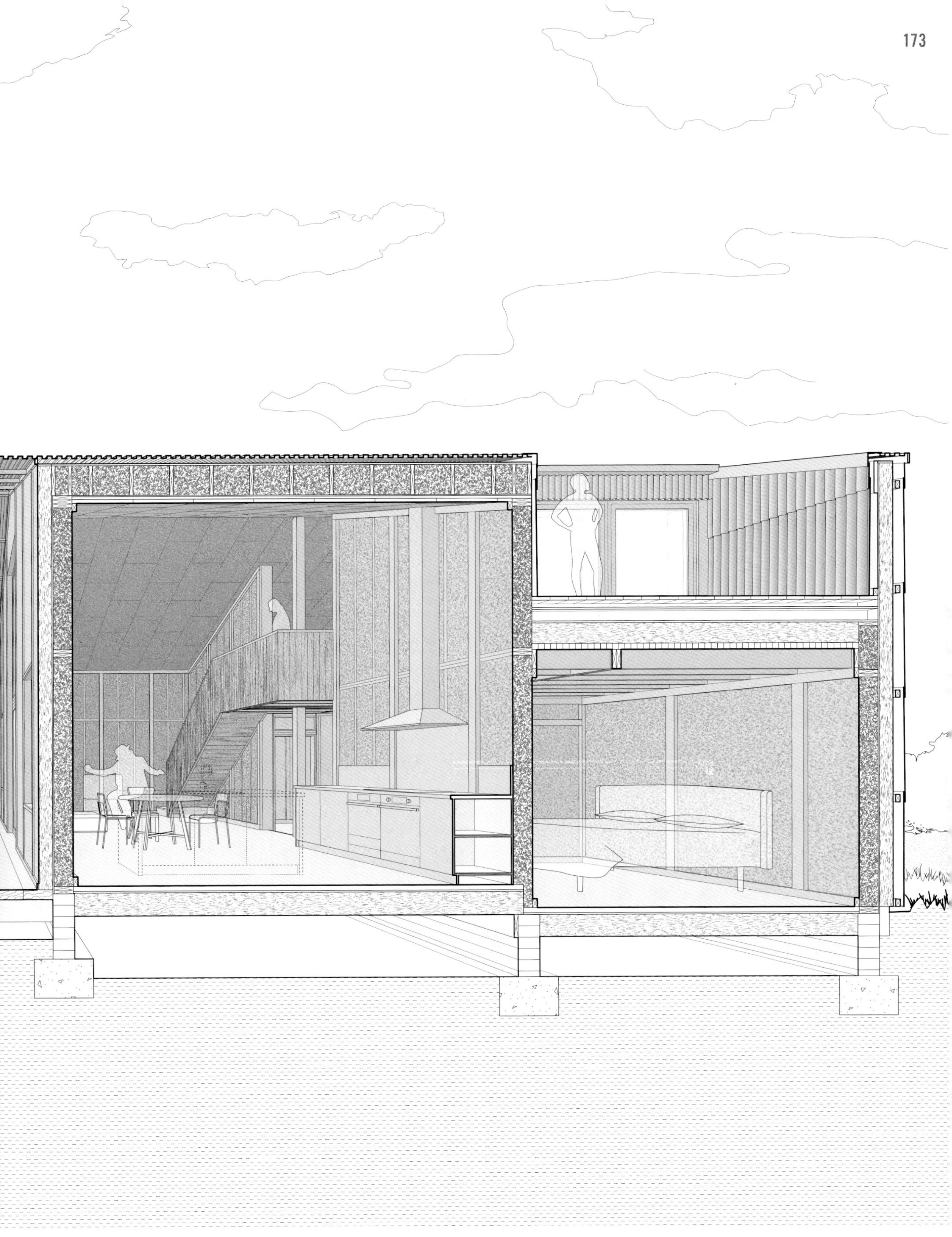

fiber rain screen cladding. The hemp- and wood-based wall system creates an elegant and high-performing exterior wall that absorbs moisture, regulates humidity within the house, and provides excellent acoustic properties. This mass wall system provides a clear alternative to multi-layered conventional wall approach that relies heavily on petroleum-based membranes, seals, and components. The house maximizes the use of the hemp plant, with the inner hurd used for insulation and the exterior fiber for the outside cladding. The use of prefabrication answers one of the main challenges of using hemp and lime, namely the time and risk of on-site curing.

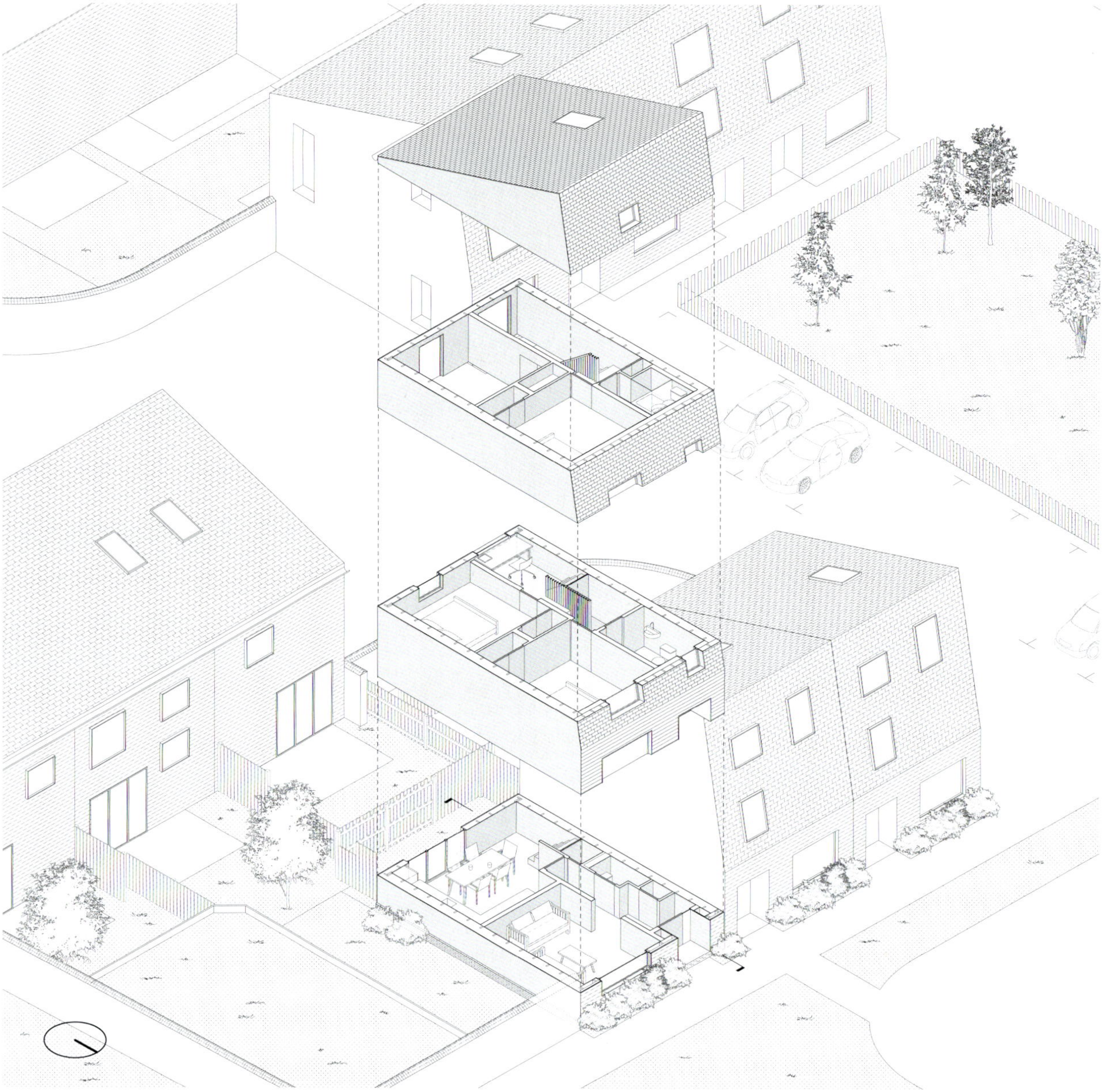

Clay Field | Riches Hawley Mikhail Architects

Clay Field demonstrates the capacity to use carbon-sequestering materials at scale in multi-unit dwellings, while engaging innovative approaches to plant-based building materials. The affordable housing project organizes 13 two-bedroom houses and nine three-bedroom and four one-bedroom apartments into a neighborhood, each unit complemented with a private back garden and collective green spaces. Clay Field was constructed using a standard timber structural frame with novel hemp and lime sprayed cavity insulation to ensure a compacted wall assembly. The houses are organized in groups of three units to minimize the number of exterior perimeter walls. Each house has a primary face to the south

Elmswell, England | 2007

where the largest windows are set to ensure passive solar benefits while also staggering the buildings to avoid casting shadows on each other. The cedar and lime stucco exterior materials perform well with the hemp-lime wall assembly, with the more textured cedar used to designate the public entrance façades.

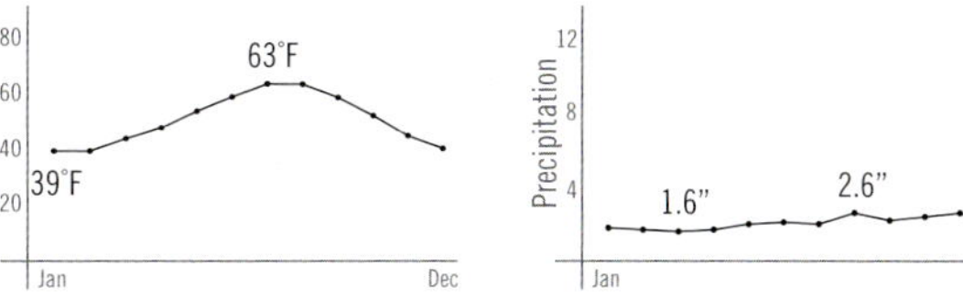

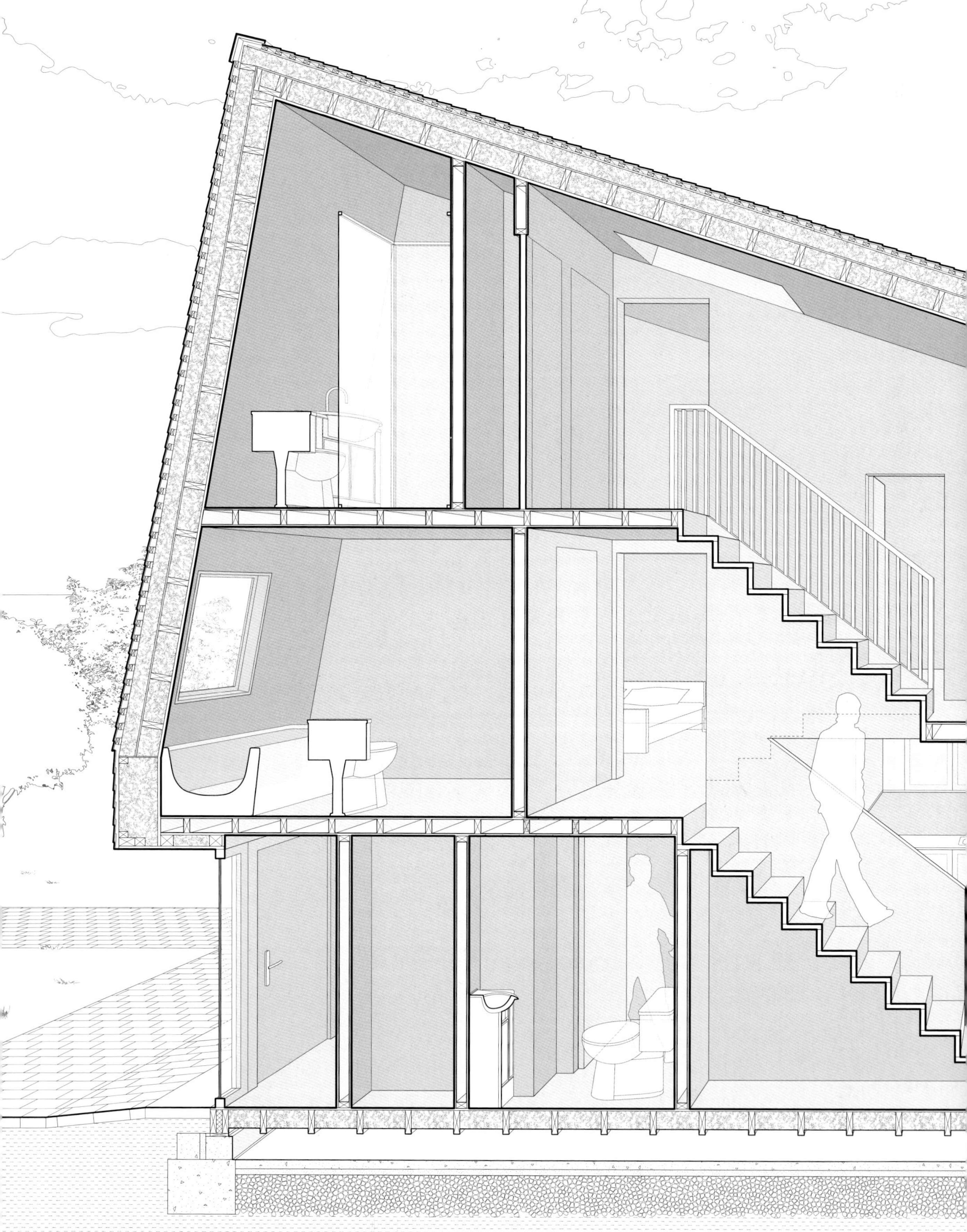

Clay Field

The compact volume of the multi-story house creates an energy-efficient form that maximizes usable space within a tight envelope. The main staircase links the three primary floors, encouraging natural ventilation, while providing additional usable space at the landing. The sloped roof follows the staircase and minimizes the shadows cast by the roof profile on the shared gardens. The foundation grade beams, made from 50% blast furnace slag, and raised wood joists lift above a ventilated void, reducing the need for a carbon-intensive solid concrete slab. A combination of hemp and recycled cotton batt insulates between the joists. The conventional wood-framed walls have a gypsum-based interior shear

wall and are packed with a mix of hemp and lime with a small amount of Portland cement to speed the drying during construction. A three-coat .75 in (20 mm) lime render is directly applied to the hemp-lime mix on the gable end walls. Western red cedar fixed to battens with a vapor barrier membrane enclose the hemp-lime walls on the north and south sides.

The wood-framed roof is insulated with two layers of hemp and recycled cotton and capped with a matrix of criss-crossed battens to ensure proper ventilation.

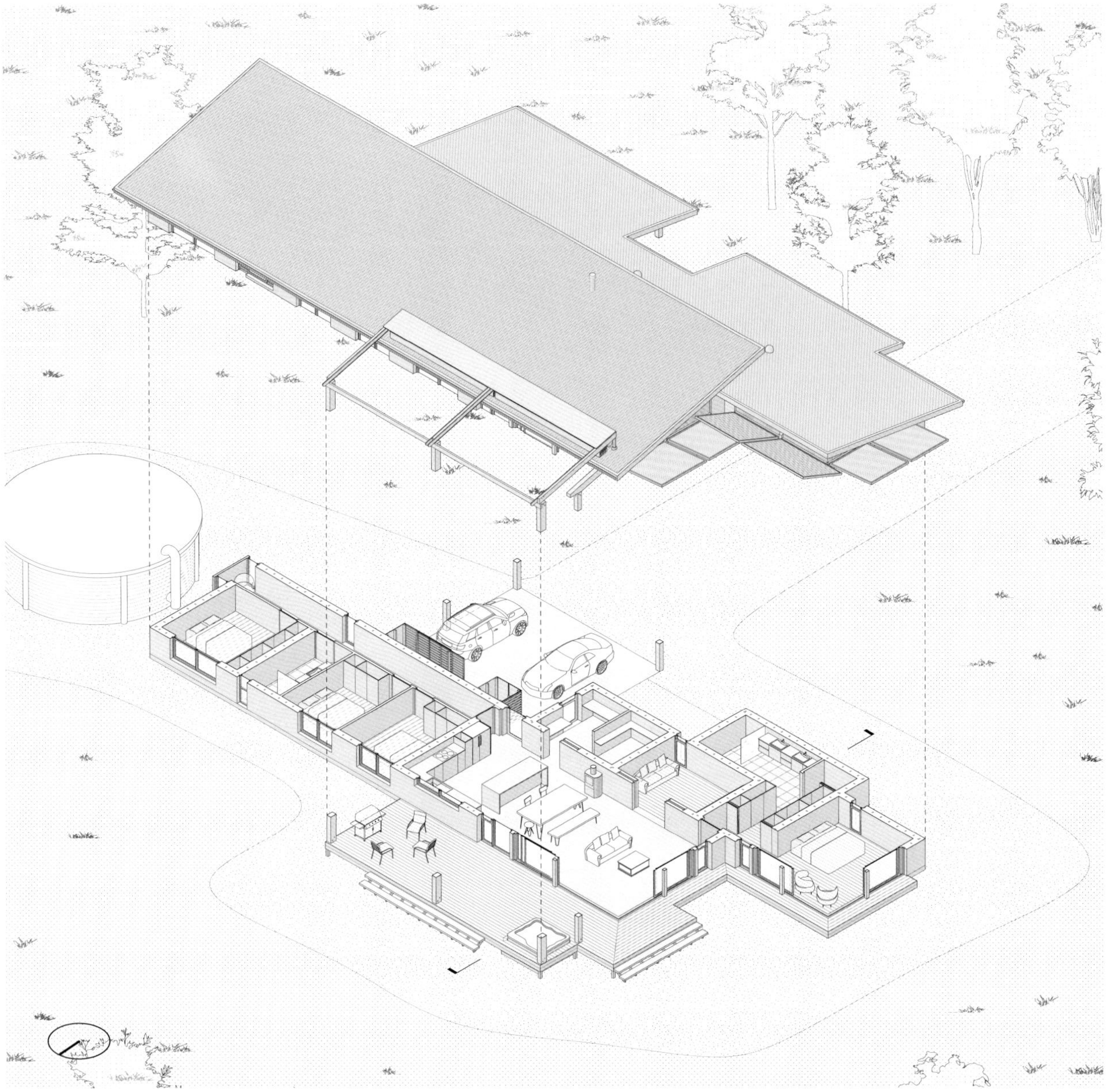

Mudgee Hempcrete House 2 | Envirotecture

Located in an area of New South Wales prone to brush fires, this project uses hemp-lime (hempcrete) walls because of its resistance to burning. An interior wood structure, anchored to the slab with steel ties, is centered in the walls and protected on both sides with hemp-lime that insulates the structure from possible fire damage. The house is elongated east and west with primary windows facing north, as is best in the southern hemisphere to maximize solar exposure. A bar of bedrooms connects to a central living area, which adjoins another zone containing the main bedroom. Situated in

Mudgee, Australia | 2015

an area of creeks, the raised foundation provides necessary elevation from the site, while enhancing views across the landscape. Manually operated metal fire shutters double as shading devices, complementing resistance provided by the thick hemp-lime walls.

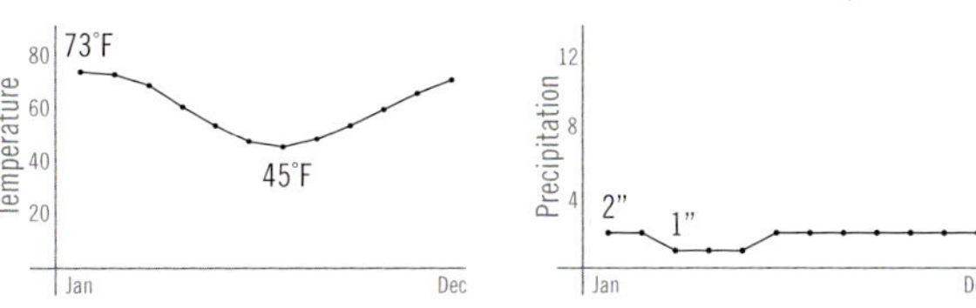

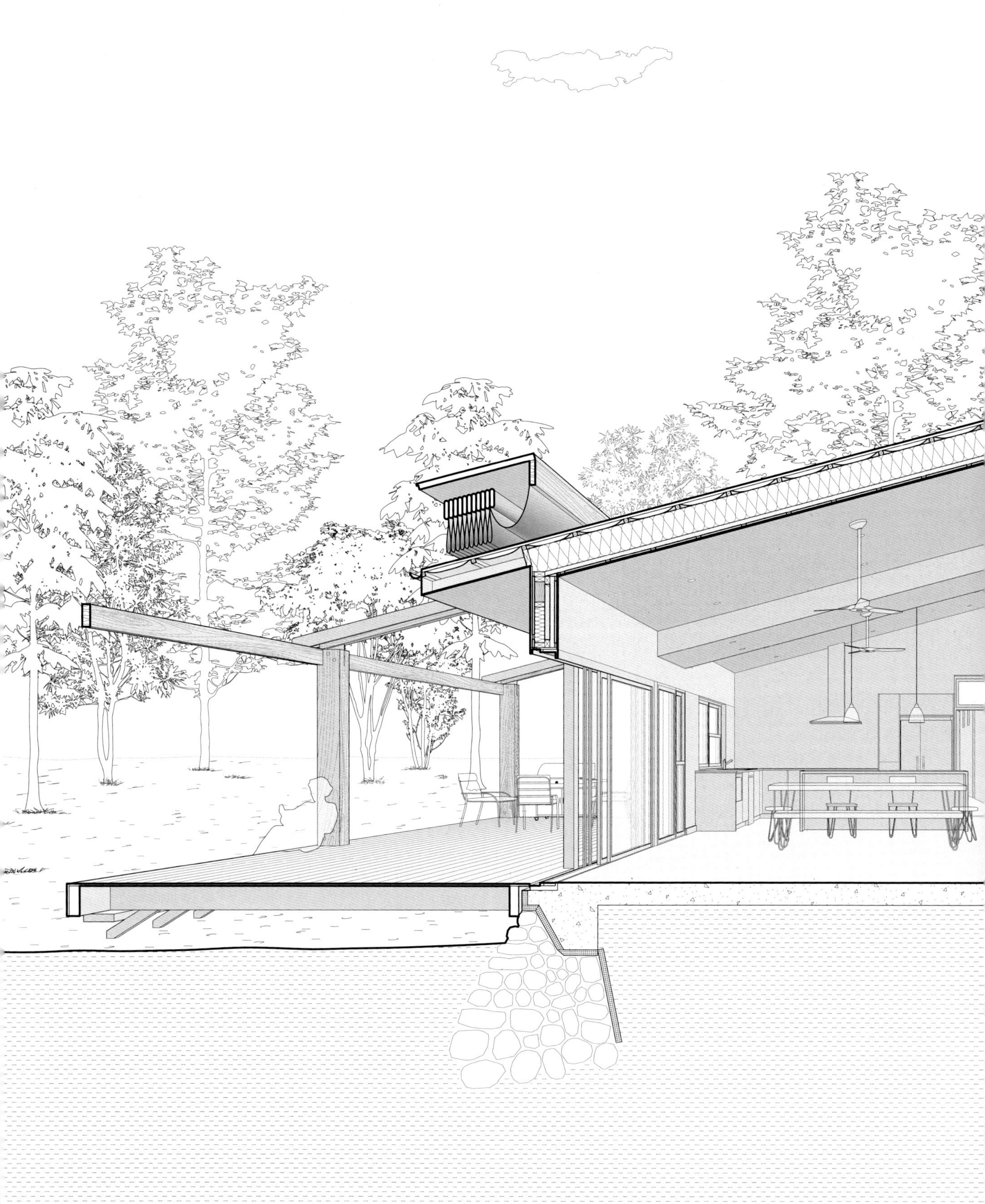

Mudgee Hempcrete House 2

This project uses hemp-lime to protect and insulate the structural walls that organize the living zones of the house. At nearly 12 in (300 mm) thick, the hemp-lime walls create a highly insulated wall at over R-30. Clad on the exterior with lime render and finished to match the interior use, the thick walls breath to mitigate unwanted condensation, while providing acoustic separation between the different areas of this house. Whereas the walls are hemp-lime, the long, gently sloped metal-clad roofs and the soffit above the large corner window to the north are more conventionally framed and insulated to address the local climatic conditions. A foil-faced fiberglass blanket provides thermal resistance, sound protection, and

condensation control directly below the metal roof. Polyester batt insulation is used in the window soffit and as fill between the long wood rafters which are notched and anchored to the wood studs in the hemp-lime walls below. Above the north porch, a large exterior retractable awning supported by recycled timber members provides solar modulation during the colder months. A central fireplace in the main living space runs on locally gathered wood, harvested to minimize bushfires, and provides the only additional heating for this thermally tuned house.

Low Energy House in Uccle | Karbon' Architecture et Urbanisme

This urban infill project embraces the challenges of its unusually narrow site at the end of a cul-de-sac and adjacent to an existing high brick wall. The design uses the significant change in topography of nearly 20 ft (6 m) across the site, from the street on the south to the garden at the north, as a catalyst for intervention, configuring a small residence that embraces each of the three façades. From the street, the house appears as a three-story narrow structure with roof, complete with garage entrance and bay windows above. Yet on the north, only two floors appear with no roof. The lower floor is unconditioned but primarily underground, taking advantage of the thermal regulating properties of the earth. The main

Brussels, Belgium | 2010

living floor is insulated with hemp-lime, while the upper two floors are built using straw-bales. Throughout, exposed wood reinforces the commitment to plant-based materials.

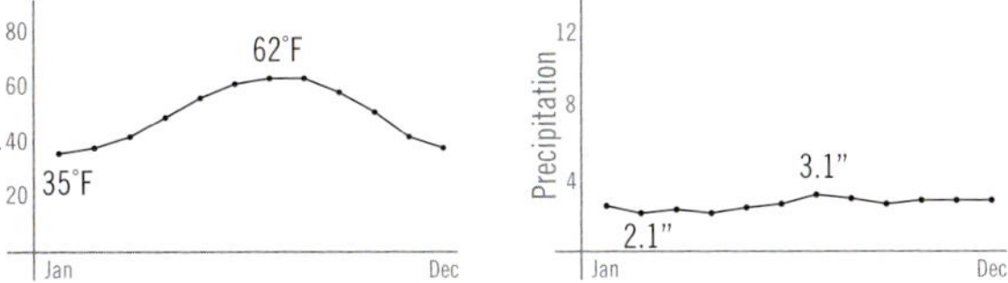

Low Energy House in Uccle

Reflecting the stacked layering of space required by the dramatic site, the project is constructed using an unusual mix of three types of mass-wall assemblies: concrete at the base, shutter cast hemp-lime for the lower floors, and prefabricated timber panels with straw-bale construction for the upper levels. On the inside, lime plaster covers the hemp-lime walls, while a thin layer of clay coats the straw walls. Zinc roofing and lime plaster over wood fiber board composes the exterior. Concrete is judiciously limited to grade and lower sitework. Additionally, the concrete blocks above grade contain an aerated clay aggregate. At the second level, an outdoor space provides separation between the retaining wall and the wood and

hemp-lime insulated wall that frames the kitchen and living space. For the top two floors, the construction system changes to thick straw-bales set into wood frames, enabling the continuity of the floor to roof bend on the south. The open staircase allows for stack ventilation by essentially creating a channel for air to circulate up through the house to the operable windows at the top level. A single wood burning stove is thus able to heat the entire structure without the use of ducts and forced mechanical ventilation.

CORK

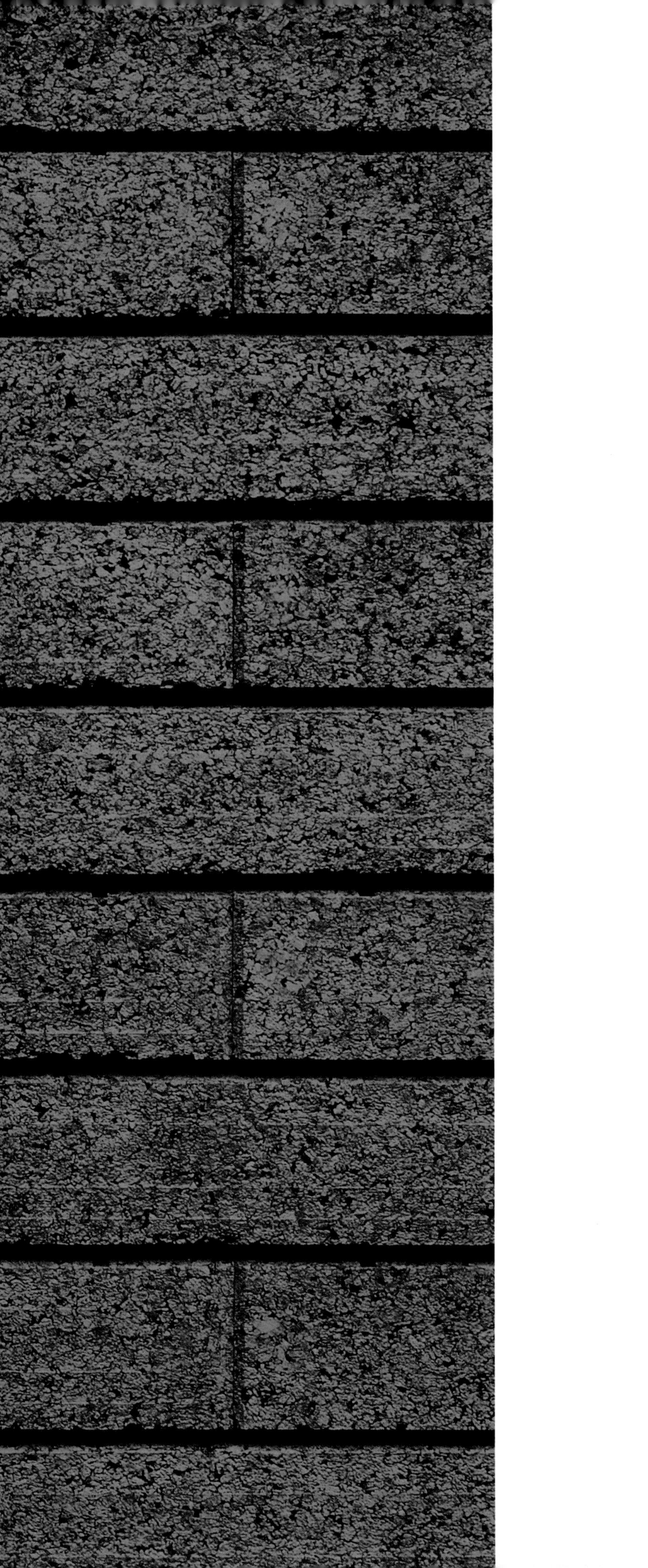

Cork

-90 $kgCO_2e/m^3$ Ökobaudat

-198 $kgCO_2e/m^3$ BEAM

Derived from the bark of the cork oak tree, this uniquely renewable material combines desirable water resistant, thermal, antifungal, acoustical, structural, and sensory qualities. Its multivalent performance can allow for mono-material tectonic assemblies while reducing reliance on multilayered, synthetic components, contributing to healthier interior atmospheres and optimizing reuse. While currently cork oak tree's growing range is limited, its cultivation provides ecosystem services to a rich agroforestry system and its use in building products recuperates waste from wine stopper production.

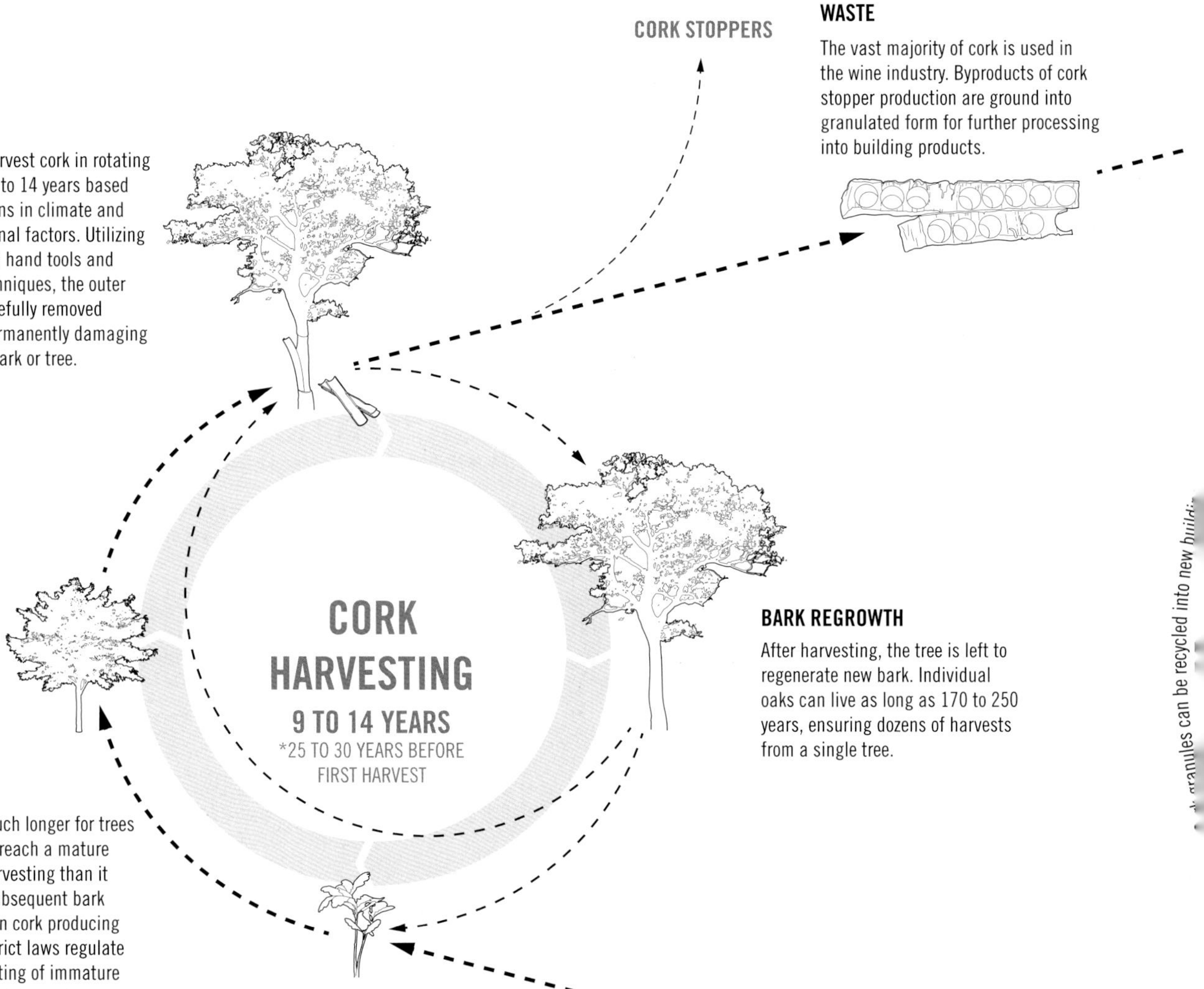

CORK STOPPERS

WASTE

The vast majority of cork is used in the wine industry. Byproducts of cork stopper production are ground into granulated form for further processing into building products.

HARVEST

Workers harvest cork in rotating cycles of 9 to 14 years based on variations in climate and other regional factors. Utilizing specialized hand tools and skilled techniques, the outer bark is carefully removed without permanently damaging the inner bark or tree.

CORK HARVESTING

9 TO 14 YEARS

*25 TO 30 YEARS BEFORE FIRST HARVEST

BARK REGROWTH

After harvesting, the tree is left to regenerate new bark. Individual oaks can live as long as 170 to 250 years, ensuring dozens of harvests from a single tree.

GROWTH

It takes much longer for trees to initially reach a mature size for harvesting than it does for subsequent bark regrowth. In cork producing regions, strict laws regulate the harvesting of immature trees, forbid damaging mature specimens, and guard against mismanagement of forests.

PLANT

Cork Oak trees are part of a centuries old agrarian ecosystem indigenous to the Iberian peninsula, known as *montados* or *dehesas* in Portugal and Spain respectively. While the geography of these woodlands presents some limits to more widespread use, their unique mix of agriculture and forestry preserves regional biodiversity and resists desertification while supporting a local economy of farmers and cork workers. While these systems have historically been self propagating, recent efforts have involved the planting of new acreage for cork cultivation to offset the effects of fire, invasive species, and encroachment by competing agricultural practices.

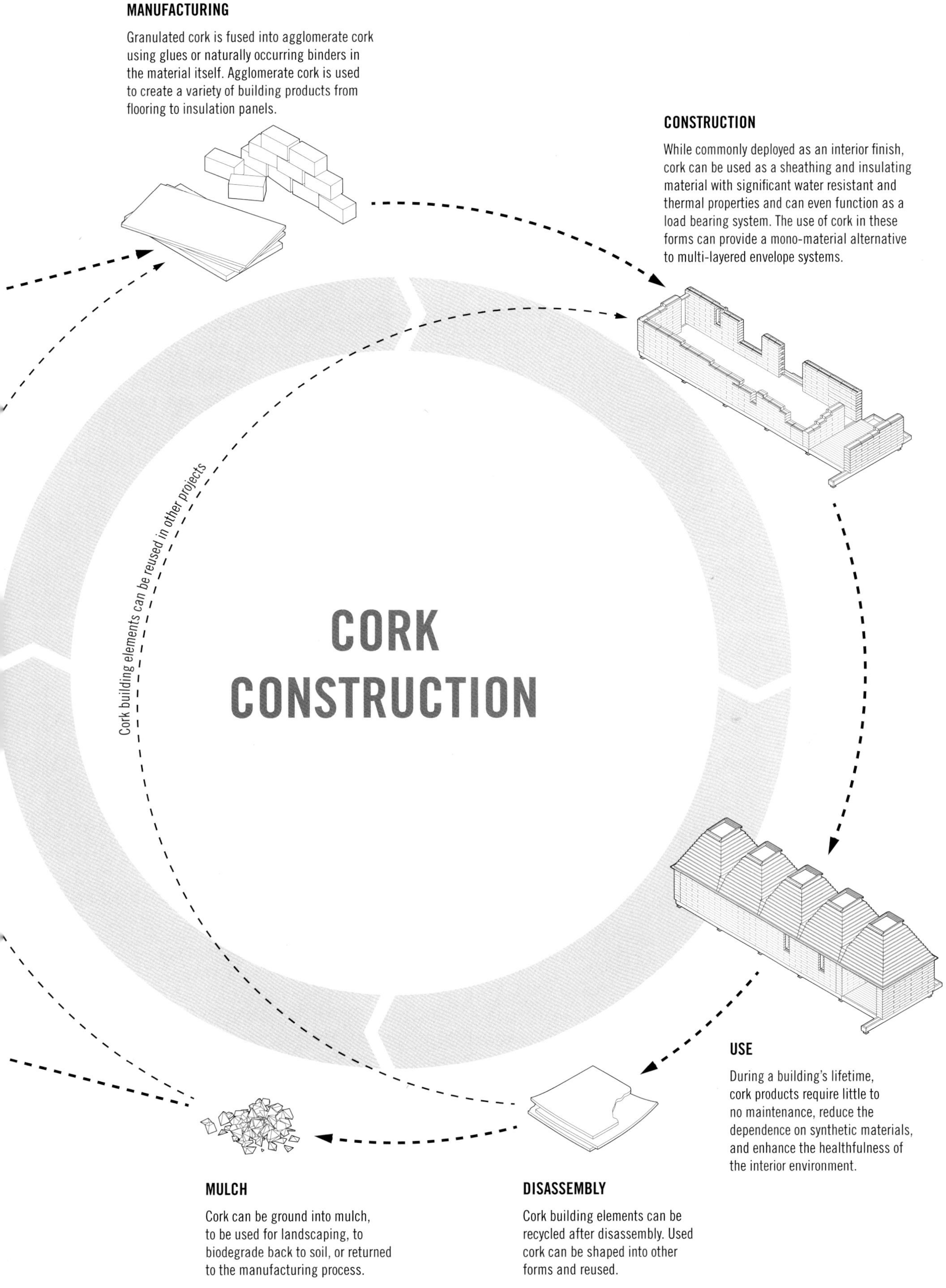

CORK CONSTRUCTION

MANUFACTURING

Granulated cork is fused into agglomerate cork using glues or naturally occurring binders in the material itself. Agglomerate cork is used to create a variety of building products from flooring to insulation panels.

CONSTRUCTION

While commonly deployed as an interior finish, cork can be used as a sheathing and insulating material with significant water resistant and thermal properties and can even function as a load bearing system. The use of cork in these forms can provide a mono-material alternative to multi-layered envelope systems.

USE

During a building's lifetime, cork products require little to no maintenance, reduce the dependence on synthetic materials, and enhance the healthfulness of the interior environment.

DISASSEMBLY

Cork building elements can be recycled after disassembly. Used cork can be shaped into other forms and reused.

MULCH

Cork can be ground into mulch, to be used for landscaping, to biodegrade back to soil, or returned to the manufacturing process.

Cork building elements can be reused in other projects

CORK

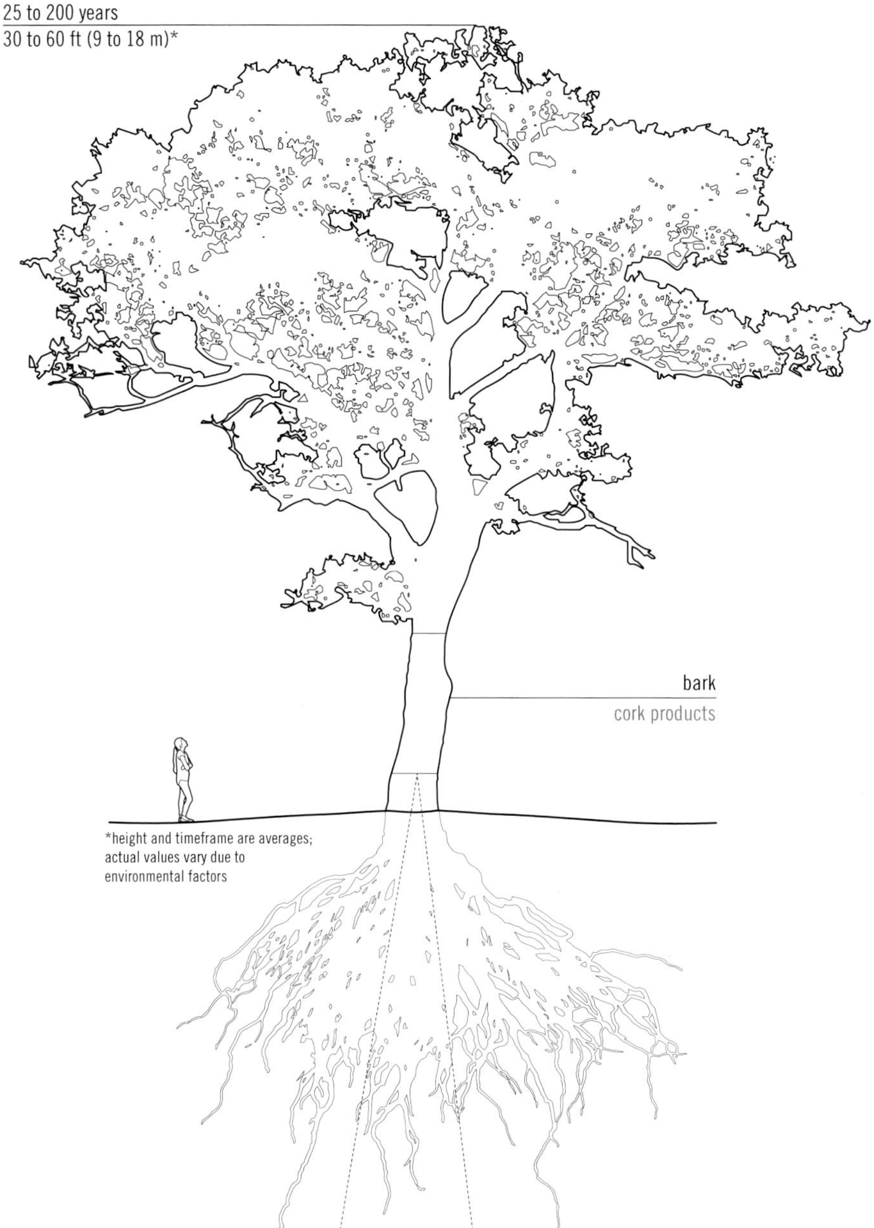

25 to 200 years
30 to 60 ft (9 to 18 m)*

bark
cork products

*height and timeframe are averages; actual values vary due to environmental factors

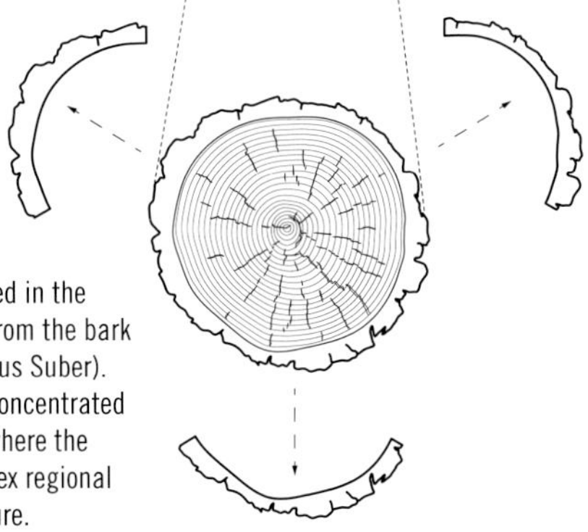

BARK

All cork, including that used in the building industry, comes from the bark of the cork oak tree (Quercus Suber). The cork oaks' habitat is concentrated on the Iberian Peninsula where the trees form part of a complex regional ecology and agrarian culture.

HARVESTING

Cork is harvested from mature trees once every 9 to 14 years. Skilled workers use specialized tools to strip off a portion of the bark such that the tree is not harmed and the bark regrows.

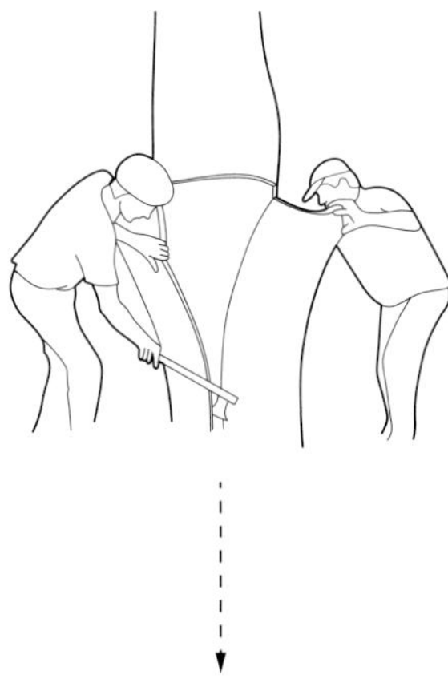

PILING

Harvested cork planks are stored in piles for several months before processing to allow for initial drying.

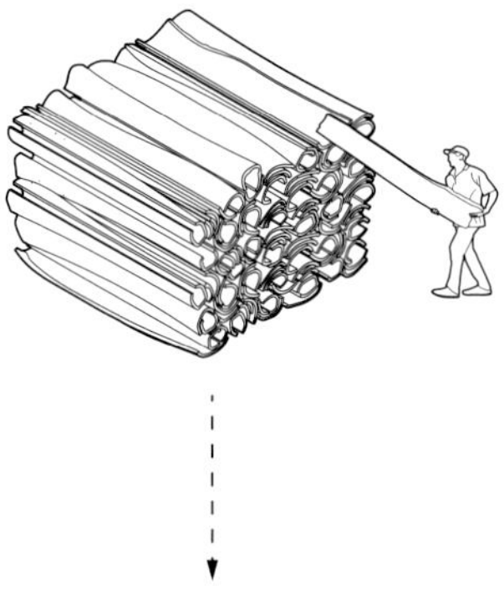

BOILING

The planks are boiled, or steamed, to soften and clean them. Boiled planks are flatter and easier to work with.

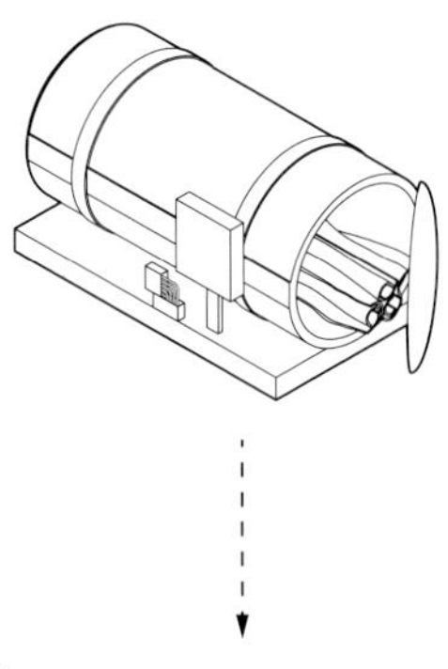

CUTTING

The planks are graded and cut into workable pieces.

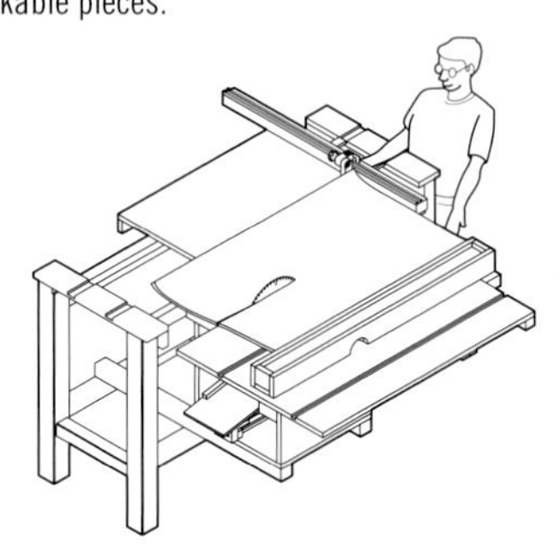

SHAPING

Cork granules are fused together into agglomerate cork using adhesives or thermal processes and then cut or formed into a variety of shapes and products. Naturally agglomerated or expanded cork is preferable from a recycling and biodegradability standpoint as it uses the naturally occurring resins in the bark itself, activated by heat, as a binder.

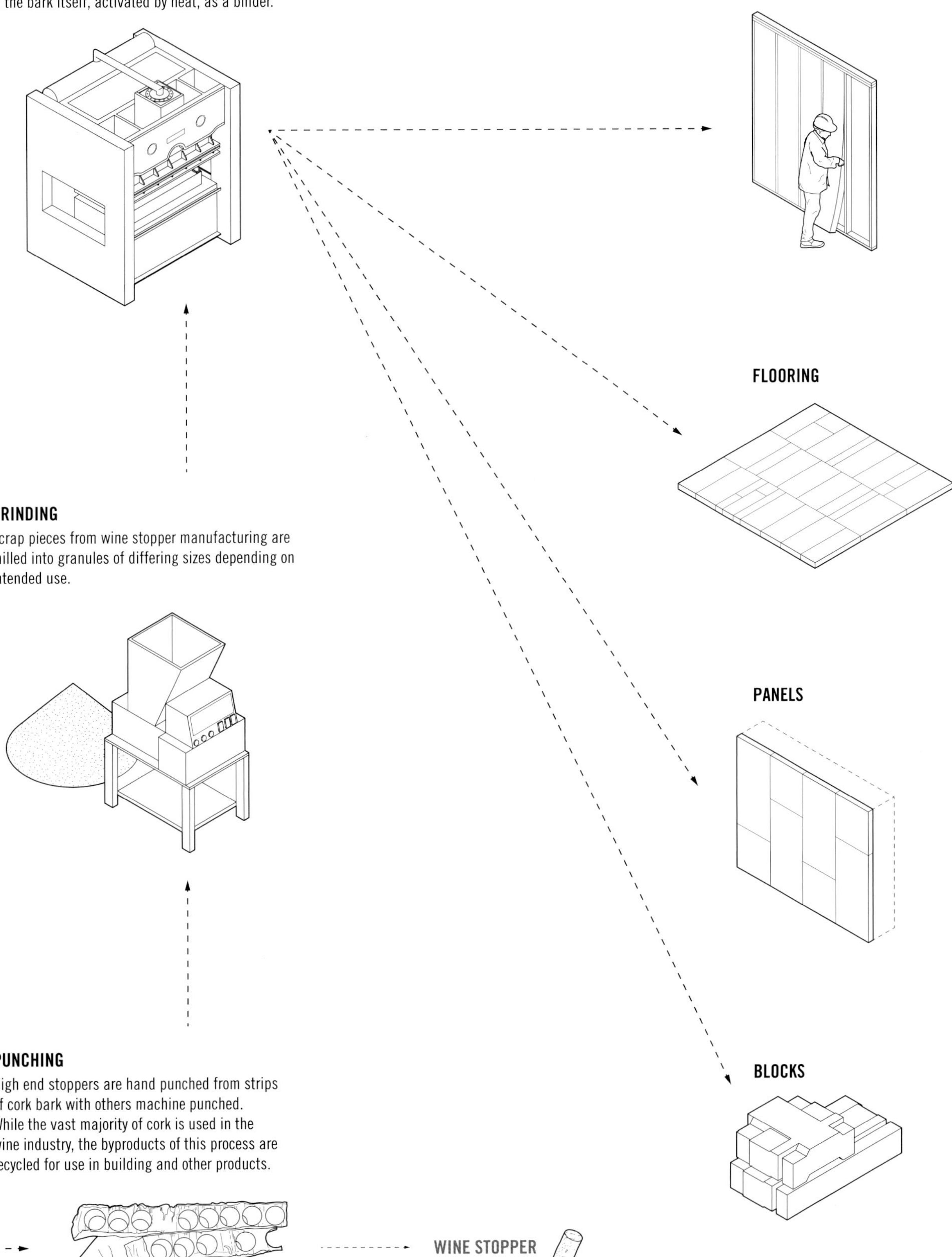

GRINDING

Scrap pieces from wine stopper manufacturing are milled into granules of differing sizes depending on intended use.

PUNCHING

High end stoppers are hand punched from strips of cork bark with others machine punched. While the vast majority of cork is used in the wine industry, the byproducts of this process are recycled for use in building and other products.

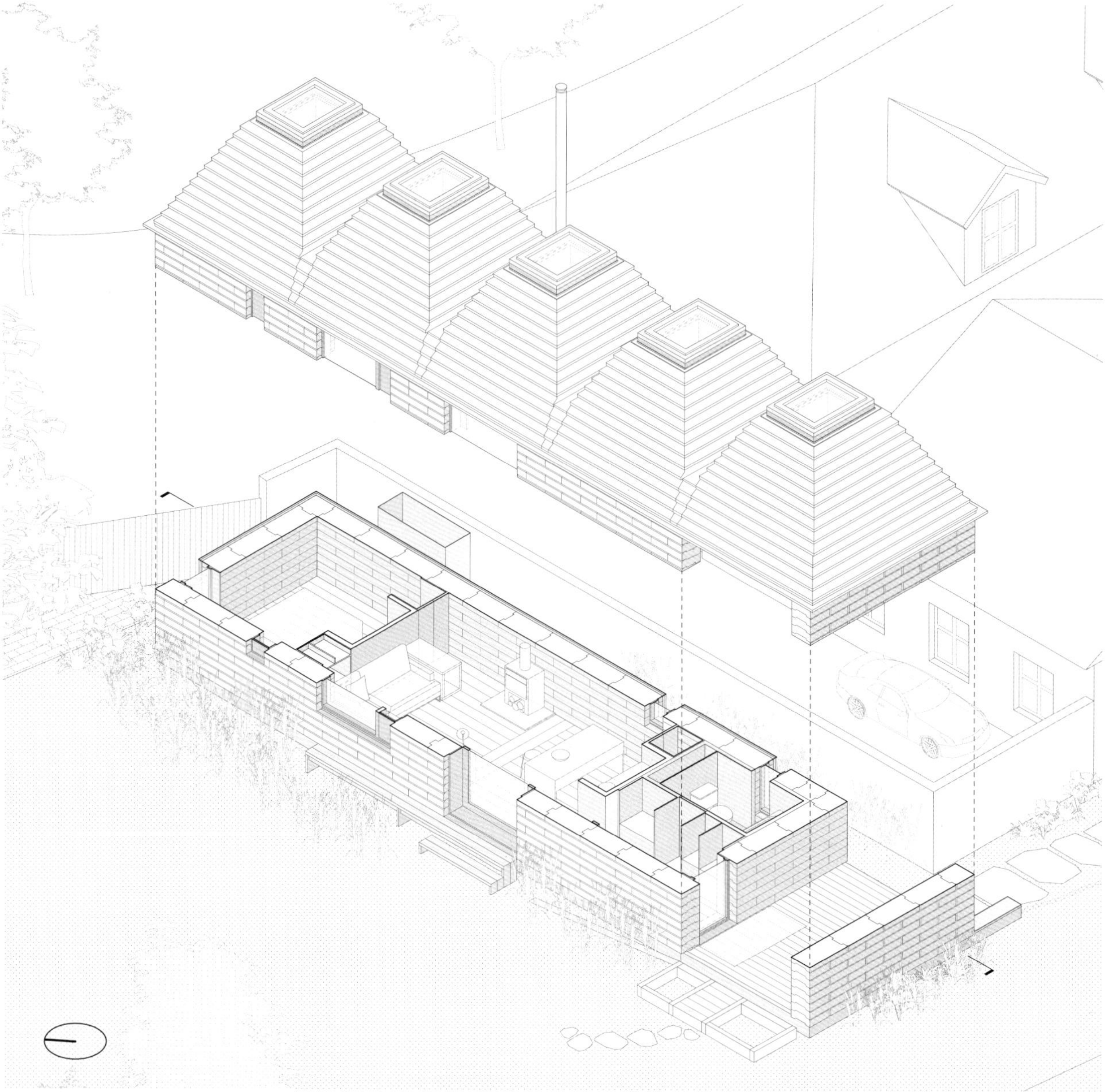

Cork House | Matthew Barnett Howland with Dido Milne and Oliver Wilton

This aptly named experimental house is constructed almost entirely of its eponymous material. Developed in conjunction with several academic institutions and engineering consultancies, the house is intended to challenge the contemporary logic of complex, layered building envelopes in favor of a monolithic system of solid cork. The house itself is a linear assemblage of five volumes, each capped by pyramidal roofs that define a sequence of living spaces below. With the exception of wood ring beams, lintels, cross-laminated timber cabinetry, and steel pilings, the house is structured by load-bearing cork blocks. Developed through an extensive R&D process, the 1,268 CNC-milled blocks, derived from byproducts of the

London, England | 2019

cork industry, take advantage of both the material's natural thermal- and moisture-resistive properties as well as its inherent aesthetic and sensory qualities.

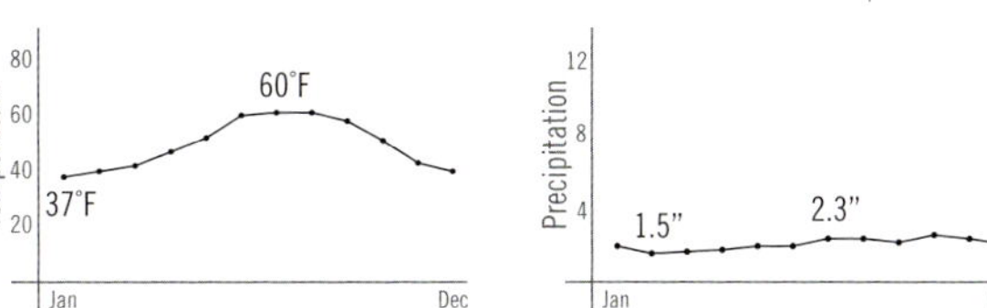

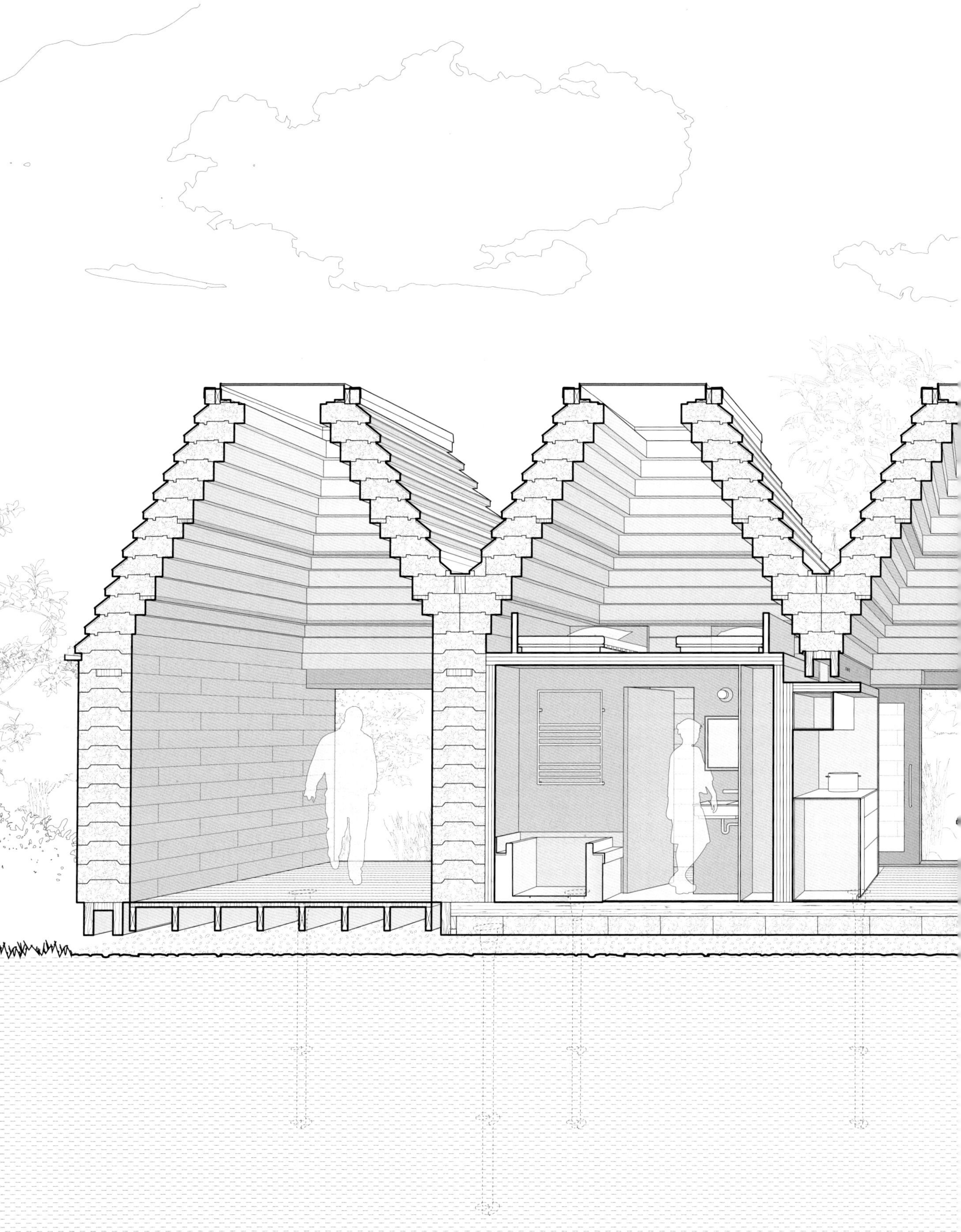

Cork House

Five interlinked volumes define the spaces of this experimental cork house: an exterior porch, entry area, bath, kitchen-dining area, living room, and bedroom respectively. A bedroom inhabits the corbeled roof volume above the bathroom. The exterior walls, comprised of interlocking blocks of solid cork, rise to a stepped pyramidal roof of the same construction, each topped by a skylight. Blocks are formed of waste material from the cork industry and CNC-milled to specific profiles that allow secure and rapid assembly without the use of adhesives or mechanical connections. This system of cork block suggests a kind of plant-based masonry; its stacked and corbeled logic is analogous to the stone construction of Celtic beehive houses. The two CLT wardrobes provide structural support to the wood ring beam and lintels that stabilize the load-bearing cork blocks, while defining more private areas of the house; the CLT floor ties to a base ring beam which is supported on steel screw piles. The project capitalizes on both the technical and sensory characteristics of this biogenic material. The fire, fungal, and moisture-resistant properties of cork are further complemented by its thermally-insulative capacity, acoustic dampening effects, and even its tactile and olfactory qualities.

Two Cork Houses | Emiliano López Mónica Rivera Arquitectos

Intended as holiday homes for three generations of the same family, two houses occupy a site dominated by pine and cork oak trees in the former cork-producing region of Costa Brava, Spain. Both buildings are rectilinear assemblies of CLT panels clad in an insulative exterior cork skin, supported atop concrete frames. The larger house nestles into the sloping terrain, while the smaller of the two extends vertically on columnar supports. Depicted here is the smaller house, which is itself formed from two intersecting cubic volumes, offset in both plan and section. Living and utility spaces occupy the lower of these two volumes, partially embedded into the hillside, whereas the bedrooms are lifted above the ground level within the

Palafrugell, Spain | 2016

more vertical, tower-like volume. The exterior and interior both reflect the flora of the surrounding site, defined by uniform insulating panels of thick cork cladding and the materiality of the pine CLT walls.

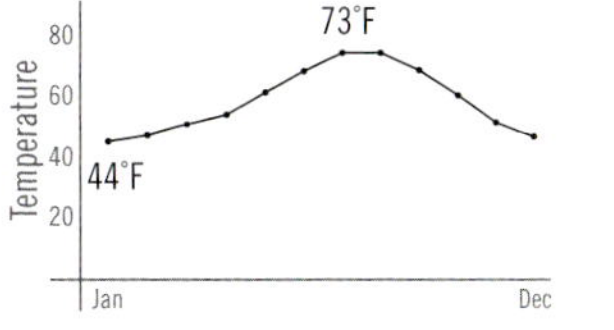

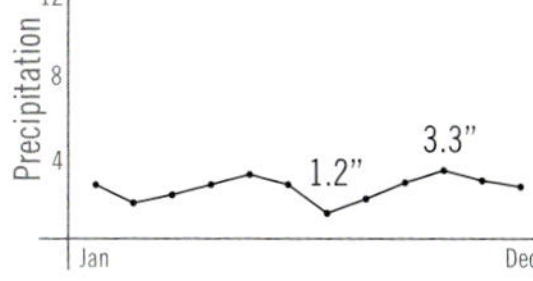

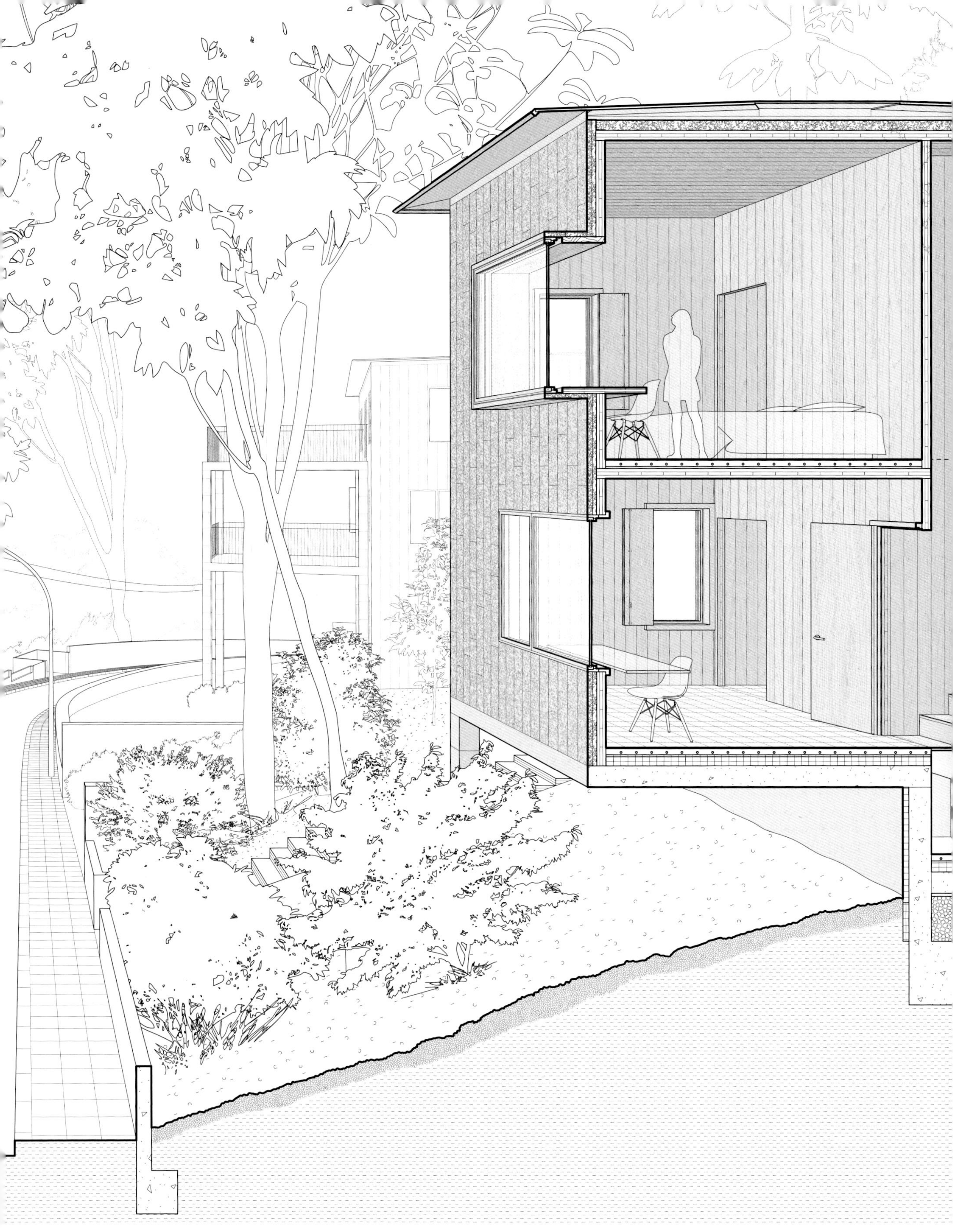

Two Cork Houses

This small holiday house comprises two interlinked rectilinear volumes sheared in section and plan, connected by a switchback stair. The more horizontal (lower) volume is embedded into the sloping landscape of the heavily wooded site while the more vertical volume is lifted above on concrete piers. A bay window in the upper-level bedroom projects outward to accommodate a built-in study, complimenting the composition of intersecting box-like forms. The house is constructed primarily of CLT panels, which comprise the walls, floor, and roof. The interior is characterized by the ubiquity of the pine finish of the panels, which extend to the connecting stair, also built of CLT. To maximize insulating qualities and provide

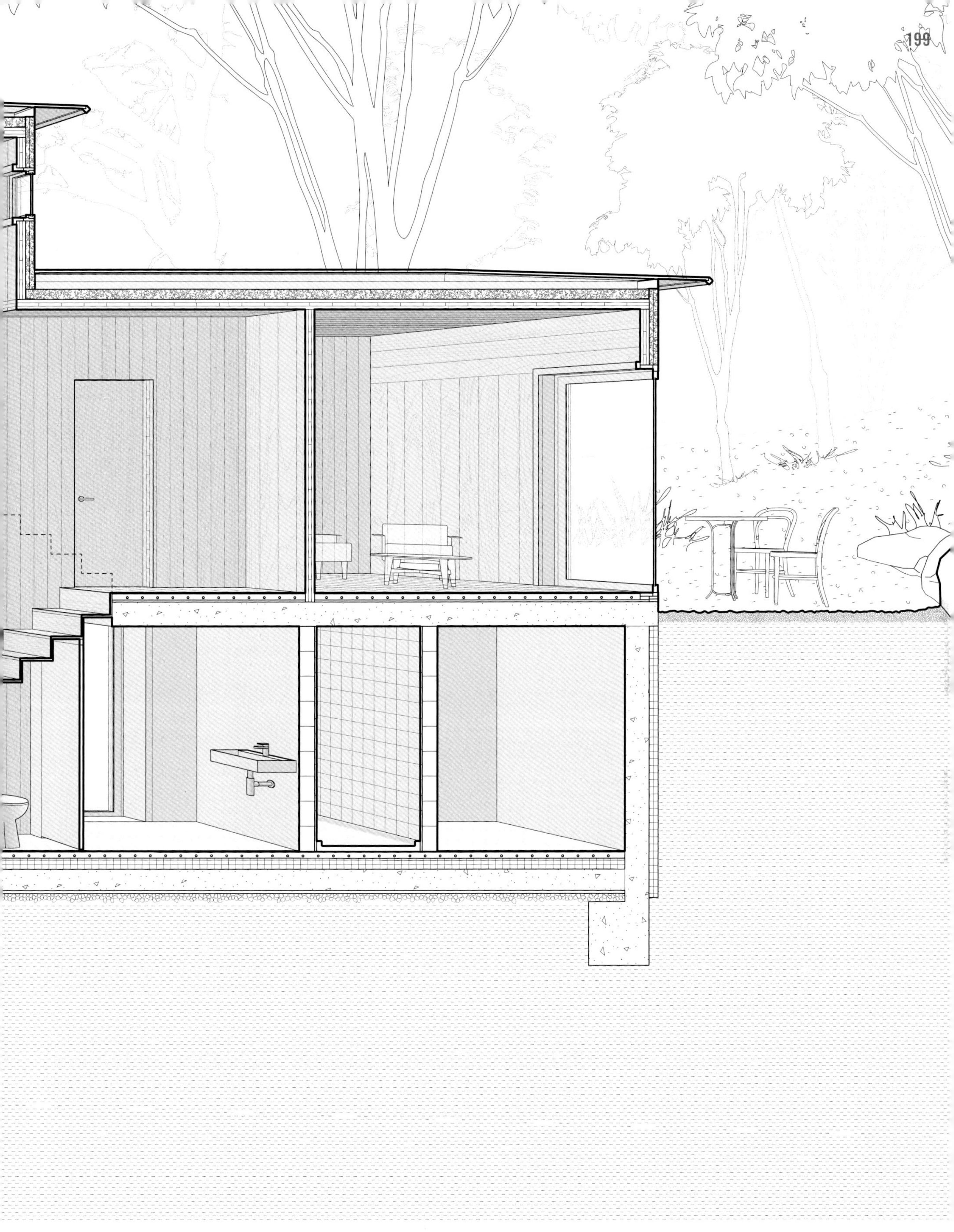

a monolithic appearance, the exterior of the house is continuously clad by layering two sizes of cork panels: one 1.6 in (40 mm) thick, pre-affixed to the mass timber walls, the other, 2 in (50 mm) thick, is attached on site with a layer of lime-mortar. With its thick exterior skin of indigenous cork and exposed CLT interior, the house's material composition references the surrounding forest of cork oaks and native pine trees, while its dynamic spatial arrangement creates a dialogue with the rugged terrain.

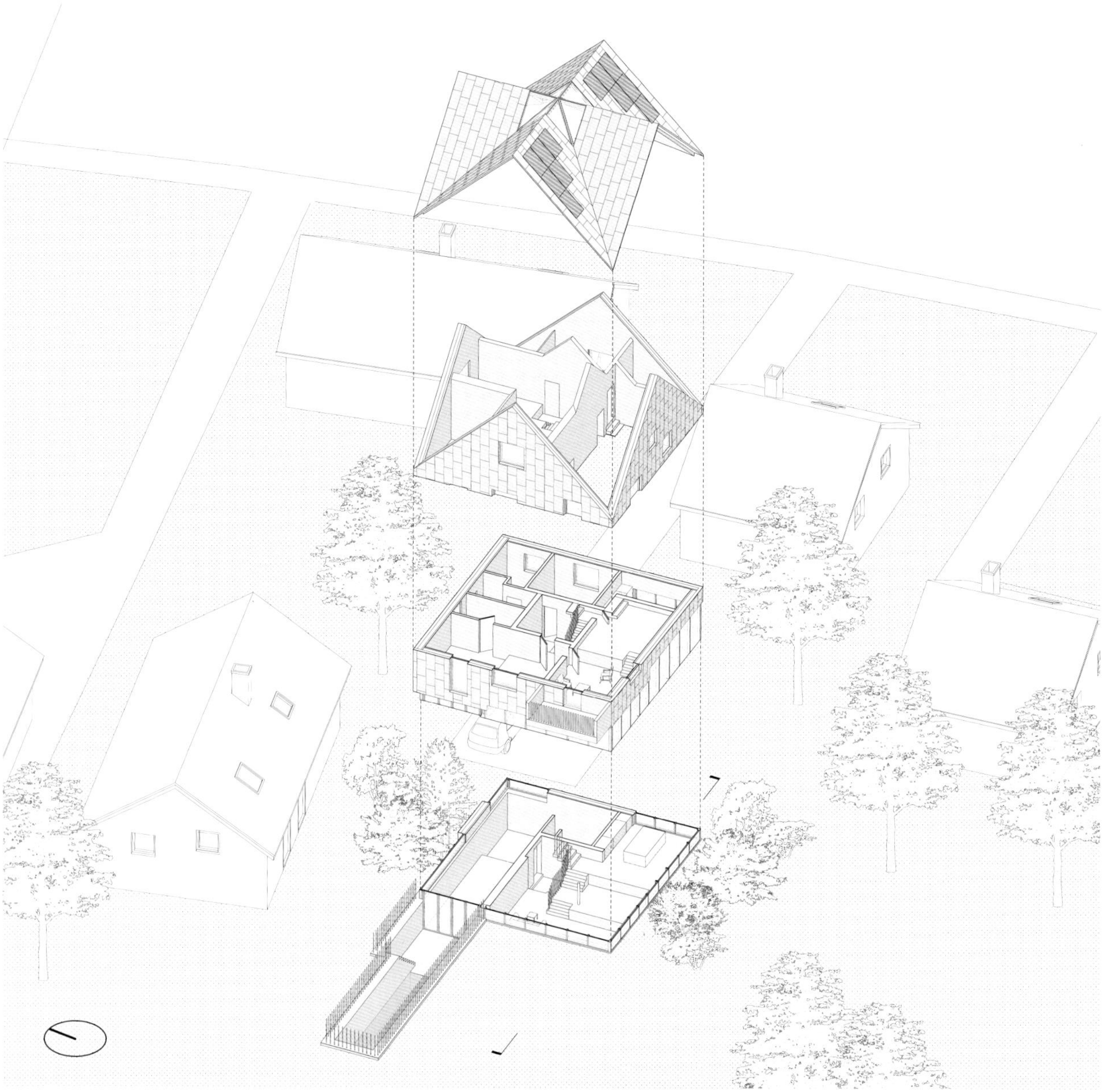

Cork Screw House | rundzwei Architekten

Situated on a typical residential plot in a Berlin suburb, the Cork Screw House can be understood as the interaction between a sculpted ground plane and an elevated cork roof volume. A series of staggered programmed levels are carved into the otherwise level terrain, including a main bedroom, living, dining, and kitchen areas. At the lowest level, the main bedroom links to a linear pool that extends into the surrounding garden, shielded from view. The upper levels comprise two additional bedrooms and baths, each with their own living and dining areas, intended to allow for future conversion of the residence into studio apartments, with a study space at the topmost level. The base and top split-level organization

Berlin, Germany | 2018

maximizes spatial efficiencies and floor area within a limited footprint. The upper volume, separated from its base by large sheets of glass, is timber-framed and clad in a monolithic skin of recycled cork. The four intersecting roof ridges, which produce the distinctive gabled façade, join at a central skylight and are partially clad with flush solar panels.

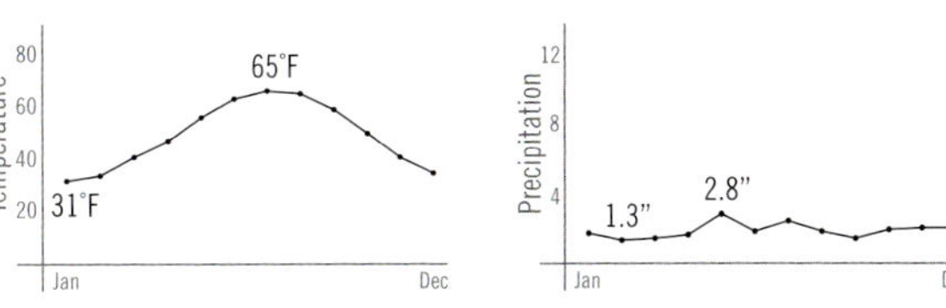

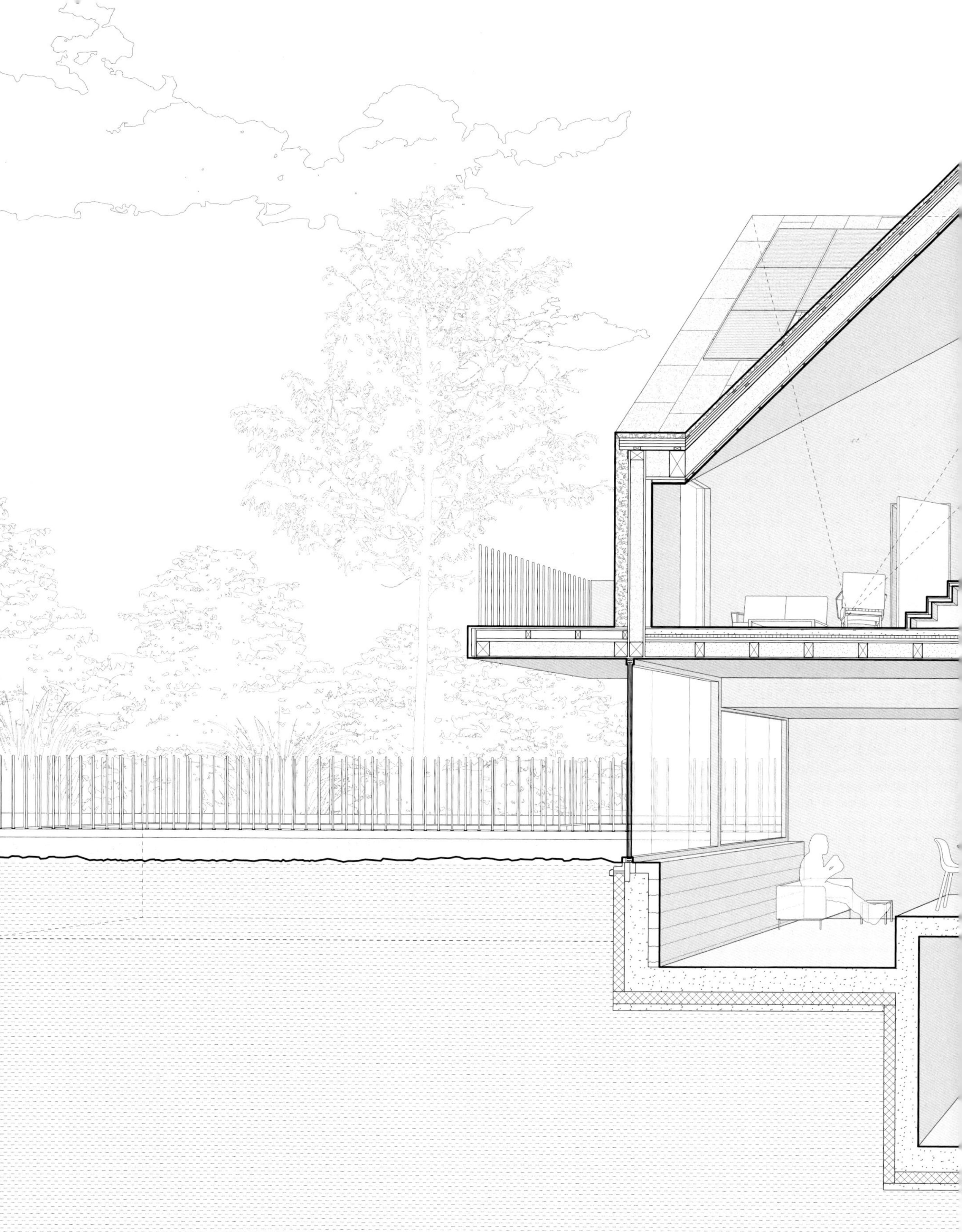

Cork Screw House

An inhabitable gabled roof appears to float above a series of staggered floor planes, carved into the suburban site. The *raumplan*-like arrangement of these sheared levels incorporates a main bedroom and allows for visual and spatial continuities between the living, dining, and kitchen areas that lead to the house's central stair. The lower levels are finished with rammed concrete walls that terminate on level with the surrounding ground. Large-scale glazing allows for ample daylight to infiltrate these earthbound levels, visually disconnecting the upper volume from the lower house while the rammed concrete walls provide textural relief. The staircase, constructed of staggered CLT planes, appears suspended from above

and continues the spiraling logic of the lower levels into the upper floors. The upper-level volume is articulated as a four-sided gable roof, framed in timber, punctuated by rectangular windows and sheathed entirely in a thick skin of cork panels. Cork was utilized for its natural moisture and mold resistance, insulative capacity, and acoustical properties as well as its monolithic appearance, allowing this hovering volume to appear paradoxically both massive and suspended.

EARTH

800
600
400
Brick
200
113 $kgCO_2e/m^3$
Block; KBOB
Stone
Earth
9 $kgCO_2e/m^3$
0
Site Mixed; Ökobaudat
Cork
Hemp
Straw
-200
-400
Bamboo
-600
Mass Timber
Wood Frame
-800

Earth is one of the oldest building materials used by humans, ubiquitous, inexpensive, and local. Earth intended for construction is a combination of clay, silt, and small stones or aggregates. This material, often called loam, is ideally absent of organic growing material. The clay acts as the binding agent and the percentage of clay is a key component to track in the long-term performance of an earth or loam construction. Loam mixes are unique and exemplify the characteristics of a given location. While additives can be used from water to lime, care should be taken to minimize, if not avoid, portland cement as the cement inhibits the ability of earth to absorb and balance humidity and reduces, if not eliminates, its ability to be reused or returned to the ground at end of life.

SITE EXCAVATION

Earth material used for construction is ideally found at or close to the building site to minimize transportation costs. Topsoil should not be used as it holds organic material which can rot over time. Digging below the topsoil, roughly two to three feet, is often required.

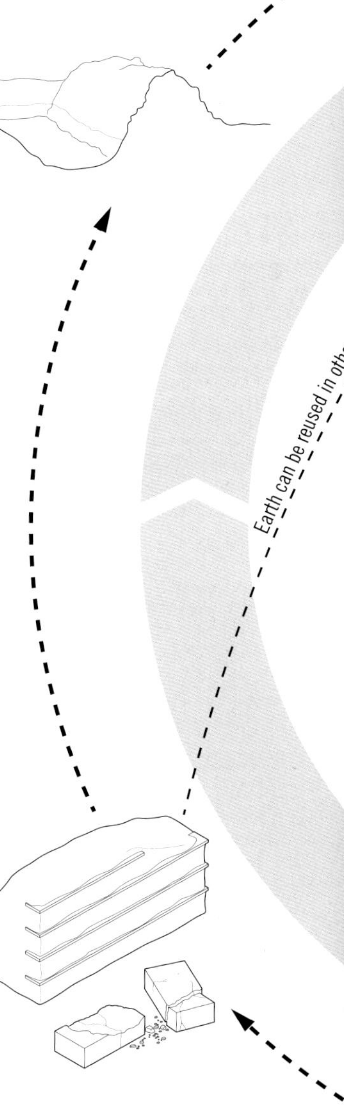

DISASSEMBLY

Earth materials can be used over and over without degradation of the quality of the material, or returned to the ground from where they came with no negative environmental impact.

MATERIAL MIXING + PREPARATION

Loam is mixed to achieve a consistency that meets the performance requirements of the construction specific to the earth of each site. Mixing breaks up the clay and distributes the components of the earth equally, with water added to cure the loam and enhance the binding forces of the clay materials. Earth mixes can be tested for water content, compaction, consistency, and cohesion.

EARTH BLOCKS

Loam placed into a form to create smaller units is a standard way of creating a unitized building material out of earth. Earth blocks can be sun dried, or compressed by hand or a mechanical press. Smaller blocks speed drying time and are a portable and flexible building unit. Dried straw or other fiber material can be added to enhance strength.

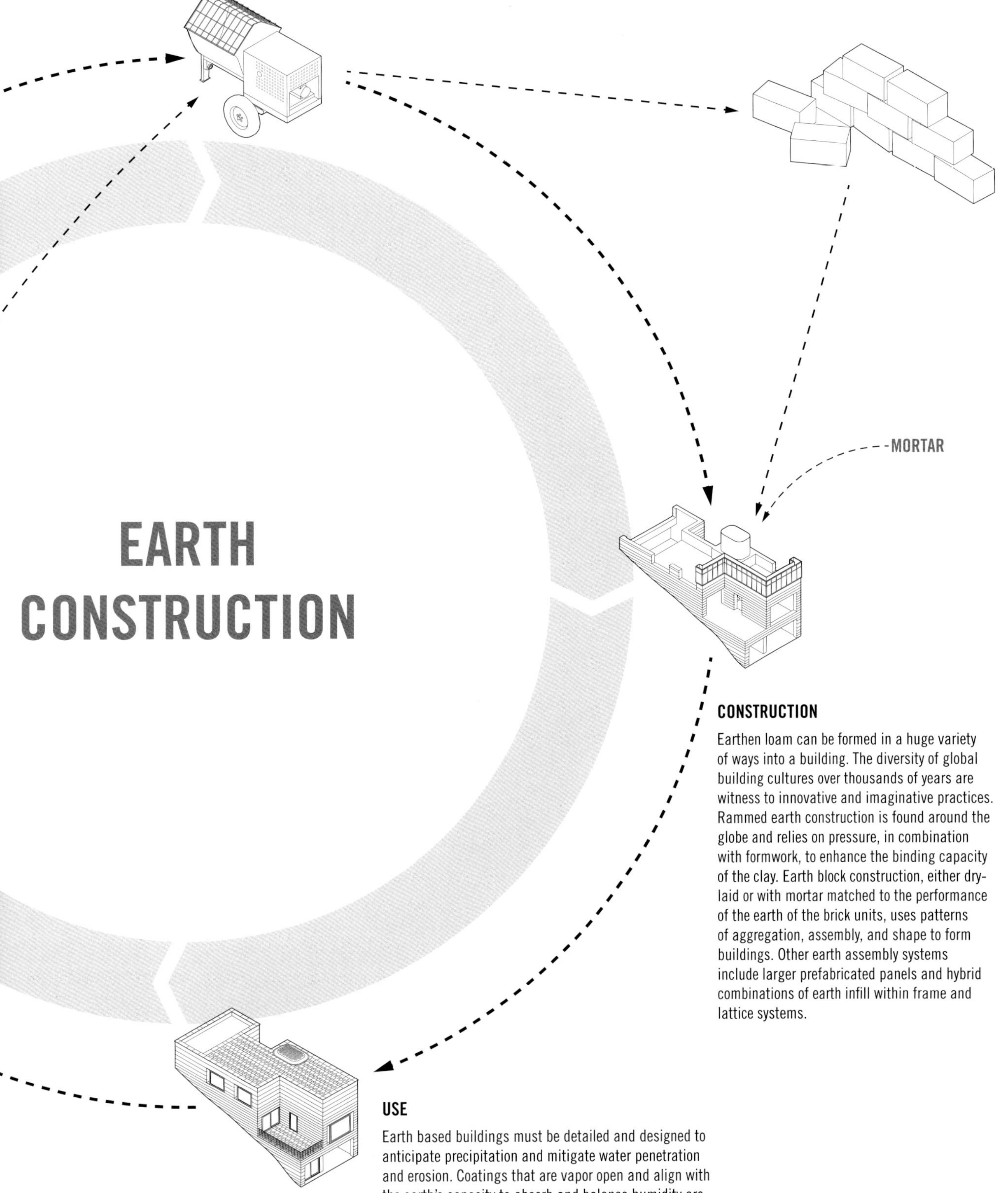

CONSTRUCTION

Earthen loam can be formed in a huge variety of ways into a building. The diversity of global building cultures over thousands of years are witness to innovative and imaginative practices. Rammed earth construction is found around the globe and relies on pressure, in combination with formwork, to enhance the binding capacity of the clay. Earth block construction, either dry-laid or with mortar matched to the performance of the earth of the brick units, uses patterns of aggregation, assembly, and shape to form buildings. Other earth assembly systems include larger prefabricated panels and hybrid combinations of earth infill within frame and lattice systems.

USE

Earth based buildings must be detailed and designed to anticipate precipitation and mitigate water penetration and erosion. Coatings that are vapor open and align with the earth's capacity to absorb and balance humidity are best. Non-permeable materials are used to isolate site groundwater from earthen materials.

SITE EXCAVATING

Earth for use in buildings should carefully examine and test soil composition prior to fabrication. Soil mixtures for construction may contain a mix of clay, silt, sand, and aggregates but mixtures should be free of organic content. Soil should be excavated below any existing topsoil.

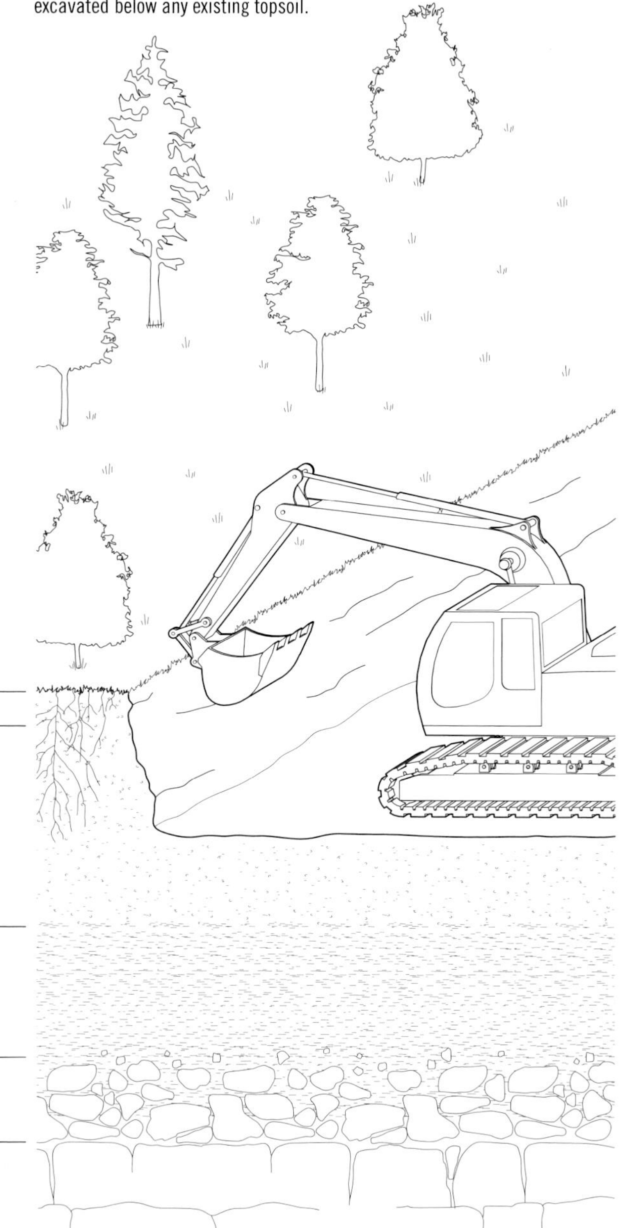

*Depths and makeup of soil horizons vary depending on location and climatic conditions.

MIXING

Depending on the makeup of the soil and the project requirements, particular ratios of loam, water, and aggregates are mixed together, either by hand or by machine.

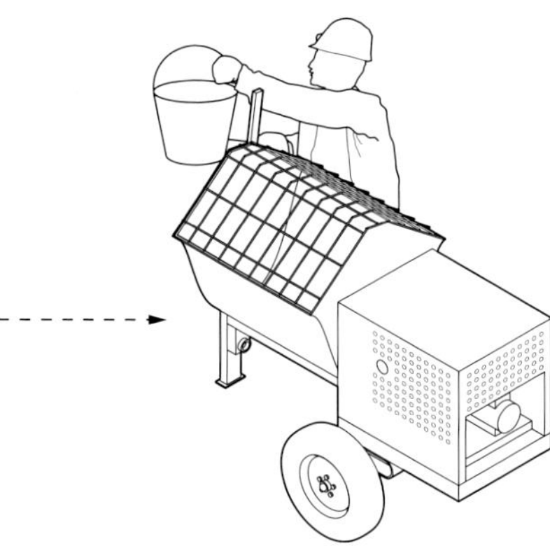

ADDITIVES

Various plant fibers or stabilizing compounds can be added to change the performance properties of the final mix.

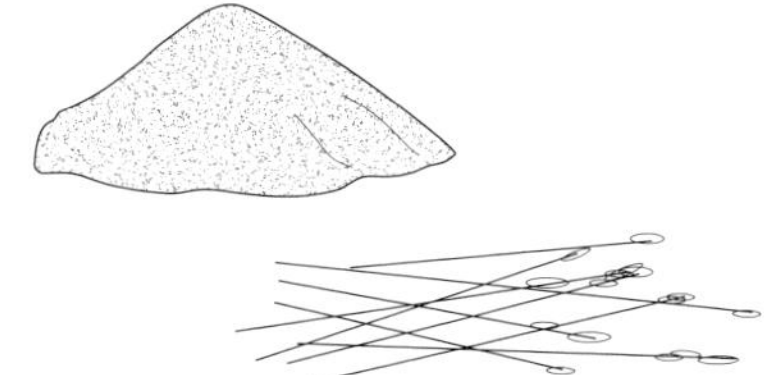

EARTH BLOCK CASTING

The soil mixture is pressed into forms to make blocks, either through manual or automated processes.

EARTH BLOCK DRYING

Blocks are cured or dried before they are used for construction. Depending on climate, no kiln drying may be required.

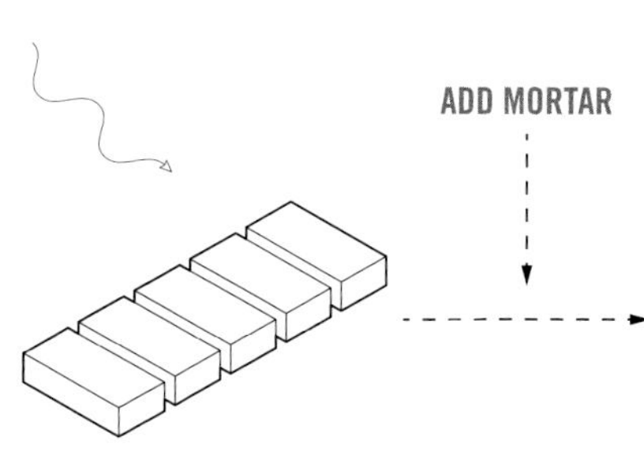

EARTH BLOCK WALL

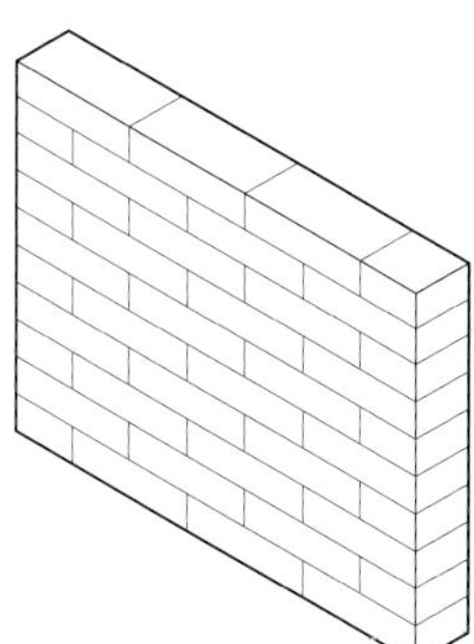

RAMMED EARTH TAMPING

After mixing, the material is pressed into temporary formwork. Successive layers are compressed, either by hand or by machine, until the final form is achieved.

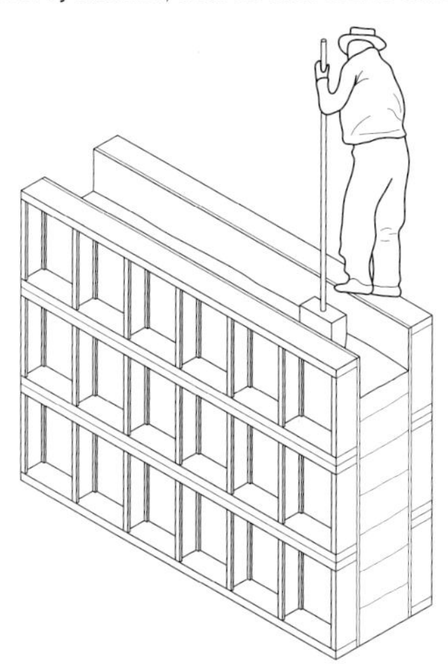

RAMMED EARTH WALL

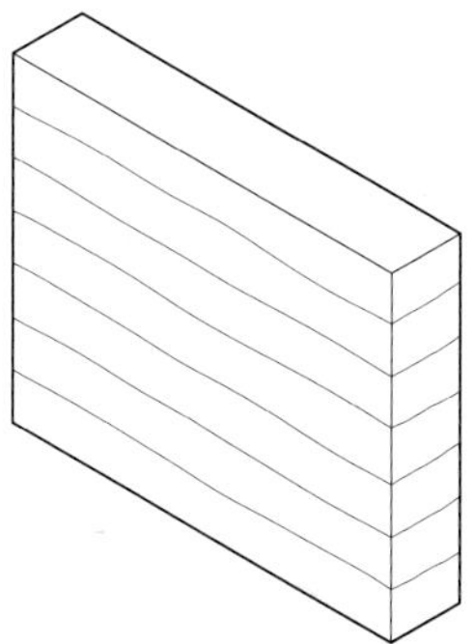

3D PRINTING

A robotic arm or 3D printer extrudes the soil mixture, slowly building a wall one thin layer at a time. Soil mixture and printing time are coordinated to ensure coherence of final form.

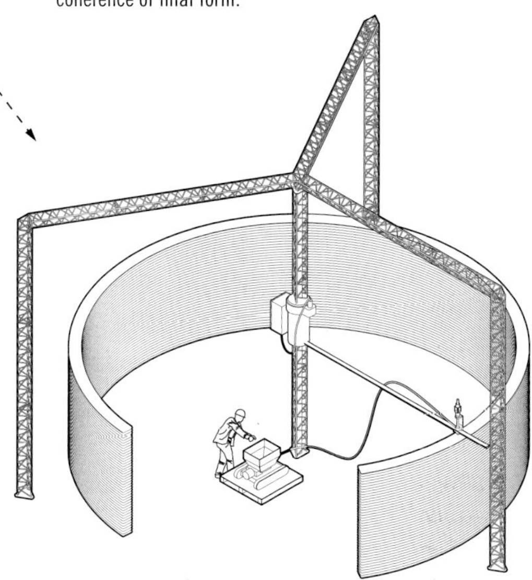

3D PRINTED WALL

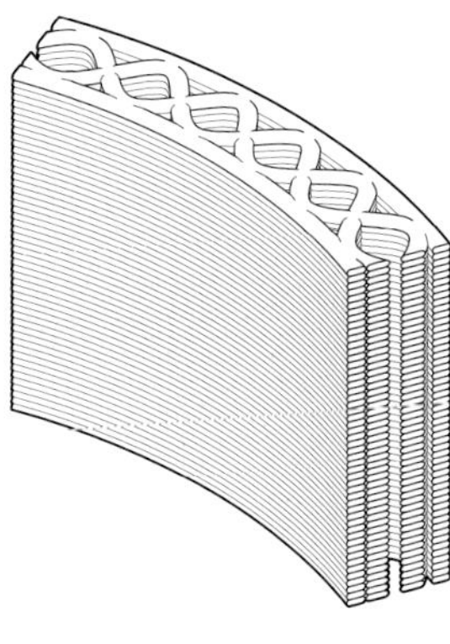

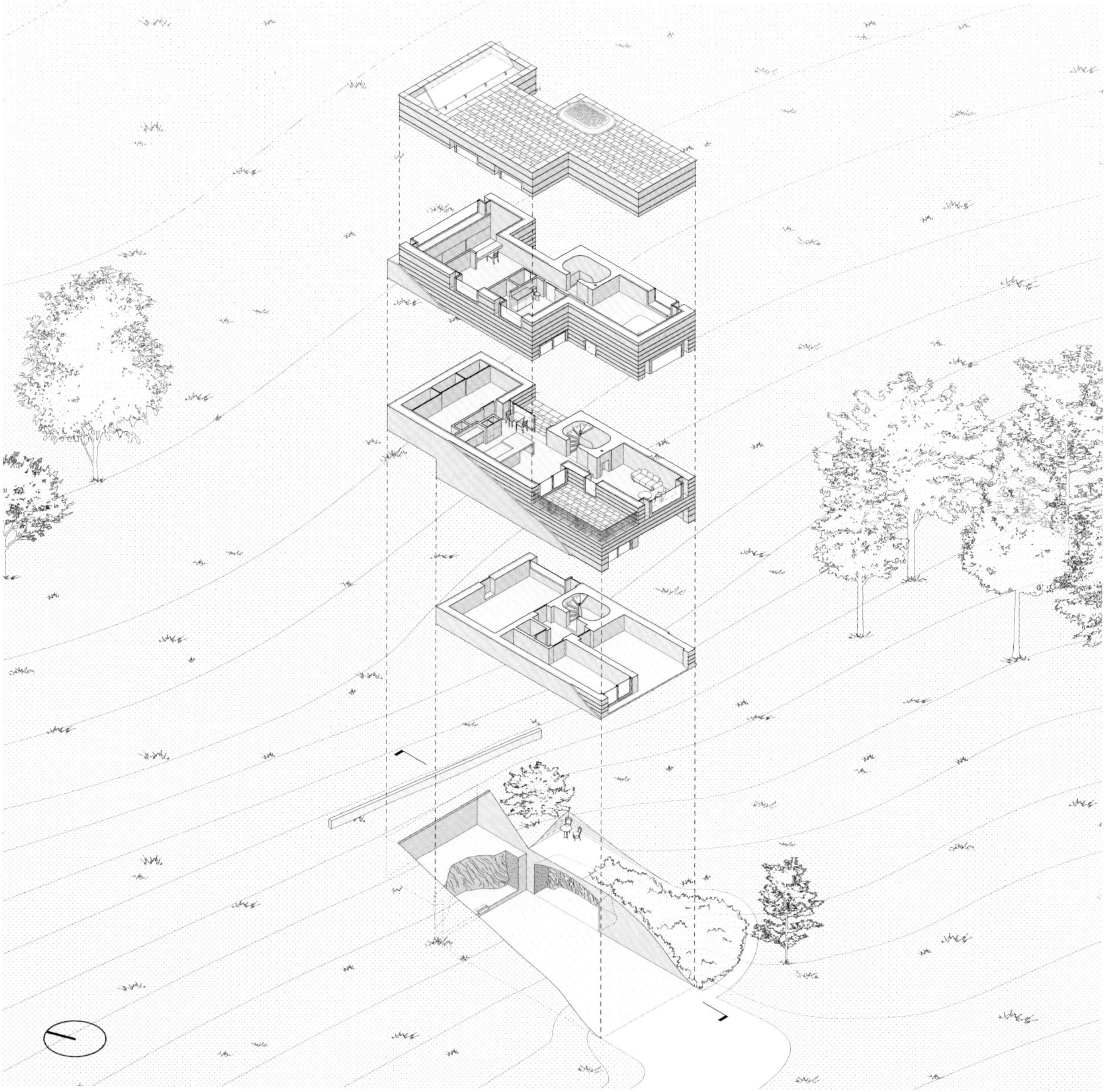

House Rauch | Boltshauser Architects, Lehm Ton Erde Baukunst

Designed for and by an expert in loam construction, this project exemplifies innovative practices in building with earth in anticipation of material end-of-life consequences. Set into the hillside, the two-bedroom house uses soil from the excavation as one of the sources of loam to construct a contemporary residence defined by clean volumes and oversized windows. This project deploys protruding fired-brick erosion checks to protect the exterior walls and realize a contemporary volume with flat roofs without the need for traditional projecting eaves. The project uses no stabilizing additives, such as portland cement, in the rammed earthen walls to ensure that the loam can return productively to the ground for reuse. Limited use of

Schlins, Austria | 2008

volcanic trass cement provides sufficient binding in reinforced ring beams, lintels, and foundations to transfer loads and allow for the unusually large window openings.

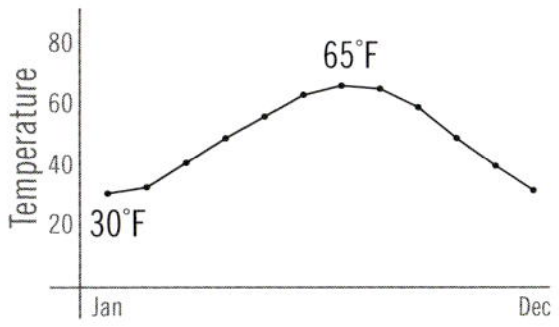

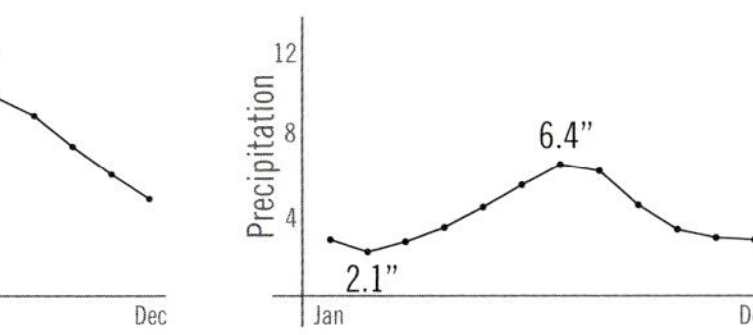

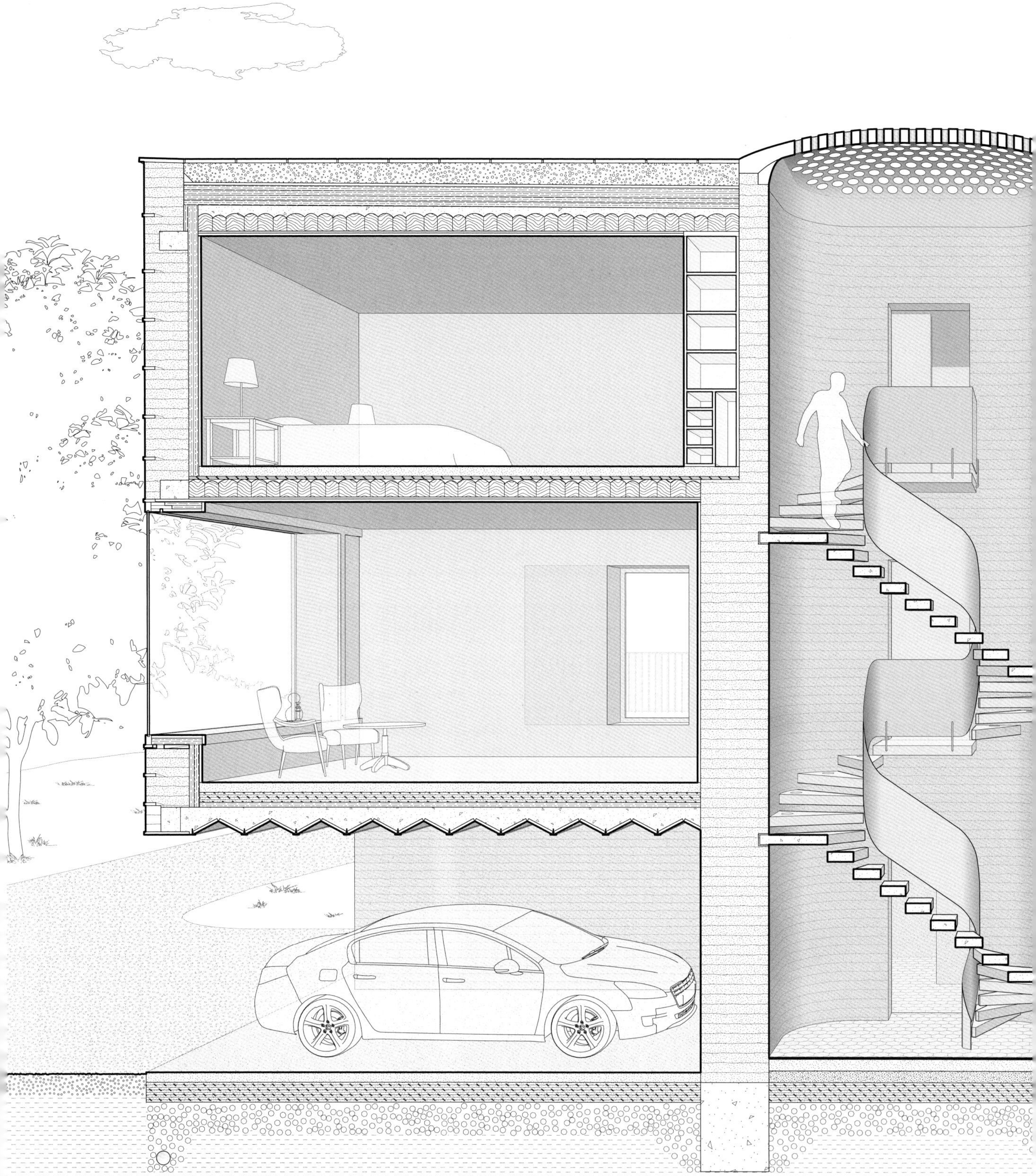

House Rauch

At 17.7 in (450 mm) thick, the rammed earth walls provide a breathable mass wall that regulates temperature and humidity, while utilizing natural loam as the primary material. Overlapping layers of reed mats adhered with fasteners and natural clay provide insulation on the inside of the walls, increasing their depth to 25.6 in (650 mm). The rammed earth walls are isolated from the ground by a reinforced trass lime and cement strip foundation set 23.6 in (600 mm) into the ground and protected from groundwater by a bitumen sheeting over glass foam insulation on the submerged earthen walls. The walls were made from carefully selected loam with no more than 1.2 (30 mm) stone granules. Cast into custom

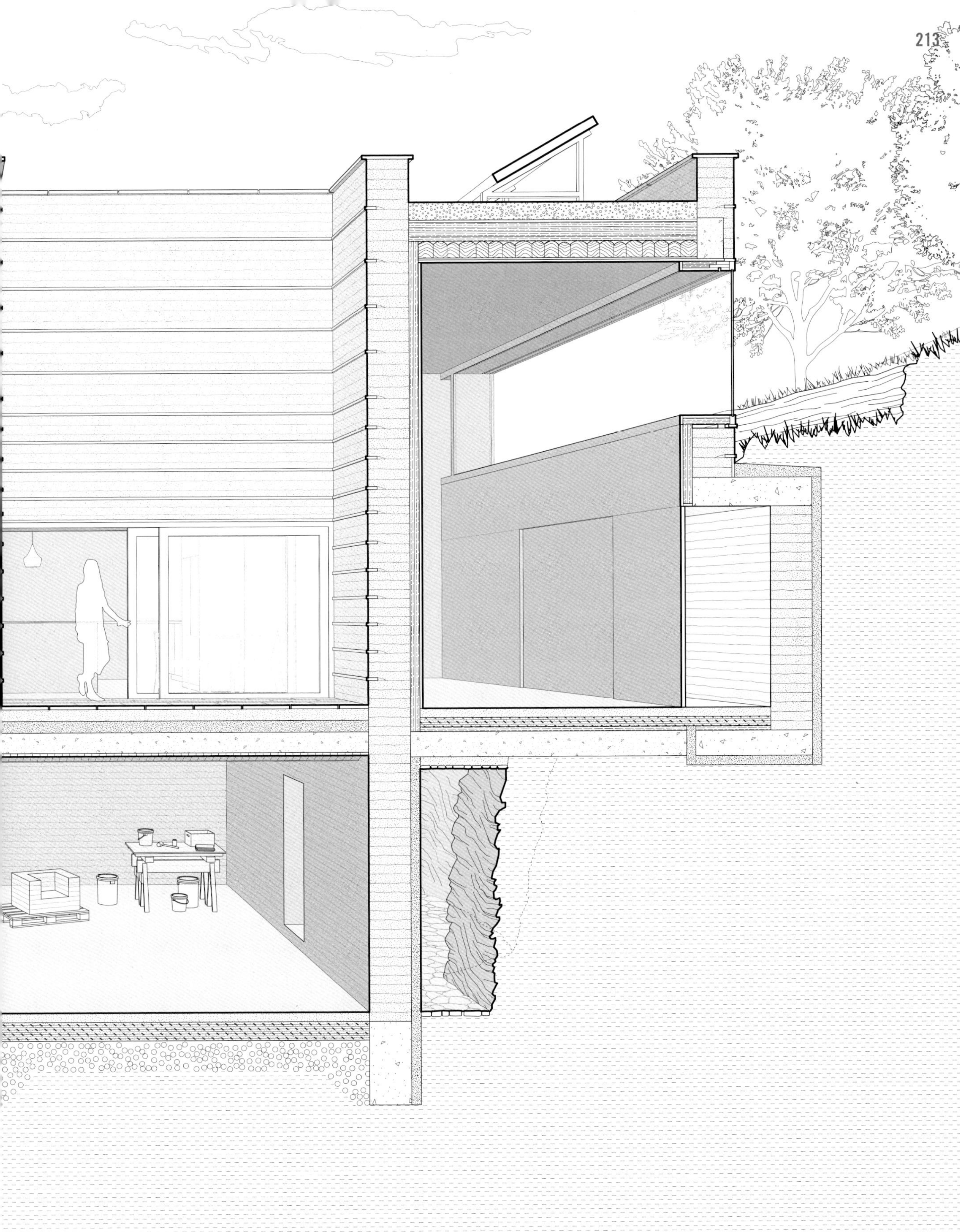

formwork, the loam is tamped down to 3.1 in (80 mm) thick from initial pours of 4 to 4.7 in (100 to 120 mm) At every third layer, fired-brick panels made from the same local loam were laid on the outer edge of the formwork. These projecting checks slow rainwater as it runs down the side of the wall, limiting the erosion of fine silt and revealing the more stable and resistant stone particles. The checks also generate the horizontal striations that articulate the building's elevations. The same brick panels arranged as folded plates provide the structure for the first floor, with the upper floors made from solid log construction; both are finished with 3.1 in (80 mm) rammed earth.

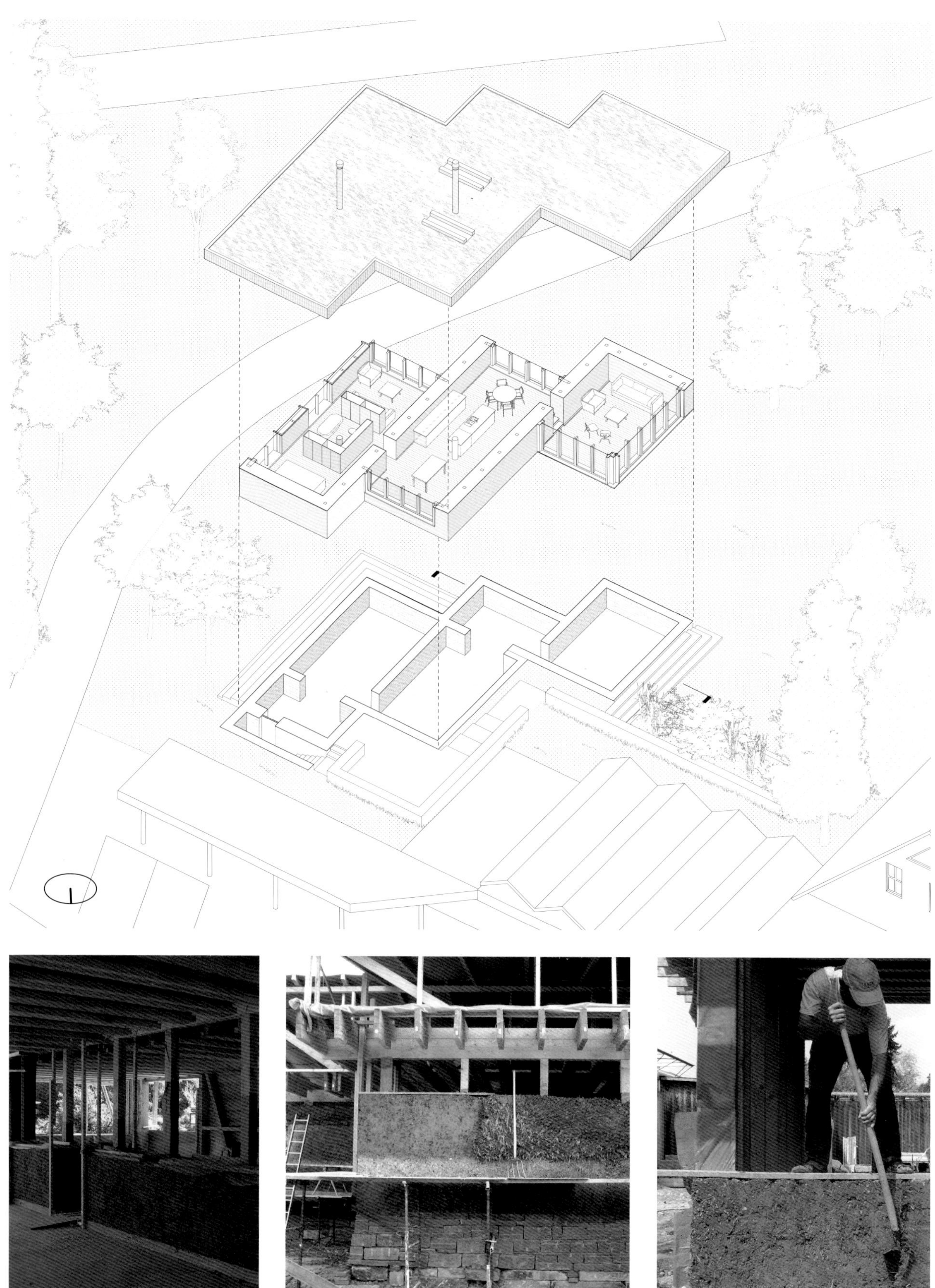

Wohnhaus Flury | spaceshop Architects

Designed to meet the client's strict material health and energy standards, this one-story house adds a private residence to a former farming complex. Slightly staggered in elevation and connected by steps, three open rectangular rooms comprise the house. The center kitchen and dining area is flanked by a smaller living space and a larger bedroom and bathroom.

These rooms are defined by two 31.5 in (800 mm) thick L-shaped earthen walls, made from cob—a combination of straw and local clay—cast by layering 24 to 36 in (600 to 900 mm) at a time, and cut straight by a spade to create the finished interior and exterior surfaces. These thick monolithic walls manage moisture, offset diurnal temperature changes,

Deitingen, Switzerland | 2010

and provide required thermal resistance to meet the Swiss climate without any chemical or concrete additives. All materials for the house are local, sourced within a 6 mi (10 km) radius.

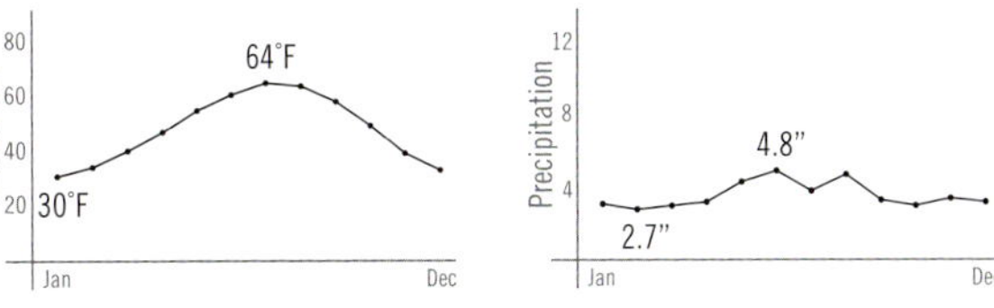

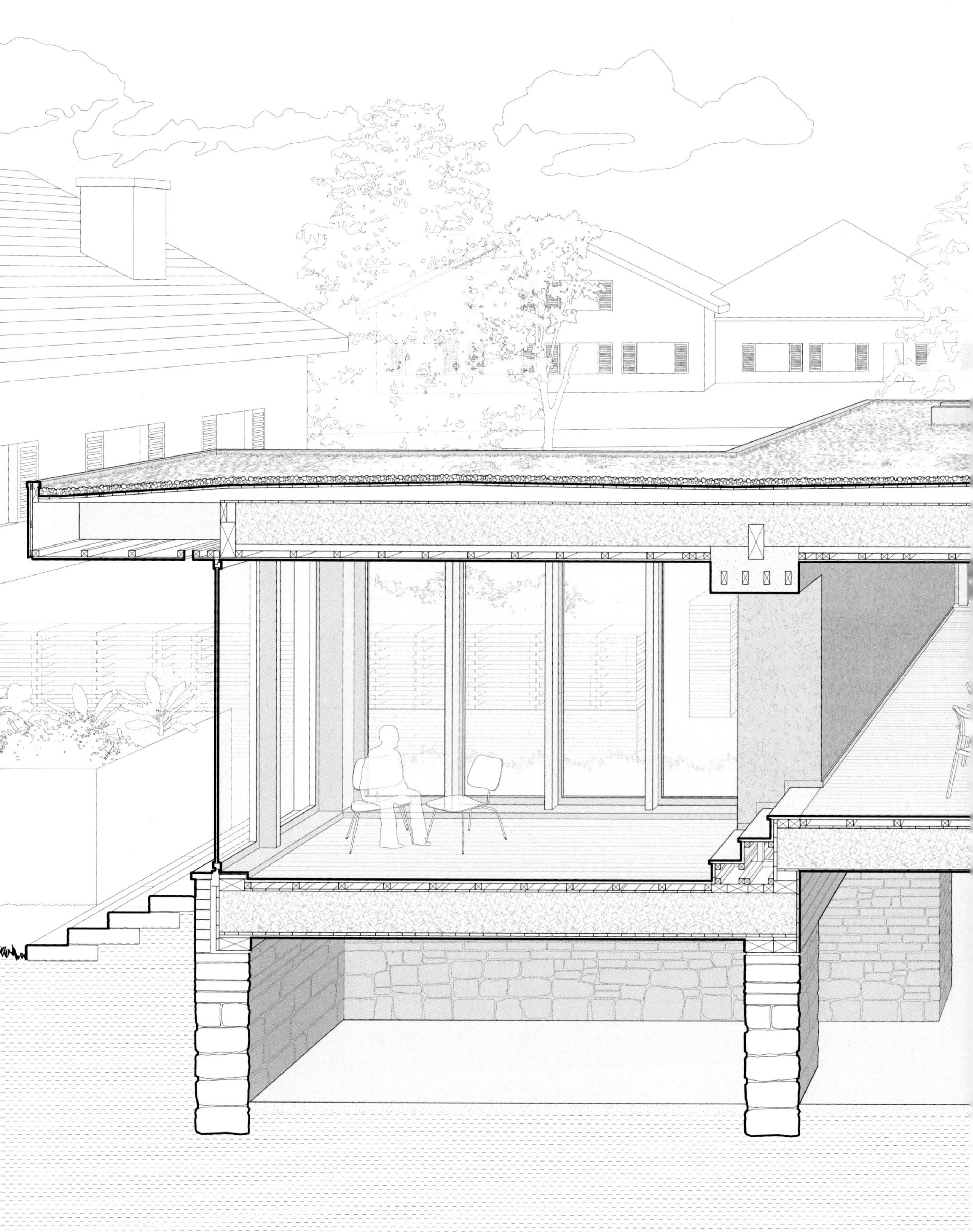

Wohnhaus Flury

The cob walls, wood, and straw materials that comprise the main house are lifted from the ground and protected from moisture by repurposed masonry and stone foundations, salvaged from demolished structures, and pieced together by lime mortar. The basement floor is compacted earth high in clays and carbonate minerals. Softwood studs, the primary structural material, are protected at the center of the cob walls. All of the wood was harvested within two kilometers and cut according to lunar cycles to minimize moisture content. The wood floor and roof joists are spaced to accommodate the dimensions of the compressed straw-bale insulation. Throughout the project, materials are primarily unprocessed

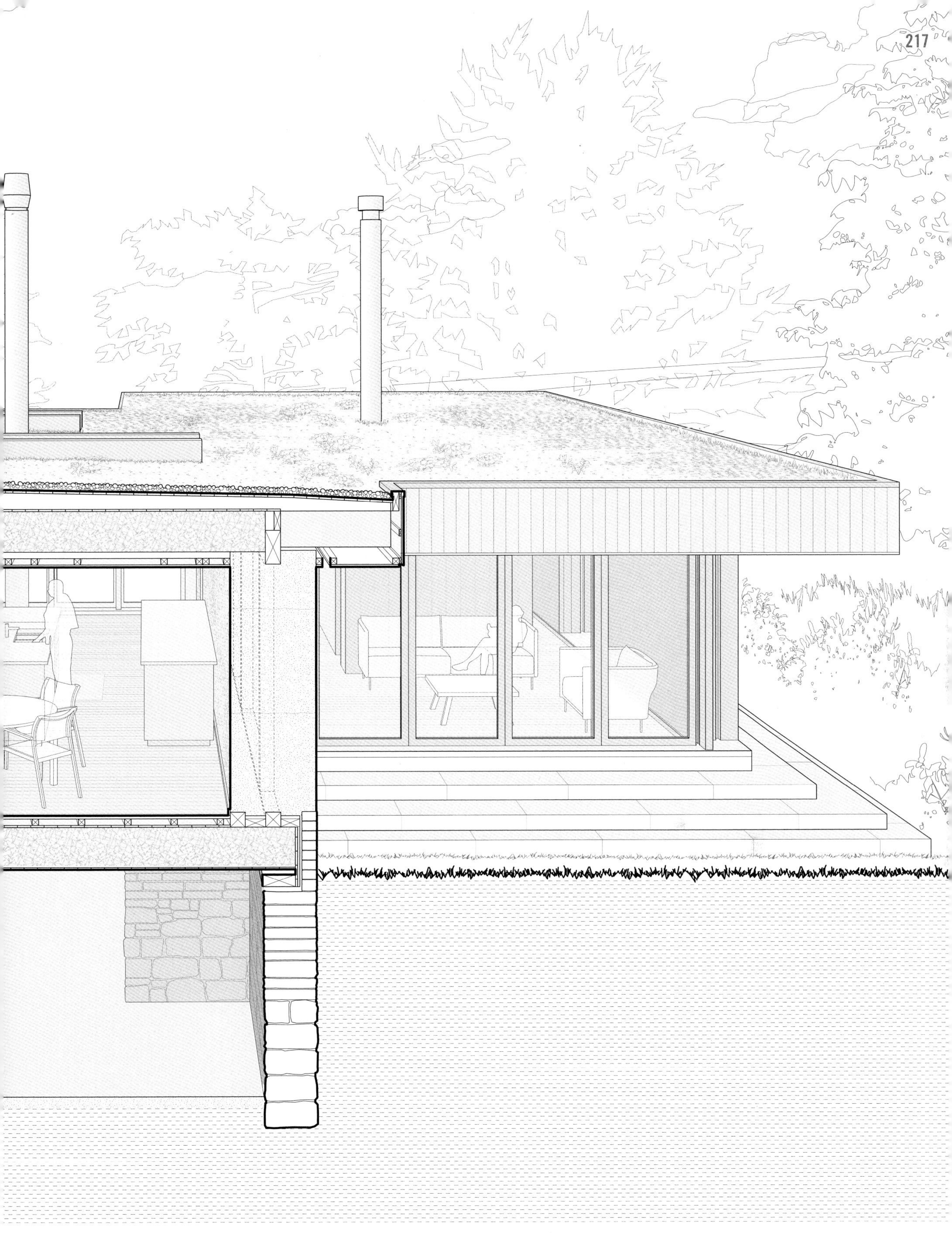

and deployed in their raw state to minimize carbon emissions and the use of petroleum products, sealants, and chemicals that can lead to poor indoor air quality and health risks. The extensive planted roof, designed to slow rainwater run-off and support biodiversity, did require a synthetic rubber roof membrane on top of the straw insulation and is ballasted by crushed recycled brick. This roof is cantilevered to protect the exposed cob walls below from rainwater erosion. Two skylight openings bring daylight into the kitchen and living room below. In a testament to the thermal performance of the project, a single wood cook stove in the middle of the central room provides the only source of supplemental heat.

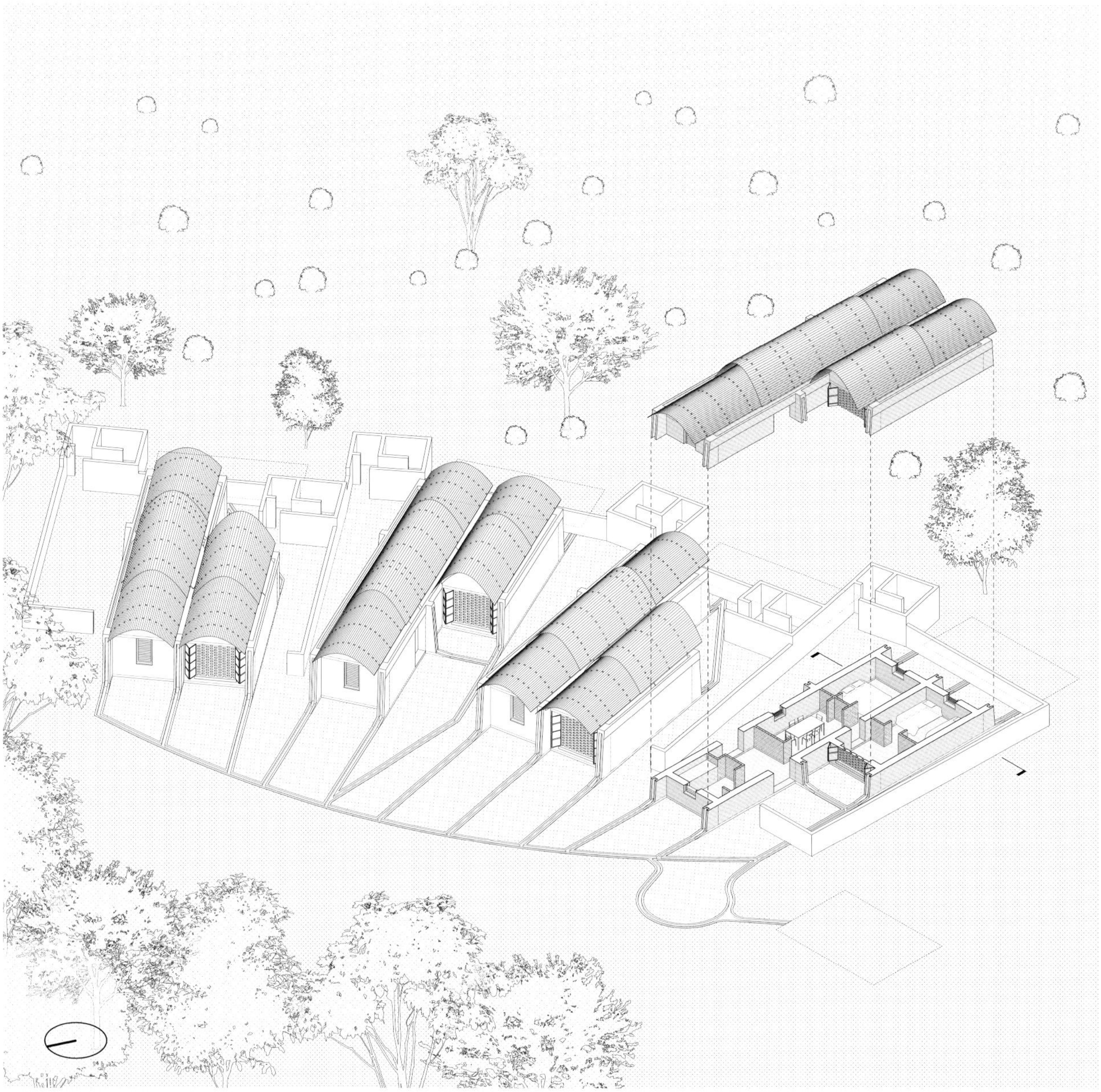

Gando Teachers' Housing | Kéré Architecture

The intent of this project was to provide new, stable housing to attract and support teachers adjacent to the recently constructed Gando Primary School in a remote area of Burkina Faso in Western Africa. Set in a curvilinear array, the four structures providing six housing units use a combination of traditional construction techniques and selective industrialized materials to create durable houses. The primary building material is 4 by 8 by 16 in (100 by 200 by 400 mm) earthen adobe blocks that were hand assembled to build the walls and vaulted ceilings, then covered with loam

Gando, Burkina Faso | 2004

on the walls and a cement-based mixture on the roof. The roofs overhang to protect the end-walls, while channeling rainwater. Sickle-shaped gaps between the walls and roof, combined with open-air spaces, facilitate cross-ventilation, adapting the residences to the local climate.

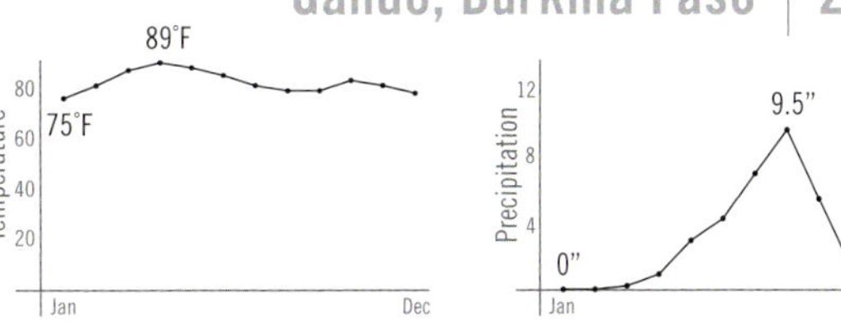

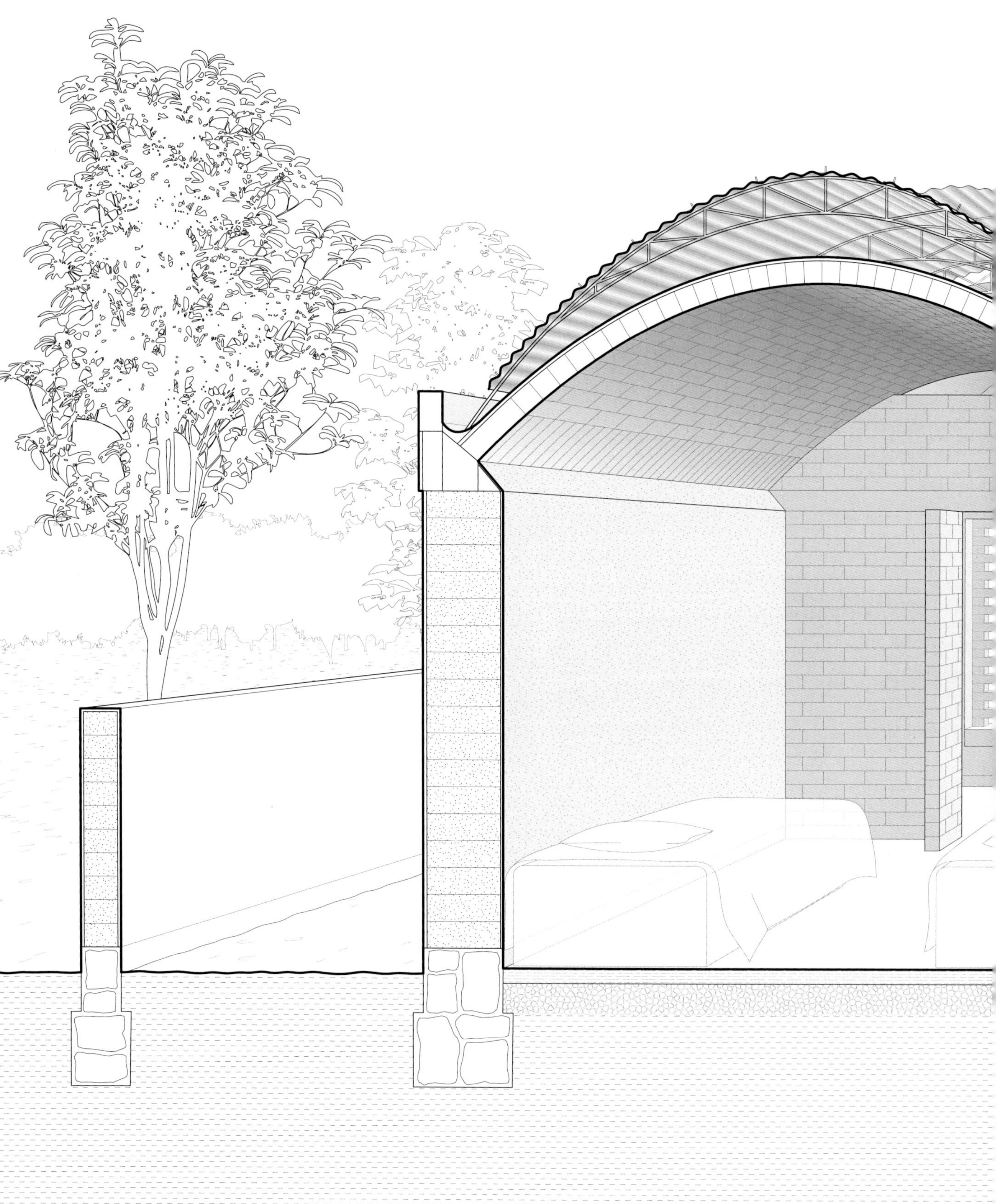

Gando Teachers' Housing

This project invested in the community and bolstered local construction knowledge through its methodology and material selection. In all, 15,000 blocks were made by the local residents at a rate of 600 to 1,000 per day and form the primary material of the assembly. The traditional mixture of cow dung and vegetable oil was updated to bitumen in the exterior loam coating for the 15.7 in (400 mm) thick block walls, creating a durable assembly that is resistant to termites and does not degrade during the rainy season. A foundation of crushed granite and cement isolate the earthen walls from groundwater. The floors are made from traditional hand-tamped earth over a crushed gravel separation layer. For the roof, the

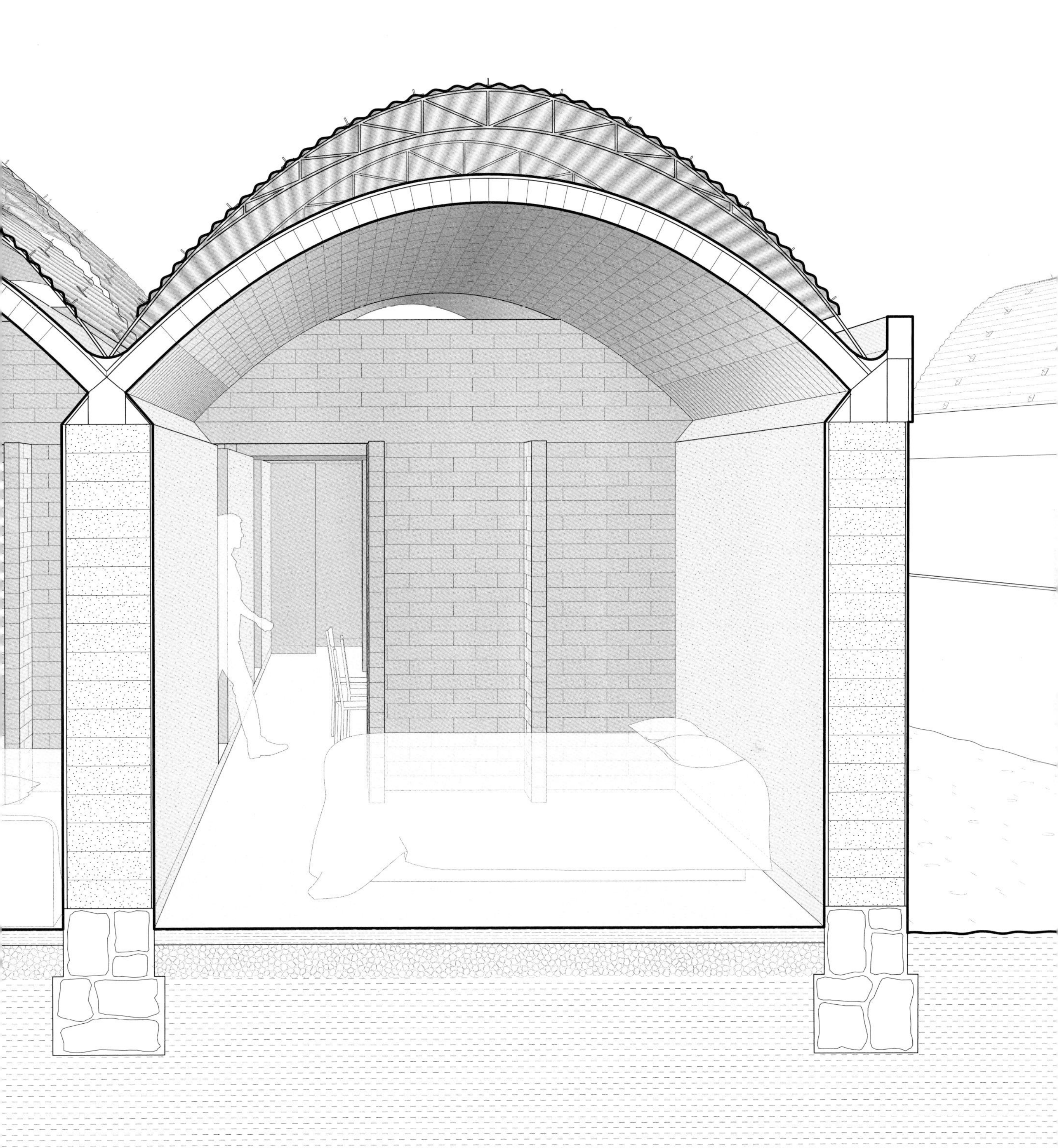

adobe blocks were hand assembled into an arch over a reusable formwork and covered with a layer of cement-stabilized loam to create a robust shell. A simple corrugated metal sheet secured to lightweight metal trusses provides water protection and creates a ventilation gap at the gables. A cast concrete ring-beam atop the adobe wall stabilizes the system, provides the transition from roof to wall, and creates a water channel to direct rainwater. The project exemplifies the combination of traditional earth construction with selective and accessible contemporary materials to build community capacity and economic development.

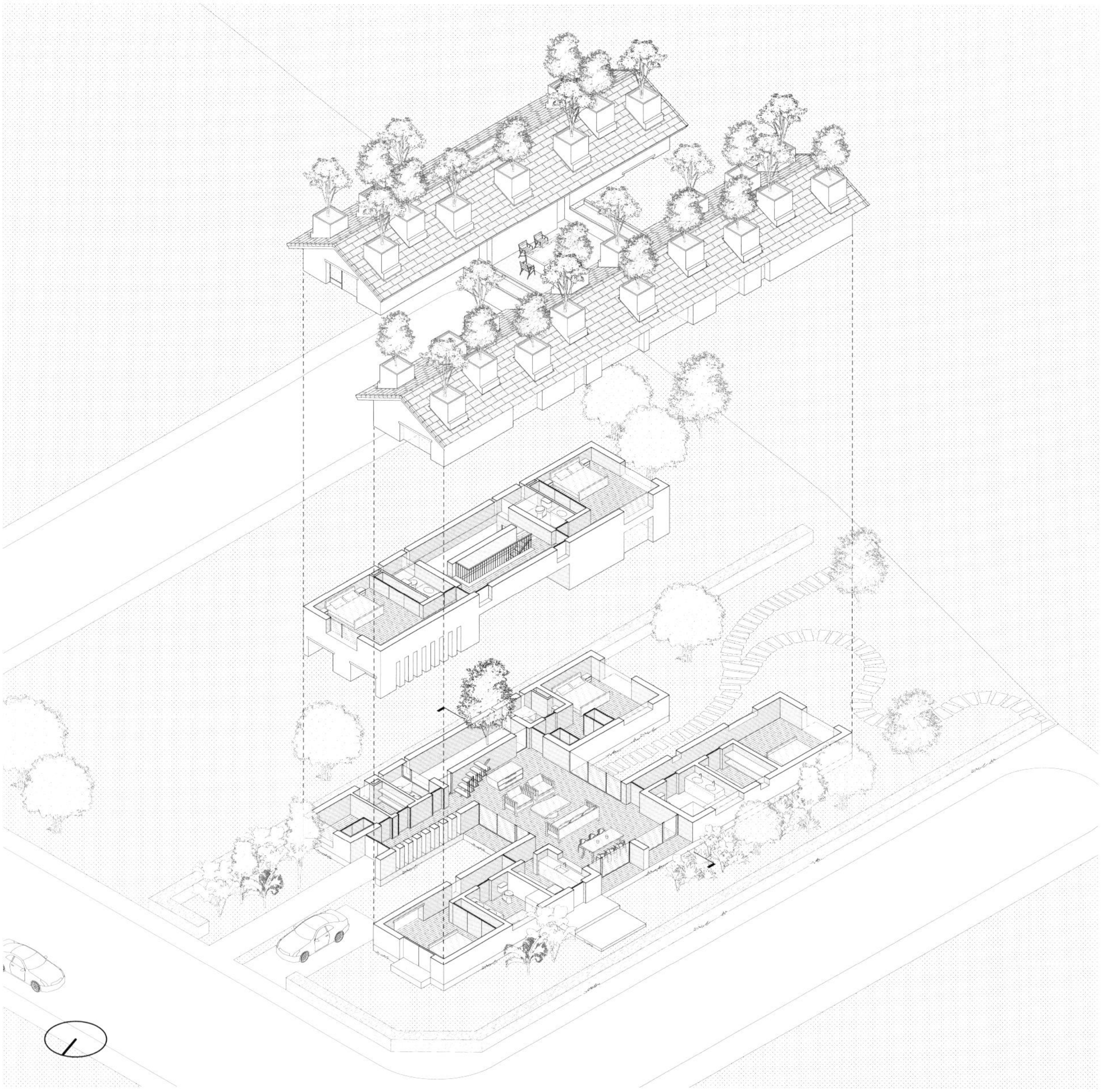

Dong Anh House | Vo Trong Nghia Architects

Located outside Hanoi, this project addresses the demands of its tropical climate through two compelling approaches to the design. The 14 in (35 cm) thick rammed earth walls provide the primary structural system to accommodate one large family. The thick earth walls act as thermal sinks, muting the diurnal temperature swings, warming the house at night and cooling it during the day. These one- and two-story walls support a roof carrying 29 fruit trees in individual planter boxes integrated into the sloped roof. The trees shade the house in the summer, and help mitigate

Hanoi, Vietnam | 2017

the impact of rain in the monsoon seasons. Extensive eaves without gutters direct the rainwater beyond the line of the earthen walls. Multiple sources for the clay mix, all within about a 20 mi (30 km) radius, create the striations of color registered during the casting process.

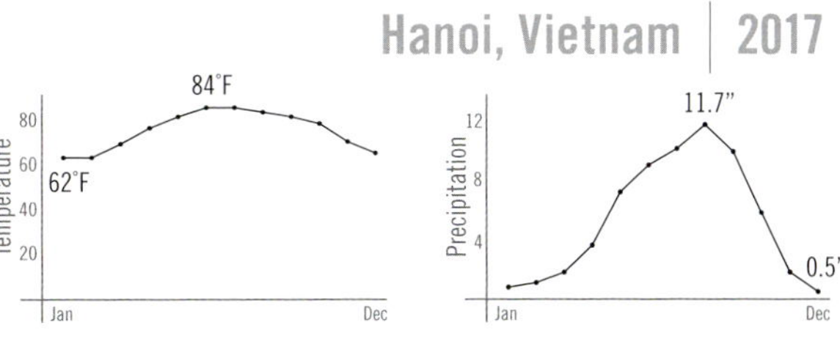

Dong Anh House

The thick rammed earth walls are made from local clay, silt, and sand. A small amount of cement was added to earthen mixture to meet the required structural demands and address the risk of erosion in the wet and moist climate. While the addition of cement limits the capacity of the earthen walls to breathe and increases the carbon footprint, it adds to the long-term durability of rammed earth in a monsoon climate. A concrete roof carries the load of the rooftop trees to the earthen walls, and provides structure supporting the outdoor gathering space located in the middle of the H-shaped house. Concrete lintels and floor beams in the earth walls support larger openings. The skylights filter ample daylight into the living

and interior garden spaces, while animating the color and imperfections inherent in the casting process of the earthen walls. A double-height, open-air courtyard framed on all sides with the rammed earth provides a delightful and contemplative garden retreat within the interior adjacent to the main staircase. At the heart of the house, a large skylight doubles as a table for the garden roof deck and a place to gather under the pomelo rooftop trees.

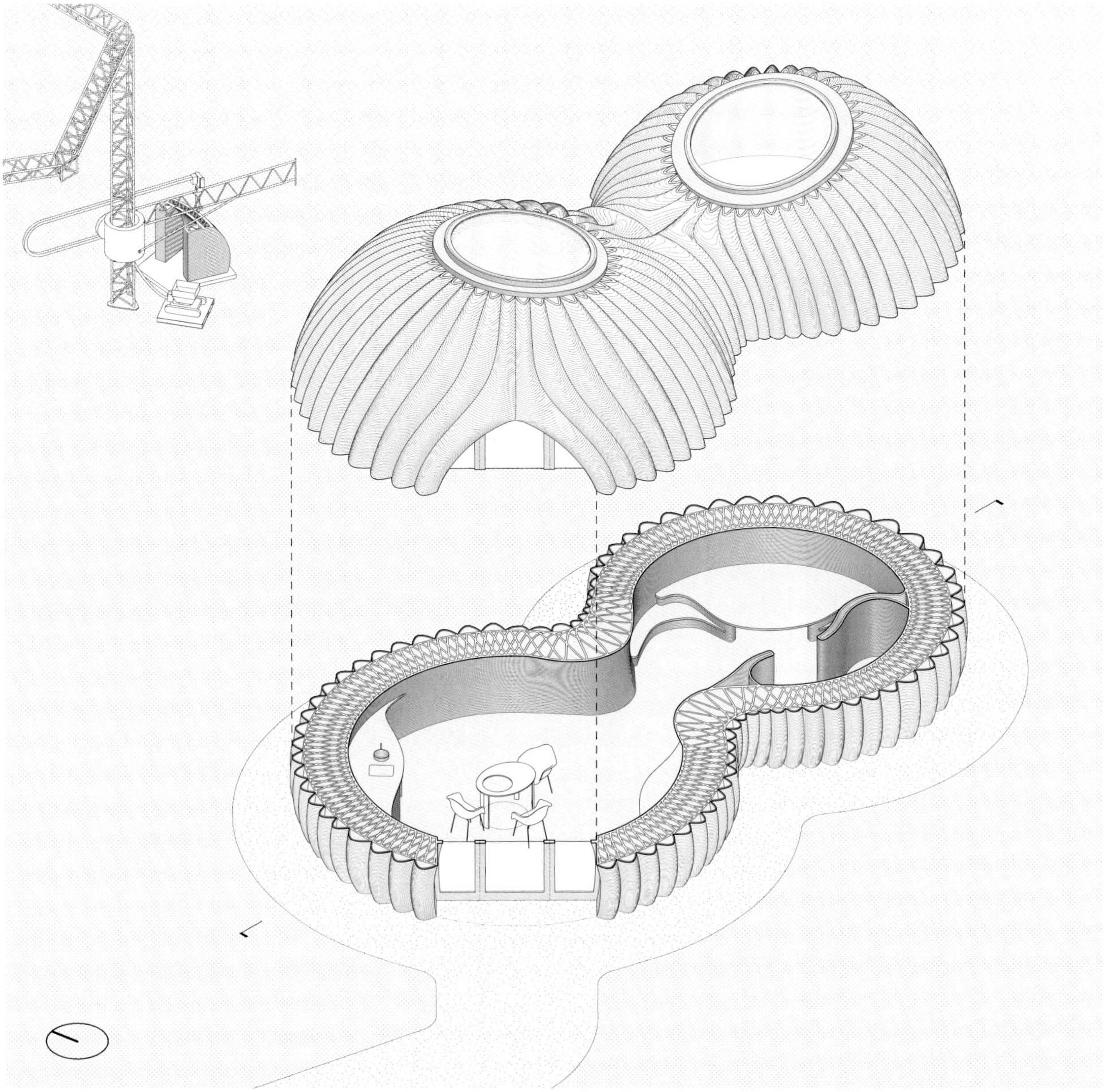

TECLA - Technology and Clay | Mario Cucinella Architects

A collaboration between the architect and WASP, a 3D-printing company, this project seeks to address one of the challenges of building with earth, namely the extensive labor required to form, compact, and layer compressed walls. In this prototype project, two digitally controlled ejection heads connected to boom cranes extrude a mixture of loam, rice husks, water, and binding agents to print the house in 0.5 in (12 mm) layers over a 200-hour period. Without using portland cement, the earthen material can be returned to the ground at end of life. The 650 sq ft (60 sq m) house

Massa Lombarda, Italy | 2021

consists of two conjoined rounded volumes topped by oculi that provide daylight and ventilation. One space serves as the primary living area with a kitchen while the other hosts the bedroom and bathing area.

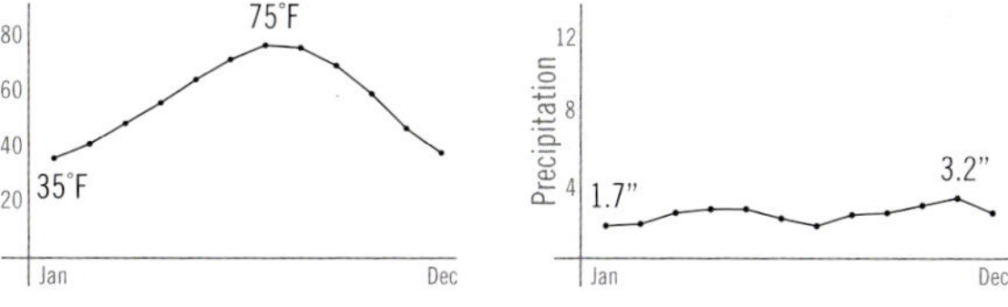

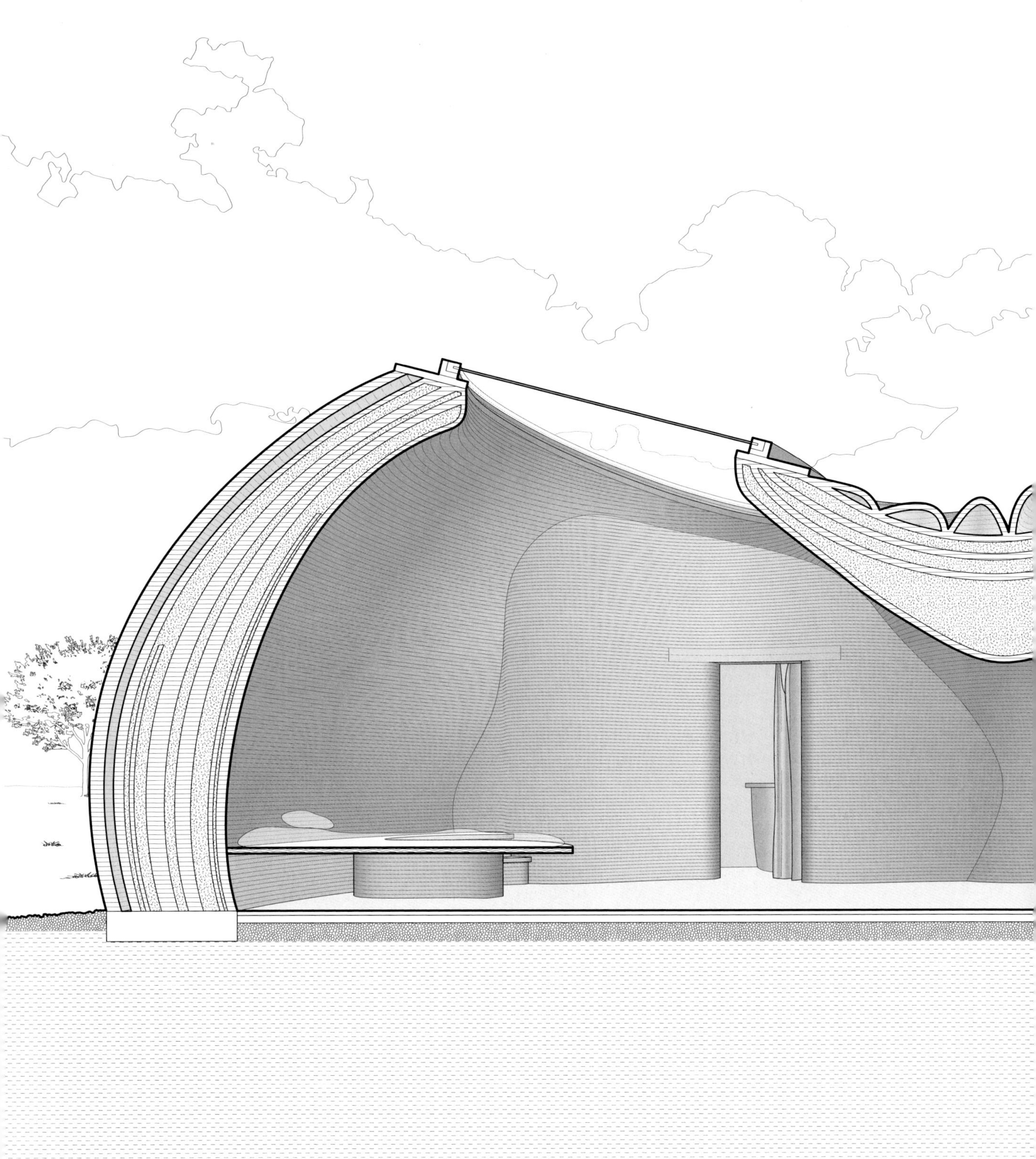

TECLA - Technology and Clay

The approximately 30 in (75 cm) thick walls are printed along courses of looping lines that connect the exterior layer to the interior through inner ribs following sine wave patterns. This reduces the amount of material required, introduces wall cavities that allow for the introduction of insulation, accelerates drying, and provides the opportunity for vertical ventilation and respiration at the exterior layer. The sloped orientation of the skylights demonstrates how to minimize heat-gain through self-shading while still providing ample daylight, eliminating the need

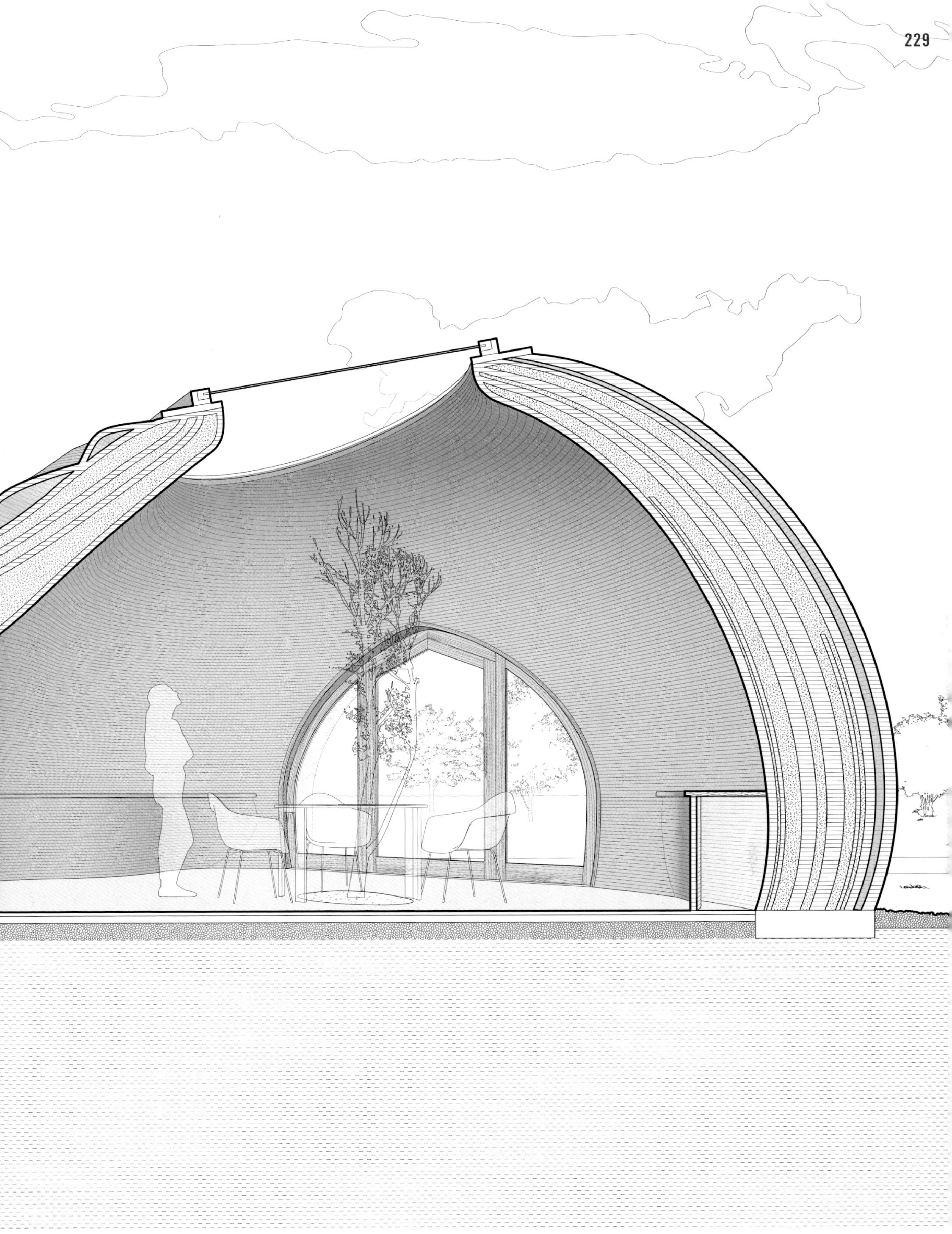

for traditional windows. As an early prototype, there are additional details to be addressed in future iterations. For example, the textured surface resulting from the layered printing inadvertently allows for water to pool and, over time, penetrate through the exterior, even with an applied waterproofing layer. Nevertheless, the combination of advanced digital technology using locally sourced earth-based materials in a building-scale 3D printer offers a tantalizing prospect for addressing the acute need for housing globally.

BRICK

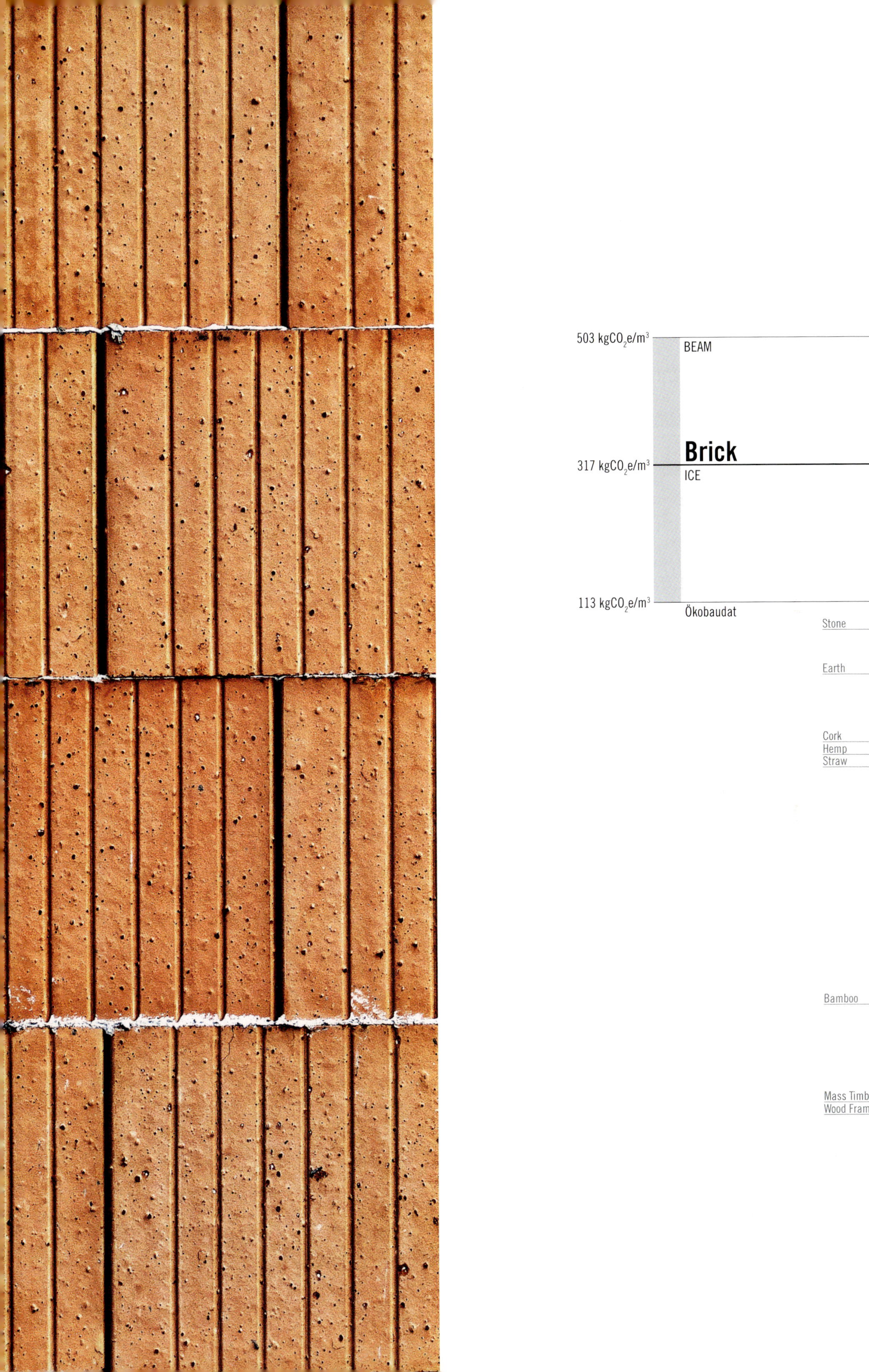

800
600
503 kgCO_2e/m^3
BEAM
400
Brick
317 kgCO_2e/m^3
ICE
200
113 kgCO_2e/m^3
Ökobaudat
Stone
Earth
0
Cork
Hemp
Straw
-200
-400
Bamboo
Mass Timber
-600
Wood Frame
-800

BRICK

While sharing similarities in their material basis, bricks are distinguished from earth blocks by their conversion under heat to create a building material that is more durable and resistant to water and weathering. Clay and shale form the primary earth-based materials of brick, with the unique properties of the source providing a diverse range. The firing process of the clay at temperatures between 1600 to 2400 F (870 to 1315 C) melts or vitrifies the material. Once fired, bricks have a long life span and can be reused, recycled back into the brick manufacturing process or crushed and downcycled for other uses. From a global warming standpoint, the largest challenge for bricks is the energy needed in the firing process. While more energy efficient kilns are available, the future of brick use will depend on the ability to use renewable resources, electric kilns, or alternative hardening processes to reduce if not eliminate the carbon emissions associated with the firing process.

CLAY MINING

The clay and shale used in the manufacturing of bricks is mined from the surface of the earth in geological deposits found throughout the globe. Both clays and shales are composed of silica, alumina, and various metallic oxides that influence the color of the brick during firing. Shales are clays that have hardened under geological pressure. Mining for bricks is relatively efficient with 95% of excavated material used.

MANUFACTURING PROCESS

Converting the earth-based materials into brick is a multi-step process. The clay and shale is first mixed and screened, and water added if needed, to form a homogeneous mass. Mass clay is then processed and cut into shapes before it is dried, and stacked and set into or through a kiln.

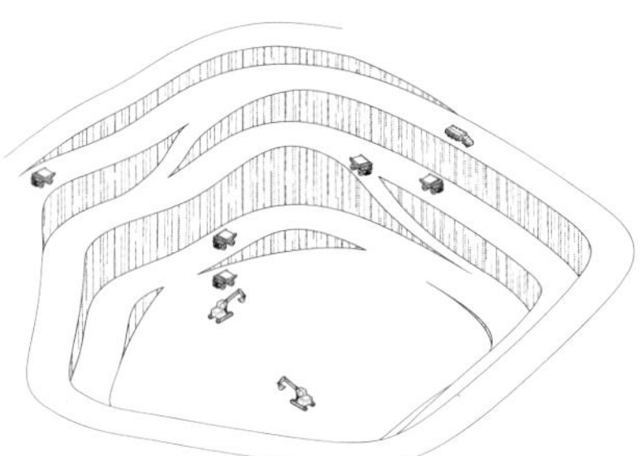

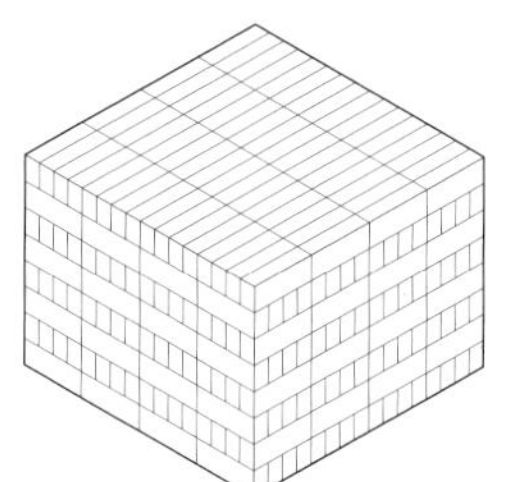

LANDFILL

Given current market and political structures, a large percentage of bricks after a building's end of life are landfilled. While non-toxic this standard practice wastes the embodied energy already spent in their making.

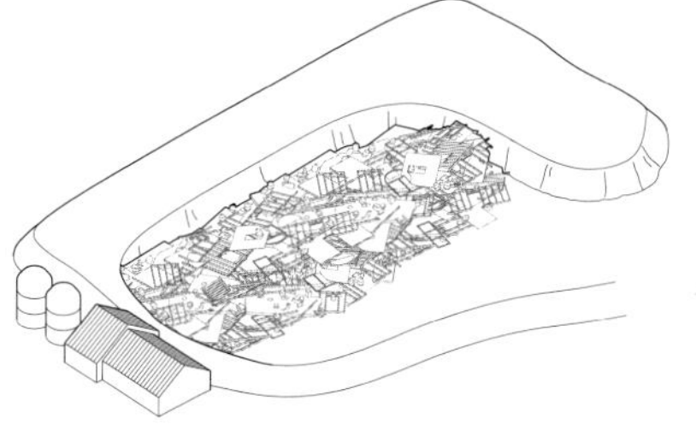

BRICK MORTAR

Various types of mortar are used to bind bricks together, and can make up a significant portion of an assembly. Mortars made from portland cement, lime, sand, and water are typical.

CONSTRUCTION

Brick-based assemblies accommodate a vast assortment of configurations in compressive load-bearing and veneer applications. Bricks enable hand assembly and labor practices.

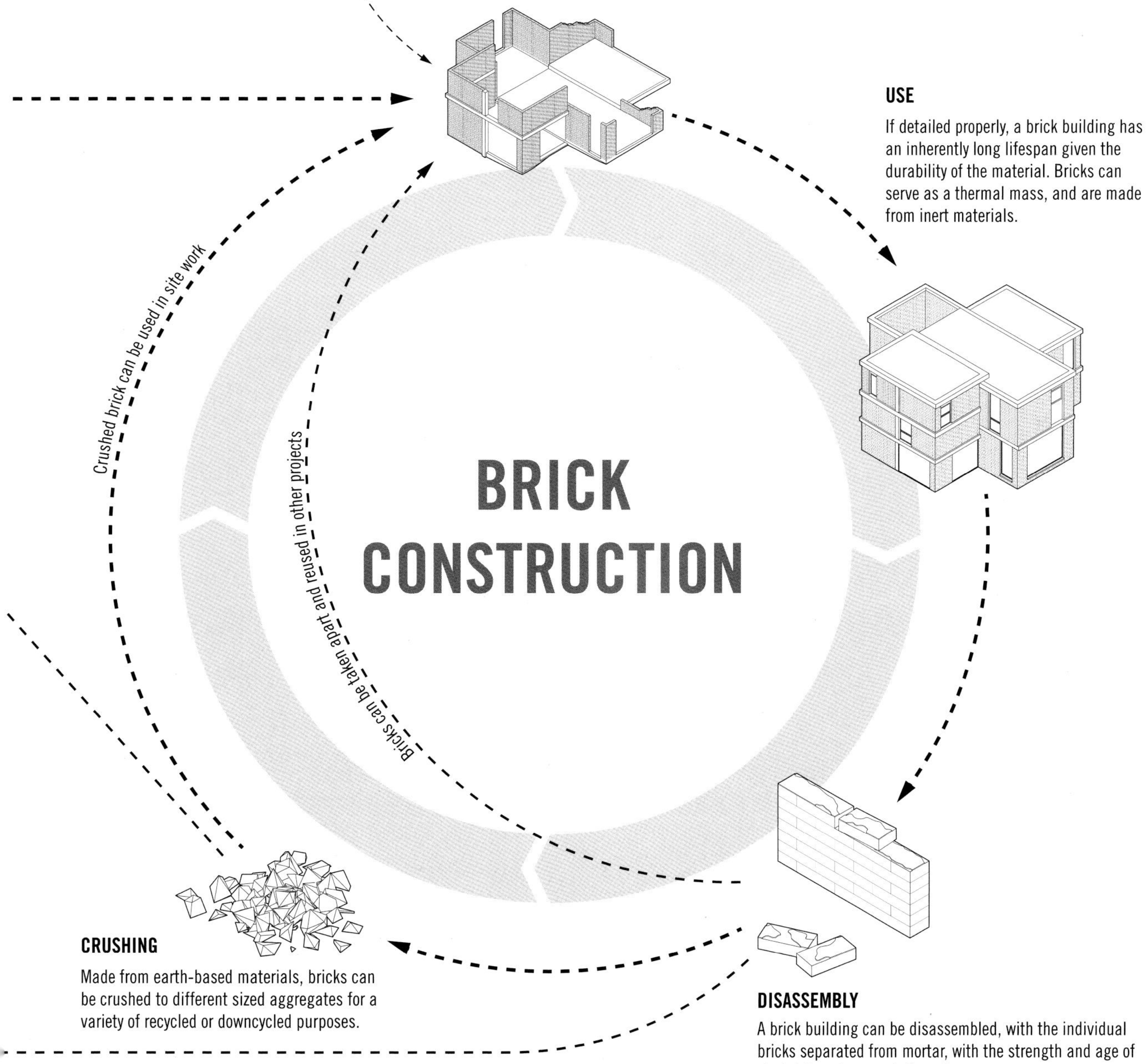

USE

If detailed properly, a brick building has an inherently long lifespan given the durability of the material. Bricks can serve as a thermal mass, and are made from inert materials.

Crushed brick can be used in site work

BRICK CONSTRUCTION

Bricks can be taken apart and reused in other projects

CRUSHING

Made from earth-based materials, bricks can be crushed to different sized aggregates for a variety of recycled or downcycled purposes.

DISASSEMBLY

A brick building can be disassembled, with the individual bricks separated from mortar, with the strength and age of the brick and mortar influencing recovery.

BRICK

HAND MIXING

Clay and shale can be prepared and mixed with water in smaller batches.

SITE EXCAVATING

Excavated clay and shale are the primary elements in standard brick.

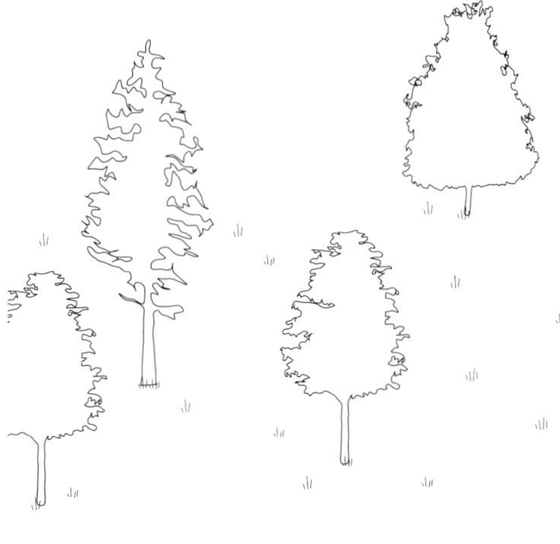

INDUSTRIAL MIXING

Extracted clay and shale is crushed, prepared, screened, and mixed with water at large scale using industrial processes to meet commercial standards.

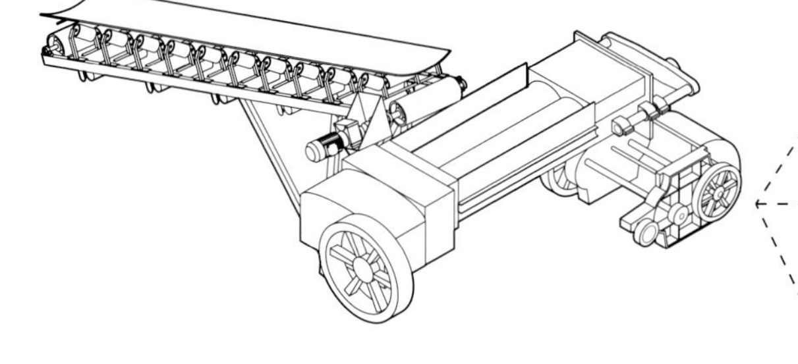

organic material

topsoil

subsoil

regolith

bedrock

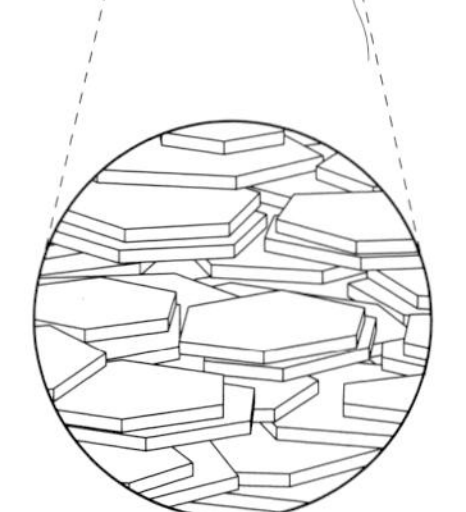

CLAY FORMATION

Clay minerals form where bedrock is weathered by water, air, or steam. Deposits occur near their source or near bodies of water where particles have been deposited over time. The particles' layered structure is what gives clay the ability to absorb water and become formable.

*Depths and makeup of soil horizons vary depending on location and climatic conditions.

HAND-MOLDED

A mold is hand-filled with the clay mixture, typically lined with sand or water to ease the release.

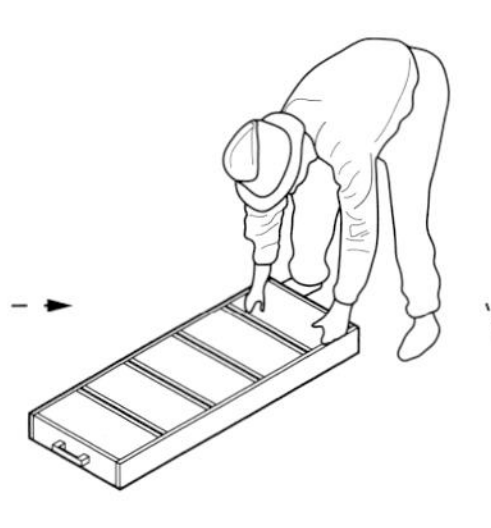

DRY-PRESS PROCESS

For more rigid clays with lower percentages of water, bricks are stamped by pressure using steel molds.

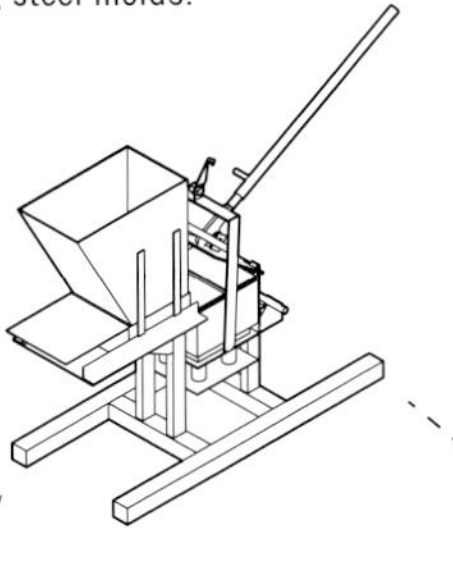

SOFT-MUD PROCESS

Clays that are too soft to be extruded or have additionally added water, a mold process is used. Sand or water are used to keep the mud from sticking to the mold, producing "sand-struck" or "water-struck" bricks.

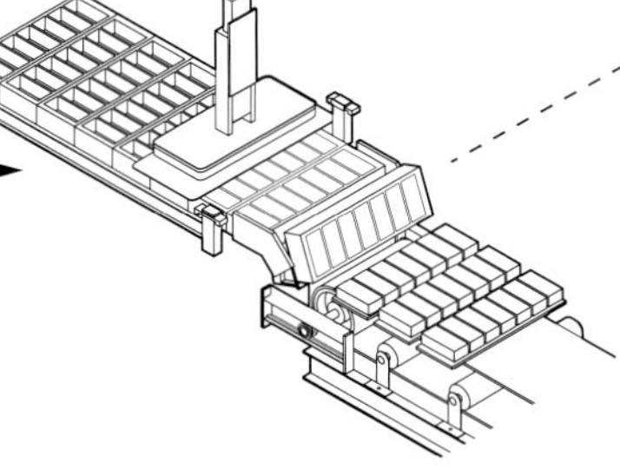

STIFF-MUD PROCESS

Clay with 10 to 15% water is pushed through a de-airing chamber before being extruded through a die. The continuous clay extrusion is then cut into different shapes and sizes. This is the dominant method of industrialized brick fabrication.

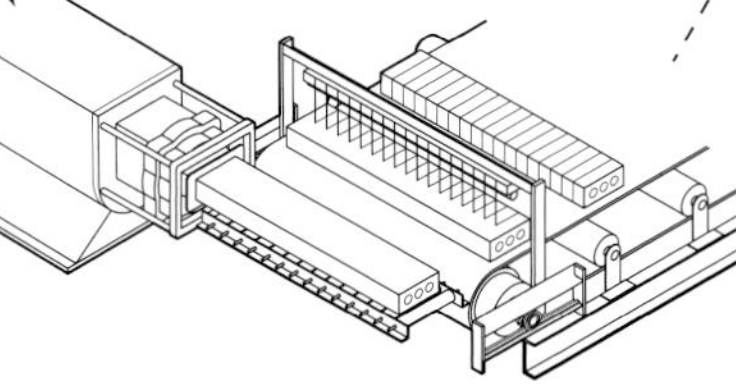

PROFILES

solid

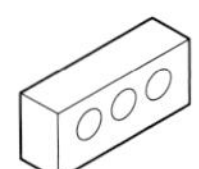

perforated

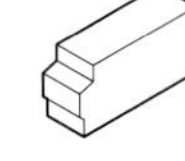

shaped

FIRED

Workable clay and shale mixes are converted into rigid and durable brick through high-temperature heating or firing in a kiln. During the firing process, the clay particles are partially melted together, or vitrified. The shape and process of the kiln impacts the variety and consistency of the brick produced. In tunnel kilns, the bricks are moved through a continuously heated process, whereas periodic kilns provide intermittent heat around stationary bricks.

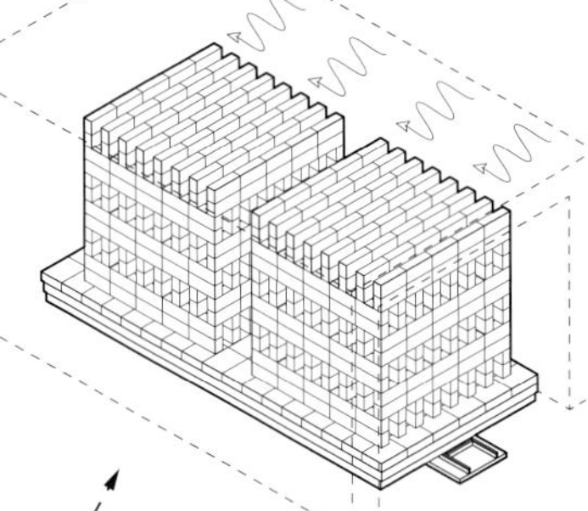

STABILIZED

While clay bricks are hardened through a firing process, lime or cement stabilizers or alternative biological processes can be used with different base materials to harden or cure building blocks. These units depart from the clay and shale basis of standard brick manufacturing, while addressing the energy issues associated with firing.

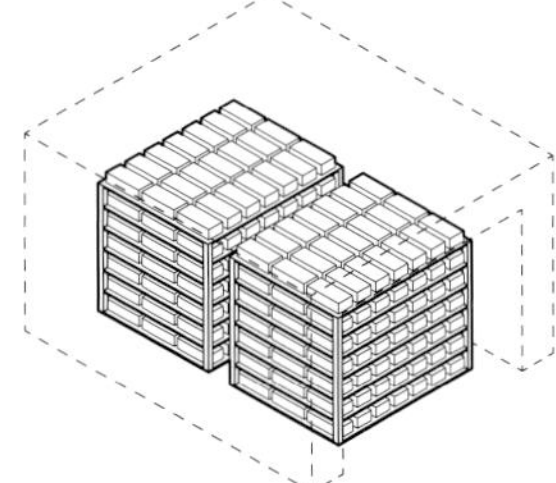

SELF-SUPPORTING WALL

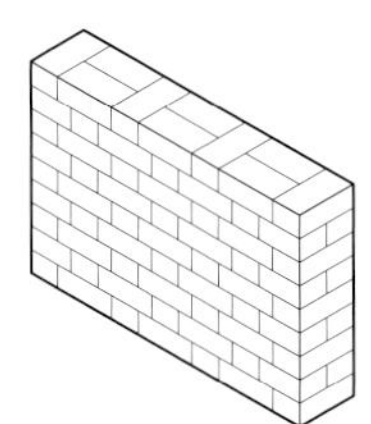

ARCH

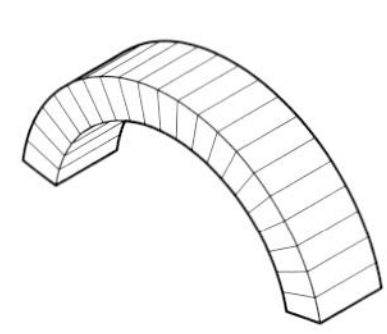

RAINSCREEN

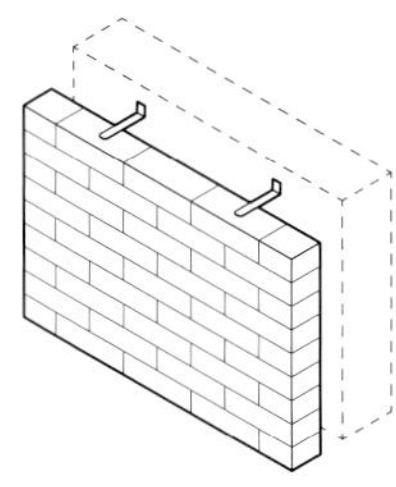

SCREEN

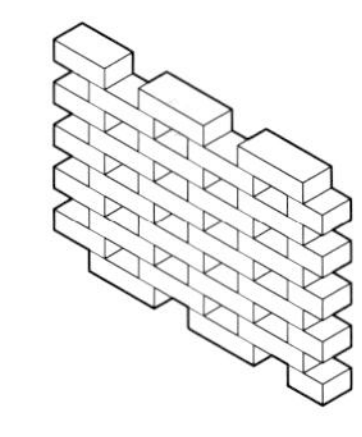

FLOOR

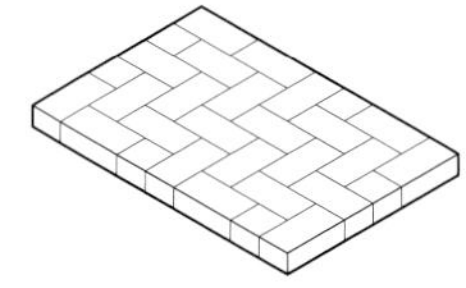

PARTITION WALL

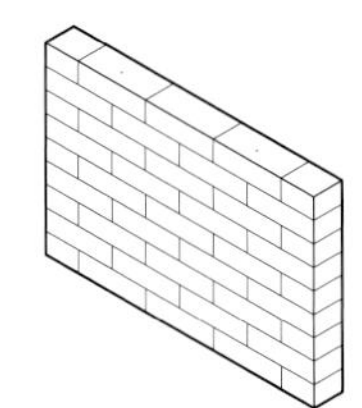

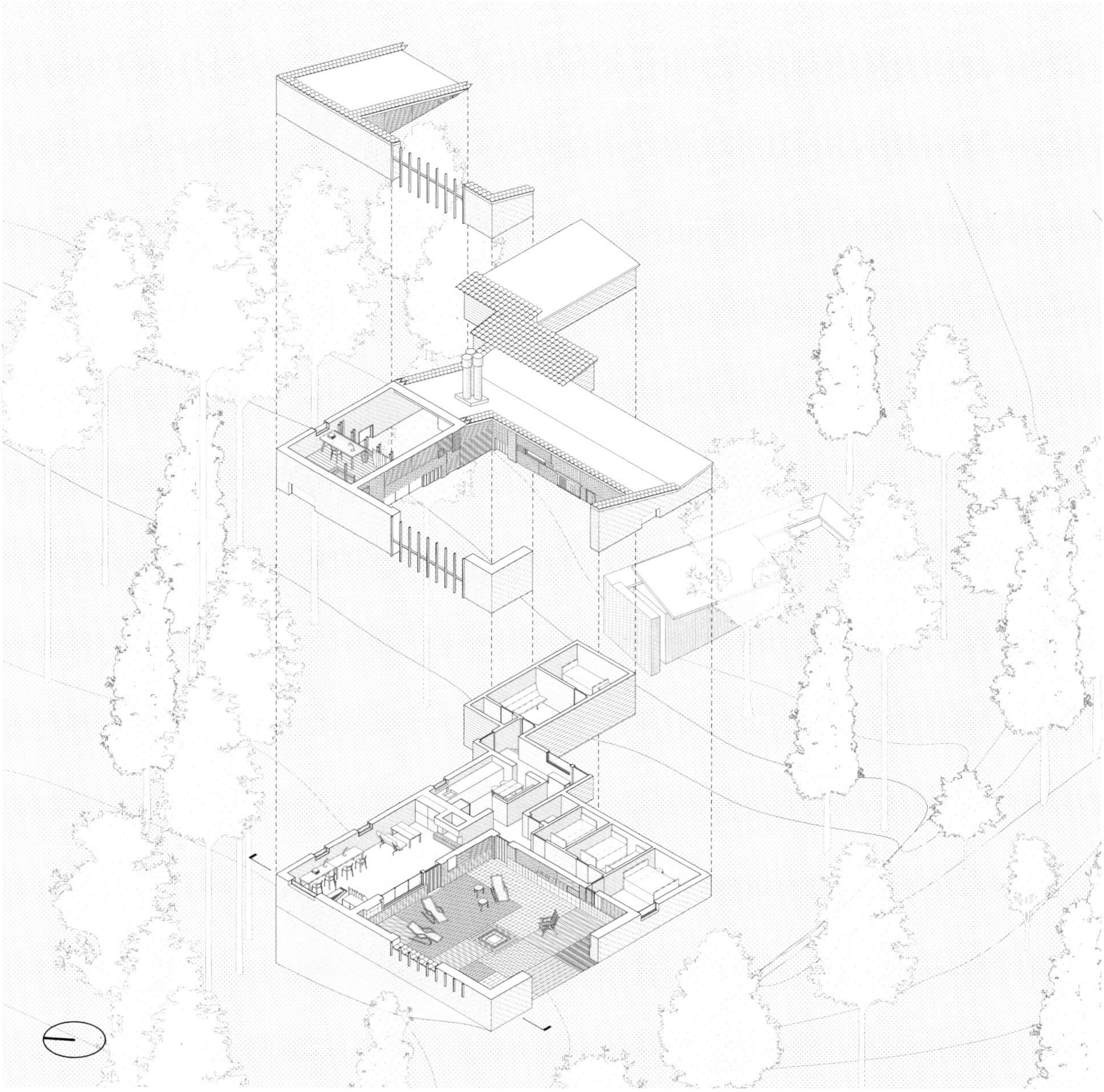

Muuratsalo Experimental House | Alvar Aalto

This summer home for the architect is primarily recognizable for the distinctive brick surfaces of its courtyard. Although it is an exterior space, the courtyard is positioned as the central heart of the building, and used as the main gathering place marked in its center by a sunken fire pit. The square plan is activated in section through the incline of the roof which is high enough to host a suspended wood painting loft in its tallest portion. This inclined plane at its lowest point inflects into a butterfly roof along the bar of kitchen, bathroom, and three bedrooms. The exterior wall surrounding the courtyard follows this roofline forming a tall opening on the side opposite the living area, framing views to the nearby water. A guest

Jyväskylä, Finland | 1953

wing stretches the building's footprint to the north, but rests only on logs above the ground in Aalto's experiment with foundationless construction.

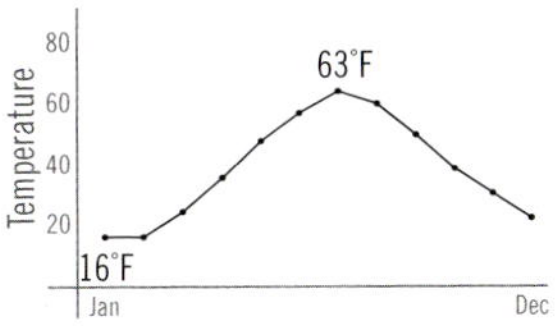

Temperature 80 60 40 20
63°F
16°F
Jan Dec

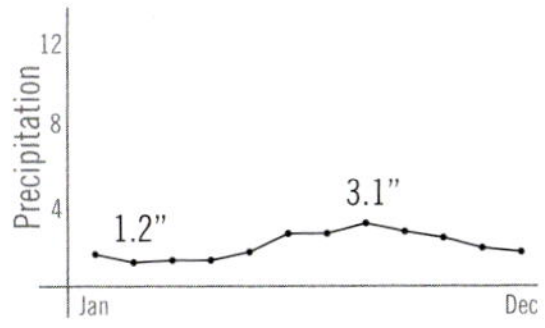

Precipitation 12 8 4
3.1"
1.2"
Jan Dec

Muuratsalo Experimental House

The house was used as a site for tectonic experimentation, testing brick assemblies and their durability in the harsh Finnish climate, in tandem with larger nearby building commissions. Although all the walls and the floor of the courtyard were covered in the nearly 50 different patterns and aggregations of bricks and tiles, the differences of those surfaces are made legible in the section. As a veneer applied to a load-bearing brick wall, the bricks visible on the face of this wall are allowed to protrude depending upon their thickness. Shadows and light enhance the reading

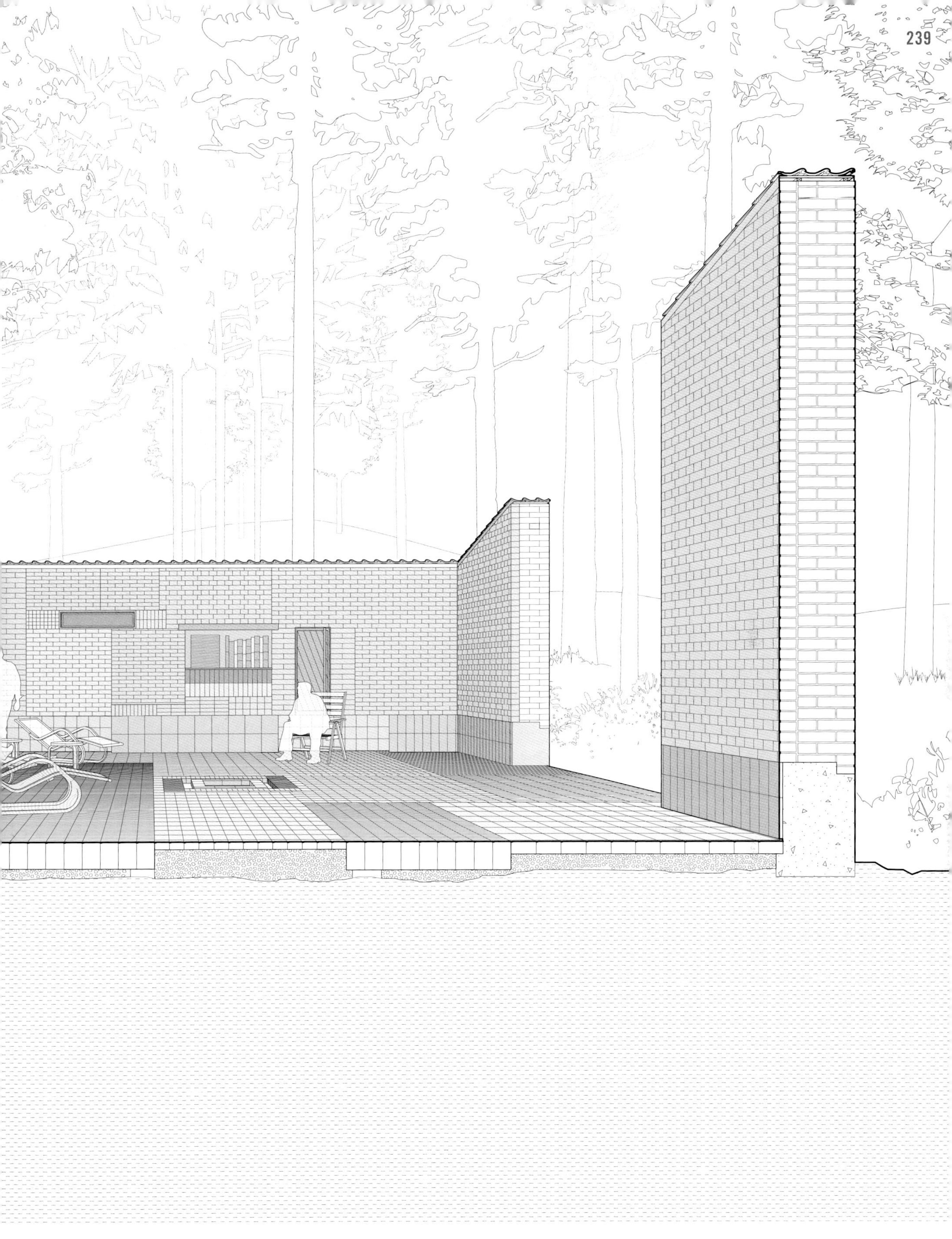

of depth and accentuate the distinctions between the fields of materials. These walls contrast with the smoothness of the flooring blocks, whose differential depths are buried. The striking quality of the courtyard is staged through a contrast with the whitewashed bricks and board-formed concrete on the more muted exterior perimeter of the house. Similarly, the brick and wall panels inside the house are also whitewashed, muting their colors in deference to the structural wood details and the material exuberance of the courtyard.

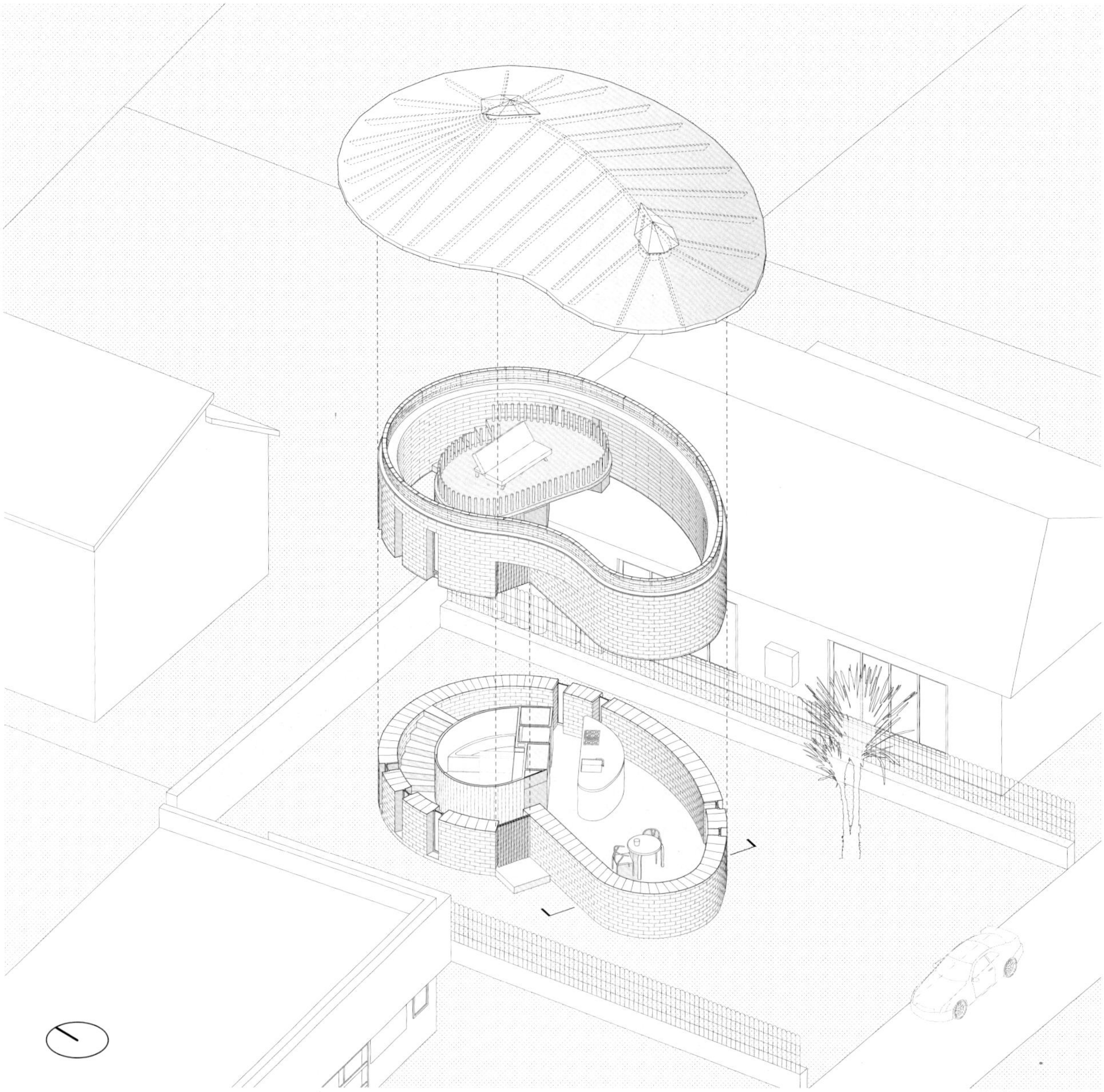

Earth Bricks | Atelier Tekuto

Made from 2,500 hand-made earth-based bricks or blocks, this prototype research project demonstrates the structural and spatial capacities of non-rectangular soil-based building units using magnesium oxide from calcinating seawater as the hardening agent. Unlike traditional earthen bricks, which require heating to solidify and harden clay, these building blocks solidified through a chemical reaction [$MgO + H_2O = Mg(OH)_2$] and continue to harden over time through a process that absorbs CO_2 [$Mg(OH)_2 + CO_2 = MgCO_3$]. With only locally sourced materials, the monolithic, single-wythe walls are an adaptable building system, creating an elegant and simple form with material resonance. The kitchen, bathing space, and

Chiba Prefecture, Japan | 2011

sleeping loft, accessed by a staircase that follows the curve of the walls, are defined through separate distinct materials and pulled away from the block walls, creating a nested section.

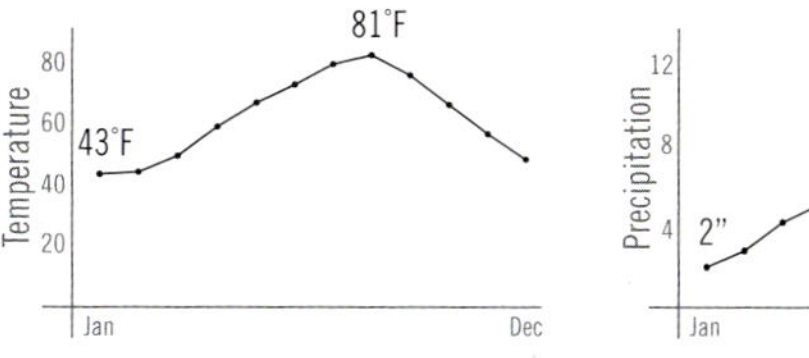

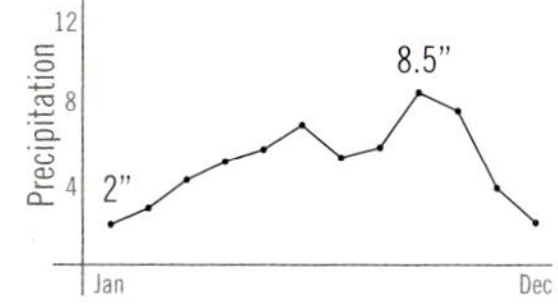

Earth Bricks

At 15.7 in (400 mm) thick, the walls meet structural code while achieving a height of 9.7 ft (2.97m) using only a single wythe. Although each block is approximately 3.9 by 9.8 by 15.7 in (100 by 250 by 400mm), straight and tapered wood molds were used to shape the brick units in order to form the curvilinear shape. To demonstrate the universality and low technology of the system, each of the blocks were hand-made with teams of four to six people, with an output of 30 bricks a day, using locally sourced earth and magnesium oxide, and assembled on site. A concrete ring beam at the top adds stability, transfers the loads from the lightweight wooden roof, and supports five courses of glass blocks to illuminate the form. Openings are

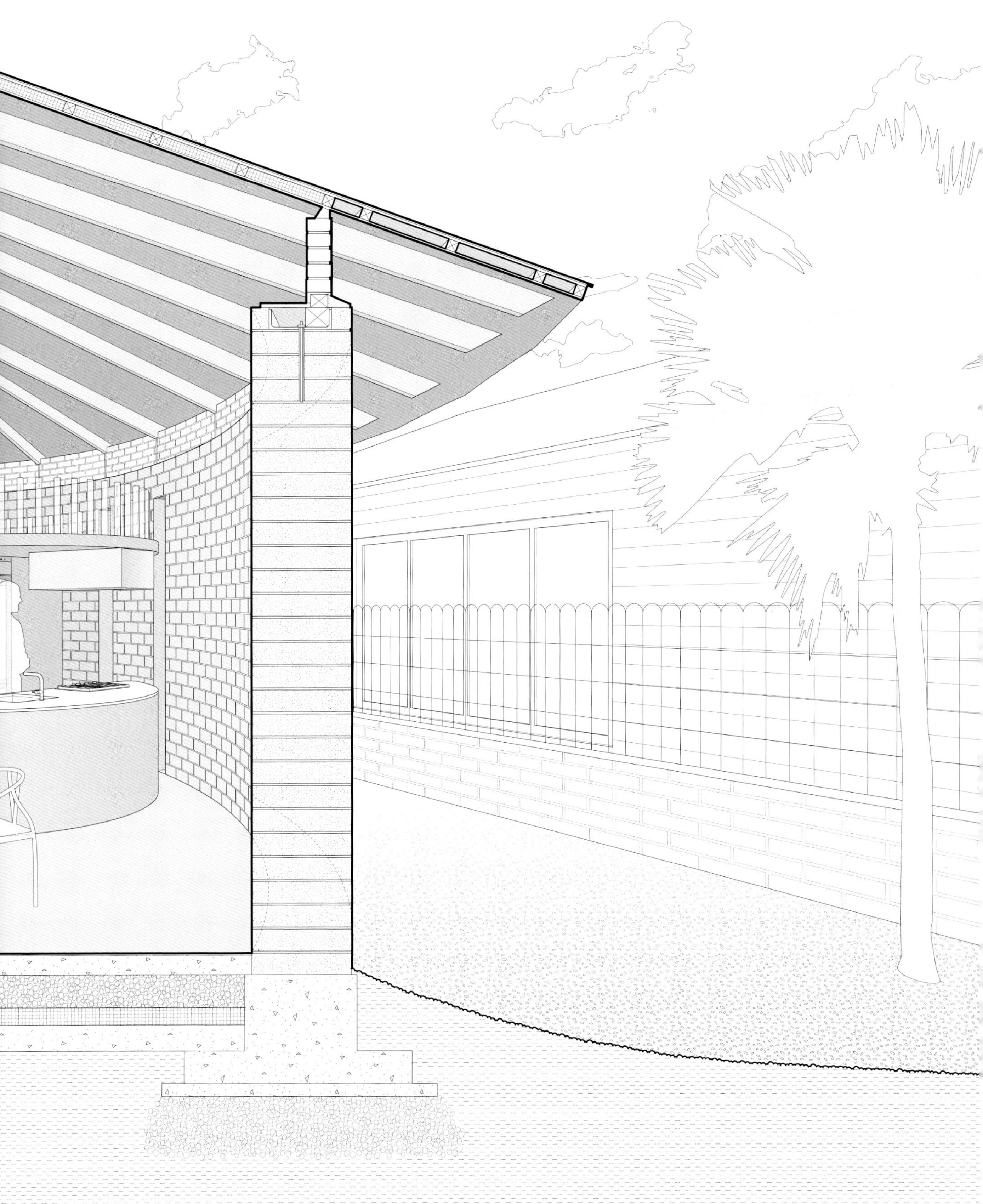

left in the earth brick wall for tall, thin windows around the perimeter of the house. The roof cantilevers past the wall protecting them from rainwater. Two skylights integrated into the ridge beam provide daylight that reflects off the white terrazzo floor and kitchen island, set in contrast to the earthen material of the walls. Importantly, at the end of the building's life, the blocks can be reused, or crushed and returned to the ground, completing a cycle without waste.

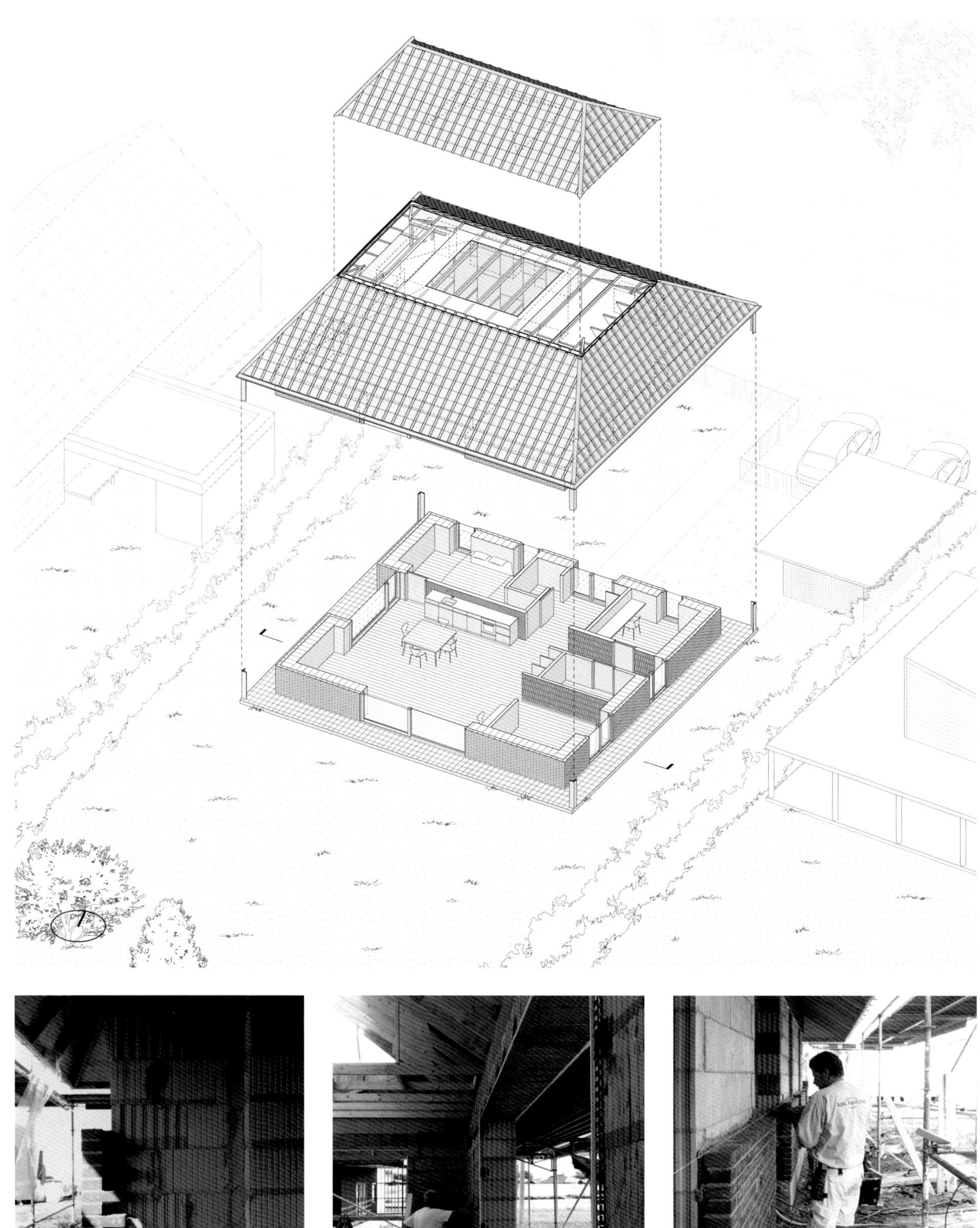

Brick House | LETH & GORI

Designed and constructed as one of six prototype houses in Nyborg to examine different approaches to affordable and low-carbon houses, this project proposes a sustainable dwelling based on longevity and durability. With a projected lifespan of 150 years, the 1,436 sq ft (133 sq m) house mitigates the impact of the embodied carbon involved in brick and terracotta by using traditional building assemblies and a limited number of materials to minimize maintenance and simplify performance. The load-bearing 22 in (560 mm) thick exterior wall is made only from fired clay blocks, creating a monolithic, single material wall that is vapor open. A lightweight wood roof, filled with ample cellulose insulation completes

Nyborg, Denmark | 2014

the house without additional vapor membranes. Drawing from traditional building practices, the simplified material assembly anticipates end-of-life reuse, extending the value of the upfront carbon.

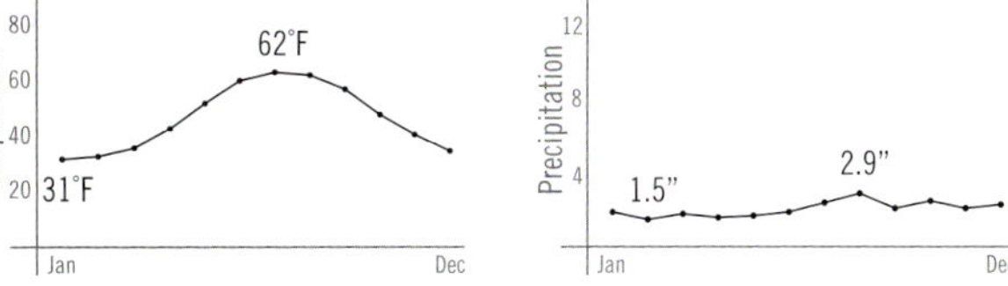

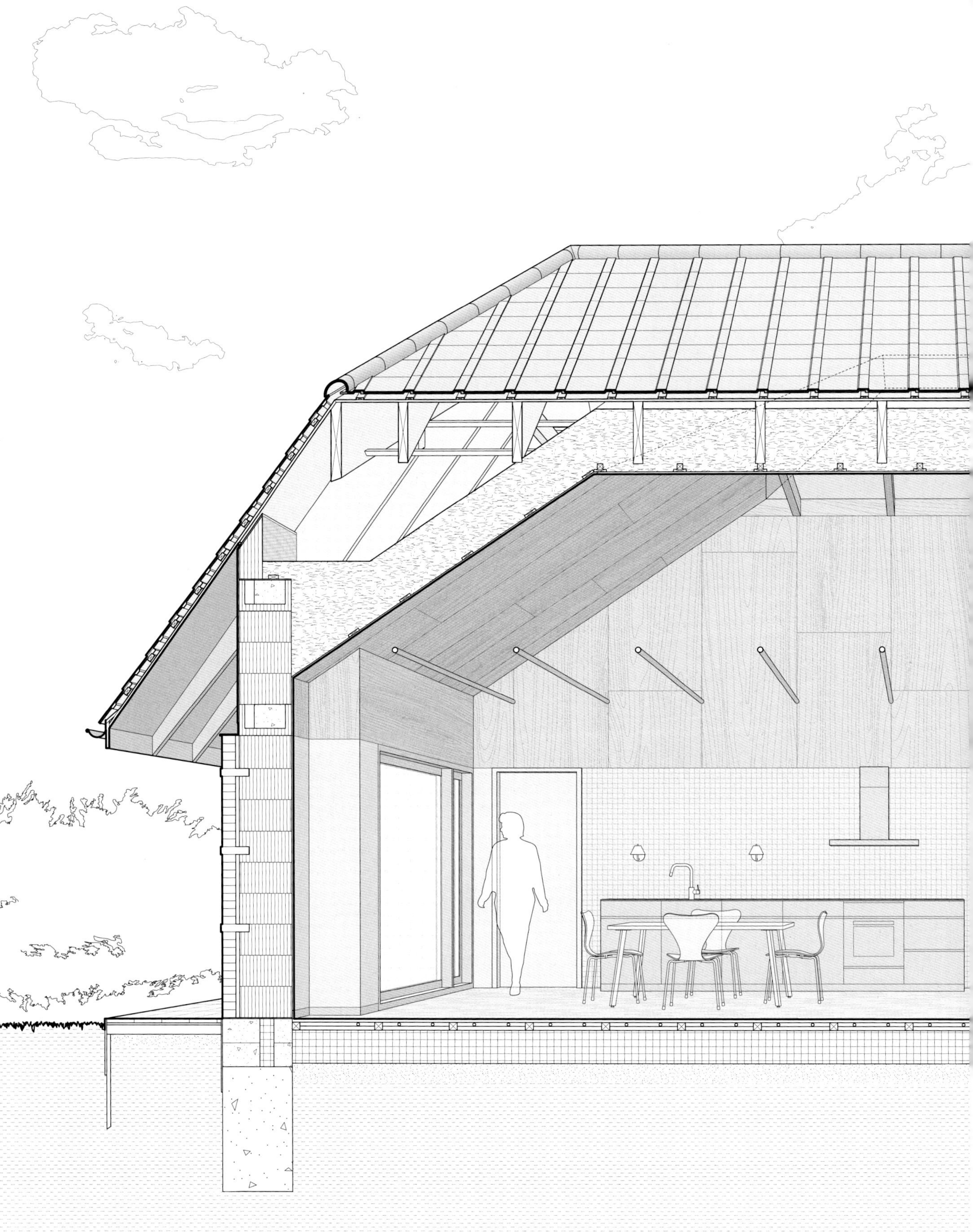

Brick House

The section of the house is animated by a second, unorthodox wood roof below the conventional hipped roof assembly, adding spatial complexity to an efficient rectangular plan. Unlike conventional brick-veneer walls that are a composite of multiple layers of materials, compromising its durability, this exterior wall is made from interlocking bricks that form an insulating terra cotta block. The single material breathes, regulates temperature with its thermal mass, and eliminates concern for cracking with a single rate of expansion. Rotated tie bricks on the façade create a decorative pattern and floor-to-ceiling windows at each façade fill the square plan with daylight. Nested individual rooms form niches for

flexibility within the dwelling, and unfinished terra cotta and exposed plywood reduce the need for redundant finishes. Encircling the house is a covered, 39 in (1 m) wide porch, extending the living spaces outward. The steeply sloped hipped roof provides long term weather performance and protects the masonry walls from direct moisture. Concrete foundations are limited to supporting the perimeter clay walls with a radiant wood floor built over insulation.

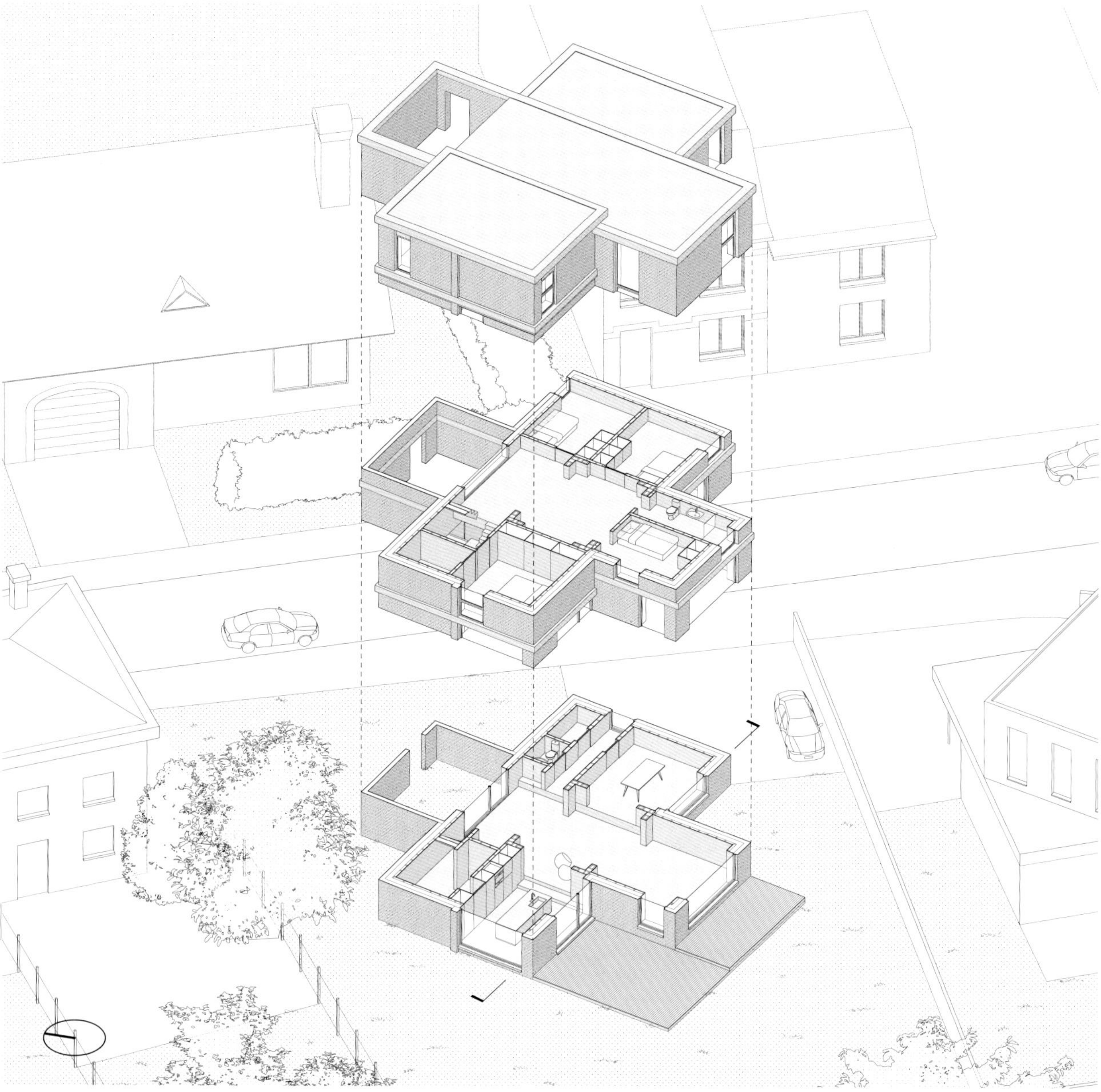

dnA House | BLAF Architecten

Located along a residential street of similarly scaled buildings in a small town in the periphery of Brussels, this house deploys bricks walls in unusual but subtle ways. Using a combination of reclaimed bricks that match the context and concrete, the walls are self-supporting but do not hold up the interior, nor are they propped up as a veneer. Instead they contain a wood-framed interior structure separated by an insulated cavity. The independence of these wall systems is made legible at the courtyard, where the two separate, revealing the flat interior of the brick. Inside the house, the wood framing is developed as a shear section, allowing the lower-level living area to cascade with the topography away from the

Asse, Belgium | 2013

street, while the upper floor splits into two levels. The cruciform plan is rotated 45 degrees to the street, enhancing the three-dimensional qualities of the house.

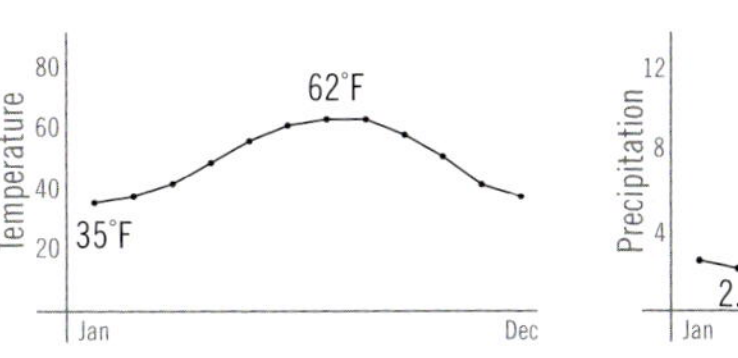

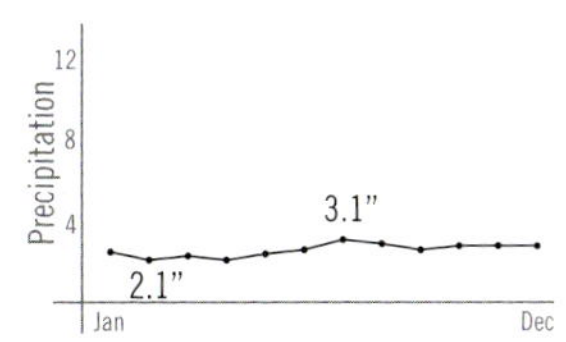

dnA House

The two structural skins allow the masonry walls to outlive its interior, with its independence being more easily adapted for a future life. The interior surface of the brick walls were designed to be smooth to simplify the detailing of the wood lining. Moreover, the design of the house differentiates the detailing of the masonry enclosure and the wood enclosure to great effect. On the exterior, the concrete frame is playfully supported by, or in other locations covered over by, corbeled bricks. Bricks form flat surfaces appearing as infill walls within the concrete beams,

while also gathering into columns flush with that concrete. Despite appearances the horizontal concrete bands are not the floor, but merely register the floor levels. On the interior, wood columns are clustered into overlapped corners, reinforcing the cruciform plan in the main room and accentuating the design as a collection of semi-discrete rectilinear boxes. Wood joists are visible throughout the ceiling, but their direction shifts from room to room underscoring each volume's relative autonomy.

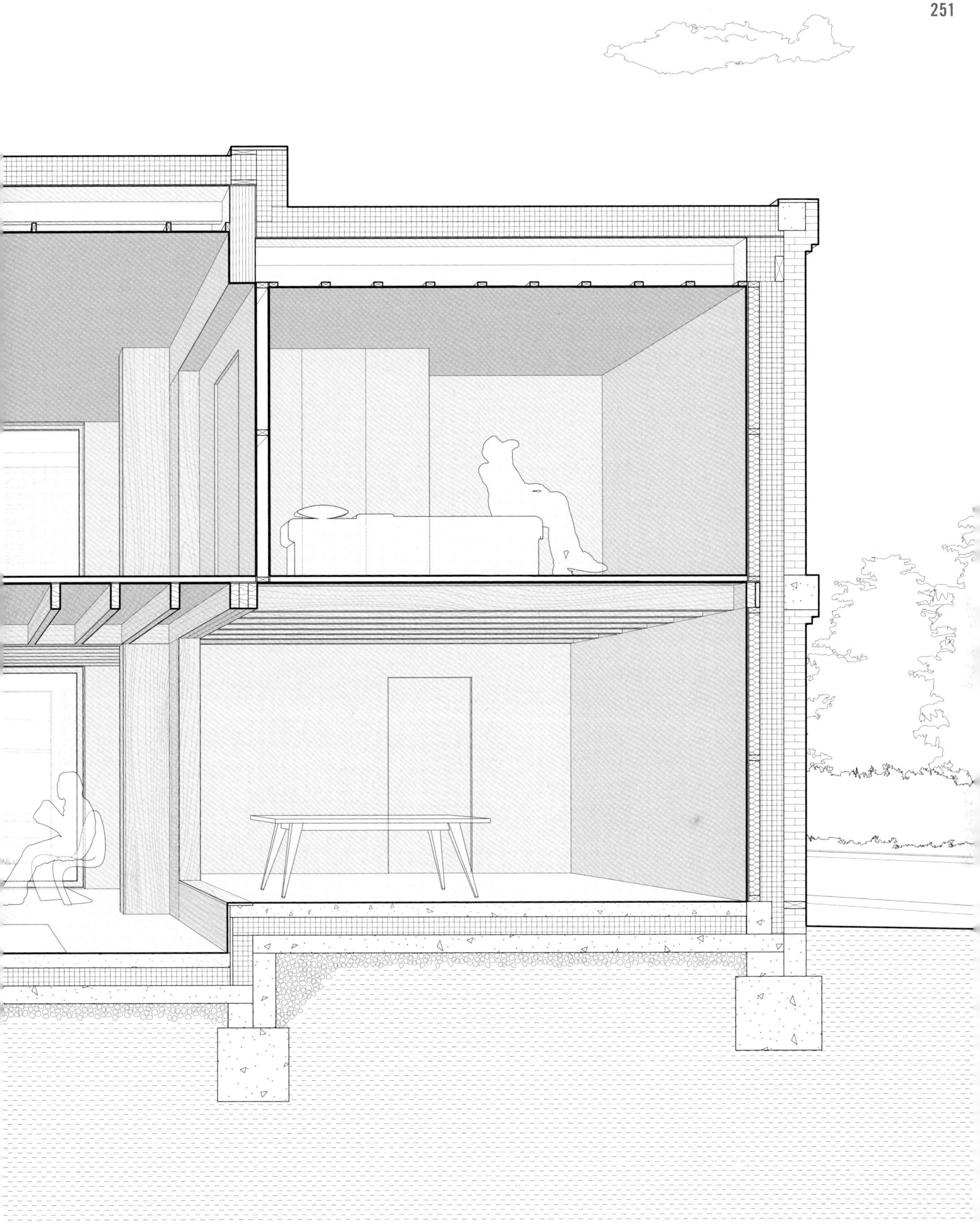

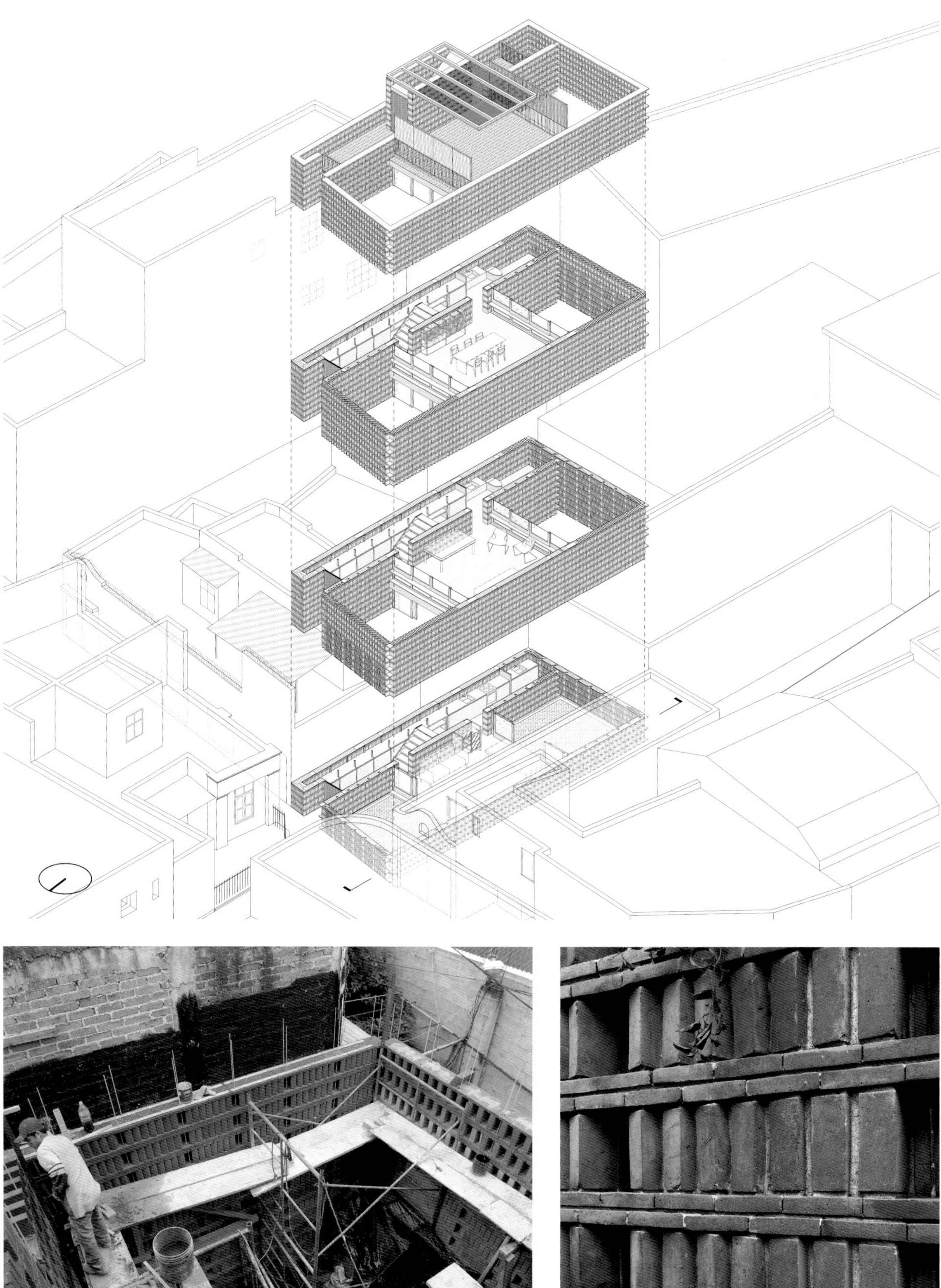

Iturbide Studio | Taller | Mauricio Rocha + Gabriela Carrillo |

Woven into a densely built area of Mexico City, on a plot measuring only 23 by 79 ft (7 by 14 m), this project uses unglazed brick as the primary material to realize spatial ambiguity and complexity through repetition and variation. Designed as a studio for a photographer, the aggregation of brick screens the inner workings of the space from outside observation, while filtering and controlling daylight to meet the client's needs. A repeated two course running bond pattern of thin horizontal bricks separated by a soldier course, varied in its density and spacing, form all walls and define the spaces. The plan is divided into three distinct areas, with a central climate-controlled living and working space nestled between two

Mexico City, Mexico | 2017

open-air courtyards that buffer the surrounding urban context. A narrow staircase volume integrated with the kitchen, bathrooms, and storage forms a thickened east wall and provides access to the three floors and open rooftop terrace.

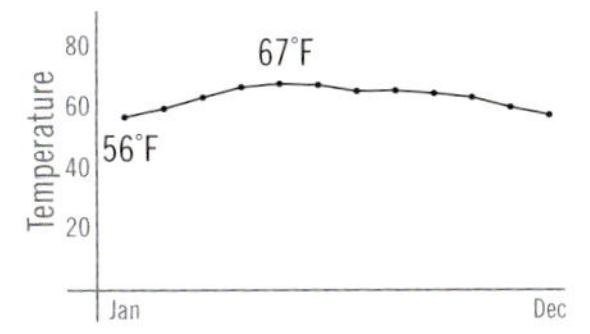

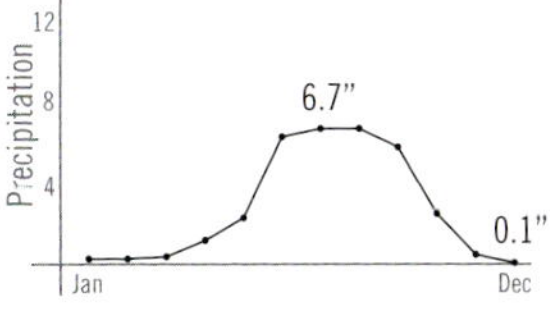

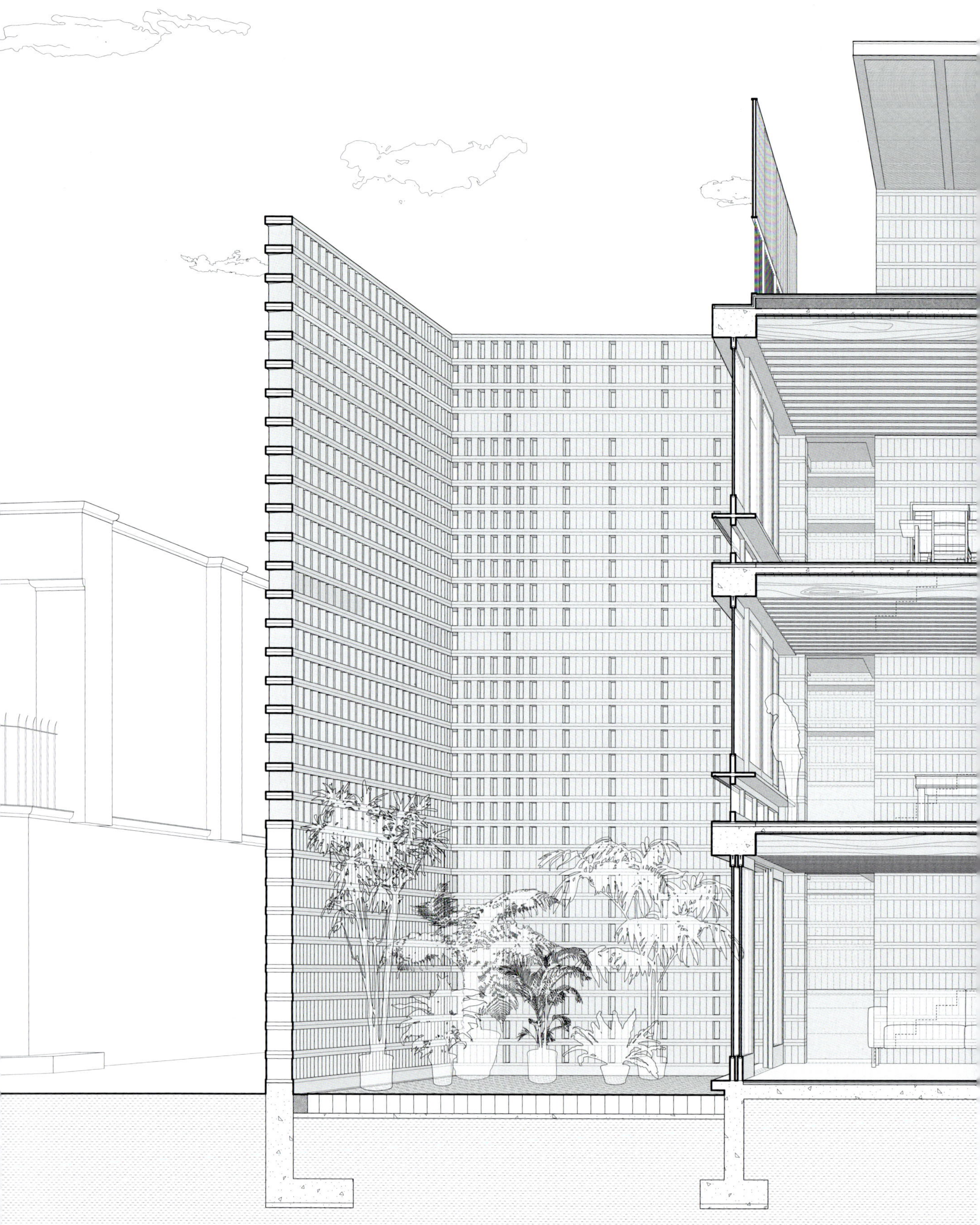

Iturbide Studio

Built in an area prone to seismic activity, the assembly of individual bricks relied on a discrete and integrated steel support system to provide stability, creating diaphanous single-wythe brick skins, without reliance on heavy concrete back-up walls. This metal lattice is woven into the masonry, underlying a dynamic structural assembly, allowing for a playful arrangement of the bricks. While the horizontal brick layers are always solid, the delight comes through the organization of the soldier-course bricks, through rotation, spacing, and orientation. At lower levels, these vertical bricks are packed tightly together to create security and privacy, yet rotated and opened on upper walls to facilitate the penetration of

air and light. Reinforcing the sense of place, the handmade bricks were all sourced from a local fabricator. Densely spaced timber joists support wooden floors, and reduce the depth of the concrete slabs, while ample arrangement of plants cool and condition the outdoor courtyards. As a result, the enclosed living quarters are insulated physically and spatially from distractions of the street, yet simultaneously the innovative use of brick ties the project back into the cultural and urban fabric and history of its site.

STONE

Stone

746 $kgCO_2e/m^3$ Interior Flooring; Ökobaudat

72 $kgCO_2e/m^3$ Exterior Slab; Ökobaudat

STONE

Arguably the most primordial of building materials, stone exists in a diversity of forms and can be readily cut, shaped, and finished into an equally wide range of architectural elements and surfaces. Although stone itself is naturally occurring, its extraction, transport, and processing have environmental consequences and its use is often reduced to surface veneers on more carbon-intensive building assemblies. Nevertheless, depending on source and method of construction, stone can provide a durable resource with intrinsic structural, water resistant, and thermal properties as well as a rich spectrum of visual and tactile qualities.

QUARRIED STONE

Large stone blocks are excavated from open quarries. Quarrying of stone can result in landform alteration, changes to surrounding hydrology, sedimentation patterns, and ground water levels, as well as impacts on plant life, animal habitat, and human health. While stone is a widely distributed resource globally, it is often transported long distances for processing prior to reaching building sites.

SHAPING + TEXTURING

Quarried blocks are cut in progressive stages into a wide variety of sizes, thicknesses, and shapes; from ashlar blocks to thin tiles. Depending on the type and use of stone, a range of profiles, geometries, and surface finishes can be achieved.

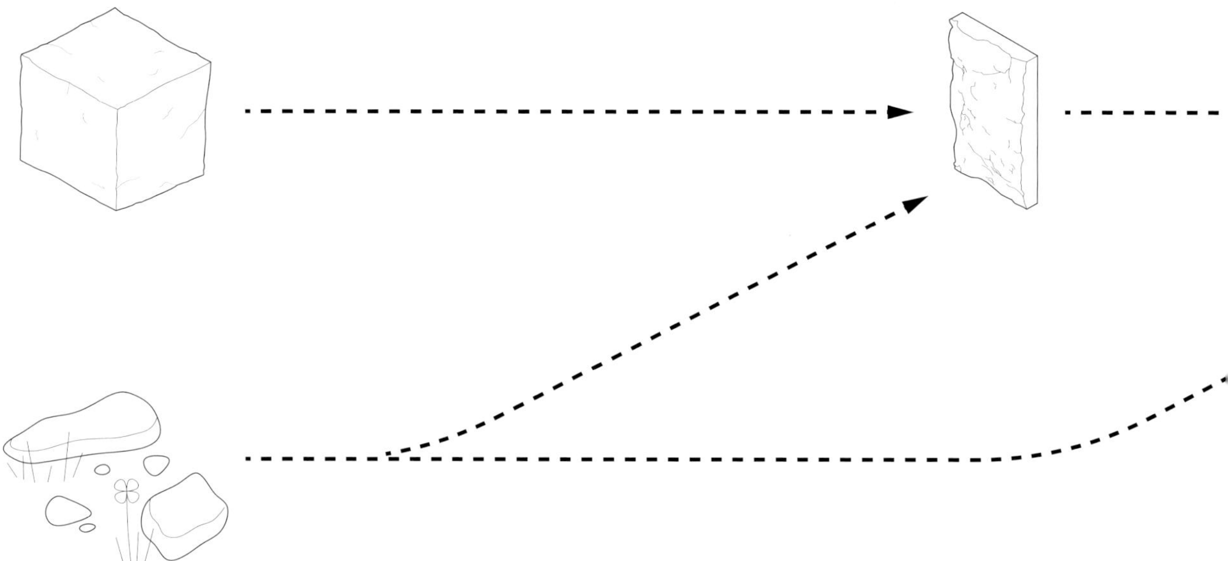

FOUND STONE

Instead of excavating stone from a quarry, usable found stones may be collected without the use of industrialized processes. Use of local stone gathered from nearby sources is most desirable to minimize disruptions to landscapes and transportation impacts.

MORTAR

Various types of mortar are used to bind stone together, and can make up a significant portion of an assembly. Mortars made from portland cement, lime, sand, and water are typical.

CONSTRUCTION

The vast majority of stone in buildings today takes the form of thin veneers applied to more typical steel and concrete structural systems. Stacked and load-bearing stone masonry is less common but can be more impactful in terms of limiting embodied carbon. The typical use of mortar as a binder limits potential reuse.

USE

If properly detailed, stone requires little to no maintenance throughout the building's lifespan.

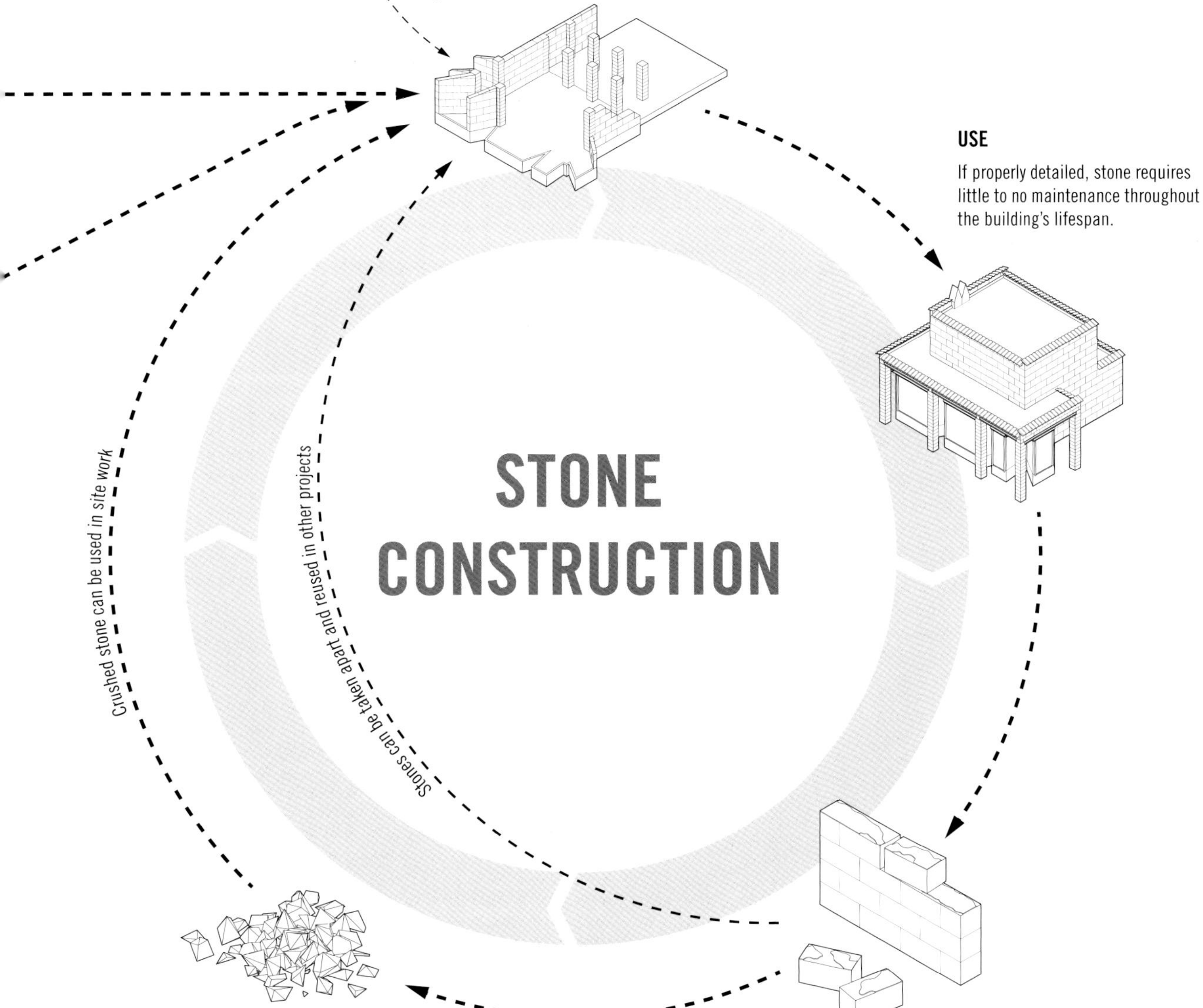

STONE CONSTRUCTION

Crushed stone can be used in *site work*

Stones can be taken apart and reused in other projects

DISASSEMBLY

With care, stone can be salvaged during demolition for later reuse. Dry stacked and mechanically fixed systems facilitate disassembly and repurposing of stone.

CRUSHING

Stone can be crushed to be downcycled in the form of aggregate or for use as fill and in landscaping. Otherwise it will naturally decompose and humify over time.

STONE

FOUND STONE COLLECTING

Loose stones of an appropriate shape and size can be collected from local sites without the negative effects associated with industrial quarrying.

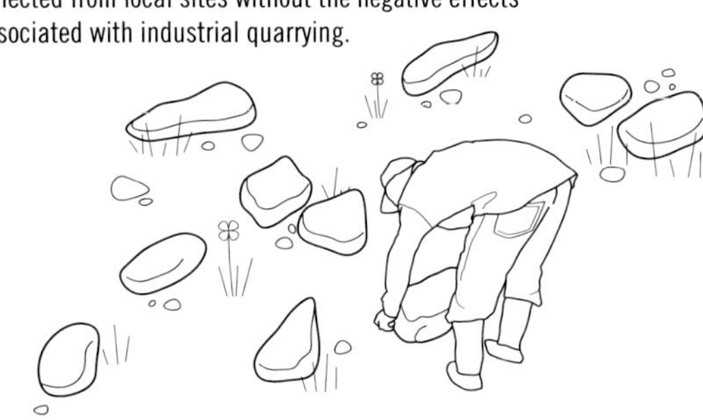

HAND SHAPING

Hand tools cut and shape stones to a usable dimension, proportion, and finish.

QUARRYING

Open quarries are the source of most stone used for construction. Heavy machinery is used to cut large blocks of stone which are progressively broken down into sizes suitable for transport and processing. Quarries have long term impacts on the surrounding landscape and ecology.

ROUGH CUTTING

The vast majority of stone used in construction is transported from quarries to stone mills for processing. Automated saws cut the large quarry stones in successive stages into slabs or blocks of more manageable scale and thickness. Since stone itself can be considered carbon neutral, it is the energy associated with mechanized processing and transportation that increase its negative environmental impacts.

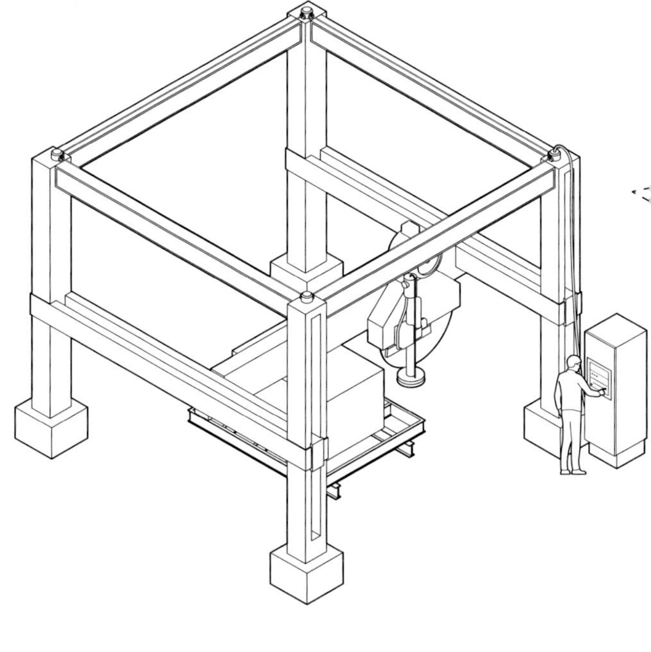

ROCK TYPES

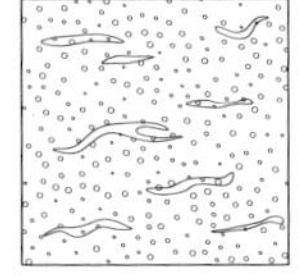

igneous
granite
basalt

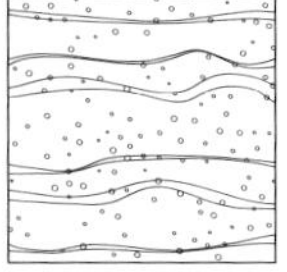

metamorphic
marble
slate

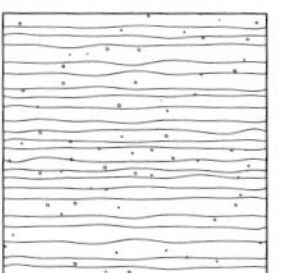

sedimentary
limestone
sandstone
travertine

GABION WALL

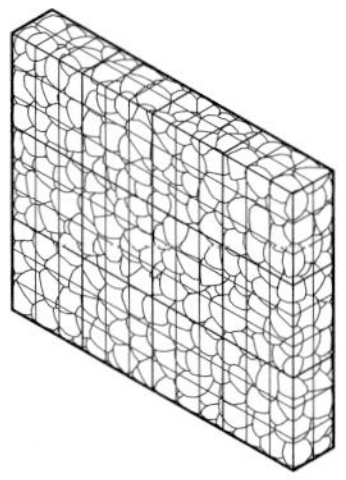

DRY STACK WALL

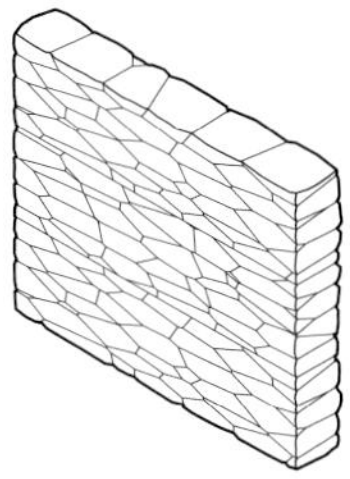

CONSTRUCTION

Larger stone blocks, whether found or dressed, are assembled following typical patterns of stacking or more complex vaulting geometries. Thinner stone veneers are often attached to a backing structure via clips or adhesives.

MORTARED WALL

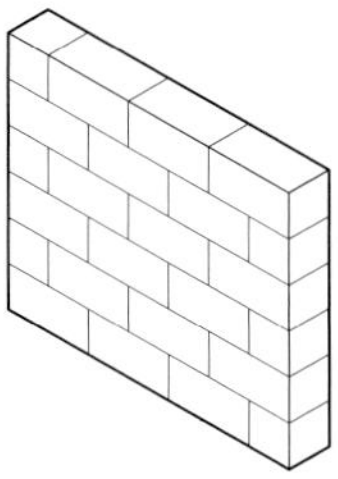

ARCH

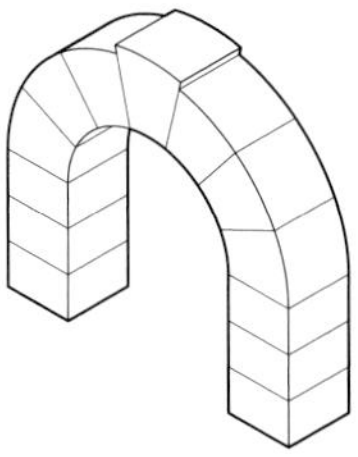

FINAL SIZING + TEXTURING

Large slabs are cut to their final dimensions and the desired finish texture is produced. A variety of digitally controlled sawing, milling, or manual processes may be deployed to achieve finished shapes and surface effects.

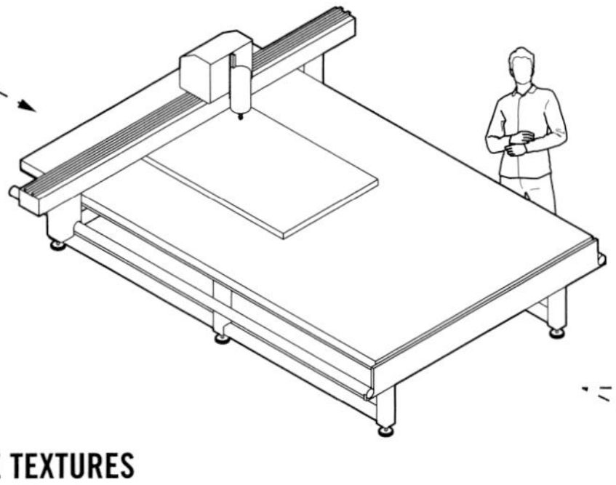

PARAPET CAP

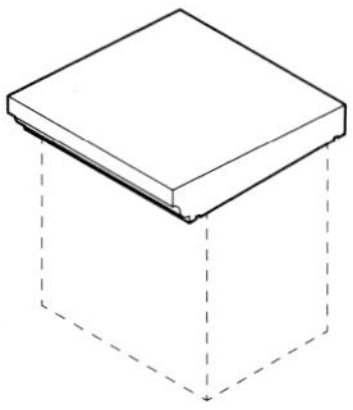

SURFACE TEXTURES

polished
honed
combed
hammered
split face

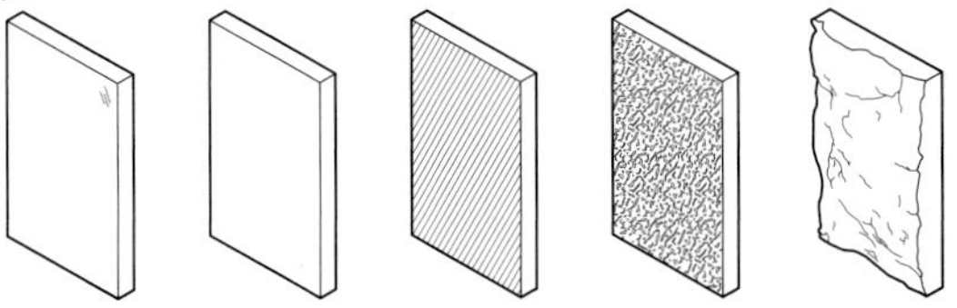

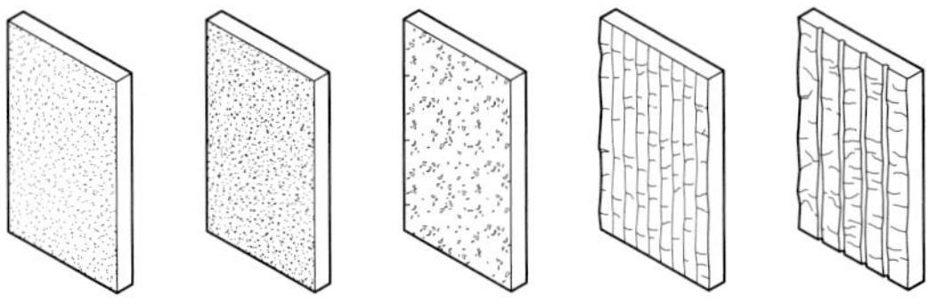

VENEER PANEL

sand blasted
flamed
tumbled
chiseled
grooved + chiseled

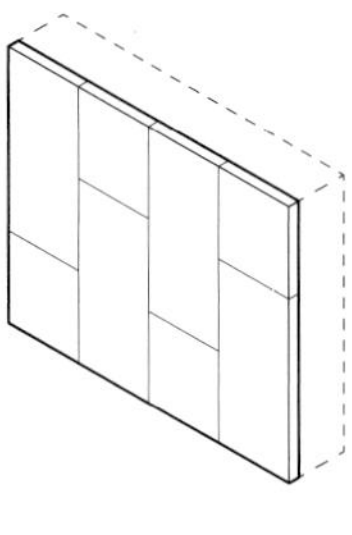

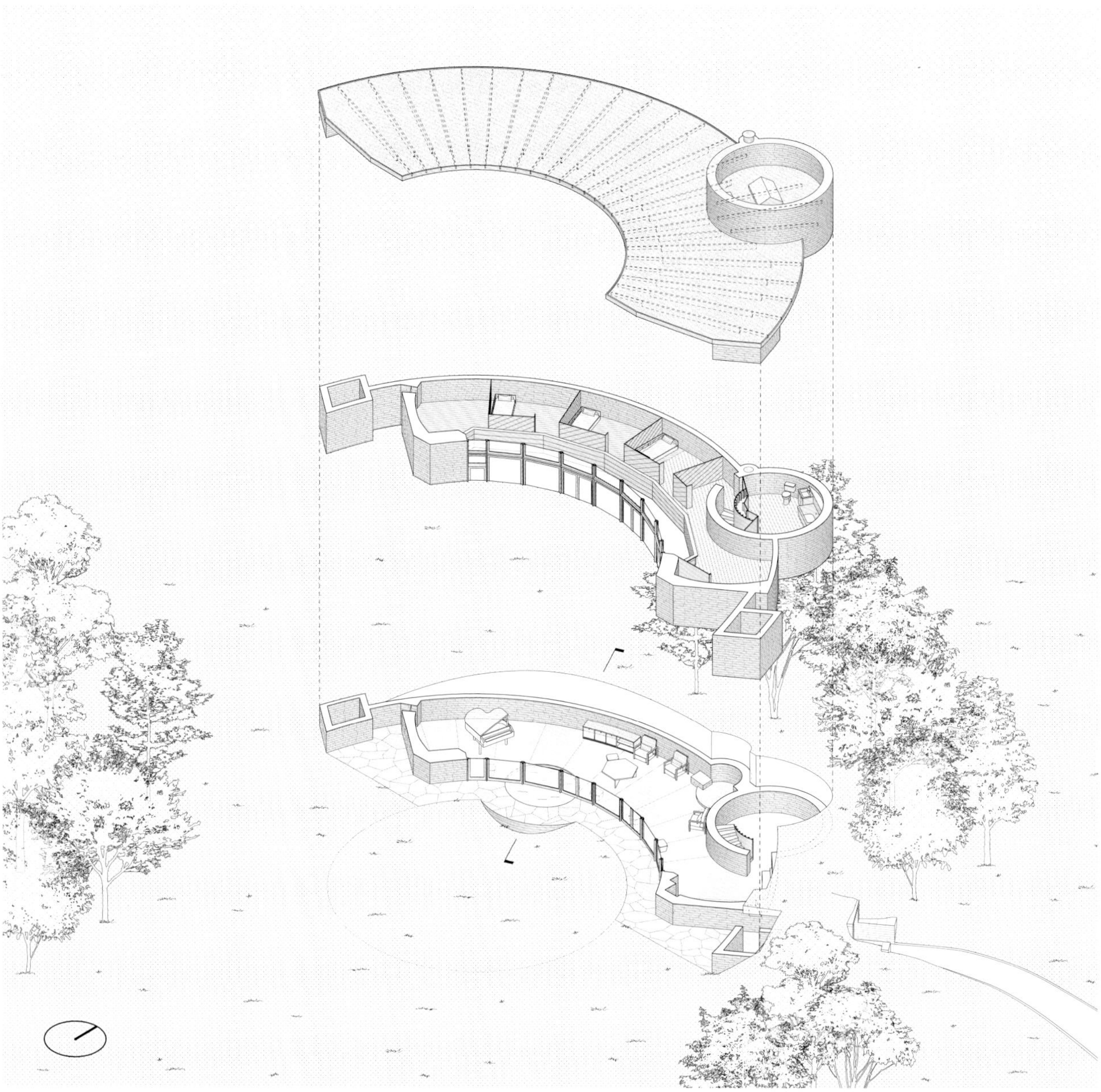

Jacobs House II | Frank Lloyd Wright

Responding to the client's demands for thermal efficiency, the Jacobs House II derives its primary geometry from the solar forces of the site, rendering them in earth, stone, glass, and wood. Also known as the Solar Hemicycle, the house is semicircular in plan, partially buried in the site and opening to a circular garden and the Wisconsin prairie beyond. While the extensive glass wall maximizes sunlight in winter, the windward side of the house is sheltered by a curving wall of local limestone, itself enclosed by an earthen berm that further embeds the house within the site.

Madison, Wisconsin | 1948

The interior is open in plan and section, with a stone cylinder and partly interiorized pond providing subtle distinctions between functions and a wood mezzanine of bedrooms pulled back from the exterior wall to allow for visual and thermal exchanges between levels.

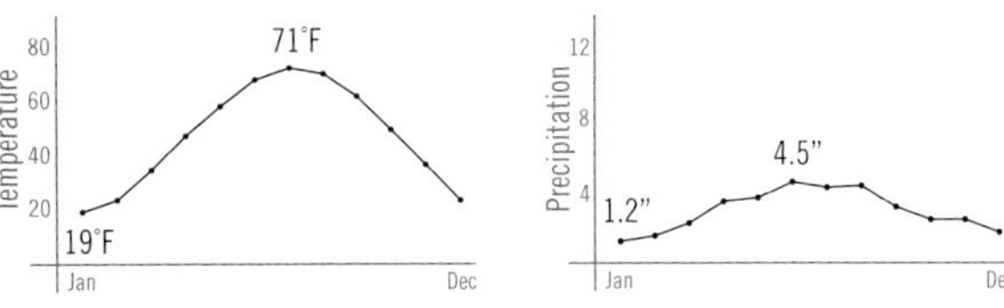

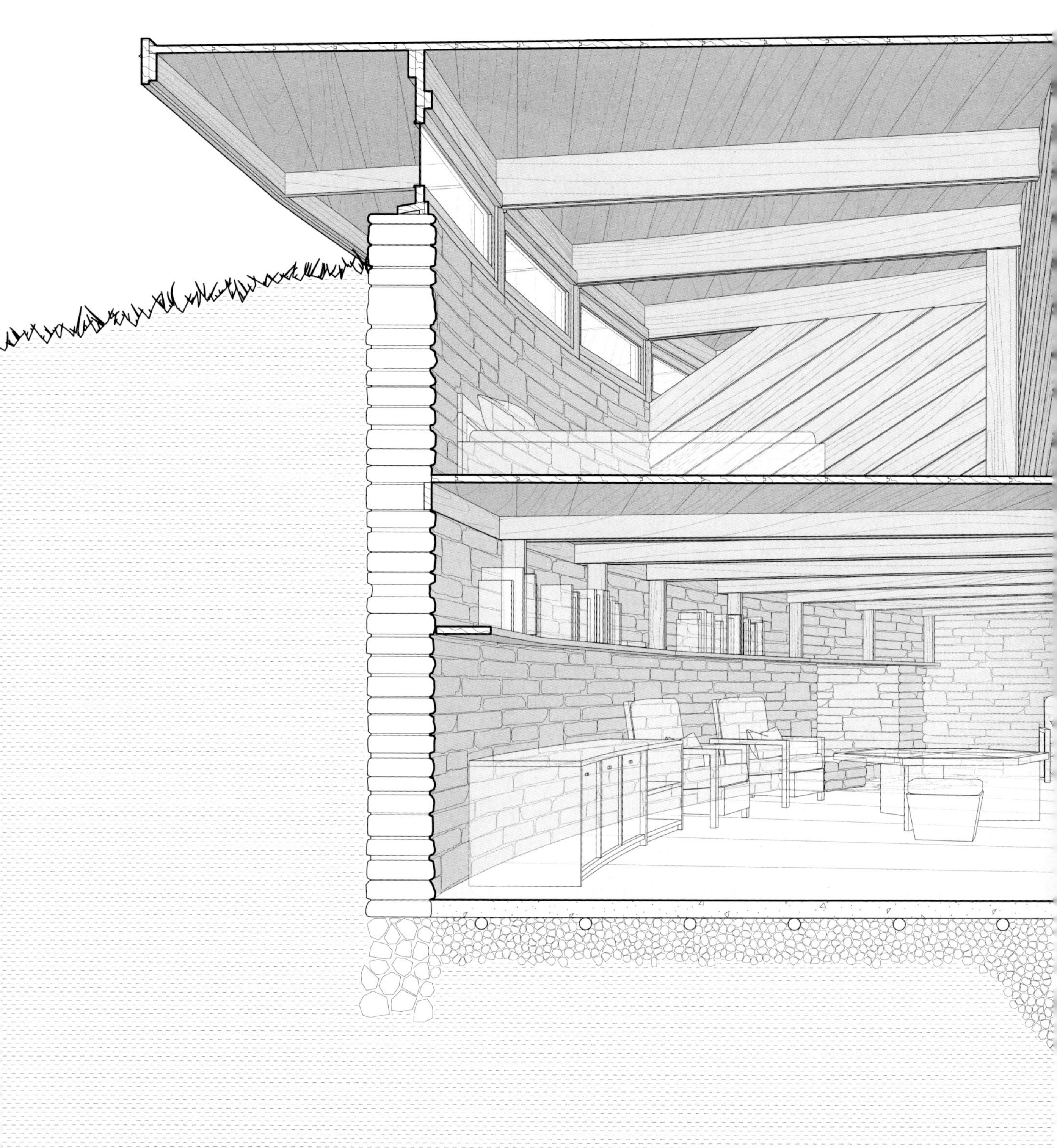

Jacobs House II

Layers of earth, stone, wood, and glass are organized to optimize thermal, spatial, and visual exchanges in this semicircular prairie-style house. The hemicycle of the plan is oriented to maximize the warming effects of winter sun via the extensive double-height glass wall, recycled from disused storefronts, and partly embraces a sunken garden. The deep overhang of the roof and bedroom mezzanine, suspended on steel rods from the wooden rafters, shields the interior from summer sun. To the north, a curving wall of stacked Wisconsin limestone, partially embedded within an enclosing earth berm, provides a protective barrier to winter winds, with the geometry of the mound shielding the open side of the house from rain and snow. The stone wall provides enclosure, structural stability, and thermal mass while acting as the architectural backdrop for the interior activity and incorporating functional elements into its irregular, tactile surface. Clerestory windows at the top of the wall provide illumination to the mezzanine bedrooms, while self-structuring planes of diagonal pine boards provide privacy from the balcony circulation. A small circular pond and plunge pool, thermally broken at the window wall, provides visual continuity between the interior space and the garden beyond, reflecting the house's balance of transparency and enclosure.

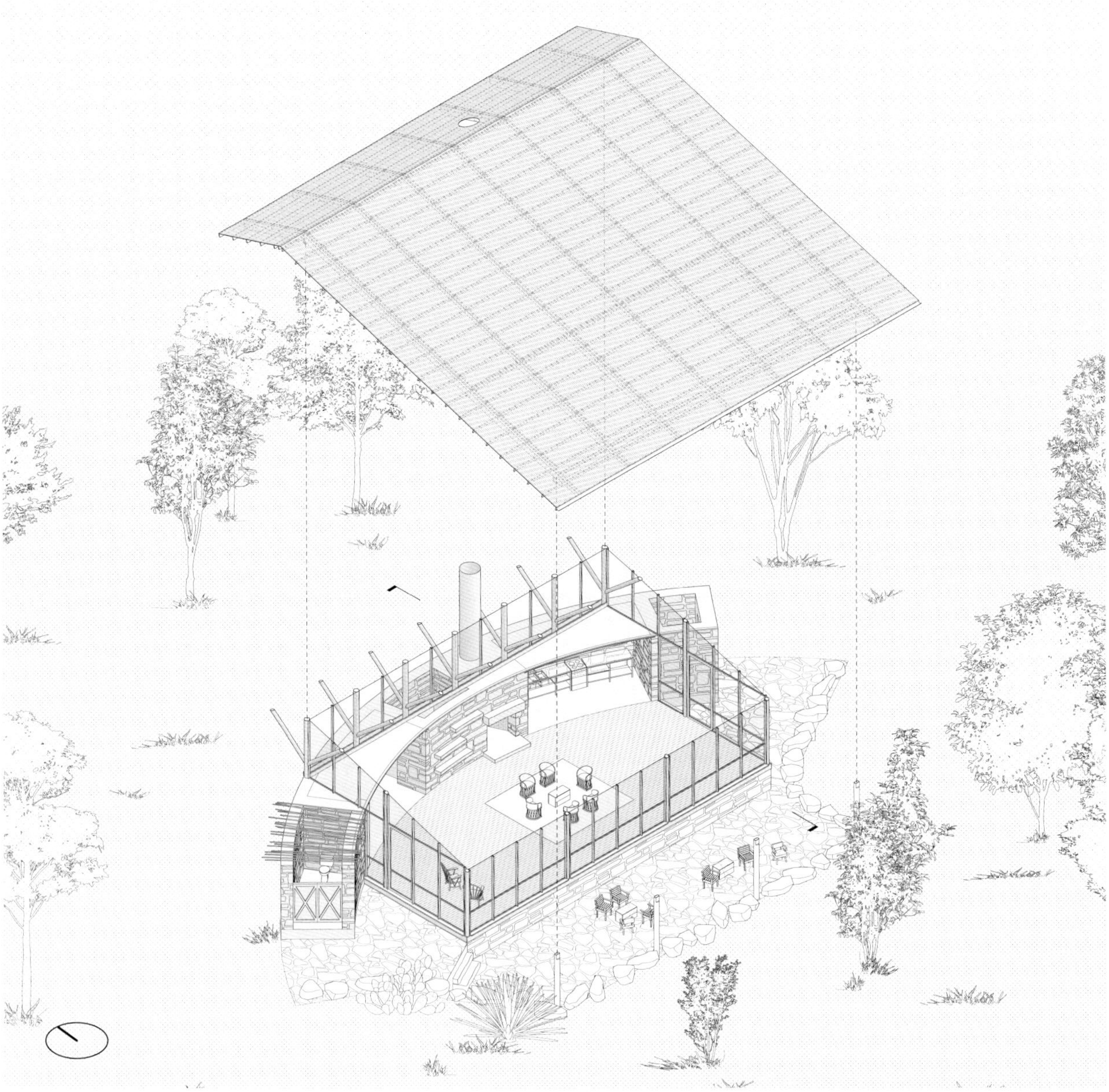

Hill Country Jacal | Lake|Flato Architects

This modest, off-the-grid retreat in rural Texas combines a thickened limestone wall with a simple, cedar pole structure supporting a sloping roof. Oriented to take advantage of the site's microclimate, the screened enclosure of the main living space opens to summer breezes while the curving stone wall shelters the interior from winter winds. The stone wall is doubled and thickened to contain a composting toilet, hearth, kitchen, and exterior shower and integrates operable flaps that facilitate cross ventilation. The main living area and exterior porch terrace exist below the timber

Pipe Creek, Texas | 1997

shed roof that parallels the incline of the surrounding terrain. Deploying minimal enclosure and intentionally reductive construction based on the primal materials of wood and stone, this dwelling distills the fundamental requirements of shelter into a rustic but paradoxically elegant mix.

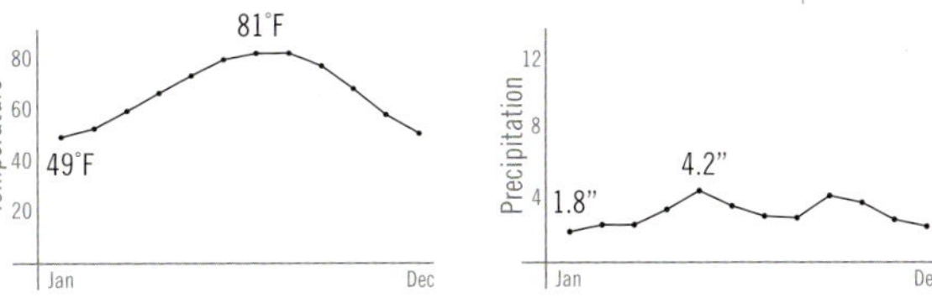

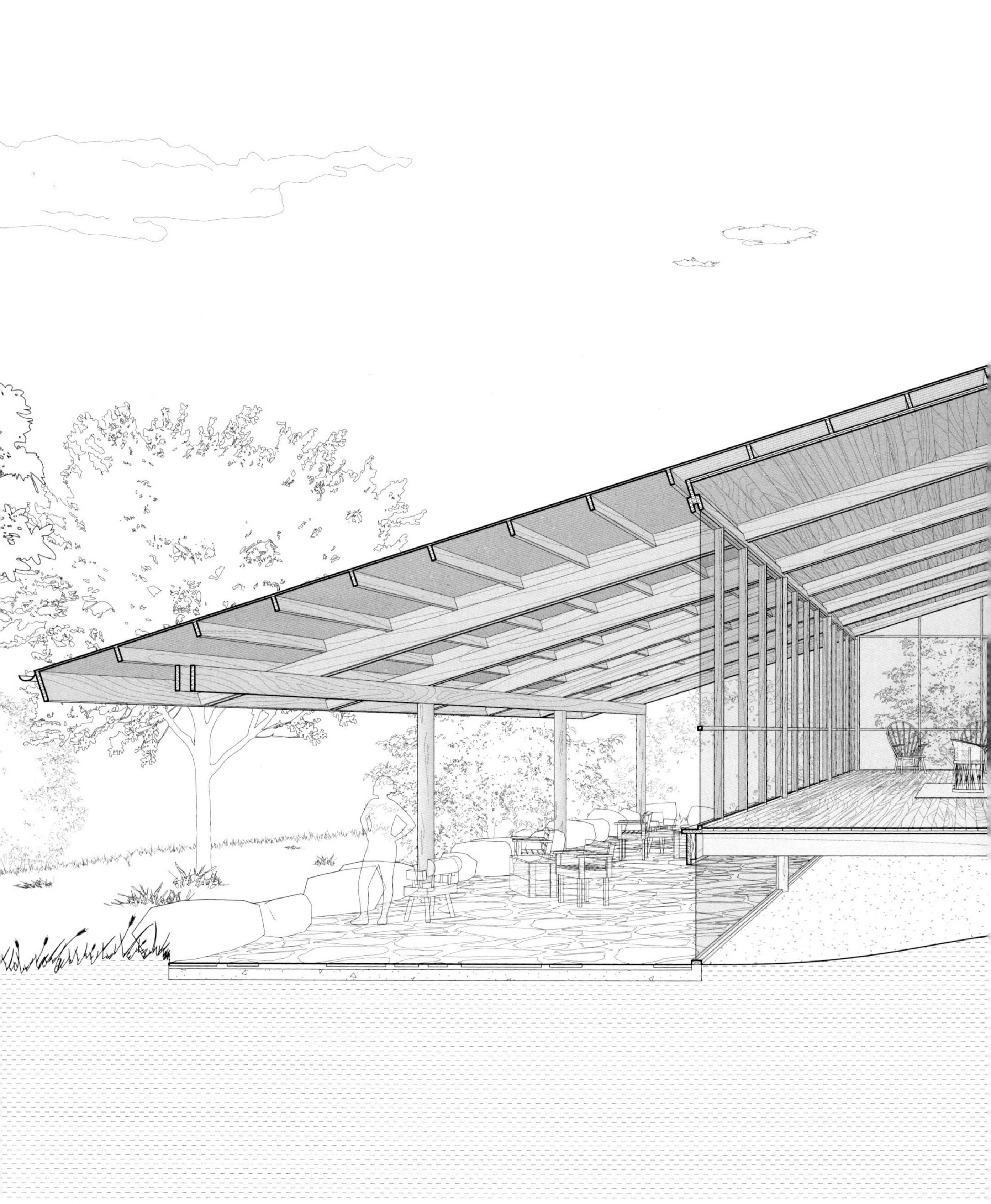

Hill Country Jacal

A sloping timber roof shelters a semi-enclosed living space and exterior porch that terrace down a gently inclined site above a creek. Open on the downhill side to take advantage of cooling breezes, the jacal or lean-to is shielded from prevailing winter winds by a semicircular stone mass on the uphill side. Carved away to accommodate a kitchen, hearth, and sleeping alcove (as well as bathing and toilet facilities), the thickened wall is constructed of irregular, rough-hewn limestone blocks. Shelving and the fireplace mantle are articulated as projecting stone ledges, while small,

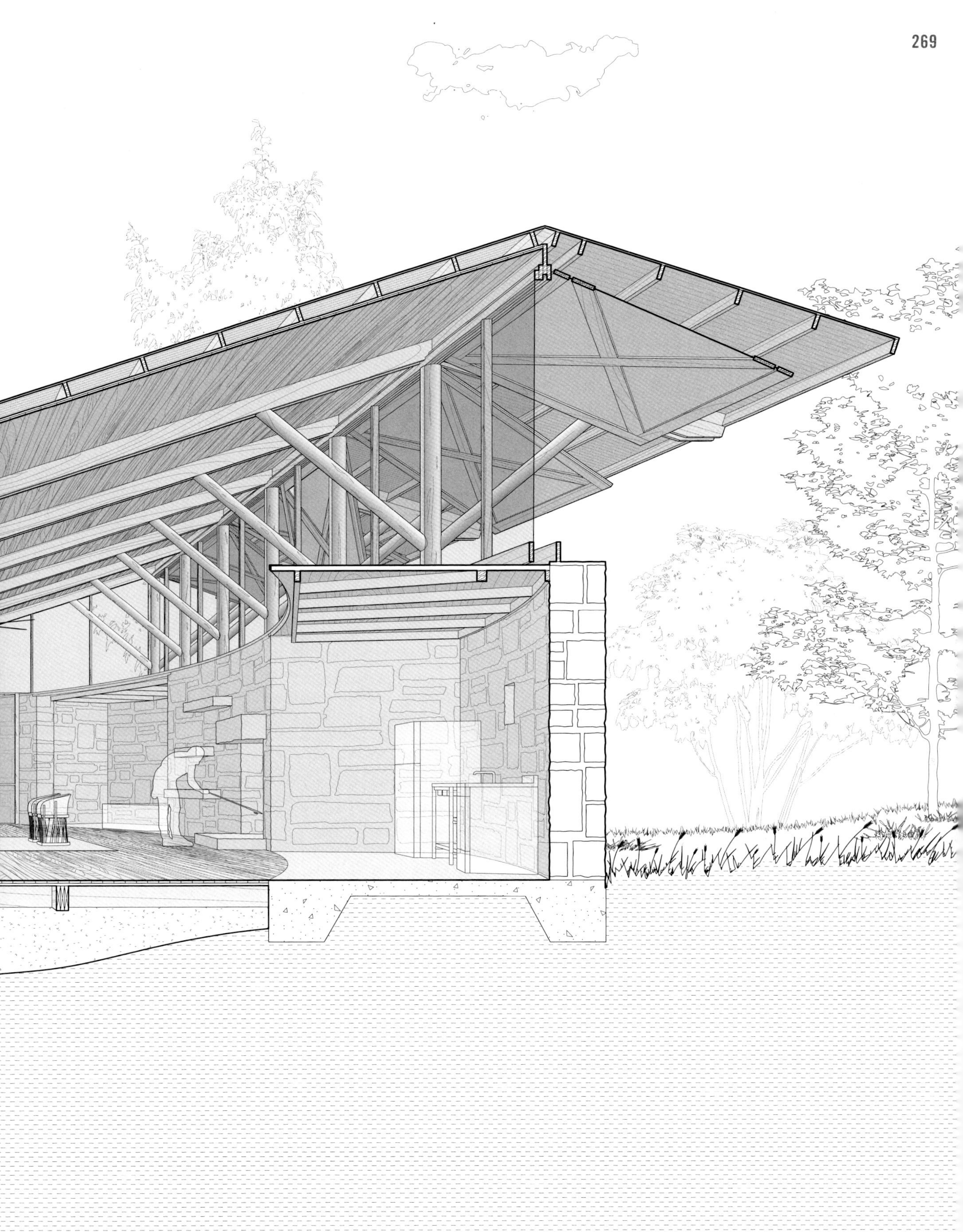

square windows allow for limited views. Operable panels at the clerestory can be opened to promote ventilation or closed in harsher weather. The timber-framed, corrugated metal roof is clad by wood boarding over the main living areas and supported on three parallel rows of cedar trunks, left in their raw, unprocessed state. A simple wood-framed screen provides the only enclosure. This minimal rural retreat, with its simplified lean-to logic, creates a reduced but refined dialogue between the tectonics of a lightweight wood roof and a massive stone wall.

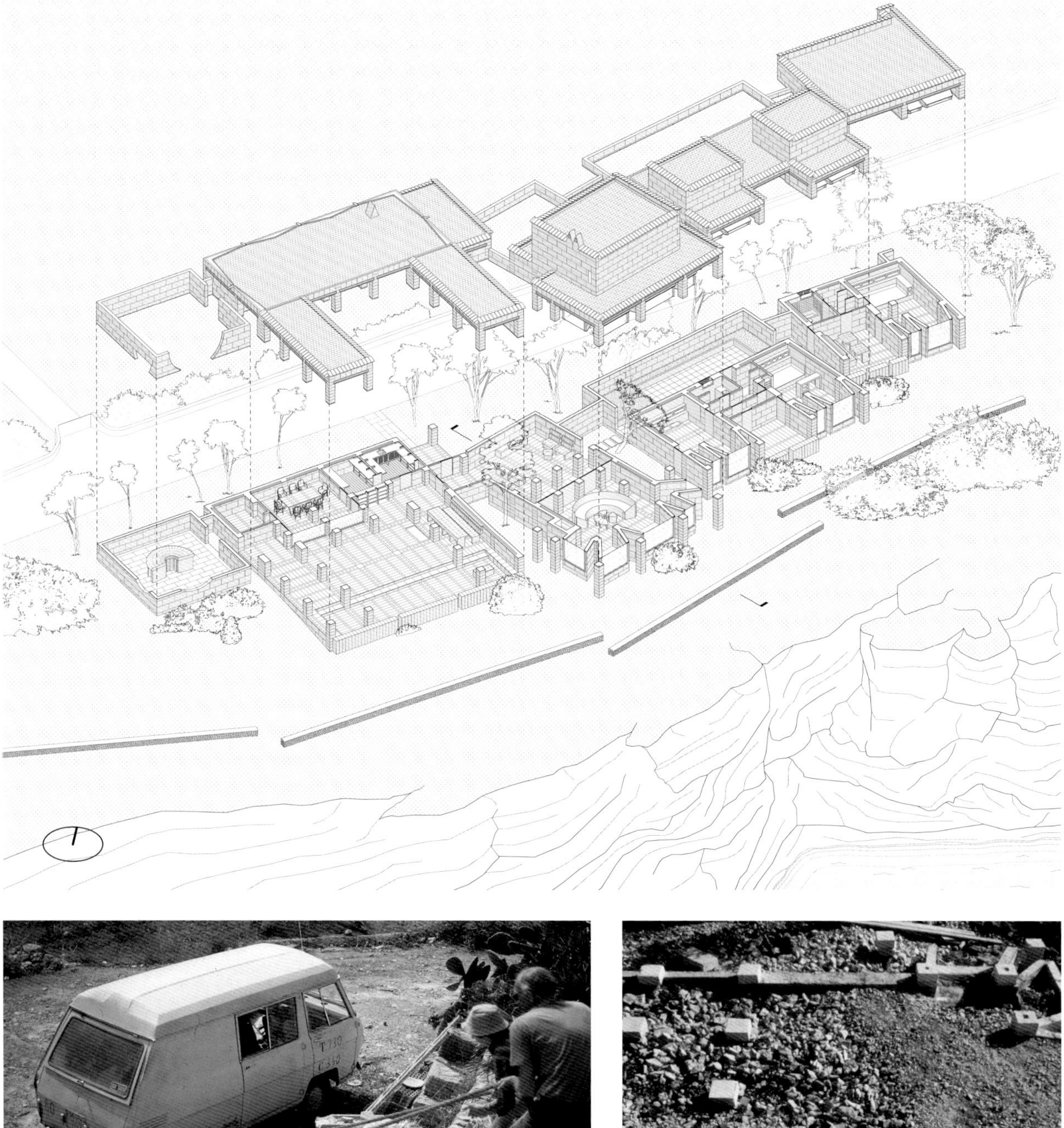

Can Lis | Jørn Utzon

This island house was built by Utzon as a family retreat. Lodged between an undistinguished street and a dramatic seaside cliff, the house is composed of five linked pavilions, each defined by a single program and constructed of indigenous sandstone. Refined by the architect and local craftsmen in situ, each pavilion is uniquely proportioned and oriented relative to the idiosyncrasies of the site and view. The kitchen/dining building forms a large courtyard oriented to the sea while the bedroom and living room buildings integrate deep, niche-like windows that contribute to a sense of both cave-like interiority and visual extension. The pavilions are linked by an irregular wall, which presents a mute façade to the street,

Portopetro, Mallorca, Spain | 1971

while exterior spaces and forecourts allow for circulation. Despite the individuation of the pavilions, a consistent tectonic logic of local stone and traditional construction techniques is deployed throughout, creating a sense of organic integration between the spectacular site and the highly calibrated interior spaces of the house.

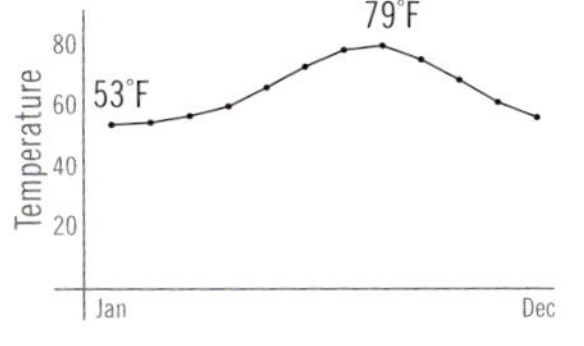

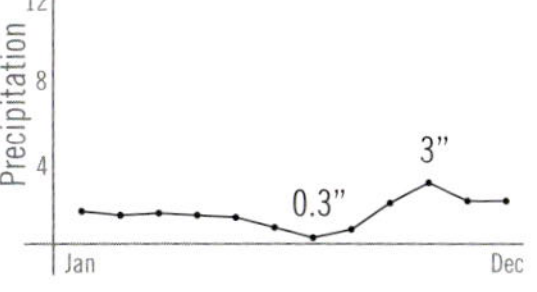

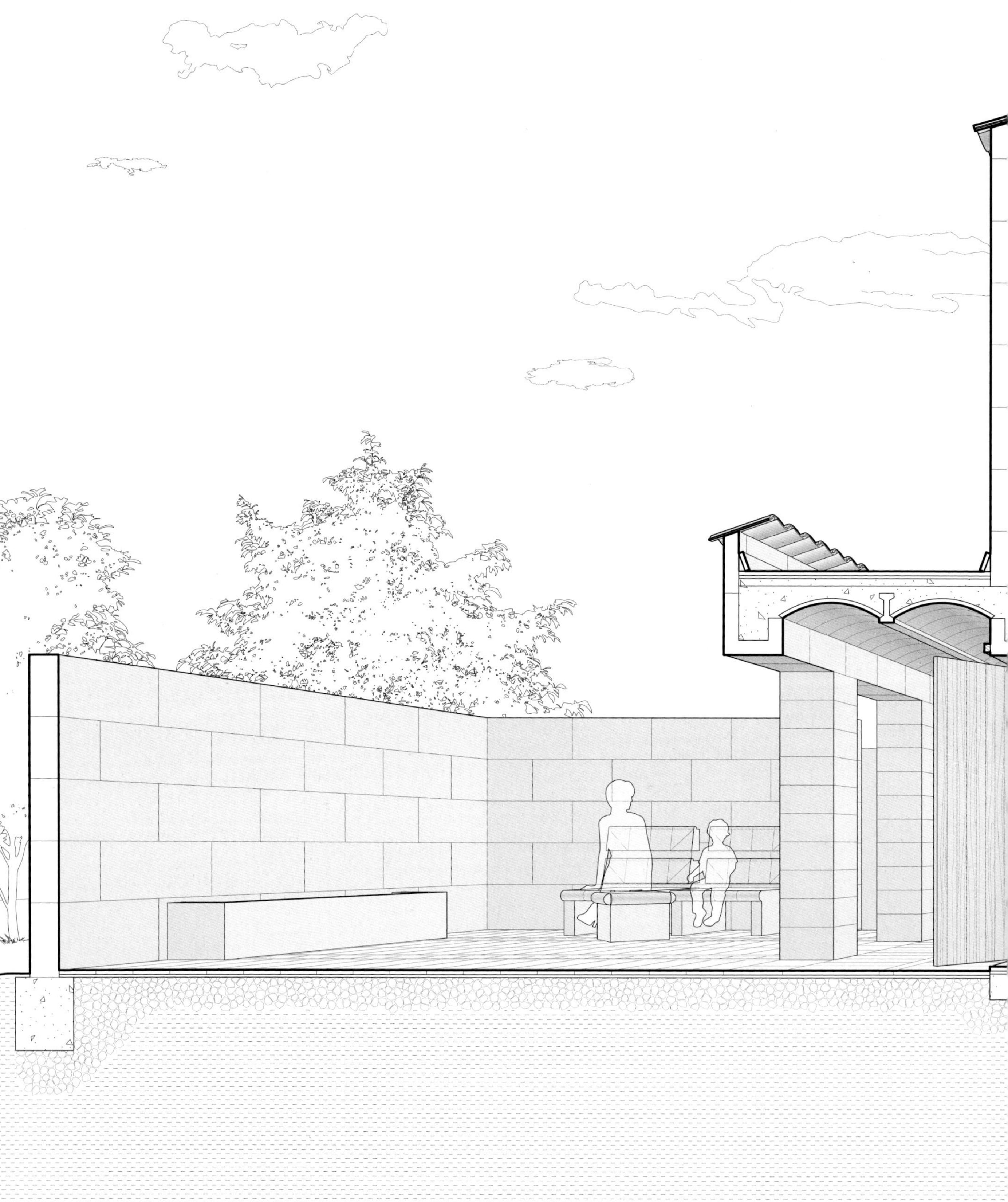

Can Lis

Entered via a forecourt through an intervening loggia, the living room of this seaside house is centered around a built-in seating crescent rotated due south. The tallest of the houses' volumes, its verticality is amplified by a single full-height column while five finger-like extensions radiate outwards from below the surrounding loggia to the horizon. These extruded windows generate differently scaled niches, intimate extensions of the main space, creating the sense of a thickened perimeter while visually linking to views of the sea. Like the rest of the house, both living room and

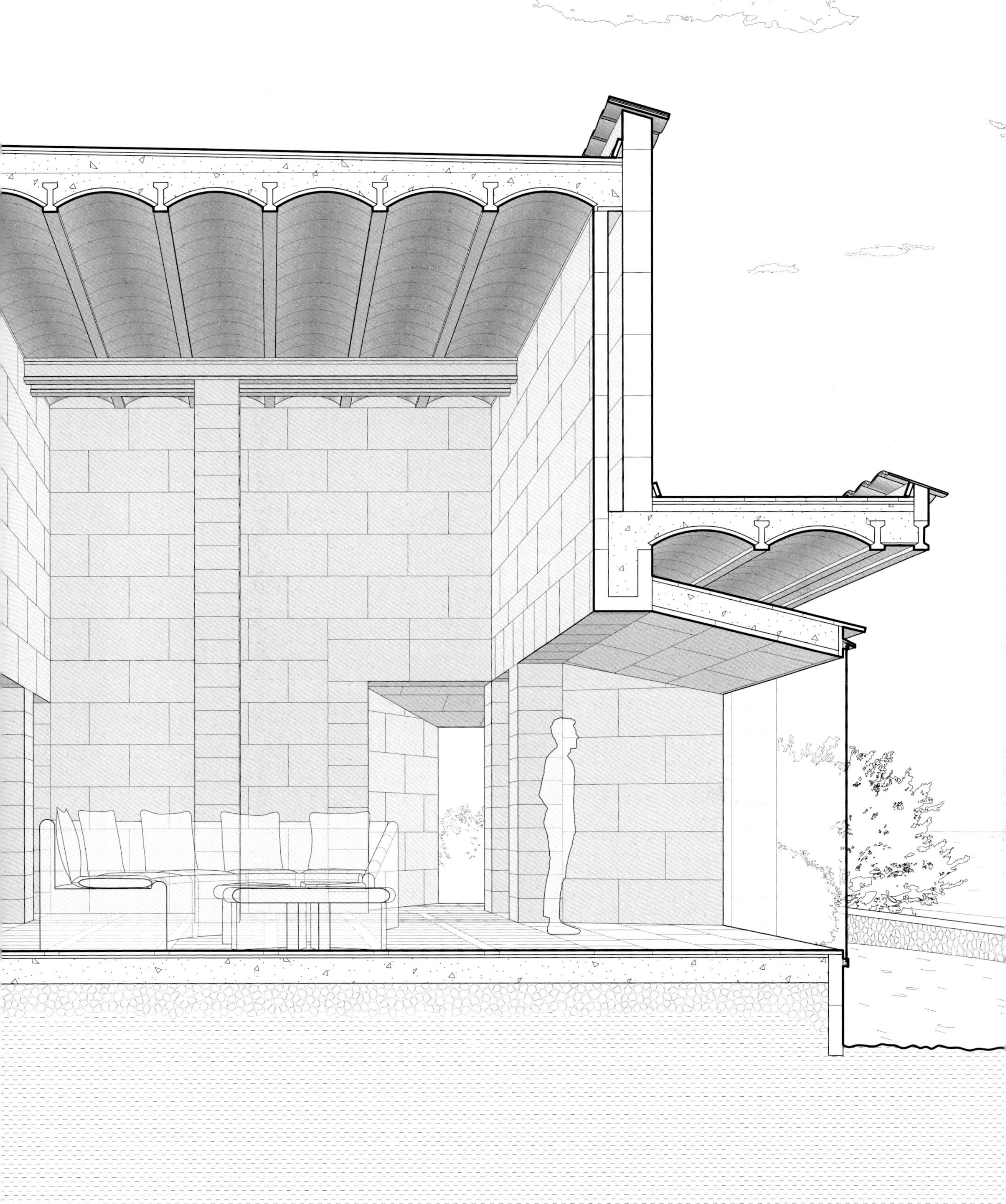

court are constructed of local, rough-sawn sandstone blocks, more porous Mares for the exterior bearing walls and columns, and denser Santanyi for the flooring and interior walls. The roofs employ a local system of vaulted tiles called *bovedillas* that span between precast concrete I-beams to produce the characteristic arched ceilings. The use of these local stone and earthen systems throughout creates a unity within the spatial diversity of this idiosyncratic seaside dwelling that weaves together inside and outside, interiority and extension.

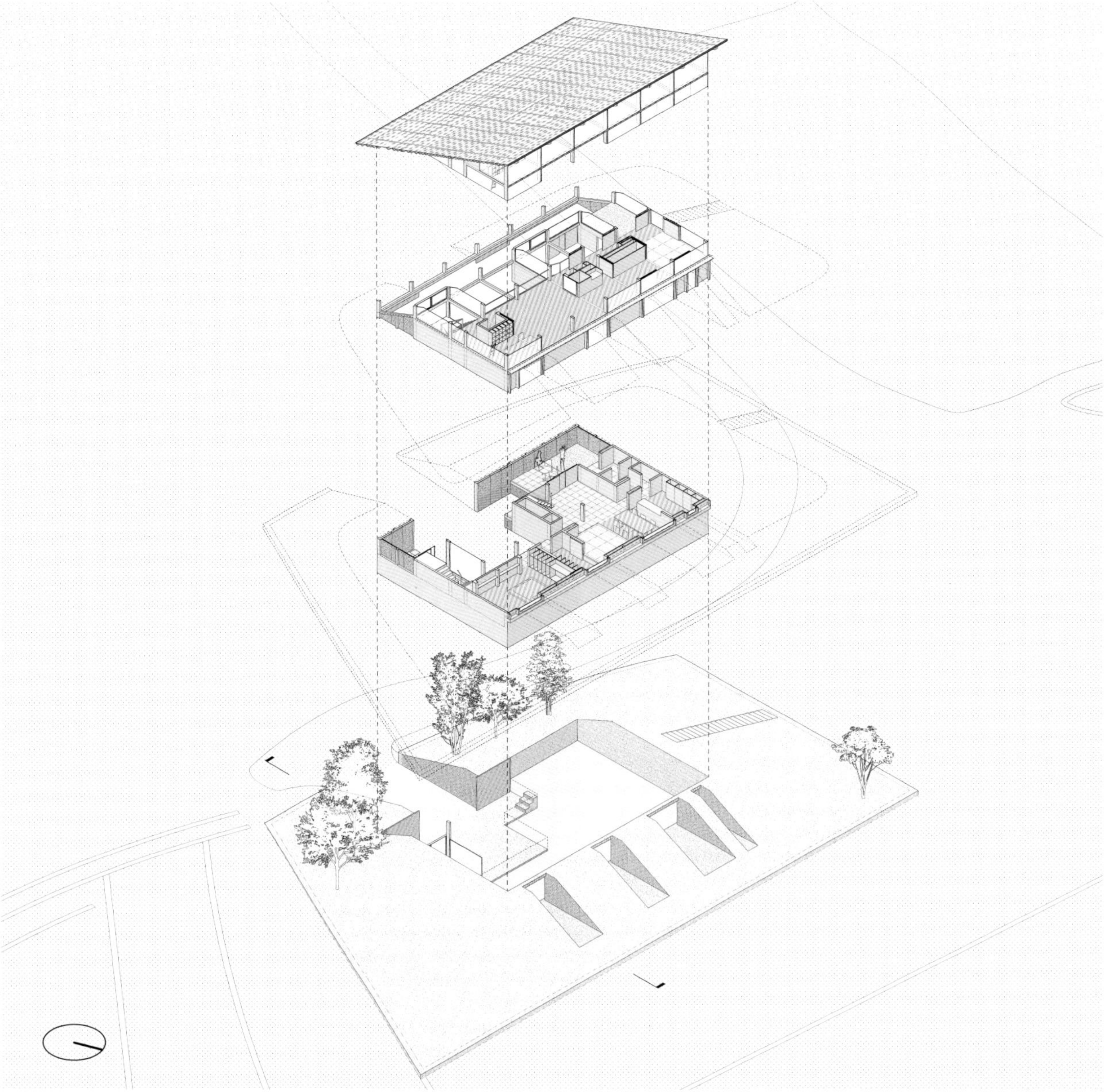

Stone House | Sambuichi Architects

Located in a region of climatic extremes, the house is designed to address both the heavy snows of the area's winters and the humid heat and rains of its summers. The primary environmental strategy was to embed a wooden house within a mound of stone. This protective mineral envelope acts as a thermal buffer; covered by snow in the winter it traps an insulating mass of tempered air. In the summer when rain and groundwater are plentiful it functions as evaporative cooling. The angled mound of local stones is echoed by the hovering wooden roof that opens to the southern sun. Nested

Shimane, Japan | 2005

within the stone, the house is articulated as a wooden frame, strategically pulled away from the gabion walls to create an internal terrace. While the owners occupy the ground floor, the more exposed upper level functions as a sectionally distinct guest house.

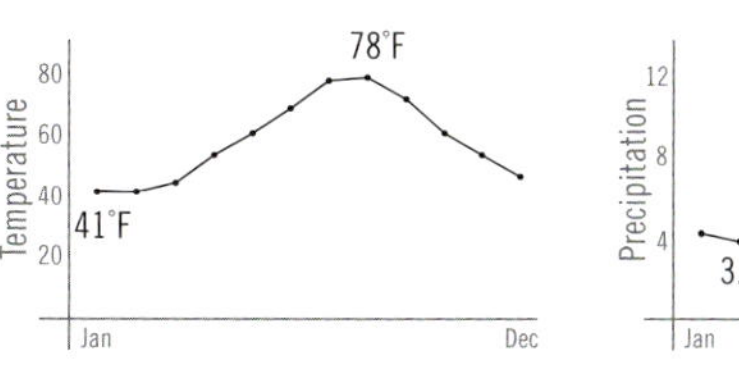

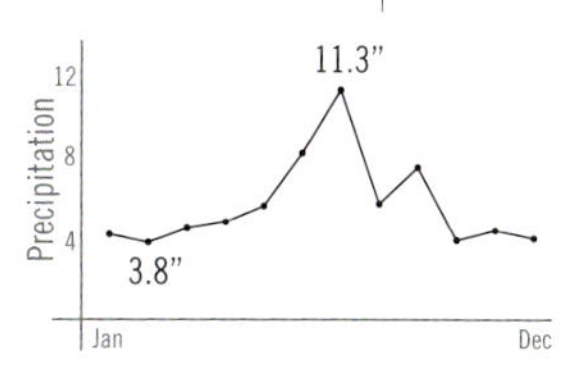

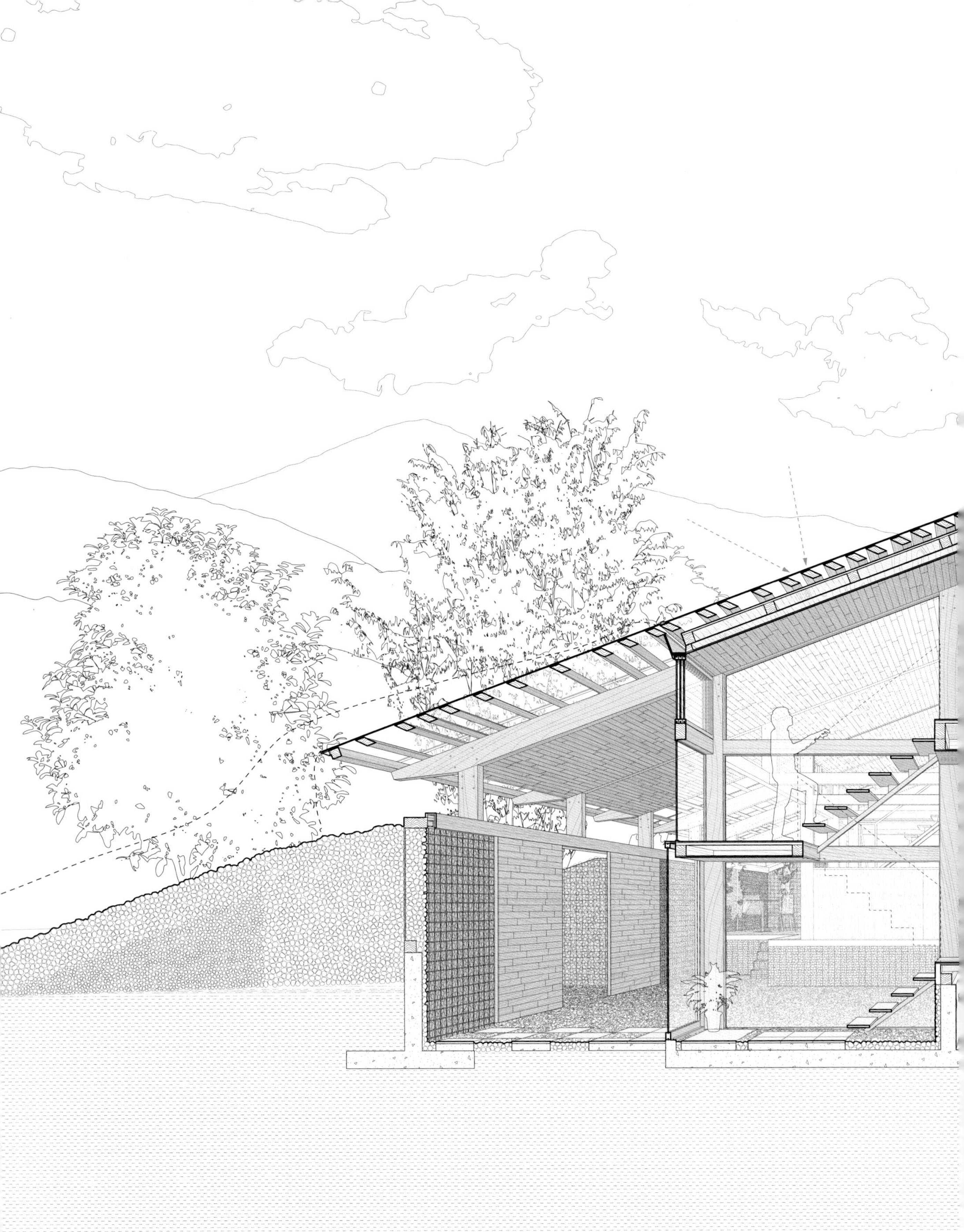

Stone House

A timber-frame house is sheltered within a mound of local stone. Composed of several scales of graded rock, collected from a nearby river and arranged in layers to optimize insulating and evaporative effects, the pyramidal stone berm is held in place by perimeter grade beams and strategically cut away by gabion walls to accommodate windows and access for circulation. While the stone mound visually ties the house to the site and creates a sense of interior privacy, its principal role is as a climatic filter. In the harsh winters of the region, the stones are covered by a deep layer of snow, creating a region of thermally insulating air, an effect the architect likens to that of an igloo. In the humid summer, the

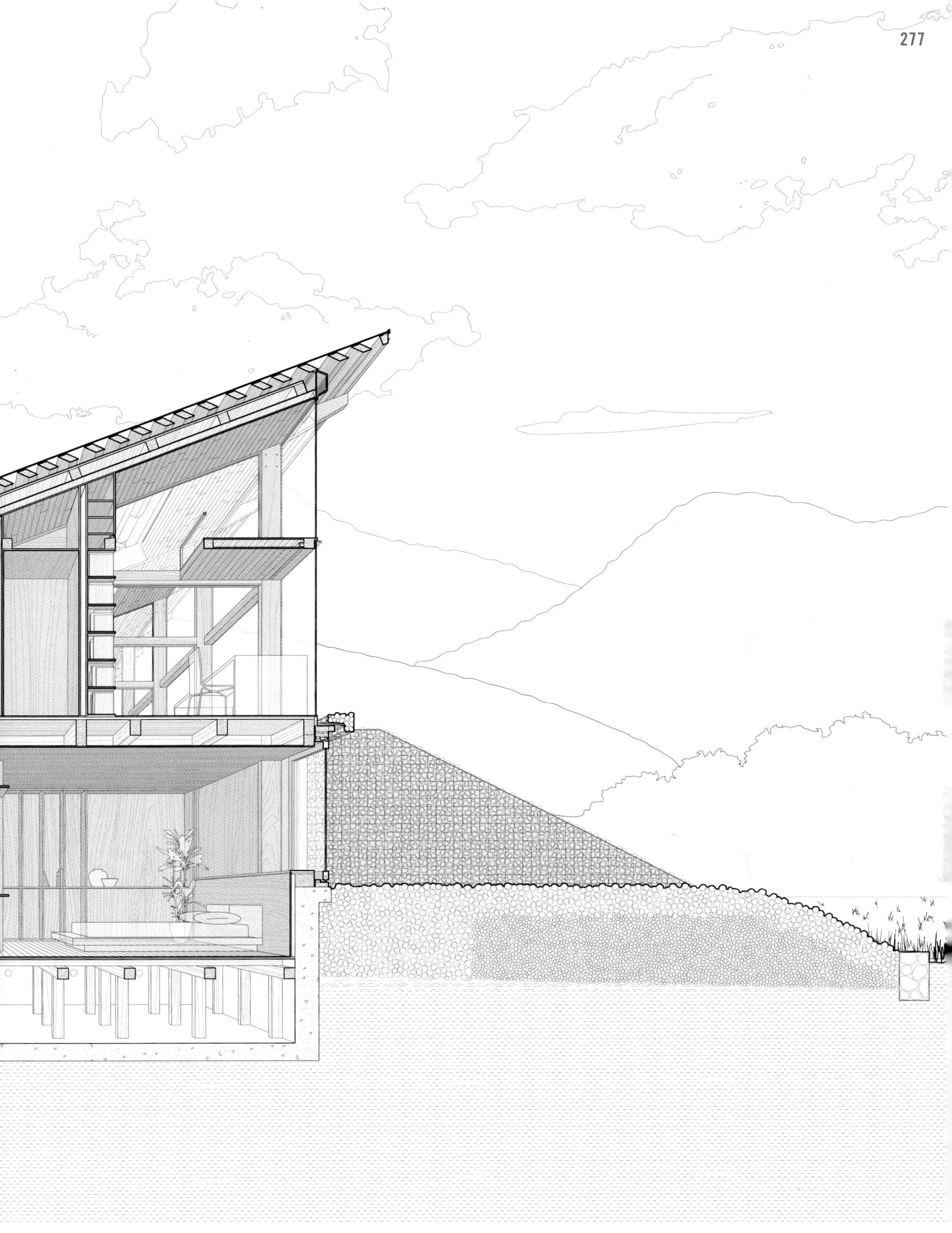

stones perform as a thermal mass and generate cooling effects as rain filters downward and evaporates upwards. The house within the piled stones is a timber frame supporting a large sloping glass and wood roof that echoes the angle of repose of the surrounding stone. Oriented south to optimize daylighting, the roof incorporates trapezoidal wooden slats that produce shading in the summer and allow sun to enter in the winter. Along the northern side a large exterior terrace acts as an entry zone and semi-enclosed patio as well as facilitating cross ventilation via sliding gates and glazing panels.

REUSE

800

600

400

Brick

200

Stone

Reuse

Earth

0 $kgCO_2e/m^3$ 0

Cork
Hemp
Straw

-200

-400

Bamboo

Mass Timber -600
Wood Frame

-800

REUSE

ADDING

RENOVATING

Renovating involves modifying interior partitions, finishes, and services as needed for a new use. The more flexibility a building has in plan and section, the more possibilities there will be for a future retrofit. Limited interior load-bearing elements, generous floor-to-floor heights for accommodating updated technical systems, and a robust shell facilitate greater adaptability over time.

WRAPPING

Wrapping involves either replacing or adding an additional layer to the existing façade. New layers can protect aging materials, improve thermal performance, or respond to changes in building function without the waste produced by demolition. Façades designed to be modular and detachable allow for the most flexibility for future change.

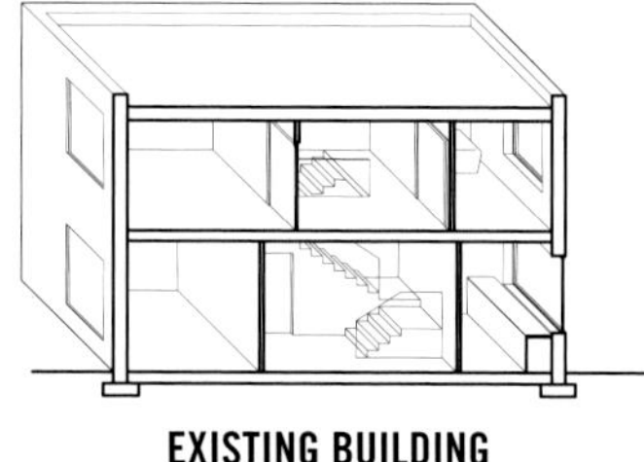

EXISTING BUILDING

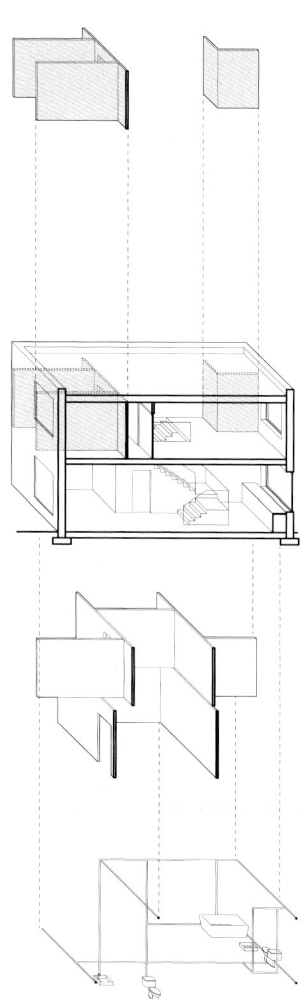

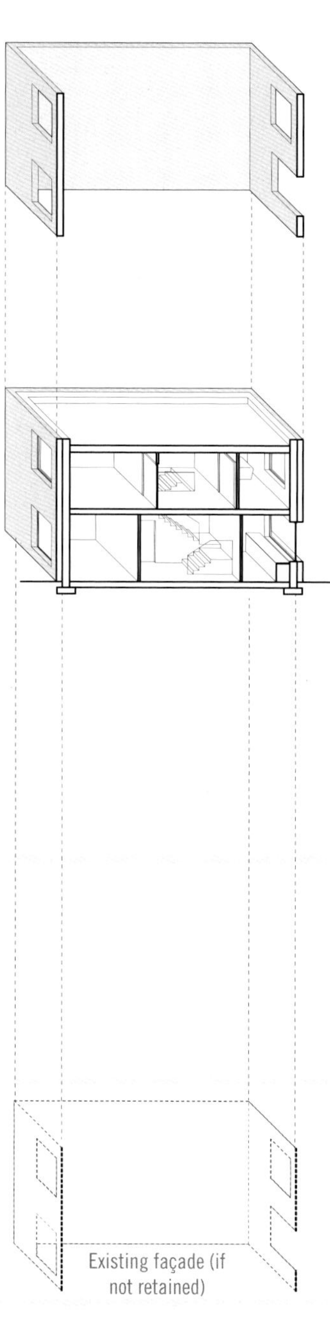

ADDING

Constructing an addition to the volume of the existing building accommodates increased spatial needs or new functions. This typically requires some modification of the original architecture, ideally optimizing existing structural capacities and material systems.

INSERTING

This is a version of renovation that involves gutting the building for the insertion of a new, semi-autonomous building within a building. This approach retains the exterior shell only, sometimes for contextual or aesthetic reasons, and creates a layering of spatial environments with thermally performative or programmatic imperatives.

RECOVERING

If the building cannot be repurposed, recovery of building materials for reuse, recycling, or downcycling becomes the priority. Reuse of materials on site with minimal processing is preferable as it avoids the use of fossil fuels for transportation, processing, or disposal. Ease of material recovery is tied to questions of disassembly: mechanically joined assemblies facilitate recovery more readily than bonding, and mono-material constructions are more easily repurposed than multi-component layered systems which impede separation and processing.

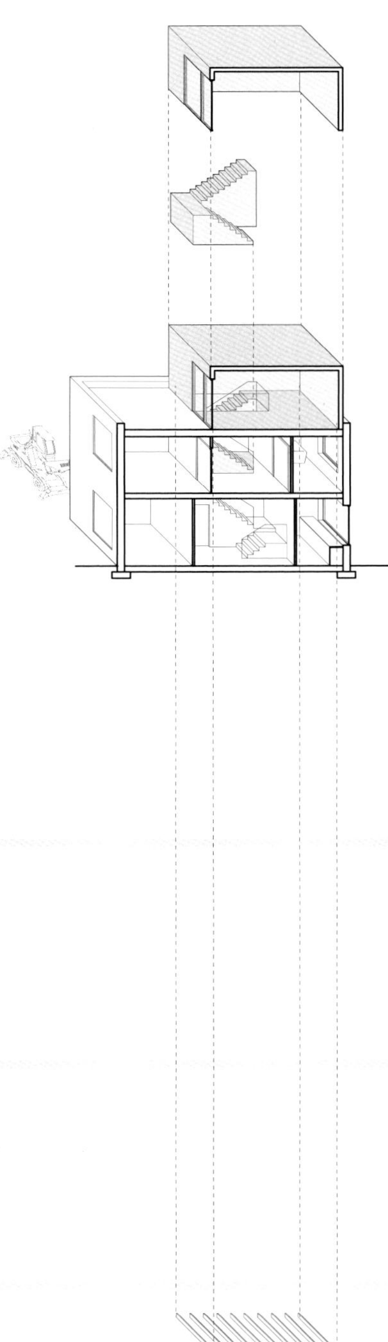

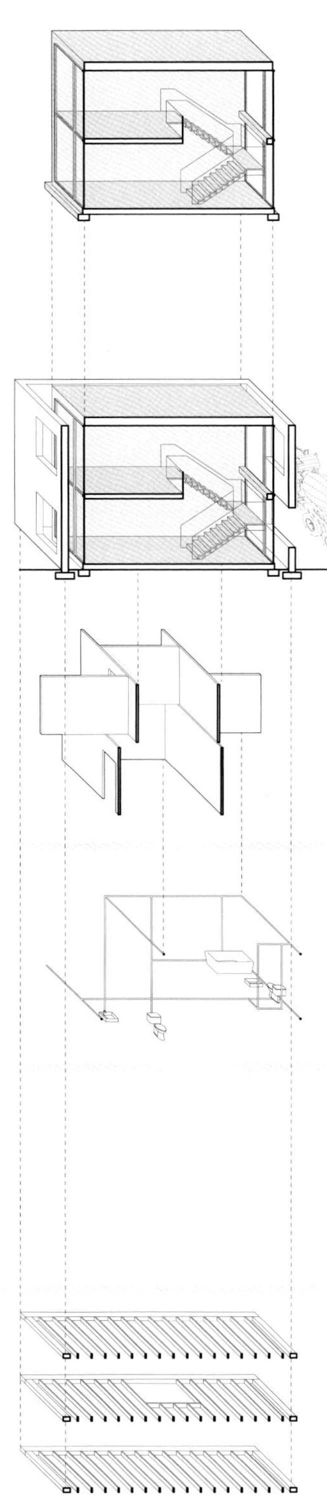

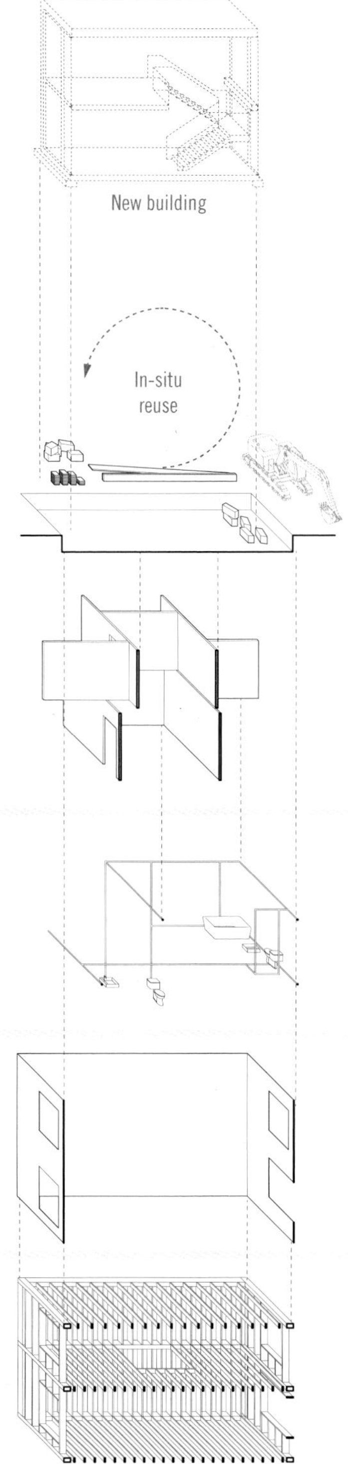

REUSE

MATERIALS - BIOTIC LOOP

Biotic materials are environmentally preferable based on their ability to sequester carbon during the lifespan of the building and their regenerative capacity. As natural products they are intrinsically biodegradable and can feed back into growth cycles as nutrients for soil. However, chemical additives, use of adhesives or metal fasteners, and binding to other materials impede humification.

REUSE

Biotic materials may not be strong enough to withstand damage during the disassembly process. Other barriers to reuse are a lack of standardization of the components and the time and cost necessary to dismantle the materials.

BIOTIC

CORK

Includes expanded cork insulation and cork façade panels. The process of expanding cork uses heat to bind cork granules together rather than using an adhesive, which makes it compostable and recyclable.

BAMBOO

Whole bamboo culms and bamboo wattle are minimally processed, making them more readily reuseable and biodegradable, while products such as bamboo plywood and flooring may contain adhesives.

STRAW

Straw is an agricultural waste product typically formed into bales or framed into prefabricated panels. Its direct reuse is limited by the natural degradation of the material, but bales can safely decompose at end of life if free of added chemicals or finishes and panels can be designed to be disassembled for composting.

HEMP

Hemp itself is compostable. However, hemp-lime uses lime as a binder and should be reused if possible. Hemp in this form may also be incinerated for energy.

LUMBER

Dimensional lumber can be repurposed, downcycled into other wood-based products, or composted at the end of its lifespan if it has not been treated with chemicals and preservatives.

MASS TIMBER

Mass timber can be reused, downcycled, or composted. However, monolithic mass timber assemblies such as dowel-laminated timber are easier to recycle and compost than products that use adhesives or mechanical fasteners.

WOOD COMPOSITE

Wood composite materials such as MDF and particle board are made from downcycled wood fibers. However, they contain adhesives that make them unable to be composted or recycled.

PLYWOOD

Plywood is formed by glue laminating thin wood veneers with perpendicular grain orientations into a sheet good. Plywood is relatively durable and can be reused. However, the use of binders and other additives makes composting problematic.

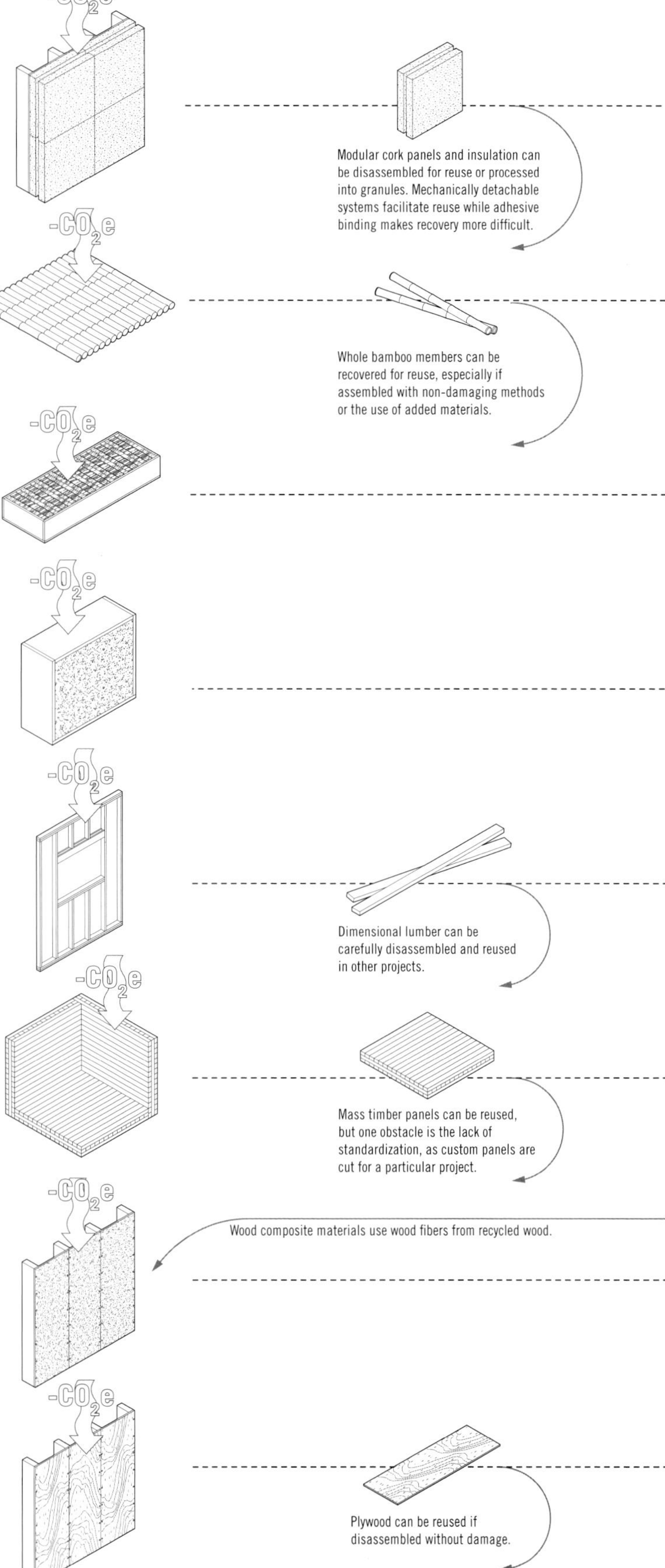

RECYCLING

Recycling involves the breaking down of a material in order to remake it into a new product of equal quality. Biotic materials like hemp-lime and cork can be recycled for use in new versions of similar or identical products depending on additives and adhesives.

DOWNCYCLING

Downcycling is when a product is made into a different product of lower quality. This is an established process in the manufacturing of wood composite products.

END OF LIFE

In a biotic loop, the preferred end-of-life scenario is incineration for the generation of energy or composting. In the case of composting, the material provides nutrients that feed back into the biotic life cycle, while in its use as biofuel it can offset more carbon consumptive fuels and processes.

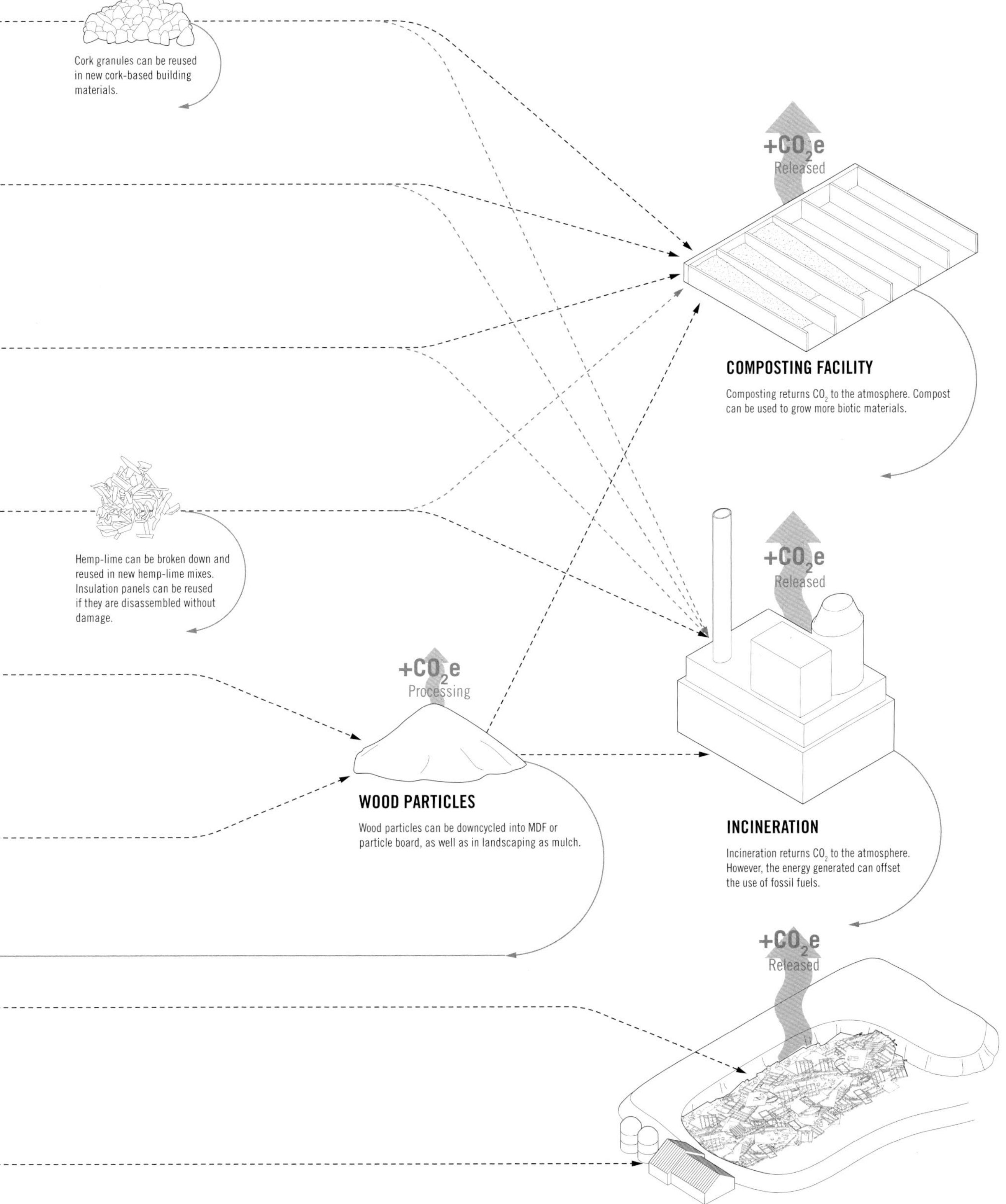

REUSE

MATERIALS - TECHNOLOGICAL LOOP

Metallic and mineral materials are all finite, non-renewable materials and therefore do not participate in organic growth cycles. However, their varying methods of extraction and processing impact the approach to reuse. Due to their energy intensive production and recyclability, metals and glass should be captured in closed loop systems. Earth, stone, and, to a lesser extent, brick are relatively plentiful resources with less intensive carbon investment upfront and can be allowed to humify without significant environmental harm.

REUSE

Reuse is preferable because it requires little processing. Barriers are a lack of standardization of the components, cost, and time to properly dismantle and separate materials at the end of a building's life, and ensuring the performance of the material in its new use.

MINERAL

EARTH

This includes rammed earth construction and earth blocks. The earth is usually taken from the project's immediate site and can be returned to the earth or used elsewhere if cementitious binders are not present.

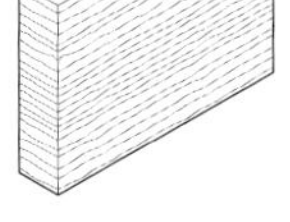

STONE

Stone can be reused as large pieces if disassembly without breakage is possible, making mechanical fastening systems preferable to mortar. Otherwise it is downcycled as aggregate.

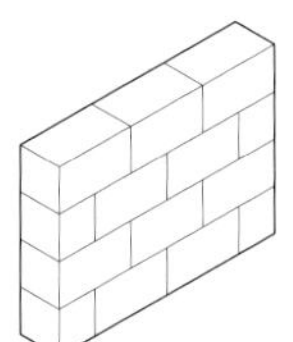

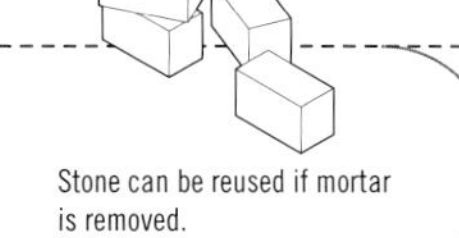

Stone can be reused if mortar is removed.

BRICK

Brick reclamation is labor-intensive. Mortar may be chiseled or saw cut to separate a brick. Brick may best be reused through direct sourcing for projects but general purpose recycling may be difficult, which results in most bricks being downcycled into aggregate.

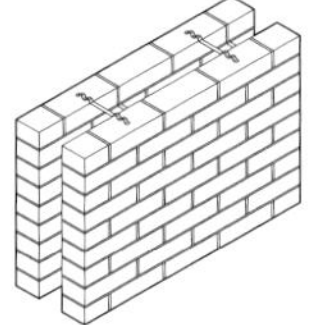

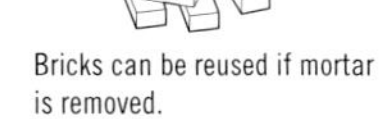

Bricks can be reused if mortar is removed.

CONCRETE

Concrete requires carbon-intensive processing for its initial production and is difficult to reclaim. Despite its ubiquity in building construction the majority of concrete ends up in landfills. Concrete may be downcycled into aggregate for reuse.

Crushed brick can be used as aggregate in new concrete mixes.

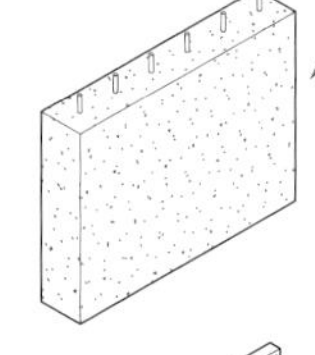

GLASS

Glass can be infinitely recycled if properly sorted. However, glass is generally downcycled into products of lesser quality. While it would seem plentiful, sand, a primary component in the manufacture of glass is fast becoming an extremely rare resource without viable substitutes, making the recycling of glass increasingly critical.

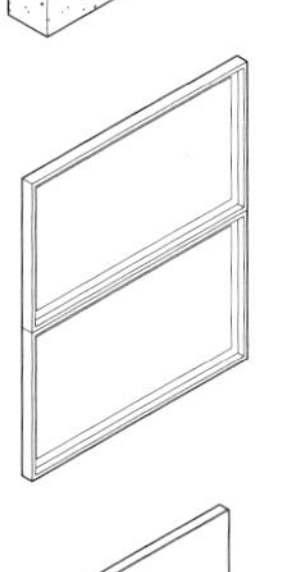

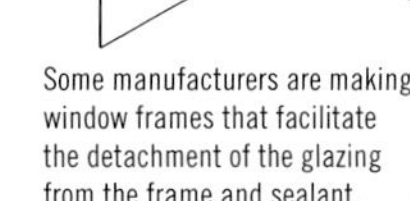

Some manufacturers are making window frames that facilitate the detachment of the glazing from the frame and sealant.

GYPSUM BOARD

Most gypsum board currently goes into landfills but there is the potential to reuse gypsum in the production of new gypsum board if properly separated during disassembly.

METALLIC

STEEL STRUCTURE

Though its initial manufacture is energy and carbon intensive, steel can be recycled or even upcycled into stainless or weathering steel when reprocessed. The recycling of steel requires 1/4 of the energy of making new steel.

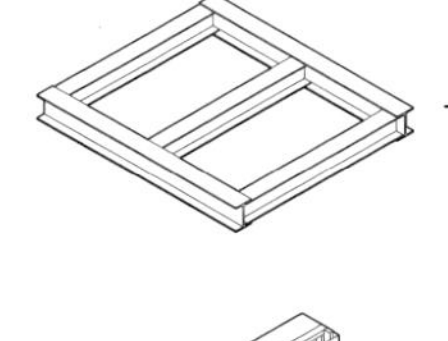

Detachable connections are common in steel frame construction. Structural members can be taken apart and reused.

METAL PLATES, EXTRUSIONS, AND CLADDING

This includes zinc, copper, aluminum, corten, stainless steel, and coated steel panels. These materials can be readily recycled, particularly if detailed for easy separation.

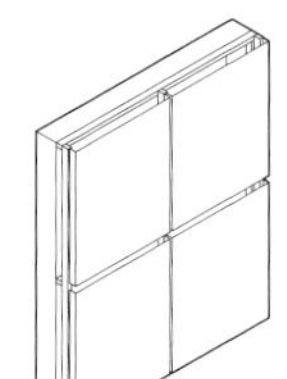

If attachments are designed for disassembly, panels can be taken apart and reused.

RECYCLING

Recycling of mineral or metallic products into new products of similar quality is preferable to their disposal in landfills, particularly for materials whose original manufacture is energetically consumptive. This approach captures anthropogenic materials in closed cycles. However, the processes that are needed in a technological loop still require energy, often from fossil fuels.

DOWNCYCLING

Like recycling, downcycling involves energy for processing and transport, with diminished return on value. Downcycling is often progressive with loss of quality leading to disposal over time.

END OF LIFE

In a technological loop, materials that aren't able to be recovered typically end up in a landfill, with little potential for energy generation. Some materials will humify or decay but at a slow rate.

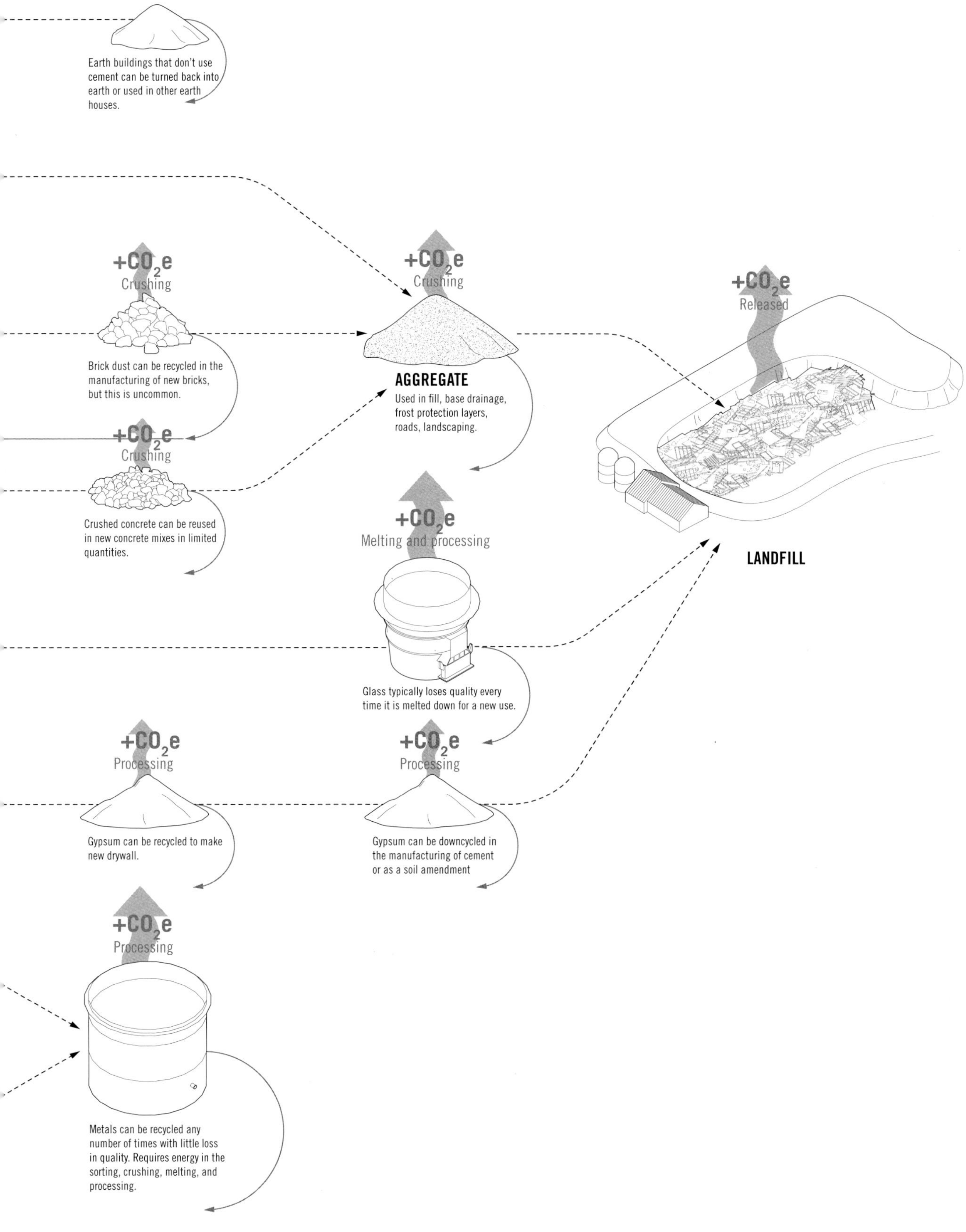

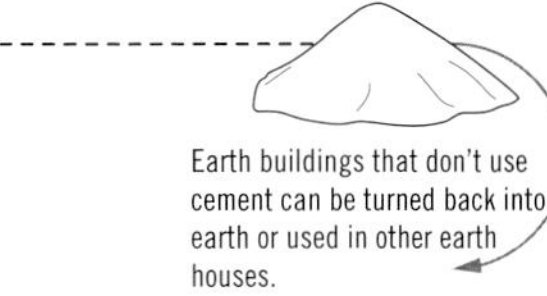

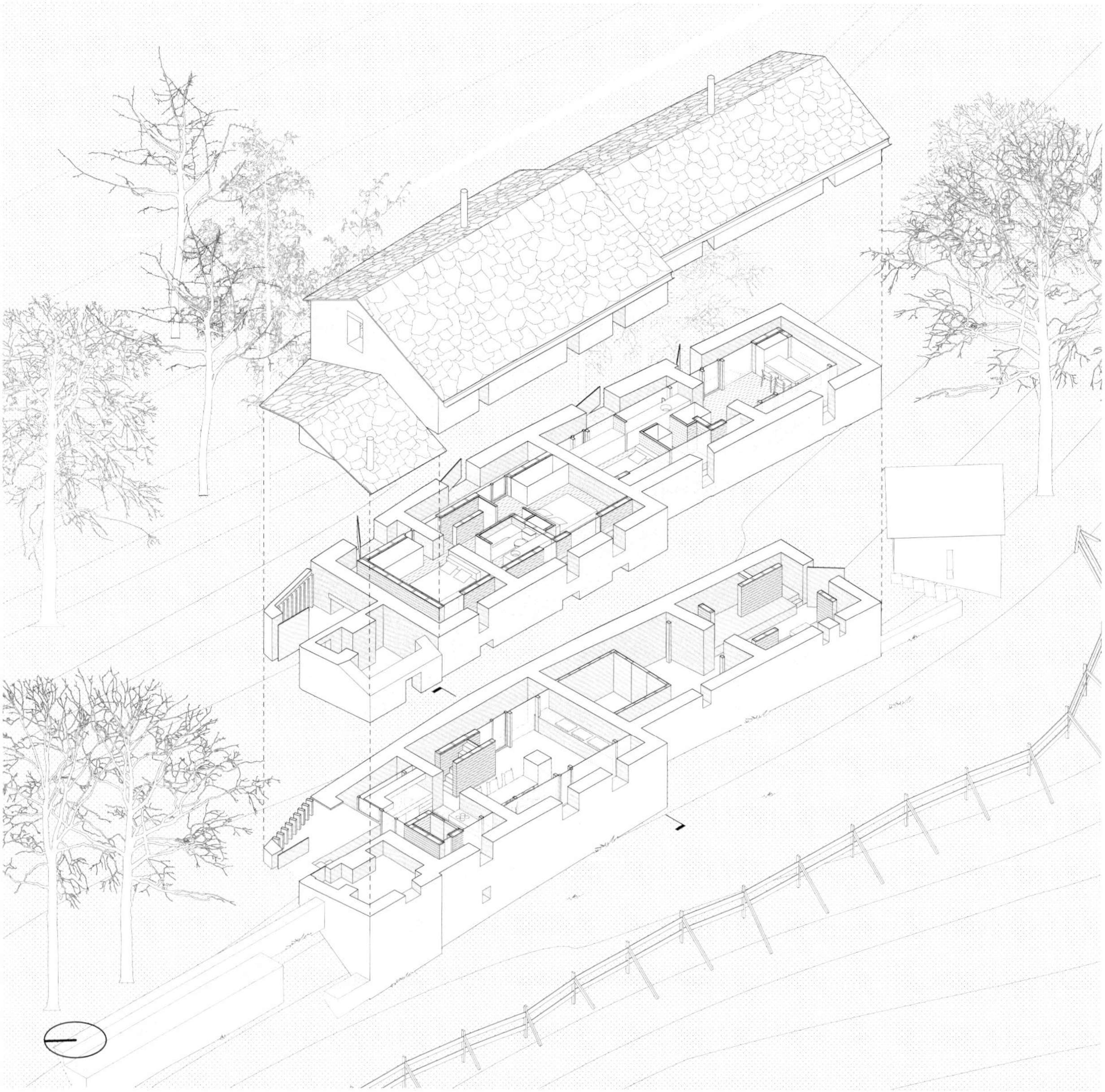

House Renovation in Scudellate | Wespi de Meuron Romeo Architects

Extant historic structures, often robust constructions of durable materials like stone, offer a rich resource and context for reuse. In this project, a contemporary timber construction nests within the outer shell of a surviving agricultural stable, built of local gneiss masonry. Due to preservation restrictions in Ticino, the architects were obligated to maintain the exterior appearance of the disused stable, repairing the walls and replacing the damaged roof. The roof replacement allowed for the insertion of a two-story unit for the owner and a single-story rental unit. These new internal forms

Scudellate, Switzerland | 2017

were made from prefabricated, insulated timber-framed boxes, sheathed in OSB and finished on site with wood boarding throughout. Treated as separate from the exterior stone walls, the new wood house remains a legible volume within its historic shell.

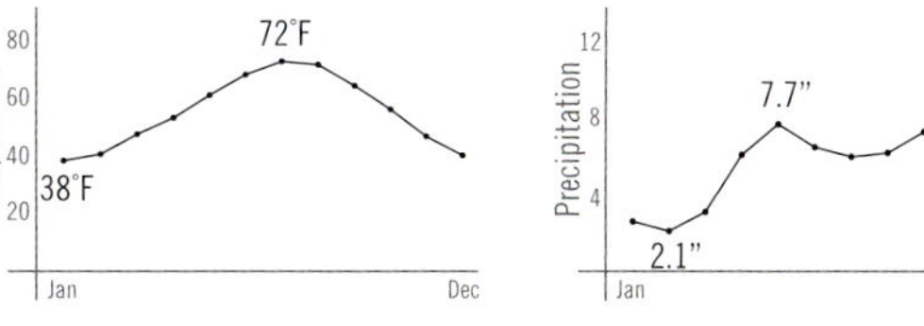

House Renovation in Scudellate

A house within a house, this project repurposes a historic agricultural building as the outer masonry shell for a newly inserted timber residence. The extant stone walls provide an outer layer of protection from snow and rain, a foothold in the sloping terrain, and establish continuity with the agricultural landscape of this protected area of the Ticino region. The inner timber-framed volume provides moisture protection and thermal insulation while enclosing wood-sheathed living spaces for two residential units, each partially bisected by perpendicular stone walls original to

the stables. This internal wood 'box' is treated as independent from the enclosing walls, maintaining an occupiable, double-height gap between the old and new structure. This interstitial space creates a semi-exterior transitional zone, open to the restored timber roof above, and acts as circulation, firewood storage, as well as the front entry to the main living unit and guest house. Large glazed panels throughout the house alternate with fir boarding, allowing views from the wood-clad interior to the outer stone walls, visually linking the historic and new.

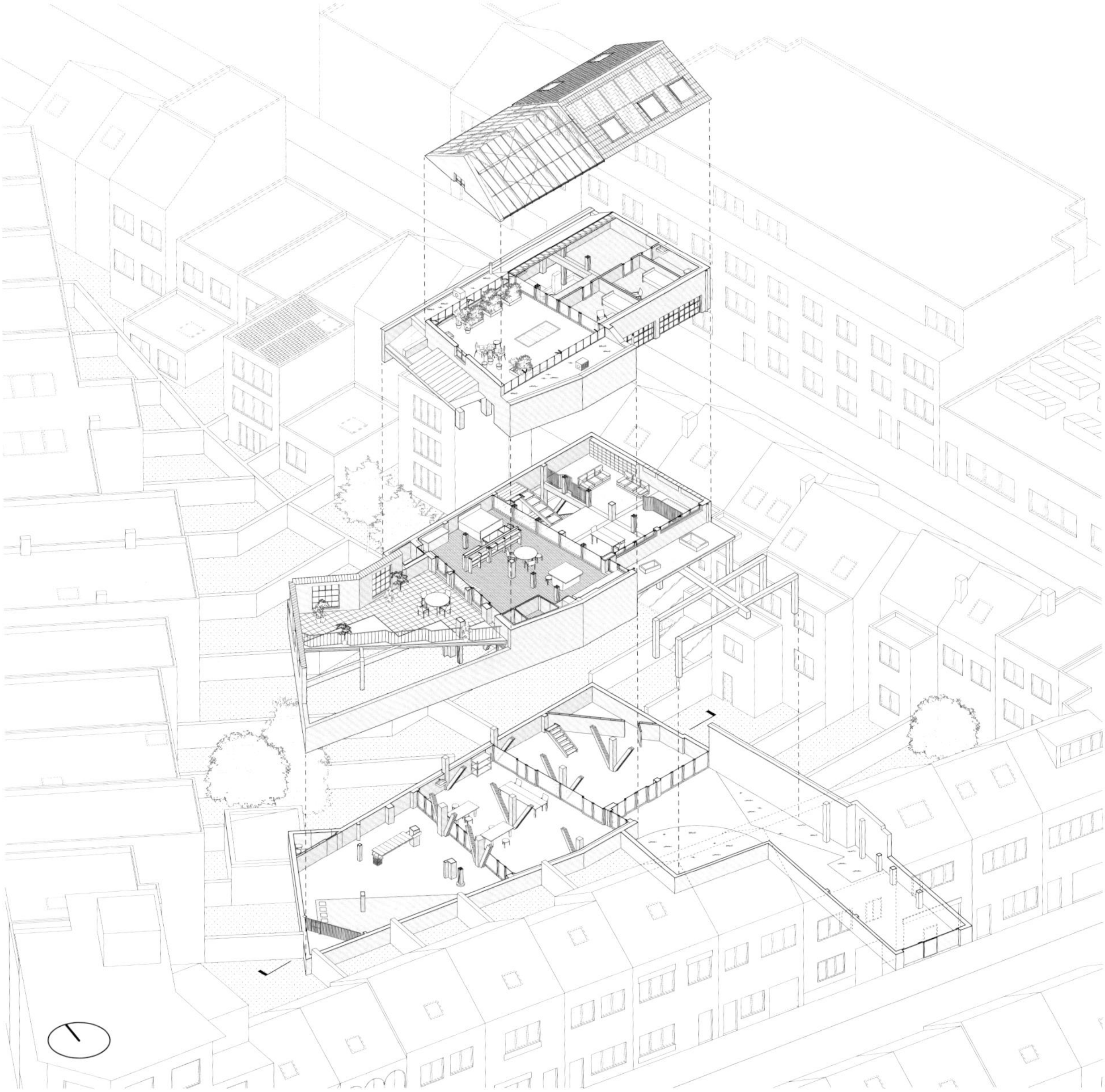

Verbiest | AgwA

Industrial buildings like this one, typically constructed of carbon-heavy materials like concrete and steel, provide a vital opportunity for reuse, since the resources needed to build them have already been spent. Located on the interior of an otherwise residential block, this project converted a sprawling factory building, built incrementally between 1900 and 1970, into a family home and shared arts workshop. Working with a 'resistance to the unnecessary,' a number of pragmatic tactics were deployed to realize the project with an attention to minimum waste and maximum effect: mining the existing structure for materials; banishing additional concrete and steel; and, when required, augmenting with low-carbon,

Brussels, Belgium | 2020

biogenic systems and materials. The resulting construction leverages the contrast between the raw found conditions and new interventions to create an intentionally heterogeneous ensemble.

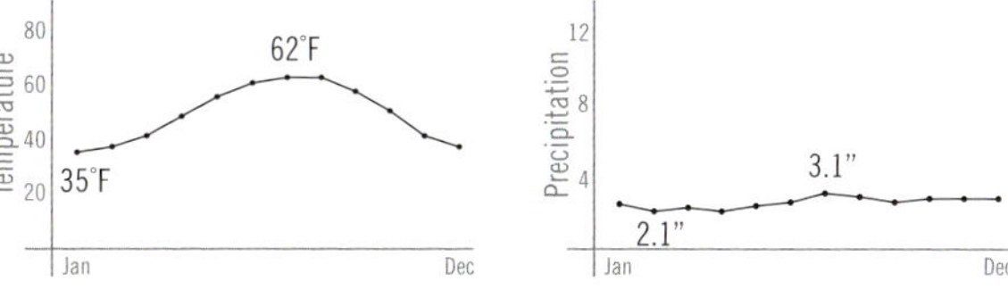

Verbiest

This repurposing of a 20th-century industrial building into a residence and arts production space takes an intentionally provisional approach that evolved over time in response to the specific conditions of the site. Demolishing as little of the existing structure as possible, the project occupies only a part of the full complex, reducing conditioned space and required energy to a minimum, taking advantage of the resulting outdoor spaces for uses like ceramics firing, terraces, or exterior recreation. Conditioned areas use locally produced hemp insulation and allow for the overflow of heating to the adjacent partially enclosed spaces. Where required, the original factory structure was reinforced without additional

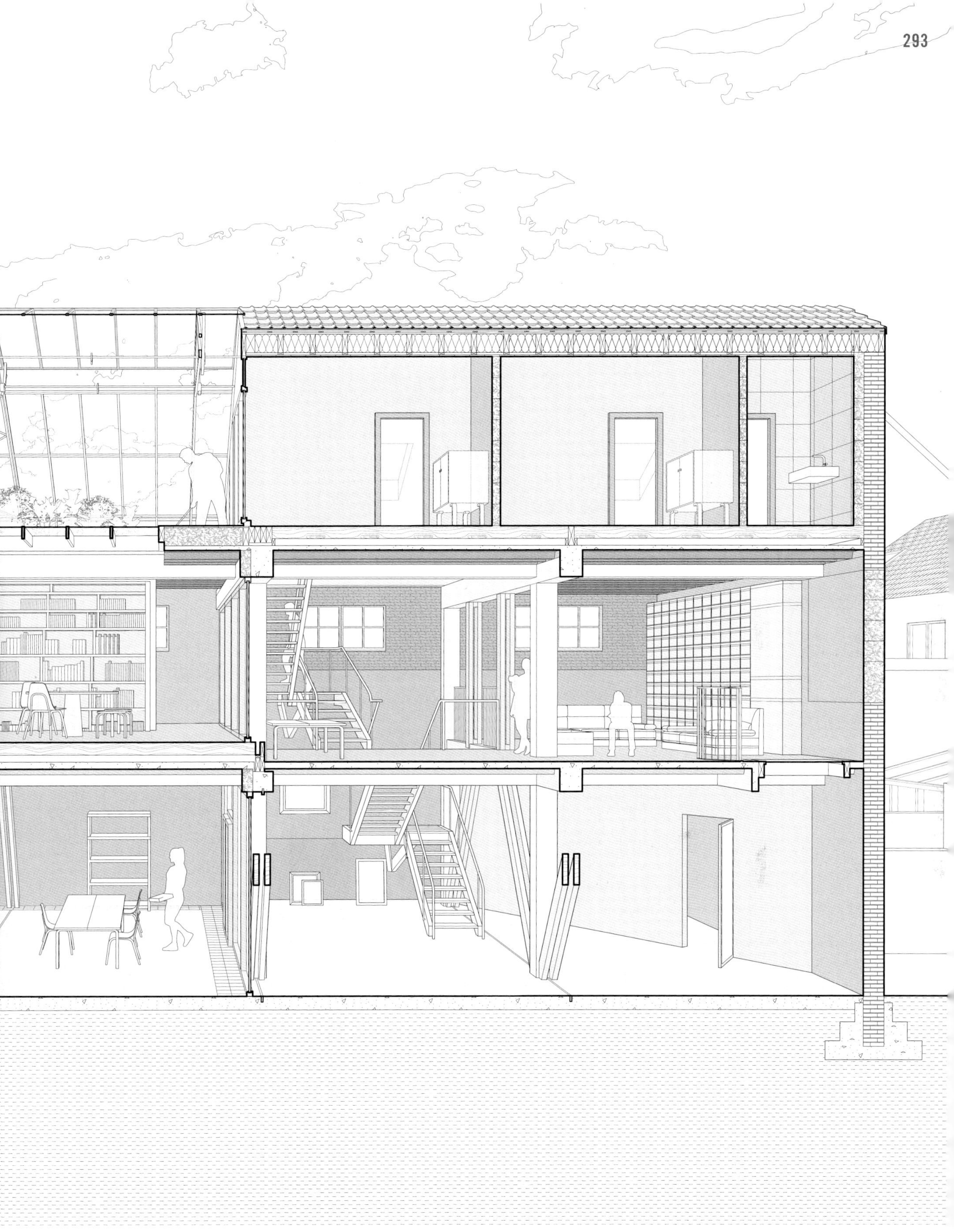

steel or concrete, counterintuitively using wood bracing to shore up the lower-level beams and columns. The original building also provided a resource for recycled materials, with roof and terrace tiles recovered from the site while railings and other elements were reused from other projects. At the upper level an agricultural greenhouse extends the pitched volume of the adjacent bedrooms and allows for productive gardening and a passive climatic buffer. Working opportunistically and utilizing the existing building as both resource and site, the project creates an architecturally rich juxtaposition of found conditions and tactical reinhabitation.

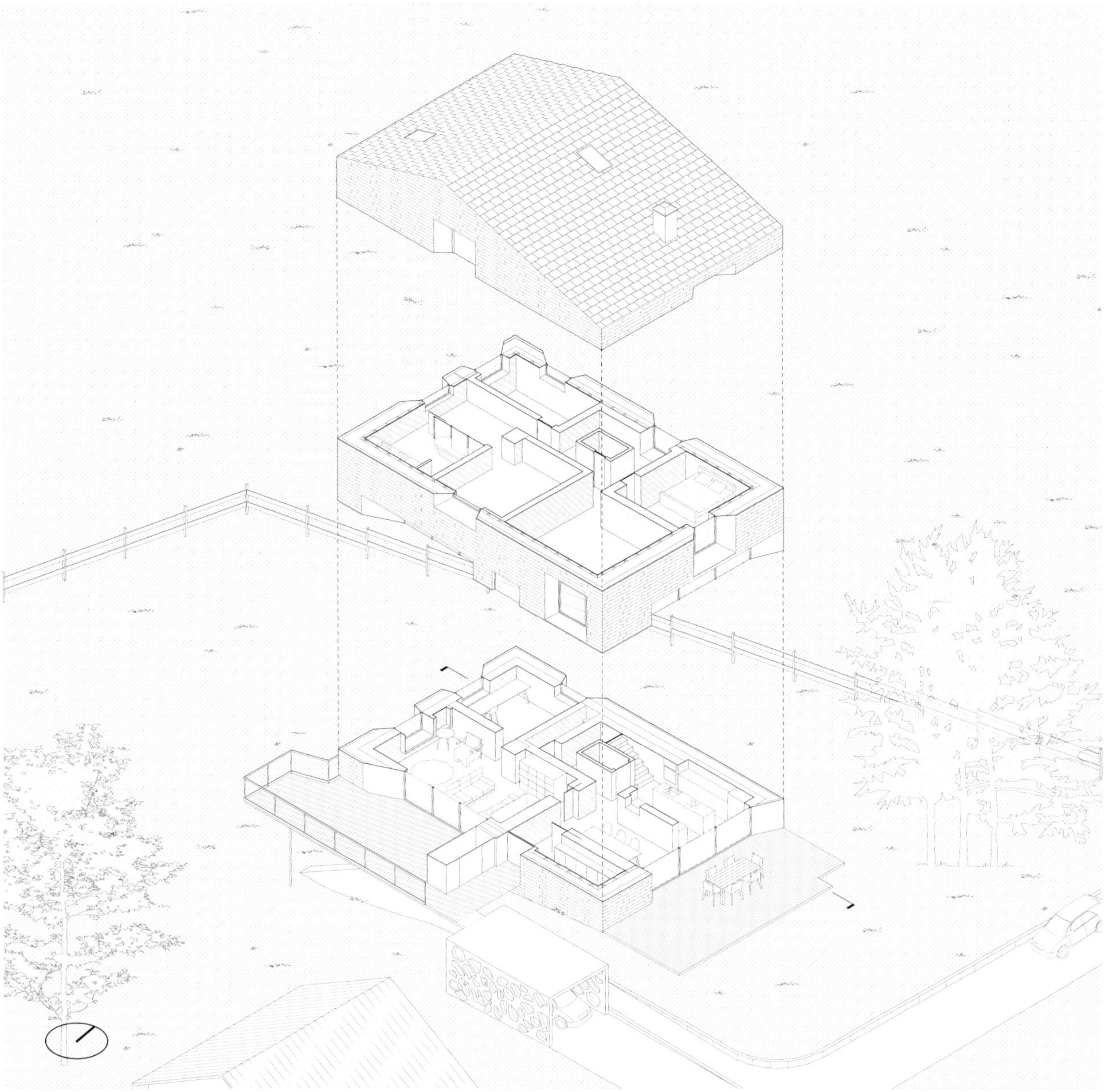

House Simma | Georg Bechter Architektur + Design

Strategically repurposing select aspects of an existing 1966 house, the project creates a unified, high-performing contemporary dwelling. The deep roof overhangs of the existing, nearly uninsulated, house were trimmed back and the upper levels rebuilt to create a consolidated, single volume while preserving the masonry construction at the lower level. This allowed the reconfigured house to be sheathed in a continuous membrane of straw-bales, maximizing the insulative capacity of the walls and roof. This new thermal envelope allows the house to be fully heated from a single

Egg, Austria | 2011

wood-burning stove. While the interior spaces were opened up to create greater spatial and visual continuity, the straw wrapper creates the thickened façade and deep walls that provide the house's unique character.

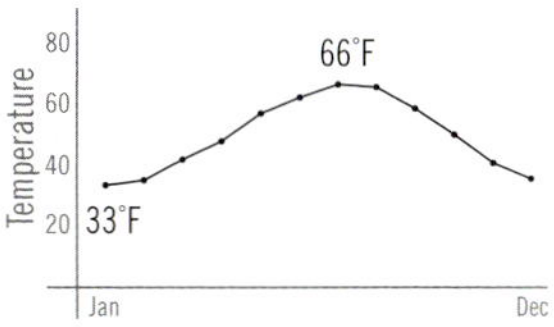

Temperature
80
60
40
20
66°F
33°F
Jan
Dec

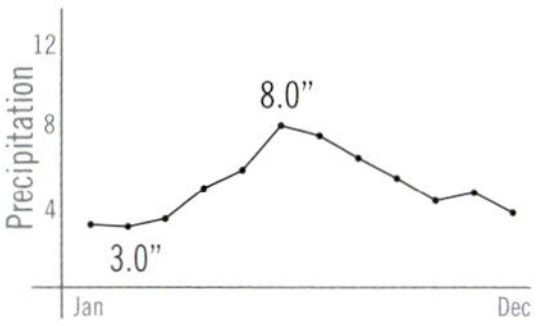

Precipitation
12
8
4
8.0"
3.0"
Jan
Dec

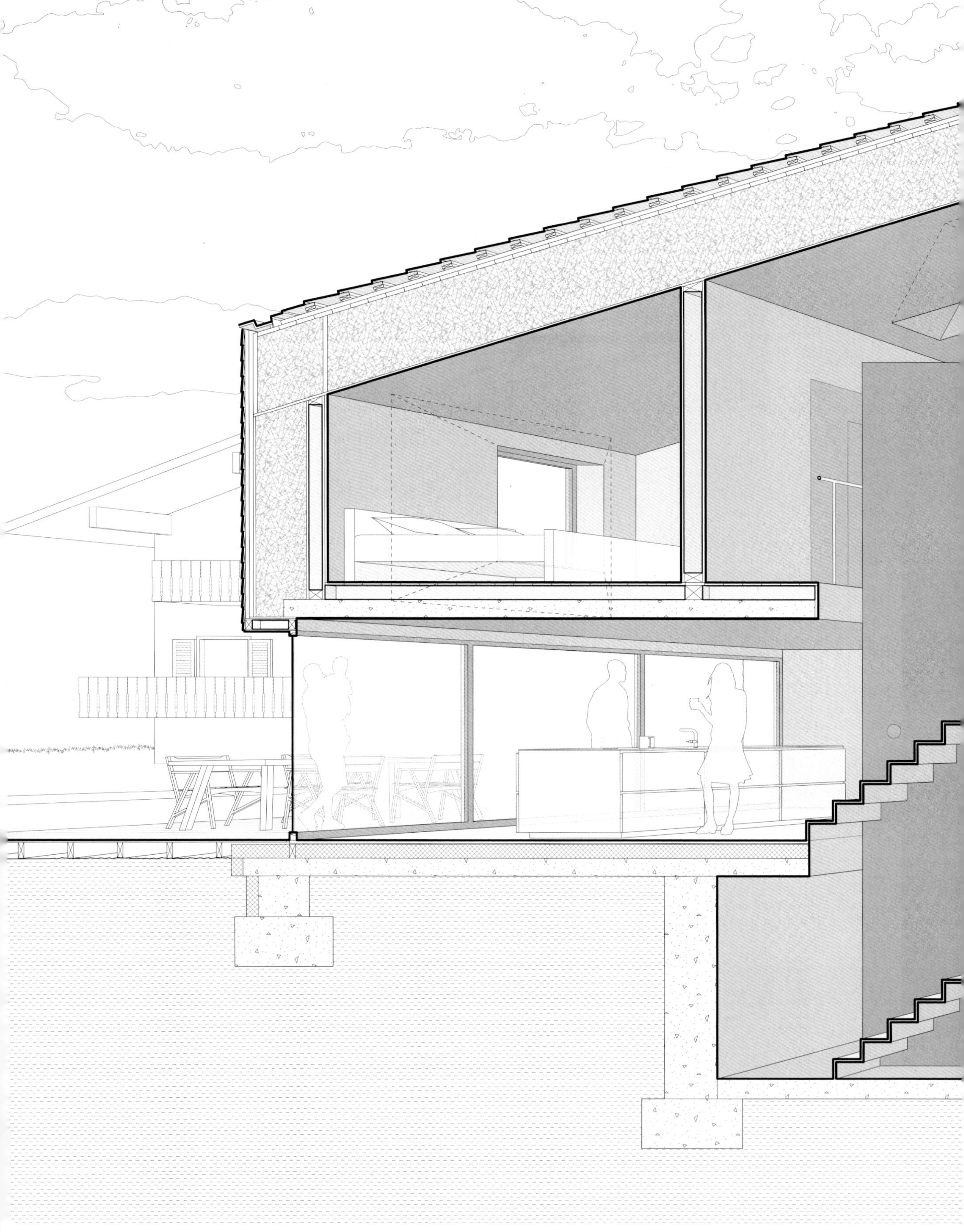

House Simma

The section makes clear how the existing house was spatially reconfigured and wrapped in a thickened envelope of insulating straw-bales. While preserving the ground-level masonry walls and basement of the original residence, a new wood-framed second story raises the original roofline by half a level to create more habitable space, reorienting the ridge line by 90 degrees and reducing overhangs in favor of a simplified pitched roof volume. This new upper level is open to the roof pitch, illuminated by skylights, and contains three enclosed bedrooms. An independent bath-room volume provides the central anchor for a wraparound stair. Similarly, the originally compartmentalized ground floor is opened up, with large glazed cuts in the exterior envelope to the south and east expanding the interior to an exterior patio and terrace. It is the exterior skin that provides the house's most distinctive feature: a 17.7 in (450 mm) thick layer of straw-bales is wrapped continuously around the outer walls and roof, creating a thermally insulative mass broken only at the windows and clad with locally sourced wood shakes. The windows, of uniform proportions but distinguished by their orientations, create tapering pyramidal apertures that intensify the legibility of the thickened envelope while maximizing daylighting.

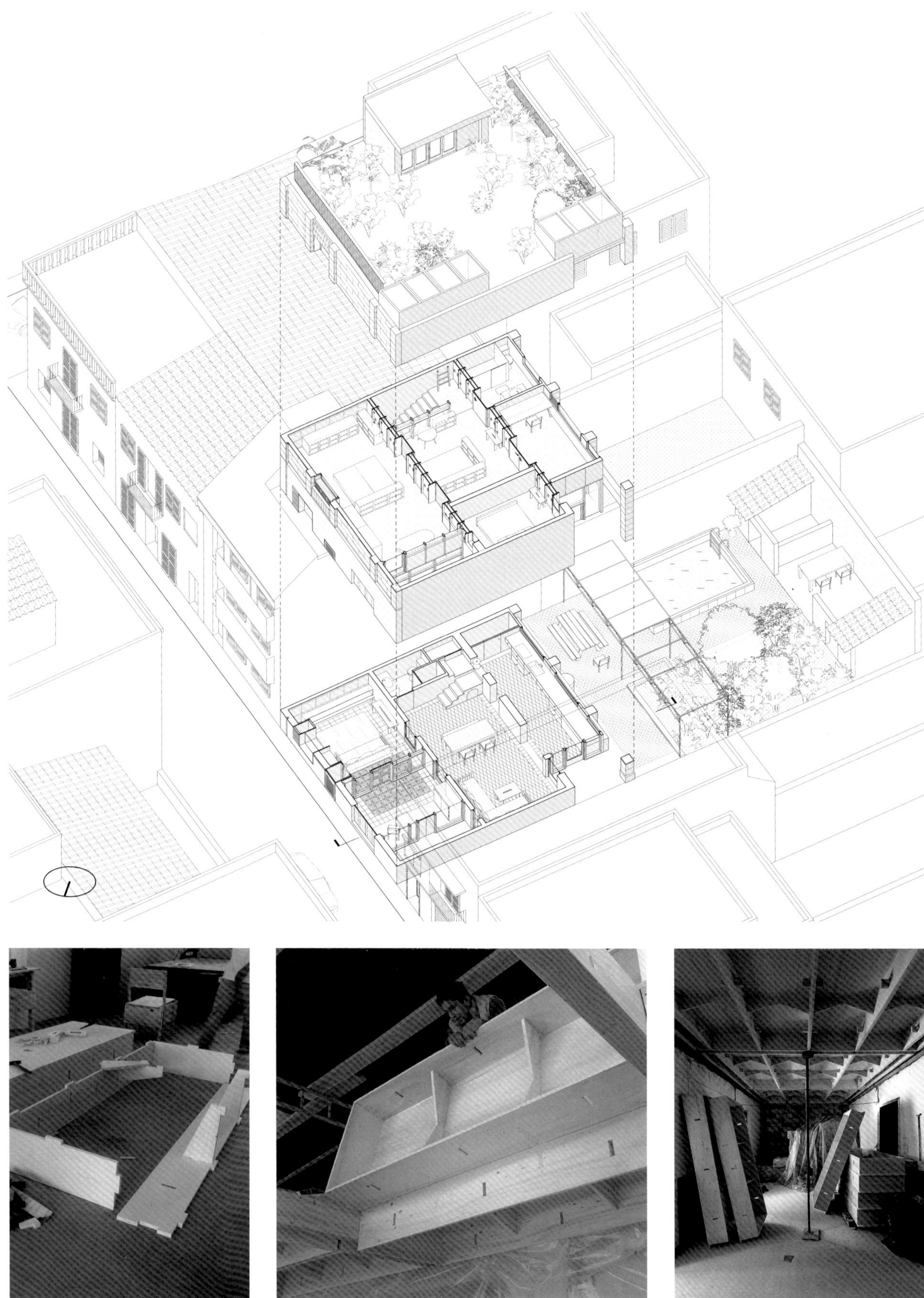

Plywood House | Feina Studio

The materially inventive reuse project vertically extends an existing one-story terrace house on an urban street. To avoid overloading the original stone walls, the architects deployed a custom system of CNC-milled plywood sheets, prefabricated and installed on site to create a lightweight box structure that forms the upper floor, walls, and roof. The digitally manufactured wood elements include the interior cabinetry and a playful staircase and is extended throughout the furniture design of the house. In contrast to the CNC-milled floor and roof, left exposed to reveal their

Palma de Mallorca, Spain | 2017

intersecting geometry of plywood plates, the ground floor and original walls are tiled in a variety of locally sourced, artisan-produced finishes, producing a clear sectional contrast of tectonic and material systems while alluding to the ornamental motifs of the region.

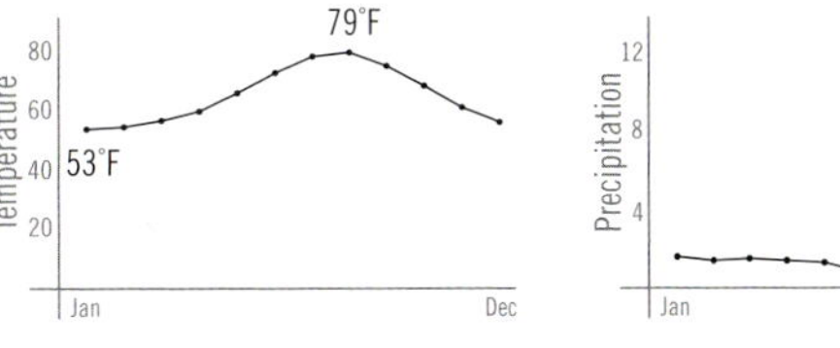

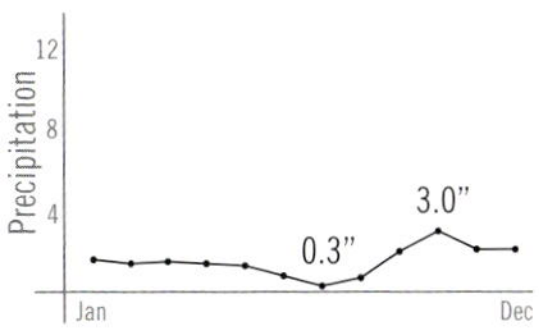

Plywood House

Combining local material resources with a process-driven logic of assembly, Plywood House adds a new second story to an existing residence on an urban street. The upper-level addition involved the development of a digitally fabricated wood system that could be shop assembled, easily transported, and installed on site. A series of box-like modules span between timber beams resting on the original masonry walls. Each module is constructed of CNC-milled poplar plywood panels assembled into a five-sided box with triangulated reinforcing plates. Slots milled into the sides allow for plywood connectors that link box to box in a modified version of a mortise and tenon joint. This assembly creates a lightweight structure for

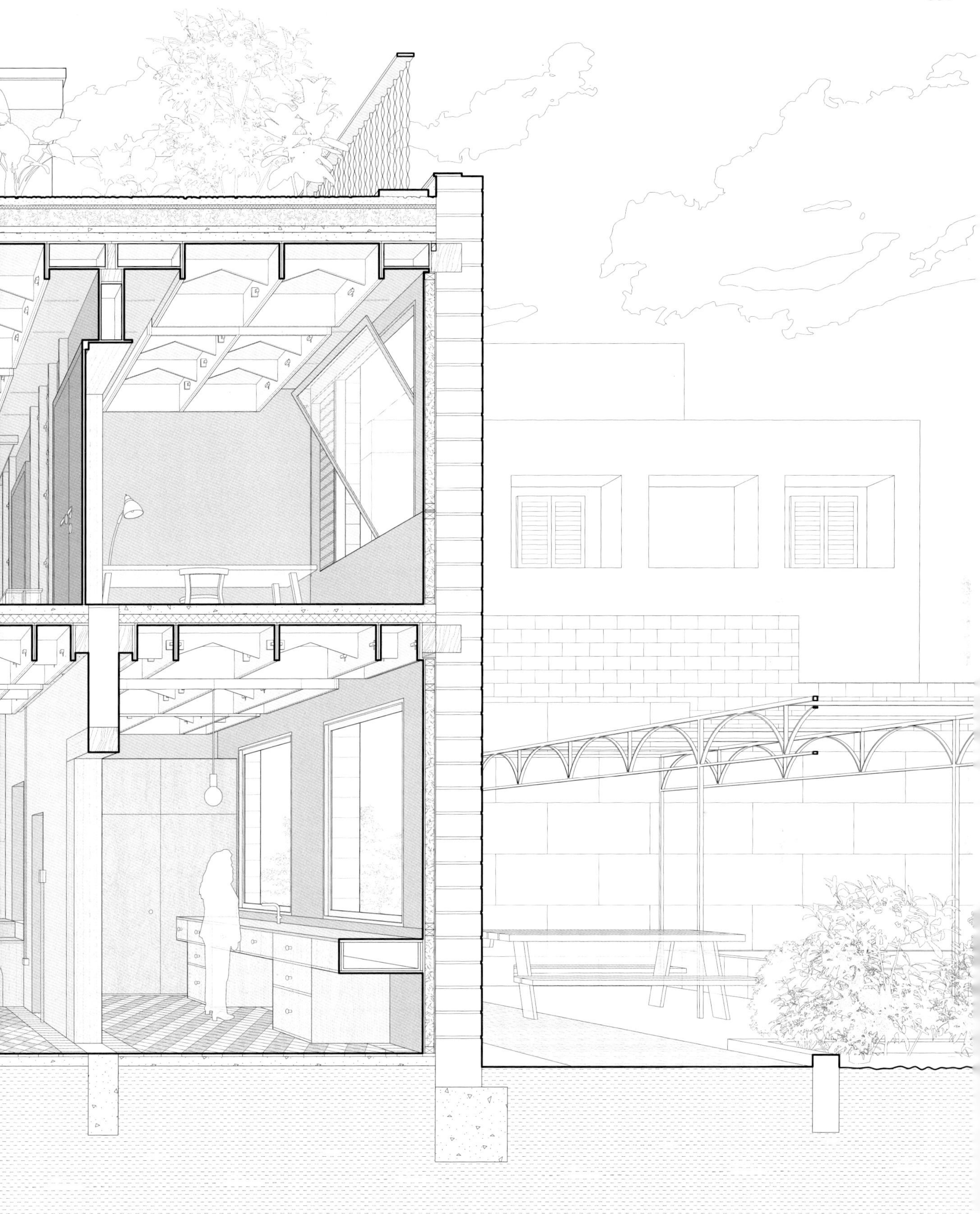

the second floor and roof while providing a geometrically complex ceiling that acts as a unifying architectural element throughout the house. A second series of internally ribbed plywood boxes, built above the existing masonry, functions as interior dividing walls at the upper level and the horizontal system is repeated to support an occupiable green roof. At the ground level, a series of programmatic layers extend from street to garden, finished in colorful patterns of artisanal concrete and terracotta tiles that create a dialogue between regional craft and emerging technologies.

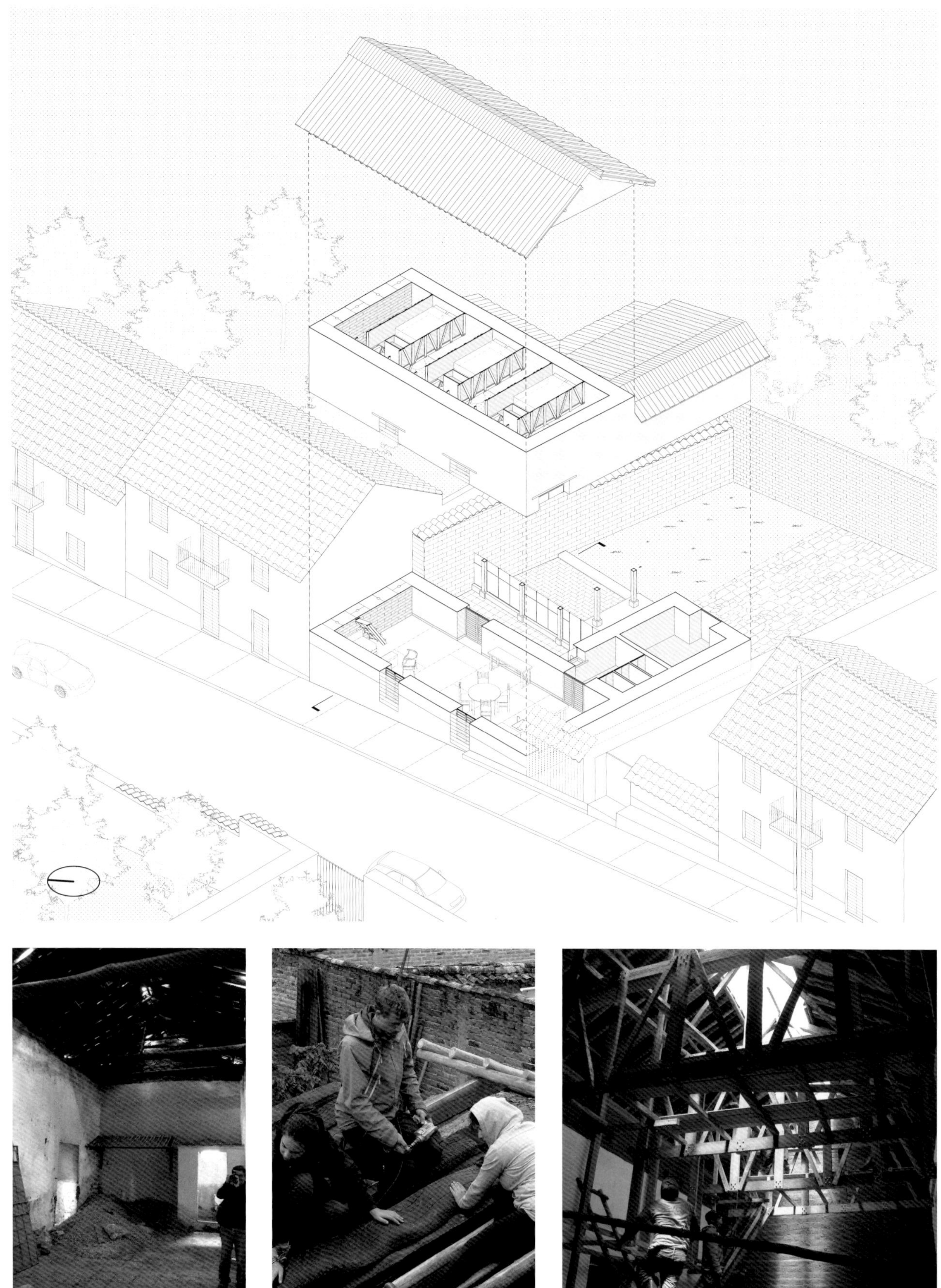

House of Flying Beds | Al Borde

The refurbishment of an 18th-century building, located along a street of similarly proportioned residences, takes a minimal approach to intervention that capitalizes on the qualities of the existing structure. Essentially a tall rectangular volume with thick walls of rammed earth and a lower L-shaped extension enclosing a rear courtyard, the house was in a state of advanced disrepair and required a new roof. A series of wooden trusses were introduced to span between the restored earthen walls while the party walls were rebuilt using site-cast adobe bricks. Taking advantage

La Esperanza, Ecuador | 2017

of this intervention, a bed was integrated between each alternating truss creating a series of suspended sleeping platforms accessible via a hanging walkway. This occupiable roof structure, containing the only private spaces in the house, shelters the single, open public area below.

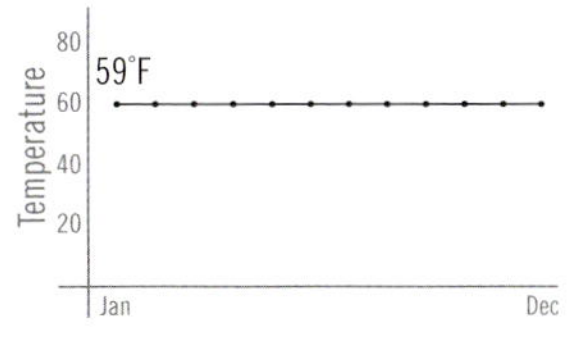

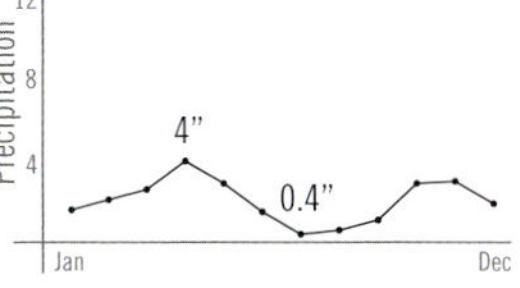

House of Flying Beds

A series of inhabitable wooden roof trusses span between the restored earthen walls of this rehabilitated house, which originally dates to the 18th century. Alternating with open zones at every other truss, these flying sleeping platforms incorporate beds and built in-wardrobes, and are accessible via a series of ladders anchored to a lower-level wooden walkway hung from the trusses and the massive outer wall of the house. The wood trusses are supported by a new concrete ring beam added atop the existing rammed earth walls. The rebuilt roof, which replaced the original rotting one, is sheathed with recycled rubber tire treads and a ridge cap of repurposed glass that allows plentiful daylight to fall between the

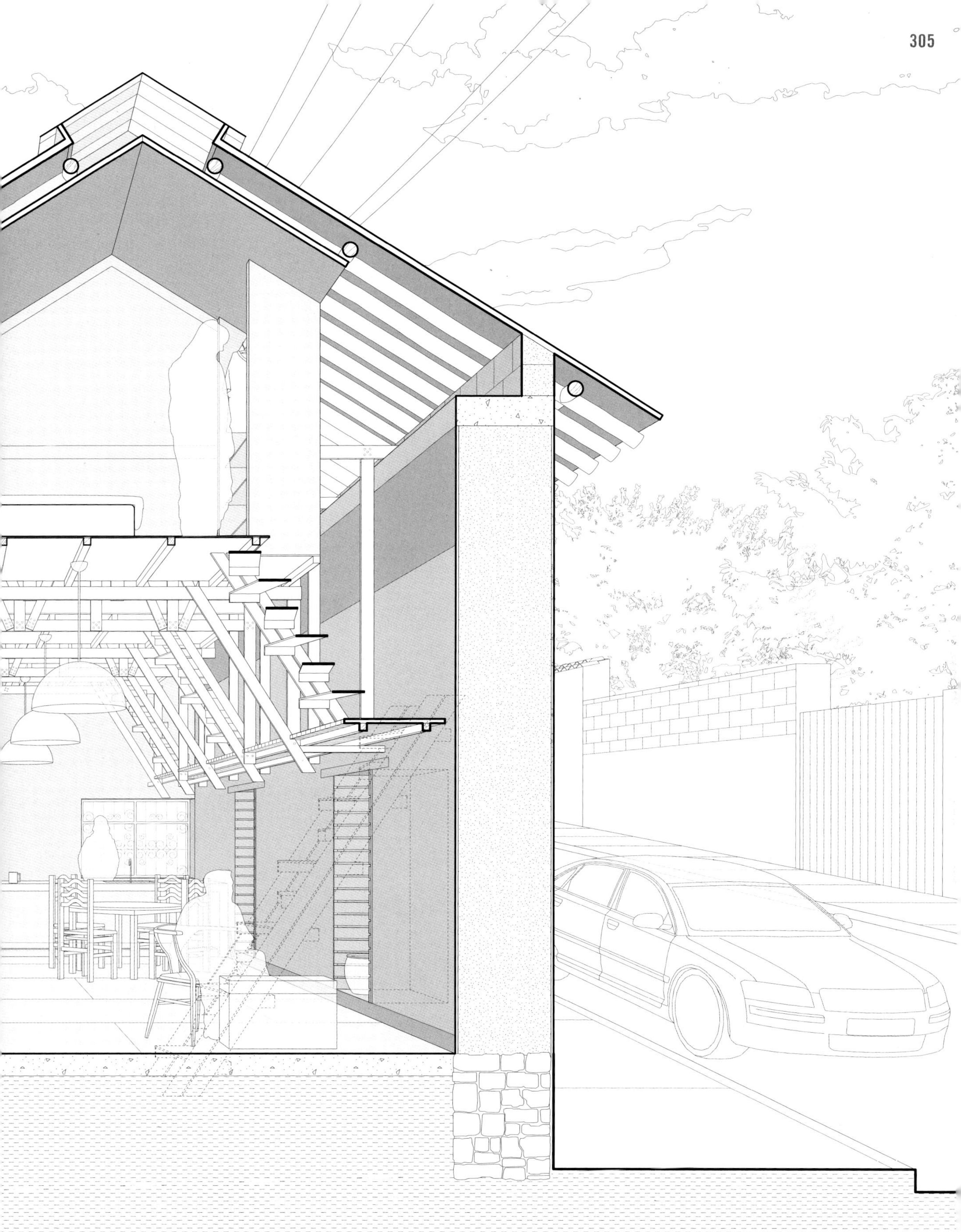

suspended platforms. The beds hang over the large main room of the house which incorporates the kitchen, dining, and living areas while a porch-like, glass-enclosed extension provides a transition space to an exterior courtyard repaved with the original roof tile. By reducing private space to the minimal accommodation of the sleeping lofts, this strategic reuse project maximizes the social utility of the existing structure in a fashion that is simultaneously pragmatic and imaginative.

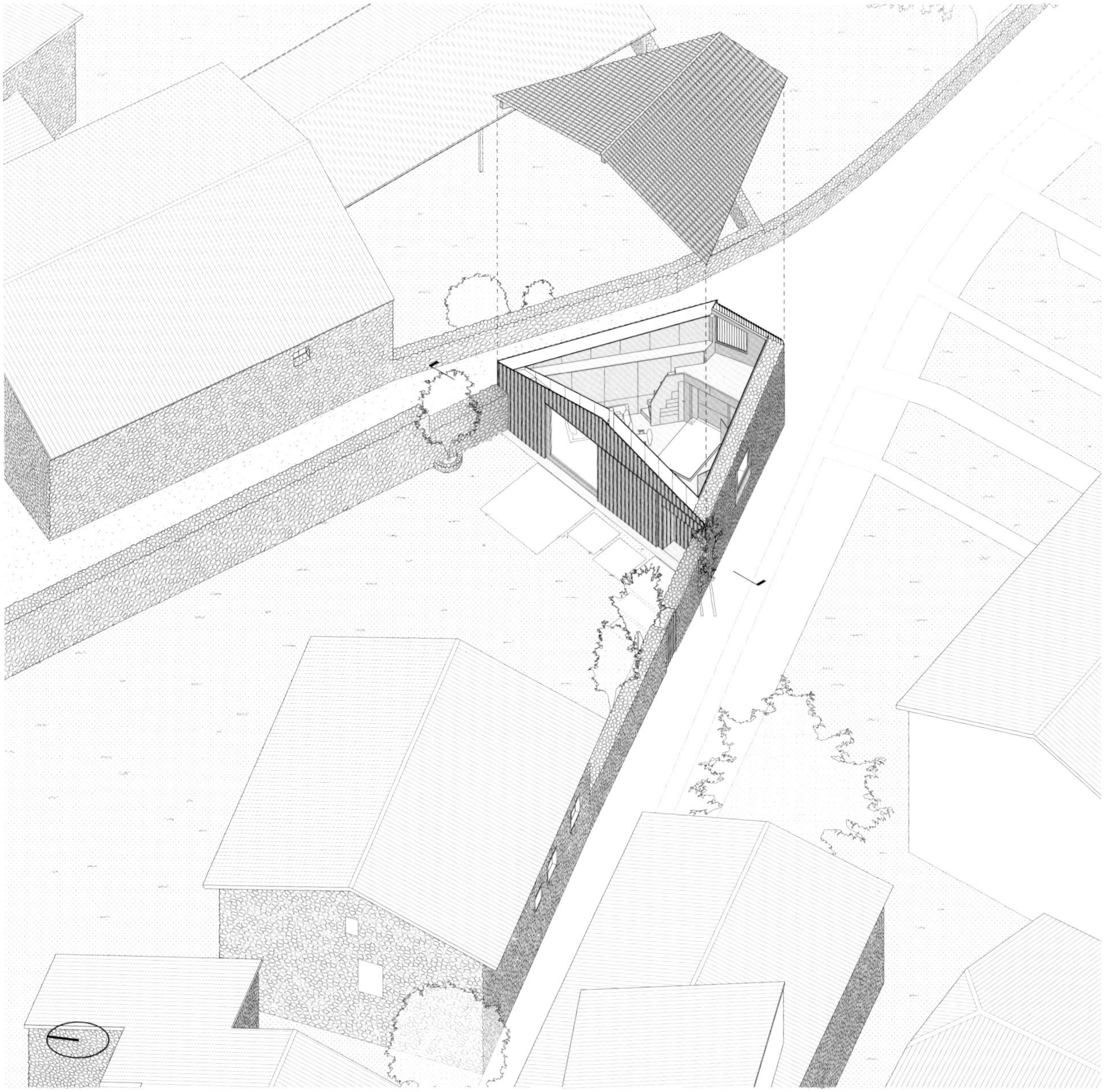

Small Cottage Ojacastro | MAAV

This refurbishment of a diminutive, dilapidating agricultural storehouse maintains a character and scale appropriate to its rural Riojan context. Occupying the convergence of two intersecting boundary walls, the project conserves and repairs the old rubble walls while replacing the decaying roof with a comparable fishbone structure of laminated wood members. The interior of the small house is treated as a single, inhabitable piece of cabinetry, with all of the functional elements—kitchen, wardrobes, a bed, and a small bathroom—concealed within the thickness of the

Ojacastro, Spain | 2020

plywood-clad walls. The interior-facing façade is articulated with wood boards and battens, and incorporates a single oversized, operable glazed panel that can also be shuttered; in the open position this extends the otherwise minimal cabin into the expanse of the adjacent enclosed field.

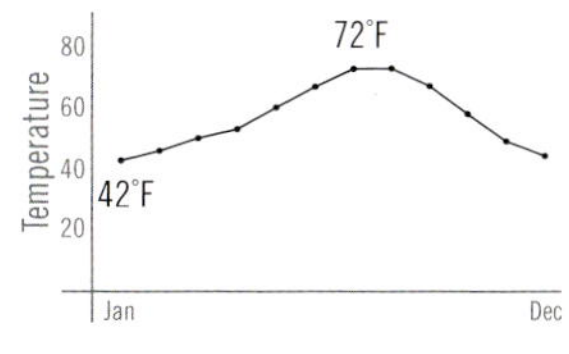

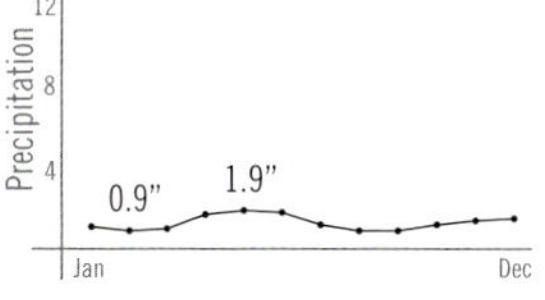

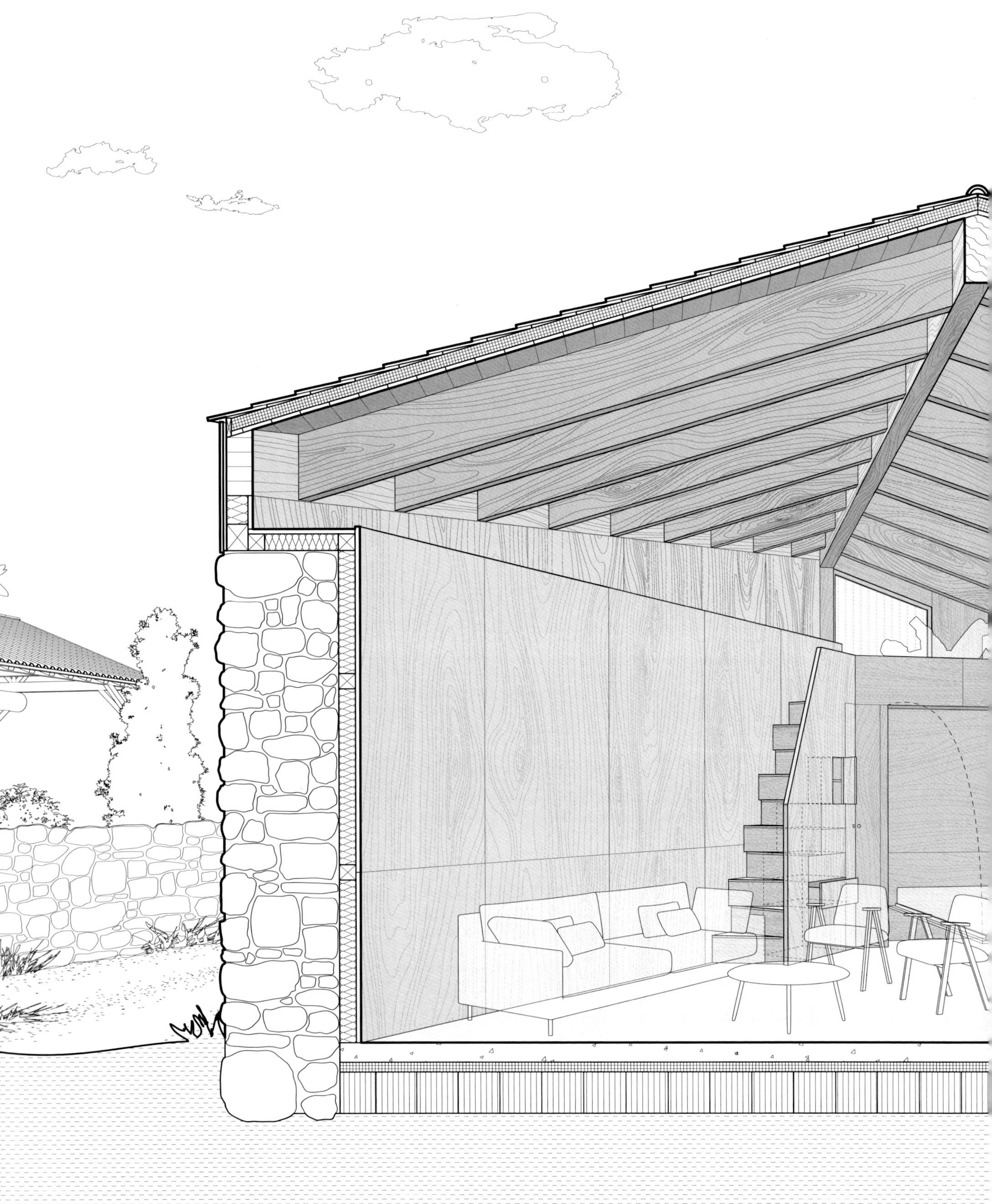

Small Cottage Ojacastro

Occupying the footprint of a former agricultural shed, this compact dwelling rehabilitates and reoccupies the space between two extant rubble walls in the rural village of Ojacastro. A lightweight, insulated wood surface lines the interior of the converging stone walls, while a new roof structure of exposed laminated timber spans between, with the roof shingles extending just past the outer edge of the stone walls. Although formed from load-bearing stone walls, the interior sensibility is lightweight and adaptable. Moreover, the depth of the triangulating walls is exploited as a functional thickness, clad on the interior with plywood panels and transformed into an architecturally scaled furniture element. Panels

open to reveal the built-in kitchen and a deployable murphy bed can be folded down from the walls to convert the single multi-functional space from living or dining into a bedroom. Above the bathroom, concealed in the thickness behind the bed, is an additional sleeping loft accessible via an alternating tread stair. Modest in scale, inventive in its planning, and thoughtful in its deployment of locally appropriate, organic materials, this small house demonstrates the architectural potentials of even the most humble of existing buildings.

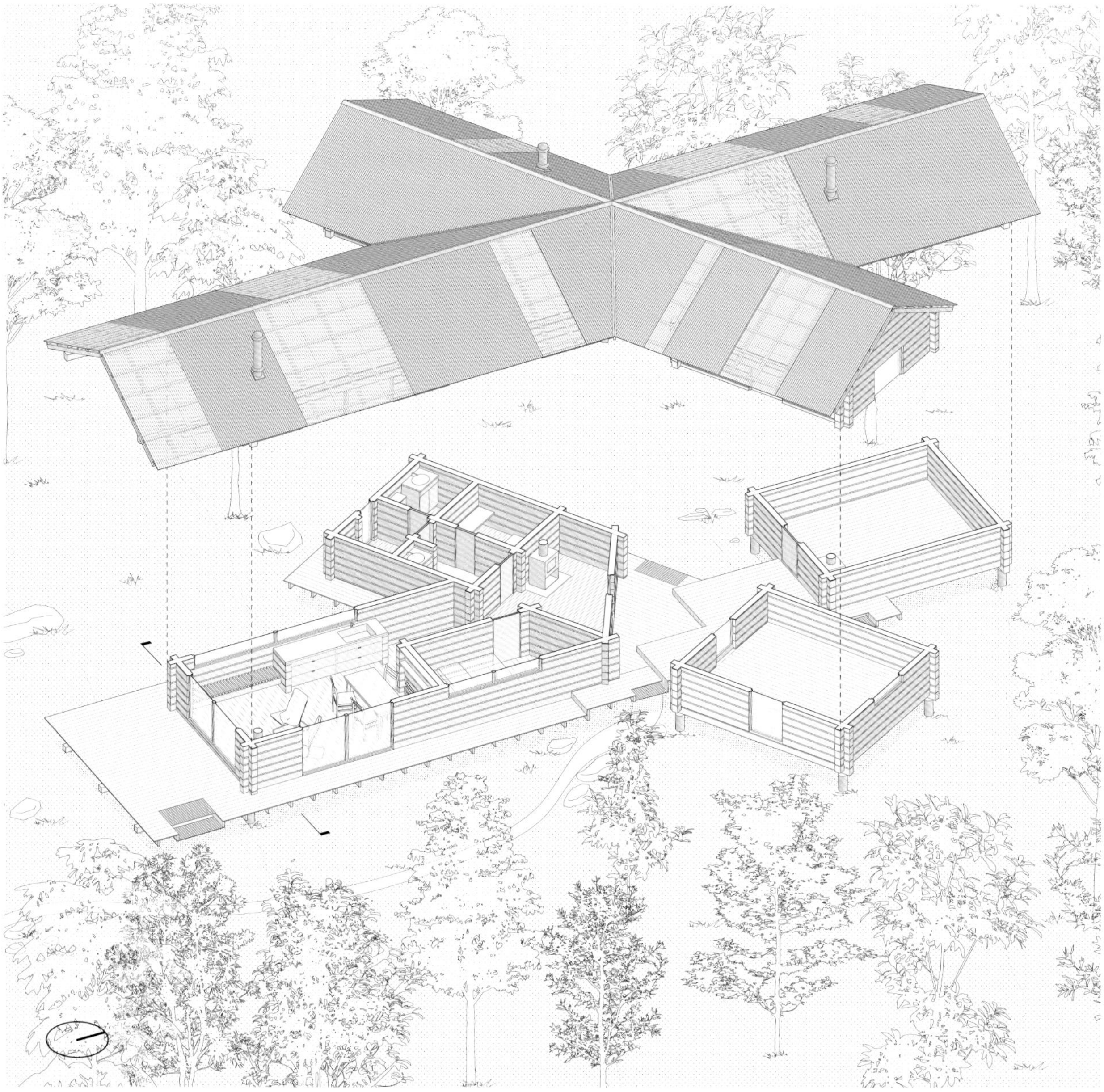

Cabin Femunden | Arkitekt Aslak Haanshuus

This repurposing and addition to two existing cabins on a wilderness site effectively blurs the distinction between new and old. The new design extends the existing axes of two isolated but adjacent log cabins already on site, creating an ensemble of intersecting pitched roof volumes.

Unexpectedly, each of the linear log volumes comprises both a newly constructed contemporary portion and one of the original structures, further unified via a new steel and polycarbonate roof and an extensive wood deck that cantilevers over the site. This X-shaped complex is conjoined at the

Femunden, Norway | 2015

middle by a covered entry court, with the main spaces located in the new portions and a guest room and storage in the original structures.

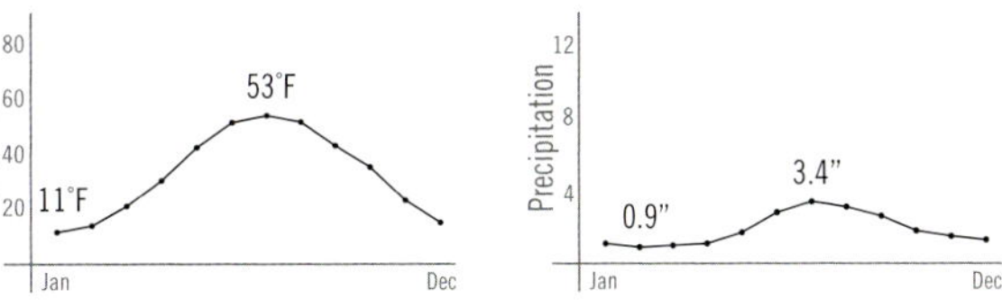

Cabin Femunden

This rural retreat recapitulates the solid timber tectonic of two extant log cabins on the lakeside site while incorporating them into a new spatial composition. Each of the new wings of the check-mark-shaped addition extends the axis of an existing log structure, extruding its dimension and shape into a newly built linear cabin. Drawing on the typical construction traditions of the area, the new portions, like the old, are assembled from locally sourced solid pine timbers, squared, staggered, and intersected at the corners, sealed with wool and serving as a single monolithic wood envelope. The longest of these cabins, shown in section, contains the primary living spaces and terminates in a large, glazed opening with

views toward Lake Femunden. An elevated deck links the new and old components together, creating an entry court at the intersection and is cantilevered above the ground on point foundations to minimize disruption to the site. An expansive new roof, clad alternately in corrugated metal or translucent polycarbonate affixed to wood battens that span exterior timber rafters, extends onto the original buildings, creating sheltered outdoor spaces while allowing for plentiful daylight. At the new portions, a second set of internal rafters provides the space for thermal insulation while large timber tie beams reinforce the log walls.

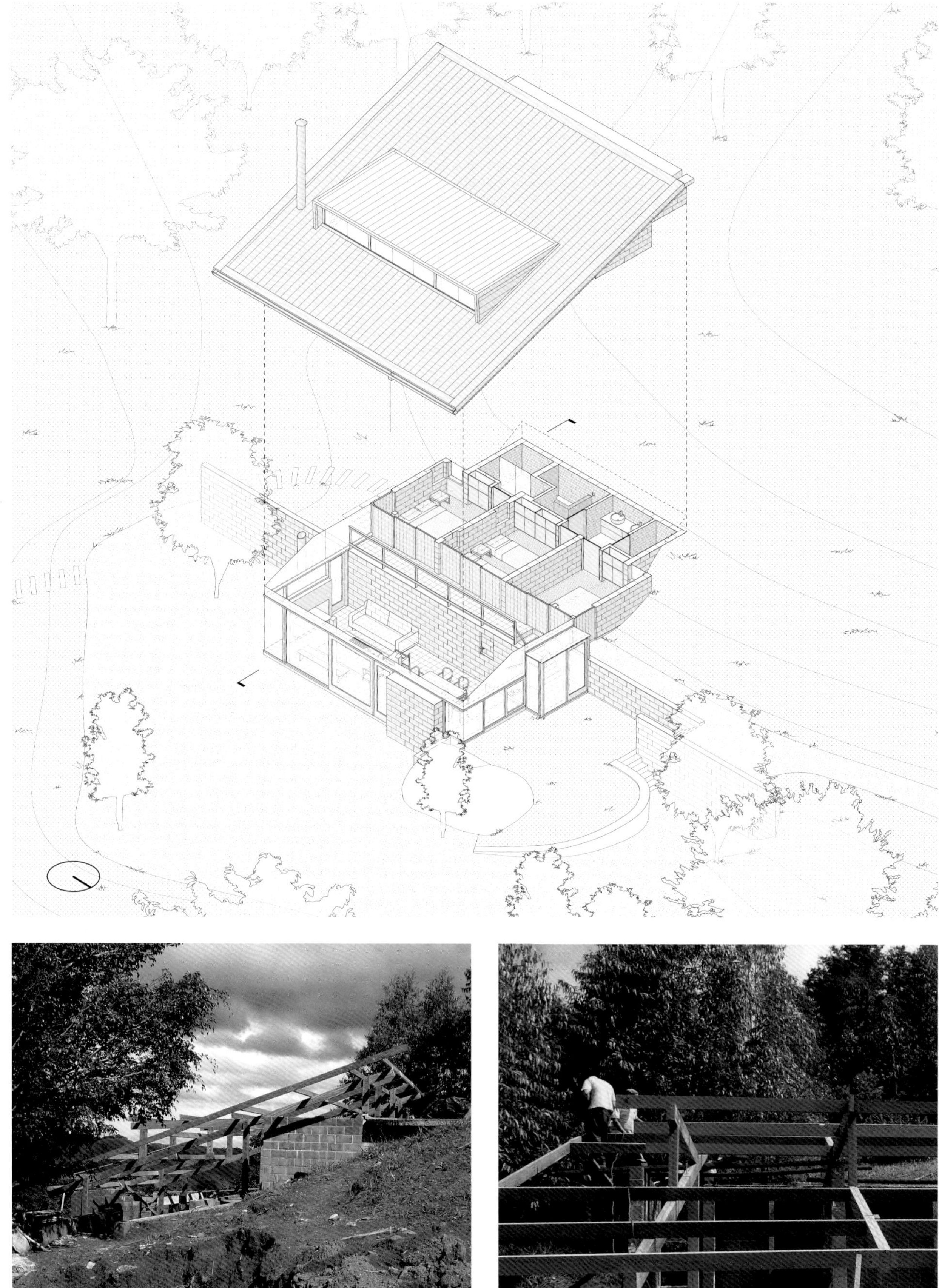

Half-Slope House | Denis Joelsons + Gabriela Baraúna Uchida

Located in a mountainous area of rural Brazil, this project recycles an existing retaining wall, the remnant of an earlier construction on the sloping site. Rather than fully occupy the artificially leveled land below the wall, the house is positioned so that the retaining wall splits the house in two, preserving a portion of the plateau for outdoor activities. Bedrooms and bathrooms are built above the wall, partly embedded in the angled terrain while the main living spaces are located below, against the masonry plane and open out onto the adjacent plateau. The shed-like

São Francisco Xavier, Brazil | 2013

timber roof echoes the slope of the ground, adding to the dialogue between house and site, human-made terrain, and natural landscape.

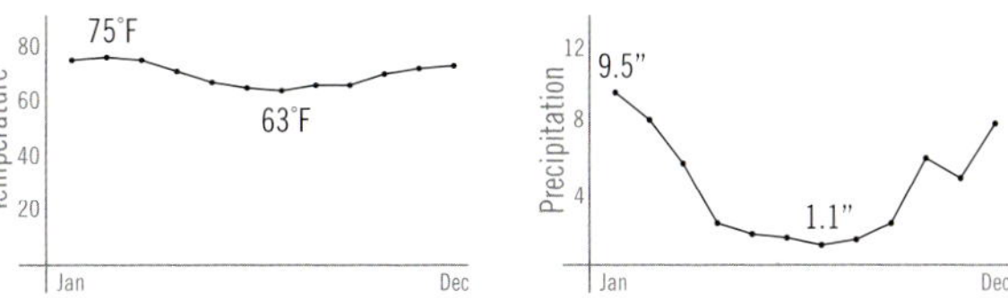

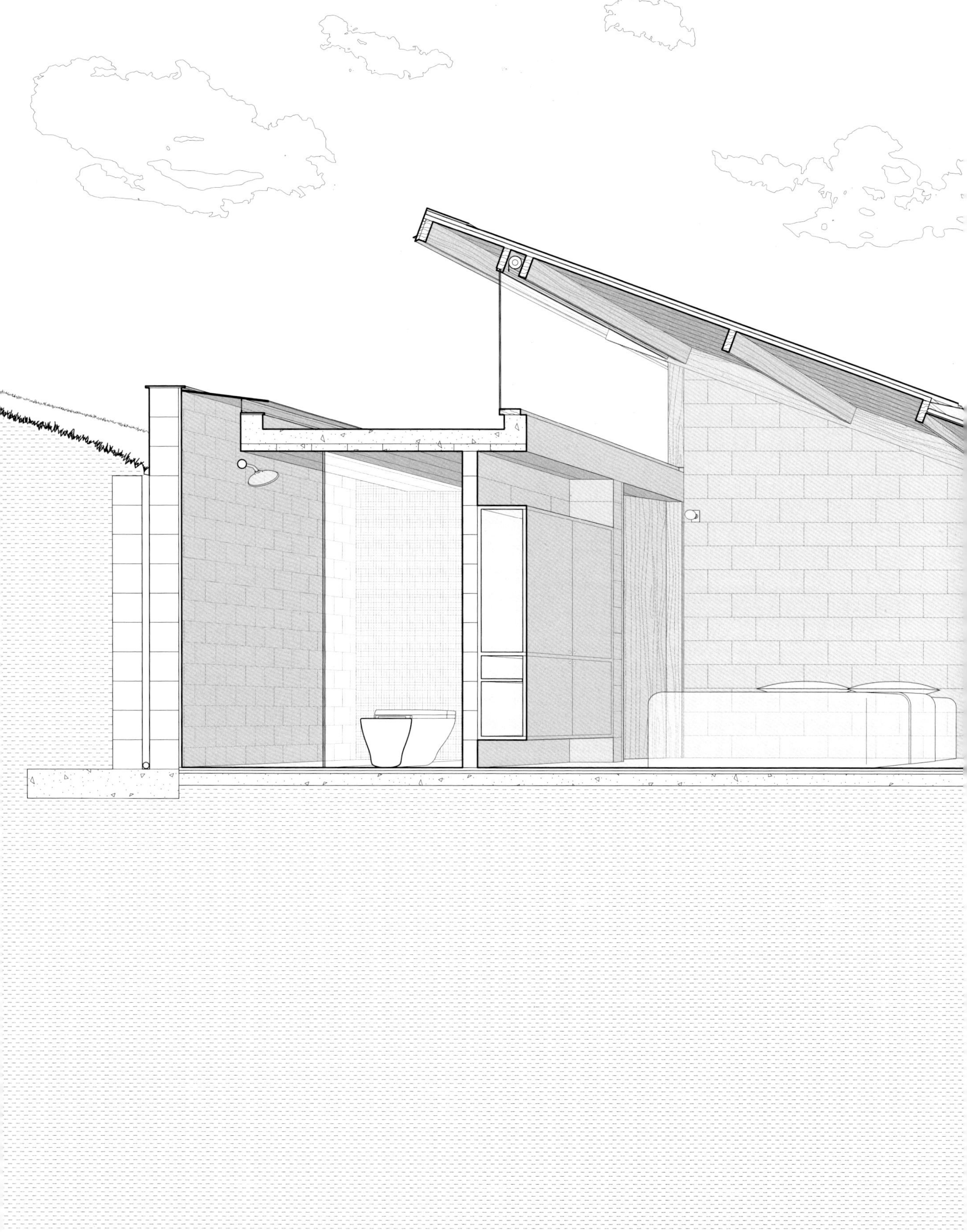

Half-Slope House

A new house is constructed around an extant retaining wall on a steeply inclined site. Half the house is located on the level plane established by the now partly internalized retaining wall, while half is located above the wall, creating a vertical shear between the two sections. The upper portion of the house contains parallel zones of bedrooms and bathrooms with circulation along the top of the original masonry wall. The upper rooms are partially embedded into the hillside, with light provided from clerestories and skylights, and linked to the adjacent site via a gravel path. The lower portion of the house comprises the main living areas, articulated as a single open room. The extensive glazing and large sliding door ensure continuity between indoor and outdoor spaces while a large site boulder and concrete hearth provide a sense of enclosure. The expansive angled roof, constructed of local timber, incorporates a counter sloping segment with operable glass panels for natural ventilation. While the sloping roof reflects the landscape, the retaining wall interrupts it, creating productive tensions that build on the original found condition.

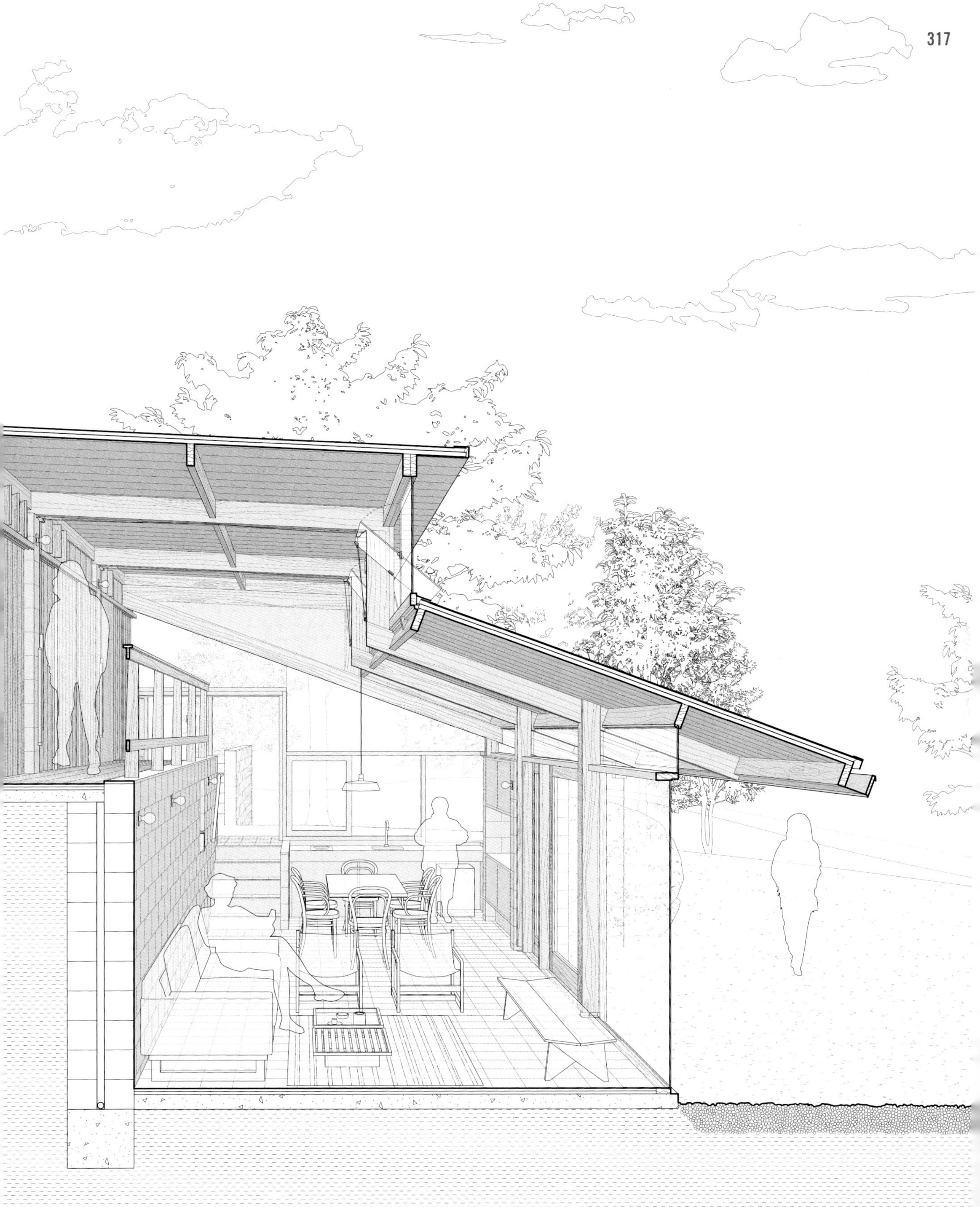

APPENDIX

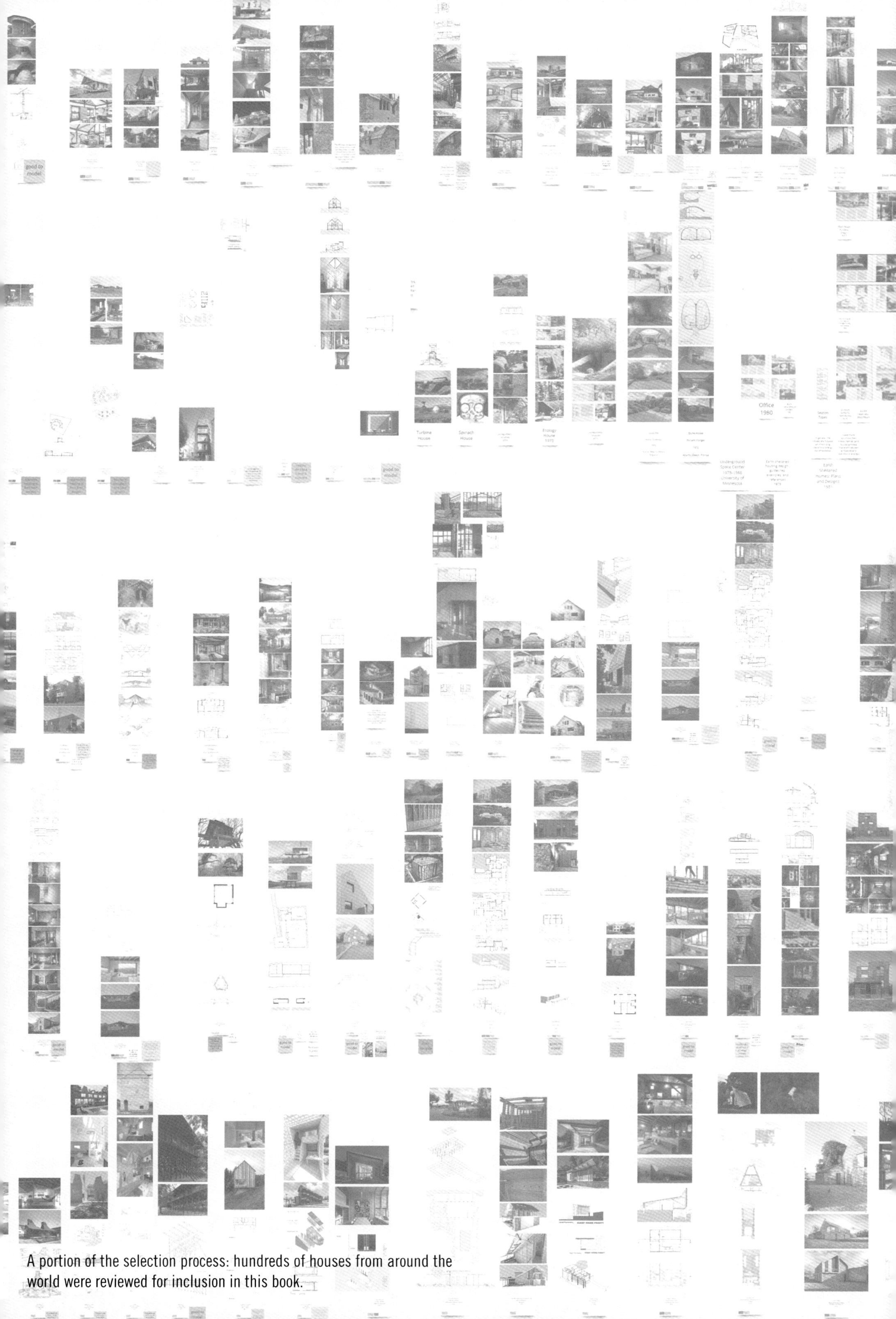

A portion of the selection process: hundreds of houses from around the world were reviewed for inclusion in this book.

Material Assemblies

Section axonometrics of the salient material tectonics of each house

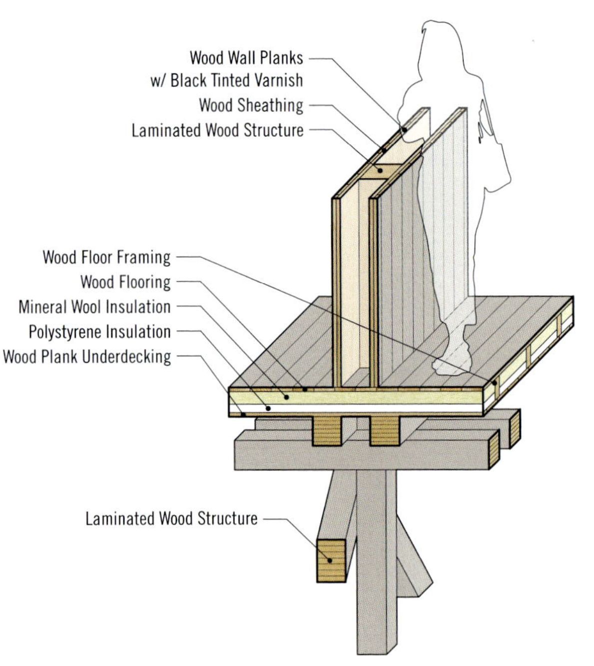

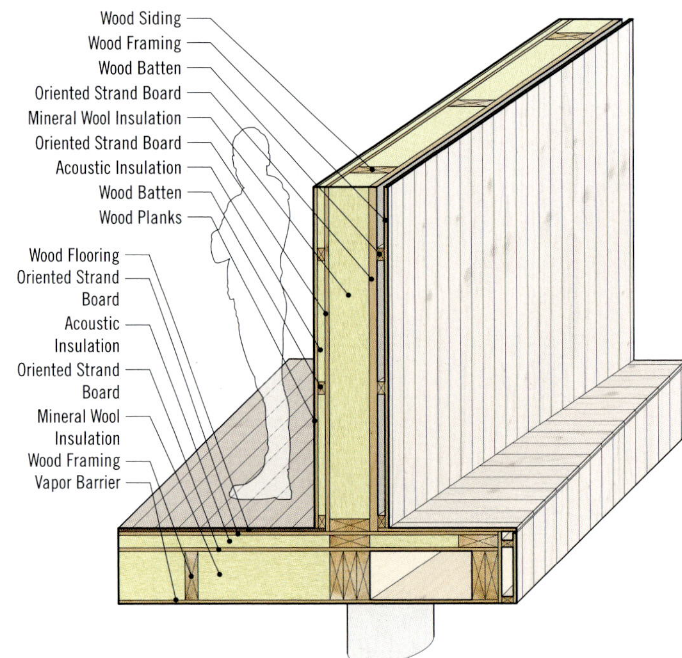

Wood Frame

Wood House
Smiljan Radic

Zilvar House
ASGK Design

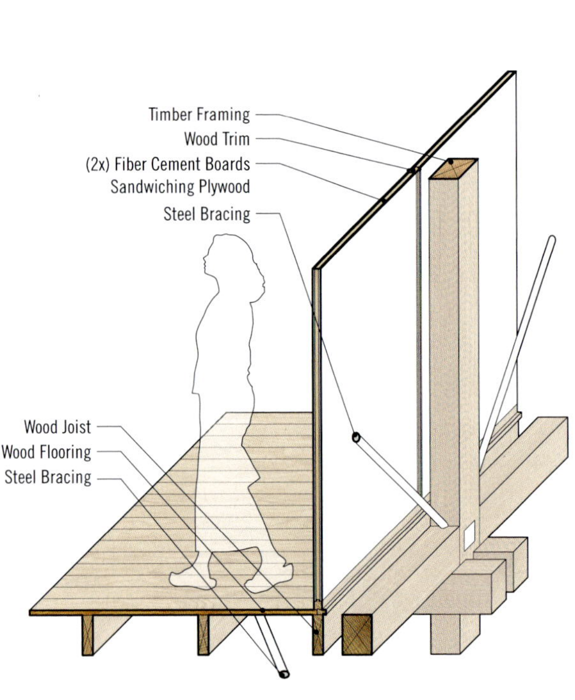

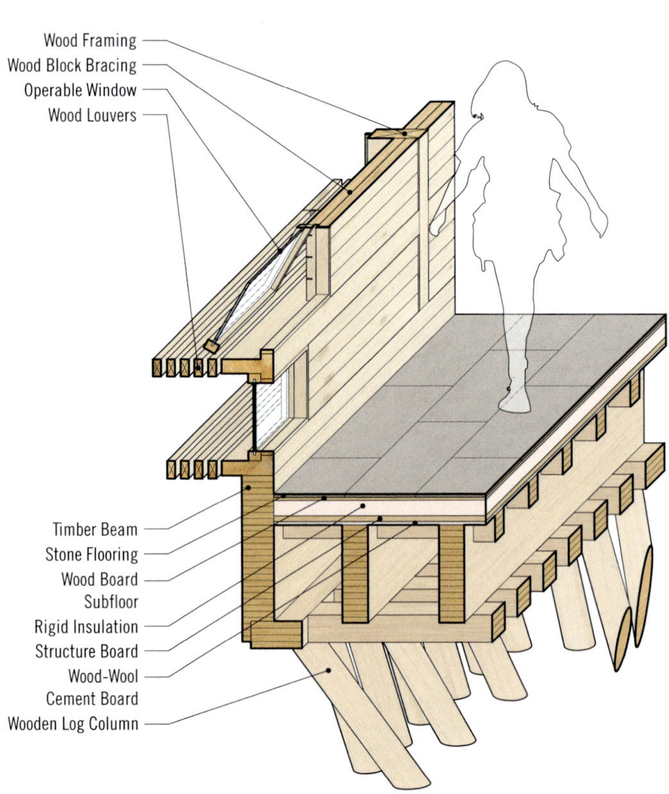

Helio Olga House
Marcos Acayaba Arquitetos

House in Itsuura
ADX

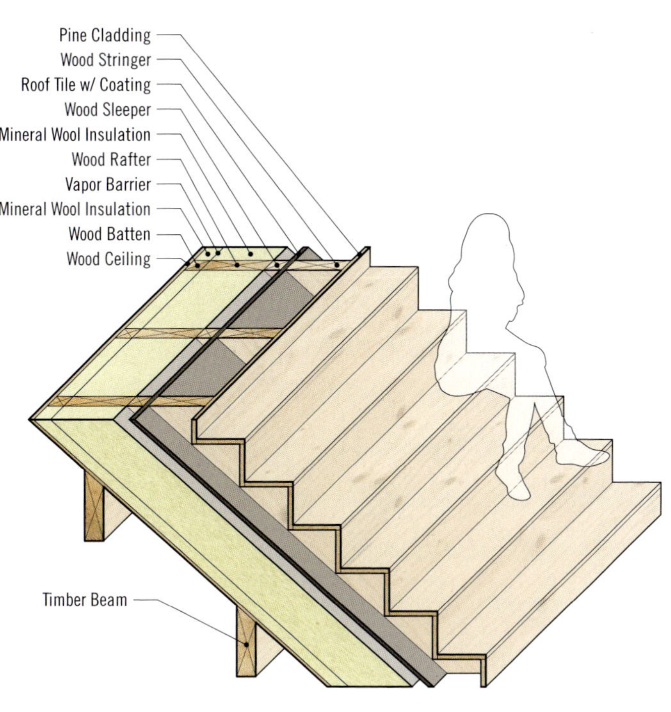

Thunder Top Cabin
Gartnerfuglen Arkitekter

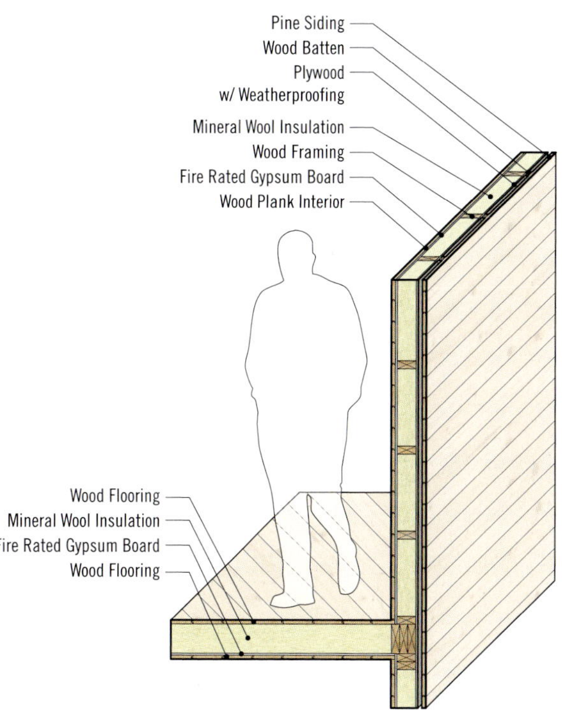

Gago House
Pezo von Ellrichshausen

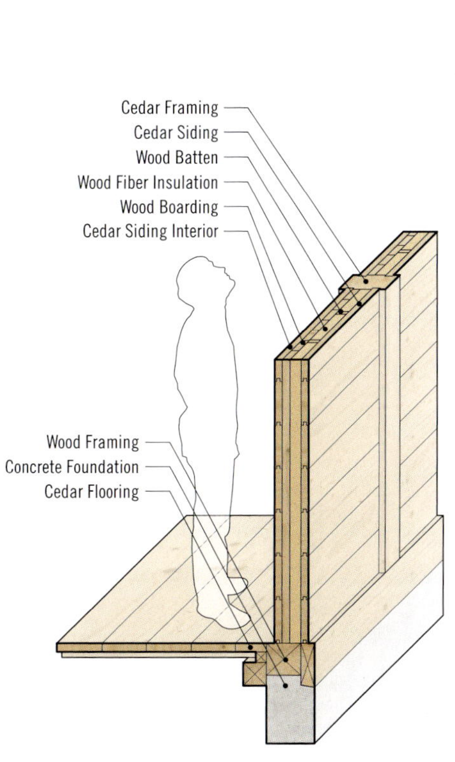

Ogimachi House
Tomoaki Uno Architects

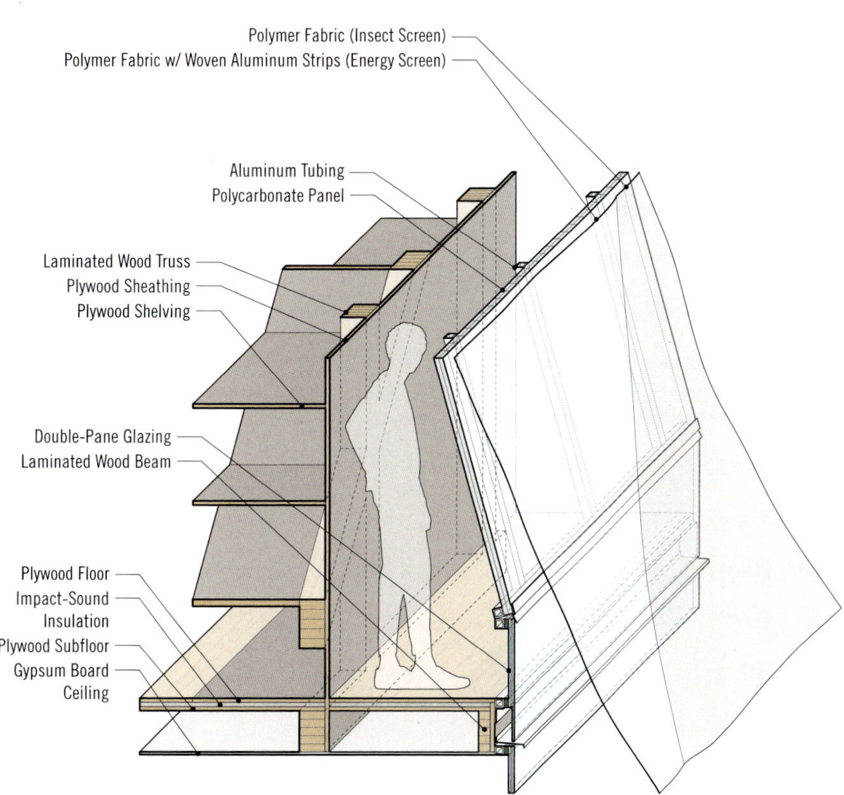

Wall House
FAR frohn&rojas

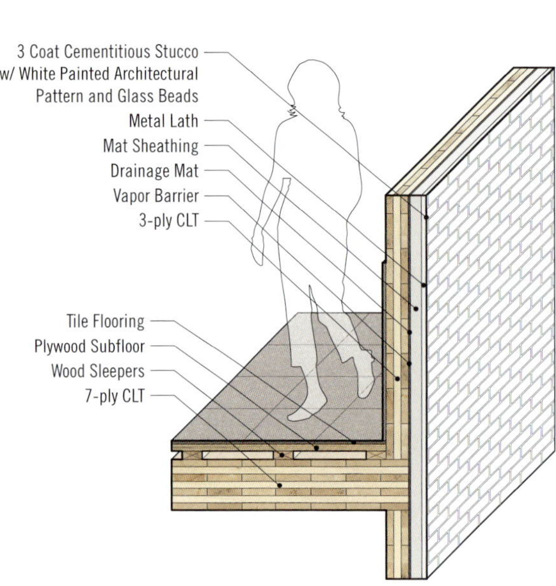

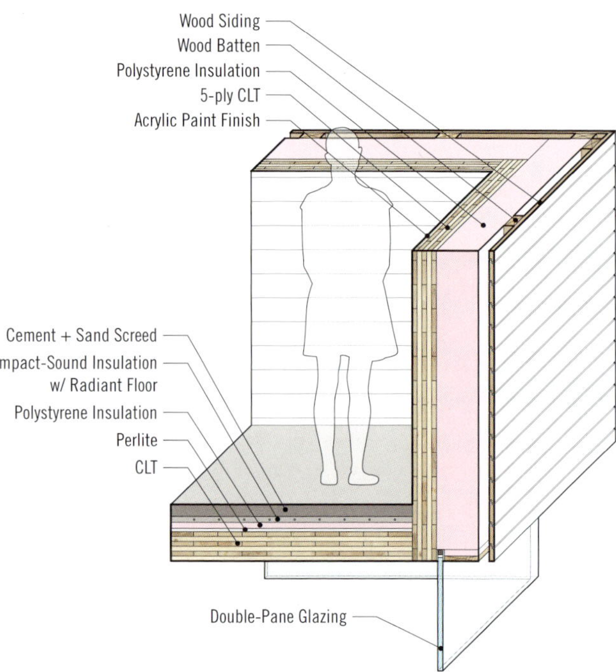

Mass Timber

Haus Gables
Jennifer Bonner / MALL

House W
Kraus Schönberg Architects

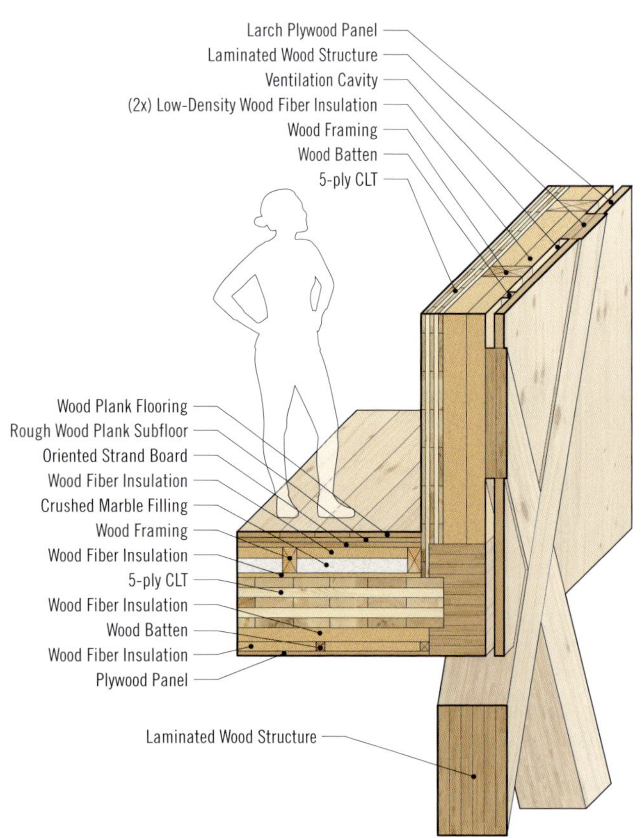

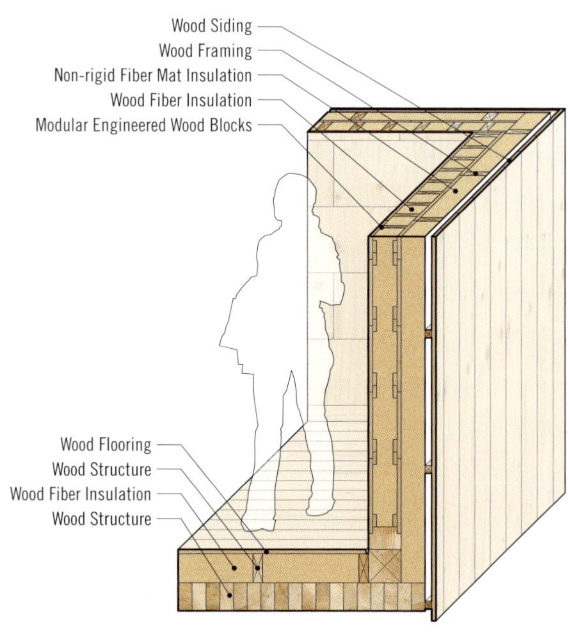

Kostner House and Studio
MoDus Architects

House Köris
Zeller & Moye

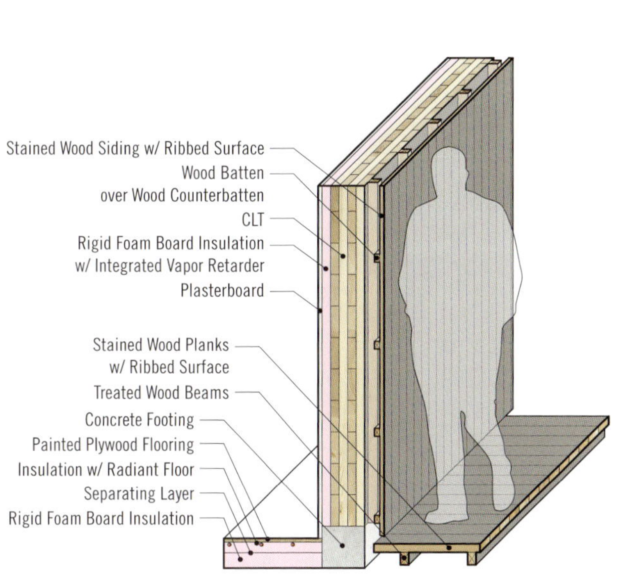

Sunken House
Adjaye Associates

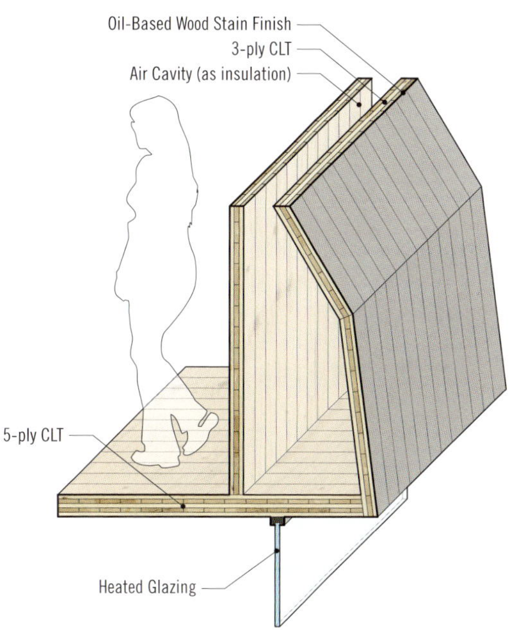

Meteorite
Ateljé Sotamaa

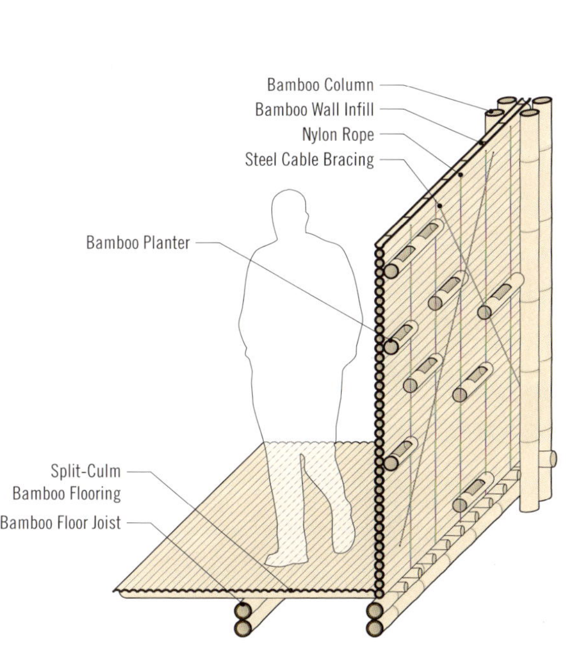

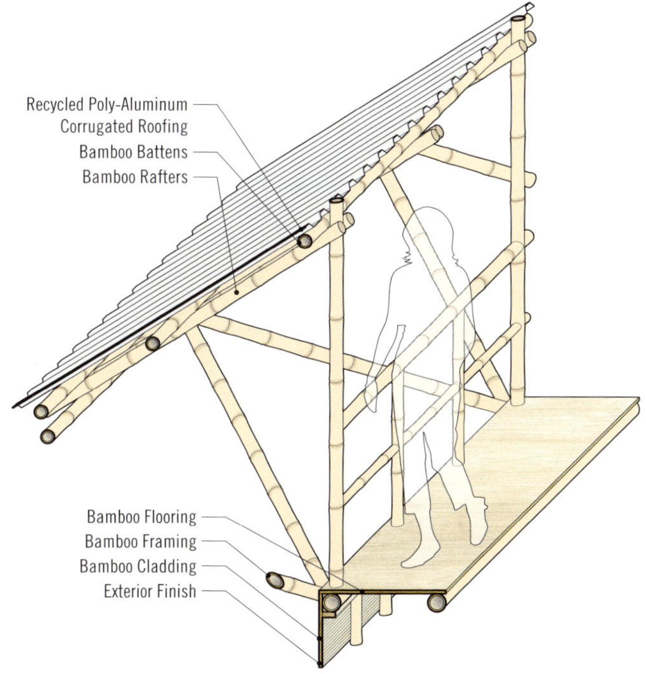

Bamboo

Blooming Bamboo Home
H&P Architects

From the Territory to the Dweller
Rozana Montiel Estudio de Arquitectura

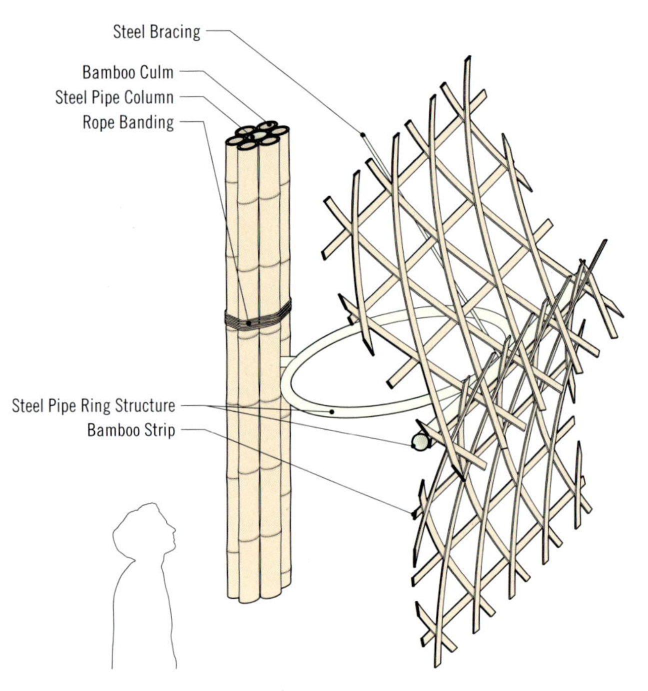

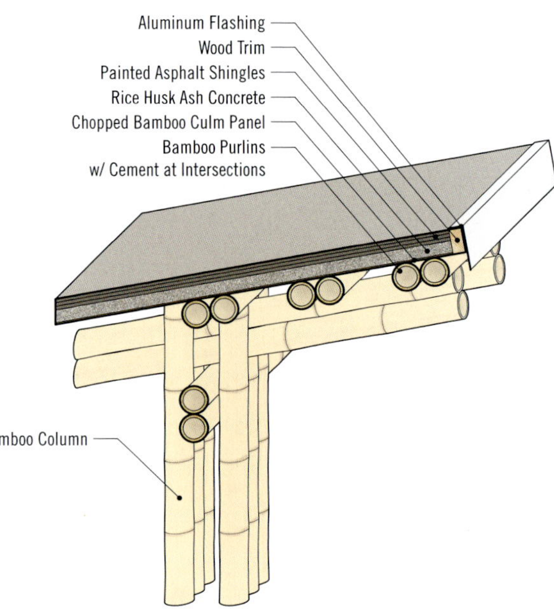

Bamboo (cont.)

Bamboo Hostels
Studio Anna Heringer

Cabañón DLPM
Juan Carlos Bamba + Ignacio de Teresa + Alejandro González

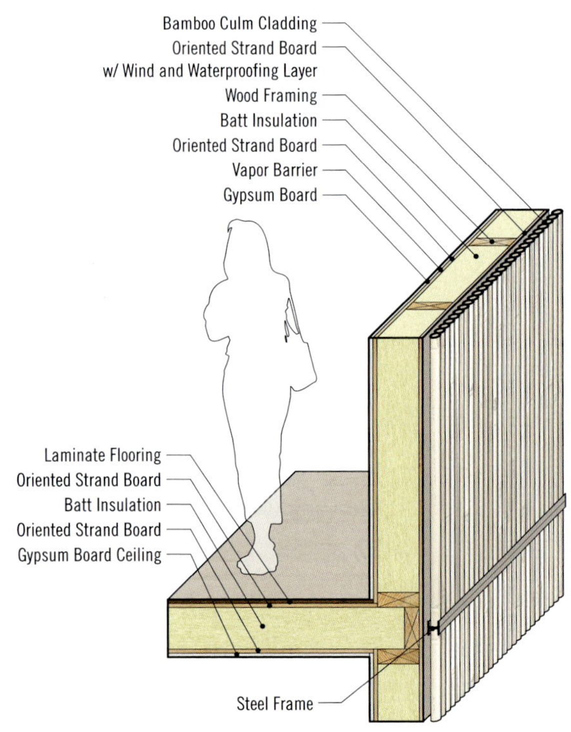

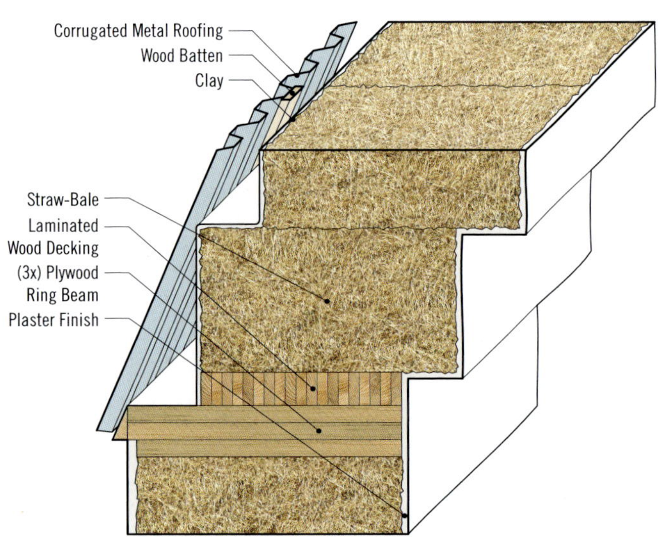

House Rotselaar
AST 77 Architecten

Straw

Gartist GmbH House
Atelier Werner Schmidt

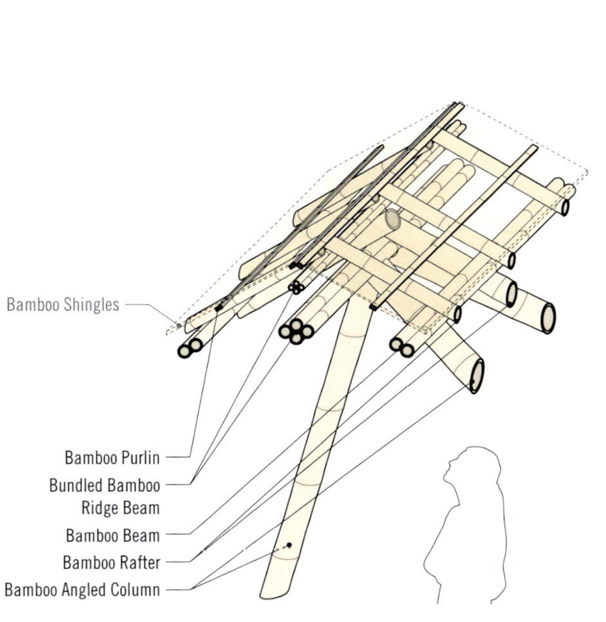

Trika Villa
Chiangmai Life Architects

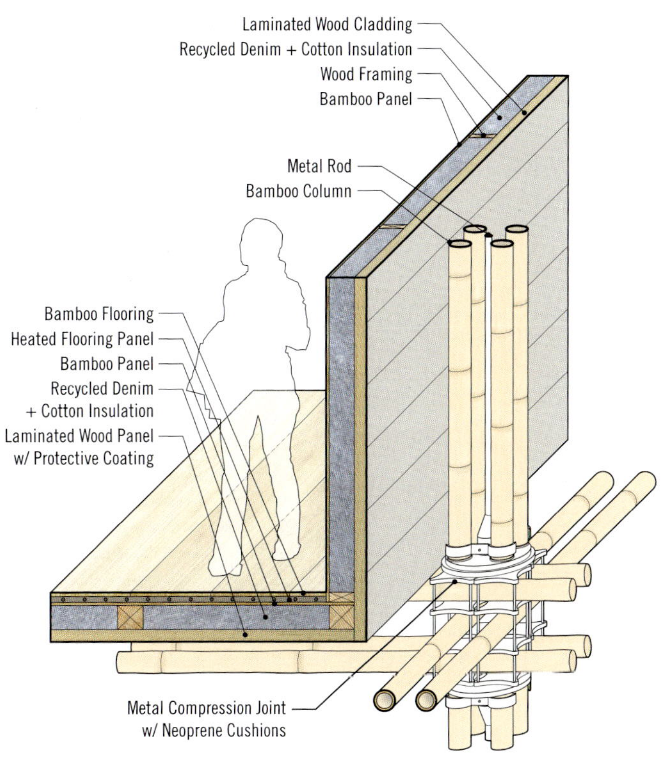

Energy Efficient Bamboo House
Studio Cardenas Conscious Design

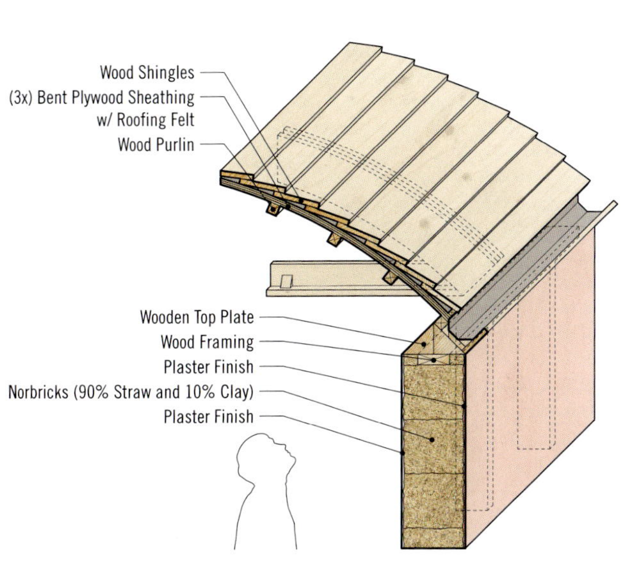

Mauritzberg Test House
Sverre Fehn

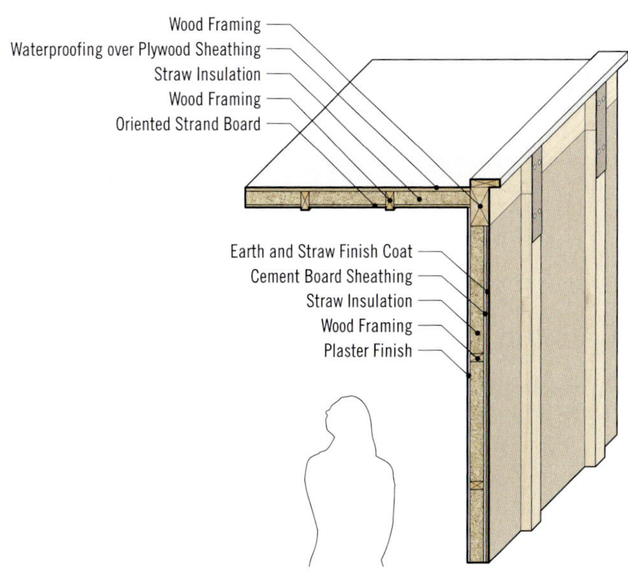

Media Perra House
Santos Bolívar

Straw (cont.)

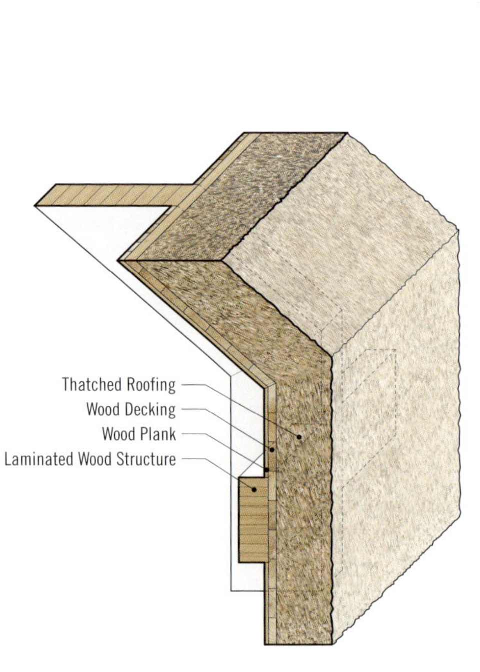

Dune House
Archispektras

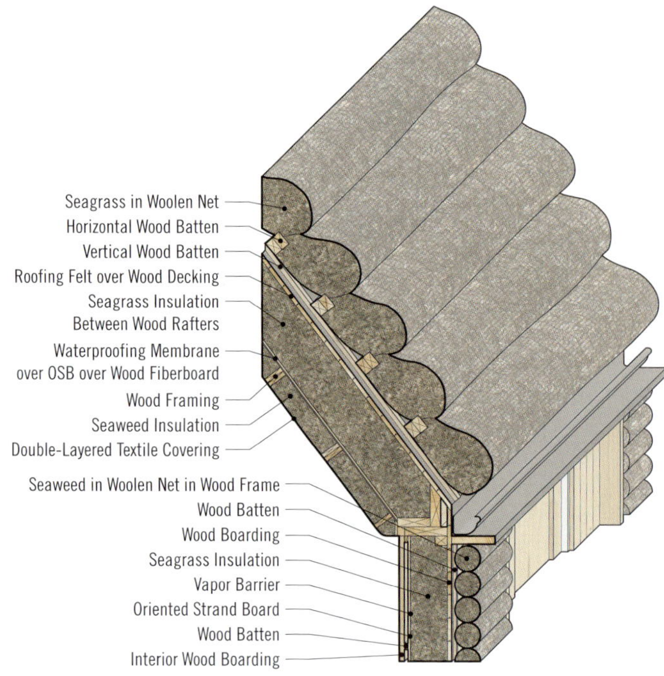

Modern Seagrass House
Vandkunsten Architects

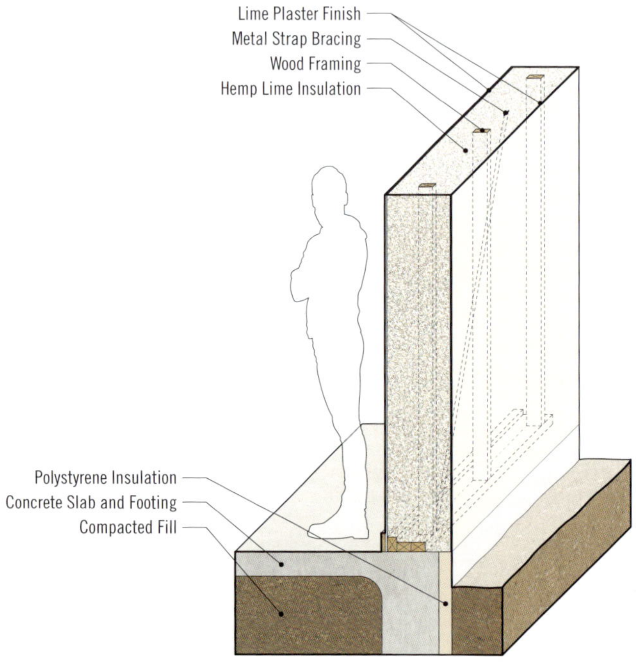

Mudgee Hempcrete House 2
Envirotecture

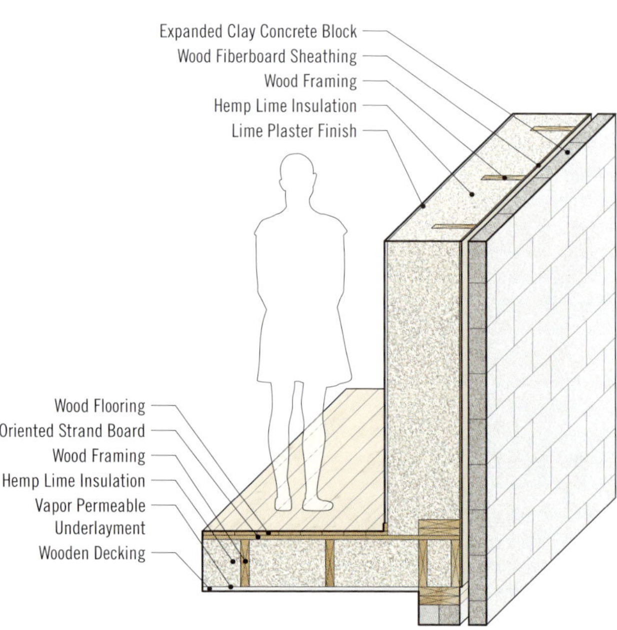

Low Energy House in Uccle
Karbon' Architecture et Urbanisme

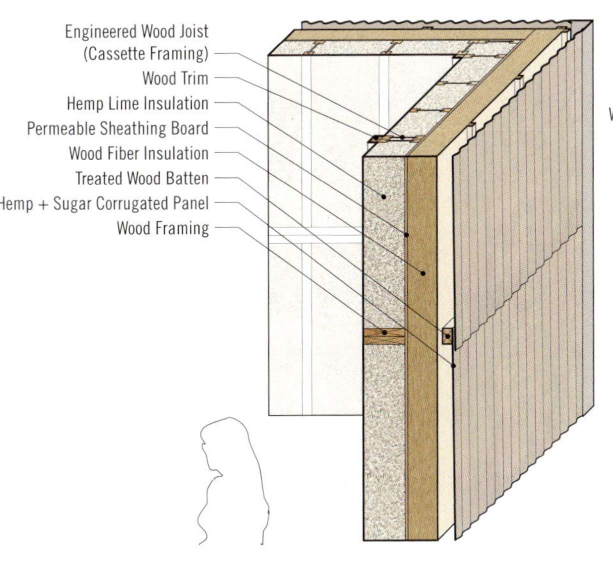

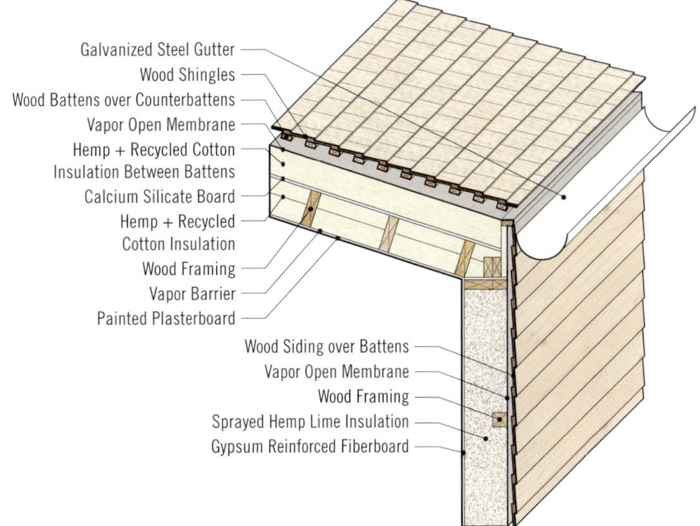

Hemp

Flat House
Practice Architecture

Clay Field
Riches Hawley Mikhail Architects

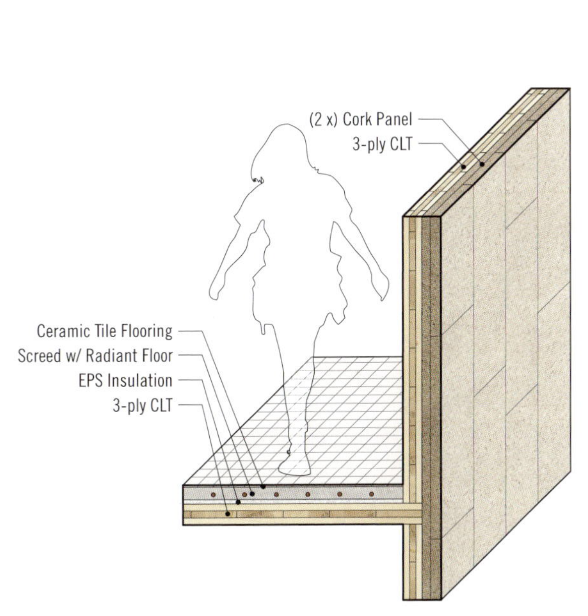

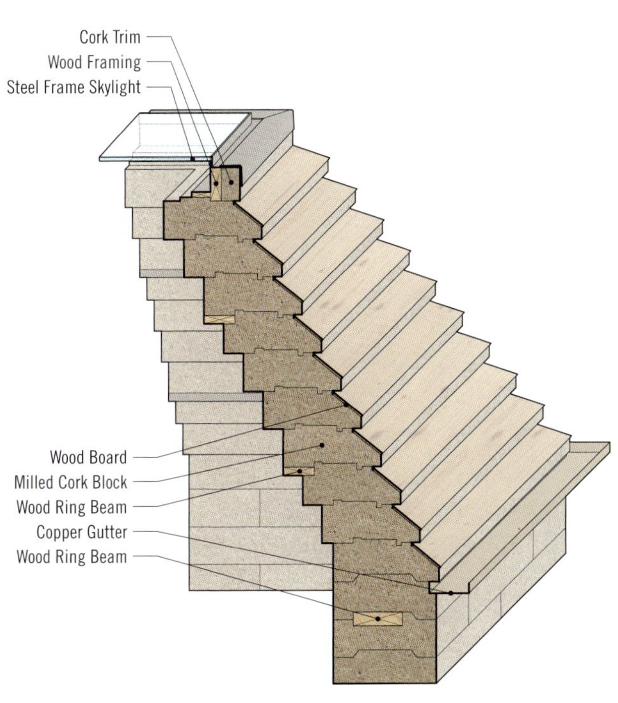

Cork

Two Cork Houses
Emiliano López Mónica Rivera Arquitectos

Cork House
Matthew Barnett Howland with
Dido Milne and Oliver Wilton

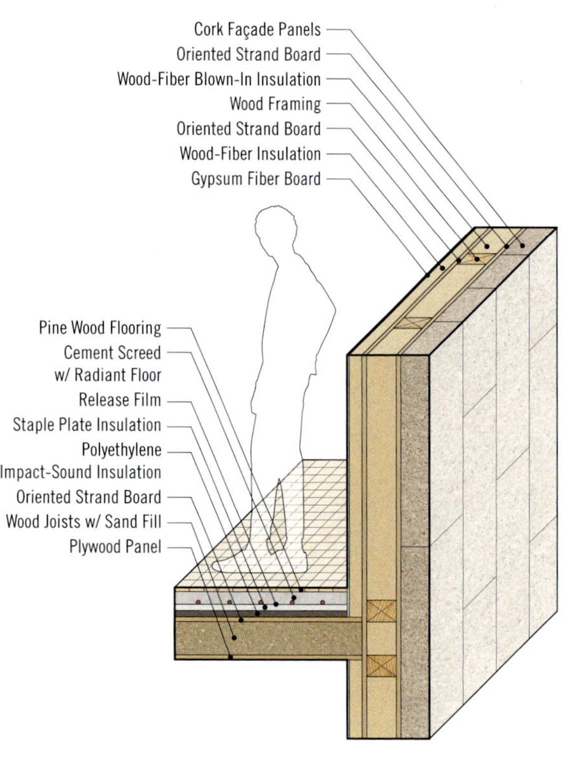

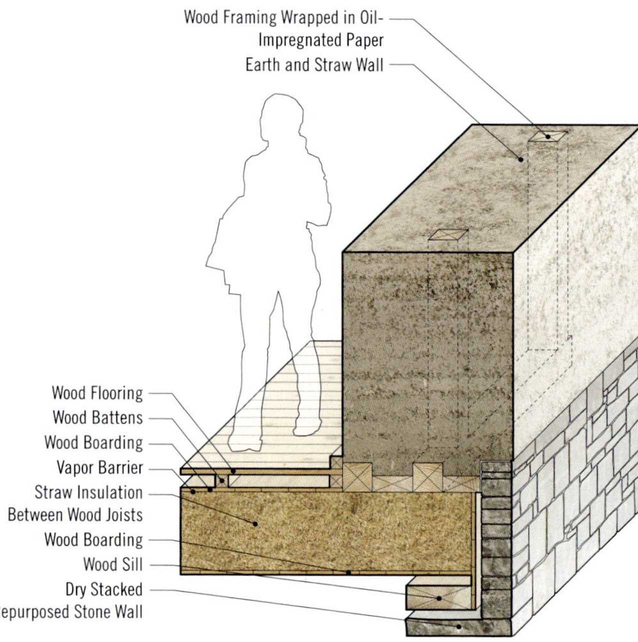

Cork (cont.)

Cork Screw House
rundzwei Architekten

Earth

Wohnhaus Flury
spaceshop Architects

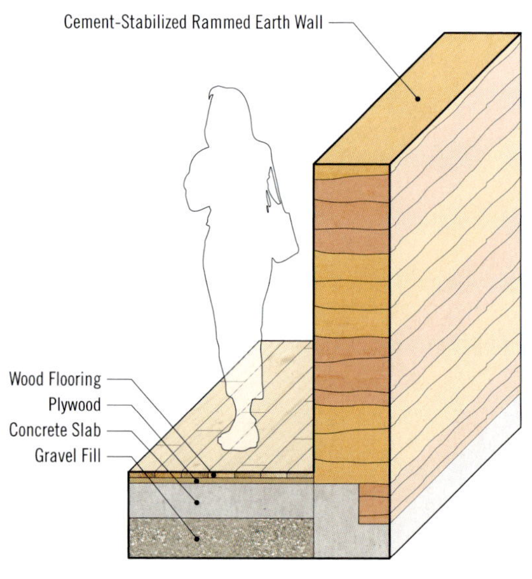

Dong Anh House
Vo Trong Nghia Architects

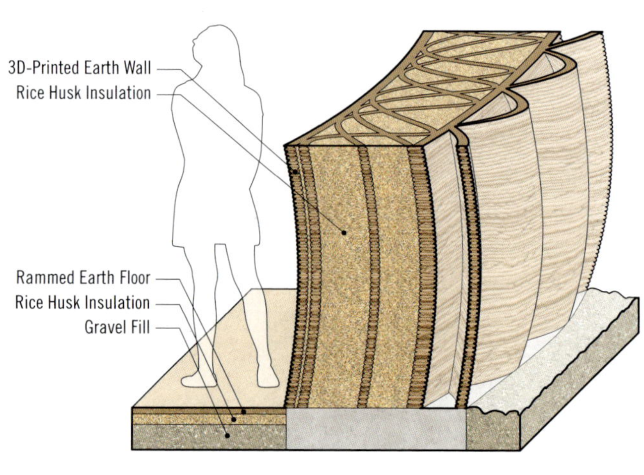

TECLA - Technology and Clay
Mario Cucinella Architects

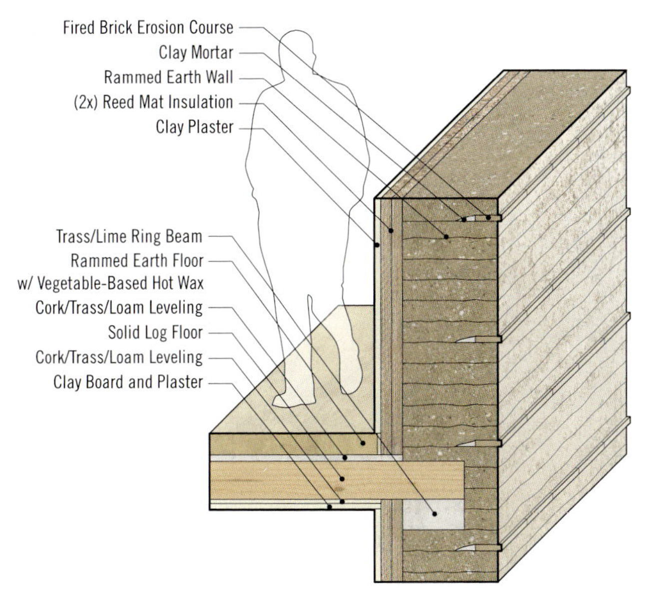

House Rauch
Boltshauser Architects, Lehm Ton Erde Baukunst

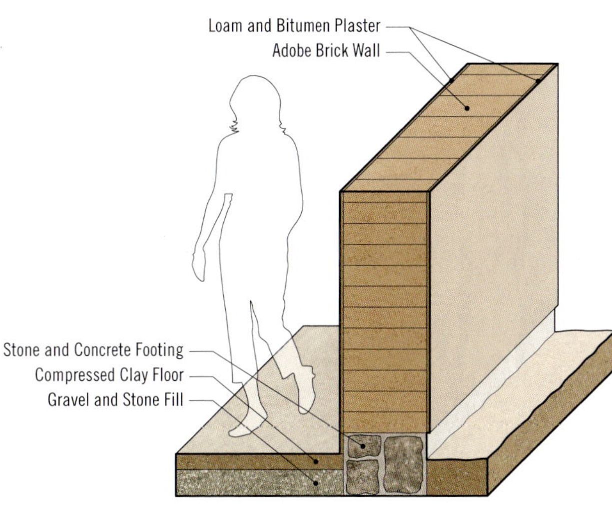

Gando Teachers' Housing
Kéré Architecture

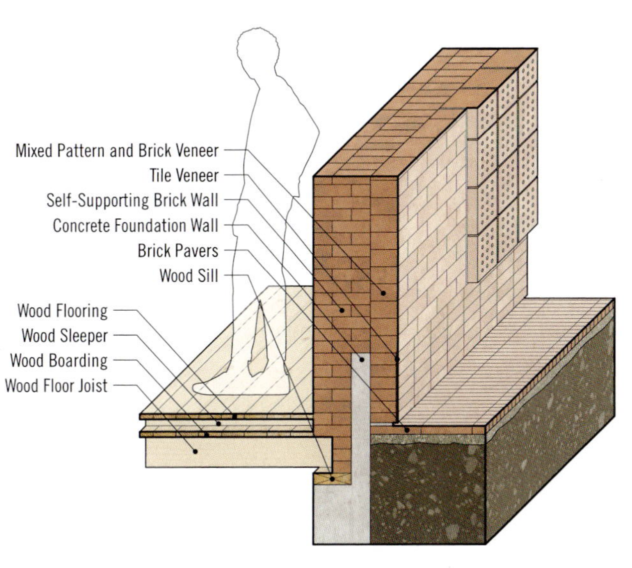

Muuratsalo Experimental House
Alvar Aalto

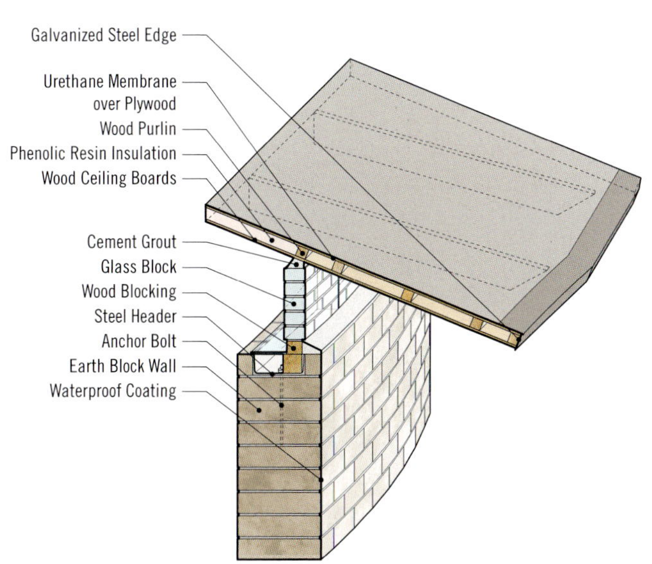

Earth Bricks
Atelier Tekuto

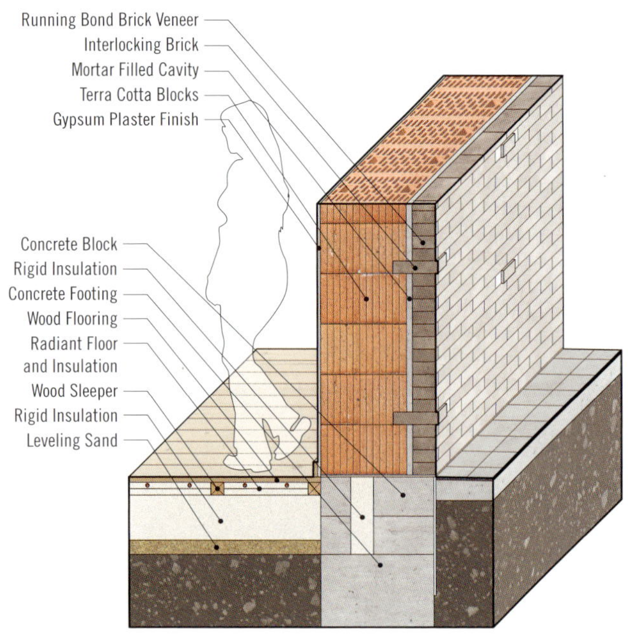

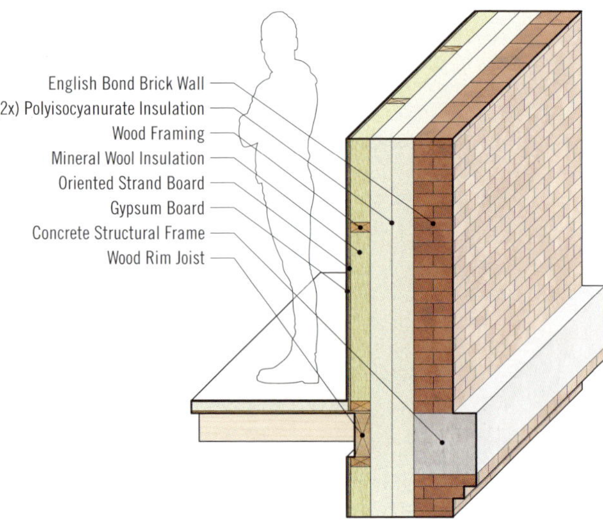

Brick (cont.)

Brick House
LETH & GORI

dnA House
BLAF Architecten

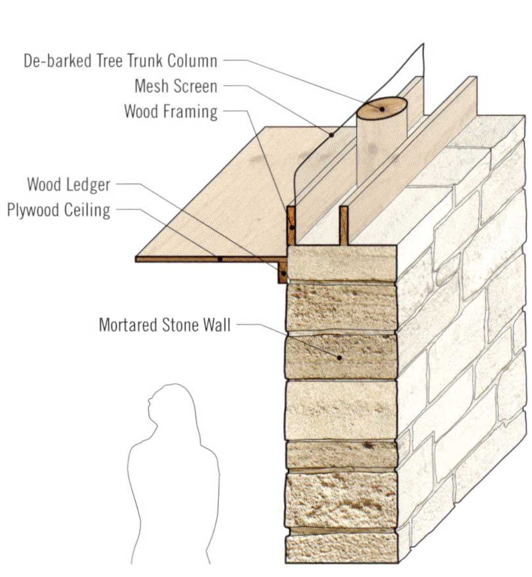

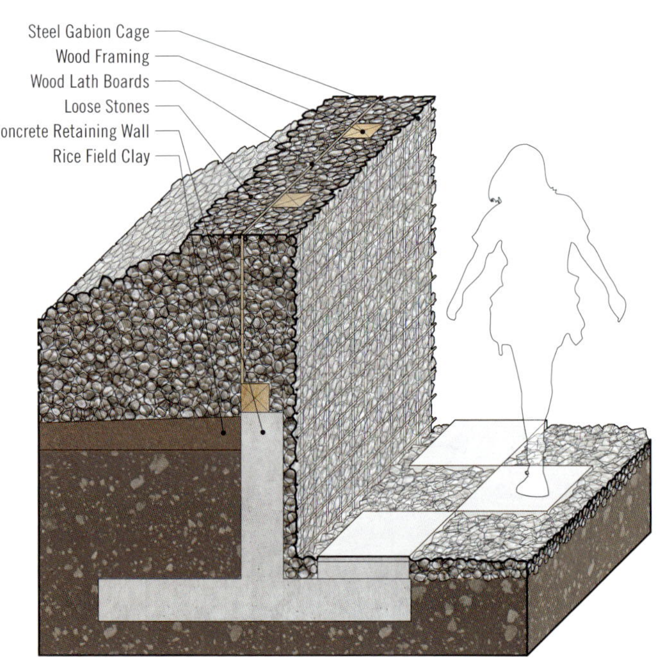

Hill Country Jacal
Lake | Flato Architects

Stone House
Sambuichi Architects

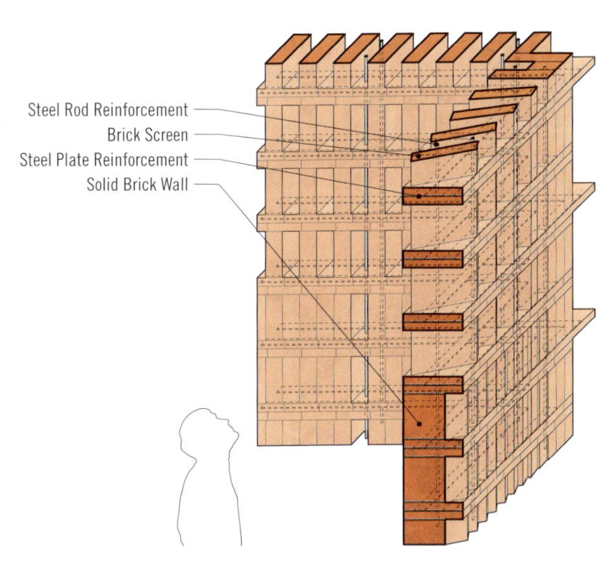

Iturbide Studio
Taller | Mauricio Rocha + Gabriela Carrillo |

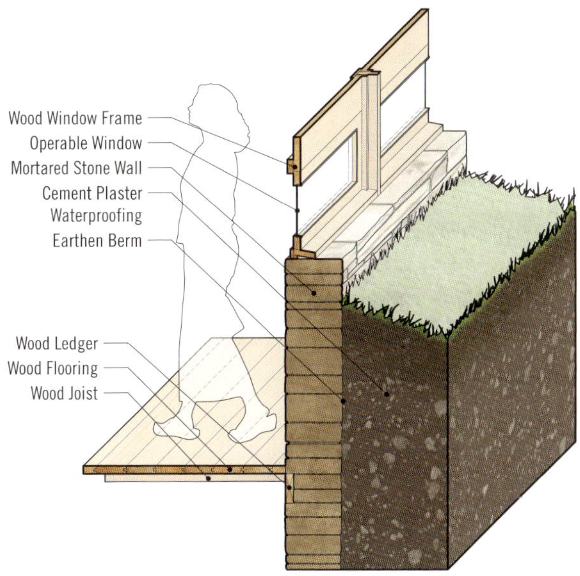

Stone

Jacobs House 2
Frank Lloyd Wright

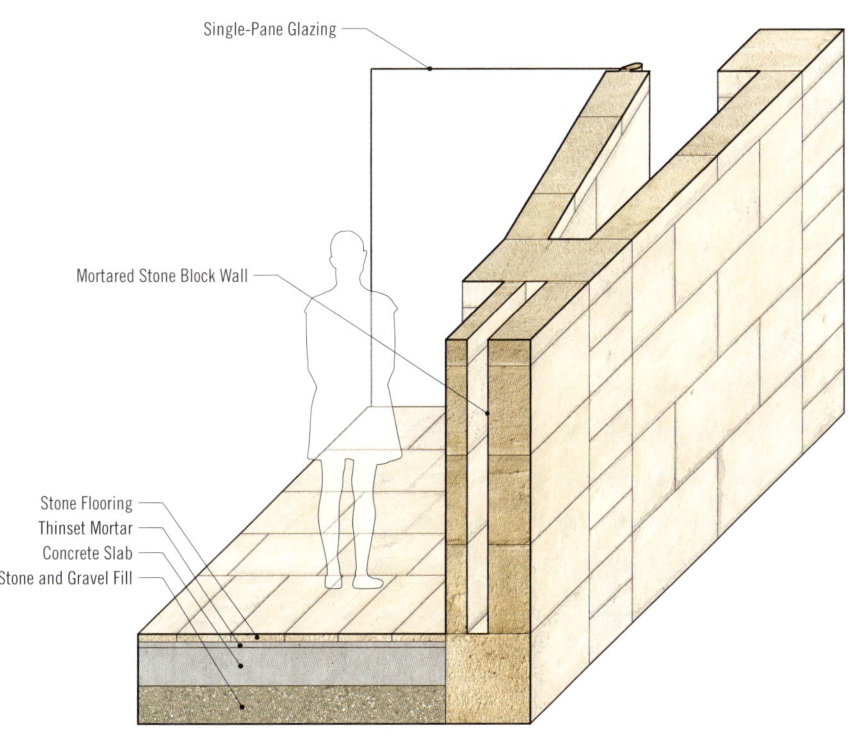

Can Lis
Jørn Utzon

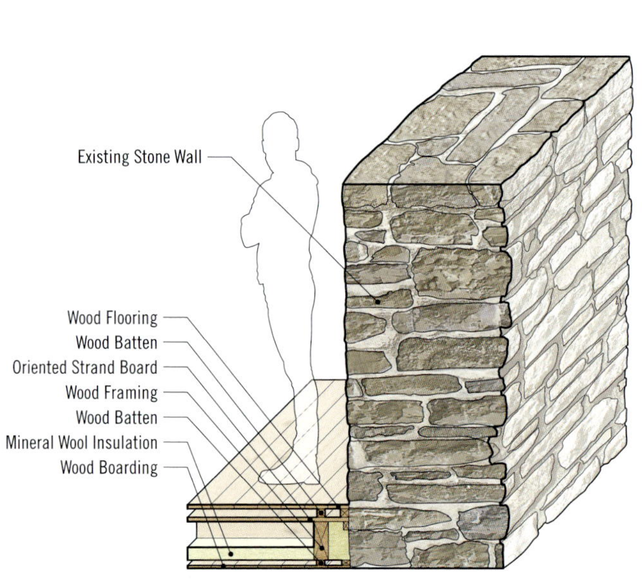

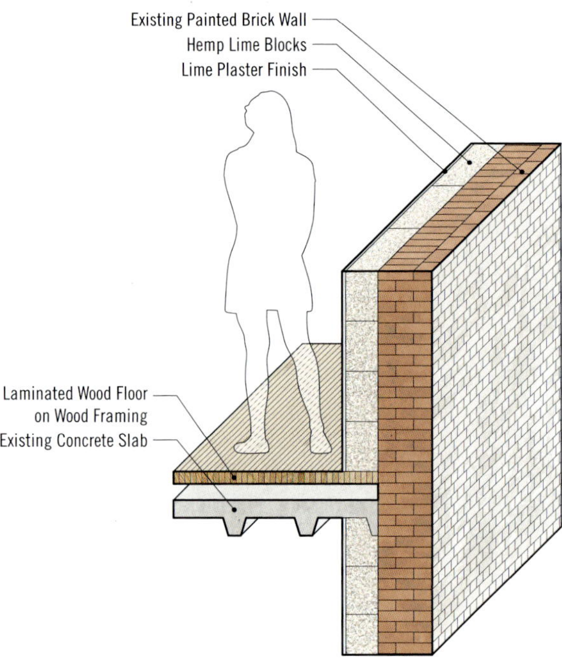

Reuse

House Renovation in Scudellate
Wespi de Meuron Romeo Architects

Verbiest
AgwA

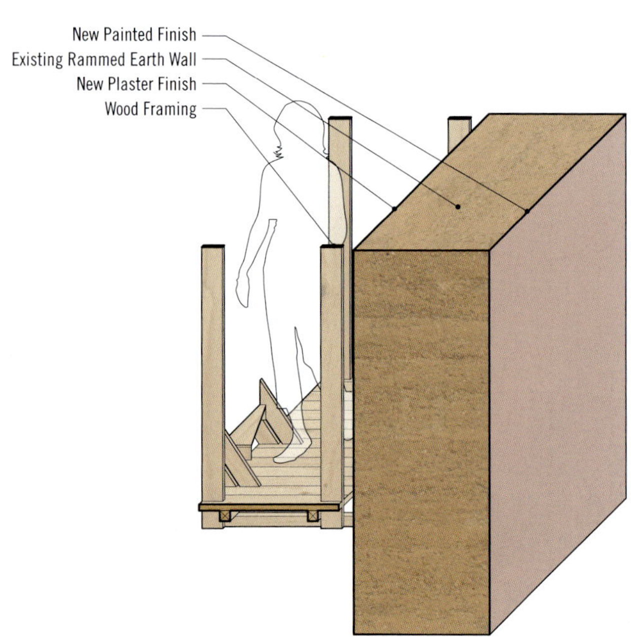

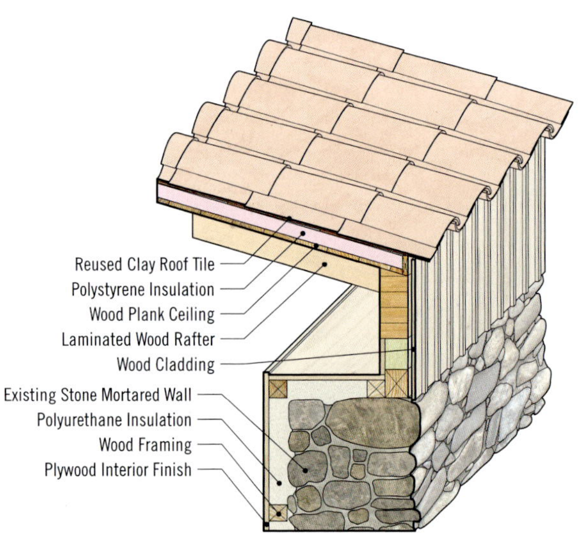

House of Flying Beds
Al Borde

Small Cottage Ojacastro
MAAV

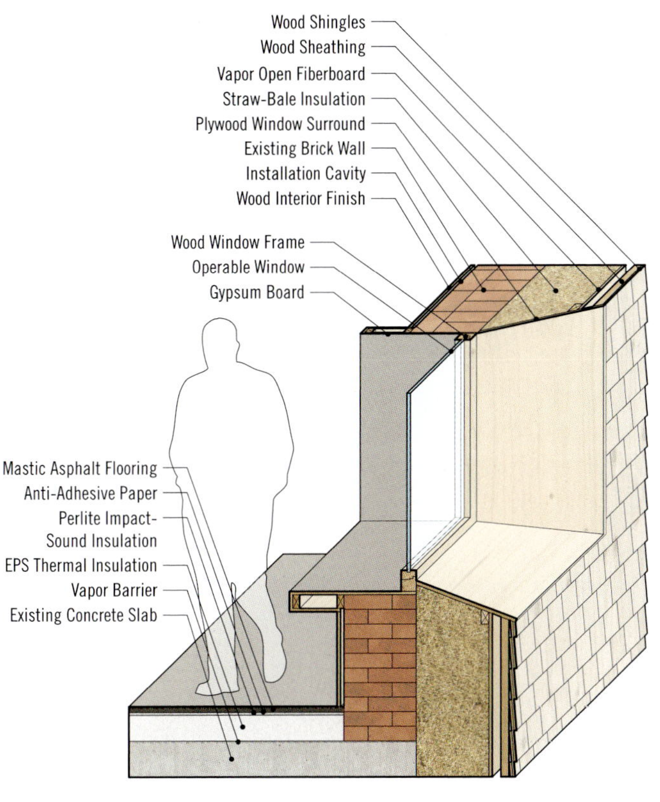

House Simma
Georg Bechter Architektur + Design

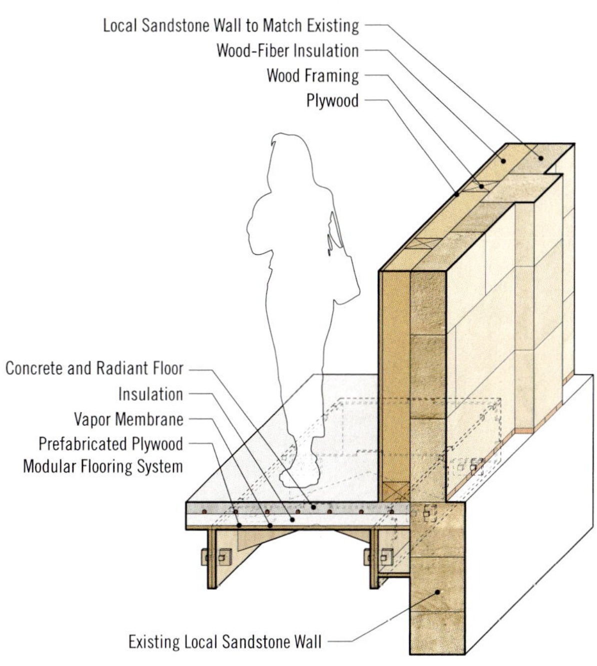

Plywood House
Feina Studio

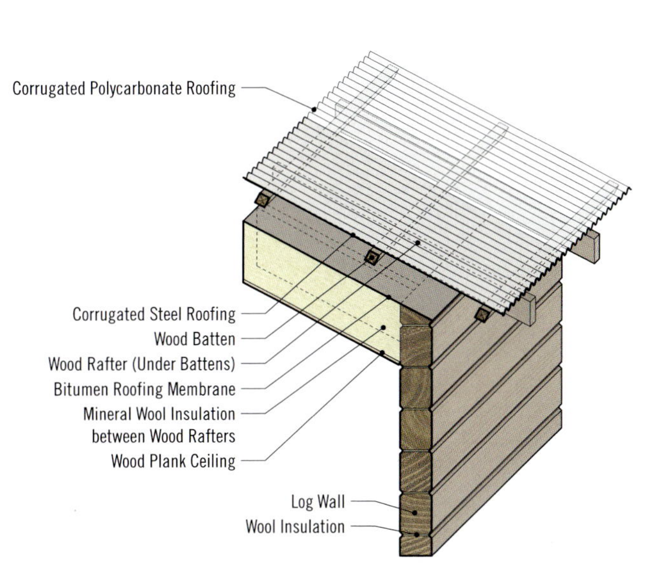

Cabin Femunden
Arkitekt Aslak Haanshuus

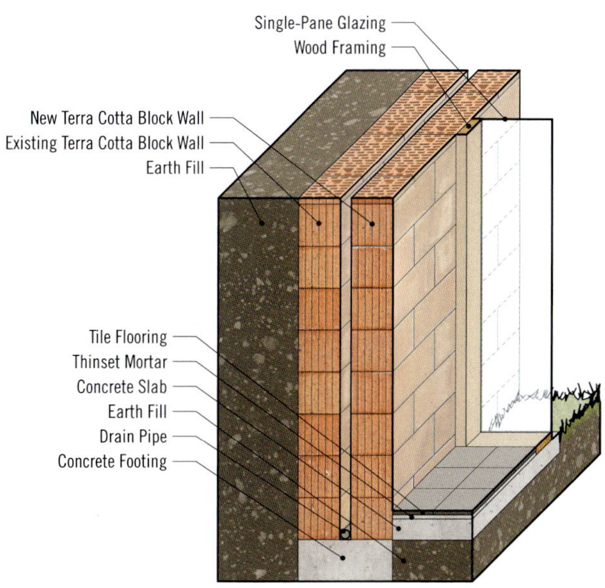

Half-Slope House
Denis Joelsons + Gabriela Baraúna Uchida

Embodied Carbon Assessment

Material choices have an impact on the environment. These impacts can and should be quantified in order to form a clear understanding of the implications of choices we make in designing and constructing houses and other buildings. The challenge in determining environmental impacts is data accuracy, transparency, and standardized reporting processes. Most materials used in construction do not yet have third-party verified environmental product declarations (EPDs) that accurately report the range of environmental impacts, including global warming potential, ozone depletion, acidification, eutrophication, abiotic depletion, and water use, and should include the impact on human health and biodiversity. EPDs are of critical importance to making informed decisions about materials. The data in an EPD is derived from life cycle assessment (LCA) methodology that calculates the environmental impact of the product from extraction through end of life. An EPD for a given product is based on agreed-upon product category rules (PCRs) so that there is a standardized basis for conducting an LCA for a given product type.

Organizing this data-driven process are the different stages of a life cycle that materials and buildings go through. The standard life cycle stages for conducting a single product LCA are defined by EN 15978 or ISO 21930:2017 and form a framework for evaluation. The primary stages of a life cycle are the product stage (A1-3), construction stage (A4-5), use stage (B1-5), use stage operational (B6-7), end-of-life stage (C1-4), and beyond life cycle (D). Different groupings of these stages are referred to by shorthand terms. For instance, cradle-to-gate stages are only those in the product stage (A1-3) and designate the impact from raw material supply, to transportation to the factory to manufacturing, but not any impacts or energy costs past the gate of the factory. A life cycle assessment that includes all stages at the scale of a structure or project is a whole building life cycle assessment (WBLCA).

For the purposes of this book, we are calculating the global warming potential of the assembled materials, quantified by kilograms of CO_2 equivalent ($kgCO_2e$). One house from each material chapter was selected and the carbon was calculated using a shared set of available and published data for the product stage (A1-3). We have derived this data set from published records and known databases, giving priority to sources that provide an aggregated value from a larger set of EPDs and studies for a given material. For each material, we used the same determination process. We started with the Inventory of Carbon & Energy (ICE), then ÖKOBAUDAT, then BEAM Estimator, and then industry average or product-specific EPDs for a few items to define the values for this exercise.

Using available construction documentation, we generated digital models of the houses to determine material quantities. In most instances, we used the volume of the material as the measurable unit, except for thin sheet goods where the area was quantified. Because the houses are so unique in their construction they do not pair well with the typical user-facing input format of many available embodied carbon calculators, which assume common contemporary forms of North American construction.

We focused on cradle-to-gate embodied carbon in $kgCO_2e$ data to demonstrate the important way in which biogenic material choices impact global warming. This intentionally eliminates the unique site of each house as a variable, removing the energy and embodied carbon cost for transportation from the factory to the site and for construction. We want to make clear that this means that the data provided are not calculations of the precise materials or products used in each specific house and do not reflect the different local energy infrastructures within which each house exists. This is intentional in order to focus the assessment on the consequences of the design and its materials as if each project were built in the same location. The goal is not the absolute accuracy of the actual embodied carbon of a given project. Not only would that require published data for a unique set of products for each house that may not exist, but the conclusions would reflect the divergence of national and local energy systems. For instance, a material made and shipped in a country with a high percentage of renewable energy could significantly outperform the same material made in a country dependent on coal. This is not to say that such an inventory isn't valid. It is and a WBLCA for all projects is needed during the design process. Rather, for the purposes of this publication, we are interested in the consequences of materials thus muting other variables intentionally.

In addition, we have chosen to include biogenic or sequestered carbon within these cradle-to-gate calculations. This practice is critical in order to recognize the positive, up-front impact of these plant-based materials made through photosynthesis. We have limited time to radically reduce and eliminate the release of greenhouse gases, and acknowledging the $kgCO_2e$ that biogenic materials sequester now is key to informing policy and transforming entrenched design and construction economies and practices. At some point, biogenic sequestered carbon will most likely be released back into the global carbon cycle. But that 30, 50, or 200 years of sequestration combined with the avoidance of commonplace emitting materials, gives us the time we all need now to reestablish our relationship with the earth.

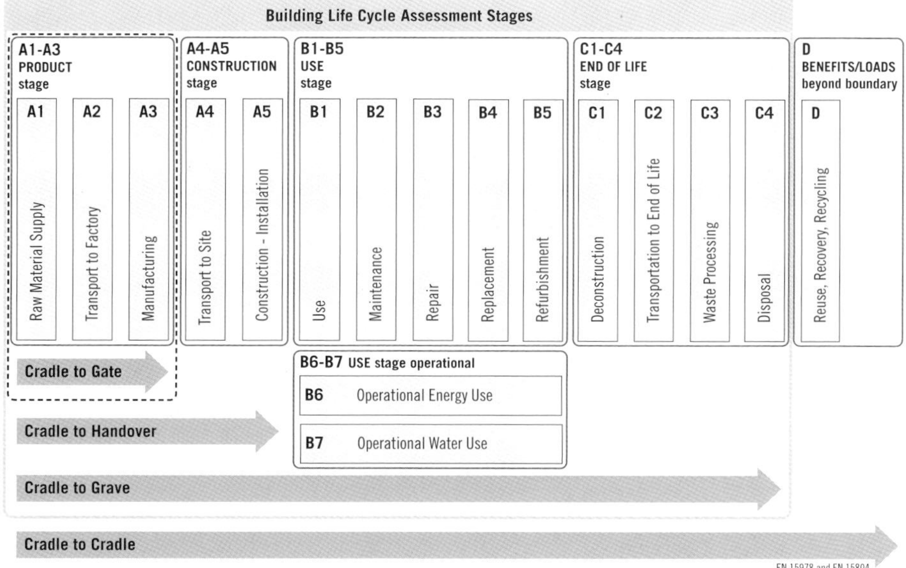

Embodied Carbon by Material

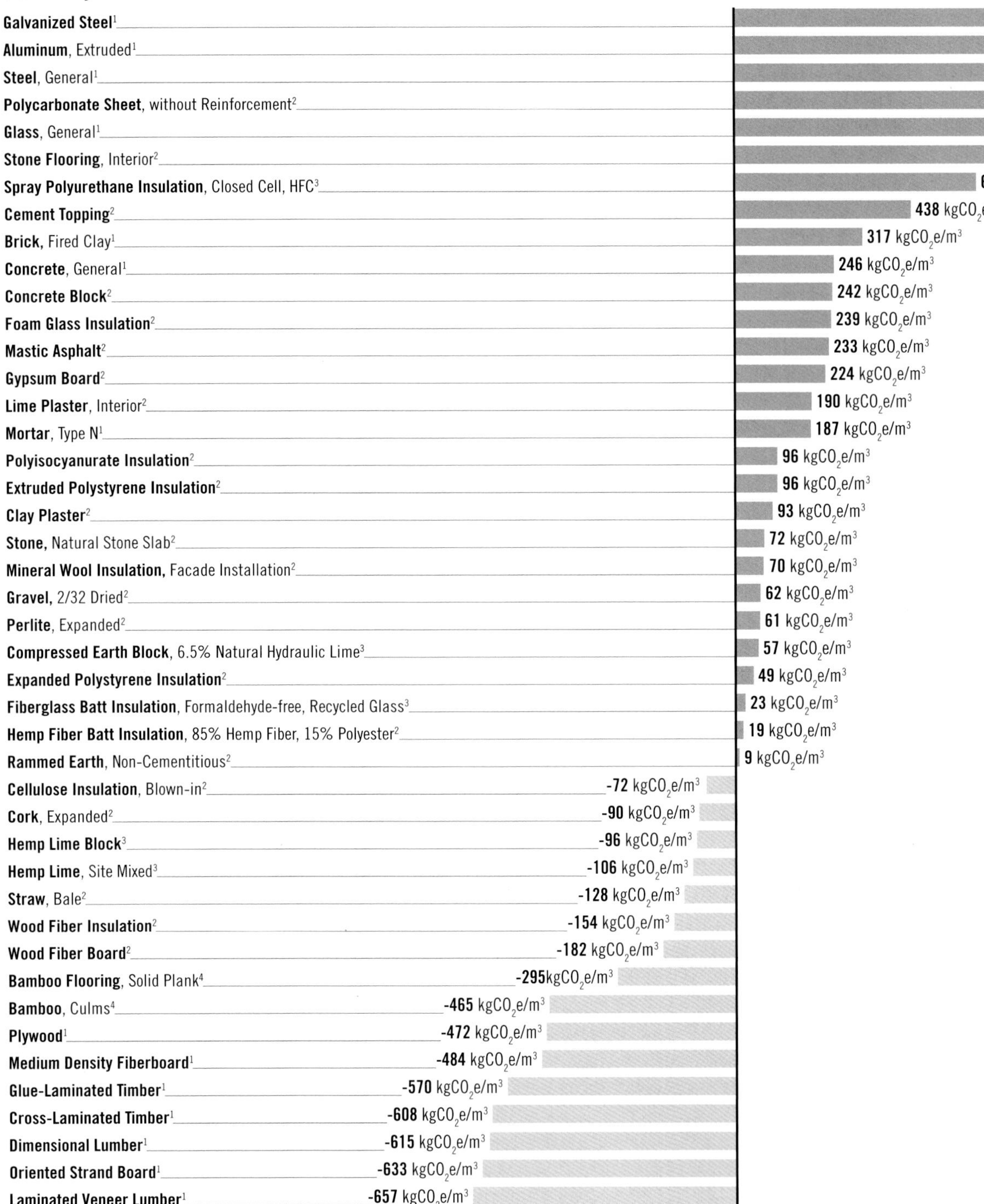

Materials by Area

Material	Embodied carbon
Clay Roof Tile[2]	**16** kgCO$_2$e/m^2
Terrazzo Flooring, Site Cast, Cement Binder[5]	**9** kgCO$_2$e/m^2
EPDM Membrane[2]	**9** kgCO$_2$e/m^2
Carpet, Nylon, Polypropylene and Polyester Blend[2]	**9** kgCO$_2$e/m^2
Polyurethane Membrane[6]	**8** kgCO$_2$e/m^2
Vinyl Tile, Heterogeneous[2]	**6** kgCO$_2$e/m^2
Vinyl Siding[7]	**5** kgCO$_2$e/m^2
Asphalt Shingles, with Underlayment[8]	**5** kgCO$_2$e/m^2
Bitumen Membrane[2]	**2** kgCO$_2$e/m^2
Vapor Barrier, Polyethylene[2]	**0.4** kgCO$_2$e/m^2

21,666 kgCO$_2$e/m^3 ►
18,373 kgCO$_2$e/m^3 ►
17,898 kgCO$_2$e/m^3 ►
7,123 kgCO$_2$e/m^3 ►
3,593 kgCO$_2$e/m^3

Notes All of the total embodied carbon numbers listed only represent life cycle assessment stages A1-A3, cradle to gate.

These numbers are estimates and reflect the best available published information as of May 2022. The use of a single number is for clarity of comparison, and should nevertheless be understood as an approximation, as specific material carbon data is subject to many variables.

The values given are drawn from publicly available carbon databases and EPDs as identified in the footnotes listed below. To be as consistent as possible, embodied carbon data was sourced from databases in the following order: Inventory of Carbon and Energy, version 3.0 2019, then Ökobaudat, then BEAM Estimator. Specific materials not contained in those databases were sourced from individual EPDs as noted.

Databases
[1] Inventory of Carbon and Energy, version 3.0, 2019
https://circularecology.com
[2] Ökobaudat
https://www.oekobaudat.de
[3] BEAM Estimator
https://www.buildersforclimateaction.org

Individual EPDs
[4] INBAR, Technical Report #35
https://www.inbar.int
[5] Herrljunga Terrazzo
https://www.epd-norge.no
[6] Sikalastic©-618
https://www.igbc.ie
[7] Vinyl Siding Institute - Industry Average
https://www.vinylsiding.org
[8] Asphalt Roofing Manufacturer's Association - Industry Average
https://www.asphaltroofing.org

Carbon Estimates

Wood Frame

Ogimachi House
Tomoaki Uno Architects

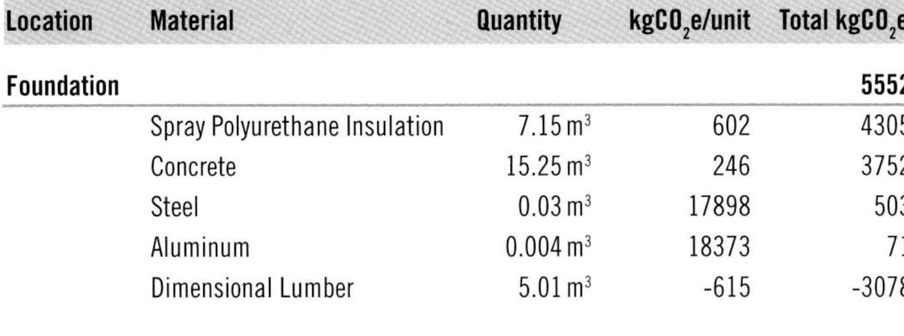

Location	Material	Quantity	$kgCO_2e$/unit	Total $kgCO_2e$
Foundation				**5552**
	Spray Polyurethane Insulation	7.15 m^3	602	4305
	Concrete	15.25 m^3	246	3752
	Steel	0.03 m^3	17898	503
	Aluminum	0.004 m^3	18373	71
	Dimensional Lumber	5.01 m^3	-615	-3078
Roof				**1013**
	Spray Polyurethane Insulation	10.95 m^3	602	6592
	Galvanized Steel	0.05 m^3	21666	1015
	Aluminum	0.03 m^3	18373	469
	Glass	0.08 m^3	3593	280
	Bitumen Membrane	71.10 m^2	2	164
	Plywood	1.43 m^3	-472	-674
	Dimensional Lumber	11.12 m^3	-615	-6832
Interior				**-8010**
	Gypsum Board	0.14 m^3	224	32
	Plywood	0.11 m^3	-472	-52
	Dimensional Lumber	13.00 m^3	-615	-7990
Exterior				**-12724**
	Galvanized Steel	0.02 m^3	21666	376
	Vapor Barrier	195.89 m^2	0.4	78
	Wood Fiber Insulation	6.12 m^3	-154	-942
	Dimensional Lumber	19.91 m^3	-615	-12235

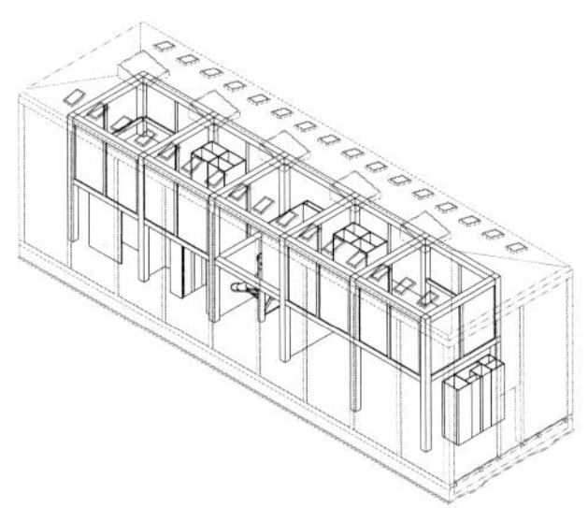

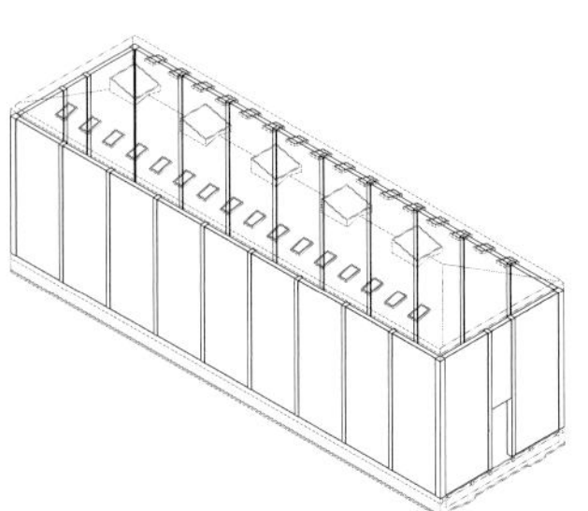

31.6k standard home

5.6k

-8.0k

-12.7k

-14.2k total

Total **-14,168 $kgCO_2e$**
Area 113 m^2
Total per Area **-125 $kgCO_2e/m^2$**

Assumptions:
Skylights are double pane glass, 4 + 4mm
Skylight frames are calculated as 20% of simplified frame volume
Roof is 29 gauge galvanized steel
Skylight frame edge is 16 gauge aluminum
Steel column footings are 7 mm thick at perimeter and 16 mm thick at the base
Foundation standoffs are 2 mm hollow tube aluminum
Balcony railing is 10 gauge galvanized steel

Exclusions:
Crushed stone underneath the foundation
Spreading silica gel in the roof
Fasteners
MEP
Fixtures
Concrete reinforcement
Flashing
Gutters and downspouts
Landscaping
Counters and casework

Mass Timber

Meteorite
Ateljé Sotamaa

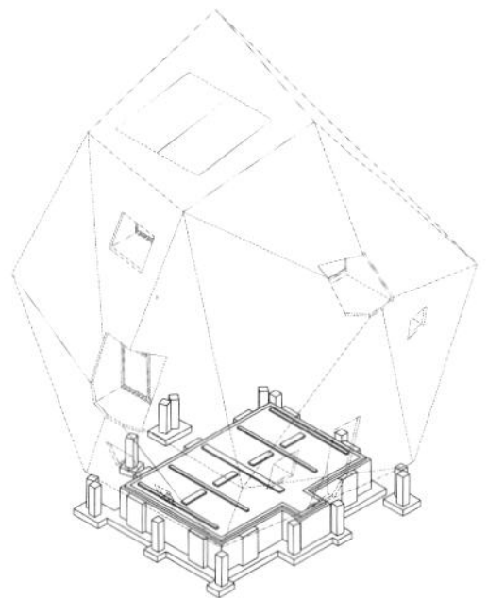

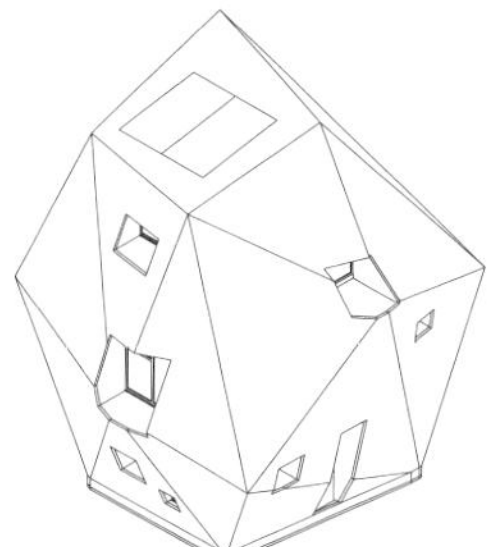

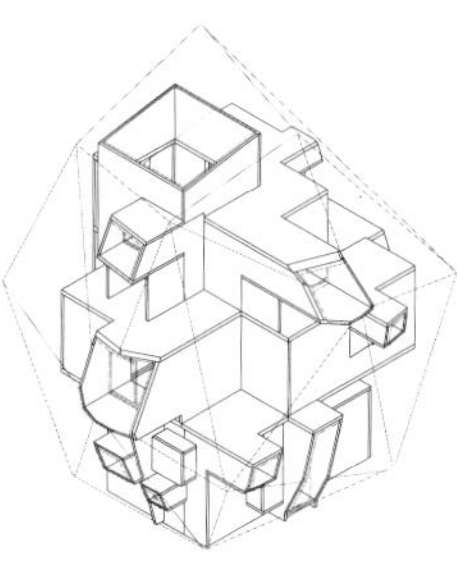

Location	Material	Quantity	$kgCO_2e$/unit	Total $kgCO_2e$
Foundation				**2862**
	Concrete	10.97 m^3	246	2699
	Expanded Polystyrene Insulation	7.10 m^3	49	348
	Dimensional Lumber	0.30 m^3	-615	-185
Exterior				**-17737**
	Aluminum	0.08 m^3	18373	1510
	Glass	0.21 m^3	3593	766
	Steel	0.01 m^3	17898	116
	Cross-Laminated Timber	33.12 m^3	-608	-20129
Interior				**-33540**
	Glass	0.21 m^3	3593	762
	Steel	0.01 m^3	17898	230
	Cement Topping	0.23 m^3	438	102
	Gypsum Board	0.22 m^3	224	49
	Dimensional Lumber	0.86 m^3	-615	-527
	Cross-Laminated Timber	56.20 m^3	-608	-34156

Total **-48,416 $kgCO_2e$**
Area 98 m^2
Total per Area **-432 $kgCO_2e/m^2$**

Assumptions:
Steel door frames are 18 gauge
Steel door panels are 24 gauge
Windows are double pane glass, 4 + 4 mm
Interior glass transom is single pane glass, 4 mm
Glass railings are 2 x 10 mm
Window frames are calculated as 20% of simplified frame volume
Floor area calculation includes space of netting and window seats

Exclusions:
Deck
Insulation beneath deck
Drainage mat
Oil-based wood stain
Fastners
Gravel in foundation
MEP
Fixtures
Concrete reinforcement
Flashing
Built-in furniture, counters, and casework

Bamboo

Blooming Bamboo Home
H&P Architects

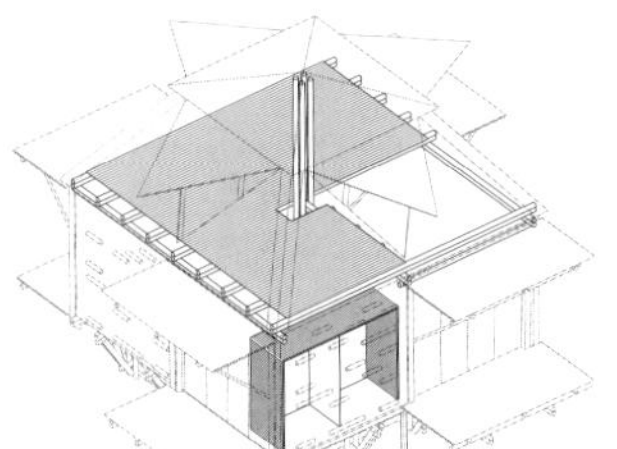

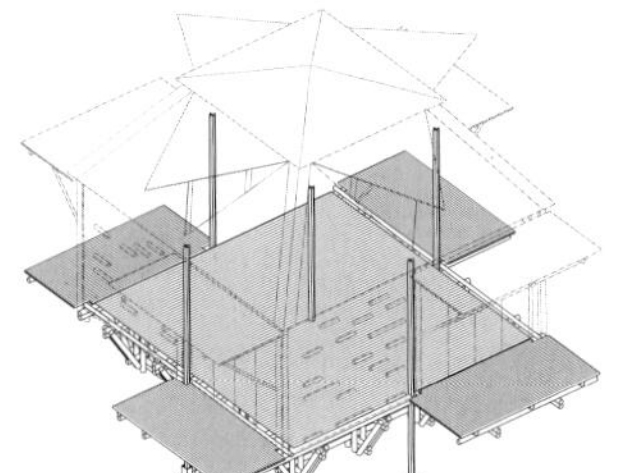

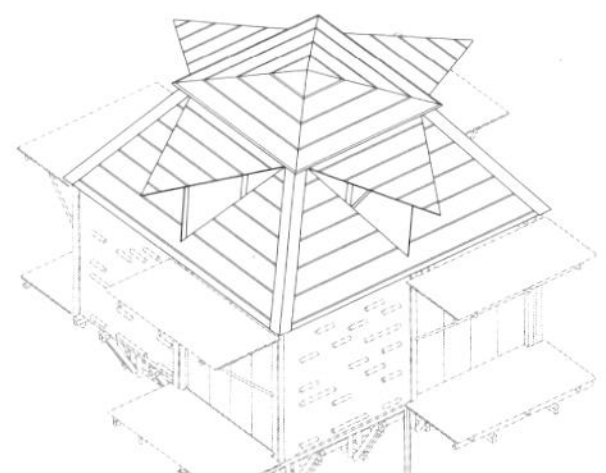

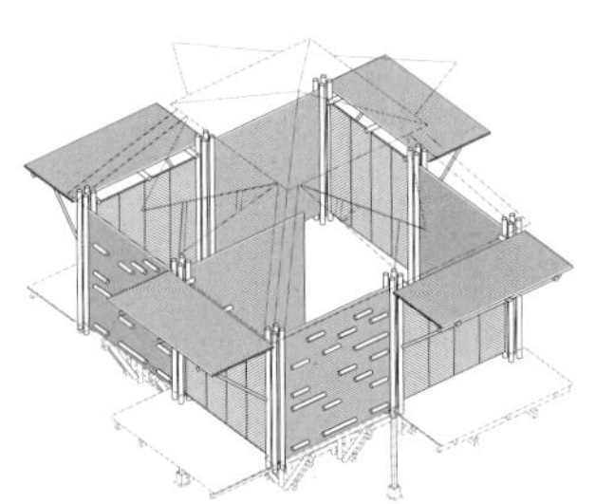

Location	Material	Quantity	$kgCO_2e$/unit	Total $kgCO_2e$
Interior				**-540**
	Bamboo	1.16 m³	-465	-540
Foundation				**-1097**
	Bamboo	2.36 m³	-465	-1098
Roof				**-1102**
	Bamboo	2.37 m³	-465	-1102
Exterior				**-1256**
	Bamboo	2.70 m³	-465	-1256

Total **-3,996 $kgCO_2e$**
Area 80 m^2
Total per Area **-45 $kgCO_2e/m^2$**

80k
60k
40k
31.6k
standard home
20k
0
-4.0k
total
-20
-40
-60
-80

Assumptions:
Whole culms have a wall thickness of 9 mm
Roof is three layers of 4 mm bamboo mat board over 9 mm of flattened culms
Flattened culms in the floors and ceiling are 9 mm thick

Exclusions:
Bamboo furniture and ladder
Rope ties
Oil drums for floatation
Steel wire
Fasteners
MEP
Fixtures
Flashing

Straw

Gartist GmbH House

Atelier Werner Schmidt

Location	Material	Quantity	$kgCO_2e$/unit	Total $kgCO_2e$
Interior				**-10198**
	Lime Plaster	1.52 m^3	190	289
	Dimensional Lumber	17.06 m^3	-615	-10486
Foundation				**-14290**
	Steel	0.16 m^3	17898	2850
	Concrete	9.82 m^3	246	2417
	Stone Flooring	2.42 m^3	746	1803
	Gravel	27.26 m^3	62	1677
	Cement Topping	2.30 m^3	438	1004
	Vapor Barrier	58.42 m^2	0.4	23
	Straw	46.09 m^3	-128	-5908
	Dimensional Lumber	29.54 m^3	-615	-18157
Exterior				**-25730**
	Lime Plaster	12.34 m^3	190	2345
	Clay Plaster	15.01 m^3	93	1398
	Glass	0.12 m^3	3593	443
	Dimensional Lumber	18.61 m^3	-615	-11439
	Straw	144.13 m^3	-128	-18478
Roof				**-33320**
	Galvanized Steel	0.14 m^3	21666	2956
	Lime Plaster	9.69 m^3	190	1841
	Aluminum	0.03 m^3	18373	498
	EPDM Membrane	39.89 m^2	9	361
	Glass	0.06 m^3	3593	233
	Bitumen Membrane	25.62 m^2	2	59
	Dimensional Lumber	20.52 m^3	-615	-12615
	Straw	207.91 m^3	-128	-26654

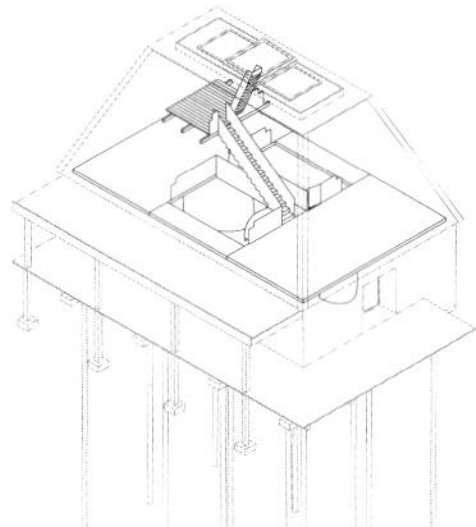

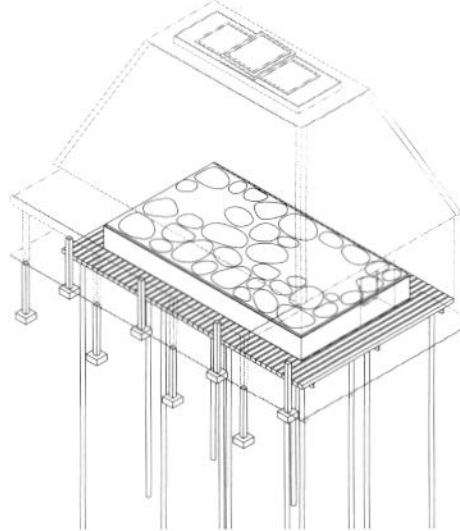

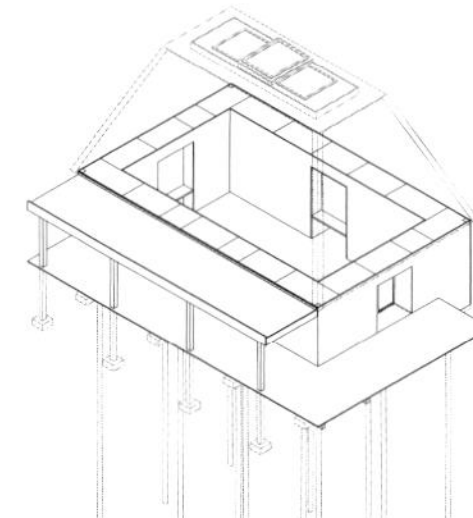

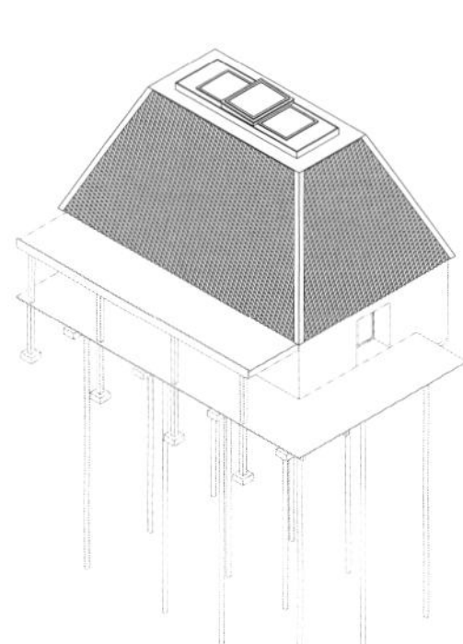

Total -83,538 $kgCO_2e$

Area 171 m^2

Total per Area -488 $kgCO_2e/m^2$

80k
60k
40k
31.6k standard home
20k
0
-10.2k
-14.3k
-20k
-25.7k
-40k
-60k
-33.3k
-83.5k total

Assumptions:

Skylight and doors are double pane glass, 4 + 4 mm
Aluminum skylight frames are calculated as 20% of simplified frame volume
Metal roofing is 29 gauge galvanized steel
Aluminum skylight edge is 16 gauge
Windows and skylights are triple pane glass, 4 + 4+ 4 mm
Lime plaster on interior and exterior surfaces is 5 cm thick
Roof deck railing is 10 gauge galvanized steel
"Stone Flooring" value is used for stone in ground floor
Skylight opening is framed with lumber
Wood-framed partitions in bathroom and kitchen volumes
Clay sprayed on exterior of straw-bales is 5 cm thick
EPDM roofing membrane is used on green roof

Exclusions:

Metal lath in kitchen and bathroom walls
Stone steps and gabion wall
Green roof soil and plantings
Uncovered portion of deck
Fasteners
MEP
Fixtures
Concrete reinforcement
Flashing
Gutters and downspouts
Stove and stove pipe
Counters and casework

Hemp

Flat House

Location	Material	Quantity	$kgCO_2e$/unit	Total $kgCO_2e$
Interior				**2447**
	Glass	1.71 m^3	3593	6136
	Anhydrite Topping	0.83 m^3	164	136
	Oriented Strand Board	0.11 m^3	-633	-71
	Hemp Lime	7.90 m^3	-106	-834
	Dimensional Lumber	4.75 m^3	-615	-2920
Foundation				**757**
	Concrete Block	27.05 m^3	242	6557
	Anhydrite Topping	3.91 m^3	164	641
	Foam Glass Insulation	1.32 m^3	239	315
	Mortar	1.47 m^3	187	275
	Oriented Strand Board	1.41 m^3	-633	-892
	Bamboo Flooring	5.97 m^3	-295	-1761
	Dimensional Lumber	3.37 m^3	-615	-2073
	Wood Fiber Insulation	14.98 m^3	-154	-2305
Exterior				**-5628**
	Aluminum	0.11 m^3	18373	2083
	Glass	0.40 m^3	3593	1447
	Galvanized Steel	0.04 m^3	21666	955
	Steel	0.00 m^3	17898	39
	Oriented Strand Board	0.41 m^3	-633	-260
	Medium Density Fiberboard	1.78 m^3	-484	-860
	Hemp Lime	20.88 m^3	-106	-2204
	Wood Fiber Insulation	19.53 m^3	-154	-3006
	Dimensional Lumber	6.22 m^3	-615	-3821
	Concrete (reused, no impact)	0.34 m^3	246	84
	Steel (reused, no impact)	0.30 m^3	17898	5352
Roof				**-5843**
	Galvanized Steel	0.06 m^3	21666	1402
	Polycarbonate Sheet	0.04 m^3	7123	269
	Medium Density Fiberboard	2.57 m^3	-484	-1244
	Dimensional Lumber	4.57 m^3	-615	-2809
	Wood Fiber Insulation	22.49 m^3	-154	-3461

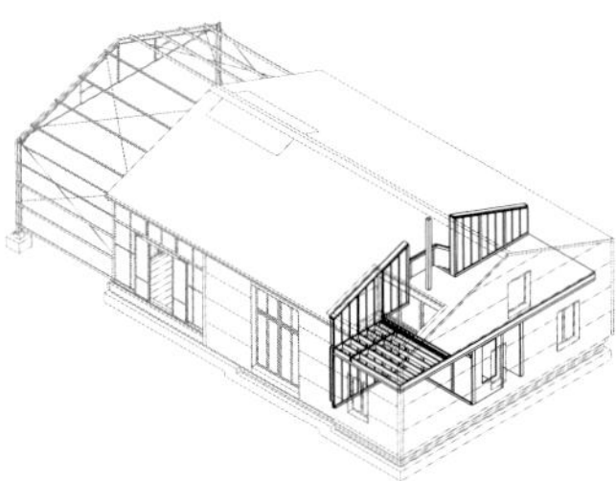

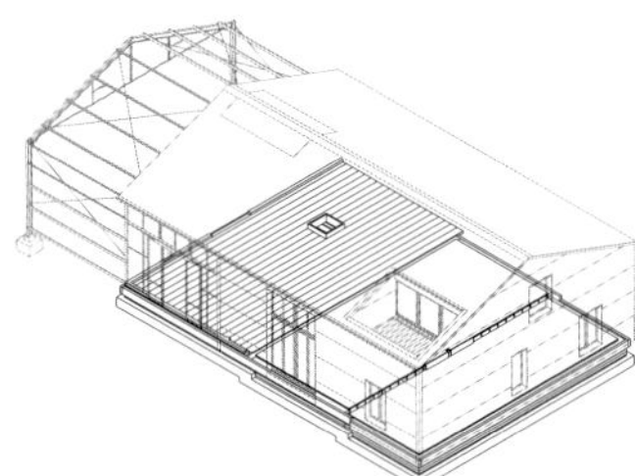

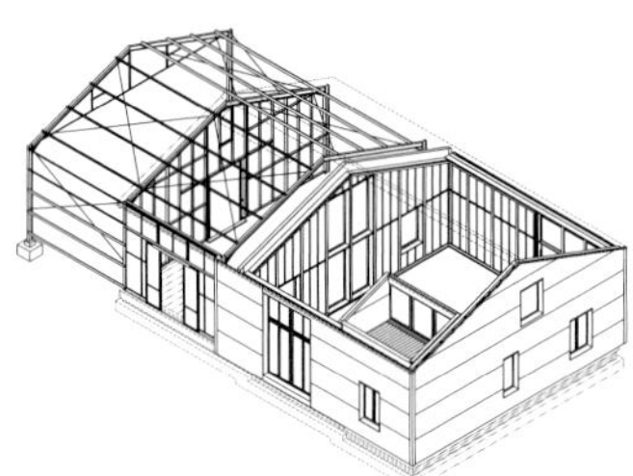

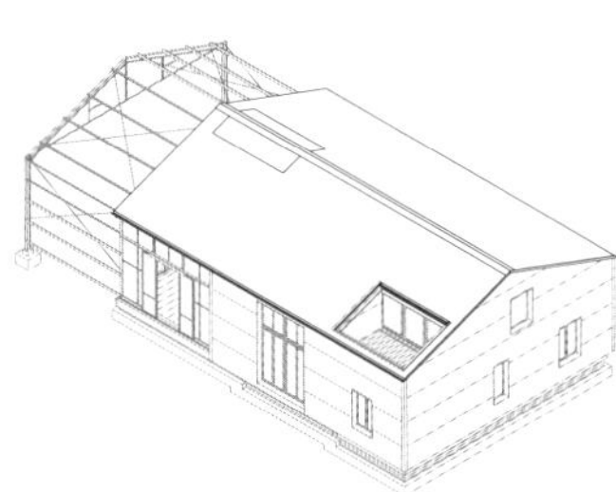

Total	**-8,268 $kgCO_2e$**
Area	177 m^2
Total per Area	**-47 $kgCO_2e/m^2$**

80k
60k
40k
31.6k standard home
20k
2.4k
0
-5.6k
-8.3k total
-5.8k
-20
-40
-60
-80

Assumptions:
Layer of sheathing underneath exposed wood fiber insulation panels
Metal roofing is 29 gauge galvanized steel with 13/3 corrugated profile
Ridge cap is 500mm wide
Square battens under metal roofing are 50 x 50 mm
Square battens below rafters are 38 x 38 mm
Polycarbonate panels are 4 mm thick, with 13/3 corrugated profile
Windows are double pane glass, 4 + 4 mm
Hot house glass panes are single pane glass, 4mm
Galvanized tube is 40 x 40 x 3 mm
Aluminum window frames calculated as 20% of total frame volume
Anhydrite topping bathroom interior is 50 mm thick
Mortar calculated as 15% of total block wall volume
Floor area calculation includes hot house
"MDF" data used for Panelvent sheathing
Assuming no additional vapor barrier is needed over wood fiber insulation

Exclusions:
Corrugated hemp fiber cladding
Metal mesh underneath floor insulation
Fastners
MEP
Fixtures
Flashing
Gutters and downspouts

Cork

Cork House

Matthew Barnett Howland with Dido Milne and Oliver Wilton

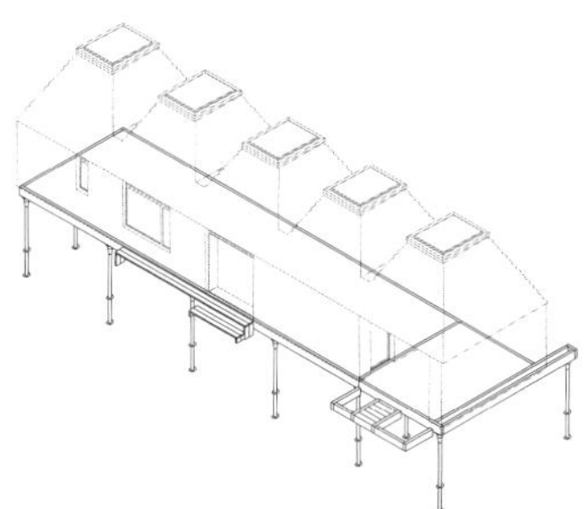

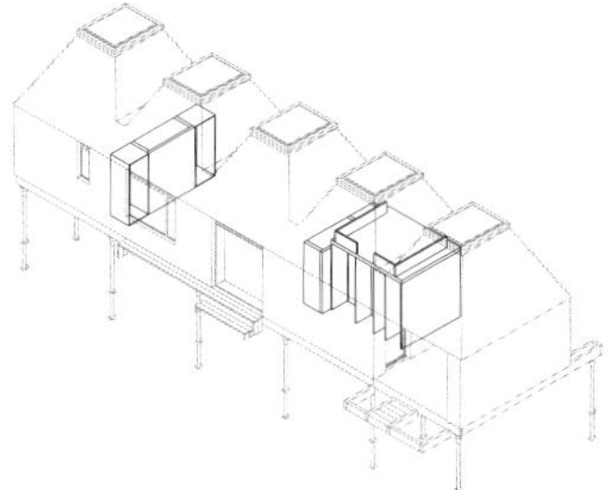

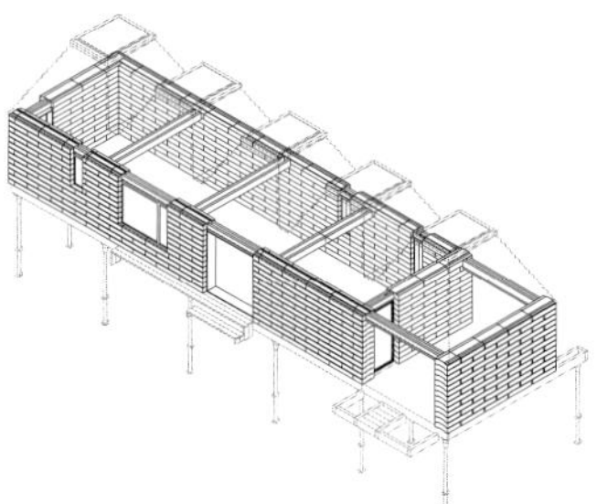

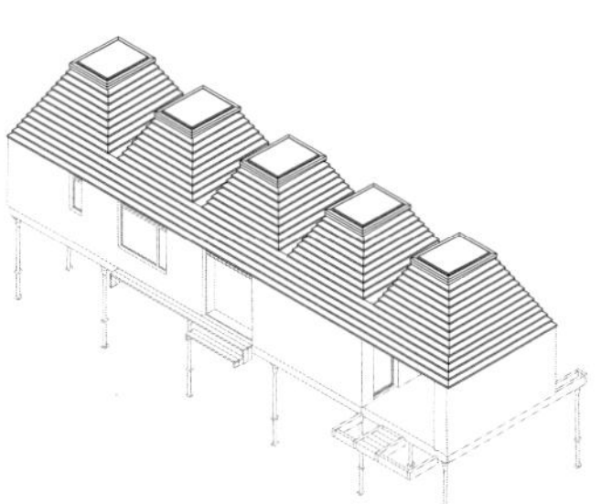

Location	Material	Quantity	$kgCO_2e$/unit	Total $kgCO_2e$
Foundation				**-2614**
	Galvanized Steel	0.17 m^3	21666	3699
	Cork	9.28 m^3	-90	-835
	Dimensional Lumber	2.40 m^3	-615	-1476
	Cross-Laminated Timber	6.59 m^3	-608	-4003
Interior				**-2644**
	Cross-Laminated Timber	4.35 m^3	-608	-2644
Exterior				**-3733**
	Glass	0.07 m^3	3593	261
	Dimensional Lumber	1.11 m^3	-615	-683
	Cork	36.83 m^3	-90	-3311
Roof				**-5787**
	Steel	0.01 m^3	17898	252
	Glass	0.07 m^3	3593	234
	Dimensional Lumber	3.40 m^3	-615	-2091
	Cork	46.52 m^3	-90	-4182

Total	**-14,778 $kgCO_2e$**
Area	63 m^2
Total per Area	**-235 $kgCO_2e/m^2$**

80k
60k
40k
31.6k
standard home
20k
0
-2.6k
-2.6k
-3.7k
-5.8k
-14.8k
total
-20k
-40k
-60k
-80k

Assumptions:
Aluminum skylight edge is 16 gauge
Exterior wood cladding is 2 cm thick
Windows and skylights are double pane glass, 4 + 4 mm
"Dimensional Lumber" value used for roof cladding, exterior cladding over the cork, and window frames
Steel piles are welded pipe with 12 mm walls, based on typical driven pile design
Partitions in bathroom and kitchen volumes are constructed out of lumber
Clay sprayed on exterior of straw is 5 cm thick
EPDM roofing membrane is used on green roof

Exclusions:
Copper interior finishes
Window sills
Outdoor deck and steps
Fasteners
MEP
Fixtures
Flashing
Gutters and downspouts
Stove and stovepipe
Counters and casework

Earth

Wohnhaus Flury
spaceshop Architects

Location	Material	Quantity	$kgCO_2e$/unit	Total $kgCO_2e$
Foundation				**705**
	Mortar	12.84 m^3	187	2401
	Dimensional Lumber	2.76 m^3	-615	-1696
	Stone (reused, no impact)	72.76 m^3	72	5216
Exterior				**-6194**
	Glass	0.41 m^3	3593	1486
	Rammed Earth	84.69 m^3	9	792
	Straw	2.86 m^3	-128	-367
	Dimensional Lumber	13.19 m^3	-615	-8105
Interior				**-20587**
	Vapor barrier	238.68 m^2	0.4	95
	Straw	45.34 m^3	-128	-5813
	Dimensional Lumber	24.19 m^3	-615	-14869
Roof				**-29252**
	EPDM Membrane	238.68 m^2	9	2161
	Bitumen Membrane	477.37 m^2	2	1104
	Glass	0.03 m^3	3593	121
	Straw	51.90 m^3	-128	-6654
	Dimensional Lumber	42.27 m^3	-615	-25984

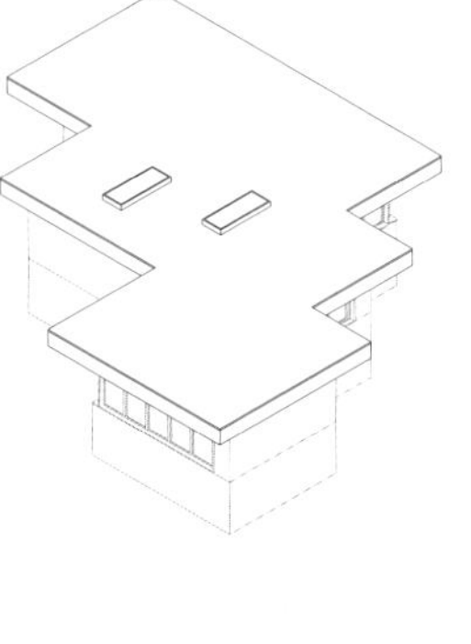

Total **-55,327 $kgCO_2e$**
Area 241 m^2
Total per Area **-229 $kgCO_2e/m^2$**

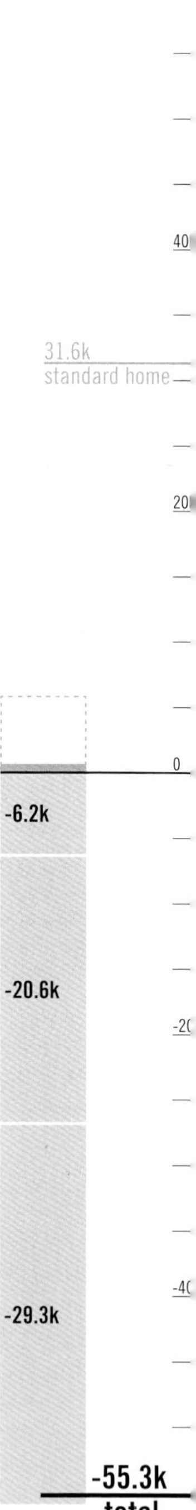

Assumptions:
Skylight is double pane glass, 4 + 4 mm
Vapor barrier and board are a combined product
Stone wall mortar is calculated as 15% of total wall volume
Extra straw in rammed earth wall not accounted for in embodied carbon data

Exclusions:
Green roof build-up above roofing membrane
Oil impregnated paper around timber posts in earth walls
Fastners
MEP
Fixtures
Flashing
Stone walls and planters on site
Stove and stovepipe
Counters and casework

Brick

Earth Bricks
Atelier Tekuto

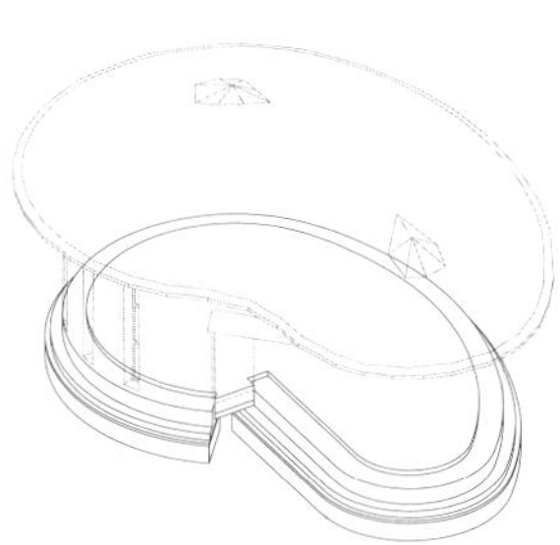

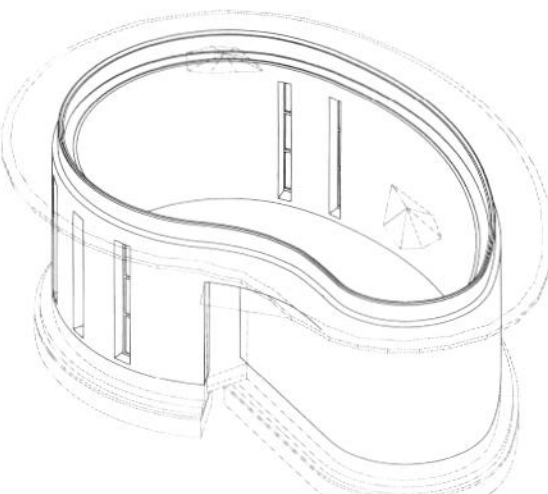

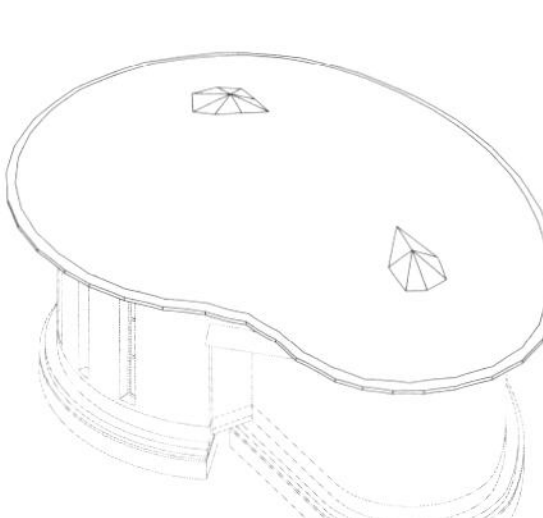

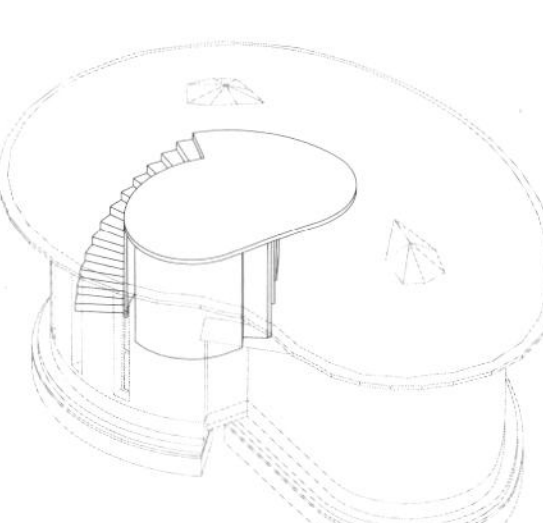

Location	Material	Quantity	$kgCO_2e$/unit	Total $kgCO_2e$
Foundation				**5487**
	Concrete	16.80 m^3	246	4135
	Foam Glass	2.86 m^3	239	684
	Terrazzo Flooring	36.39 m^2	9	337
	Gravel	5.36 m^3	62	330
Exterior				**4222**
	Glass (Block)	0.78 m^3	3305	2585
	Compressed Earth Block	31.71 m^3	57	1794
	Glass	0.03 m^3	3593	119
	Mortar	0.35 m^3	187	65
	Dimensional Lumber	0.56 m^3	-615	-341
Roof				**824**
	Galvanized Steel	0.07 m^3	21666	1577
	Polyurethane Membrane	74.36 m^2	8	619
	Phenolic Resin Insulation	3.01 m^3	87	262
	Glass	0.02 m^3	3593	63
	Dimensional Lumber	1.35 m^3	-615	-829
	Plywood	1.84 m^3	-472	-869
Interior				**-1862**
	Glass	0.03 m^3	3593	95
	Laminated Veneer Lumber	2.98 m^3	-657	-1957

Total	**8,670 $kgCO_2e$**
Area	48 m^2
Total per Area	**181 $kgCO_2e/m^2$**

80k
60k
40k
31.6k standard home
20k
5.5k
4.2k
-1.9k
8.7k total
0
-20k
-40k
-60k
-80k

Assumptions:
Galvanized steel roof structure is 29 gauge
Metal roof edge is 29 gauge galvanized steel
3 mm thickness for steel ridge structure
20 mm thickness for steel structure nodes (underneath the skylights)
10 mm thickness for steel rafter supports
"Glass" generic value used for solid glass blocks, with modified density per specification
Regular mortar used between glass blocks, calculated as 20% of wall volume
"Compressed Earth Block" data used for architect's patented earth block mixture
Glass partition in bathroom is 12 mm thick
Windows and skylights are double pane glass, 4 + 4 mm
Solid LVL interior wall and floor construction.
LVL construction for stair and load-bearing stair framing
"Gravel" value is used for crushed rock in foundation

Exclusions:
Exterior wall waterproofing
Acrylic silicone spray on roof
Roof vent
Perimeter gravel landscaping
Gravel beneath concrete foundation
Fastners
MEP
Fixtures
Counters and casework

Stone

Jacobs House II

Frank Lloyd Wright

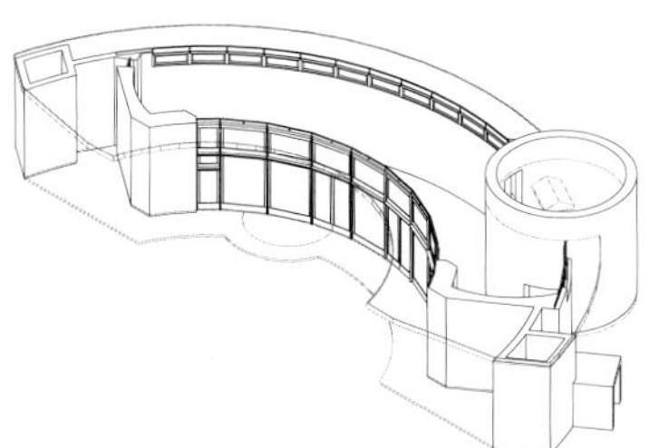

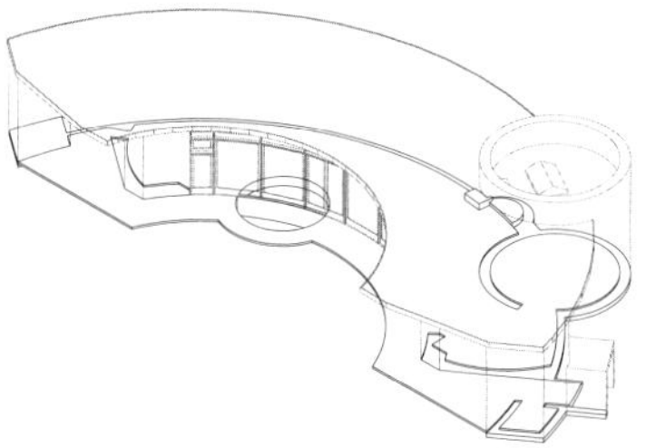

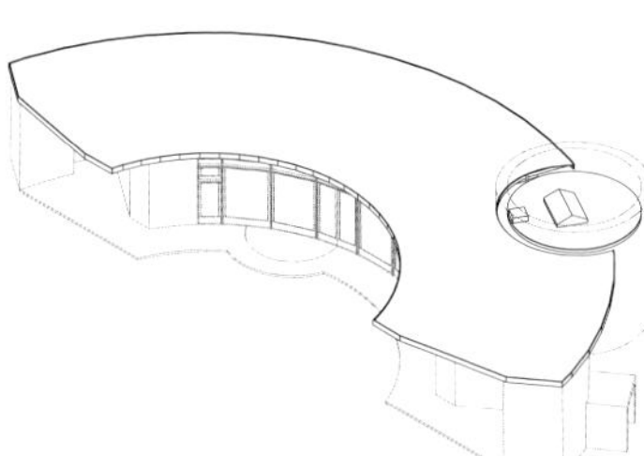

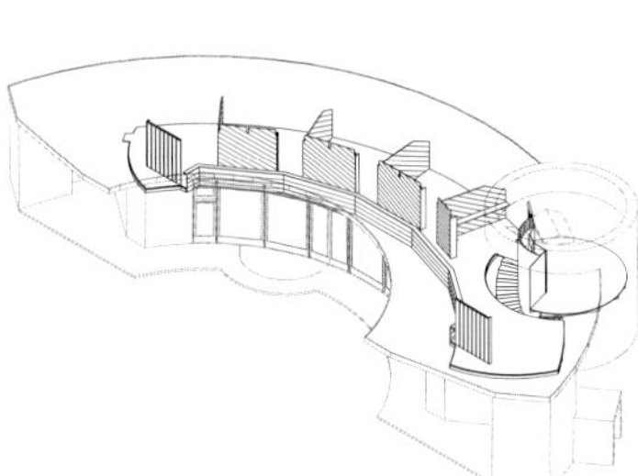

Location	Material	Quantity	$kgCO_2e$/unit	Total $kgCO_2e$
Exterior				**9839**
	Stone	109.13 m^3	72	7823
	Mortar	19.26 m^3	187	3601
	Steel	0.004 m^3	17898	72
	Dimensional Lumber	2.70 m^3	-615	-1657
	Glass (reused, no impact)	0.32 m^3	3593	1160
Foundation				**3169**
	Concrete	12.54 m^3	246	3087
	Stone	0.56 m^3	72	40
	Cement Topping	0.10 m^3	438	24
	Mortar	0.06 m^3	187	18
Roof				**-5204**
	Bitumen Membrane	752.03 m^2	2	1739
	Steel	0.06 m^3	17898	984
	Dimensional Lumber	12.90 m^3	-615	-7928
Interior				**-5213**
	Steel	0.003 m^3	17898	54
	Dimensional Lumber	8.57 m^3	-615	-5267

Total	**2,591 $kgCO_2e$**
Area	240 m^2
Total per Area	**11 $kgCO_2e/m^2$**

31.6k standard home

9.8k 3.2k -5.2k -5.2k

2.6k total

Assumptions:
Stone wall mortar is calculated as 15% of total wall volume
"Cement Topping" value used for aquella, with 1 coat equal to 1.5 m^2 per kg of aquella.

Exclusions:
Glass reused from local storefronts
Vermiculite insulation in stone wall
Patio and landscaping
Tunnel retaining walls
Crushed stone foundation base
Fasteners
MEP
Fixtures
Concrete reinforcement
Flashing
Gutters
Casework and shelving

House Simma

Georg Bechter Architektur + Design

Reuse

Location	Material	Quantity	$kgCO_2e$/unit	Total $kgCO_2e$
Foundation				**2108**
	Expanded Polystyrene Insulation	26.81 m³	49	1314
	Mastic Asphalt	2.97 m³	233	694
	Perlite	0.99 m³	61	61
	Vapor Barrier	99.07 m²	0.4	40
	Concrete (reused, no impact)	75.10 m³	246	18482
Interior				**-12696**
	Concrete	15.00 m³	246	3690
	Gypsum Board	4.22 m³	224	944
	Lime Plaster	4.49 m³	190	853
	Glass	0.05 m³	3593	162
	Mastic Asphalt	0.31 m³	233	73
	Dimensional Lumber	29.96 m³	-615	-18418
Roof				**-14217**
	Clay Roof Tile	279.91 m²	16	4445
	Bitumen Membrane	279.91 m²	2	647
	Vapor Barrier	279.91 m²	0.4	112
	Glass	0.02 m³	3593	64
	Gypsum Board	0.17 m³	224	37
	Dimensional lumber	6.43 m³	-615	-3955
	Plywood	10.43 m³	-472	-4920
	Straw	83.05 m³	-128	-10647
Exterior				**-20970**
	Glass	0.55 m³	3593	1982
	Vapor Barrier	478.85 m²	0.4	191
	Gypsum Board	0.65 m³	224	145
	Wood Fiber Board	2.73 m³	-182	-498
	Plywood	1.41 m³	-472	-667
	Straw	66.02 m³	-128	-8464
	Dimensional Lumber	22.22 m³	-615	-13660
	Brick (reused, no impact)	28.36 m³	242	6873
	Mortar (reused, no impact)	7.09 m³	187	1325

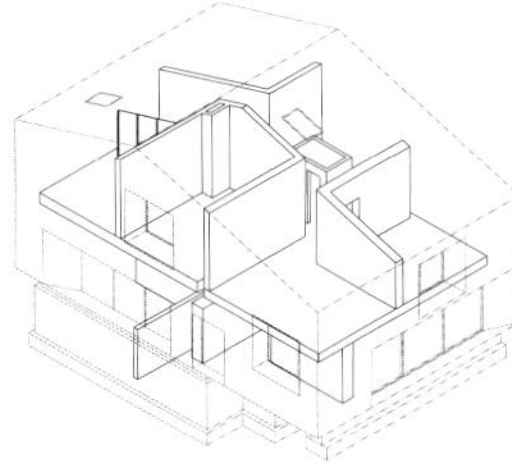

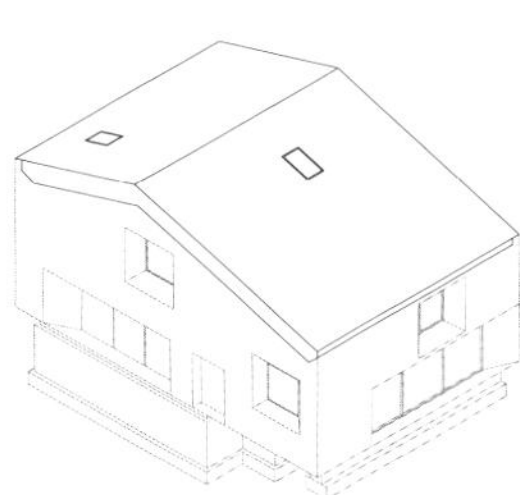

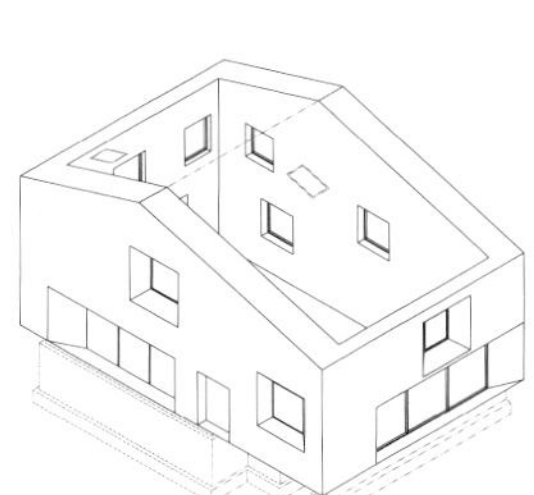

Total -45,776 $kgCO_2e$

Area 251 m²

Total per Area -182 $kgCO_2e/m^2$

80k

60k

40k

31.6k
standard home

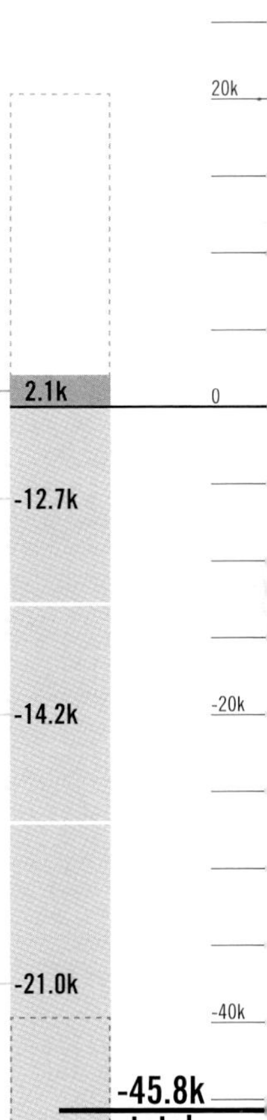

-60k

-80k

Assumptions:

"Dimensional Lumber" value used for boarding, window frames, and wooden roof structure

Existing walls of first floor are brick and existing foundation walls, footings, and floors are cast-in place concrete

First floor interior walls in living room and study are part of existing structure

Wood framing for interior walls calculated as 25% of wall volume

Basement walls have added 15 cm of EPS

Timber studs on exterior walls of the second floor are 60 cm O.C.

Skylight openings are clad in gypsum board

Interior walls are finished with 30mm of wood, except bedroom walls which are left as plastered straw

Interior shaft is concrete

Gypsum board over wood framing for basement interior walls and stair core interior

"Plywood" value used for 3-ply board

Windows and skylights are triple pane glass, 4 + 4 + 4mm

Bathroom glass partition is single pane, 4 mm

Wood framing for interior walls calculated as 25% of wall volume

Interior doors are hollow core, wood volume is calculated by 20% of full door volume, front door is solid wood

Exclusions:

Storage room on the exterior

Deck around the house and the carport

Fasteners

MEP

Fixtures

Gutters and downspouts

Flashing

Paint

Counters and casework

Index of Architects

Photography Credits

42 **Gago House** Construction photographs by Pezo von Ellrichshausen; Building photographs by Cristóbal Palma
46 **Zilvar House** Construction and bottom building photographs by ASGK Design s.r.o., Gabriela Kaprálová; Top building photograph © Petra Hájská
50 **Thunder Top Cabin** Construction photographs by Gartnerfuglen Arkitekter; Building photographs © Ivar Kvaal
54 **Wood House** (54) Left photograph by Cristóbal Palma; All other photographs © Hisao Suzuki
58 **Helio Olga House** Construction photographs © Marcos Acayaba; Building photographs by Nelson Kon
62 **Ogimachi House** Construction photographs © Tomoaki Uno; Building photographs © Benjamin Hosking
66 **House in Itsuura** Construction photographs by Kotaro Anzai; Building photographs by Osamu Abe
70 **Wall House** Construction photographs by FAR frohn&rojas; Building photographs by Cristóbal Palma
80 **House W** Construction photographs by Kraus Schönberg Architects; Building photographs by Iona Marinescu
84 **Sunken House** Construction photographs by Adjaye Associates; Building photographs by Ed Reeve
88 **Haus Gables** Construction photographs by Jennifer Bonner / MALL; Bottom building photographs by NAARO; Top building photograph by Tim Hursley
92 **Meteorite** Construction and top building photographs by Kivi Sotamaa; Bottom building photographs by Tuukka Koski
96 **Kostner House and Studio** Construction photographs by MoDus Architects; Top and bottom left building photographs by Marco Zanta; Bottom right building photograph by Niccolò Morgan Gandolfi
100 **House Köris** Construction photographs by Zeller & Moye; Building photographs by César Béjar Studio
110 **Blooming Bamboo Home** All photographs by Doan Thanh Ha
114 **From the Territory to the Dweller** Construction photographs courtesy of Rozana Montiel Estudio de Arquitectura; Building photographs © Sandra Pereznieto
118 **Bamboo Hostels** Construction photographs by Jenny Ji/Studio Anna Heringer; Building photographs Julien Lanoo © - 2007
122 **Cabañón DLPM** Construction photographs by the architect; Building photographs by JAG Studio: Juan Alberto Andrade + Cuqui Rodríguez
126 **Trika Villa** Construction photographs by Chiangmai Life Architects: Markus Roselieb, Tosapon Sittiwong; Building photographs by Alberto Cosi
130 **Energy Efficient Bamboo House** Construction and bottom right building photographs © Ping Ji; Top and bottom left building photographs by Mauricio Cardenas Laverde
134 **House Rotselaar** Construction photographs © AST 77; Building photographs © Steven Massart
144 **Gartist GmbH House** Construction and left interior photographs by Atelier Schmidt GmbH; Bottom right building photograph by Gartist GmbH
148 **Mauritzberg Test House** (148) Model, construction, and (149) top photographs from Nasjonalmuseet; (149) Bottom photographs by Lars Hallén/ Nordiska museet
152 **Media Perra House** All photographs by Miguel Mayoral
156 **Dune House** All photographs by Juozas Kamenskas
160 **Modern Seagrass House** Left construction photograph and building photographs by Helene Høyer Mikkelsen; Right construction photograph by Vandkunsten Architects
164 All photos by Jonsara Ruth
170 **Flat House** Construction photographs by Practice Architecture; Building photographs by Oskar Proctor
174 **Clay Field** (174) Left and (175) bottom photographs by Nick Kane; (174) Right and (175) top photographs © Tim Crocker
178 **Mudgee Hempcrete House 2** Construction photographs by Andy Marlow; Building photographs by Amber Hooper
182 **Low Energy House in Uccle** All photographs © Karbon'
186 Right photograph by David Grandorge
192 **Cork House** Construction photographs by Matthew Barnett Howland; Top building photograph by Ricky Jones; Bottom left building photograph by Alex de Rijke; Bottom right building photograph by Magnus Dennis
196 **Two Cork Houses** Construction photographs by Juande Jarrillo; Building photographs © José Hevia
200 **Cork Screw House** Construction photographs by rundzwei Architekten BDA; Building photographs by Gui Rebelo/Elephant Studio Photography
204 All photographs by Hanno Mackowitz
210 **House Rauch** Construction photographs by Lehm Ton Erde Baukunst; Building photographs by Beat Bühler
214 **Wohnhaus Flury** Construction photographs © spaceshop.ch; Building photographs © swebfoto.ch
218 **Gando Teachers' Housing** Construction photographs © Kéré Architecture; Top building photograph by Erik-Jan Ouwerkerk © Kéré Architecture; Bottom building photographs by Iwan Baan
222 **Dong Anh House** All photographs by Oki Hiroyuki
226 **TECLA - Technology and Clay** Construction photographs © Wasp; Building photographs © Iago Corazza
230 Center photograph by LTL Architects, with permission from the Alvar Aalto Foundation
236 **Muuratsalo Experimental House** All photographs by LTL Architects, with permission from the Alvar Aalto Foundation
240 **Earth Bricks** Construction photographs by Atelier Tekuto; Building photographs by Toshihiro Sobajima
244 **Brick House** Construction photographs by LETH & GORI; Building photographs by Laura Stamer
248 **dnA House** Construction photographs © BLAF architecten; Building photographs by Stijn Bollaert
252 **Iturbide Studio** Left construction photograph courtesy of Taller I Mauricio Rocha+Gabriela Carrillo I; Building photographs © Rafael Gamo
262 **Jacobs House II** Construction photographs: Herbert and Katherine Jacobs Residence, Middleton, WI, 1948. Frank Lloyd Wright. Herbert and Katherine Jacobs Residence and Frank Lloyd Wright Records, Ryerson and Burnham Art and Architecture Archives, The Art Institute of Chicago. Digital Files #197701_220331-001 and #197701_220331-002; Building photographs © Ezra Stoller/Esto.
266 **Hill Country Jacal** All photographs © Leigh Christian
270 **Can Lis** Construction photographs © The Utzon Archives/The Utzon Center; Top building photograph by Chen Hao; Bottom building photographs by Pedro Pegenaute
274 **Stone House** Construction photographs © Sambuichi Architects; Building photographs by Shinkenchiku-sha
286 **House Renovation in Scudellate** Construction photographs by Wespi de Meuron Romeo Architects; Building photographs © Albrecht Imanuel Schnabel
290 **Verbiest** All photographs © Séverin Malaud
294 **House Simma** Construction photographs by Georg Bechter Architektur + Design; Building photographs © Adolf Bereuter
298 **Plywood House** Left and center construction photographs by Feina Studio; Right construction photograph by Jaume Rebassa; Building photographs by Luis Díaz Díaz
302 **House of Flying Beds** Construction photographs © Al Borde; Building photographs by JAG Studio: Juan Alberto Andrade + Cuqui Rodríguez
306 **Small Cottage Ojacastro** All photographs by MAAV. Guillermo Avanzini Alcibar; Adrián Martínez Muñoz
310 **Cabin Femunden** Construction photographs by Aslak Haanshuus; Building photographs by Tom Gustavsen © Aslak Haanshuus
314 **Half-Slope House** Construction photographs by Denis Joelsons e Gabriela Baraúna

Acknowledgments

This publication is the product of several years of collective effort and would not have been possible without the generosity and support of institutions, colleagues, friends, and families. The talents and intelligence of our staff at LTL Architects were a constant resource in its development. In particular, Celia Chaussabel and Kyle Reich were instrumental to the realization of this book, using their visual talents to bring the drawings to fruition, and their analytical abilities to unpack and make legible the material life cycles and carbon assessments. In addition, Anna Knoell, Shane Algiere, and Lana Licciardi provided timely editorial feedback.

We are indebted to the material expertise of Martha Lewis and Jonsara Ruth, who not only provided specific feedback on the book's content, but also were catalysts for the book. We are privileged to be guided by their passion for a healthier material future, by their ethical compass, and by their ongoing support as members of our family.

Throughout this book's development, we have been inspired and influenced by the ideas and discussions at the academic institutions where we teach: Princeton University School of Architecture, Columbia University Graduate School of Architecture, Planning and Preservation, and Parsons School of Constructed Environments. In particular, we are thankful for the many years of support from Dean Monica Ponce de Leon, Dean Amale Andraos, Dean Robert Kirkbride, and Dean Joel Towers. Crucial to this book's existence were also the dialogues that emerged from a range of other institutions and initiatives, including The Architectural League of New York, Parson's Healthy Materials Lab, US Architects Declare, and Architecture Camp. We want to thank a number of colleagues who directly influenced this book: Lucia Allais, Sunil Bald, David Benjamin, Leila Behjet, Andrew Bernheimer, Fred Bernstein, Stella Betts, Tatiana Bilbao, Merritt Bucholz, Eric Bunge, Stephanie Carlisle, Debbie Chen, Fiona Cousins, Roy Decker, Sarah Dunn, Anna Dyson, Martin Felsen, Andrew Freear, Rosalie Genevro, Leslie Gill, Lisa Gray, Mimi Hoang, Oded Horodniceanu, Eric Höweler, Joyce Hwang, Florian Idenburg, David Leven, Alexandra (Xan) Lillehei, Astrid Lipka, Jing Liu, Chris Magwood, Karen McEvoy, V. Mitch McEwen, Alison Mears, Forrest Meggers, Michael Meredith, Ana Miljacki, Kiel Moe, Lee Moreau, Guy Nordenson, Nat Oppenheimer, Alan Organschi, Peter Pelsinski, Mahadev Raman, Lyn Rice, Hilary Sample, Catherine Seavitt Nordenson, Kate Orff, Anne Reiselbach, Karen Stonely, Caitlin Watson, Dan Wood, and Meejin Yoon.

This content of this book was dependent on innovative houses from around the world, and the creativity and intelligence of their design and realization. The development and accuracy of the detailed cross-sectional perspective and the axonometric of these houses would not have been possible without the cooperation, information, and feedback from these architects: AgwA, Al Borde, Alvar Aalto Foundation, Marcos Acayaba Arquitetos, ADX, Adjaye Associates, ASGK Design, AST 77 Architecten, Juan Carlos Bamba + Ignacio de Teresa + Alejandro González, Georg Bechter Architektur + Design, BLAF Architecten, Boltshauser Architects, Jennifer Bonner / MALL, Studio Cardenas Conscious Design, Chiangmai Life Architects, Mario Cucinella Architects, Pezo von Ellrichshausen, Envirotecture, FAR frohn&rojas, Feina Studio, Gartnerfuglen Arkitekter, Arkitekt Aslak Haanshuus, Studio Anna Heringer, Hille Strandskogen Arkitekter, Matthew Barnett Howland with Dido Milne (CSK Architects) and Oliver Wilton (UCL), Denis Joelsons + Gabriela Baraúna Uchida, Karbon' Architecture et Urbanisme, Kéré Architecture, Kraus Schönberg Architects, Lehm Ton Erde Baukunst, LETH & GORI, Emiliano López Mónica Rivera Arquitectos, MAAV, Mikhail Riches Architects, MoDus Architects, Rozana Montiel Estudio de Arquitectura, Santos Bolívar, The National Museum of Art, Architecture and Design (Norway), Practice Architecture, Taller I Mauricio Rocha + Gabriela Carrillo I, rundzwei Architekten, Sambuichi Architects, Atelier Werner Schmidt, Ateljé Sotamaa, spaceshop Architects, Atelier Tekuto, Tomoaki Uno Architects, Utzon Center, Vandkunsten Architects, Wespi de Meuron Romeo Architects, Frank Lloyd Wright Foundation, and Zeller & Moye.

We thank ORO Editions Press, Publisher Gordon Goff, and COO Jake Anderson for their enthusiastic and unwavering support, and their continued contributions to architectural discourse through the printed medium. The coherence of our introductory essay, with its three writers, is a tribute to the expeditious editorial skill of Jessie Williams Burns.

Finally, we offer heartfelt gratitude to our families for encouraging and enabling the completion of this work. The cautionary optimism we hope it reflects regarding not only the practice of architecture but a more conscious and circular relationship to our shared planet, grows directly from their presence and support.

This book is dedicated to:
Kim Yao, Sarabeth Lewis Yao, and Maximo Lewis Yao
—Paul Lewis
Carmen Lenzi, Kai Luca Tsurumaki, and Lucia Alise Tsurumaki
—Marc Tsurumaki
Jonsara Ruth and Quinn Arnold Lewis
—David J. Lewis

Publication is made possible in part by a grant from the Barr Ferree Foundation Publication Fund, Department of Art and Archaeology, Princeton University and by the Graham Foundation for Advanced Studies in the Fine Arts.

Drawing Credits

This book continues the visual scholarship from our previous publication *Manual of Section*, with the smaller scale of the included houses allowing a more detailed articulation of the materials that comprise the houses' wall sections. In order to produce both the cross-sectional perspectives and the exploded axonometrics, each house in this book was developed as a precise model in Rhinoceros 3D from research and careful examination of drawings and photographs. Wherever possible, construction drawings were used to provide detail and dimensional specificity about each house's material assembly. This level of information, literally concealed within the walls of the house, often remains less prominent in a building's documentation and history due to its absence in completed project photography. The section cut makes these invisible components legible. The 3D model was then used to test and select a specific two-dimensional section and to refine its alignment with a carefully composed perspective drawing, linking the abstract orthogonal cut with a specific interior view. The model was also translated into the exploded axonometric of each house to illustrate its relation to the site and context while simultaneously showing the key plans. The articulation of each drawing was further fleshed out in Adobe Illustrator through an iterative process, which involved the direct feedback and redline adjustments from many of the buildings' architects or archivists. Nevertheless, all the drawings in this book are the work and interpretation of LTL Architects.

We would like to thank the following people for their contributions to the making of the drawings in this book, which unfolded over four years: Andrew Cornelis, Hailey Craft, and Sophie Buteau helped produce an initial spatial taxonomy of domestic section types; Adam Ainslie shifted this spatial taxonomy into one based on materials and continued the selection process that expanded to over 500 houses from around the world reviewed for inclusion in the book; Celia Chaussabel, Max Heintz, Grace Lee, Austin Madrigale, Julia Medina, Alena Nagornaia, Kyle Reich, Zhiqian Xu, and Jingyuan Zhang refined the selections and developed the initial digital models. The drawings based on the models were the work of Austin, Celia, Grace, Jingyuan, Julia, and Kyle. The life cycle and process diagrams for each material were the work of Adam, Celia, Kyle, and Jingyuan. Celia Chaussabel and Kyle Reich generated the material assembly drawings, edited and refined all the drawings to completion, and were responsible for diligently shepherding the book through the last year of its creation. Following is the specific attribution of the work on the drawings found on the listed page numbers:

Celia Chaussabel
Models: 34, 54, 96, 144, 174, 286, 2902, 294, 302
Drawings: 34, 54, 56, 88, 90, 96, 98, 110, 112, 130, 132, 144, 146, 160, 162, 174, 176, 192, 214, 216, 222, 224, 236, 238, 240, 242, 286, 288, 290, 292, 294, 296, 298, 300, 302, 304
Drawing edits: 36, 52, 54, 56, 58, 64, 66, 68, 70, 86, 88, 90, 92, 98, 100, 102, 104, 112, 114, 124, 126, 132, 134, 146, 148, 162, 164, 176, 178, 194, 196, 202, 204, 216, 218, 224, 226, 238, 240, 242, 244, 288, 290, 292, 294, 296, 298, 300, 302, 304, 306

Max Heintz
Models: 58, 62, 84, 88, 110, 114, 122, 148, 152, 160, 222, 236, 262, 298

Grace Lee
Drawings: 50, 52, 62, 64, 134, 136, 244, 246, 314, 316

Austin Madrigale
Drawings: 44, 102, 194

Julia Medina
Model: 170
Drawing: 44

Alena Nagornaia
Models: 42, 50, 66, 92, 100, 118, 126, 130, 192, 200, 214, 240, 244, 252, 266, 306

Kyle Reich
Models: 46, 58, 70, 80, 118, 126, 134, 156, 170, 178, 182, 210, 218, 226, 252, 262, 266, 270, 274, 314
Drawings: 42, 46, 48, 60, 70, 72, 80, 82, 126, 128, 156, 158, 170, 172, 178, 180, 182, 184, 196, 198, 210, 212, 222, 224, 226, 228, 252, 254, 266, 268, 270, 272, 274, 276, 306, 308, 310, 312
Drawing edits: 42, 44, 46, 48, 58, 60, 70, 72, 80, 82, 92, 94, 114, 116, 118, 120, 126, 128, 134, 136, 148, 150, 152, 154, 156, 158, 170, 172, 178, 180, 182, 184, 196, 198, 210, 212, 218, 220, 226, 228, 244, 246, 248, 250, 252, 254, 262, 264, 266, 268, 270, 272, 274, 276, 306, 308, 310, 312, 314, 316

Jingyuan Zhang
Models: 248, 310
Drawings: 58, 60, 66, 68, 84, 86, 92, 94, 100, 114, 116, 118, 120, 148, 150, 152, 154, 200, 202, 248, 250, 262, 264

Zhiqian Xu
Models: 96, 196

No unpaid intern labor was used in the production of this work, and all the work was executed within the offices of LTL Architects.

ORO Editions
Publishers of Architecture, Art, and Design
Gordon Goff: Publisher

www.oroeditions.com
info@oroeditions.com

Published by ORO Editions

Design: Lewis.Tsurumaki.Lewis Architects
Book Project Managers: Celia Chaussabel and Kyle Reich
Introduction Editor: Jessie Williams Burns
ORO Project Manager: Jake Anderson

Library of Congress Cataloging-in-Publication Data:

10 9 8 7 6 5 4 3 2 First Edition

ISBN: 978-1-957183-09-1

Color Separations and Printing: ORO Group Inc.
Printed in China

ORO Editions makes a continuous effort to minimize the overall carbon foot-printof its publications. As part of this goal, ORO, in association with Global ReLeaf, arranges to plant trees to replace those used in the manufacturing of the paper produced for its books. Global ReLeaf is an international campaig run by American Forests, one of the world's oldest nonprofit conservation organizations. Global ReLeaf is American Forests' education and action program that helps individuals, organizations, agencies, and corporations improve the local and global environment by planting and caring for trees.

Publication is made possible in part by a grant from the Barr Ferree Foundation Publication Fund, Department of Art and Archaeology, Princeton University and by the Graham Foundation for Advanced Studies in the Fine Arts.